The Arizona Guide

SECOND EDITION

Judy Wade

Fulcrum Publishing
Golden, Colorado

This book is dedicated to my sister, Karen, the principal.

*Although she gave me only an "A-" on the manuscript,
she did say that she thinks
I have great potential as a writer.
Thank you, Karen. Next time I'll try harder.*

Text copyright © 2000 Judy Wade
Cover and interior photographs copyright © 2000 Bill Baker

The Arizona Guide, Second Edition provides many safety tips about weather and travel, but good decision-making and sound judgment are the responsibility of the individual. Neither the publisher nor the author assumes any liability for injury that may arise from the use of this book.

Library of Congress Cataloging-in-Publication Data

Wade, Judy.
   The Arizona guide / Judy Wade.— 2nd ed.
     p.   cm.
Includes index.
   ISBN 1-55591-051-3
   1. Arizona—Guidebooks. I. Title.
   F809.3 .W33 2000
   917.9104'54—dc21   00-009957

Printed in China
0 9 8 7 6 5 4 3 2 1

Editorial: *Kris Fulsaas, Daniel Forrest-Bank*
Design: *Bill Spahr*
Maps: *Marge Mueller, Gray Mouse Graphics*
Cover photograph: *Saguaro cactus in an Arizona sunset by Bill Baker*
Back cover photograph: *Grand Canyon lookouts like this one on the South Rim offer myriad vistas of the world-famous natural wonder. Photograph by Bill Baker.*

Fulcrum Publishing
16100 Table Mountain Parkway, Suite 300
Golden, Colorado 80403
800-992-2908 • (303) 277-1623
www.fulcrum-books.com

Contents

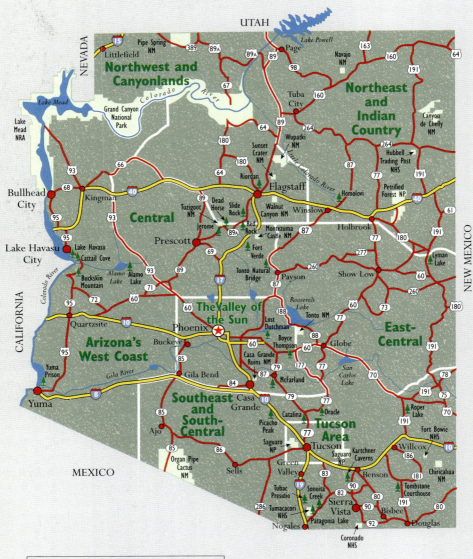

UTAH

NEVADA

Littlefield

Pipe Spring NM

389   89A

89A   89   Page

Lake Powell

Navajo NM   163   160   64

Northwest and Canyonlands

Colorado   River   67

98

Tuba City   160

Northeast and Indian Country

Canyon de Chelly NM

Lake Mead

Grand Canyon National Park

Lake Mead NRA

64   89

Wupatki NM

180

Sunset Crater NM   264

Hubbell Trading Post NHS   264

Little Colorado River

180   Riordan   Flagstaff

Homolovi   77   Petrified Forest NP   191

87

40

Bullhead City   68   Kingman

93   66   64

89   Dead Horse   Walnut Canyon NM

Winslow   Holbrook   61

Tuzigoot NM   Slide Rock

Central   Jerome   89A   Red Rock   Montezuma Castle NM   87   277   77   180   191

95   93   Prescott   69   Fort Verde   260   Show Low   Lyman Lake

Lake Havasu City   Lake Havasu   93   89   Tonto Natural Bridge   Payson   87   260   60

Cattail Cove   17   260

Alamo Lake   71   Roosevelt Lake   73   180

Buckskin Mountain   Alamo Lake   60   The Valley of   188   Tonto NM

95   72   60   the Sun   Lost Dutchman   60   77   East-Central

Quartzsite   10   Phoenix   Boyce   88   191

Arizona's West Coast   Buckeye   60   Thompson   60   Globe

95   85   Casa Grande Ruins NM   177   77   70   78

Yuma Prison   Gila River   Gila Bend   79   San Carlos Lake   75

Yuma   8   84   87   McFarland   191   70

10   79   Roper Lake   70

Casa Grande   77   Oracle   191

Southeast and South-Central   Catalina   Fort Bowie NHS

Ajo   85   Picacho Peak   77   Tucson Area   Kartchner Caverns   Willcox   10

95   Saguaro NP   Tucson   186

85   86   Saguaro NP   181   Chiricahua NM

Organ Pipe Cactus NM   Sells   Green Valley   83   Benson   Tombstone Courthouse

MEXICO   Tubac Presidio   19   82   90   80

Sonoita Creek   90   Bisbee   80

286   Tumacacori NHS   Sierra Vista   90

Nogales   Patagonia Lake   92   Douglas

Coronado NHS

CALIFORNIA

NEW MEXICO

Arizona

N

0   25   50 Miles

☐ National Park or Monument
▲ State Park
🛡 Interstate Highway
◯ 93 U.S. Highway
◯ 89 State Highway

Introduction

Background Information

Multifaceted Arizona has been credited with having more personalities than almost any state in the union. From the cactus-dotted sands of the low desert to peaks in excess of 12,000 feet, covered with snow even in summer, Arizona's diversity is celebrated in all aspects of nature. It is home to nearly 5 million residents.

Dry sandy washes, placid lakes, shimmering rivers, and dramatic canyons provide backdrops for appreciating the land in its natural state as well as for enjoying the improvements made by humankind. The red rocks of Sedona, Canyon de Chelly's well-preserved Indian ruins, the eerie beauty of Monument Valley, Window Rock's sacred history, and the developing wine country of Sonoita/Patagonia all are part of Arizona's outdoor treasures.

Almost 30 million visitors come to the state each year, most of them arriving during winter months to take advantage of superb sunshine in Phoenix; others are drawn by the Grand Canyon, one of the seven natural wonders of the world, which by itself hosts more than 5 million visitors each year.

History

Admitted to the Union on February 14, 1912, as the nation's 48th state, Arizona is a U.S. youngster. To many it seems in a hurry to create the history it doesn't yet have. Others point to the ancient ones, whose residence in what is now Arizona dates to prehistory, as validation of a valuable past.

Three tribal groups—the Anasazi in the northern plateau regions, the Mogollon people

Saguaro cactus against a dramatic Arizona sunset.

who inhabited the northeastern and eastern mountain ranges, and the Hohokam who had an agrarian culture and dwelled primarily on desert plains near rivers—lived honestly and well for centuries. The state's diversity of creatures, climate, and resources furnished them with an affluence of life's necessities. Understanding the survival techniques of desert plants helps to comprehend the lives of these early Native Americans, who have left traces of their cultures in Montezuma Castle, Tuzigoot, Pueblo Grande, and other ruins.

The peaceful desert began to change in the 1500s when the Spanish Conquistadors arrived. The introduction of horses and guns had a huge impact on the lives of the Native Americans, as did new crops and growing techniques. By the early 1800s, settlers from the East began to discover the state's mining riches, farming possibilities, and animal resources. Beavers in the Gila River Valley soon were hunted to extinction. Native Americans who had lived in the state for centuries were perceived as a nuisance as they resisted encroachment on their hunting and farming lands, and the military was called in. The bloody Indian wars of the 1800s permanently subdued them. President Abraham Lincoln created the Arizona Territory in 1862. Today, Native Americans in the state number more than 100,000, many living on 23 reservations that are home to 21 distinct tribes.

For decades Arizona has been known for its Five Cs—copper, citrus, cattle, cotton, and cactus. Despite the fact that developers are gobbling up fields at a great rate, irrigation sustains cotton as the state's number-one cash crop. Fewer acres are planted, but technology allows higher yields per acre, so bottom-line production remains stable. You still can see cotton in the Phoenix area near Litchfield Park, along rural roads south of Chandler, and in great quantity flanking US 70 west of Thatcher and Safford. October, a harvest month, is a good time to see the fluffy white bolls ready for picking. Yuma, on the Colorado River bordering California, and areas around Willcox in the state's southern region, produce vast fruit and vegetable crops.

Arizona has produced celebrities at least as exciting as those from any longer-lived state. Baseball great Reggie Jackson attended Arizona State University on a football scholarship in 1964, then went on to fame with the Oakland A's in 1967, the Orioles in 1976, and the New York Yankees in 1977. Ghoulish rock musician Alice Cooper played with a Phoenix band in his 1964 high school days. Arizona has had a woman governor (Rose Mofford in 1988), an impeached governor (Evan Mecham in 1988), and a governor found guilty of bank fraud (Fife Symington in 1997). Presently it has another woman governor, Jane Dee Hull.

State Symbols

In a state whose history is filled with the symbolism of Native American cultures, it's not surprising that symbols still are an important part of Arizona's identity. In 1985 the state's schoolchildren were asked to vote on their choices for state mammal, fish, reptile, and amphibian, choosing from a group preselected by the Arizona Department of Game and Fish. The Arizona Legislature already had chosen the state bird, flower, and tree. So in 1986 the following plants and animals became official emblems of the State of Arizona.

State Flower: Saguaro Cactus Blossom

This famous plant was a slam dunk in the flower category, mainly because it is the most recognizable cactus on earth. With its many arms and lovely waxy white flowers, it grows naturally only in Arizona and in a small portion of California, along the Colorado River where the two states share a border. Saguaro bloom in May, with each blossom opening for just a few hours. You have to catch them in early morning because usually by noon they're closed, never to reopen. If the bats, bees, and moths have done their pollinating job, fruit will appear in about a month. It is considered a great delicacy by finches, sparrows, cactus wrens, and other desert birds, and within hours of turning pink will be pecked full of holes.

State Bird: Cactus Wren

You might hear the scratchy, strident call of this pretty desert bird long before you spot the bird itself. The largest member of the wren family, it is not colorful but is attractively patterned with shades of brown and white, and is interesting to watch for its flitty behavior. Cactus wrens are so-called because they depend on cactuses as a nest-building site, for protection, and as a food source. Besides cactus fruit, they also eat the bugs and insects that live on the spiny plants.

State Tree: Paloverde

This green-trunked tree is a classic example of how plants survive in the desert. Tiny leaves conserve water that is lost by broader-leafed plants. The green bark encourages photosynthesis as do leaves in other plants. In April and May it is covered with tiny yellow flowers that create a dramatic explosion of color.

State Mammal: Ringtail

A relative of the raccoon and about the size of a gray squirrel, the ringtail has a long, bushy tail that, at about 15 inches, is the same length as its body. It prefers rocky cliffs, caves, crevices, and hollow trees and is nocturnal, so chances of spotting one are pretty slim. But you'll know if one has been in the area because of the vile, skunklike smell it emits when threatened or frightened.

State Reptile: Arizona Ridge-Nosed Rattlesnake

The beautiful white stripes on this snake's brown face are said to be the inspiration for war paint worn by the Chiricahua Apaches. This small 24-inch snake is one of 11 rattler species that live in Arizona. Found at 5,000- to 8,000-foot altitudes in mountain ranges in south-central Arizona, it has a row of scales on its nose that give it its name. As with all rattlers, it's wise to give these a wide berth. They are protected, and it is illegal to kill or possess one.

State Fish: Arizona Apache Trout

Presently listed as threatened under the Endangered Species Act, this colorful fish readily breeds with other trout species such as rainbow, which have been introduced to Apache trout's natural habitat. It lives in high mountain streams in central and eastern Arizona and is gaining ground again as a pure species as non-native trout are removed. The Apache trout is yellowish with dark spots and has an orange slash on its lower jaw.

State Amphibian: Tree Frog

The only time you'll probably ever be aware of this little hopper is during summer rains when it is very vocally looking for a mate. It rarely gets more than 2 inches long and lives above 5,000 feet in pine, oak, and fir forests, using circular pads at the end of its toes to crawl into treetops and out along branches.

State Gem: Turquoise

This warm blue-green stone, used for centuries in Indian jewelry, now is a popular semiprecious stone often combined with silver.

State Flag

The state's copper industry and continued growth (which seems assured) are symbolized by a copper star rising from a blue field of honor in the face of the setting sun.

State Seal

The state motto, "Ditat Deus," which in Latin means "God Enriches," is interwoven with the state's original major enterprises—reclamation, farming, cattle raising, and mining—along with the date 1912, when Arizona was admitted to the Union.

State Name

Two Native American words, *Aleh-zon,* meaning "Little Spring," are the derivative for the state name.

Geology and Geography

The nation's sixth-largest state, Arizona covers 113,417 square miles that encompass three distinct geographical zones. The northern plateaus that we refer to as Canyonlands and Indian Country in this book bear signs of the volcanic activity that formed their peaks and valleys. The central mountains, where the Mogollon Rim marks the abrupt end of the plateaus, are covered with fragrant pine forests. High mountain lakes, winter resorts, and hiking trails have made the rim the state's playground. We cover this in sections called East-Central—Above and Below the Rim and Central Region. The southern deserts, where Phoenix and Tucson have grown up, create the image that most out-of-towners have of the state. This is where saguaro cactuses grow in abundance, and where reliable sunshine and extensive irrigation systems sustain the bulk of the state's population. The sections called Valley of the Sun, Tucson, Southeast and South-Central—Old West Country, and Arizona's West Coast deal with the southern deserts.

Arizona is the only state in which all four

North American deserts are found. Within this abundance of aridity, there is great diversity of plant and animal life. The **Sonoran Desert,** located in the southwestern part of the state, extends into California and is sometimes subdivided as the **Colorado Desert** and the **Arizona Desert.** It has more birds, plants, and animals than any other desert, making up a species list that includes graceful fan palms, green-trunked paloverde, and brushy mesquite. From magnificent bighorn sheep to little kangaroo rats, the range of species is enormous.

The **Chihuahuan Desert** gets more rain and has more limestone in its pale soil than the Sonoran Desert, and is characterized by generally small, stubby growth except near riparian areas. It reaches north into Arizona from Mexico and is dotted with yucca and agave.

The **Mojave Desert,** the most arid of the deserts, stark and sparsely vegetated, touches the state's western edge where it adjoins California, extending into Nevada. Higher elevations make it the coldest of the deserts.

Flora and Fauna

One of the state's biggest wildlife claims to fame is bird-watching, particularly for hummingbirds in Ramsey Canyon south of Sierra Vista. But opportunities for viewing other wildlife, including fleet-footed pronghorns, desert bighorn sheep, white-tailed deer, coatimundi, javelinas, and more exist almost everywhere.

Arizona's terrain ranges from close to sea level in the southwestern deserts to 12,643 feet at the top of Mount Humphreys near Flagstaff, providing fertile growing conditions for many varieties of flora. More than 60 species of cactuses are found in Arizona's desert regions, while fir, juniper, and pine conifers are common at higher elevations. Riparian areas and canyons usually are home to cottonwood and maple. Spring rains bring wildflowers in abundance.

See individual chapters (under Outdoor Activities or Wildlife Viewing in Seeing and Doing) for places to go and resources for more information. An excellent starting point to see what the state has to offer is the **Arizona-Sonora Desert Museum** in Tucson (see Major Attractions in the Tucson chapter).

Recommended Reading

Arizona Wildlife Viewing Guide (Falcon Press, 1995) by John N. Carr not only tells you where to go to see neat animals, but gives directions on how to get there.

70 Common Cacti of the Southwest, 100 Desert Wildflowers of the Southwest, and *100 Roadside Wildflowers* (Southwest Parks and Monuments Association, Tucson) are part of a series of small books with excellent color photographs that help you identify the state's plants.

Climate and Weather

In Arizona it is quite possible to ski in the morning and play golf in the afternoon. In the Tucson area, for example, an early winter morning glide down the slopes of Mount Lemmon easily can be followed by a quick 18 holes on a local course. In the Phoenix area, there's no question that summers are hot, and getting hotter. Weather bureau records show that as more and more people move into the Valley of the Sun, as more air conditioners and more cars blow off increasing quantities of hot air, and more desert is paved over to create highways and urban areas, temperatures go higher and higher, and stay there. Summer nights, which used to bring cooling relief to even the hottest August mornings, are not cooling off as much as they used to. *The Arizona Republic* labels it a phenomenon called "urban heat island," a problem that exists not only in Phoenix but in most large cities. So far the power is available to keep those air conditioners humming, and although it's pricey, there's no shortage of gasoline to fuel cars and their air conditioners. You can come to Phoenix assured of a cool experience, no matter what time of year.

THE HEAT INDEX

If you're from a part of the country where winter is hard, you're familiar with windchill factors.

The Arizona equivalent is the heat index. You'll hear it in weather reports, and it often is referred to in newspaper weather columns. Basically it is an indicator of humidity. As moisture increases, the air temperature is perceived to be even hotter than it really is. For example, a 90°F day with 60 percent humidity (which sometimes happens during the July and August monsoons) feels like the temperature really is 120°F. But a normal 100°F summer day in Phoenix, with only 10 percent humidity, is felt at just what it is—about 100°F.

Ditat Deus, *or "God Enriches," is the centerpiece of Arizona's state seal, pictured with the state's three main industries—farming, cattle ranching, and mining.*

Statewide, temperatures have a huge variance. A January day in Flagstaff or the Grand Canyon averages about 41°F, while in Phoenix it will be shirtsleeve weather with a temperature averaging about 65°F, easily slipping into the 80s by midafternoon. Flagstaff and the Grand Canyon regularly experience below-freezing temps Nov.–Apr., while Phoenix and Tucson may only occasionally dip below the 32°F mark. Flagstaff has the summer advantage, with averages in the 70s and 80s, while Phoenix averages triple digits for much of June–Sept.

For state weather information visit "The Weather Channel" website: www.weather.com/weather/us/cities/AZ.

Visitor Information

General Information

Individual chambers of commerce and visitor centers are your best source of information for the specific areas you want to see. They're included in the Services section at the end of each chapter. Overall state information and a comprehensive Travel Planner will be sent if, at least four weeks in advance, you contact the **Arizona Office of Tourism, 2702 N. Third St., No. 4015, Phoenix, 85004; 888-520-3444 or 602-230-7733. Website: arizonaguide.com.**

The State of Arizona website, **arizona guide.com,** links you to hundreds of sites within the state. **AccessArizona.com** also has

loads of useful information. Other handy websites are those for Arizona's two major metropolises: the City of Tucson's website is **www.visittucson.org;** the City of Phoenix's website is **www.phoenixcvb.com.**

NATIONAL PARK SERVICE UNITS IN ARIZONA

See the index to locate these parks and monuments in their geographical sections within the book, where addresses and phone numbers are given. Website: **www.nps.gov.**

National Monuments

Canyon de Chelly
Casa Grande Ruins
Chiricahua
Montezuma Castle
Navajo
Organ Pipe Cactus
Pipe Spring
Sunset Crater
Tonto
Tuzigoot
Walnut Canyon
Wupatki

National Parks

Grand Canyon
Petrified Forest
Saguaro

National Historic Sites

Coronado
Fort Bowie
Hubbell Trading Post
Tumacacori

National Recreation Areas

National recreation areas are defined by the lakes and reservoirs they encompass, most of which were created by dams. Lake Mead, on the Arizona–California border, was the first.

Glen Canyon
Lake Mead

STATE PARKS

Arizona has some of the loveliest, best-kept state parks in the country, mainly because the State Lottery system generates adequate funding. Most Arizona state parks charge an entry fee, usually nominal, but if you're traveling as a family, fees can add up. You may purchase a $40 family pass, valid for a year, at the first park you visit or from the **Arizona State Parks Dept., 1300 W. Washington, Phoenix, 85007; 602-542-4174. Website: www.pr.state.az.us.** The State Park Service says it is very important that you call and verify camping availabilities and open hours before setting out, because sites fill up and hours change.

Alamo Lake State Park (near Lake Havasu), P.O. Box 38, Wenden, 85357; phone and fax 520-669-2088.

Boyce Thompson Southwest Arboretum (east of Phoenix), 37615 E. Hwy. 60, Superior, 85273; 520-689-2723, fax 520-689-5858.

Buckskin Mountain State Park (near Lake Havasu), 54751 Hwy. 95, Parker, 85344; 520-667-3231, River Island phone 520-667-3387, fax 520-667-3387.

Catalina State Park, P.O. Box 36986, Tucson, 85740; 520-628-5798, fax 520-628-5797.

Cattail Cove State Park, P.O. Box 1990, Lake Havasu City, 86405; 520-855-1223, fax 520-855-1730.

Dead Horse Ranch State Park, 675 Dead Horse Ranch Rd., Cottonwood, 86326; 520-634-5283.

Fool Hollow Lake State Recreation Area, P.O. Box 2588, Show Low, 85901; 520-537-3680, fax 520-537 4349.

Fort Verde State Historic Park, Box 397, Camp Verde, 86322; 520-567-3275, fax 520-567-4036.

Homolovi Ruins State Park, HC63, Box 5 (Hwy. 87 N.), Winslow, 86047; 520-289-4106, fax 520-289-2021.

Jerome State Historic Park, P.O. Box D, Jerome, 83331; 520-634-5381, fax 520-639-3132.

Kartchner Caverns State Park, I-10 at Benson, Benson, 85602; reservations 520-586-CAVE, Mon.–Fri. 8:00 A.M.–6:00 P.M.

Lake Havasu State Park, 1801 Hwy. 95, Lake Havasu City, 86406; 520-855-2784, fax 520-855-7423.

Lost Dutchman State Park, 6109 N. Apache Trail, Apache Junction, 85219; phone and fax 602-982-4485.

Lyman Lake State Park, P.O. Box 1428, St. Johns, 85936; 520-337-4441, fax 520-337-4649.

McFarland State Historic Park, P.O. Box 109, Florence, 85232; phone and fax 520-868-5216.

Patagonia Lake State Park, P.O. Box 274, Patagonia, 85624; 520-287-6965, fax 520-287-5618.

Picacho Peak State Park, P.O. Box 275, Picacho, 85241; phone and fax 520-466-3183.

Red Rock State Park, HC-02, Box 886, Sedona, 86336; 520-282-6907, fax 520-282-5972.

Riordan State Historic Park, 1300 Riordan Ranch St., Flagstaff, 86001; phone and fax 520-779-4395.

Roper Lake State Park, Route 2, Box 712, Safford, 85546; phone and fax 520-428-6760.

Slide Rock State Park, P.O. Box 10358, Sedona, 86339; 520-282-3034, fax 520-282-0245.

Tombstone Courthouse State Historic Park, P.O. Box 216, Tombstone, 85638; 520-457-3311, fax 520-457-2565.

Tonto Natural Bridge State Park, P.O. Box 1245, Payson, 85638; 520-476-4202, fax 520-476-2264.

Tubac Presidio State Historic Park, P.O. Box 1296, Tubac, 85646; phone and fax 520-398-2252.

Yuma Crossing State Historic Park, 201 N. Fourth Ave., Yuma, 85364; 520-329-0471.

Yuma Territorial Prison State Historic Park, Box 10792, Yuma, 85366; 520-783-4771, fax 520-783-7442.

NATIONAL FOREST UNITS

There are six national forests in Arizona: the Apache-Sitgreaves, Coconino, Kaibab, Coronado, Prescott, and Tonto. Detailed maps of national forests and wilderness areas can be purchased from the U.S. Forest Service's Southwestern Regional Office. For a listing of available maps, including scale and cost, contact USDA Forest Service, Public Affairs Office, 517 Gold Ave. SW, Albuquerque, NM 87102; 505-842-3292. Website: www.fs.fed.us.

Apache-Sitgreaves National Forest

Forest Supervisor, P.O. Box 640, Springerville, 85938; 520-333-4301, TTY 520-333-6292.

Alpine Ranger District, P.O. Box, 4619, Alpine, 85920; 520-339-4384, TTY 520-339-4566.

Chevelon Ranger District, HC 62, Box 600, Winslow, 86047; voice and TTY 520-289-2471.

Clifton Ranger District, HC 1, Box 733, Duncan, 85534; voice and TTY 520-687-1301.

Heber Ranger District, P.O. Box 968, Overgaard, 85933; 520-535-4481.

Lakeside Ranger District, Rural Route 3, Box B-50, Pinetop-Lakeside, 85929; voice and TTY 520-368-5111.

Springerville Ranger District, P.O. Box 760, Springerville, 85938; 520-333-4372, TTY 520-333-6335.

Coconino National Forest

Forest Supervisor, 2323 E. Greenlaw Ln., Flagstaff, 86004; 520- 527-3600.

Beaver Creek Ranger District, HC 64, Box 240, Rimrock, 86335; 520-567-4121.

Blue Ridge Ranger District, HC 31, Box 300 Happy Jack, 86024; 520-477-2255.

Long Valley Ranger District, HC 31, Box 68, Happy Jack, 86024; 520-354-2216.

Mormon Lake Ranger District, 4373 S. Lake Mary Rd., Flagstaff, 86001; 520-774-1147.

Peaks Ranger District, 5075 N. Hwy. 89, Flagstaff, 86004; 520-526-0866.

Sedona Ranger District, P.O. Box 300, Sedona, 86339; 520-282-4119.

Coronado National Forest

Forest Supervisor, Federal Bldg., 300 W. Congress, Tucson, 85701; 520-670-4552.

Douglas Ranger District, 3081 N. Leslie Canyon Rd., Douglas, 85607; 520-364-3468.

Nogales Ranger District, 303 Old Tucson Rd., Nogales, 85621; 520-281-2296.

Safford Ranger District, P.O. Box 709, Safford, 85548; 520-428-4150.

Santa Catalina Ranger District, 5700 N. Sabino Canyon Rd., Tucson, 85750; 520-749-8700.

Sierra Vista Ranger District, 5990 S. Hwy. 92, Hereford, 85615; 520-378-0311.

Kaibab National Forest

Forest Supervisor, 800 S. Sixth St., Williams, 86046; 520-635-8200.

Chalender Ranger District, 501 W. Bill Williams Ave., Williams, 86046; 520-635-2575.

Kaibab Plateau Visitor Center, HC 64, Jacob Lake, 86022; 520-643-7298.

North Kaibab Ranger District, P.O. Box 248, Fredonia, 86022; 520-643-7395.

Tusayan Ranger District, P.O. Box 3088, Tusayan, 86023; 520-638-2443.

USDA Forest Service/City of Williams Visitor Center, 200 Railroad Ave., Williams, 86046; 520-635-4707.

Although it belonged to the Sinagua people, Montezuma's Castle is named for someone else.

Williams Ranger District, Route 1, Box 142, Williams, 86046; 520-635-2633.

Prescott National Forest

Forest Supervisor, 344 S. Cortez St., Prescott, 86303; 520-771- 4700.

Bradshaw Ranger District, 2230 E. Hwy. 69, Prescott, 86301; 520-445-7253.

Chino Valley Ranger District, 735 N. Hwy 89, Chino Valley, 86323; 520-636-2302.

Verde Ranger District, 300 E. Hwy. 260, Camp Verde, 86322; 520-567-4121.

Tonto National Forest

Forest Supervisor, 2324 E. McDowell Rd., Phoenix, 85006; 602-225- 5200.

Cave Creek Ranger District, 40202 N. Cave Creek Rd., Scottsdale 85262; 480-595-3300.

Globe Ranger District, Route 1, Box 33, Globe, 85501; 520-402-6200.

Mesa Ranger District, 26 N. Mac-Donald, Mesa, 85211; 480-379-6446.

Payson Ranger District, 1009 E. Hwy. 260, Payson, 85541; 520-474-7900.

Pleasant Valley Ranger District, P.O. Box 450, Young, 85554; 520-462-4300.

Tonto Basin Ranger District, Hwy. 88, HC 02, Box 4800, Roosevelt, 85545; 520-467-3200.

NATIVE AMERICAN INFORMATION

Native American Tourist Center

The center will send pamphlets, brochures, and information on Native American sites, casinos, and other areas of interest in the state. There are 21 Native American tribes represented in Arizona, with 17 active casinos. There probably will be more, because some tribes have authorized sites but have not yet opened casinos on all of them. Note that when driving on a reservation, road signs may be few and far between. It's best to ask directions. 4130 N. Goldwater Blvd., No. 114, Scottsdale, 85251; 480-945-0771.

Tips for Visitors

Health

Not surprisingly, it's the sun that causes many

of the health problems that visitors to Arizona encounter. **Sunburn** is typical, especially among winter visitors who want to return home with a trademark Arizona tan. Use a lotion with a sun protection factor (SPF) of at least 15 when going outdoors. **Dehydration** is common among hikers, cyclists, and even golfers who, because of the dry climate in which perspiration evaporates quickly, lose fluids before they even realize they're perspiring. Symptoms can be dizziness, lightheadedness, intense thirst, and a general feeling of weakness. If these occur, get into the shade as quickly as possible and drink water. To prevent dehydration, always carry water with you, even if you're just going for a one-hour stroll. Drink before you get thirsty. In addition to air-conditioning, some establishments have misters. For the uninitiated, misters are cooling systems that periodically emit a blast of superfine water vapor that evaporates almost instantly in Arizona's dry air. The cooling effect, sometimes as much as 20°F below the ambient temperature, is instant and refreshing.

Telephones

Phoenix recently activated new area codes: 602 covers Phoenix and the metro area; 480 covers Scottsdale, Mesa, Tempe, Ahwatukee, Chandler, Gilbert, and other communities to the east and south; 623 covers areas mainly west of Central Avenue in Phoenix; and 520 covers regions outside the Phoenix area, including Tucson.

Getting There

By Plane

Phoenix's **Sky Harbor International Airport** is served by 20 major carriers: Aeromexico, Air Canada, Alaska, America West, American, American Trans Air, British Airways, Continental, Delta, Frontier, Mesa, Midwest Express, Northwest/KLM, Scenic, Southwest, Sun Country, Sunrise, TWA, United, and US Airways. The airport is 15 minutes from downtown, and within 15 to 30 minutes of major area hotels and resorts. British Airways has daily nonstop service from Gatwick Airport, and Air Canada

offers daily nonstops to Toronto. From Sky Harbor, many airlines serve Tucson, and there are some that connect from Phoenix to even smaller cities such as Sierra Vista, Page, Lake Havasu, Flagstaff, and Prescott.

By Train

There is no Amtrak service directly to Phoenix; Amtrak discontinued train service to Phoenix in 1996. The Southwest Chief, between Chicago and Los Angeles, stops at Winslow, Flagstaff, and Kingman. The Sunset Limited, between Florida and Los Angeles, serves Benson, Tucson, and Yuma. **Amtrak, 800-872-7245. Website: www.amtrak.com.**

By Car

Arizona is about as car-dependent as it gets. All major rental car companies have offices at or near Sky Harbor International Airport. In addition, check the Yellow Pages once you're here for companies that may have good off-airport car-rental rates. I-40 bisects the northern third of the state east to west, through Flagstaff and Kingman. I-10 bisects the southern third of the state east to west, through Tucson and Phoenix. I-8 connects Yuma to I-10 south of Phoenix; I-17 runs north from Phoenix to I-40 at Flagstaff.

By Bus

Greyhound provides bus service to Phoenix, where the main terminal is located at 2115 E. Buckeye Rd. Suburban stations are in Apache Junction, Chandler, Mesa, and Tempe. For fare and schedule information call **800-231-2222.**

Cybercafes

Cybercafes in Arizona serve up the opportunity to check your e-mail, surf the Web, or just get your computer fixed while you're away. Although many public libraries offer on-line services, the following sites often do it with a bit more atmosphere. For a completely up-to-the-minute list, see this website: **www.cybercafe.com.**

   CyberCafe, **1520 S. Riordan Ranch Rd., Flagstaff; 520-774-0005. Website:**

www.bookmans.com. Located in Bookmans Used Books. Four computers. $3 for 30 minutes.

Den of the Red Bear, 2801 S. Fourth Ave., No. 14, Yuma; 520-344-1415. Website: red-bear.com. A computer store, closed Sun. Two computers. $2 per hour.

Gypsy Java, 3321 E. Bell Rd., Phoenix; 602-404-9779. Website: www.gypsyjava. com. Coffee, board games, friendly atmosphere. Three computers. $9 per hour.

Innhouse Video & Cybercafe, 160 A Coffee Pot Dr., Sedona; 520-282-7368 Website: www.innhousevideo.com. $9 per hour.

Library of Congress, 311 E. Congress St., Tucson; 520-622-2708. Website: www. hotcong.com/libcong/art/cybar_on.gif. Located in the bowels of the Hotel Congress downtown, it claims to be the world's oldest continuously operating cybercafe. $5 per hour.

Netspresso Coffee House, 1949 Beverly, No. C-104, Kingman; 520-692-5277. Website: www.netspresso.com. Full line of gourmet coffee drinks, sandwiches, pastries, desserts. $6 per hour.

Information for Disabled Visitors

In many cases, this guide indicates when a trail or venue is wheelchair-accessible, but in general, Arizona complies with the Americans with Disabilities Act (ADA), and there is no shortage of hotel rooms that can accommodate visitors with various disabilities, from wheelchair users to those who are sight or hearing impaired.

How This Book Is Organized

The Arizona Office of Tourism graciously agreed to share its sensible way of dividing the state. The only change we have made is to single out Tucson as an area all its own. There are eight geographic regions: (1) Northwest and Canyonlands; (2) Northeast and Indian Country; (3) East-

Central—Above and Below the Rim; (4) Central Region; (5) The Valley of the Sun (Phoenix and environs); (6) Tucson Area; (7) Southeast and South-Central—Old West Country; and (8) Arizona's West Coast. Each region is divided into cities or destinations and is decribed in a geographical sequence, in the way one might cover it in a car. Especially in the Phoenix region, which is made up of more than 30 smaller towns and communities, the text is organized in a logical geographical flow.

Because Arizona is an exceptionally fast-growing state, roads are being extended and freeways are being added at a brisk clip. You may be pleasantly surprised to find that a route may extend farther than indicated on the maps in this book.

Major Attractions

These are places or things that most travelers put on their "must-see" list. Often, they've made an area famous and are widely known in and out of the state. Tonto Natural Bridge north of Payson, for example, is studied by geologists from around the world and attracts visitors with its unusual beauty.

Festivals and Events

We have highlighted what we think are the most important events in each area, although there usually are many more. Contact local visitor centers and chambers of commerce for full calendars of events. A statewide calendar also is available from the **Arizona Office of Tourism** at **800-842-8257.**

Outdoor Activities

BICYCLING
Some areas, like Sierra Vista, Sedona, and Tucson, are particularly off-road friendly for **mountain biking.** See Outdoor Activities in those areas for details. Many trails welcome mountain bikers, but riding in wilderness areas is prohibited.

In Tucson and Phoenix there are many bike

lanes designated on city streets for **road cycling**. In addition, you can ride just about anywhere that is safe. Sierra Vista has some interesting road rides, and there are good paved rides in Saguaro National Park in Tucson. Your best bet is to hook up with a local bike shop for information on friendly places to ride.

BIRDING

Southern Arizona is at the northern tip of Mexico's Sierra Madre and the southern end of the Rockies, which accounts for an amazing diversity of bird species. Arizona attracts birders from all over the world who are drawn to the state's southern parts. Wings over Willcox, held in January, celebrates overwintering sandhill cranes. The August Southwest Wings Birding Festival in Sierra Vista includes owl prowls and lectures by Audubon experts. The elegant trogon and a number of flycatchers are among southern Arizona's attractions. A good birding resource is the **Maricopa Audubon Society**. The lengthy recording will answer most of your questions. 480-829-8209, **birding hot line 480-832-8745. Website: www.amug.org/~drowley/mas.** You can also contact the **Tucson Audubon Society website: www.audubon.org/chapter/az/tucson;** and the **White Mountain Audubon Society website: www.audubon.org/chapter/az/whitemtn.**

BOATING

River Rafting and Tubing

Arizona has some great white-water rafting and equally good float trips. Snow runoff flows from the White Mountains into the Salt River in the early spring, creating great conditions, and the Colorado River is legendary. See Outdoor Activities in the Valley of the Sun region (Phoenix and environs) and Grand Canyon chapter for rafting opportunities.

FISHING

The sports section of the Thursday edition of *The Arizona Republic* (Phoenix's morning daily newspaper, sold all over the state) carries a rating of how the fish (and what kinds) are biting at local lakes. Ratings include good, fair, and poor destinations, with comments on which baits are successful, which fish are biting best, where in the lake they're hitting, and what time of day to try for best results. Local lakes that are covered include Alamo, Apache, Bartlett, Canyon, Horseshoe, Pleasant, Roosevelt, Saguaro, and San Carlos Lakes, as well as the Colorado River. It also lists the mountain lakes where anglers can expect to have good luck.

GOLF

Golfing is a huge sport in Arizona. We have listed favorite courses in just about every area, but many more are not mentioned, or there would be no room in this book to mention anything else. For a listing of hundreds of Arizona courses, by area and difficulty, log on to **accessarizona.com** and click on golf.

HIKING

Because so much of Arizona is wide-open space, it is prime territory for hiking. See individual chapters for hikes of varying difficulties, including a spectacular Lost Dutchman Moonlight Hike listed in the Apache Junction chapter.

Although they are used for many types of recreation, state and national parks are usually listed under Hiking within each chapter because most (not the historic ones) offer hiking and backpacking. If you plan to use the parks a lot, check out the **Golden Eagle Passport** that admits the holder and passengers in a private vehicle for $50 a year. The **Golden Age Passport,** available to those 62 and older, is a lifetime entrance pass to most national parks. Both may be purchased at any federal area where an entrance fee is charged. The best way to get information quickly is to go to the National Park Service's official website: **www.nps.gov.** Once you reach it, you may search by name for the park you're interested in, listed above in the General Information section.

HORSEBACK RIDING

Because this is the Old West, of course there are many opportunities to ride. See individual chapters, as well as dude ranches listed under Where to Stay.

SKIING

Arizona's main ski areas—the SnowBowl near Flagstaff in the Coconino National Forest, Sunrise on the White Mountain Apache Reservation, and Mount Lemmon near Tucson—generally get enough snow to have successful seasons. See individual chapters for specifics on downhill and cross-country.

Seeing and Doing

MUSEUMS AND ART GALLERIES

These range from small-town one-room affairs that may be interesting for their local perspective to huge, nationally acclaimed institutions that take a day to explore. Both have merit. We have listed the reasons we like each one and have tried to include enough information for you to make a decision. Galleries are a different matter. A few are listed, but art is so subjective that we hesitate to make any specific recommendations.

SCENIC DRIVES

As with art, what is "scenic" is somewhat subjective, so we've pretty much stuck with pointing out drives that others have designated as scenic. Some are AAA-designated, and others are posted with the attractive little signs that the State of Arizona uses to tell you that what

you're seeing is scenic—whether you think so or not. We love the desert, and so naturally think almost everything here is scenic.

Four-Wheel-Drive and Motorcycle Trips

Though they're not usually called out as separate trips, when a four-wheel-drive vehicle is necessary to travel a particular route, we indicate this.

Arizona is also a great state for motorcycling, and many riders consider this mode of travel about as close to seeing the state from horseback as you can get without actually getting on a horse. In Phoenix, **Western States Motorcycle Tours** rents Harley-Davidson, BMW, and Suzuki motorcycles; stores your extra luggage; and sends you on your way. **9401 N. Seventh Ave., Phoenix, 85021; 602-943-9030. E-mail: members.aol.com/AzMcRent** (this is a really helpful home page that answers your questions quickly and with humor).

Recommended Reading

Western States Motorcycle Tours owner Frank Del Monte has written a helpful 144-page guide called *Motorcycle Arizona!* that lists tours of one day to one week throughout the state. Accompanied by easy-to-read maps and very specific directions, this guide is essential if you're biking the state for the first time. It's available for $9.95 in bookstores, by calling **602-943-9030,** or by visiting the above website.

Where to Stay

Although most of the accommodations in Arizona are very special, some are included simply because they're the only ones in a particular town. In some cases, we refer to the fact that chain accommodations are available, occasionally highlighting one if it provides particularly good services, is an unusual value, or is the best of a limited number of accommodations in a given area.

Besh-Ba-Gowah, a Salado Indian village in Globe, has been partially restored to its A.D. 1450 original state.

HOTELS, MOTELS, AND INNS

Our favorites are the historic hotels, and they

seem to be all over Arizona. From the elegant old Copper Queen in Bisbee to Flagstaff's Weatherford, to the venerable Arizona Biltmore in Phoenix, they run the gamut from a bit dowdy to unsurpassed luxury. There are few youth hostels, and we have listed those we know about. The following scale approximates what a night's lodgings costs based on double occupancy (keep in mind that in popular resort areas, during the main season prices can soar above $400 per night):

$	Less than $25
$$	$25–$50
$$$	$50–$100
$$$$	$100 on up

NATIONAL HOTEL/MOTEL CHAINS
Best Western—800-528-1234. Website: www.bestwestern.com.

Clarion—800-221-2222. Website: www.hotelchoice.com.

Comfort Inn Choice Hotels—800-221-2222. Website: www.hotelchoice.com.

Days Inn—800-325-2525. Website: www.daysinn.com.

Econo-Lodge—800-553-2666. Website: www.econolodge.com.

Hampton Inn—800-426-7866. Website: www.hamptoninn.com.

Holiday Inn—800-465-4329. Website: www.basshotels.com.

Motel 6—800-466-8356. Website: www.motel6.com.

Quality Inn—800-221-2222. Website: www.hotelchoice.com.

Sleep Inn—800-221-2222. Website: www.hotelchoice.com.

Super 8—800-800-8000. Website: www.super8.com.

CAMPING
Campgrounds and RV parks are all over the place. Camping is popular because of the state's mild weather. In most parts you can camp year-round in relative comfort. Many RV parks specialize in accommodating the snowbirds who flock here to escape tough winters elsewhere.

State parks often have great facilities, and many take reservations (see the listing under General Information, above).

There are many ElderHostel programs in Arizona. Check them out by contacting **ElderHostel, 80 Boylston St., Boston, MA 02116; 877-426-8056. Website: www.elderhostel.org.**

There are 12 national forests in the Southwest, six of which are in Arizona. The Apache-Sitgreaves, Coconino, Coronado, Kaibab, Prescott, and Tonto National Forests all lie within state boundaries. For all national forests in Arizona except Kaibab, you can reserve a camp unit that usually has a parking space for a vehicle, table, and fire pit or fireplace. Spaces may be reserved up to 240 days in advance, but you must call at least five days ahead of the time you want to be there. With this number you can reserve a campsite in 24 national forest campgrounds in Arizona: 800-280-2267. Website: www.reserveusa.com.

Recommended Reading
Local author James Tallon's book, *Arizona's 144 Best Campgrounds* (An Arizona Highways Book), has good details on what the sites look like and what else there is to do in each area.

Where to Eat
We've tried to find independently owned family-run restaurants that always are more interesting than the chains. In some areas there isn't much of a choice; it's fast food on the highway or no food at all. But if you take time to pull off the interstates, the chances of chatting with locals while you eat and discovering something new are greatly increased. Meal costs indicated are based on the following categories and are exclusive of beverages, desserts, and tips:

$	Under $5
$$	$5–$10
$$$	$10–$20
$$$$	$20 on up

UTAH

NEVADA

St. George
Littlefield
Colorado City
Kanab
Fredonia
Kaibab Reservation
Pipe Spring National Monument
Jacob Lake
Kaibab National Forest
Mt. Trumbull
Tuweep
Toroweap
Grand Canyon National Park
Supai
Havasupai Reservation
Hualapai Hilltop
Hermits Rest
Phantom Ranch
Desert View
Colorado River
Colorado River
Vermillion Cliffs
Cliff Dwellers Lodge
Glen Canyon Dam
Page
Lake Powell
Bitter Springs
The Gap
Navajo Reservation
Tusayan
Grand Canyon Village
Kaibab National Forest
Cameron
Valle
Wupatki National Monument
Hualapai Reservation
Peach Springs
Seligman
Ash Fork
Williams
Bill Williams Mountain
Kaibab National Forest
Cataract Lake
Humphreys Peak
Lowell Observatory
San Francisco Mts.
Sunset Crater NM
Leupp
Navajo Reservation
Flagstaff
Walnut Canyon NM
Lake Mary
To Winslow
Meteor Crater
Ashurst Lake
Slide Rock SP
Riordan SP
Munds Park
Kinnickinnick Lake
Mormon Lake
Sedona
Red Rock SP
Verde R.
Clarkdale
Jerome
Cotton-wood

Northwest and Canyonlands

N

- National or State Forest
- National Park or Monument
- Indian Reservation
- ▲ State Park
- 🛣 Interstate Highway
- U.S. Highway
- State Highway
- Indian Route

0   10   20   30   40 Miles

Northwest and Canyonlands

A wind-twisted tree tells of decades of weathering on the Grand Canyon's West Rim.

The Arizona Strip

The 3.2 million acres of undeveloped land south of the Utah state line and north of the Grand Canyon is considered the Arizona Strip. This remote, wild, and lovely area in the state's northwest corner is little known and lesser explored, not because of a lack of riches, but because access is difficult. To get to other parts of the state from the strip, you have to drive around either end of the Grand Canyon. It contains eight wilderness areas: Beaver Dam Mountains, Cottonwood Point, Grand Wash Cliffs, Kanab Creek, Mount Logan, Mount Trumbull, Paiute, and Paria Canyon–Vermilion Cliffs. One of the advantages of being so remote is that the Vermilion Cliffs area provides habitat for the California condor (see sidebar in this chapter). The Bureau of Land Management (BLM), the largest landowner in terms of acres, strictly limits development to keep the strip a pristine wilderness. The strip also includes jurisdictions of the National Park Service, National Forest Service, and some Kaibab Indian Reservation land.

Although there are 5,000 miles of open roads, only I-15 (in the uppermost northwest corner of the state) and US 89A (between Page and Fredonia) are paved. Some of the dirt routes seem to meander to nowhere, disappearing into washes, cliffs, and canyons. Driving, however, is the chief means of exploring the Arizona Strip, but you must come prepared because it is a long time between gas stations and eateries. The BLM cautions that the winding, rough, and rocky roads are not appropriate for motor homes and travel trailers. If you're going off the paved roads at all, you should have a four-wheel-drive vehicle. The brown road signs belong to the BLM; the yellow oval ones are county road signs.

For those uninitiated to the strip, the BLM has created Recreation Management Zones ranging from Zone 1, "Scenic and Historic Highways," which directs you to paved highways, to Zone 4, "Primitive Passages," which requires a four-wheel-drive or all-terrain vehicle, with the likelihood of getting help if stranded rated as "very low." Rangers say that being current on road and weather conditions is a must for safety.

If you're thinking about spending time in this area, it's essential to have the Arizona Strip Visitor Map, a detailed chart of tiny roads and obscure places. It's printed on weatherproof stock, so it will take a beating without falling apart. It is available for moderate cost at the BLM Arizona Strip field office (see Services), or in the BLM Phoenix office (see the Phoenix chapter).

The largest community in the Arizona Strip is Fredonia, on Hwy. 389; it has fewer than 1,500 hardy souls and a few low-key motels and eateries that cluster along Main St. To the southeast, at the junction of US 89A and Hwy. 67, is Jacob Lake, a tiny community at an elevation of close to 8,000 feet, which has a population figure that depends on what season it is and who's home. It's the gateway to the Grand Canyon's North Rim. Littlefield, on I-15 in the state's northwest corner, is accessible only by looping north into Utah, then coming southwest.

History

This remote area is little known because access

is difficult. It was one of the last places in Arizona to be inhabited by modern-day people. In 1776 Spanish priests Francisco Dominguez and Silvestre Escalante slogged on foot from Santa Fe, through Colorado to Utah, then back through northern Arizona to Santa Fe. Later, Fredonia was established as a Mormon pioneer community.

Major Attractions

Lees Ferry

About 15 miles below Glen Canyon Dam, this historic town is the jumping-off point for river-rafting trips through the Grand Canyon and for backpackers hiking the Paria Canyon Primitive Area. A dozen or so companies offer white-water trips on the Colorado River through the canyon. The May–Sept. season is heavily booked for these three- to eight-day motorized and oar trips. Check the Grand Canyon National Park website: **www.nps.gov/grca.**

Nampaweap Petroglyph Site

You have to walk about 0.5 mile from the parking area, but it's worth it to see hundreds of boulders covered with thousands of rock art images along a 0.5-mile basalt cliff. There are no services, but hiking is not terribly difficult. Located about 55 miles southeast of St. George, Utah (on I-15), off a gravel road (BLM Rd. 1069 or County Rd. 5) that goes through Wolf Hole to the Mount Trumbull area. Roads from Pipe Spring National Monument and Colorado City (on Hwy. 389) also lead to the site, but a good map is essential.

Pipe Spring National Monument

One of the least-known national monuments, Pipe Spring is an oasis named for its four springs. Native Americans and Mormon settlers were attracted by the springs and the grasslands that once were here. The remains of a Mormon cattle

> ### Getting There
> The Fredonia–Vermilion Cliffs Scenic Rd. is generally considered the entrance to the Arizona Strip. From the Navajo community of Bitter Springs on US 89 south of Lee's Ferry, it follows US 89A past magnificent Echo Cliffs to Fredonia, 85 miles to the west near the Utah state line.

ranch and a historic fort, Winsor Castle, provide a taste of pioneer life. The visitor center is open daily 8:00 A.M.–4:30 P.M. Oct.–May; 7:30 A.M.–3:30 P.M. June–Sept. Except Christmas, Thanksgiving, and New Year's days. Located 14 miles west of Fredonia. **520-643-7105.** Website: **www.nps.gov.**

Seeing and Doing

Historic Sites

Dominguez-Escalante

At a roadside turnoff, interpretive signs explain the grueling journey undertaken by Spanish priests in 1776. There are trailheads for a number of hiking and equestrian trails, and a picnic area, but no services or water. Located about 21 miles east of Jacob Lake off US 89A, near Paria Canyon and the Vermilion Cliffs Wilderness.

Scenic Drives

The Fredonia–Vermilion Cliffs Scenic Rd.

From Bitter Springs on US 89 south of Lees Ferry, this route follows US 89A 85 miles to the west near the Utah state line. Approximately 3 miles south of Lees Ferry, you cross the historic Navajo Bridge at Marble Canyon. It has been converted to a pedestrian bridge, with cars now using a larger and stronger bridge, completed in 1997. The Navajo Bridge is famous for the views it provides of the Colorado River

The Arizona Strip is known for its remote wilderness areas.

almost 500 feet below. Stop at the **Navajo Bridge Interpretive Center** at the west end of the bridge for more great views and information. It has rest rooms and a large patio. The route passes through the Vermilion Cliffs area, where condors recently have been released (see Wildlife Viewing and sidebar), and continues on to House Rock Valley, a wide grassland where elk, antelope, and bison frequently are spotted. At Jacob Lake, US 89A connects to Hwy. 67, which leads south to the Grand Canyon's North Rim. From Jacob Lake the road begins to climb with a series of sometimes unnerving switchbacks to the heavily forested Kaibab Plateau, leading to Fredonia.

Wildlife Viewing

Condors

On the brink of extinction, these magnificent birds are getting a new lease on life in the Vermilion Cliffs area of the Arizona Strip. The gigantic grayish-brown creatures are the largest land birds in North America, with a wingspan of more than 9 feet and body weight of 17 to 24 pounds. Although condors were last sighted in the Arizona wilds in 1924, condor bones that date back 11,000 years have been found near the Vermilion Cliffs. It seems a natural site for releasing condors today.

In 1987 the last free-flying condors were captured in an attempt to save the species. There were just 27 birds remaining. Programs rebuilt the population so that in 1997, 15 condors were released in the Vermilion Cliffs area. As of this writing, 27 are still flying high, not all of them part of the original group. Each bird wears a tiny transmitter so that biologists can track it, not just for research but for the bird's safety. Their social nature encourages them to readily accept human handouts, an event that may encourage them not to return to the wilds. The closer condors are to civilization, the greater the danger of encounters with power lines and other hazards. The Vermilion Cliffs provide young condors with the good thermals critical for their flight development. Also, the cliffs are pockmarked with caves and ledges for roosting and nesting.

Visitors can drive dirt roads and hike the area, high-powered binoculars poised for possible sightings. Often the condors may be seen from the pullout parking places along US 89A between Lees Ferry and House Rock Valley Rd. Rangers say that travel off the highway is unnecessary and ill advised. See also the sidebar at the end of this chapter.

Where to Stay

Hotels and motels with varying degrees of comfort are located in Mesquite, Nevada (on I-15), at Jacob Lake and Fredonia, and in St. George, Utah (also on I-15). You'll find a few motels and restaurants in Littlefield as well. The **Crazy Jug Motel** (520-643-7753) in Fredonia is open all year, but its restaurant closes Nov.–Mar. The **Jacob Lake Inn** (520-643-7232) offers basic motel rooms year-round, and cabins during the summer.

Condors

These birds do not generally fit the romantic notion of endangered species, like the enormous gray whale, elegant peregrine falcon, or diminutive spotted owl. The huge red-headed vulture is ugly, it feasts on carrion, and so far efforts to re-introduce it to the wilds have consumed more than $20 million in federal, state, and local funding. Animal lovers maintain, however, that there is much romanticism in the great bird's soaring, graceful flight and its inquisitive, gregarious nature. Its feathers and bones have been a part of legend and ceremony within Indian mythology for generations. And scientists point out there is still so much we don't know about the world's creatures that it is foolish to think that any of them are disposable.

Those who remember seeing condors in the wild attest to the fact that they rely on soaring, rather than flapping, flight. A condor roosts in a spot where it can launch itself easily with just a few wing beats, using uplifting winds along mountain ridges to stay aloft. Graceful spiraling means that the bird is using a warm thermal updraft to gain altitude, after which it can glide for long distances before seeking another uplifting thermal.

Condors raise only one young every other year from a single pale aqua-colored egg placed in a remote cave, sheltered outcrop, or crevice on a cliff. No nesting material is added. Baby condors develop slowly, not perfecting flying skills until they're almost a year old. Parents may continue to feed a chick for more than a year. Condors do not breed until age five or six.

To find likely spots for seeing condors, check out the California Condor Notes from the Field, website: **www.peregrinefund.org/notes_condor.html.** A chatty narrative traces each bird by number, so soon you feel you know them as individuals. The release of the condors is a joint project of The Peregrine Fund, the U.S. Fish and Wildlife Service, the BLM, and the Arizona Game and Fish Department. For more information contact **The Peregrine Fund, 566 W. Flying Hawk Ln., Boise, ID 83709; 800- 377-3708 or (208) 362-3716.** See also Wildlife Viewing in this chapter.

Camping

Backcountry camping in undeveloped areas without a permit is allowed for a total of 14 days. The only full-service campground, with 75 developed sites, is in the **Virgin River Canyon Recreation Area**, about 20 miles southwest of St. George in Arizona's far northwest corner. Located between the Paiute and Beaver Dam Mountains Wilderness Areas, set deep down in the gorge's multicolored walls, the campground has rest rooms, a picnic area, drinking water, showers, a dump station, electrical hookups, hiking trails, canoeing, and fishing in the Virgin River. You might have to wade across the river to get to some of the trails. Fee for overnight camping. Located just off I-15 where it cuts briefly across Arizona between St. George, Utah, and Mesquite, Nevada, before you reach the town of Littlefield.

Services

BLM Arizona Strip Field Office

The office is located in St. George, Utah, about 5 miles north of the Arizona border. There is no Strip office in Arizona because there is no town to house employees and provide support services for the office. Open Mon.–Fri., 8:00 A.M.–5:00 P.M.; Sat., 9:00 A.M.–4:00 P.M. 345 E. Riverside Dr., St. George, UT 84790; (435) 688-3200.

Page and Lake Powell

Page is a Main Street town with a tidy, new look. A grassy city park, just behind the Chamber of Commerce office, provides a pleasant picnic place, alive with glossy black ravens that eye your lunch hopefully but keep a respectful distance. On Lake Powell Boulevard, "Church Row" is a ribbon of 11 places of worship, created when each congregation was offered a free plot of ground if it would build a church.

From an elevation of 4,300 feet on Manson Mesa, Page overlooks Glen Canyon Dam and Lake Powell. While some consider its landscape bleak, others find majestic beauty in its sweeping vistas and low vegetation. During June, July, and Aug., high temperatures hover in the 90s, retreating to the chilly 40s and 50s in Jan. and Feb. Summer is high season here, but many visitors prefer the serene and sunny days of May and Oct., free of the frenzy of kids out of school.

Glen Canyon Bridge, 700 feet above the Colorado River, offers a good view of the Glen Canyon Dam. When it opened in 1959, the bridge cut the driving distance from one side of the canyon to the other by 197 miles. With 250 square miles of blue water, Lake Powell, the reservoir created by the dam, is a maze of backwater canyons, quiet bays, and tiny inlets. It is 186 miles long and has 1,986 miles of shoreline and 96 water-filled side canyons. It took until 1980 to fill the lake to its capacity, which puts its glossy surface 3,700 feet above sea level. Maximum depth at the dam is 560 feet. Lake Powell's easy-to-take, 75°F summer water temp dips as low as 42°F in winter, its sheer mass keeping it warm enough to prevent freeze-over.

From the vantage point of a boat, great cliffs rise as much as 400 feet from the water's surface. Gray waterlines on canyon walls mark the lake's ever-changing level. High and low watermarks can have a 90-foot spread. What look like ancient hieroglyphics really are the marks of erosion. At one point, man-made cutouts in the rock, called Prospector's Steps or Miner's Stairs, rise from the water's edge, remnants of days when the canyon was mined. Two flights are visible. Locals say there are an additional four flights underwater that reach down to what was the canyon floor before the lake was filled. "Navajo tapestry" is the term given to the intricate stains on the canyon walls. Porous sandstone absorbs the colors created by minerals such as iron (red), manganese (black), and calcium (white) to create the rich patterns.

History

Glen Canyon dates back 310 million years, a history that can be traced visually through the layers of sandstone that make up its walls. During the Cretaceous period, which began 135 million years ago, the sandstone cliffs on the canyon's north edge were formed, as were layers of tropic shale that bear fossil oysters, snails, sharks, and other sea life. They confirm that Lake Powell is not the first body of water to fill the canyon.

The canyon's earliest residents were prehistoric Indians who hunted the plentiful bison and mammoth that lived here 11,000 years ago. By 200 B.C., as the climate became drier, the Anasazi moved in and began to cultivate corn. These resourceful people left evidence of their culture in baskets, pottery, and ruins that include Defiance House, located in the lake's Forgotten Canyon in Utah. Major John Wesley Powell, a Civil War veteran, explored the Colorado River in the late 1800s; the lake created by Glen Canyon Dam was named after him. For decades the canyon was undisturbed except for a few gold prospectors and adventurous river runners.

In 1956 the U.S. Congress authorized the Bureau of Reclamation to build a dam on the Colorado River to supply water to the lower basin states of California, Arizona, and Nevada. A construction camp was established to house workers. By the time the Glen Canyon Dam was completed in 1965, the camp, now known as Page, was an established city and the gateway to a new aquatic playground. Page is named for John C. Page, a past commissioner of the Bureau of Reclamation who oversaw the construction of Hoover Dam. On a map Page and Lake Powell, a dot and a spidery patch of blue, respectively, hang across the middle of Arizona's border with Utah; they have a population of about 8,200, a figure that swells considerably during pleasant summer months when visitors come to enjoy water activities.

Major Attractions

Glen Canyon National Recreation Area

Everything that happens out of doors near Page happens in this enormous park. Established in 1972 as part of the national park system, it cov-

---

Getting There

Page is about 280 miles north of Phoenix and 125 miles north of Flagstaff on US 89. Most visitors make the easy drive by private car. By air, Great Lakes Air serves Page from Phoenix. During summer months, Scenic Airlines operates a daily flight from Las Vegas, Nevada, to Page. Other airlines offer service seasonally.

---

ers more than 1 million acres. Glen Canyon is the center point of the Grand Circle, an ecological aggregate of seven national parks and seven national monuments, as well as state parks and historic sites that encompass Indian ruins and geologic formations. National Park Service rangers are at most marinas, ready to answer questions. Vegetation in the recreation area is brushy, consisting of junipers and piñon pines at higher elevations, with yucca and prickly pear cactus farther down. Seeps or springs from overhanging cliffs sometimes support gardens of maidenhair fern, monkey flower, and (watch out!) poison ivy. Red-tailed hawks, ravens, and peregrine falcons catch thermals near cliffs. Seldom seen, but in the area, are bighorn sheep and bobcats. You're more likely to catch a glimpse of a coyote or deer as you hike the area. **Glen Canyon National Recreation Area, P.O. Box 1507, Page, 86040; 520-608-6404 general information, 520-608-6200 headquarters. Website: www.nps.gov/glca.**

Glen Canyon Dam

This massively impressive 710-foot wall of concrete, crossing a deep sandstone gorge, holds back the mighty Colorado River. It is the last of eight dams built on the river. The site was chosen because the reservoir basin could safely hold an enormous amount of water, the canyon walls and bedrock foundation were strong and stable, and nearby Wahweap Creek supplied good rock and sand for making concrete aggregate. Power produced at the dam is sold to hundreds of cities

Lake Powell's Gunsight Bay has a gently sloping beach so houseboats may nudge up to land for easy shoreside exploration and picnicking. Boats that sleep as many as 12 are for rent, completely furnished.

in a six-state area. Much of it goes south for the summer to run air conditioners and to pump water for irrigation. In winter months the power goes north to help supply heating loads. Free self-guided tours of the dam and power plant take about 30–45 minutes. Scheduled guided tours that descend 53 stories into the dam are offered during the summer. Pick up a tour booklet at the **Carl Hayden Visitor Center, P.O. Box 1507, Page, 86040; 520-608-6404.**

Rainbow Natural Bridge

About 8 land miles north of the Arizona-Utah border and approximately 50 lake miles north of Wahweap Marina, it is the world's tallest known natural bridge. It was featured in a 1909 *National Geographic* and by the following year it was declared a national monument. The bridge remained relatively obscure until Lake Powell was filled in 1963, but today is one of the lake's most popular sites. Its 275-foot span arches to 290 feet, created over the centuries by a swift-flowing stream, forcing its way to the Colorado from Navajo Mountain. The best way to see this

amazing sandstone formation is by water, either on a five-hour tour (see Tours under Seeing and Doing) or in a private boat. You disembark on a sturdy floating dock, and from there it is an easy 0.25-mile walk to the bridge. The inspiring spectacle has deep spiritual meaning to Native Americans. Please be respectful, and do not walk under the bridge or beyond the viewing area.

Festivals and Events

Page Attacks Trash/Earth Day

mid-Apr.

More than 4,000 residents and visitors spread out over Page and clean up the town, then come back to the central park to collect their T-shirt reward. Anti-trashers feast on barbecue provided by Salt River Project, the local utilities company, and cooked by the Elks Club. It's such an event that former President George Bush declared it one of his Points of Light. **520-645-6210.**

Lake Powell Air Affaire

early Oct.

Billed as "The Best Little Air Show" in the Southwest, past celebrations have featured the Canadian Snowbirds, the Canadian Air Force's nine-plane precision jet team, as well as the U.S. Navy Leap Frog parachute team. Wing walkers, hot-air balloons, radio-controlled models, and more are part of this two-day event. Spectators sprawl in bleachers and rental chairs, slathered with sunscreen and protected with brimmed hats. 520-645-9373.

Outdoor Activities

Bicycling

Within the national recreation area, bicycles are permitted only on established trails and roads. An excellent park map and guide is available at the Carl Hayden Visitor Center, where helpful rangers will point you in the right direction to find the best trails for riding. The center is located at Glen Canyon Dam. **Carl Hayden Visitor Center, P.O. Box 1507, Page, 86040; 520-608-6404.**

Boating

HOUSEBOATING

Houseboating and Lake Powell were made for each other, and in fact there are more than 500 of the floating condos available for rent, some of which are handicapped-accessible. The lake's placid waters sometimes are upset by testy weather, so boaters have to be alert for the occasional storm that brings high winds and ocean-force waves. A good navigational map is essential for quick access to the closest arm as a protective retreat. These secluded inlets also make it possible for boaters to stay fairly remote even in the middle of summer. Much of the fun is simply anchoring for an on-deck barbecue, then watching stars appear in a smog-free sky.

A rock formation creates a natural frame for a couple enjoying some solitude on the shores of Lake Powell.

Usually several couples or families get together to rent a houseboat, not only for the camaraderie but in order to have more than one boat driver. Houseboats can be as long as 59 feet with bunks for 12. Full briefings are held before anyone is allowed out on the lake. Piloting, navigating, docking, anchoring, refueling, and pumping out are essential skills that must be learned.

Houseboats may be rented for as few as two days during the off-season Oct.–mid-May, but three-day minimums are usual the rest of the year. Most houseboaters rent a tag-along powerboat for water skiing or exploring places too small to accommodate the houseboat. If you're thinking about renting a houseboat during summer months, book as far ahead as possible. Some categories of boats are reserved during peak seasons up to a year in advance. For reservations call **Lake Powell Resorts & Marinas, 520-645-2433.**

Marinas

Although most of the Glen Canyon Recreation Area is in Utah, one of its most important jumping-off points is **Wahweap Marina (520-645-2433)**, the largest of the lake's five marinas, 6 miles north of Page. Here you can rent houseboats and powerboats, fuel up, and find fishing and water sports gear, groceries, and general merchandise. Wahweap Lodge is a top-notch place to overnight (see Where to Stay) and the center of marina activities.

Bullfrog Resort & Marina (435-684-3000), **Halls Crossing Marina (435-684-7000)**, and **Hite Marina (435-684-2278)** are in Utah. You may find yourself stopping at any of them if you're cruising the lake.

Dangling Rope Marina (520-645-2969) has an Arizona area code because it is in the middle of Lake Powell and gets its calls by cellular phone, but it is in Utah, about 40 miles up the lake from Wahweap. Accessible only by boat, it offers a year-round gas dock and pump-out station.

KAYAKING

Lake Powell is a great place for this shore-hugging sport because it has close to 2,000 miles of shoreline. Best time to paddle is Sept.–May, when boat traffic is at a minimum yet the weather is reliably sunny. Many places have kayak rentals, including **Twin Finn Dive Center** (see Diving).

RIVER RAFTING

There's no white water on this last undammed section of the Colorado that winds south from Glen Canyon Dam. Usually a leisurely 15-mile float, it meanders past ancient Anasazi petroglyphs, affording great views of the Colorado's handiwork as it carved the canyon out of high desert plateaus. Sandstone cliffs hunker 2,400 feet above river level. Half-day and all-day (with lunch) tours are available. A number of companies do full motor and oar trips that range from four to 12 days. **Wilderness River Adventures** does seven- or eight-day oar and motor trips that cover 188 miles. **P.O. Box 717, Page, 86040; 800-992-8022 or 520-645-3296. Website: www.riveradventures.com.** To book tours with a number of companies, contact **Rivers & Oceans , P.O. Box 40321, Flagstaff, 86004; 800-473-4576 or 520-526-4575.**

Diving

Those accustomed to Caribbean diving may find Lake Powell's dive sites a tad under-whelming, while others really get into the austere beauty of underwater pinnacles and sheer vertical walls. It is definitely worth at least a onetime dive, just for comparison's sake. These are altitude dives, so take that into consideration when calculating depth and time limits. Even beginning divers can wade into the water from a gently sloped shoreline to look at rock formations, walls, cracks, crevices, cliffs, and an amazing array of articles dropped from boats (see the sidebar Tracking the Trash in this chapter). Sagebrush, blown into the water, replaces the coral reefs of the Caribbean. Local fish that reliably swim into view include smallmouth bass, bluegill, crappie, walleye, catfish, and striped bass. Shad, the small inch-long feeder fish that provide meals for larger species, are especially spectacular on a night dive when they come close to shore in huge schools. For boat dives, **Navajo Canyon** has good year-round visibility. **Antelope Island** has easy access. Visibility can be as little as 7 feet in warmer water near the surface, with 60–80 feet of visibility usual at cooler depths during late fall and early spring when water temps are around 55–60°F. Wet or dry suits are a definite requirement. For truly hardy souls, drift diving in the Colorado River below the Glen Canyon Dam is available year-round. For information and gear rental contact **Twin Finn Dive Center, P.O. Box 4780, 811 Vista Ave., Page, 86040; 520-645-3114. Website: www.twinfinn.com.**

Fishing

Lake Powell attracts anglers after largemouth, smallmouth, and striped bass, as well as walleye, pike, and scrappy little bluegill and crappie. There always seems to be a local tournament in progress, which is not surprising considering the great fishing on the lake and on the river below the dam. You must have an Arizona fishing license, as well as a Utah license if you plan to fish farther north. Purchase them at marina stores (see Boating).

Bubba's Guide Service offers a nine-hour fishing day to pursue largemouth, smallmouth, or striped bass and includes a guide, bass boat and gas, bait and tackle, lunch, and soft drinks. **P.O. Box 3778, Page, 86040; 520-645-5785.**

Golf

Glen Canyon Golf and Country Club
The older nine-hole Glen Canyon course has been around for more than 30 years. Playable and open to the public all year, daily. Greens fees take a drop Oct.–Mar. Tee times, recommended, are given seven days in advance. **Adjacent to the Marriott. Glen Canyon Golf and Country Club, 520-645-2715.**

Lake Powell National Golf Course
The new 18-hole National course brings total available holes to 27. The new course is a masterpiece of planning, incorporating the best of natural surroundings. It is set picturesquely on rolling dunes overlooking Lake Powell, with views so spectacular it's hard to keep an eye on the ball and off the vistas. Some golfers come here just to play what's billed as the "longest and steepest hole in the Southwest." Four tees on each hole cater to a variety of skill levels. It has a pro shop, restaurant, and grill. Playable and open to the public all year, daily. Greens fees take a drop Oct.–Mar. Tee times, recommended, are given seven days in advance. **Adjacent to the Marriott. Lake Powell National Golf Course, 520-645-2023.**

Hiking

Glen Canyon provides many areas for brief strolls, challenging day hikes, and multiday backpack forays. It can be tough going, however, because it is a slickrock area with few marked trails. But orienteering is made somewhat easier because the lake often is in view.

Nonetheless, hikers should be proficient with a compass and should have a good updated map, available from the **National Park Service (520-608-6404)** or at the **Carl Hayden Visitor Center** (see Services). Best hiking months are Mar.–June and Sept.–Oct. In summer, water may be scarce so carry your own. If you drink found water, boil or treat it first because it may contain *Giardia*. Gnats and flies can be a problem in spring, so bring repellent.

The Horseshoe Bend View
This 0.75-mile moderate day hike winds to a spectacular view of the Colorado River as it makes a looping curve around a sandstone escarpment. Starts at milepost 545 on US 89.

Wiregrass Canyon
A mellow 3-mile hike (it gets hot in summer, so do it early in the morning), it traces an easy-to-follow wash, passing a little natural bridge, balanced rocks, and small arches. Side canyons offer good exploring. If there's a storm brewing, rethink your hike, because flash floods have been known to gush through the canyon. The trailhead is 10 minutes north of Glen Canyon Dam. From Page, follow US 89 to Big Water, Utah, turn right onto Hwy. 277, then right onto Hwy. 12 and go 4.5 miles south on Warm Creek Rd. Park where you see the sign "Wiregrass Canyon Backcountry."

Swimming

Lake Powell is considered swimmable June–Oct., and terrific in Aug. when the average water temperature is close to 80°F. Be careful when swimming or diving because the water level frequently fluctuates. When it is particularly low, submerged salt cedar (tamarisk) trees and cactuses become formidable deadheads. A 0.5-mile-long beach west of Wahweap Lodge is open to the public.

Water Skiing

Lake Powell's placid surface is ideal for water skiing. It is prohibited in marked channels with

Sun-warmed canyon walls at Lake Powell form a dramatic background for a runabout heading home.

heavy boat traffic and in narrow side canyons. Boats and equipment can be rented at many local shops (see Boating).

Seeing and Doing

Museums

John Wesley Powell Memorial Museum

At this museum in downtown Page, you can not only check out history, but make reservations for lake, river, air, and ground tours and get general visitor information. Greeting visitors on the front lawn is an oversized, yet accurately scaled, replica of the long boat used by John Wesley Powell on his rugged and grueling exploration of the Colorado River. The boat was featured in the Disney movie *Ten Who Dared.* The area's past is illustrated in a sequence of black-and-white archival photos from the days when the river was first explored.

The museum includes Powell's family history, his adventures exploring the Colorado, along with Indian artifacts and an explanation of the canyon's geologic structure. If you don't think your camera adequately captured the grandeur of Antelope Canyon, professional photographs are available here along with a good selection of books on the area. Nominal fee. Open Mon.–Fri. 9:00 A.M.– 5:00 P.M. Located at the corner of **Lake Powell Blvd. and N. Navajo, P.O. Box 547, Page, 86040; 888-597-6873 or 520-645-9496. Website: www.powellmuseum.org.**

Nightlife

Ken's Old West Dining and Dancing, the local hangout, is so crowded most nights that you can't even get in. The rustic, wood-front place usually has a country western band. Locals recommend the steaks and prime rib. 718 **Vista, Page;** 520-645-5160.

Tracking the Trash

Anytime there's an aggregate of humanity at a special site, it's to be expected that a certain percentage of visitors will be insensitive to the garbage, refuse, trash, waste, and debris that they leave behind. At Lake Powell, sudden gusts of wind can carry unsecured hats and towels into the lake, and items accidently dropped from boats find their way to sandy shores. They end up as unsightly, unwelcome intrusions on an area that should be scenic and unspoiled.

Enter the Trash Tracker. This well-equipped houseboat scours the lake on 26 weekly trips each year, staffed by volunteers who devote their days to corralling the visitor-generated junk that mars the lake's lovely beaches. Golf balls, swimsuits, towels, shotgun shells, cans and bottles, motor parts, even barbecue grills, baby pacifiers, and coins are among the "treasures" that the volunteers stuff into huge biodegradable garbage bags. Each volunteer has a "quota" of five bags per day. They often fill more.

The Tracker leaves from Wahweap Marina, towing the Eliminator (a bargelike craft in which retrieved refuse is stored) and a small runabout for forays away from the "mother ship." Volunteers, usually four per trip, plus a captain who doubles as a guide, sleep in bunks and share a head (bathroom). Each volunteer brings a sleeping bag and some groceries and assumes cooking duties for one night.

The privately funded program is a huge asset to the underfunded National Park Service, which otherwise is charged with lake cleanup. Lake Powell Resorts and Marinas provides the houseboat, pilot, and trash barge, with other donators picking up the tab for trash bags and motors. Volunteers work hard and should come prepared with hats, gloves, sunscreen, hiking boots, and long pants. Days are spent on the pick-up brigade, but evenings allow plenty of time for comparing the day's finds, relaxing, and enjoying the lake.

The Trash Tracker makes 26 runs Apr.–Nov. each year. The program is enormously popular and takes just four volunteers per trip. Each must be 18 years old (many are seniors), and in good enough shape to bend, lift, and walk in summer temps that can top 100°F. Volunteer applications are considered on July 15 for the following year. Don't be surprised if there is a waiting list of a year or more, although last-minute cancellations do happen. You're welcome to join if you can do so at a moment's notice. For more information, and to apply, contact **Trash Tracker Coordinator, Glen Canyon National Recreation Area, P.O. Box 1507, Page, 86040; 520-608-6404.**

Windy Mesa Bar has some of the best entertainment, varying from country to reggae to pop. Sunday is jam night. Pool tables and pinball machines keep an eclectic clientele entertained. **800 N. Navajo Dr., Page; 520-645-2186.**

Gunsmoke Saloon offers dining, dancing, and cocktails. During prime tourist months, May–Oct., a country and western music show is presented nightly. At 9:00 P.M. the saloon turns into a nightclub. Adjacent to **The Dam Bar and Grille,** which offers good steaks and seafood in a setting that's a sort of shrine to Glen Canyon Dam. An etched-glass dam and a 60-foot-by-5-foot replica of the dam graces one wall. 644 N. Navajo, Page; 520-645-2161 **dinner reservations or 520-645-1888 show reservations. Website: www.damplaza.com.**

Scenic Drives

FOUR-WHEEL-DRIVE TRIPS

Antelope Canyon

One of the most photographed (and most difficult to photograph) spots in the area, Antelope Canyon, also called Slot and Corkscrew Canyon, is a cavelike passage of petrified sand that winds for 0.5 mile. Formed when rushing water swirled and curled through the soft pink sandstone to pour onto the canyon floor, it is a shadowy, ethereal place where the temperature stays about 70°F even during the heat of summer. Water-sculpted rock, impregnated with quartz crystals, reflects shafts of sunlight, creating ever-shifting rainbows and deep blue shadows. Clearly outlined against the sky 150 feet above the canyon floor, the formations called Weeping Eye and Eagles Head need no explanation.

Although the corkscrew portion covers barely 0.25 mile, the canyon itself extends more than 25 miles from Lake Powell. Bring a flashlight for the darkest parts. May–July are the best times to photograph because the sun is high enough to shine down inside the canyon. The jeep trip leaves from downtown Page and heads past six steaming strobe-lighted stacks on the horizon, belonging to the 2,250-megawatt Navajo Generating Station. So much coal is produced on the Navajo and Hopi Reservations that much of it is transported 275 miles to Laughlin, Nevada, through a unique coal and water slurry pipeline. Where the jeep leaves paved Hwy. 98 for the canyon turnoff, members of the Navajo tribe staff the gate into the canyon. You must be with a licensed guide to go into the canyon. No private hikers or autos are allowed. At the end of 3.5 miles of shifty, sandy road, jeep tracks end at the canyon's mouth and you'll begin your stroll. This spot was in the news in August 1997 when 11 hikers were killed by a flash flood that swept through it. If there is rain anywhere in the area, postpone your trip. Companies with permits to tour the canyon include **Lake Powell Jeep Tours, 104 S. Lake Powell Blvd., P.O. Box 1144, Page, 86040; 520-645-5501. Website:** www.jeeptour. com. For more information on tours and other Lake Powell goings-on, go to their website: **www.canyon-country.com.**

Tours

BOAT TOURS

Canyon King

This 95-foot paddle wheeler makes one-hour rides from Wahweap Marina to Castle Rock and nearby sights. Some cruises include dinner. Other half- and all-day boat trips explore remote and beautiful canyons at a leisurely pace. For information and reservations call **Wahweap Boat Tours, 520-645-2741 or 520-645-2433.**

Rainbow Natural Bridge

Approximately 50 lake miles north of Wahweap Marina, this national monument (see Major Attractions) is visited on a five-hour tour. Along the way, as your tour boat traverses the lake, you'll see natural rock sculptures that include Sleeping Indian and Eighteen Wheeler. On Antelope Island there are no antelope even though the National Park Service wanted to introduce them. They discovered that vegetation on the island is insufficient to support a herd. You disembark on a sturdy floating dock, from where it is an easy 0.25-mile walk to the bridge. Tours leave from **Wahweap Marina, 800-528-6154 or 520-645-2741 for reservations.**

Where to Stay

Hotels, Motels, and Inns

With the exception of Wahweap Lodge, all of Page's motels are in about a 3-mile radius. During summer months, reservations are a must. In the winter, if they stay open, most motels cut their rates by about half. Days Inn, two Best Westerns, Holiday Inn Express, Super 8, Ramada, Motel 6, Comfort Inn, and Econo-Lodge are all on US 89 or within the city.

Wahweap Marina at Lake Powell shelters houseboats against cliffs warmed by the evening sun.

Courtyard by Marriott—$$$-$$$$

This attractive place definitely is a number of notches above the basic small-town motel. The territorial adobe-look hostelry offers lovely canyon, golf course, or lake views from the balcony of each of its 153 rooms. The Southwest-style lobby has a huge fireplace and massive mission furnishings that invite settling in to watch the flames. A workout room and heated outdoor pool and whirlpool are welcome amenities. A well-stocked gift shop carries sundries and reading material. In-room coffee means you don't have to traipse to the restaurant for your morning caffeine jolt. Rates June–Sept. are highest, going down during low season Nov.–June. **600 Clubhouse Dr., P.O. Box 4128, Page, 86040; 800-851-3855 or 520-645-5000.**

Wahweap Lodge—$$$-$$$$

This is Arizona's only resort on the shores of Lake Powell, offering great lake views from many of its 350 rooms. The fine-dining Rainbow Room and Itza Pizza, open summer months only (see Where to Eat), make it possible for you never to have to leave the resort and marina for your entire stay. Rooms are comfortable and well furnished, ideal base camps for exploring the area. Higher rates prevail Apr.–Oct., falling Nov.–Mar. **100 Lake Shore Dr., Page, 86040; 520-645-2433 or reservations 800-528-6154.**

Hostels

Lake Powell International Hostel—$-$$

As its name implies, in this friendly place you'll rub elbows with an interesting international clientele. Accommodations, in three different buildings, can handle up to about 100 guests at a time. On warm summer evenings, everyone's out playing volleyball and badminton, and making plans for the next day's hikes. There are bunks in dorms, private rooms, and a few private suites, all with linens furnished. Coffee and tea are always available, and guests can use a number of complete kitchens and an outdoor cooking area. 141 **Eighth Ave., P.O. Box 1077, Page, 86040; 520-645-3898.**

Camping

Camp just across the border in Utah, or anywhere on BLM land north of Glen Canyon Dam and west of US 89. You can camp almost anywhere in Glen Canyon National Recreation Area except within 1 mile of the marinas and Lees Ferry, or at Rainbow Bridge National Monument.

Lake Powell Resorts and Marinas Wahweap RV Park

Full utility hookups are available all year, along with water, groceries, rest rooms, showers, a coin-operated laundry, and LP gas. No reservations needed in winter, but they are essential during the summer. Located **at Wahweap Marina. 800-528-6154.**

Wahweap Campground

Great vistas and proximity to water-based activities attract swarms of folks during summer months, who quickly fill the 180 spaces here. Open mid-Mar.–Oct. for dry camping with no hookups. On the **shores of Lake Powell. P.O. Box 1597, Page, 86040; 520-645-1004.**

Where to Eat

If you're putting together a picnic, try Safeway or Basha's, the two major grocery stores, for good deli items. (*Note:* That small refrigerator near the door as you leave Basha's isn't full of dark spaghetti. Those are live fishing worms, chilled so they stay calm and last longer.)

Rainbow Room—$$$$

At Wahweap Lodge, this elegant glass-walled restaurant has reliably good food as well as sweeping views of the marina and its goings-on, Wahweap Bay, and Castle Rock beyond. The adjacent **Driftwood Lounge,** looking out over the swimming pool, is a gathering spot for boat-

ers coming off the lake. **100 Lake Shore Dr.; 520-645-2433.**

Peppers Cantina—$$$–$$$$

Inside the Courtyard by Marriott, this pleasant restaurant has a menu with a definite Southwest style, with spicy dishes a feature. Steaks come with a corn and cilantro garnish, and traditional pasta dishes always are reliable choices. During summer months, ask to dine on the attractive patio. **Lake Powell Blvd. and US 89; 520-645-5000.**

Navajo Room—$$$

Also at Wahweap Lodge. June–Sept., an expansive dinner buffet precedes colorful Native American dance entertainment. Buffet is at 6:00 P.M., entertainment begins at 8:00 P.M. **100 Lake Shore Dr.; 520-645-2433.**

Strombolli's—$$

The outdoor deck is the place to be for people-watching and to be in the thick of what's happening in Page. Hand-tossed pizza and micro-brew draft beers are among its most popular fare, but baked calzones are the favorite of many. Don't be in a hurry. Relaxed service is just part of the ambiance. **711 N. Navajo Dr., Page; 520-645-2605.**

Services

Carl Hayden Visitor Center

Serving the Glen Canyon National Recreation Area, the center is located at the Glen Canyon Dam in a building used jointly by the Bureau of Reclamation and the National Park Service. Hiking and trails, camping, weather, and other area information is available. The Park Service provides an information center here to help with outdoor activities in the Glen Canyon Recreation Area. In summer open daily, 7:00 A.M.–7:00 P.M.; other months, 8:00 A.M.–5:00 P.M. **Box 1507, Page, 86040; 520-608-6404.** The Natural History Association operates a **bookstore** in the center, filled with good reference material, including topographical maps, hiking books, and sources for the history of the area. **P.O. Box 581, Page, 86040; 520-645-3532.**

Lake Powell Resorts and Marinas

Page–Lake Powell Visitor Center, 888-261-PAGE or reservations 800-528-6154. Website: www.visitlakepowell.com (awesome).

Page–Lake Powell Chamber of Commerce Visitor and Convention Bureau

Information on area activities and events, and also for booking tours. Open mid-May–mid-Oct., daily, 8:00 A.M.–7:00 P.M.; mid-Oct.–mid-May, Mon.–Sat., 8:00 A.M.–5:30 P.M. Located in **Page Plaza,** facing the road, near Safeway. **P.O. Box 72, Page, 86040; 888-261-PAGE (7243) or 520-645-2741.** Website: www.visitlakepowell.com.

Flagstaff

This remarkably lovely, clean, entertaining, and altogether appealing town once was nothing more than a pit stop on Route 66. It was the place for an overnight in a neon-signed motor court on the way to the Grand Canyon or Las Vegas. And then visitors began to linger to enjoy crisp, pine-scented air and explore the surrounding forests. Phoenix residents realized that Flagstaff's 7,000-foot elevation made for much more pleasant temperatures during July and Aug. when the Valley of the Sun sweltered in triple-digit temps for weeks without relief. Flagstaff has a distinct four-season climate, with the first snow usually appearing in Nov. and lasting into Apr. Because 20 inches of the white fluffy stuff generally fall in Mar., spring skiing is reliably good.

Today Flagstaff remains the seat of Coconino County, the country's second-largest county, with an area of more than 11 million acres. This city of about 53,000 is surrounded by the Coconino National Forest, 1.8 million acres of pine trees, lakes, and picturesque gorges that afford outstanding opportunities for recreation. The area boasts the highest point in the state, 12,643-foot Humphreys Peak, one of the San Francisco Peaks, which have become Flagstaff landmarks.

Flagstaff narrowly missed being the motion-picture capital of the world. Although accounts differ, the general story says that Cecil B. DeMille and producer Jesse D. Lasky came through Flagstaff on the train from New York in 1912, looking for locations to make *The Squaw Man,* as well as a venue suitable for a permanent studio. They loved the scenery, the fresh air, the tall pines, and the climate. But

History

Settled in 1876, Flagstaff gets its name from a tall pine tree that was a trail marker for early travelers on their way to California. By 1882 the Atlantic & Pacific Railroad reached the town and a depot was built. The adjacent street became known as Railroad Ave. (it's now Route 66 or Santa Fe Ave.), and businesses flourished along its busy length. Saloons and houses of ill repute flourished as well, supplying entertainment for mill workers and railroad construction crews. By 1891 Flagstaff was named county seat of newly created Coconino County.

Getting There

Flagstaff is situated at the junction of I-17 and I-40. It is 146 miles or about two and a half hours north of Phoenix on I-17. Amtrak **(800-872-7245)** *arrives and departs daily, eastbound in the morning, westbound in the evening. America West Express* **(800-235-9292)** *has scheduled air service to Phoenix Sky Harbor International Airport from the new Pulliam Airport 4 miles south of Flagstaff.*

while they were there it started to snow. Coming from the East Coast with the express goal of finding a place with weather that would let them film in every season, the flurry rendered the town unsuitable. They proceeded to a small West Coast real estate development called Hollywoodland, and the rest, as they say, is history. Nonetheless, many movies and television programs have been shot in the Flagstaff area, which continues to attract filmmakers for the same reasons that DeMille and Lasky found it appealing.

Major Attractions

Lowell Observatory

Forever niched in the annals of astronomy as the site from which the planet Pluto was discovered by Clyde W. Tombaugh in 1930, this is an active research observatory that also shares its facilities with an interested public. The one-and-a-half-hour tour starts with a half-hour slide show narrated by energetic students. Visitors usually are amazed to learn of the observatory's genesis as a place for Percival Lowell to pursue verification for what he thought were canals on the surface of Mars. He believed they were built by intelligent life to harvest water from polar ice caps. Only when V. M. Silpher used a spectrograph in conjunction with the enormous Clark telescope to document the theory of an expanding universe was the canal theory proved false. To set myths to rest concerning the planet Pluto being named after Disney's daffy dog, guides explain that it was an English schoolgirl who suggested Pluto in honor of the Greek god of the underworld. Since it fit with the progressive sequence of Jupiter and Neptune, it was adopted. It also appeased those who thought the new discovery should bear the name of Percival Lowell, as the planet's astronomical symbol became P with a sub-L, which are Lowell's initials.

Each tour visits the site's 1916 library that houses Lowell's collection of books, memorabilia from his life, and the original spectrograph used

During spring and summer, fields of wildflowers are part of the landscape near Flagstaff.

in the expanding cosmos study. Take a look at the "Saturn" chandelier, a precursor of the art deco style. Guests are introduced to the huge Clark refractor telescope and are able to walk past Lowell's grave on a pine-covered hill. If viewing conditions are right on the nighttime tours, visitors can peer through a telescope at the fascinating celestial bodies in the night sky. The 103-year-old observatory was heavily involved in the Apollo program, hosting Buzz Aldrin and Neil Armstrong as students. Armstrong's signature is displayed in the library guest book. A gallery with interactive displays and a gift shop well stocked with trinkets as well as useful research books is in the main visitor center. Small fee. Open Apr.–Oct., daily, 9:00 A.M.–5:00 P.M.; Nov.–Mar., daily, noon–5:00 P.M. From City Hall, where all main roads entering Flagstaff converge, drive west on Aspen St. four blocks to Thorpe Park. Turn left at the park, proceed one block, then turn right and follow the road up the hill. Lowell Observatory is located on Mars Hill; 520-774-2096. Website: www.lowell.edu.

Walnut Canyon National Monument

Just east of Flagstaff, one of the loveliest canyons in the state is open for hiking and exploring. The Sinagua, canyon dwellers from A.D. 1120 to 1250, left a well-documented history in more than 300 cliff dwellings, two dozen of which may be viewed from groomed trails. Artifacts found in the canyon verify that its residents were skilled traders. Bones of birds from Mexico, seashells, and distinctive jewelry were no doubt traded for Sinagua pottery and obsidian. The canyon provided a comfortable living for its early residents, with freshwater flowing along its floor for drinking and to nourish fertile garden plots. Limestone cliffs, eroded by centuries of creek action, wind, and rain, are layered with ledges that provided building sites for Sinagua cliff dwellings. Niched safely above the canyon bottom, families could keep a watchful eye for enemies as they caught cooling breezes.

The **Island Trail,** the monument's most challenging, descends 185 feet into the canyon for a 1-mile round trip. Although most hikers dread the uphill return (you're at an elevation of 6,690 feet here), if your legs are not in great shape you may find that going down 240 steps is just as difficult as coming back up. However, the trail is paved and unless it is snowing, it should not be difficult to navigate. The 25-plus cliff dwellings that it winds past are an ample reward. Another option is the **Rim Trail,** a mostly level 0.75-mile hike along the edge of the canyon that meanders through a special community of plants and animals. There is an elevation gain of only 20–30 feet, and the surface is smooth enough so that the trail can be negotiated in a wheelchair, along with someone to help brake and back up. You'll see flashes of blue Steller's jays among the pines, through which breezes truly do whisper. The Rim and Island

Trails are the only two that are self-guided.

A ranger-led **Ledge Hike** leaves Wed. and Sun. at 10:00 A.M. for a one-and-a-half-hour hike that covers 0.75 mile off-trail, going to a number of cliff dwellings that are not usually open to the public. For somewhat of a challenge, show up Sat. at 10:00 A.M. for the two-hour, 2-mile **Ranger Cabin hike.** Slopes are steep and you have to deal with loose footing and brush, so wear long pants. The reward is seeing the historic cabin first used by the National Park Service as ranger housing, then later as the original visitor center until 1939. You hike down a side canyon formed by one of the tributaries of Walnut Creek, then come back along a ledge past 30 cliff ruins that are closed to the public without a ranger escort. Reservations are a must for this hike.

From the visitor center there is a spectacular view of the San Francisco Peaks. From left to right they are Mount Eden, 9,280 feet; Mount Agassiz, 12,300 feet; Mount Fremont, 11,900 feet; Mount Humphreys, 12,643 feet; and Mount Doyle, 11,460 feet. The center has a good selection of books and exhibits on the canyon's former residents. If you don't want to hike and prefer to simply sit and bird-watch, there are pleasant shady benches just for that purpose. There is no food sold here, but you can bring a picnic to enjoy at convenient tables. Weather can be very changeable. It is not unusual in the spring for a sunny day to turn into sleeting snow. Small fee per vehicle. Open during summer, daily, 8:00 A.M.–6:00 P.M.; during winter, daily, 9:00 A.M.–5:00 P.M.; trails close an hour before the park closes. Walnut Canyon is 7 miles east of Flagstaff off I-40. Take exit 204 and go south 3 miles on a paved road to the visitor center. 520-526-3367. Website: www.nps.gov/waca.

Riordan Mansion State Historic Park

This unusual mansion will seem like a real step back in time to youngsters, but older visitors will no doubt remember many of the furnishings, especially in the kitchen, that were very much in use when they were kids. The whole story behind this quirky home seems like a set of mirror images, with brothers Timothy and Michael Riordan, prominent Flagstaff logging scions, marrying sisters Caroline and Elizabeth Metz. They built a sort of mansion-duplex, with private living quarters in separate wings for each family and a large central living room with fireplace and billiards table where the families gathered together.

Built in 1904, it was designed in the American Craftsman style by Charles Whittlesey, who also designed El Tovar Lodge at the Grand Canyon. The rustic 13,000-square-foot log-slab building, with volcanic-stone arches and wood shingles, was ahead of its time in many ways. It had a refrigerator, not an icebox, long before refrigerators were common. Interior "wells," open to the roof, provided natural air conditioning. Much of the original furniture remains, including a high-sided "jail chair" in which naughty children were made to sit quietly as they contemplated the error of their ways. Within an oval dining room, an elliptical table with no head or foot democratically assured that guests had clear views of each other and no one was seated in any particular place of honor. A wicker swing moves freely in the living room where Mary Riordan, in an oil portrait, has the unusual ability to follow visitors with her eyes wherever they move in the room. Mary, daughter of Timothy and Caroline, is the namesake of upper and lower Lake Mary, 10 miles southeast of Flagstaff. A Steinway piano is ready to be played, and Tiffany stained-glass windows accent a number of rooms. Bedrooms look as though the occupants had left just moments ago, with clothing draped casually over chairs, and personal photos and the accouterments of private lives displayed on dresser tops. Only Timothy's half of the house currently is open to the public, as a family member lived in the other half until recently. It is being refurbished and is expected to be open to the public sometime in 2001.

You can pick up a pamphlet for a self-guided tour of the estate grounds, where there are tables for picnicking, but you are permitted in the home only on a guided tour. When the guide instructs you to stay on the red carpet, pay attention. If so much as an errant toe slides off, you will be admonished in front of the group. The home is lavishly decorated for the holiday season. Small fee. Open May–Sept., daily, 8:30 A.M.–5:00 P.M., with guided tours on the hour 9:00 A.M.–4:00 P.M.; Oct.–Apr., daily, 11:00 A.M.–5:00 P.M., with guided tours on the hour noon–4:00 P.M. Reservations are recommended. **1300 Riordan Ranch St., Flagstaff, 86001; 520-779-4395. Website: www.pr.state.az.us.**

Northern Arizona University

This respected university contributes a great deal to Flagstaff's sense of being a "young" town. Besides the nearby outdoor recreational opportunities, the university's excellent reputation and strong emphasis on teacher preparation draw students here. It began in 1899 as Northern Arizona Normal School, a teacher prep institution. In 1925 it became Northern Arizona State Teachers College, and in 1966 was accorded university status. Old Main was built even before that, in 1894, as a reform school. Seven university buildings are on the National Register of Historic Places. Today the campus covers 666 acres, plus more than 4,000 acres that the School of Forestry uses as a lab forest. For information on visiting the campus call **Student Union Information (520-523-4636)** or the general switchboard **(520-523-9011)**, from where you can be transferred to other departments.

Sunset Crater Volcano National Monument

About 15 miles north of Flagstaff, this extinct (at least it has been since A.D. 1065) volcano is part of the vast volcanic field that covers much of the terrain north of Flagstaff. It took 200 years from the last eruption for the field to calm down, and when it did it left this thousand-foot classic cinder cone. The lava has had a great influence on plant and animal life, which have had to adapt to a harsh environment at about 8,000 feet. Some have evolved to become distinct species. Endemic to the area is a type of white or blue scorpion weed with a blossom that curves like a scorpion's tail. It blooms during the late-summer rainy season, as does the pink penstemon, also endemic, which was removed from the endangered species list in 1986. Aug. is the month to see fabulous wildflowers. Moderate fee for admission to both Sunset Crater and nearby Wupatki National Monument. Open in summer, daily, 8:00 A.M.–6:00 P.M.; during winter, daily, 9:00 A.M.–5:00 P.M. Follow US 89 north to the signs; you can also continue on Forest Service Rd. 545, a paved 35-mile scenic loop that connects Sunset Crater with Wupatki. 520-526-0502. Website: www. nps.gov/sucr.

Wupatki National Monument

The fields and meadows that make up this monument immediately say that the people who once lived here were agrarian. Located on the southern Colorado Plateau in the rain shadow of the San Francisco Peaks, the area is studded with the remains of pueblos and small structures that once held stores of grain. The Anasazi and Sinaguan people settled here in about A.D. 1110, but within 200 years were gone. Legends and artifacts point to a migration to the Verde Valley and possibly to the Hopi mesas. Today the area is rich in archaeological sites.

The 35-mile scenic loop that connects Sunset Crater with Wupatki starts at about 8,000 feet, and descends to about 4,500 feet at the onetime agricultural fields of Wupatki. From the crater's rough and rugged lava landscape you'll pass through ponderosa forests and serene grasslands. Pick up a brochure guide in the visitor center. Although the ruins are widespread, all are within walking distance of parking areas, along short trails.

Located just behind the visitor center, **Wupatki Ruin** is the largest, with about 85 rooms that probably housed 200 residents when fully occupied. If the winds are right, you'll feel air rushing in or out of an interesting blowhole that is connected through a network of underground crevices to other blowholes. From the visitor center, drive less than five minutes to a smaller pueblo called **Wukoki Ruin** that may have accommodated just a few families. Follow the park road to well-preserved **Lomaki Ruin,** which once had two stories and six to eight rooms. From the **Citadel Ruin** on top of a volcanically formed rise, there is a good view of other ruins in the area. It gives a sense of how this once well-populated place must have functioned.

The visitor center has a museum with artifacts from the site and a bookstore. Open in summer, daily, 8:00 A.M.–6:00 P.M.; during winter, daily, 9:00 A.M.–5:00 P.M. Located about **35 miles north of Flagstaff.** Follow US 89 north to the signs, or follow Forest Service Rd. 545, a paved 35-mile scenic loop that continues to Wupatki from Sunset Crater. 520-679-2365. Website: www.nps.gov/wupa.

Festivals and Events

Flagstaff Winterfest

Feb.

When the temps are in the 70s in Phoenix and the Valley of the Sun, Flagstaff is reveling in the snow that makes this annual event possible. Going on for more than a decade, Winterfest showcases Flagstaff as a mountain snow-fun destination. As one of Arizona's truly wintery sites, the city takes its position seriously, putting on nearly 100 snow-related events that include dogsled races, nordic and alpine skiing competitions, snowmobile drag racing, and snowboard and snowshoe events. Sleigh rides, historic walking tours, stargazing, special children's activities, concerts, cultural events, outdoor hikes, and family snow games are part of the festivities that begin with the Winterfest parade. **Flagstaff Chamber of Commerce, 520-774-4505 or 800-842-7293.**

Flagstaff's Museum of Northern Arizona gift shop purveys Native American arts and crafts.

A Celebration of Native American Art

end of May–Sept.

This summerlong celebration honors the creativity of Native American artists and the Museum of Arizona's legacy of support for the Native arts of the Colorado Plateau. The exhibit features arts and crafts of the Hopi, Navajo, Pai, and Zuni. In recent years, Hispanic representation has been included. **Museum of Northern Arizona, 3101 Fort Valley Rd., Flagstaff, 86001; 520-774-5213.**

Pine Country Pro Rodeo

third weekend in June

If you've never been to a rodeo, this is about as pleasant a setting as you'll find to view this favorite western festivity in which top national contenders gather to compete in classic rodeo events. June in Flagstaff is reliably sunny and warm without being hot. Held at the **Coconino County Fairgrounds. 520-556-2276. Website: www.pinecountryprorodeo.com.**

Flagstaff SummerFest

first weekend in Aug.

More than 75,000 visitors throng from hot parts of the state to this cool, piney-mountain arts-and-crafts festival. The three-day event features 200 juried artists, 40 musical groups performing continuous live entertainment on three stages, and an assortment of food vendors purveying their specialties. A hands-on creative activity area for children is called the Mini Monet. Moderate entrance fee. Held **at Fort Tuthill on Coconino Country Fairgrounds,** which is part of a 350-acre wooded park. For information call **520-774-5139.**

Outdoor Activities

Bicycling

MOUNTAIN BIKING

Flagstaff's Urban Trail System (FUTS) for nonmotorized transportation is a great way to get around town and the area. The network of trails offers ready access to the campus of Northern Arizona University, forested areas, canyons, national monuments, cultural centers, and historic downtown. FUTS interconnects with the Arizona State Trail, the Coconino National Forest trail system, and the Flagstaff Bikeways System. You'll see recreational users, as well as the occasional business-dressed cyclist obviously on the way to work. The basic 18-mile trail, of bladed aggregate, is soft enough for runners and sturdy enough for mountain bikers. Cross-country skiers use it in winter. 520-774-9541.

Many of the trails used by skiers become hiking and **cycling trails** once the weather warms. **The Nordic Center,** 16 miles north of Flagstaff on US 180, doubles as a mountain-bike park May–Oct. Use fee for trails is waived during the summer, and bike rentals are available on-site. For information call **520-779-1951.**

Maps of **forest service roads,** many of which are great ways to explore backcountry on a mountain bike, are available from **Peaks Ranger District, Coconino National Forest, 5075 N. Hwy. 89, Flagstaff, 86004; 520-527-3600.**

Fishing

Mormon Lake

Although it's the largest lake in Coconino County, it has a tendency to go dry, which is probably why the Mormon colony that tried to settle here in the late 1800s finally gave up. In good years, there are reports of large bullheads being pulled from its waters, but in bad years it can be a bog. There are trails for hiking around the lake, and camping at two campgrounds. A circle drive around the lake takes you through the town of Mormon Lake, where a small grocery store, restaurant, and other businesses serve the large, seasonal RV population. Located **25 miles southeast of Flagstaff on Lake Mary Rd.**

Stoneman Lake

You might find yourself completely alone at this ancient water-filled crater, which is reason enough to seek out the secluded little lake. Duck hunters frequented the place up until the early 1970s, and now anglers come to bag large northern pike and yellow perch. It is named for Gen. George Stoneman, who was part of the Mormon Battalion that crossed the state in 1846. Bring your own boat or canoe because there are no services and no camping. Private cabins surrounding the lake are occupied seasonally. The lake is **south of Mormon Lake on Forest Route 213,** which also may be reached from I-17 by taking the Stoneman Lake exit (exit 306) about 35 miles south of Flagstaff.

Golf

Elden Hills Golf Course

The area's only full-length public course, its pine-flanked fairways are breezy and pleasant, a cool alternative to courses in the Valley of the Sun during the summer. Here golf season generally extends Mar.–Nov. Located in the old Fairfield Continental area in east Flagstaff, the par-72, 6,100-yard layout is a challenge for anyone who has a tendency to stray into the rough. **2380 N. Oakmont Dr., Flagstaff; 520-527-7997, tee times 520-527-7999.**

Hiking

The relatively flat cross-country ski trails of Nordic Center become agreeable hiking trails when it gets warm. At the **Arizona Snowbowl Scenic Skyride,** the chair lift transports hikers through the Coconino National Forest to 11,500 feet at the top of Mount Agassiz for fabulous views that on clear days extend to the Grand Canyon, 80 miles away. Riders can hike back down the mountain or take the lift. Tickets are moderately priced, with discounts for seniors; children five and younger riding with an adult are free. Open mid-June–Labor Day, daily; after Labor Day, Sat.–Sun. Follow US 180 for about 7.5 miles to Snowbowl Rd. on the right. Follow Snowbowl Rd. for 7 miles to the top parking lot and look for the ski lift. For Skyride information call **520-779-1951.**

Humphreys Peak Trail

This is the most popular trail within the Kachina Peaks Wilderness, a super area because there are no roads and no motorized vehicles. Even mountain bikes are not permitted. A number of trails are accessible from Flagstaff, with the most popular, the 4.5-mile Humphreys Peak Trail, starting at the base of the ski area at the Snowbowl. The trail starts at 9,500 feet and hits 12,643 feet at the summit, the state's highest point. This is Arizona's Mount Everest. Air is fresh and cool, but thin, so don't even think about this hike unless you're in good cardiovascular shape. The hike begins in forested territory, which becomes a field of volcanic rock that authenticates the peak's origins by fire. Signs caution you not to stray from the trail lest you damage delicate plant species that grow in the alpine tundra. It takes three to four hours to reach the summit. Most say the spectacular views are worth the effort. It's not difficult to understand why the Hopis and Navajos consider these peaks sacred. You can document your ascent by leaving a written comment in the metal ammo box that rests against a pile of rocks at the top. The trail is accessible from late spring to early fall, but expect to find snow almost all the time except perhaps Sept.

Also starting from the Snowbowl parking lot, the **Kachina Trail** is a wonderful hike among shadowy tall timber that includes Douglas fir and ponderosa pine. The whole hike is at about 9,000 feet, so don't be surprised if you have to take things more slowly than you normally do. The trail is 5 miles one-way, and makes a good day hike up to Schultz Tank and back. It connects with the Humphreys Trail and Weatherford Trail, which gives you a tougher and longer way back if you want more of a challenge. **Inner Basin Trail** is an easy 4-mile round-trip hike with a 1,000-foot elevation gain. **Weatherford Trail** is a good 12-mile day hike to the saddle between Fremont and Doyle Peaks with about a 2,000-foot elevation gain. The **Bear Jaw** and **Aubineau Trails** also are favored for day hikes. For more information, contact the **Coconino National Forest, Supervisor's Office, 2323 E. Greenlaw Ln., Flagstaff, 86004; 520-527-3600,** or the **Peaks Ranger Station, 520-526-0866.**

Skiing

There are no overnight accommodations in any of Flagstaff's ski areas, but many hotels and motels in town offer ski packages that combine accommodations and more with lift tickets. Call the **Flagstaff Visitors Bureau (800-842-7293)** for a list of hotels in town. For more information call the **Coconino National Forest Supervisor, 520-527-3600.**

CROSS-COUNTRY

Flagstaff Nordic Center

For cross-country skiers, there are 25 miles of groomed trails for all skill levels. The center has

a ski school, equipment rentals, guided tours, and races. Located **16 miles north of Flagstaff on US 180. 520-779-1951.**

DOWNHILL

Arizona Snowbowl

This popular area among the San Francisco Peaks 14 miles north of Flagstaff has two mountain day-lodges with restaurants and lounges, four chair lifts, a 2,300-foot vertical drop, 32 trails, a rental shop, and ski instruction for adults and kids. There are 50 miles of beginner terrain and a special area for snowboarders. Two new expert runs, Volcano and Lava, recently were added, giving the Snowbowl more advanced runs than any other state ski area. The season is generally mid-Dec.– early Mar. During summer months the area offers scenic chair-lift rides and mountain biking. Lift tickets are moderately priced; kids seven and under and seniors over 70 ski free. Take **I-17 north to US 180 and exit on Snowbowl Rd. 8 miles north of Flagstaff. P.O. Box 40, Flagstaff, 86002; 520-779-1951, 520-779-4577 snow report, 602-957-0404 from Phoenix. Website: www.arizona snowbowl.com.**

Sledding and Snowplay

Along US 180

If you simply want to play in the snow and build a snowman, there are a variety of locations close to Flagstaff where you can bury yourself in the chilly white stuff. Toboggans and saucers are ideal for the small slopes that line US 180, between Flagstaff and Valle at the foot of the San Francisco Peaks. **Wing Mountain,** at milepost 226, is a good one, as is **Crowley,** at milepost 223. Parking lots usually are plowed at these two spots, but if the snow is really fresh, the plows may not have gotten there yet. Just be sure you park well off the road to be safe. For more information call the **Coconino National Forest Supervisor, 520-527-3600.**

Seeing and Doing

Gardens and Arboreta

The Arboretum at Flagstaff

This huge 200-acre arboretum has a fascinating array of plants, from alpine tundra to high desert. A magnificent ponderosa pine forest, part of the arboretum, flourishes at this 7,150-foot altitude. Stroll nature trails, a wildflower meadow, and an herb garden, then settle in at one of the shady picnic tables to enjoy the lunch you've brought. Guided tours offered daily, 11:00 A.M. and 1:00 P.M. Open Apr. 1–Dec. 15, daily, 9:00 A.M.–5:00 P.M. Located **3.8 miles south of W. Route 66. Woody Mountain Rd., Flagstaff, 86002-0670; 520-774-1442.** Website: www.thearb.org.

Museums

Museum of Northern Arizona

One of the outstanding museums in the state, this one requires at least two hours, more if possible, to truly appreciate everything here. Even before entering, take a moment outdoors to stand at the Rio de Flag Canyon overlook to enjoy the crisp air scented with ponderosa pine.

In front of the museum, a little nature trail starts at the flagpole and follows the canyon rim to the east, then descends to the canyon floor via easy-to-negotiate steps, where it follows a creek. Placards dispense nature tidbits, such as how to recognize a ponderosa (needles cluster in threes). Heed the markers for poison ivy and poison hemlock. If you touch the former or ingest the latter, you'll either end up with a horrible case of the itches, or dead, like poor Socrates.

When you walk into the museum you face a large window that overlooks a courtyard, with at least a dozen wild bird species flocking to the feeders. Broad-tailed hummingbirds, glossy black ravens, red-headed house finches, dramatic blue-crested Steller's jays, and colorful hairy woodpeckers are among regular diners.

Founded in 1928, the museum focuses on the Colorado Plateau and its biology, geology, anthropology, and fine arts. Always a crowd-pleaser, the life-size model skeleton of Dilophosarus, a flesh-eating dinosaur that once roamed these woods, greets visitors in the **Geology Gallery.** For a rest, curl up in front of the fireplace in the living room-like **Babbitt Gallery** to contemplate historic paintings donated by the pioneer Babbitt family of northern Arizona.

In one of the best museum gift shops anywhere, you'll find an extensive collection of books on museum-related subjects and excellent pieces of Native American art, including Navajo rugs, Hopi pottery, fetishes, and an outstanding selection of well-priced turquoise and silver jewelry. Besides assuring authenticity (kachina dolls are made of genuine cottonwood roots, for example), the gift shop charges no sales tax. Moderate admission. Open daily, 9:00 A.M.–5:00 P.M.; closed New Year's Day, Easter, Thanksgiving, and Christmas. **3101 N. Fort Valley Rd., Flagstaff, 86001; 520-774-5213.** Website: www.musnaz.org.

Pioneer Museum

One of four branches of the Arizona Historical Society (Tempe, Yuma, and Tucson have the other three), the museum is in the building that served as the county hospital 1908–1938. Known then as the "poor farm" for the number of elderly men without families who ended up there, it has been a museum since 1963. A horse barn, root cellar, and settler's cabin also are on the property. The collection, which gives a sense of the explorers, lumber magnates, and railroad developers in Flagstaff's history, includes vehicles, farm machinery, and other pioneer memorabilia. A 1929 Baldwin articulated locomotive and a Santa Fe caboose are favorites with children. During winter months the exhibit called "Playthings of the Past" draws together toys, games, dolls, and children's books from years past. Another exhibit features medical instruments and equipment used by early Flagstaff physicians.

Donations appreciated. Open Mon.–Sat., 9:00 A.M.–5:00 P.M.; closed New Year's Day, Easter, Thanksgiving, and Christmas. Located on Fort Valley Rd. next to Sechrist School. **2340 N. Fort Valley Rd., Flagstaff, 86001; 520-774-6272.**

Nature Centers

The Nature Conservancy
Hart Prairie Preserve

Established in 1994 these 245 beautifully undisturbed acres contain a globally rare community of Bebb's willow trees. Herds of elk often pass through the preserve. At an elevation of 8,600 feet, golden aspens create spectacular fall color. In winter, the area is blanketed with snow. An 1877 lodge called the Homestead may be reserved for groups of up to 20; individual reservations also are often available. At present this is a closed preserve, which means you can't simply wander onto it at will. Winter cross-country ski weekends and summer hiking weekends are regularly scheduled. Free guided hikes that last about one and a half hours are offered about June 1–Oct. 15, Wed. and Sun., 10:00 A.M. Located about 12 miles from Flagstaff. From the preserve office on US 180, you carpool for the half-hour drive on Forest Service roads to the preserve itself. **2601 N. Fort Valley Rd. (US 180), Flagstaff, 86001; 520-774-8892.** Website: www.tnc.org.

Nightlife

The Museum Club

"The Zoo," as it is affectionately known, is a Flagstaff landmark and not to be missed. It's a bar, a dance club, a roadhouse, and unquestionably a museum, with so much history that it has been listed on the National Register of Historic Places. Noisy, rowdy, and fun, it is constructed of native ponderosa pine logs around five ponderosa tree trunks, complete with branches, that have become part of the interior decor. When it was built in 1931, it was the largest log cabin in the state.

The Museum Club in Flagstaff is better known as "The Zoo" for all the stuffed creatures inside.

You enter under the inverted forked trunk of a ponderosa, past the watchful eyes of a door person who makes sure you're not under age, you're suitably dressed (shirt and shoes), and you won't cause problems. The reason it's called The Zoo is immediately obvious. A stuffed bear, bobcat, owls, and peacock perch in tree branches above the dance floor, and a javelina snarls down at imbibers at the bar. The Zoo's former owner built it to house his collection of taxidermied animals, Indian artifacts, and rifles. He apparently stuffed anything, from fish to fowl, that moved. Only a few of his original mounts remain today, but others have taken over, assuring that the zoolike ambiance endures.

It's almost impossible not to have a good time here. If you don't know the dances being done on the floor, a resident dance instructor will gladly introduce you to the intricacies of the two-step. More than 10 years ago the club's owner instituted "Friendly Cab," providing a free trip home to imbibers who need it. There is a well-stocked shop with Route 66 souvenirs, and of course Museum Club T-shirts, some with big red Corvettes zooming across the front. The Museum Club is open daily, 11:00 A.M.–1:00 A.M. **3404 E. Route 66, Flagstaff; 520-526-9434. Website: www.museumclub.com.**

Scenic Drives

Flagstaff to Valle

Along US 180 between Flagstaff and its junction with Hwy. 64 leading to the Grand Canyon, a section designated as a scenic road passes through tall pines and alpine meadows. Depending on season and rainfall, the roadside could be carpeted with brown-eyed goldeneye, yellow rabbitbrush, and scarlet penstemon mixed in with piñon pines. During the winter, the road often is banked with snow, pushed to the sides by diligent plows. The San Francisco Peaks in the distance look as though someone should put a cherry on top. About 20 miles from Flagstaff the Kendrick Picnic Area has tables among the trees. Follow US 180 northwest from Flagstaff to the town of Valle, about 45 miles.

Hart Prairie Rd.

This is really a side trip from the Peaks Loop Drive (see below) and is very popular in the fall. Besides great views of the San Francisco Peaks, all along the roadside aspen groves turn a brilliant golden yellow. There are plenty of places to pull off for a picnic or short hike. From Flagstaff, go to Hart Prairie Rd., take US 180 north to milepost 235 and turn right onto Hart Prairie Rd. (Forest Rd. 151). Follow it until it returns to US 180, turn left, and you'll be headed back to Flagstaff. From the Peaks Loop Drive on Forest Rd. 418, at Forest Rd. 151 simply turn left for a tour south.

Peaks Loop Drive

Great in fall because of the aspen, but also good almost any summer day when you're looking for a place to cool off, this 60-mile trip loops around the impressive San Francisco Peaks. From Flagstaff head north on US 89 and turn left onto Forest Rd. 418 just past the Sunset Crater turnoff. You'll start climbing, and it's hard to keep

your eyes on the road and off the scenery. It's best just to pull off at a safe point and savor the ponderosas and canyons from afoot. Follow the road until it joins US 180; turn left to return to Flagstaff.

Where to Stay

Flagstaff has many types of accommodations in all price ranges, from budget chains to historic inns to cabins and bed-and-breakfasts. On I-40 east of town, there are close to a dozen chain motels.

Bed-and-Breakfasts

The Inn at 410—$$$$

Elegant by most b-and-b standards, this 110-year-old brick California Craftsman home's nine rooms are filled with antiques and personal treasures that make you think the real occupants could reappear at any moment. Everything here is well thought out for the comfort of guests, including a garden room with a private entrance that is completely wheelchair-accessible. You'll wonder how the tree-trunk bed frame ever was placed in the Dakota Suite, because doors and windows are way too small. The room is paneled in weathered barn siding and has a wood-burning fireplace. Besides a full, truly fabulous breakfast, cookies fresh from the oven are set out each afternoon. **410 N. Leroux St., Flagstaff, 86001; 800-774-2008 or 520-774-0088. Website: www.inn410.com.**

Birch Tree Inn—$$$

Just around the corner from Comfi Cottages, this 1917 country Victorian home once was a fraternity house. Two energetic couples took it over, refurbished the whole place, and kept it low-key with no TVs or phones in the rooms. A pool table, reading material, and TV are in the main-floor parlor. In the summertime, arriving guests are offered iced tea and hors d'oeuvres on the veranda. Five comfortable, homey second-floor guest rooms all have queen beds, except the Southwest room, which has a king. Two rooms have a shared bath. **824 W. Birch Ave., Flagstaff, 86001; 888-774-1042 or 520-774-1042. Website: www.birchtreeinn.com.**

Comfi Cottages of Flagstaff—$$$

Six individual cottages built in the 1920s and 1930s (one is from the 1950s) are scattered along quiet streets in an older residential neighborhood. One-, two-, or three-bedroom places are completely equipped with the comforts of daily living, including cable TV, phone, bicycles, even a picnic basket. When you check in, you'll find the fixings for breakfast in your refrigerator. A favorite is the cottage at 710 Birch, one block from the city park and forest; the bathroom has a claw-foot tub, and there's a fireplace in the living room. **1612 N. Aztec, Flagstaff, 86001; 888-774-0731 or 520-774-0731. Website: www.virtualflagstaff.com/comfi.**

Hotels and Motels

Hotel Monte Vista—$-$$

Brochures invite you to "Kick off your boots in Gary Cooper's room, sleep in Carole Lombard's bed, and make a little history of your own" at this 1920s hotel in historic downtown. Its 50 rooms are furnished with reminders of the past that include ceiling fans, brass detailing, and antique reproductions. Phones and cable TV, however, are definitely touches for today. Pleasant lounge and coffee shop, too. Want to sleep where Humphrey Bogart slept? Ask for Rm. 408. **100 N. San Francisco St., Flagstaff 86001; 800-545-3068 or 520-779-6971, fax 520-779-2904. Website: www.hotelmontevista.com.**

Hotel Weatherford—$-$$

This historic landmark is a combination of dining, live entertainment, and lodging, with eight quaint rooms decorated in early 1900s style. Five private rooms have baths, three share a bath. One of the first brick structures in Flagstaff, the hotel was built by Texas cattleman John W. Weatherford in 1898 and enlarged the follow-ing year. Once the crown jewel of Flagstaff's hotels, the three-story structure had a conservatory, dance pavilion, roof garden, and sun parlor. It hosted William Randolph Hearst, Zane Grey, and artist Thomas Moran. Carley Burch and Glenn Kilbourne, characters that Grey created for the novel *The Call of the Canyon,* came alive as the author toiled away in one of the hotel's upstairs rooms. William Boyd, better known as Hopalong Cassidy, worked here as a desk clerk.

In 1929 fire destroyed the Weatherford's ornate wood balconies, and during the next 40 years it went through a number of structural and ownership changes. In 1975 it was purchased and saved from destruction, and today is still in the process of being renovated. Layers of stucco have been removed to reveal a lovely old fireplace, and the third-floor ballroom has been carefully restored. The mirrored Brunswick bar is an antique from Tombstone, wood floors gleam with their original luster, and stained-glass windows have been added. If you call in advance, whether you stay there or not, the management will arrange a free tour. Also in the building is Charly's Pub and Grill (see Where to Eat). **23 N. Leroux St., Flagstaff, 86001; 520-774-2731. Website: www.weatherfordhotel.com.**

Inns and Resorts

Arizona Mountain Inn—$$$

On 13 ponderosa pine-blanketed acres surrounded by national forest, this inn is ideal for families or a group of friends. Accommodations range from bed-and-breakfast rooms in a main lodge to separate cottages with one to five bedrooms, appropriate for up to 16 people. Rustic cottages with fireplaces are furnished with kitchen utensils and a barbecue. Pricing is according to the number of guests in the unit, with a four-night minimum during the summer. From Flagstaff, take I-17 southeast about five minutes, exit at Lake Mary Rd., and follow it 1 mile; the inn is on the left. **4200 Lake Mary Rd., Flagstaff, 86001; 520-774-8959 or 800-239-5236. Website: www.arizonamountaininn.com.**

The Hotel Weatherford is one of Flagstaff's historic hostelries. Hopalong Cassidy once was the desk clerk here.

Montezuma Lodge at Mormon Lake—$$$

If you grew up "going to the cabin" during summer months, you'll love this quintessential lodge, with 18 rustic cottages scattered among 16 acres of densely wooded pine forest overlooking Mormon Lake. Squirrels pitter-patter across the cabin roof, jays and nuthatches chatter noisily just above your porch, and there isn't a civilized sound to be heard, except perhaps the slam of a car door. The Audubon Society recently identified 286 bird species in the area. Mismatched dishes, crisp little curtains that possibly were once flour sacks, braided rugs, and knotty pine walls darkened by the years are part of what makes this lodge such a delight. Resident skunks, although not de-scented, will approach for a handout and refrain from turning their backs unless offended. The trailhead for three area hikes is just below the lodge. If you're there in the late summer and fall, you're almost certain to hear elk bugling in the distance. Open May 1–Dec. 1; rates Mon.–Thurs. are slightly lower than weekends. Located about 25 miles southeast of Flagstaff, about a 35-minute drive. From Flagstaff, take I-17 southeast about five minutes, exit at Lake Mary Rd., and take it 20 miles south to milepost 324; 0.5 mile past the marker, turn right onto Mormon Lake Rd. Follow the road about 4 miles until you see the sign for Montezuma Lodge. Turn right at the sign and proceed 0.5 mile to the main lodge. **H.C. 31, Box 342, Mormon Lake, 86038; 520-354-2220, fax 520-354-2555. Website: www.arizonamountainresort.com**

Mormon Lake Lodge—$$–$$$

Another great in-the-woods kind of place, this one has genuine log cabins, horseback riding through the pines, and mountain-bike rentals among its reasons to stay. There's cross-country skiing and snowmobile rentals during the winter. All cabins have full baths, and some have kitchenettes and fireplaces. Family cabins, with one and two bedrooms, are great for kids or for two couples. The Lodge has one of the few open-pit steak houses still in operation; besides the best beef available, the menu also features game and fish choices. On Fri. and Sat. nights there's live country music in the 1880 Saloon, and the

Cowboy Dinner Theater is really good, corny fun. There is a considerable price difference between weeknights and weekends. Located about 30 minutes south of Flagstaff. From Flagstaff take I-17 southeast to Lake Mary Rd., then head 21 miles to the Mormon Lake turnoff. P.O. Box 38012, Mormon Lake, 86038; 520-354-2227. Website: www.foreverresorts. com/mormon.

Hostels

Grand Canyon International Hostel—$
This clean, cheerful place has dorms and private rooms in a historic building in old Flagstaff just south of the Amtrak station downtown. It's hard to miss. Just look for the 142-foot Downtowner neon sign. Linens and breakfast are included, and there are phones in every room. It has two big kitchens, a barbecue, a laundry room, and free tea and coffee. No lockout during the day, no curfew at night, and no chores. Guests seem to gather in the cable TV room in the evening to chat over the day's experiences. 19 S. San Francisco St., Flagstaff, 86001; 520-779-9421, reservations 888-442-2696. Website: www.info@grandcanyonhostel.com.

Camping

National Forest Service campgrounds **Dairy Spring** and **Double Springs** at Mormon Lake have water, rest rooms, showers, and dump stations, but no hookups. At this 7,000-foot elevation, camping is comfortable only May–Sept. Located 25 miles southeast of Flagstaff on Lake Mary Rd.

Bonito Campground
This unusual campground is in the middle of a grove of gorgeous ponderosa pines. You actually camp on cinders catapulted thousand years ago out of a volcano that later became Sunset Crater Volcano National Monument (see Major Attractions). At an elevation of almost 7,000 feet, it is a cool summer haven run by the Forest Service, with 44 developed sites, drinking water,

and rest rooms, but no hookups. Its charm is in its remote primitiveness. About **18 miles northeast of Flagstaff just off US 89.** For information call the **Coconino National Forest, 520-526-0866.**

J & H RV Park
This popular park is tidy, well kept, and up to date. It has 55 full hookups, a general store, laundry, showers, recreation and TV rooms, and 24-hour security. Open Apr. 1–Nov. 1. Located 1 mile past Townsend-Wynona Rd. on US 89. 7901 N. Hwy. 89, Flagstaff, 86004; 520-526-1829.

Where to Eat

Flagstaff has a wealth of eateries with truly outstanding food. That's not to say you can't find a Denny's, Domino's Pizza, or Jack in the Box. They're there, but they definitely are secondary to the great grills, delicatessens, and bakeries that dominate the dining scene.

Charly's Pub & Grill—$$–$$$
In the historic Hotel Weatherford (see Where to Stay), this lively pub is likely to be crowded with students and young people from all over the world. Three different eating venues, all serving the same menu, have very different atmospheres. The pub part, with pool tables and a bar, is by far the most active. If you're looking to settle in for a nice, leisurely dinner, you'll probably want to go through the French doors into the quieter dining room with a fireplace. Or move to the next room, the Exchange Pub, which once housed Flagstaff's telephone exchange. A blackened-chicken Caesar salad has just enough garlic, and the sun-dried tomato, spinach, and cheese appetizer is outstanding. The *posole,* a stew of pork, hominy, and green chile served in a flour tortilla shell, is certainly worth a try, especially since it's likely to be awhile before you'll see it on another menu. In historic downtown. **23 N. Leroux St.; 520-779-1919.**

Pasto—$$-$$$

"Fun Italian dining" is the way this place bills itself, but it's a lot more. Creative, imaginative food comes in portions so huge, you'd do well to consider splitting any order. Or be prepared to ask for a doggie bag, assuming your dog eats things like Southwestern black-bean ravioli, tortelloni florentine, chicken vesuvio, or artichoke orzo—just a few of the menu items that keep local patrons coming back (always a good sign) and hook newcomers for good. Downtown. 19 E. Aspen; 520-779-1937.

Beaver Street Brewery and Whistle Stop Cafe—$$

Wood-fired pizza and boutique beers are the drawing card to this lively brew pub set in a building that dates to 1938. Painted wall signs are remnants of its days as a market. Opened in 1994, the Brewery has become a local favorite, especially for its rich, full-bodied Railhead Red Ale. Nut Brown and Indian Ales also are popular. Almost everyone opts for an appetizer fondue. The vegetable version, fragrant with sharp cheddar, caramelized onion, and ale, is served with bread cubes and chunks of squash, carrot, and whatever else is fresh. A classic Swiss fondue made with Gruyère, white wine, and a splash of kirsch is served with bread cubes and fresh fruit. Their Caesar salad is garlicky and tasty, and the chili is not shy. You come here as much to try the great beer as you do to eat, but both experiences are reliably good fun. 11 S. Beaver St.; 520-779-0079.

Cafe Espress—$$

An antidote to The Place (see below), Cafe Espress has a casual vegetarian and otherwise health-conscious menu that includes low-fat turkey dishes with nary a smidge of beef or pork. The bakery/gallery has ever-changing works by local artists. Open daily, 7:00 A.M.–9:00 P.M. Downtown. 16 N. San Francisco St.; 520-774-0541.

The Place Mike & Ronda's Restaurant—$-$$

For years Flagstaffers have been getting their morning cholesterol fixes with the enormous breakfasts, served all day, at this all-American diner-type restaurant. Prices are straight out of the '70s. Open daily, 6:00 A.M.–3:00 P.M. On the West Side. 21 S. Milton Rd.; 520-774-7008.

Salsa Brava—$-$$

This restaurant comes highly recommended by a reader who says the Guadalajaran-style Mexican food is "delightful, and they know how to make some decent margaritas." He goes on to praise large portions and reasonable prices. Open Sun.–Thurs., 11:00 A.M.–9:00 P.M.; Fri.–Sat., 11:00 A.M.–10:00 P.M. 1800 S. Milton; 520-774-1083.

Services

CyberCafe

Four computers, $3 for 30 minutes. Located in Bookmans Used Books. 1520 S. Riordan Ranch Rd.; 520-774-0005. Website: www.bookmans.com and click on CyberCafe.

Flagstaff Convention & Visitors Bureau

800-217-2367.

Flagstaff Visitor Center

This is worth a stop not only to pick up lots of good information, but to see the historic train station in which it is housed. Amtrak passengers arrive daily at the Tudor revival–style station built in 1926. 1 E. Route 66, Flagstaff, 86011; 800-842-7293 or 520-774-9541. Website: wwwflagstaff.az.us or www.flagstaff arizona.org.

Fall Color

The annual burst of color produced by broad-leafed deciduous trees has been immortalized in songs like "Autumn Leaves" and idolized by dazzled spectators. Arizona's arid climate would seem unencouraging to trees that autumn's cool temperatures can oxidize into the spectacular rusts and golds that prevail in the East and Midwest. In much of the state there are no distinguishable four seasons. But when fall comes to the Arizona mountains, there is a change in the way the air smells and in how sunlight filters through the trees, creating elongated shadows even at midday. Colors are at their best from end of Sept.–Oct.

In northern Arizona, cottonwoods in **Canyon de Chelly National Monument** near Chinle take on a golden hue that changes to a vivid orange. Yellow quaking aspen shimmer in golden stands near **Flagstaff** at the Snowbowl. You can view them from aloft by riding the chair lift that operates Fri.–Sun. The **Arboretum at Flagstaff** has an herb garden with Virginia creeper that displays rich shades of red, while sumac, bigtooth maple, willow, and aspen flourish elsewhere. The riparian area along **Oak Creek Canyon** near Sedona is thick with aspen, oak, and sycamore. The reds are created by Rocky Mountain maple and bigtooth maple. Follow Hwy. 89A north of Sedona. During Oct., ranger-led walks are offered at **Slide Rock State Park** in Sedona. The **Payson** area is networked with hiking trails that include Horton Creek and Pine Creek Trails, where sycamores, maples, and box elders flourish. Near **Pinetop/Lakeside,** the Woodland Lake Loop is an easy and colorful hike.

Central Arizona's **Verde Valley** glows with fall color from about mid-Oct. on. A good vantage point is the Verde Canyon Railroad. Even if it's quite late in Oct., you probably haven't missed the color show at **Boyce Thompson Southwestern Arboretum** near Superior. During Nov. and even early Dec. cottonwoods, willows, and sycamores brighten the landscape.

In southern Arizona in the **Chiricahua Mountains** near Willcox, oak, aspen, ash, and burgundy bigtooth maples put on reliably colorful displays. In this same area, along the **San Pedro River,** cottonwoods acquire a classic autumn gold. The Nature Conservancy's **Ramsey Canyon** near Sierra Vista is brilliant with the reds of bigtooth maples.

The **Arizona Office of Tourism** has information on the best places to see autumn at work. Call **888-520-3444** and ask for the week's fall foliage report.

Williams

At 6,780 feet, the landscape around Williams is dotted with small piñon pines and distant dark cinder cones. Williams, close to the Grand Canyon (just 60 miles north), was once known as "The Gateway to the Grand Canyon." Today the business loop through Williams follows old Route 66, which is split into two one-way streets to alleviate traffic congestion. The entire downtown area is on the National Register of Historic Places. A number of original 1940s neon signs dating to the heyday of Route 66 still light up old Motel Row in East Williams.

History

Named for legendary mountain man Bill Williams, whose statue greets travelers coming from the west, the town began along the Beale Wagon Rd. and the Overland Rd., early exploration routes. Williams received the boost it needed to put it on the map when the railroad reached there in 1882, making it possible to ship lumber, cattle, and sheep from the formerly remote area.

It didn't take long for residents to realize that Williams' proximity to the Grand Canyon gave it a unique position in the tourism industry. By 1901 a spur line reached the scenic wonder, with a paved road following in 1929. When the Fray Marcos, one of the famous Harvey Houses, was built by the Santa Fe Railroad, Williams was securely niched as "The Gateway to the Grand Canyon." Fray Marcos is named for Fray Marcos de Niza, a Franciscan monk traveling with Spanish explorer Coronado, who is said to be the first white man to visit what is now Arizona.

By the time Route 66 went through in the 1930s, Williams' Wild West image had been shed, and tourists found a warm welcome in the dozens of family restaurants and neon signs of Motel Row. Williams became a "tourism town."

But as a traveling public began to rely more heavily on automobiles than trains, rail service to the canyon ended in 1968.

In 1984 Williams was bypassed by the new interstate highway system. Even as a special ceremony was being held to mark the historic event, a wave of nostalgia was beginning. Although many of the gas stations and other businesses suffered terribly, and even closed, others began capitalizing on a trend that had begun with the very first Route 66 bypass.

Festivals and Events

Rendezvous Days

Memorial Day weekend
Formerly called Bill Williams Days, an old-time mountain men encampment is re-enacted with black-powder shooting contests and a parade featuring the famous Bill Williams Mountain Men. It commemorates the days when these rowdy guys were Indian scouts, trappers, and guides for the military. A parade, covered wagon ride, arts and crafts booths, a street dance on

Sun. night with live music, and a Sat. steak fry and dance are part of the festivities. **Held downtown. 520-635-4061.**

Mountain Village Holiday

mid-Nov.–New Year's
The whole town literally glows during the holidays as more than a half million architectural lights outline buildings, businesses, and structures downtown. Do your Christmas shopping in galleries, antique shops, specialty stores, and historic buildings decked out in holiday finery. The celebration includes a night parade with decorated RVs, trucks, military vehicles, and private cars. On weekends, local merchants sponsor free hayrides, and Santa welcomes children in the Youth Center next to the Williams Visitor Center, **200 W. Railroad Ave.; 520-635-4061.**

Outdoor Activities

Bicycling

MOUNTAIN BIKING
There are two short but challenging mountain-bike rides on abandoned sections of old Route 66, at the top and bottom of Ash Fork Hill. Ash Fork Hill Trail is north of I-40 at an elevation of 5,500 feet; Devil Dog Trail is south of I-40 at 6,500 feet. You can easily do both trails in the same day.

It can be hot during summer, so take plenty of water and sunscreen because there are no services. In the winter, mud and snow may make the routes impassable, so check with the Forest Service before starting out. The Forest Service also has an excellent trail map. **Williams Ranger District, USDA Forest Service, Route 1, Box 142, Williams, 86046; 520-635-5600.**

Ash Fork Hill Trail
This ride loops along a 1922 section of Route 66 for 6 miles. A rough downhill is followed by a smooth but steep uphill. Rewards are great views of Picacho Peak and Bill Williams Mountain. You

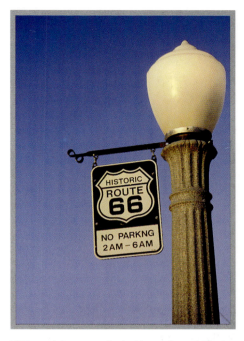

Williams, Arizona, was the last town along old Route 66 to be bypassed by Interstate 40 in 1984.

can add 2 miles to your ride by following Forest Rd. 6 through piñon and juniper woodland, where you may see red-tailed hawks and golden eagles soaring overhead, as well as deer and antelope moving slowly through the forest shadows. This hour-long ride can be longer if you take the time to enjoy your surroundings. To access the trail, take I-40 12 miles west of Williams to exit 151. Take Forest Rd. 106 north to the parking area.

Devil Dog Trail
This route begins on Forest Rd. 108 and loops for 5 miles at the top of Ash Fork Hill through cool pines. Where it becomes Forest Rd. 45,

Getting There
From Phoenix, take I-10 west to I-17 and go north 146 miles to Flagstaff, to the junction with I-40. Follow I-40 west for 32 miles to Williams.

you're on a section of Route 66 built in 1922. You have the option of charging up Bixler Mountain for a side trip (only the hardy should try it), following Forest Rd. 45 at the point where it leaves the 1922 road. The old road then loops back to the starting point along a 1932 portion of Route 66 that at one time was paved. The whole ride can take as little as 30 minutes if you don't do Bixler Mountain. To access the trail, take I-40 6 miles west of Williams to exit 157. Bear right under the underpass and turn left to the parking area on Forest Rd. 108.

Golf

Elephant Rock Golf Course

The recent addition of another nine holes brings this pretty 18-hole course to a par 72. The mature layout is named for a nearby rock formation. The back nine were built in the 1920s on the town's north side by railroad workers. Open seasonally, closing "when the snow sticks," says the pro. **2200 Country Club Dr., Williams; 520-635-4935.**

Skiing

The slopes at **Williams Ski Area** will be slightly underwhelming if you're into extreme skiing, but they are wonderful family slopes with a T-bar and a rope tow. They're also safe and secure for beginners who might be intimidated by larger areas. In addition to five usually uncrowded runs, there are marked cross-country ski trails. Equipment rental is near the snack bar and warming lounge. When there's snow, it's open Thu.–Sun. Go **south from Williams on I-40 to the ski area. 520-635-9330.**

Seeing and Doing

Museums

Williams Depot

The 1908 depot is the jumping-off point for the **Grand Canyon Railway.** Built of solid-poured concrete, its sturdy construction saved it from demolition. Most such buildings, made of wood, are razed to avoid paying taxes on them when they've outlived their usefulness. Since it would have cost more to demolish the building than to pay its taxes, it was spared. The **Railway Museum,** located in what used to be the hotel dining room, is crammed with artifacts and photos that trace the line's history. Try your hand at sending Morse code over the wires. The museum is free. Open 7:30 A.M.–5:30 P.M. **233 N. Grand Canyon Blvd, Williams, 86001; 800-THETRAIN.**

Outdoors, **Locomotive Number 20,** built in 1910, its tender, and a restored 1923 Harriman coach car testify to the elegance of turn-of-the-century rail travel. The gift shop has an above-average selection of actually useful railroad souvenirs, including model train equipment and guidebooks. If you missed breakfast, you can grab a quick continental version in the Santa Fe room before boarding. The sound of gunfire will draw you outdoors to the **Old West Village** and theme show, presented on scheduled train days.

Tours

Grand Canyon Railway

The classic way to see the Grand Canyon is to start in Williams and ride this historic train through forest and high desert plains to the South Rim. Its history dates to 1901 when the Santa Fe Railroad built a spur from Williams to the Canyon, thereby opening passenger service. The steam train chugged along the route for 67 years, opening to the world a wonder that previously had been visited mainly by miners. But with the popularization of the automobile and construction of reliable roads, the train made its last run on July 30, 1968, with just three passengers aboard. In 1989, environmental awareness and a desire to avoid serious traffic congestion at the canyon gave the train a new life.

Today, refurbished steam engines with original gauges and whistles pull restored vintage railcars that a responsive public keeps full. Three of the venerable locomotives were built in 1910. Turn-of-the-century steam engines are in service Memorial Day weekend–Sept. Diesel locomotives, which pulled passengers and freight from the 1940s to 1960s, are used from Oct.–Memorial Day weekend. The Harriman coach cars were built by Pullman in 1923, and the Coconino dome coach was built in 1954 for the Chicago, Burlington and Quincy, and Northern Pacific Railways. A number of classes of service include coach cars with conventional train seating, a club car with mahogany bar, and a domed observation car. The Chief has overstuffed club chairs and divans, an open platform, and oversize windows. In this first-class car, a continental breakfast is served on the way up, with hors d'oeuvres and champagne on the return trip. Singing cowboys provide onboard entertainment, and there is an almost guaranteed "holdup," complete with masked bandits, on every journey.

Amtrak's Southwest Chief has daily connecting service with the Grand Canyon Railway. Call **Amtrak (800-872-7245)** for reservations. The Grand Canyon Railway runs daily except Dec. 24–25. The morning Grand Canyon Railway train leaves Williams Depot at 10:00 A.M. and arrives at the South Rim at 12:15 A.M. The return trip leaves the Grand Canyon Depot at 3:30 P.M., arriving in Williams at 5:45 P.M. If you think that three and a half hours at the canyon are enough for you, this can be a great day trip. Otherwise, book into a hotel (see the Grand Canyon chapter, Where to Stay), take your time exploring, and return the next day. There are many train and lodging packages that offer good value. For information call **800- THETRAIN.** Website: www.thetrain.com.

Where to Stay

Hotels, Motels, and Inns

Sheridan Inn—$$$–$$$$
Poised on a hillside among a thick stand of pines,

the Sheridan Inn's 11 gorgeous rooms have been filled by hosts Steve and Evelyn Gardner with every possible comfort, like night lights in bathrooms, fridges filled with beer and sodas, and hair dryers. There's genuine privacy, too, because some rooms are in an adjacent annex. Happy hour (which could be dinner) includes vintage wines, martinis mixed with Absolut vodka, and generously splashed Chivas Regal over the rocks. All rooms have cable television with HBO videotape players and a CD-equipped stereo system along with a telephone. Full breakfasts are far more than you can eat. **460 E. Sheridan Ave., Williams; 86046; 520-635-9441 or 888-635-9345. Website: www.the grandcanyon.com/sheridan/.**

Mountain Country Lodge—$$$
Cozy bed-and-breakfast, built as a private mansion in 1909, has nine guestrooms with private baths. On Route 66 in the center of town, it's within walking distance of the Williams historic district and the Grand Canyon Railroad. Rooms have cable television, refrigerators, and VCRs with plenty of tapes in the communal library. Rates include an extensive continental breakfast. 437 West Route 66, Williams, 86046; 520-635-4341 or 800-973-6210. Website: www.the grandcanyon.com/mclodge.

Fray Marcos Hotel—$$$
This impressive hostelry, built in 1995, re-creates the style of the historic Williams Depot next door. It follows the same architectural theme as the original 1908 Fray Marcos built by the Santa Fe Railroad. The hotel's large, high-ceilinged lobby has a massive Arizona flagstone fireplace flanked by enormous paintings of the Grand Canyon by southwestern artist Kenneth McKenna. The dark-wood balcony and wrought-iron chandelier contribute to an old-time look. Don't miss the three lovely Remington bronzes in lobby niches. The one called *Rattlesnake,* with horse and rider both in the air, is remarkable. Rates are seasonal, with the lowest offered Nov.–Feb.; high season is Apr.–Labor Day. **235 N. Grand Canyon Blvd.,**

The Grand Canyon Railway takes passengers in historic luxury from Williams to the Grand Canyon daily.

Williams, 86046; 520-635-4010 or 800-843-8724.

Red Garter Bed & Bakery—$$$

This delightfully restored 1897 onetime bordello and saloon offers four rooms with private baths in a two-story Victorian Romanesque-style brick structure. The breakfast that's included is worth the stay. Don't miss the oat scones and sticky buns, served with coffee, juice, and fresh fruit. They also offer homemade soups and fresh-baked bread, and will pack a picnic lunch for the rest of your journey. Bakery is closed Mon. 137 W. Railroad Ave., P.O. Box 95, Williams, 86046; 800-328-1484 or 520-635-1484. Website: www.redgarter.com.

Hostels and Camping

Grand Canyon Red Lake
Hostel & Campground

This is the closest hostel to the Grand Canyon, so it's always busy. Reservations are a must May 1–Oct. 15. There are eight rooms that sleep four,

but may be reserved privately for an extra charge. It has 14 RV hookups and 10 tent sites. A gas station and country store with a good selection of Indian crafts and jewelry are next door. **On Hwy. 64, 8 miles north of junction with I-40. 520- 635-9122 or 800-581-4753. E-mail: Redlake@infomagic.com.**

Where to Eat

Cruisers Cafe 66—$$–$$$

In downtown Williams, this lively eatery is obviously the '50s re-created, but it's actually more like the '50s never left. It reveals its roots as a gas station with the front end of a '66 Chevy blasting through a wall, old gas pumps, wall-size paintings of postcards and travel maps from the Neon Road's heyday, and chairs uphol-stered in Route 66 tapestry. Fajitas and grilled steaks are great, and cajun prime rib is superb. Open daily, 3:00 P.M.–10 P.M. 233 W. Route 66; 520-635-2445. Website: www.thegrand canyon.com/cruisers.

Max & Thelma's—$$-$$$

Handy new restaurant right at the train depot serves a typically American menu. An all-you-can-eat breakfast buffet, dinner buffet, and lunch specials are always fresh and good. Open daily, 6:00 A.M.–9:00 P.M. **235 N. Grand Canyon Blvd.; 520-635-8970.**

Miss Kitty's Steak House and Saloon—$$-$$$

You can ride your horse up to the hitching post at this large, noisy, friendly place where wagon-wheel lamps light up a busy dining room and dance floor. In summer a great breakfast buffet is available 7:00–10:00 A.M. Lunch and dinner entrees include lots of steak and prime rib, as well as chicken, ribs, and salmon. If you're yearning to try jalapeño chile beer, with a real chile pepper inside the bottle, this is the place. Open Sun.–Thur., 5:00 P.M.–9:00 P.M.; Fri.–Sat., 5:00 P.M.–10:00 P.M. Located next to the Ramada Inn. **642 E. Route 66; 520-635-9161.**

Rod's Steak House—$$-$$$

A Williams landmark for half a century, with Domino, a huge fiberglass steer. His "girlfriend," Dominique, greets patrons at the entrance. Owners Stella and Lawrence Sanchez have created a steer-shaped menu that offers an enormous top sirloin with all the trimmings. Named for original owner Rodney Graves, who organized the town's first rodeo, Rod's is filled with memorabilia and has a great gift shop. Don't miss the oversize margaritas. Open Mar.–Oct., daily, 11:30 A.M.–9:30 P.M.; Nov.–Feb., Mon.–Sat., 11:30 A.M.–9:30 P.M. **301 E. Route 66; 520-635-2671. Website: www.rods-steakhouse.com.**

Spenser's—$-$$

Inside the Fray Marcos Hotel, Spenser's is worth

Cruisers Cafe #66 in Williams celebrates Route 66 with vintage road signs, maps, postcards, and more.

a stop just to see its amazing solid oak bar. It was crafted in 1887 in Shepherd's Bush, a small English village, for a pub called the Lion's Den. The pub proprietor paid cabinetmaker George O. Spenser 200 pounds to make the bar, with the promise that he'd never have to pay for another drink. Spenser fared well, as he lived to age 84 and never missed a day at the Lion's Den. The light menu here at Spenser's includes salads, soup, sandwiches, and pizza. Open daily, 4:00 P.M.–10:00 P.M. **235 N. Grand Canyon Blvd.; 520-635-4010.**

Services

Williams–Grand Canyon Chamber of Commerce

200 W. Railroad Ave., Williams, 86046-2556; 520-635-4061 or 800-863-0546. Website: www.thegrandcanyon.com.

Grand Canyon

On its 1,450-mile journey from Colorado's Rocky Mountains to the Sea of Cortez in Mexico, the Colorado River has left a legacy of sublime beauty. Nowhere is that more evident than in the Grand Canyon. Each year more than 5 million visitors are drawn by the canyon's incomparable panoramas and unique history. Some visitors come just for the day, but to truly appreciate all the canyon has to offer, plan an overnight stay. A tour of the South Rim's many overlooks can take the better part of a day. To visit both the North and South Rims requires a very long drive, and so most people visit either the South or the North Rim, not both.

A master plan has been approved by the National Park Service that will change forever the character of visits to the South Rim. For at least two decades it has been apparent that the huge number of visitors, topping 5 million in recent years, is taking its toll on the experience. Where once the biggest traffic problem was a "deer jam," waits of several hours just to enter the park have become commonplace. Among the plan's components is to remove 80 percent of private vehicles that now enter the park. A year-round shuttle system will be put in place to bring guests from remote parking lots, and a nonpolluting, in-park shuttle will quietly and efficiently take visitors from place to place once they're in the park. The 20 percent of private vehicles still allowed inside the park will belong to employees and hotel guests.

In its effort to save all national parks, the National Park Service has increased fees at many of them. The Grand Canyon entrance fee for vehicles doubled in 1997, and a new backcountry permit of $20 plus a $4-per-person charge each night is now levied. The new auto entrance fee hasn't slowed visitors a bit. Eighty percent of the fees stay at the canyon, with the rest going to help bail out less affluent parks.

Fall is undisputably a lovely time to visit either the North or South Rim. But winter's

another story. The North Rim, oftentimes completely snowed in, closes end Oct.–mid-May. Backcountry skiers and snowshoe trekkers may find it an accessible challenge, but should not proceed without first checking with the National Park Service regarding weather.

History

The canyon's history is layered in its geology. Light-colored Kaibab limestone, filled with ancient fossils, caps the rim. A dozen layers down, black Vishnu schist is striped with pink granite formed by fire more than 2 billion years ago. Over millions of years, the Colorado River cut the canyon's depth, while erosion created its width, a vista-making 18 miles at the South Rim.

Since prehistory, when paleo-hunters drifted across the Southwest in search of game, the Grand Canyon has been home to someone. The Desert Archaic culture lived there 10 centuries before the birth of Christ, and the Anasazi tended corn and bean fields as recently as 800 years ago. Spanish explorers, U.S. Army surveyors, and Catholic missionaries also passed through the canyon.

Present-day hikers often follow trails created by miners searching for silver and copper shortly before the turn of the century. But it was tourism that would ultimately bring the canyon its greatest recognition. By 1883 visitors began arriving by stagecoach, and miners became tour guides who introduced Easterners to natural wonders they'd seen only in picture books. In 1893 the canyon area became a forest reserve, and in 1908, through the efforts of President Theodore Roosevelt, it was named a national monument. In 1919 it became one of the first national parks.

In times past, the Navajo raised crops along the friendly Colorado River on the canyon floor. And today the Havasupai tend cattle and produce highly collectible basketry and beadwork on a reservation that is picturesquely niched in the western Grand Canyon.

North Rim

A thousand feet higher than the South Rim and much less crowded, a highlight of the North Rim is 8,803-foot Point Imperial. From Grand Canyon Lodge there is a 46-mile round-trip drive to the point, which looks out over the Navajo reservation. For hiking along the rim, take the 3-mile roundtrip Transept Trail from the Lodge to the campground.

The Department of Transportation closes the Grand Canyon North Rim Parkway (Hwy. 67) around Oct. 15 and reopens it May 15, which coincides with the closing of National Park facilities at the North Rim. Most people visit

Getting There

North Rim
To get to the North Rim, take Hwy. 67 south from Jacob Lake, which is on US 89A west of Page.

South Rim
To get to the South Rim from Phoenix, take I-17 north 146 miles to Flagstaff, to the junction with I-40. Follow I-40 west for 32 miles to Williams. From Williams take Hwy. 64 north for 63 miles to the South Rim. Or take the Grand Canyon Railway from Williams (see Williams chapter).

West Rim
To get to the West Rim, from Williams, continue west on I-40 to either Ashfork or Seligman, and drive northwest on Route 66 to Peach Springs. From here, take Hwy. 18 northeast.

during summer months, when services can really be overstressed. Portable rest rooms usually are available but are not always clean, so plan your rest stops. Yet the serene loveliness of the North Rim, in sharp contrast to the South Rim's hubbub, draws many hardy souls, most often in RVs or with tenting equipment. At the rim, near the Grand Canyon Lodge, you'll find a campground, camper store, service station, and self-service laundry.

OUTDOOR ACTIVITIES

Boating
Canyoneers is a river-rafting outfitter that does white-water pontoon boat and hiking trips from the North Rim. **Website: www.canyoneers.com** (links to Kaibab Lodge).

Horseback Riding
Choose from short rim rides or half-day and full-

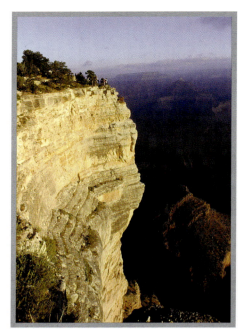

Yavapai Point on the Grand Canyon's South Rim offers spectacular views.

day **mule rides** into the canyon. Make reservations at the desk in the Grand Canyon Lodge lobby (see Where to Stay on the North Rim), or call **520-638-9875, before June 1 call 435-679-8665.**

WHERE TO STAY ON THE NORTH RIM

Grand Canyon Lodge—$$$
This resort is a National Historic Landmark with cabins and motel rooms. The homey lodge has a western-style dining room with canyon views, as well as a sun room, snack shop, saloon, and gift shop. You can book mule rides and bus tours at the hotel. Its 200 rooms fill up quickly, and no waiting list is kept, but sometimes there are last-minute cancellations, so it's always worth a call. Open mid-May–mid-Oct. 303-297-2757. Website: www.amfac.com.

Kaibab Lodge—$$$
Located 18 miles from the North Rim and 5 miles from the park boundary, this truly rustic lodge has a series of cabin-style rooms with private baths and showers. There are no private cabins. There also are eight rooms in the Longhouse. Owners stress that this is basic lodging with nothing larger than a double bed—no phones, no TVs. The lodge has a dining room where a large continental breakfast is served along with a dinner menu that changes nightly. Open mid-May–mid-Oct., coinciding with park openings on the North Rim. **P.O. Box 2997, Flagstaff, 86003; summer 520-638-2389, winter 520-526-0924, outside Arizona 800-525-0924.** Website: www.canyoneers.com.

Camping
Kaibab Camper Village near Jacob Lake is the closest full-hookup camper and RV park to the North Rim. Tent space available. Open May 15–Oct. 15. Located **44 miles north of the North Rim. Summer 520-643-7804, winter 520-526-0924. Website: www.canyoneers.com.**

Jacob Lake Campground in Kaibab National Forest at 7,920 feet has 53 sites without hookups, as well as a visitor center, nature trails, and handicapped facilities. Guided hikes and naturalist programs are offered, as well as horseback riding and chuckwagon rides and meals. Services nearby include a restaurant, supplies, telephone, and dumping station. Open May 15–Nov 1, depending on snowfall. Located 30 miles southeast of Fredonia **at US 89A and Hwy. 67. North Kaibab Ranger District, Box 248, Fredonia, 86022; 602-643-7395.**

South Rim

The South Rim, while open during winter months, often has below-freezing temps and blustery winds. On the other hand, a brilliantly crisp day that's cold but sunny, with a fraction of the touristy crowds that accumulate during the summer, has a lot of appeal. Most services such as bus trips and hikes with a ranger continue during the winter. Campgrounds remain open as do lodges and hotels.

A proposed Heritage Educational Center

will replace a parking lot and utility building, and an Orientation Center at Mather Point is expected to be operational by the year 2001. Two recently constructed lodges, Kachina and Thunderbird, are scheduled for demolition by about 2002 so that the area at the canyon's South Rim can become a true historic district, with major buildings all dating to the canyon's early days. The pace at which this plan proceeds is largely dependent on funding, which is expected to require $350 billion. But, say project creators, it ultimately will enhance the experience at the Grand Canyon and will encourage visitors to stay for a number of days rather than a number of hours as many now do.

The signature musical interpretation of the Grand Canyon, Ferde Grofe's *Grand Canyon Suite,* makes interesting listening as you hike or simply sit and view the spectacular chasm. It is divided into movements called "Sunrise," "Painted Desert," "On the Trail" (most familiar as the orchestra imitates the bray of a burro and the clip-clopping of hooves) and "Sunset and Cloudburst." This pleasant work of humankind is an apt accompaniment to a remarkable work of nature.

Festivals and Events on the South Rim

Grand Canyon Music Festival

first three weeks of Sept.

Since 1984 this concert series has been held in the park on the South Rim, usually featuring chamber music, often including jazz and blues. Recently concerts have been presented at the Shrine of the Ages auditorium, an enchanting, intimate setting that accommodates just 310 patrons. The auditorium has a wall of glass that looks out onto the forest, while the music presents a perfect complement to the setting. The event typically attracts the nation's best chamber musicians. **P.O. Box 1332, Grand Canyon, 86023; 520-638-9215.**

Outdoor Activities on the South Rim

Hiking

Bright Angel Trail

The park's most popular trail, it was constructed in 1891 so that miners could get from the South Rim to their claims. It involves a series of switchbacks that make the return ascent longer but less strenuous than the Kaibab Trail. It is a 19-mile hike round trip, so a stay at the bottom is just about mandatory unless you're doing it by mule. The elevation change is 4,500 feet. The descent takes four to five hours; coming out takes twice as long. There are stop-off stations at various points along the trail, and during summer months rangers patrol regularly, hoping to head off heat-related incidents. On the canyon floor at Indian Garden, a grove of cottonwoods tell you there is water here. At this point, water from the North Rim's Roaring Springs is pumped up to the South Rim and is its only water supply.

South Kaibab Trail

Great views are the attraction on this ridgeline trail. But it's a challenge, dropping almost 5,000 feet in just over 6 miles. You can do a portion of the trail as a day hike, starting from the trailhead at Yaki Point on the South Rim and turning around at Cedar Ridge for a 3-mile round trip, which is tough because even here the elevation drop is almost 1,500 feet.

Horseback Riding

Canyon Mule Trips

For more than 100 years, the classic way to descend into the canyon has been astride a sure-footed, unflappable mule, a cross between a female horse and a male donkey. The four-legged taxis are used because they are more sure-footed than horses. More than 100 mules are trained for canyon trekking, each with a 10- to 12-year worklife expectancy. When they retire, they are sold to petting zoos where they become "canyon celebrities." The animals are educated at special mule schools in Tennessee, where each one undergoes three years of training. Canyon officials boast that there has never been a mule with rider lost over the edge. Single-day and overnight trips are extremely popular, so it is essential to book early. Sometimes it is possible to snag a last-minute reservation because of a cancellation, so don't hesitate to put your name on a waiting list. To see the mules, go to the Bright Angel trailhead on the South Rim where they're corralled. **For rides fewer than four days in advance, go to the Bright Angel transportation desk; 520-638-3283. For reservations more than four days in advance, call 303-297-2757 in Aurora, Colorado.**

Seeing and Doing on the South Rim

Museums and Historic Sites

Hopi House

At the South Rim, this historic gift shop recently underwent a 10-year restoration. Constructed in 1904, it was designated a National Historic Landmark in 1987. It was the first building designed by Mary Elizabeth Jane Colter, the renowned architect who is responsible for the look of many of the original Fred Harvey-owned buildings in the West. The structure was designed to present Hopi tribal arts and crafts in roomlike settings, and is built of native stone and wood. Stone from the original quarry, which had been weathered by exposure to the elements, was a perfect match for the stone it replaced in reconstruction. Located **across from main entrance to El Tovar Hotel; no public phone.**

Kolb Studio

Built on the very lip of the canyon's South Rim in 1904 and enlarged in 1926, Ellsworth and Emery Kolb's photography studio was one of the canyon's earliest entrepreneurial endeavors.

The industrious brothers would photograph mule riders as they began their descent into the canyon. But because the water supply at the rim was so restricted, the Kolbs had to run the 4.5 miles to the bottom of the canyon to Indian Garden where there was sufficient water to process the film. Then they'd charge back up, developed prints in hand, to sell them to mule riders as they returned to the rim. In 1911 the brothers made a daring river trip down the Colorado, which they filmed. Copies of the film are still being shown today. **Located at the canyon's edge near the Bright Angel trailhead. No public phone.**

Nightlife

The club scene is not exactly why you come to the Grand Canyon, and you won't find it here. But on the South Rim there are a number of pleasant places to go for a nightcap and conviviality. The **Bright Angel Lounge,** open daily, 11:00 A.M.–12:30 A.M., in the Bright Angel Lodge has a full-service bar and live entertainment in the evenings Wed.–Sat. **Maswik Sports Lounge** in the Maswik Lodge has a big-screen TV aglow with whatever sporting event is of the moment. Seven additional sets are scattered throughout the room. Open daily, 11:00 A.M.–12:30 A.M. **El Tovar Lounge** in the El Tovar Hotel overlooks the canyon and when it's warm, drinks are served on the veranda. Settle in here while you're waiting for your dinner reservations. Open 11:00 A.M.–12:30 A.M. Call **303-29-PARKS** for all three nightspots.

Tours

AERIAL TOURS

Strict regulations as to when and where aircraft can fly over the Grand Canyon have decreased noise impact to that of a bus operating within the park area. The only helicopters that you as a visitor will see (unless you take a helicopter tour) are those operated by the National Park Service on rescue flights, or flights to bring supplies to the bottom of the canyon.

Among the half-dozen companies that fly, **AirStar Helicopters** does a particularly good job of showing off the canyon. Non-English-speaking guests are given a taped simultaneous translation of the English narration that they may patch into their camcorders to precisely accompany the video they are shooting. Tours of 25–30 minutes cover the Dragon Corridor and Central Canyon; 40- to 45-minute tours also take in the Colorado River at the point where it merges with the Little Colorado; 50- to 60-minute flights add even more pinnacles, buttes, and spires. Flights **leave from the Grand Canyon Airport near Tusayan,** near the South Rim and just south of the park boundary **on US 180.** 800-962-3869 or 520-638-2622. Website: www.airstar.com.

Where to Stay on the South Rim

Hotels, Motels, and Inns

All of the Grand Canyon National Park lodges are operated by **Amfac Parks and Resorts (website: www.amfac.com),** the official National Park Service concessionaire on the South Rim. Of the eight properties, four are located on the canyon's rim, three are within the park, and one is just outside the park's south entrance. All rooms have phones and TVs, but there are no housekeeping units. Some accommodations close during winter months. Usually packages are available during winter months that can considerably lower the price of a room. Individuals can book as many as 23 months in advance. For reservations at all Grand Canyon properties, call (303) 29-PARKS. If you're staying at any park hotel or lodge, just dial the operator to be connected to any other park facility.

El Tovar Hotel—$$$$

Built by the Fred Harvey Company in 1905 and now a National Historic Landmark, it is the only

Condors, recently re-introduced to their original habitat near Vermilion Cliffs, have been spotted at Grand Canyon lookouts like this one.

lodging at the canyon that's considered a true hotel because it has room service and a concierge. All 77 rooms have just undergone renovation to restore the decor to its original soft pastels. Located right on the South Rim and fashioned after hunting lodges in Europe, it is constructed of native stone and Oregon pine. Lovely and dignified, it is the most upscale of all accommodations at the Grand Canyon. It has a gift shop, elegant restaurant, and lounge. Breakfast or lunch here, looking out over the canyon, is a must.

Kachina and Thunderbird Lodges—$$$$

These twin 104-room buildings have rooms facing the canyon or the park, and are right in the middle of everything that's going on at the South Rim. They may not exist much longer because they do not fit the historic ambiance of this part of the rim, but for the next few years, they offer modern motel-type accommodations.

Maswik Lodge—$$$

Located at the southwest end of Grand Canyon Village, it was named for a Hopi Kachina who is said to guard the canyon. It has 278 rooms, and sometimes is the last to fill up, so try here if all else fails. Rustic cabins also are available during summer months. It has a gift shop, restaurant, and lounge.

Yavapai Lodge—$$$

With 385 rooms, this is the park's largest lodge. Actually it's a series of lodge buildings in a piñon and juniper forest about a mile from the South Rim, adjacent to the visitor center and the village business area. It is not unusual to see mule deer grazing outside your window, jays and nuthatches in the trees, and squirrels and chipmunks being adorable in hopes of a snack. Don't feed them. It's against park regulations. If you don't want to be in the middle of the South Rim hubbub, try Yavapai Lodge for peace and quiet.

Bright Angel Lodge and Cabins—$$–$$$

Almost everyone who stays overnight at the canyon wants to book here because the name Bright Angel is so well known. But because it has just 37 rooms and 49 cabins, you should reserve early. It overlooks the South Rim and provides dramatic views from many rooms. Designed in 1935 and built of log and native stone, it is the point from which mule rides depart for descents into the canyon. In the lobby, a carved wood thunderbird was named the "bright angel of the sky" by architects. It has a restaurant and lounge.

Phantom Ranch—$

At the bottom of the canyon, accessible only by mule, foot, or river raft, Phantom Ranch has dormitory-type accommodations, segregated for male or female hikers. Hikers also can reserve meals at the Phantom Ranch Dining Hall. If you're even thinking of doing this, reserve well ahead because accommodations fill up more than a year in advance. You also can book overnight mule trips that include three meals and cabin accommodations.

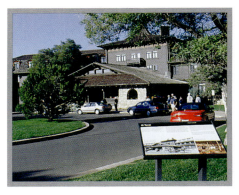

For years, the historic El Tovar, built in 1905, has welcomed Grand Canyon guests with elegance and luxury.

Where to Eat on the South Rim

There are several good choices for mealtimes at the South Rim, ranging from fine dining to basic fast fare. Although there are no dress codes, you probably won't be comfortable showing up for dinner at El Tovar or Arizona Steak House in shorts and a T-shirt. For dinner reservations, from any of the hotels or lodges inside the park, use a house phone and dial 6431.

Arizona Steak House—$$$–$$$$

Located on the South Rim with huge windows affording a canyon view, the specialty here is steak. A fresh catch of the day is also reliably good. Open seasonally, 5:00 P.M.–10:00 P.M. Reservations are not accepted, so during busy summer months show up before 5:00 P.M. or you could have a wait of up to an hour. **In Bright Angel Lodge.**

El Tovar—$$$–$$$$

The elegant dining room in this famous hotel is lined with murals depicting the Hopi, Apache, Mojave, and Navajo cultures. Service is still as impeccable as it was when crisply clad Harvey Girls served fresh oysters and imported Roquefort to well-heeled diners. Truly a fine dining experience with canyon views from many tables, dinner reservations are in high demand. Reservations are not accepted for breakfast (try the asparagus and boursin omelet) or lunch. For dinner reservations call 520-638-2631, ext. 6431 from outside the park. **In El Tovar Hotel.**

Bright Angel Coffee Shop—$$–$$$

This is a good family restaurant, open for three meals a day. Though always busy, it doesn't have the long waits that build up at the Arizona Steak House. Well-prepared fare includes Southwestern entrees, sandwiches, pasta, omelets, and vegetarian dishes. Reservations not accepted. Open 6:30 A.M.–10:00 P.M. **At Bright Angel Lodge.**

Maswik Cafeteria—$–$$

This food court offers lunch and dinner with daily specials that feature pasta, Mexican food, and sandwiches to go. Beer and wine are available. Opens at 6:00 A.M. to accommodate guests taking the many tours and rafting trips with early departures. Closes at 11:00 P.M. **In Maswik Lodge.**

Yavapai Cafeteria—$–$$

The spacious, bright dining room has greenhouse window seating. You feel like you're eating under a waterfall when it rains. Lines move quickly and efficiently, and the cafeteria serves up fare that ranges from pancakes and pizza to burgers and fried chicken. Beer and wine are available. Open seasonally, 6:00 A.M.–11:00 P.M. **In Yavapai Lodge.**

Babbitt's—$

This market and deli has groceries and will make sandwiches to go. Open 7:00 A.M.–7:00 P.M. Located **across from Yavapai Lodge.** There are also Babbitt's in Tusayan and Desert View (east on Hwy. 64).

Outside the South Rim

Tusayan

This little town just beyond the park's southern boundaries in the Kaibab National Forest exists primarily to supply visitor support for the national park. The **Imax Theatre** presents a 34-minute film, *The Grand Canyon—The Hidden Secrets,* every hour on the half-hour, 8:30 A.M.–8:30 P.M. There is a post office at the Babbitt's store, which also carries groceries, general supplies, books, magazines, and take-out deli food (see Where to Eat). For more information on Tusayan, log on to the website: **www.gcanyon.com.** It has a number of lodging options (see Where to Stay Outside the South Rim).

Valle

This small town 25 miles south of the canyon at the intersections of US 180 and Hwy. 64 has a Days Inn, restaurant, gas station, and small market. **Bedrock City,** that oh-so-blue-walled area to the west of Hwy. 64, is a Flintstones-themed "prehistoric park" where kids can ride a train through an "active volcano." The Flintstone and Rubble houses are there, as is a gift shop with more Flintstones stuff than ever you imagined. Fred's Diner is open for three meals, serving Bronto Burgers, Dino Dogs, Gravelberry Pie, and other themed fare.

SEEING AND DOING

Museums

Open since 1995 and growing every year, **Planes of Fame Air Museum** is part of the much larger Planes of Fame Museum in Chino, California. Many of the vintage aircraft are flyable, with others being restored. In the collection is a Lockheed C-121A Constellation, the old "Connie" that was the VIP transport for Gen. Douglas MacArthur during the Korean War. You can tour its interior. Morbid but interesting is the Japanese-piloted World War II suicide rocket called the Yokosuka Ohka, whose name means "cherry blossom." The one at the museum was captured on the island of Okinawa. A Hawker Hunter, the first genuinely transsonic British service aircraft, had its initial flight in 1951. The airport itself sometimes accommodates overflow traffic from the Grand Canyon Airport, and often gets traffic that has been diverted because of weather conditions. Small fee. Open in summer, daily, 9:00 A.M.–6:00 P.M.;

in winter, daily, 9:00 A.M.–5:00 P.M.; closed Thanksgiving and Christmas. Located in Valle, at US 180 and Hwy. 64. **HCR 34, Box B, Valle, Williams, 86046; 520-635-1000. Website: www.planesoffame.org.**

WHERE TO STAY OUTSIDE THE SOUTH RIM

Grand Hotel—$$$

This new hotel has an indoor pool, plus king or queen beds in its 120 rooms. The adjacent Canyon Star Restaurant prides itself on perfectly grilled steaks. **In Tusayan. P.O. Box 3319, Grand Canyon, 86023; 888-63-GRAND.** Website: thegrand@gcanyon.com.

Holiday Inn Express Hotel and Suites—$$$

Spacious Arizona Rooms (two-bedroom suites) have coffeemaker, microwave, and refrigerator. Continental breakfast included. **In Tusayan. P.O. Box 3245, Grand Canyon, 86023; 520-638-3000 or 888-473-2269. Website: HI@gcanyon.com.**

Moqui Lodge—$$$

With 136 rooms, this is sometimes a good bet if lodging right at the canyon is full. It is the headquarters for the Apache Stables horseback riding facilities. A breakfast buffet is included with the room rate. **On Hwy. 64, 0.5 miles before the south entrance to the Grand Canyon; 520-638-2424.**

Camping

The AAA-approved **campground at Valle** south of the South Rim has pull-through sites with full hookups, and also has tent camping with showers and rest rooms. Once closed during winter months, it now is open all year. **520-635-2600.**

West Rim

Peach Springs

Situated on the Hualapai (say "WALL-a-pie") Indian Reservation where Grand Canyon National Park reaches its southernmost point, for years Peach Springs was visited only by those who wanted to get permits for backcountry trips. When I-40 bypassed Peach Springs in the early 1970s, everything pretty much closed except a deli and a service station. But for the last 10 years this area has been re-emerging as the jumping-off point for exploring the canyon's West Rim, which is uniquely different from the tourist-jammed South Rim more than 100 miles to the northeast. There is little traffic, few buildings, and almost no commercial enterprises or other signs of humanity's intrusion. Here, the Hualapai have stewardship over almost 1 million acres of land, 108 miles of which is Grand Canyon frontage.

OUTDOOR ACTIVITIES

River Rafting

The Native American-owned and -operated company **Hualapai River Runners** does one- and two-day raft trips on the lower Colorado. Trips include navigating nine rapids in motorized pontoon boats, hiking to Travertine Falls, and lunch at Separation Canyon. The trip travels through the Lower Granite Gorge from Diamond Creek to Pierce Ferry. Hualapai guides share legends about their culture and point out sights in nature. Offered Apr.–Oct. Leaves **from Hualapai Lodge near Peach Springs in the West Rim area; for reservations call 800-622-4409 or 520-769-2219. Website: www.river-runners.com.**

SEEING AND DOING

Tours

Along Old Route 66 near Peach Springs, you'll see huge signs for **Grand Canyon Caverns.** Don't bother if you're claustrophobic. But if you are a truly spunky spelunker, you'll enjoy a look at the largest registered dry caverns in the country. They have been documented at 345 million years old. With a guide, you'll take an elevator underground 21 stories, then walk along lighted trails with handrails through lovely limestone caves. Ancient fossilized fish and the replica of a giant ground sloth are evidence of onetime cave dwellers. A mummified bobcat suggests a more recent casualty. The underground labyrinth can't rival the caverns at Carlsbad, New Mexico, but they are interesting for their "cave snow," a murky coating that covers rocks with soft white stuff, and for the oddly lovely flowstone, stalactites, stalagmites, and helectites that give the caverns their personality. A restaurant and little market are at this stop, too. Guided 45-minute tours leave every half hour. Moderate fee. Open Memorial Day–Oct. 15., daily, 8:00 A.M.–6:00 P.M.; winter, daily, 10:00 A.M.–5:00 P.M. Located **about 10 miles east of Peach Springs on old Route 66.** Watch for the turnoff signs. **P.O. Box 180, Peach Springs, 86434; 520-422-3223.**

The West Rim is the starting point for a 4.5-mile **bus tour** that proceeds to Eagle Point for a look at rock formations, then to Guano Point to see remains of tram towers used in the 1950s as part of a system to harvest bat guano from a mine on the canyon's north face. The location, on a sharp bend in the Colorado, creates a spectacular view, much wider than on most rim sites. At Guano Point, a lunch of chicken or beef barbecue, tortillas, beans, and corn is served as part of the tour. There are picnic tables, or if it's windy, you can eat inside the little tramworks house. Located **92 miles northwest of Peach Springs via some paved and some unimproved county roads and about 3 miles from the rim; 520-699-0269.**

WHERE TO STAY ON THE WEST RIM

Hualapai Lodge—$$$

Opened in 1997 in Peach Springs, it has 60 large, comfortable rooms; a restaurant open for three meals; and a gift shop occupy a two-story building. **Located between Kingman and Seligman on the longest remaining stretch of Route 66. For reservations call 888-255-9550 or 520-769-2230.** For automated information call **520-638-7888 (website: the canyon.com/nps). Website: www.hualapai tours.com.**

The Arizona Trail

Just as Route 66 bisects Arizona horizontally, providing a historic path for motorized vehicles, the Arizona Trail reaches from north to south in a swath designed for nonmotorized use. About 500 miles of the total 780 miles opened at the beginning of 1998.

It begins at the Coronado National Memorial close to the Mexican border near Sierra Vista and ends on the Utah state line just north of Jacob Lake. It links special places that include the Huachuca Mountains, Saguaro National Monument, Mount Lemmon, the Superstition Mountains, the Mogollon Rim, Mazatzal Wilderness, Four Peaks, Walnut Canyon, San Francisco Peaks, and the Grand Canyon. It spans seven mountain ranges and crosses seven life zones, from Sonoran Desert to Canadian Alpine. It is designed to accommodate hikers, backpackers, cross-country skiers, mountain bikers (outside of wilderness or other specially managed areas), and equestrians.

Besides scenic wonders, the trail provides access to old stagecoach routes, ghost towns, Native American ruins, and trails used by early explorers. It is divided into 44 sections called passages that go from trailhead to trailhead. Maps and information are available for completed passages. Some portions may be extremely hot in summer, others can be covered with snow in winter. The entire trail is expected to be complete by the end of 2002. For more information, contact **Arizona Trail Association, P.O. Box 36736, Phoenix, 85067; 602-252-4794. Website: www.aztrail.org.**

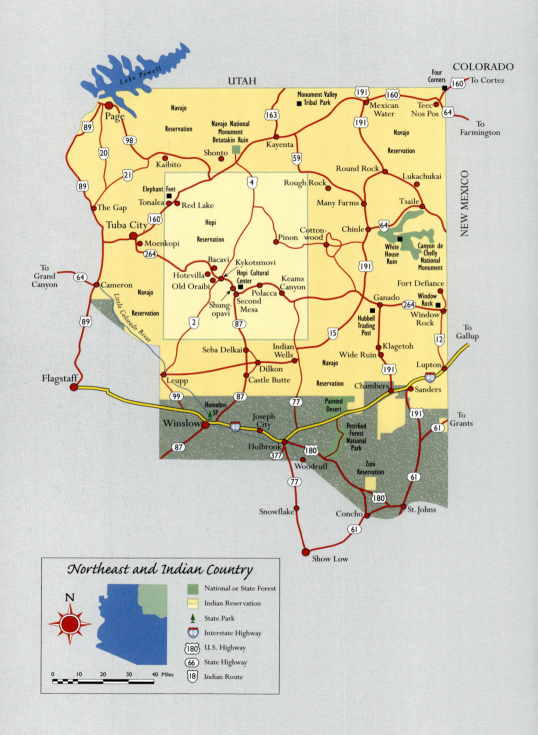

Northeast and Indian Country

Northeast and Indian Country

Merrick Butte is easy to pick out among other giant monoliths in Monument Valley.

Navajo Reservation and Environs

On a map, Arizona's far northeastern corner appears bare and featureless. In its center, the vast 27,543-square-mile Navajo Reservation wraps around the Hopi Reservation in a giant cartographic hug. The 16-million-acre Navajo Reservation is located primarily in Arizona, but extends into Utah and New Mexico. The entire expanse is crossed by only a few main roads, their wiggly courses dotted with isolated Indian-named towns. Yet this is an area that reflects Mother Nature's smile. She took her time as she molded, sculpted, and composed. Some believe that she purposefully situated this stunningly beautiful area in a place that the elements treat harshly.

This is an enigmatic part of the state, filled with hidden places waiting to be discovered. The Navajo people, called Diné, say that there are dozens of things here that no white person has ever seen. Exploring even those that are known is truly a journey to foreign-seeming lands. When given to the Navajos, the land was thought to be practically valueless. But discovery of oil and other mineral resources, and development of tourism in recent years, have proven the land's richness.

About 200,000 Navajo live on the 16-million-acre reservation, which is larger than the entire state of West Virginia. The reservation is a unique blend of traditional and modern ways. You will hear Navajo spoken as often as English, sometimes mingling in a single conversation.

The Navajo Reservation observes daylight savings time, while the rest of Arizona doesn't. The reservation is on Mountain Daylight Time, which means that May–Oct. it is on New Mexico, not Arizona, time. If you're on the res-ervation in the summer, remember that the time in Phoenix, the Grand Canyon, and elsewhere is an hour earlier. Alcoholic beverages are prohibited on the reservation. Most of the land is open range, so watch for cattle when driving. The accommodations mentioned in this chapter are not necessarily favorites, but we list them because there are so few places to camp and to stay in this area.

History

On the Navajo Reservation, spires, buttes, and mesas have been shaped over 50 million years as wind, rain, and temperature changes chafed away at layers of crumbling rock. The cliff-dwelling Anasazi lived in many areas of northeastern Arizona more than 1,500 years ago, niched among ridges and protected ledges. For them the canyons were welcoming places, sheltering rich, moist soil that produced reliable crops of corn. These peaceful people mysteriously abandoning their homes in the 1300s. The extensive pictographs (painted pictures) and petroglyphs (carved or incised symbols) found in Monument Valley and Canyon de Chelly were left by both Anasazi and the later Navajo. Rock art with horses dates to the 16th century and later, when the Spanish introduced ponies to the Anasazi. Others clearly date to the Spanish era, such as a pictograph in Canyon de Chelly that shows a rider with a cross on his cape, and riders with what appear to be rifles.

The Navajos have lived in this area for some 700 years, in traditional dome-shaped dwellings made of sticks and mud called hogans. In the traditional eight-sided hogan, each side has a use. The cooking area is in the center, and sleeping quarters are on the west. The door faces the sunrise so occupants can welcome the new day. The traditional way to enter a hogan is to walk around to the left. Navajos tended herds of cattle and sheep, spinning wool by hand to create treasured Navajo rugs. Trading posts date to the 1850s when wool, hides, meat, woven materials, whatever the Navajos had to convert to money, were exchanged by traders for cash. Trading posts were the contact point at which the Navajo culture and newcomers became acquainted with each other. They became social centers and journey's end for Native Americans who traveled on horseback to exchange their wares for supplies and trade tokens. The trading and socializing often lasted several days, with overnight guests staying in hogans built especially for that purpose.

This was a difficult time for Native Americans, who were being herded onto reservations and struggling to adjust to a new way of life. Arizona's first military outpost, Fort Defiance, was built in 1851 by Col. Edwin Sumner, on Bonito Creek. He named it Fort Defiance because it flew in the face of the Navajo desire for it not to be there. The Navajo did their best to discourage it, but the Army prevailed. It

Getting There

Kayenta and Four Corners

From Page, Hwy. 98 leads southeast into the reservation to US 160. US 160 runs east-west through the reservation, from US 89 just west of Tuba City to the Four Corners region. Kayenta is at the junction of US 160 and US 163, 20 miles south of the Utah border.

Chinle and Tsaile

From US 160 at Mexican Water, US 191 runs north into Utah and heads south through all of the eastern portion of the reservation. From US 160, go south on US 191 to Chinle; from Chinle, Tsaile is about 30 miles northeast on Navajo Route 64.

Ganado and Window Rock

Ganado is on US 191 34 miles south of Chinle and 30 miles north of I-40 at Chambers. Window Rock is 29 miles east of Ganado on Hwy. 264. From I-40 on the south, other highways also lead north into the reservation: Hwys. 99 and 87 from near Winslow, and Hwy. 77 east of Holbrook.

served as headquarters for Col. Kit Carson's Navajo Campaign in the summer of 1863, during which the Native Americans were removed from the area. The treaty of 1868 establishing the Navajo Reservation was signed on June 1 of that year. Three weeks later, the Navajo who had been imprisoned at Fort Sumner near the Mexican border were released, to return to their homeland. In 1920, oil was discovered on the reservation. A 1922 treaty between the Navajo and the U.S. government allowed the U.S. to drill the oil.

The Navajo language is so complicated that during World War II, Navajo men were employed as Code Talkers to communicate in their native

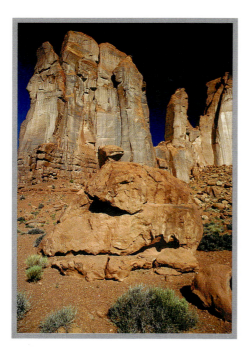

In Monument Valley, on the Navajo Reservation, sandstone monoliths have been sculpted by nature.

language to baffle the Japanese during the war in the Pacific. The "code" was never broken.

Although differences between Navajo and European-American cultures rapidly are being erased, some old customs prevail. Generations ago, photographing or sketching a Navajo would have been offensive, and the person would have edged away. Some still will, so the courteous thing to do is to request permission before photographing. Don't be surprised if you are asked for a small fee. Eye contact may be considered rude, and touching usually is reserved for close friends and family. Open friendliness may not be forthcoming. Don't be put off. Just remember that you are on the Navajos' land; they were here first, and their culture deserves respect.

Navajo National Monument

About an hour and a half east of Page off US 160, west of Kayenta, the Navajo National

Monument protects cliff ruins hidden in deep canyons, built and occupied 700 years ago by the Anasazi. If you visit in winter, be prepared for strong winds and snow at this 7,300-foot elevation. Summers are warm and pleasant. The elaborate cliff dwellings at Keet Seel and Betatakin Ruins are both remarkably well preserved. A third, Inscription House, is closed to the public. Take US 160 to 18 miles south of Kayenta and turn northwest on Hwy. 564 to the park. **HC-71, Box 3, Tonalea, 86044; 520-672-2366.**

Hiking
Most visitors simply hike the 1-mile round-trip paved **Sandal Trail** that goes to an overlook facing the Betatakin Ruin. Bring your binoculars because you won't get very close. The walk takes about 45 minutes with frequent stops to catch your breath if you're not in shape. Open year-round during daylight hours. For more hiking and a lovely view of the piñon and juniper forest, veer off onto the **Aspen Forest Trail** that descends partway into Betatakin Canyon.

For a close-up look at the **Betatakin Ruins,** you must take a 5-mile-round-trip, ranger-guided tour that's fairly strenuous, and descends 700 feet into the canyon (remember, that's 700 feet that you also have to come back up). First-come tours are limited to 25; this is a very popular hike, so show up early to claim a free ticket. Beginning in early May, daily, at 10:00 A.M.; Memorial Day–Labor Day, daily, two hikes at 9:00 A.M. and noon; Labor Day–Oct., daily, 11:00 A.M.

The only way to get to the dramatic cliff dwelling called the **Keet Seel Ruin,** located 8.5 miles from the visitor center, is by hiking or on horseback. Those who have done it say it is well worth the effort. A National Park Service backcountry permit is necessary. A local Navajo family provides horses for the day trip to the ruin for a fee, but hiking permits are free.

Museums and Historic Sites
The visitor center at Navajo National Monument has lovely Native American jewelry of excellent quality, including pieces of snowflake obsidian. The museum has a walk-in replica of

a Betatakin family home, an example of a living unit within a pueblo. Open mid-Dec.–Mar., 8:00 A.M.–4:30 P.M.; Mar.–May, 8:00 A.M.–5:00 P.M.; May–early Sept., 8:00 A.M.–6:00 P.M; early Sept.–mid-Dec., 8:00 A.M.–5:00 P.M.

Kayenta

In the northeastern part of Navajo County, the small, weathered town of Kayenta is generally considered the jumping-off point for visiting Navajo National Monument, 20 miles to the west, and Monument Valley to the north. Peabody Coal Company owns and operates two mines in the area, which fuel electric power plants.

SEEING AND DOING

Museums and Historic Sites
At the **Navajo Cultural Center,** stroll through 2.5 acres of open-air exhibits that include authentic examples of hogans, a sweathouse, and a typical shade house. Native artisans often are on hand to show how they create their famous rugs, jewelry, and sand paintings. Located **next to the Hampton Inn in Kayenta, 0.25 mile south of US 160 and US 163; no phone.**

Scenic Drives
Driving the **23-mile stretch of US 163** that extends from Kayenta through the magnificent rock formations of Monument Valley and on to the Utah state line, recently designated a scenic highway by the Arizona Department of Transportation, is an hour well spent. The paved, two-lane highway passes 7,101-foot-high Agathla Peak on the east and wanders through small Navajo communities, where in summer the residents often sell arts and crafts along the roadside.

WHERE TO STAY IN KAYENTA

Hampton Inn—$$$–$$$$
This new motel holds no surprises; it has comfortable rooms with cable TV and coffeemakers, plus a gift shop. Rate includes a good breakfast

A hogan, the traditional Navajo mud dwelling, provides protection against blowing dust and heat.

buffet; rates are lower in winter. Located **0.25 mile south of US 160 and US 163. P.O. Box 1217, Kayenta 86033; 800-428-7866 or 520-697-3170. Website: www.hamptoninn.com.**

Holiday Inn—$$$–$$$$
Rates are high (lower in winter) for basic accommodations at this 162-room property, but places to stay are few and far between near Monument Valley, and summer months are busy. The restaurant serves three meals a day and has a good breakfast buffet. Located **about 25 miles south of Monument Valley, at US 160 and US 163. Box 307, Kayenta, 86033; 800-465-4329 or 520-697-3221. Website: www.basshotels.com.**

Best Western Wetherill Inn—$$$
At this recently refurbished motel near Monument Valley, 54 rooms have cable TV and coffeemakers. The gift shop has a good selection of Native American arts and crafts. **P.O. Box 175, Kayenta, 86033; 800-528-1234 or 520-697-3231. Website: www.bestwestern.com.**

WHERE TO EAT IN KAYENTA
You can get groceries at two markets. Burger

King and McDonald's, along with the low-key Blue Coffee Pot Cafe, are on US 160.

Monument Valley Navajo Tribal Park

Located on Arizona's border and extending north into Utah, this magnificent expanse of red sandstone is a 30,000-acre Navajo Tribal Park within the reservation. Its layers of crumbling rock create stone creatures in the mind's eye—Bear and Rabbit, the King on his Throne, Three Sisters, Elephant Butte—all are clearly discernible on a monolith-studded landscape beneath a crisp, dazzling sky. The cliff-dwelling Anasazi lived in Monument Valley more than 1,500 years ago, until the 1300s. Today close to 300 Navajos are settled here, some in traditional hogans, others in present-day manufactured homes, some with electricity and running water. Navajo-escorted tours that range from three hours to all day may be booked at the visitor center. Small entrance fee. The valley is about 320 miles from Phoenix. From US 160 in Kayenta, take US 163 north about 25 miles. **Monument Valley Navajo Tribal Park, P.O. Box 360289, Monument Valley, UT 84536; 801-727-3353.**

Scenic Drives

A 17-mile dirt loop road winds through Monument Valley and is open to private vehicles, which do quite well by avoiding patches of loose sand that can envelop a tire and devour it whole. A plus for traveling by car is that you can roll up windows and turn on air conditioners in defense against the fine red dust that blows, scratching eyes and penetrating cameras. To see the valley thoroughly, plan to spend at least two and a half hours. An alternate plan is to take one of the open-air trams that leave from the visitor center. Driven by local Navajo guides, they stop at all the scenic sites and have the advantage of being allowed into shadowy canyons and remote spots that prohibit private cars. There are no rest rooms and no water on the loop drive.

A classic stop for all visitors is **John Ford Point,** named for the famous director of 1930s and 1940s westerns, beginning with *Stagecoach*, released in 1939. Many of these early flicks featured the scenic spit of land as a backdrop. *How the West Was Won,* released in 1962, and the 1988 film *Back to the Future III* all were filmed here. Another landmark, **Right Mitten,** has had luxury automobiles helicoptered to its flat top to create dramatic footage for television commercials. **Rain God Mesa** was the altar at which medicine men prayed for life-sustaining moisture and which shelters a sacred burial ground.

Sometimes it is possible to stop at a traditional hogan where Navajos offer rugs and jewelry for sale. The atmosphere is low-key and respectful, with no pressure put on the visitor to make a purchase. Along the winding road, it is common to see herds of wild horses, untamed for generations. They race beside towering cliffs, impossible to catch, savoring the sheer pleasure of running free. They belong to no one, but somehow belong to everyone who appreciates the captivating loveliness of Monument Valley.

WHERE TO STAY IN MONUMENT VALLEY

Goulding's Lodge—$$$–$$$$

It's the only hotel in Monument Valley; balcony rooms have majestic views. It has a small indoor pool, restaurant, gas station, and general store. The land once belonged to Harry Goulding, who started a trading post there in the 1920s. His home and store, adjacent to the current motel, now are a **small museum.** Rates are lower after mid-Oct. Located **about 4 miles west of entrance to Monument Valley,** just inches over Utah state line. **Box 360001, Monument Valley, UT 84536; 800-874-0902 or 801-727-3231.**

Camping

Goulding's Campground is a camping and RV option near Goulding's Lodge that has 60 RV hookups, showers, and a children's playground. Facilities, including the laundry and pool, are closed during winter months, but visitors are still welcome to park there. **Box 360001, Monument Valley, UT 84536; 435-727-3231.**

Also near Monument Valley, at **Mitten View Campground** you'll find tent and RV sites with showers and 64 hookups. Spaces are on a first-come, first-served basis. Located at the entrance to the 17-mile trail that loops through Monument Valley. **Monument Valley Tribal Park, 435-727-3353.**

Four Corners Monument Navajo Tribal Park

The northeast corner of the Navajo Reservation is the only place in the country where it's possible to stand in four states at the same time. A concrete monument marks the point where Utah, Colorado, New Mexico, and Arizona meet. Incorporating the seals of all four states and bearing the inscription "Four States Here Meet in Freedom Under God," it rests on a corner of each state, all of which are on Indian land. At the visitor center, Navajo craftspeople sell jewelry and traditional Navajo food. There are picnic tables and rest rooms, but no water. Small fee. Open May–Aug., daily, 7:00 A.M.–8:00 P.M.; late Aug.–Apr., daily, 8:00 A.M.–5:00 P.M. Located **0.25 mile west of US 160, 6 miles north of Teec Nos Pos. Navajo Parks and Recreation Dept., P.O. Box 9000, Window Rock, 86515; 520-871-6647.**

Chinle and Tsaile

SEEING AND DOING

Museums and Historic Sites

The best reason to stop at the reservation town of Tsaile is to visit the **Diné College,** used as much to educate Navajo youth as it is to preserve the culture. Two-year courses prepare students for life off the reservation. The four-story, hogan-shaped building is constructed around a traditional eight-sided hogan, the college's

center. Students come to this peaceful room to study and to reflect. By taking the time to spend a few quiet moments here, it is easy to feel the influence of an ancient culture and religion. The third and fourth floors house a terrific **museum** with works by Navajo artists that include silverwork, rugs, wool, baskets, and pottery. The **bookstore** is a treasure trove of information on the Navajo culture. The college grounds themselves have the traditional hogan layout, with each side having a use, like a room. The dining hall (corresponding to a hogan cooking area) is in the center, for example, and sleeping quarters (dorms) are on the west. Students and personnel are proud of their college and glad to take the time to explain it, so don't hesitate to ask. You usually may walk around the campus any time. The museum and gallery are open weekdays, 8:30 A.M.–4:30 P.M. Located **on Navajo Route 64 at Route 12,** about 30 miles northeast of US 191 near Canyon de Chelly. **Diné College, Tsaile, 86556; 520-724-6600.**

Canyon de Chelly National Monument

Take a look at a map and you'll see that Canyon de Chelly (pronounced "Shay") National Monument spreads like the talons of an eagle, with the two fingers of Canyon de Chelly on the south and Canyon del Muerto (Canyon of the Dead) on the north. For 50 million years, streams from the nearby Chuska Mountains have followed their courses, creating sheer, sculpted red sandstone passages that trace history in their many layers. Other elements—probing tree roots, seeping water that freezes, soil acids, and wind—continue the process of change. Glossy ravens and red-tailed hawks joyride on updrafts along terra-cotta cliffs. The spirits of the Anasazi, whose frequent ceremonies gave thanks for the reliable crops of corn, linger in petroglyphs and dwellings niched among ridges and protected ledges.

The best way to see Canyon de Chelly is to first view it from the north and south rims by

John Ford Point in Monument Valley is named for one of the famous film director's favorite vantage points.

car, to get a sense of its enormity. Then, the safest means of exploring its depths is on a tour in a tram or jeep equipped with large tires, specifically adapted to foil the canyon's shifting, sandy bottom. Brief, late-afternoon rains are common in summer, and can turn the canyon floor into quicksand.

The most widely photographed ruin is **Junction House,** which lies at the point where the canyons converge. Its 15 rooms are easy to see from below as well as from across the canyon at Junction Overlook. Hand- and toeholds are clearly visible, carved into the cliff by the Anasazi so they could reach this lofty dwelling. Farther into Canyon de Chelly, the **White House Ruin,** so called because some walls still bear traces of the original white plaster, once consisted of approximately 60 rooms and four kivas, which are ceremonial chambers evolved from pit-house structures. The ruin overlooks a shady spot alongside a cottonwood-lined creek, a favored rest stop for jeep tours where Navajos often spread blankets to display jewelry and crafts. In Canyon del Muerto **Standing Cow Ruin,** named for the white cow pictograph on the canyon wall beside a Navajo stone hogan, befuddles archaeologists because it is situated on the site of an Anasazi ruin. Usually the Navajo shun places of the Anasazi, which in Navajo means something like "ancient ones." The cow probably is of Navajo origin.

A few Navajo families live in the canyon, but most are here just during summer months, making a living by selling crafts and jewelry to visitors. Most come into the canyon during the day, returning to homes in the nearby town of Chinle at night.

The extensive pictographs and petroglyphs found in Canyon de Chelly were left by both Anasazi and Navajo cultures. Believed to have intricate meanings, they in fact express a language of their own. Some clearly date to the Spanish era, such as the pictograph near Standing Cow Ruin that shows a rider with a cross on his cape, and riders with what appear to be rifles. Whatever these enigmatic markings say, they are just part of the spectacle of towering cliffs and memorable dwellings that honor nature and an ancient way of life. Some speculate their messages are best left uncovered, permitting them to keep shadowy secrets that perhaps were never meant to be revealed. Canyon de Chelly is located 96 miles southeast of Monument Valley. **From US 191 at Chinle, drive 3.5 miles east on Navajo Route 64. Visitor Center, Box 588, Chinle, 86503; 520-674-5500. Website: www.canyondechelly.com.**

Horseback Riding

Justin's Stables provides spirited horses that, along with a guide, will take you into the canyon. Located at the mouth of the canyon. **P.O. Box 881, Chinle, 86503; 520-674-5678.**

Tours

Hiking (with a guide) and four- and six-wheel-drive vehicle tours may be booked at historic **Thunderbird Lodge (800-679-2437 or 520-674-5841)**, 0.5 mile from the visitor center. Private individual cars are not permitted.

WHERE TO STAY IN CHINLE AND TSAILE

Best Western Canyon de Chelly Inn—$$$

In downtown Chinle, 3 miles from the Canyon de Chelly National Park visitor center, this motel has an indoor swimming pool and a full-service restaurant. Located **one block east of US 191. P.O. Box 295, Chinle, 86503; 800-327-0354 or 520-674-5874, fax 520-674-3715.**

Holiday Inn—$$$

This motel at the mouth of Canyon de Chelly has a pool, cable TV, and restaurant. **P.O. Box 1889, Navajo Route 7, Chinle, 86503; 800-465-4329 reservations or 520-674-5000, fax (520) 674-8264.**

Thunderbird Lodge—$$$

This historic property within 0.5 mile of Canyon de Chelly originally was a trading post built around 1902. It simply grew, with successive owners, to accommodate the increasing flow of visitors to the spectacular canyon. The surround-

Wild horses in Canyon de Chelly run free and unbridled and are seldom tamed, even though some try.

ing massive cottonwood trees are reminders of that era. It has a restaurant and gift shop with a separate "rug room" filled with beautiful Navajo rugs. The cafeteria is open daily, 6:30 A.M.–9:30 P.M. **P.O. Box 548, Chinle, 86503; 800-679-BIRD or 520-674-5841, fax 520-674-5844.**

Bed-and-Breakfasts

Coyote Pass Hospitality, a hogan-style bed-and-breakfast, for lack of a better way to categorize it, is designed to let visitors sample the Navajo culture by actually living it. Coyote Pass's literature cautions that it is not for everyone, and it surely isn't. In a single-room hogan, mattresses lie on a dirt floor, water comes from a pail and dipper, there may be rudimentary electricity, and bathrooms are out back. The upside is that the personal request of each guest is thoughtfully considered. Recently a pair of British sisters who wanted to learn Navajo weaving techniques were introduced to a pair of Navajo sisters who taught them. You may be faxed an advance book list so you can prepare for your visit. This isn't just an overnight stop. You plan a stay that is then styled around your desired method of learning about the Navajo culture and of experiencing life as a Native

American. **P.O. Box 91-B, Tsaile, 86558; 520-724-3383.**

Camping

Spider Rock RV and Camping Too has 50 RV sites and 20 regular campsites on natural land with no hookups as of this writing. It is nothing special, but is one of the few campgrounds in the Canyon de Chelly area. Located **10 miles east of the visitor center on South Rim Dr.** 520-674-8261.

Ganado

SEEING AND DOING

Museums and Historic Sites

The **Hubbell Trading Post National Historic Site** is the oldest continuously operated trading post on the Navajo Reservation. John Lorenzo Hubbell was born in 1853 in Pajarito, New Mexico, and quickly assimilated the Navajo lifestyle and language, which put him in demand as a Navajo interpreter. He bought the post when he was just 23, and soon gained a reputation of being fair and honest with all comers. His insistence on superior craftsmanship influenced the high quality of rugs and silver jewelry for which his post became famous. He helped develop the Ganado-style rug, today a classic Navajo design. At one time he and his sons owned 24 trading posts in Arizona and New Mexico. During the difficult time when Native Americans were being herded onto reservations and struggling to adjust to a new way of life, Hubbell helped ease the way by acting as a spokesman and go-between with a world that to the Navajo was completely foreign. In 1912, when Arizona was admitted to the Union, he was elected one of the state's first senators.

The post hasn't changed much over the past half century. Declared a National Historic Site in 1967, its shelves are stocked with canned goods, flour, sugar, and coffee, with hardware hanging from the ceiling. Counters are built higher than those in a conventional store, to prevent a customer from reaching across and grabbing, and to allow the trader to duck down behind in case bullets started flying. In the rug room, intricately woven products of Navajo looms are casually stacked, each tagged with a weaver's name and a price. A single mound may hold tens of thousands of dollars' worth of rugs (see Navajo Rugs sidebar). As you enter the main store, you walk into a room dubbed the "bull pen," where trading and socializing had equal importance. Although John Hubbell has been gone since 1930, buried on Hubbell Hill overlooking the trading post, things still operate much as they did in the old days. Navajo weavers bring their wares and leave with needed supplies. The post has some of the state's best prices on rugs and jewelry.

Next door to the store is the **Hubbell home,** an adobe built in 1902, where Hubbell lived with his wife and four children. The home, with a massive-beamed ceiling, baskets tacked between the beams, and amazingly beautiful rugs everywhere, is a showplace of fine books and paintings that are unexpected in this remote place. Tours are conducted during summer months when there is enough visitor demand.

The **visitor center** usually has rug weavers and silversmiths demonstrating their craft, who will graciously pose for photos. Picnic tables are just outside the center, but there is no overnight camping. Open in summer, daily, 8:00 A.M.–6:00 P.M.; in winter, daily, 8:00 A.M.–5:00 P.M.; closed Thanksgiving, Christmas, and New Year's Day. Located 1 mile west of Ganado on Hwy. 264 (Navajo Route 3), the main east-west road through the reservation. From the south, take I-40 to US 191 and head north to Hwy. 264. **P.O. Box 150, Ganado, 86505; 520-755-3475. Website: www.wmonline.com or www.nps.gov/hutr.**

Window Rock

The geological formation that gives this place its name once had water flowing through it. Centuries of wind and blowing sand also have helped to sculpt this 47-foot opening. Navajo legend says it was made by the Giant Snake, who once crawled along the expanse of sandstone, eventually creating a passage through it. You can't climb up to the hole, but you can hike around it. The rubble at the foot of the window is the remainder of a prehistoric pueblo. To get there, from I-40 at Lupton near the New Mexico border, take Navajo Route 12 north about 20 miles. Window Rock is on Hwy. 264 about 25 miles east of Ganado (on US 191).

The small town of Window Rock is the capital of the Navajo Nation, which is governed by an elected tribal council headed by a tribal chairman. The council is made up of representatives of various election districts. This is in keeping with the Navajo heritage, which never has had hereditary chiefs. When in session, delegates call each other by traditional clan names, and proceedings are mannerly and polite. The 88-member council, which includes a number of women, has 110 chapters and meets four times a year.

SEEING AND DOING

Crafts Centers

Navajo Arts & Crafts Enterprise is a large retail store that promotes and nurtures Navajo art. Rugs, silver, jewelry, paintings, kachinas, baskets, sand paintings, and more, all authentic and of top quality, are for sale. The Enterprise brings materials at wholesale prices to artists in communities all over the reservation, which it buys back in the form of finished goods. Craftspeople are encouraged to develop marketable ideas, so you're pretty well assured of finding something new each time you visit. Designs here tend to be traditional because most customers are Navajo, but more experimental designs are creeping in. The Enterprise also purchases from other Nations, including Zuni, Hopi, and Santo Domingo. Anything you purchase here has its authenticity guaranteed. There also are shops in Kayenta and Chinle, and there is an especially large and well-stocked store in Cameron, near the junction of US 89 and Hwy. 64 between Page and Flagstaff. Open Mon.–Fri., 8:00 A.M.–5:00 P.M.; possibly Sat.,

but call first. Located **a stone's throw east of Hwy. 264 and Navajo Route 12 in Window Rock. 520-871-4090.**

Museums and Historic Sites

At the small town of **Fort Defiance,** nothing of the old fort remains, although an Indian school and Bureau of Indian Affairs Administrative Office are there. Located **6 miles north of Window Rock at Navajo Routes 12 and 7; no phone.**

Recently relocated into new, expanded quarters in Window Rock, the **Navajo Nation Museum, Library, and Visitor Center** is a repository of bits of Navajo history that include the development of the designs and symbols used in silver and weaving techniques. Historical displays explain the evolution of the Navajo culture. Open May–Sept., Mon.–Tues. and Thurs.–Fri., 8 A.M.–5:00 P.M.; Wed., 8 A.M.–8:00 P.M.; Sat., 9:00 A.M.–5:00 P.M. Located **a block east of Navajo Nation Inn at Hwy. 264 and Loop Rd. P.O. Box 1840, Window Rock, 86515; 520-871-6673.**

The hogan-shaped **Navajo Tribal Council Chambers,** located in Window Rock Tribal Park (see Parks), is made of sandstone quarried from the same type of rocks that surround it; the Window Rock formation presides over all. Ponderosa pine beams came from higher elevations, and wall-sized murals by Navajo artist Gerald Nailor were completed in 1935. They depict the history and progress of the Navajo Nation. The Santa Fe Railroad donated the bell at the entrance, used to call members to session. It commemorates the service of the Navajos who worked on the Santa Fe line. Although tours aren't scheduled regularly, if the chamber's front door is open, come in and take a look. If it is locked, come around to the back and perhaps a worker will give you a brief peek. **Navajo Council Chambers, P.O. Box 1400, Window Rock, 86515; 520-871-6417.**

Parks

Known locally in Window Rock as The Zoo, the small **Navajo Nation Zoo and Botanical**

Window Rock remains the capital of the Navajo Nation. The town of Window Rock is named for this geologic formation. Navajo legend says the 47-foot opening was sculpted by the Giant Snake.

Park differs decidedly from what you might expect. Don't look for manicured lawns and high-tech exhibits. Rather, in this area of just 12 inches of rainfall a year and a frost-free season of only 100 or so days, it's apparent that nature is harsh. Sturdy junipers, Indian rice grass, lupine, and other high-desert plants do well, however. Animals include those that figure in Navajo history and culture, as well as native and domestic creatures that exist in the area today. Bears, cougars, Mexican wolves, coyotes, deer, elk, bobcats, raccoons, prairie dogs, and a pronghorn live here. Goats, Navajo *churro* sheep, and rabbits represent domestic stock. Birds of prey, a roadrunner, a sandhill crane, wild turkeys, snakes, lizards, and turtles are at home here. Exhibits and examples of traditional Navajo dwellings, along with the animals, educate schoolchildren. Free. Open year-round, daily, 8:00 A.M.–5:00 P.M., except Christmas and New Year's Day. Located on north side of Hwy.

264, 0.25 mile east of intersection with Navajo Route 12 N. Follow the pink bears from the turnoff to the entrance. **P.O. Box 9000, Window Rock, 86515; 520-871-6573.**

Window Rock Tribal Park has trails, water, rest rooms, and picnic tables. It is also the location of Navajo Tribal Council Chambers. Located **at the Window Rock formation. Navajo Parks and Recreation Dept., P.O. Box 9000, Window Rock, 86515; 520-871-6647. Website: www.navajonationparks.org.**

WHERE TO STAY IN WINDOW ROCK

Navajo Nation Inn—$$$

This place is unremarkable except that it is the only game in Window Rock. It has a restaurant and plainly furnished standard, double, and king rooms. **48 W. Hwy. 264, Window Rock, 86515; 800-662-6189 or 520-871-4108, fax 520-871-5466.**

Navajo Rugs

Navajo rugs are one of the most beautiful Native American traditions. Each is a unique work, a product of the weaver's talent, patience, and imagination. Although modern dyes and yarns influence the finished products, many weavers still use wool from their own and neighbors' sheep, carding and spinning it themselves.

Quality of each rug differs. A crisp, flat, tightly woven design brings more money than one made of nubby, poorly carded wool with loosely woven spots. However, traders will tell you that it is important to choose a rug that you love, one whose appeal will endure. If you are attracted to a nubby, textured surface, you can see beauty in the fact that the rug was made by older hands that may have lost some of their strength, and guided by aging eyes that may not see designs as sharply as they once did.

Among the easiest-to-recognize Navajo rug designs is **Ganado,** which always has a red background. Geometric crosses and zigzags, often with emblems that look like Greek keys, a central design, and a solid border are characteristic. It is named for the town of Ganado, home of the Hubbell Trading Post.

Similar to a Ganado is a **Klagetoh,** which usually has a gray background with black, red, and white in an uncomplicated main design. **Chief** is the oldest recognized design, characterized by simple bands of red and black. It usually is square so that when the rug is folded, the design looks the same as when the rug is fully open.

Two Grey Hills and **Burntwater** are very different from the Ganado design because they contain no red, are much subtler, and generally are more intricate. Two Grey Hills are among the most expensive because the wool is natural and undyed. The shadings of brown, white, and black are created by using

Some Navajo women shear the sheep, card and dye the wool, then spin the yarn to make their rugs.

wool from different sheep, which requires a time-consuming carding process. Lovely Burntwater rugs are particularly in vogue now because of trends in decorating to pastels and natural tones. Subdued geometric patterns are interwoven in murky yellow, brown, terracotta, even rose, lilac, and pastel blue.

Yei and **Yeibichai** designs contain human figures. The Yei are intermediaries between the gods and the Navajos, and Yeibichai are human dancers who represent Yei. Both patterns are particularly appealing because they are among the few Navajo designs that feature recognizable human figures, although greatly stylized. **Pictorial** rugs also may have human figures but the design is present-day, similar to the naive or naif designs of other cultures. It is not unusual for Pictorial rugs to show pickup trucks and trains, along with trees, flowers, sky, and other natural elements.

For more information and to see rugs for sale, log on to this website: **navajorugs. spma.org.**

Hopi Reservation

Completely surrounded by the Navajo Reservation, the Hopi Reservation covers 1.6 million acres. Twelve Hopi villages are poised on, or located at the bottom of, a series of three mesas that project out from Black Mesa to the north. Loosely strung along Hwy. 264, these villages are where most Hopis live. Today there are close to 10,000 tribal Hopi members, about 7,000 of whom live on the reservation. About 70 percent rely on the sale of arts and crafts for part of their living, constantly striving to weed out bogus products.

Proper behavior when visiting any village means *no photographing, recording, or sketching of villages or ceremonies*. Please heed the restrictions, because in the past, actions of thoughtless tourists have resulted in the closure of various areas, some of which have just recently been reopened to visitors. The Hopi Reservation is highly sacred to those who live there. The feathered sticks you may see along the roadside are Hopi prayer sticks, called *pahoes*. There are no areas set aside for visitors to hike, bike, or walk, so in this chapter you'll find no section for Outdoor Activities. Please do not attempt to explore on your own, and leave an area immediately if asked to do so.

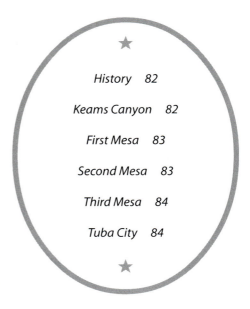

History

The Hopis represent one of the oldest cultures in North America, predating the Navajos, Apaches, and certainly whites. Oral tradition says that they came originally from South America. At one time their lands extended from the Grand Canyon east to the New Mexico border and south to the Mogollon Rim. They had a highly developed agricultural society, an amazing feat considering the harsh desert climate.

The Hopis acquired horses, burros, sheep, and cattle from the Spanish during the 1500s and 1600s, although contact was limited. Smallpox was an unwelcome Spanish acquisition, devastating the Hopi population and reducing it from about 10,000 in 1634 to fewer than 3,000 several years later. Navajo marauding, unchecked by ruling Mexico in the early 19th century, also decimated their numbers and further reduced Hopi lands.

The village of Oraibi dates to A.D. 1100 and is generally considered the oldest continually inhabited settlement in the country. Following an altercation between two chiefs in Old Oraibi in 1906, the group supporting the loser, You-ke-oma, broke off and set up its own village, Hotevilla. Near the bottom of Third Mesa, Kykotsmovi, one of the youngest villages, branched from Oraibi in the 1800s.

In 1962, as a result of a lawsuit brought by the Hopi, they were given exclusive use of a specific area, and joint use with the Navajo of a larger area, to which the Navajo previously had prevented Hopi access. To this day the conflict is ongoing, say many Hopis.

Keams Canyon

Keams Canyon, the first town you reach if you

head west into Hopi territory from US 191 just west of Ganado, isn't one of the Hopi villages; it's a government town with the Bureau of Indian Affairs Hopi Administrative Agency headquarters at its center.

SEEING AND DOING

Art Museums and Galleries

McGee's Indian Art Gallery, originally a trading post dating to 1874, once was owned by Lorenzo Hubbell of Hubbell Trading Post fame. The McGee family purchased the post in 1938. The collections of rugs, jewelry, and other crafts are genuine Hopi and Navajo arts and crafts, most of which are made within a few miles of the gallery. Located **on the Hopi Reservation. P.O. Box 607, Hwy. 264, Keams Canyon, 86034; 520-738-2295. Website: www.hopiart.com.**

Scenic Drives

Lined with cottonwoods, the 2-mile **Keams Canyon** portion of Hwy. 264 can be a cool place to picnic.

First Mesa

At the foot of First Mesa, **Polacca** is an access point to a steep, winding road that snakes up the side of the mesa. Three Hopi villages are poised on top of First Mesa, 15 miles west of the town of Keams Canyon.

The most spectacular and the most restricted of the First Mesa villages is **Walpi**, which dates to A.D. 1100. On a narrow promontory that drops off steeply on three sides, ancient stone buildings sit next to structures of concrete block in an amazing juxtaposition of centuries. Stones in the ancient buildings, brought by hand to this remote place, are smaller than those in the two more recent villages, which were brought by cart. The 360-degree views are breathtaking. The peace-loving residents planned it that way, so that anyone approaching from any direction was visible when still miles away.

Getting There

Hwy. 264 passes through the middle of the reservation, from Keams Canyon in the east to Tuba City on the west at US 160. From Keams Canyon heading west are First Mesa, Second Mesa, and Third Mesa. Hwy. 87 from I-40 just east of Winslow heads north to Second Mesa. US 160 travels a short way through the northwest corner of the reservation, through the towns of Tonalea and Red Lake.

As you walk you'll see patterned pottery shards, remnants of the work of artists of centuries ago who plied a craft that the Hopis of First Mesa are famous for today. Kachina dolls and weavings also are among their art forms. You also may find a tiny shell or a bit of a feather that has fallen from a ceremonial costume during a lively dance. If you pick up anything, be sure you replace it once you've examined it. It is strictly forbidden to take anything from the mesa. A handful of families still live in Walpi, mostly older Hopis who were born in the low-ceilinged houses. A few sell arts and crafts to visitors, but with neither electricity nor water, life is primitive. A **half-hour walking tour** of Walpi is conducted on request (you're not allowed in without a guide), led by a Hopi guide who knows the history and nuances of this ancient place.

You can drive to **Hano/Tewa** and then to **Sichomovi,** the other two villages on First Mesa, and leave your car at Ponsi Hall where you arrange for a guided walking tour. For information contact **First Mesa Consolidated Villages, c/o Tourist Office, P.O. Box 260, Polacca, 86042; 520-737-2262.**

Second Mesa

The villages of **Shungopavi, Sipaulovi,** and **Mishongnovi** are 10 miles west of First Mesa, at the junction of Hwys. 87 and 264. Hopis living here are known for their coiled baskets, kachina dolls, and silver overlay jewelry. The Hopi Cultural Center is on this mesa (see Museums and Historic Sites).

Art Museums and Galleries

A good selection of well-crafted jewelry can be found at **The Honani Gallery** on Second Mesa. 520-737-2238.

Museums and Historical Sites

The **Hopi Cultural Center Museum** on Second Mesa has a good representation of Hopi ceremonial objects and dress, and the baskets and pottery for which Hopis are famous. A restaurant and motel are connected to the museum and gift shop. Open year-round, Mon.–Fri., 8:00 A.M.–5:00 P.M.; mid-Apr.–mid-Oct., Sat.–Sun., 9:00 A.M.–3:00 P.M. **P.O. Box 67, Second Mesa, 86043; 520-734-2401. Website: www.psvcom/hopi.**

WHERE TO STAY ON SECOND MESA

Hopi Cultural Center Motel—$$$

This 33-room hostelry is the only motel in the area, so reservations usually are needed. Rates go down during winter. **P.O. Box 67, Second Mesa, 86043; 520-734-2401.**

WHERE TO EAT ON SECOND MESA

Secakuku Trading Post (520-737-2632) has a grocery store for basic supplies. The **Hopi Cultural Center's restaurant (520-734-2401)** has good basic fare as well as Hopi tacos, and tostadas served on fry bread.

Casual little 30-seat **LKD's Restaurant** used to be part of Secakuku's, but now is on its own, serving American and Mexican food that includes fry bread. Open Mon.–Fri., 11:00 A.M.–9:00 P.M.; Sat., 3:30 P.M.–7:00 P.M. Located at Hwys. 87 and 264. 520-737-2717.

Third Mesa

Another 10 miles west, Third Mesa has villages scattered throughout the western part of the Hopi reservation. Here craftspeople excel at making wicker baskets, kachina dolls, fine weavings, and silver overlay jewelry. **Oraibi** is the oldest village. **Hotevilla,** the most recently established village, is 47 miles from the Navajo Reservation town of Tuba City. Village men in Hotevilla plant vegetables along the slopes of the mesa. **Bacavi,** located just across from Hotevilla, was established by clans from Hotevilla as a result of a village clash. Near the bottom of Third Mesa is **Kykotsmovi,** one of the youngest villages, where the Hopi Tribal Offices are located. Although there is no formal visitor center, information usually is available at the public relations office within the tribal offices. Call **520-734-2441, ext. 106** to reach the Public Relations Dept.

WHERE TO EAT ON THIRD MESA

In Kykotsmovi, you can get groceries and some supplies at **Kykotsmovi Village Store; no phone.**

Tuba City

Tuba City is located on the Navajo Reservation, yet named for a Hopi chief. The Hopi village of Moenkopi, just 2 miles southeast of Tuba City, was once a Mormon settlement.

WHERE TO STAY IN TUBA CITY

Tuba City Quality Inn—$$$

This 80-room motel can be a good base for exploring the Third Mesa area of the Hopi Reservation. Reservations are necessary in summer. Located 1 mile north of US 160 and Hwy. 264 at Main St. and Moenave. **P.O. Box 247, Tuba City, 86045; 520-283-4545 or 800-644-8383. Website: www.qualityinn.com.**

WHERE TO EAT IN TUBA CITY

Eateries include Dairy Queen, Taco Bell, and McDonald's, with Basha's Market for picnic fixin's. The Hogan Restaurant next to the Quality Inn serves Mexican and American fare. **520-283-5260.** Open daily, 6:00 A.M. –9:00 P.M.

Winslow

With a population of about 11,500, Winslow sits at an elevation of 4,850 feet. It owes its existence to the railroad. Reminders of these days exist side by side with authentic cowboys who attest to the town's enduring ranching importance. Winslow State Prison sprawls beside Hwy. 87 just south of town. Between Winslow and Holbrook, I-40 parallels old Route 66 for most of the way, but the historic road's personality has been submerged by the new highway.

History

A number of Native American tribes crossed the Little Colorado River at what is now Winslow as they ventured south and west to trade. In 1876 a group of families built a settlement (Brigham City—now the northeast edge of Winslow), along the Little Colorado River, to attract additional pioneers. But within two years, it was clear they'd built on a floodplain. After a number of washouts and an ongoing struggle with alkaline water, the community was abandoned. In 1881 Atlantic and Pacific Railway sited a terminal here and named it after Gen. Edward Francis Winslow, railroad president. The post office was established in 1882. Post–World War II, Winslow's streets were lined with motor courts and diners that catered to a motoring public. But in 1979 Winslow was

In Winslow, Standin' on a Corner Park has a painting of "…a girl, my lord, in a flatbed Ford…" of Eagles fame.

bypassed by I-40, and the town languished. But with the reopening of La Posada (see Where to Stay), and the addition of the Standin' on a Corner Park, Winslow is pulling itself up by its bootstraps and emerging as a new destination.

Festivals and Events

West's Best Rodeo

mid-Sept.

In addition to the sanctioned rodeo events, festivities include an International Gallery of Taste featuring ethnic dishes with local origins and a display and sale of quilting, carving, silversmithing, and more by local artists and craftspeople. Local groups, including gospel singers, Native American dancers, Mexican folk dancers, and others, usually perform. Held **in City Park, four blocks north of historic Route 66.** 520-289-2434.

Standin' on a Corner in Winslow Arizona Celebration

late Sept.

This two-day weekend celebration features vendors, crafts, fun for the kids, and lots of music. You can count on many of the groups to play the famous song, written by Jackson Browne and recorded by the Eagles, for which the celebration is named. Events focus around the Standin' on a Corner in Winslow Arizona Park and downtown Winslow. **Second St. and Kinsley. 520-289-2434.**

Christmas Parade

Sat. before Thanksgiving

For more than half a century, Winslow has been home to the state's largest Christmas parade. It draws more than 100 entries, and the town in general is packed with bands and equestrian groups. Shriners from all over the state don classic makeup and costumes to become clowns. If you long for the style in which a small town celebrates, this is the place to be. **520-289-2434.**

Seeing and Doing

Museums and Historic Sites

Brigham City

Restoration is in progress to bring this slice of history back to the point where it can adequately convey what life once was in this former Mormon community. Very little is left of the 7-foot-high fort walls, sawmill, crockery plant, and homes. Check at the **Old Trails Museum, 212 N. Kinsley, Winslow, 86047; 520-289-5861,** to find out how the project is progressing.

Homolovi Ruins State Park

More than 300 archaeological sites include four major 14th-century pueblos of the Homolovis, called Anasazi by archaeologists. These people were ancestors of the Hopis. As with many such sites, much has been lost to collectors and antiquities dealers, but enough crumbling walls and pottery shards remain to paint a vivid picture of the civilization as it once was. Hopis consider this a sacred site. It is illegal to remove anything. The visitor center has good background information on the park and conducts a number of programs and activities, mainly during summer months. You can hike among pueblo ruins, and bring a picnic to the day-use area, where there are grills and tables; camping is also available. From Winslow **take I-40 east 3 miles to exit 257 and continue 1.3 miles north on Hwy. 87. HC 63, Box 5, Winslow, 86047; 520-289-4106. Website: pr.state.az.us.**

Meteor Crater and Museum of Astro-geology

This gigantic, privately owned hole in the ground was created 49,000 years ago when a massive meteor impacted the earth at nearly 45,000 miles per hour. You'll be awed by the enormous chasm, which you can view from observation decks that overhang the rim. If you think the topography looks like a moonscape, so did NASA, which used the site to train Apollo astronauts. The Museum of Astro-geology at the crater has excellent information on the crater's formation and the role it plays in earth and space sciences. You can touch a 1,406-pound meteorite, the largest piece of the main rock that has been found. Snacks may be purchased to enjoy in **Astronaut Park**, where tables and picnic facilities invite relaxing (you aren't allowed to bring in your own food). Moderate fee. Open daily May–Sept., 6:00 A.M.–6:00 P.M.; Sept. 16–May 14, 8:00 A.M.–5:00 P.M. From Winslow **take I-40 west 20 miles to Meteor Crater exit (exit 239) and travel 6 miles south.** P.O. Box 181, Flagstaff, 86002-0070; 520-289-5898 offices, 520-289-2362 crater. Website: www.meteorcrater.com.

Old Trails Museum

This eclectic place holds one of the best collections of Route 66 memorabilia around. You'll find a little bit of everything, including an original Route 66 sign studded with "reflector marbles," precursors of today's reflective paint. Just inside the door is a copy of the famous Eagles album on which Winslow is mentioned. Train buffs appreciate the tableware, timetables, and posters from the Santa Fe Railroad and the days when passengers stopped at luxurious La Posada Harvey House. Hours vary, so check first. 212 N. Kinsley, Winslow, 86047; 520-289-5861.

Parks

Standin' on a Corner in Winslow, Arizona, Park

When the Eagles sang about Winslow in the 1970s on their "Take It Easy" album, the lyrics "Standin' on a corner in Winslow, Arizona" gave the town a bit of tourism cachet. A large mural, quite literally built for a song, illustrates more lyrics. "It's a girl, my lord, in a flatbed Ford, slowin' down to take a look at me" comes to life in a colorful painting of a blond in a flatbed Ford reflected in a window. A statue of a young man leaning on his guitar represents the boy she's watching. One of the Eagles, Don Henley, donated $25,000 to get the park started, and patrons purchased bricks bearing their names to fund the rest. It prob-

Getting There
Winslow is located on I-40 at the junction of Hwy. 87, 50 miles from the Petrified Forest and Painted Desert, and 58 miles east of Flagstaff.

ably is the most photographed spot in Winslow. Second St. and Kinsley.

Where to Stay

Hotels, Motels, and Inns

There are plenty of good budget chain accommodations out on I-40. Days Inn, Best Western, EconoLodge and Super 8 are in the area.

La Posada—$$$

Built in 1930 as the last of the chain of luxury resorts along the route of the Santa Fe Railroad's excursion trains, this former Harvey House is getting a second chance at life and has become a catalyst for Winslow as a whole to revitalize. It closed in 1957 when the popularity of railroads succumbed to burgeoning automobile travel, and the railroad made it the office headquarters. It was designed by Mary Colter, an innovative architect now considered ahead of her time for her environmentally sensitive structures. She also created most of the other Harvey Houses, including Bright Angel Lodge at the Grand Canyon. The rambling Spanish tile–roofed building, made of steel, brick, and concrete, is structurally perfect, say its new owners. Fluorescent lights and dropped ceilings added in the 1950s have been removed to reveal graceful arches, murals, and lovely structural details. Rooms are being renovated in their former colors and style. Many have original fixtures and floors. La Posada recently was placed on the National Register of Historic Places. Although a fraction of the original number of trains now tootle past, the charming inn appeals to a new generation of travelers fascinated by how the

West used to be. Still an exciting work in progress, 20 lovely rooms are ready for guests. 303 E. Second St., Winslow, 86047; 520-289-4366. Website: www.laposada.org.

Camping

Homolovi Ruins State Park

This attractive but underused park has 52 spaces with hookups, plus rest rooms and showers (no water in winter). From Winslow **take I-40 east 3 miles to exit 257 and continue 1.3 miles north on Hwy. 87.** HC 63, Box 5, Winslow, 86047; 520-289-4106; Website: www.pr.state.az.us.

Meteor Crater RV Park

This newer park offers desert-landscaped pull-through spaces and full hookups. Facilities including showers, a rec room, playground, laundry, country store, and gas station, all new and clean. Spaces usually are available, but in prime summer months reservations are recommended. Tent spaces available. From Winslow **take I-40 west 20 miles to Meteor Crater exit (exit 239) and travel 6 miles south.** 520-289-4002 or 800-478-4002.

Where to Eat

The Turquoise Room—$$$–$$$$

Located at La Posada, Winslow's restored Harvey House, this restaurant is scheduled to open in fall 2000. It has been restored with the original viga ceiling and interior details, and is named for the famous Santa Fe Railway dining car, considered the finest Fred Harvey dining on rails. It will undoubtedly be the premier dining venue in the area, with reinterpreted Fred Harvey Continental and Native American–inspired cuisine. 303 E. Second St.; 520-289-4366. Website: www.laposada.org.

Port Java—$$

This fun and funky cafe serves excellent food in the local private airport's original 1929 adobe ter-

minal. The building was constructed by Transcontinental Air Transport (which become TWA) for use by its coast-to-coast flights. Port Java is run by self-admitted "frustrated gourmet" Rev. Dr. John Cox and his wife, Gigi. It is probably the only small-airport cafe that has a chef and sous-chef, an espresso bar, and entertainment at breakfast. Coq a l'orange is a special, along with meat loaf and spaghetti. "We also have beef Bourguignon, which actually sells a lot better when we list it as beef with gravy and mushrooms," jokes Cox, who with a little urging will pick up his guitar for an impromptu performance. Open Tues.–Fri., 10:00 A.M.–8:00 P.M.; Sat.–Sun., 8:00 A.M.–8:00 P.M. Located at **703 Airport Road** the Winslow-Lindbergh Regional Airfield. From Hwy. 87, take Airport Road east about 1.4 miles. Port Java is under the airport beacon. 520-289-0850.

Falcon, The Family Restaurant—$–$$

When Pete Kretsedemos traveled through Arizona by train as he returned from the service after World War II, he fell in love with the state and vowed to come back. He opened this homey eatery in 1955, selling thick hamburgers for 45 cents. Travelers along Route 66 gobbled them up, and now the children of these travelers return to the Falcon, along with the locals, who have eaten here for generations. Although Pete no longer owns the place, his traditions continue. A complete lunch for under $5, including soup and dessert, can consist of meat loaf, chicken and noodles, liver and onions, or other home-style fare. Homemade soups and pies are a specialty. Adjacent cocktail lounge. Open daily, 6:00 A.M.–8:30 P.M. 1113 E. Third St.; 520-289-2342.

Services

Winslow Chamber of Commerce

A small room displays area Indian cultures, as well as a good selection of printed material on regional places of interest. Open Mon.–Fri., 8:00 A.M.–5:00 P.M. 300 W. North Rd., P.O. Box 460, Winslow, 86047; 520-289-2434. Website: www.winslowarizona.org.

Holbrook

This little town of about 5,000, at a 5,000-foot high-desert elevation along historic Route 66, has a rich western history and remains a ranching center today, although on a smaller scale than in years past. Holbrook also serves as a jumping-off point for Petrified Forest National Park and the Hopi, Navajo, and Apache Reservations to the northeast.

History

Formerly known as Horsehead Crossing, Holbrook is named for Henry Randolph Holbrook, who was the chief engineer for the Atlantic and Pacific Railroad when it reached the town. When the railroad extended to Holbrook in 1881, it brought savvy money men who recognized the land's potential to nourish livestock. It became part of the Aztec Land & Cattle Company, which owned more than 2 million acres of prime grazing land. Nicknamed the Hashknife Outfit because its curved-T cattle brand looked like the chopping utensil used by the ranch cook, its cowboys were the roughest, toughest hombres ever to invade the West, so goes the legend.

Major Attractions

Petrified Forest National Park

Millions of years ago, the forces of nature replaced the woody pulp of ancient trees with bright jasper and quartz crystals, as well as iron and manganese, creating a rainbow forest of petrified logs and fossils. The dusky reds, pinks, and coppery yellows echo the shades used by present-day Southwestern Indian artisans. This 146-square-mile park is one of breathtaking scenery and is a respected center for scientific discovery and archaeological research. Es-

tablished as a national monument by Teddy Roosevelt in 1906 and elevated to national park status in 1962, its protection put an end to decades of destruction by visitors who saw the unusual logs as decorative accents for yards and gardens. Once viewed as simply a lovely curiosity, the Petrified Forest continues to reveal fossil beds, petroglyphs, and other elements that help scientists understand the history of the earth.

The 100,000-acre park's ecosystem dates back 230 million years to the Triassic period of the Mesozoic era, when bizarre, early life-forms worked their way toward becoming dinosaurs. The park's Chinle Formation is recognized as one of the world's most complete examples of the Triassic period.

The 27-mile drive through the park from I-40 on the north to US 180 on the south takes 45 minutes if you don't stop. The visitor center at the park's north entrance (see Painted Desert, below) is a good place to get an overview of what you're going to see, and to learn about recent dinosaur discoveries. Highlights are the **Puerco Indian Ruins,** where foundations of rooms and a kiva are remnants of a large agrarian culture

Native American dancers perform nightly during the summer months on the courthouse lawn.

that lived along the Puerco River. **Agate House,** dating to A.D. 1150, is an easy 0.5-mile walk from the main-road parking lot along a path studded with huge logs. Built about 900 years ago of chunks of petrified wood, it is partially reconstructed. The **Rainbow Museum,** just inside the park's southern entrance, is filled with Triassic skeletons. Also at the southern entrance is **Rainbow Forest.**

Be prepared for rarified air at the park's 5,400-foot elevation, and be sure to take water, especially during summer months when temperatures can be an arid 100°F-plus. Although

it is forbidden by law to remove any pieces of petrified wood from the park (rangers estimate they lose a ton of petrified wood a month to visitor thievery, some of which comes back when the takers realize it brings bad luck), you can purchase them for a very small amount at several Holbrook shops. Since only 10 percent of the forest is protected, there is plenty on private land. Small park entry fee. Open daily, 8:00 A.M.–5:00 P.M., with extended summer hours when budget and staffing permit. The **southern entrance, at Rainbow Forest, is 20 miles southeast of Holbrook on US 180. 520-524-6822. Website: www.nps.gov.**

Getting There

Holbrook is off I-40, 91 miles east of Flagstaff, between Winslow and St. Johns. US 180 and Hwys. 77 and 377 all converge in Holbrook. Hwy. 77 goes north to Keams Canyon, gateway to the Hopi Reservation.

The Painted Desert

The northern reaches of Petrified Forest National Park have become known as the Painted Desert for its multicolored formations pigmented by minerals that reflect light. Although all part of the same geologic formation, the Painted Desert portion has spectacular overlooks and particularly vivid colorations. Try to visit in the early morning or late afternoon when the less direct rays of the sun bring out exceptional richness of color. **Painted Desert Visitor Center,** at the park's north end, is smaller than the center and museum at Rainbow Forest at the south entrance, but has a good video that introduces you to the park. Usually open daily, 8:00 A.M.–5:00 P.M., but that can change, so call first. The **northern entrance is off I-40, 25 miles northeast of Holbrook. P.O. Box 2217, Petrified Forest, 86028; 520-524-6228. Website: www.nps.gov.**

Festivals and Events

Old West Days

first Sat. in June
A quilt auction, arts and crafts sales, roping demonstrations, a Bucket of Blood 21-mile bike race, a 10K run, and more make this one-day festival a favorite annual event. **All over town.** 800-524-2459 or 520-524-6558.

Indian Dances

June–Aug.
Young people of Navajo and Hopi ancestry perform culturally related dances Accompanied by drum music and dressed in native costumes, presenting colorful powwow-type performances. Mon.–Fri., early evening. On the Navajo County Courthouse lawn, **E. Arizona St. and Navajo Blvd.; 800-524-2459 or 520-524-6558.**

Seeing and Doing

Museums and Historic Sites

Navajo County Museum/ Holbrook Visitor Center

The 1898 Navajo County Courthouse, now a well-planned visitor center, was the oracle from which justice was dispensed for 78 years. In 1976 all county offices were moved to a location south of Holbrook. For five years the stolid building was vacant. Then it was rescued by the Navajo County Historical Society, which encour-

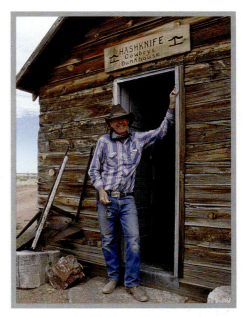

Rock Art Ranch owner Brantley Baird shows off the last remaining bunkhouse of the Hashknife Outfit.

aged local residents to donate furniture, keepsakes, and photos to chronicle area history. More than a dozen exhibits depict early Holbrook life, including a drugstore and soda fountain complete with prescriptions, wire-back chairs, and soda glasses. It looks as if the guests have just finished slurping up a sweet concoction. Upstairs, the original courtroom, judges' chambers, and law library remain much as they were when in use. Don't miss the jail cell near the entrance. It was shipped to Holbrook from St. Louis and used until the building closed. Prisoners' graffiti still decorates the walls, verifying that this grim, dark place afforded little in the way of entertainment. No one ever escaped. Donations accepted. Open daily, 8:00 A.M.–5:00 P.M.; in winter, may be closed weekends. **E. Arizona St. and Navajo Blvd.; 520- 524-6558.**

Shopping

Jack Rabbit Trading Post

This is one of those "Hey dad, we wanna stop" places, hyped by an endless succession of signs with the silhouette of a huge black and yellow jackrabbit poised for a giant leap. It's filled with the expected souvenirs and jackrabbit-shaped gewgaws, but also has a good selection of turquoise jewelry, various rocks, geodes and crystals, and books about Route 66. Its claim to fame is cherry cider. Open Mon.–Sat., 7:00 A.M.–sundown; Sun., 10:00 A.M.–sundown. Located on Route 66 near Joseph City, 15 miles west of Holbrook. P.O. Box 38, Joseph City, 86032; 520-288-3230.

Tours

Rock Art Ranch

About 19 miles from Holbrook is a remote area with some of the finest Anasazi petroglyphs in the Southwest. Cowboys take you on a tramlike vehicle to Chevelon Canyon, which at one time supported a large pre-Columbian population. On the walls of this spectacularly lovely gorge, with the river a gentle flow at its bottom, are hundreds of well-preserved petroglyphs. The Baird family, owners and stewards of this natural treasure, are multigenerational residents of the area and delightful hosts. You can do a whole-day excursion, adding hiking and a wagon ride to your petroglyph excursion, or you can go for just half a day, tailoring the time to your desires. For groups, a barbecue dinner may be served in a building filled with artifacts. The ranch has the last remaining bunkhouse of the Hashknife Outfit, now restored. The important thing to the Bairds is that you have an interesting, relaxing time, and come away with an appreciation of an area and a lifestyle that exists in very few places. Open year-round for tours, Mon.–Sat.; May 1–Oct. 30 for meals, Mon.–Sat. You'll definitely need directions on how to reach the remote ranch, so be sure to call or write first. Brantley Baird, P.O. Box 224, Joseph City, 86032-9999; 520-288-3260.

Where to Stay

Hotels, Motels, and Inns

There are two Best Westerns, a Budget Inn, Comfort Inn, Days' Inn, Holiday Inn Express, EconoLodge, and Ramada Limited in Holbrook. Off-season (winter) rates are a bargain in this area, if you aren't afraid of cold and snow.

Wigwam Motel—$$

This is one of those "Hey Dad, we wanna stay in a teepee, can we please, please, please?" places. There's no question that this village of conical overnight accommodations appeals to the spirit of adventure in every child's heart, and the kitsch buried in many adults'. It's Holbrook's most photographed site. Never mind that it was only the Plains Indians who used teepees, and this sort of structure historically was not found in this area. The concrete and wood wigwams were opened in 1950 along what was then Route 66 by Chester Lewis, and still are in the family. They mimic other similar wigwam villages that appeared across the country in the 1940s and 1950s, as a postwar public responded to the end of gasoline rationing and took to the road. Recently renovated, the wigwams have one or two double beds, a private bath, and simple furnishings. During summer months, advance reservations are essential. 811 W. Hopi Dr., Holbrook, 86025; 520-524-3048.

Camping

Cholla Lake Park

The largest body of water in northeastern Arizona, the 360-acre Cholla (say "CHOY-ah") Lake is leased to Navajo County by Arizona Public Service, a state power company. Swimming, boating, and fishing are among the activities, but most people come to use the campground because it is close to the Petrified Forest. There are full hookups, a dump station, and rest rooms. Showers are available mid-Mar.–Nov. 1. A ranger is on-site. Located 8 miles west of Holbrook, 1 mile off I-40 at exit 277. For reservations call 520-288-3717.

Holbrook Petrified Forest KOA

This is the closest campground to the Petrified Forest and Painted Desert, which are 17–22 miles away. The 132-site park has long, level pull-through spaces and a pleasant grassy tent area. Open year-round, but pool is swimmable only May 1–Oct. 15. From I-40/Hwy. 77 take exit 289 and go south 1.4 miles to Hermosa Dr., turn left (east), and go 200 yards to the entrance. **102 Hermosa Dr., Holbrook, 86025; 800-562-3389.**

Where to Eat

Burger King, Denny's, and Pizza Hut dominate the dining scene.

Jerry's—$$–$$$

Homestyle cooking that includes pastas and fish are part of the basic American menu here. Open Sun.–Thurs. 5 A.M.–10 P.M.; Fri. and Sat. 5 A.M.–

11 P.M. **2600 Navajo Blvd.; 520-524-2364.**

Mr. Maestas—$$–$$$

Decorated with antiques and collectibles, this place has served reliably tasty homemade American and Mexican food for 18 years. Open daily 6 A.M.–10 P.M. **502 Navajo Blvd.; 520-524-6000.**

Services

Holbrook Chamber of Commerce

Located in the same building as the Navajo County Museum. Open daily, 8:00 A.M.–5:00 P.M. **100 E. Arizona St., Holbrook, 86025; 520-524-6558 or 800-524-2459, fax (520) 524-1719.**

Petroglyphs and Pictographs

Arizona in is filled with marvelous expressions of the communications skills of ancient cultures. They are thought to be the maps of the ancients, recordings of special events, messages left for those who would follow, and simple decorative interpretations of life as it existed at the time.

Petroglyphs are carvings on rocks. They were carefully chiseled with stone-on-stone precision, sometimes incised using the hard, dried bones of animals, even etched with the powerful juices of native plants.

Pictographs are drawings, not as permanent as petroglyphs because they are created by marking on the surface of a rock rather than digging into its substance. Many, however, have survived well because the artists placed them in sheltered places such as on a ledge beneath an overhanging rock or inside a cave.

There are some excellent ones in South Mountain Park in Phoenix. Others, such as those in Lyman Lake State Park near St.

Johns, require a moderately strenuous hike. Still others, including some in the Petrified Forest, are best seen with binoculars.

Some are quite obvious, such as the figures of men wearing garments emblazoned with a cross that are found in Canyon de Chelly, along with men on horseback. These are the Spanish, astride the horses they introduced to the canyon's residents. A simple figure with a cross between its legs, such as is found in Chevelon Canyon at Rock Art Ranch near Holbrook, is probably a birthing scene. It has been theorized that a conglomeration of glyphs could be an ancient "scrapbook," possibly tracing the history of a village or a tribe.

Places to learn more about the artwork of the ancients include the Deer Valley Rock Art Center north of Phoenix (see Seeing and Doing under Around Phoenix: North) The Pueblo Grande Museum and Cultural Park near downtown Phoenix (see Phoenix and Environs) often offers petroglyph hikes.

St. Johns

St. Johns, population about 3,500, is located on the banks of the Little Colorado River 26 miles north of Springerville in the southeastern part of Indian Country at an altitude of 5,725 feet. It is located at the junction of Hwys. 180 and 191. If you approach this little town from the south, you'll drive through rolling grasslands that supplied early ranchers with unlimited grazing land. You can see for more than 50 miles in any direction.

History

St. Johns is the site of a 16,000-pound woolly mammoth discovery, and dinosaur bones found in the area attest to its ancient dwellers. More recently, in 1540, Coronado crossed the Little Colorado River here; generations later, descendants of the conquistadors returned to settle. Originally St. Johns was called El Vadito, which means "little crossing" in Spanish. In 1879 Mormon pioneers changed it to San Juan, which was almost immediately anglicized to its present form. In 1915 the Little Colorado was dammed to create an irrigation reservoir, named for Mormon Bishop Francis M. Lyman.

Outdoor Activities

Boating/Fishing

Lyman Lake State Park

Boaters love this 1,200-acre park between St. Johns and Springerville because the 1,500-acre lake is so large that there is no restriction on boat size. There is, however, a no-wake (5-mile-per-hour) restriction at the lake's west end to accommodate anglers who regularly pull limits of walleye, largemouth bass, and channel catfish from the clear waters. Lyman Lake is stocked around Memorial Day by Arizona Game and Fish with 30,000 rainbow trout and channel

catfish, thus assuring good summertime catches. So far as aesthetics go, some people are unsettled by the otherworldly landscape, perceiving it as desolate. Others appreciate the pristine contours and sparse vegetation, interrupted only by scattered stands of cottonwoods. The park is in the far south reaches of the Painted Desert (see Major Attractions in the Holbrook chapter) and in the ancient past was a vast lake. Today's lake is filled by snowmelt from Mount Baldy and the Escudillo Mountains. Best seasons to visit are spring through fall. At this 6,000-foot elevation, winters can be brutal.

The park pontoon boat takes a maximum of 14 visitors across the lake for a **Petroglyph Hike** that covers a moderate 1.5-mile petroglyph trail leading to a number of rock art sites; Memorial Day–Labor Day, Sat.–Sun., 10:00 A.M. The park van goes to **Rattlesnake Point Pueblo Ruin**, a 14th-century excavated site consisting of several rooms; Memorial Day–Labor Day, Sat.–Sun., 2:00 P.M. And, yes, those are genuine buffalo at the entrance, correctly called American bison, a herd of five at this writing. They were introduced by the St. Johns Chamber of Commerce in the 1960s simply to add a bit of local interest. The stock is rotated regularly to keep the herd viable.

The park has paved boat ramps, rest rooms

Visitors at Lyman Lake can take a ranger-guided hike to see ancient petroglyphs.

with showers, a campground, and a pleasant picnic area with tables and shelters. Located 10 miles south of St. Johns on US 180/191. **P.O. Box 1428, St. Johns, 85936; 520-337-4441, fax 520-337-4649. Website: www.pr.state.az.us.**

Golf

Concho Valley Country Club

Surprisingly popular considering its relatively remote location, this little club is about 15 miles southwest of St. Johns. The 18-hole, 6,656-yard course (from the championship tees) plays to a par 72 and has a number of tricky water hazards created by a spring-fed stream that wanders among greens and juniper-framed fairways. The year-round course and adjacent lounge attract out-of-the-area players with golf packages that include overnight accommodations. Located **on Hwy. 61 near the town of Concho. 800-658-8071 or 520-337-2622.**

Seeing and Doing

Museums and Historic Sites

Apache County Historical Society Museum

As the seat of Apache County, St. Johns's history is preserved in the Apache County Historical Society Museum. Its displays include mammoth tusks, miniature dioramas that depict Navajo life, lovely old handmade quilts,

Getting There

St. Johns is near the junction of US 180, US 191, and Hwy. 61, about 58 miles southeast of Holbrook via US 180 and about 27 miles north of Springerville via US 91.

and other trappings of daily life in early St. Johns. Donations accepted. Open Mon.–Fri., 9:00 A.M.–5:00 P.M. **180 W. Cleveland, P.O. Box 146, St. Johns, 85936; 520-337-4737.**

Raven Site Ruin/White Mountain Archaeological Center

Part of an active archaeological dig, this 800-room pueblo was a major pottery production and trade site during its occupied days from around A.D. 1000 to 1450. It is named Raven Site for the images of the glossy birds found on excavated pottery, proving that the ancestors of today's noisy creatures lived in the area centuries ago. Prehistoric cultures often had bird names for their clans. One of the site's most interesting programs involves inviting the public to participate in **hands-on archaeology projects** to learn the processes of restoration, reconstruction, and preservation that help ancient people tell their tale. You may participate in one-day or weeklong digs, which include bunkhouse lodging and meals. Special two-hour and half-day **hikes** into the fossil beds and petroglyph areas may be arranged. Reservations are required. Small fee. Guided petroglyph hikes daily, 9:00 A.M. and 1:30 P.M. Site is open, with self-guided tours, May–mid-Oct., daily, 10:00 A.M.–5:00 P.M.; guided tours daily, 11:00 A.M. and 2:00 P.M.

At the Raven Site **museum,** two ancient trucks that long since saw their last flat tire are now display stands for petrified wood, which may be purchased. The museum has a truly fascinating display of pottery, ladles, arrowheads, deer and antelope bones fashioned into awls and weaving tools, and other artifacts obtained from the Raven Site. If you can stand the overwhelming smell of mothballs, pop into the door marked "Insect Room" to see a display of the creepy crawlies, including tarantulas and scorpions, that are part of the state's insect population. They're all safely skewered behind glass. The knotty pine–paneled gift shop has good handcrafts, carvings, baskets, jewelry, and, on the second floor, a fine selection of kachinas and Navajo rugs. Museum and gift shop open daily, 10:00 A.M.–5:00 P.M. There is space available for tenters and self-contained RVs for a small fee. Located **16 miles south of St. Johns on US 180/191. HC 30, St. Johns, 85936; 888-333-5859 or 520-333-5857. Website: www. ravensite.com.**

Sports

The Equestrian Center of St. Johns

This is a renowned mecca for horse shows, dressage and hunter-jumper competitions, as well as ongoing clinics and camps. The annual High Country Stampede is held here on Memorial Day weekend. Located **at county fairgrounds in St. Johns on US 180. 520-337-2677.**

Where to Stay

Chain motels include Super 8 and Days Inn.

Camping

Lyman Lake State Park

The park campground has 38 hookups with shelters, 40 developed campsites, as well as beach camping with few facilities. Located 10 miles south of St. Johns on US 180/191. **P.O. Box 1428, St. Johns, 85936; 520-337-4441, fax 520-337-4649.**

Services

St. Johns Regional Chamber of Commerce

Located in the same building as Apache County Historical Society Museum. Open Mon.–Fri., 9:00 A.M.–5:00 P.M. **180 W. Cleveland; P.O. Box 178, St. Johns, 85936; 520-337-2000.**

Turkey Vultures

These are the birds everyone loves to hate. They circled ominously over Humphrey Bogart as he lay parched and dying in the film Treasure of the Sierra Madre. Their favorite meal is something dead. When frightened or challenged they often regurgitate the evil-smelling contents of their stomachs. And if that weren't enough, they are as ugly as warts. They appear to be birds with few endearing features.

Not so, say turkey vulture lovers. Cathartes aura, relative of the California condor (see sidebar in Northwest & Canyonlands), is an immense bird with a 3-foot body and a 6-foot wingspan. Its admirers point to its soaring techniques, which enable it to hover on thermals for hours as it searches for the carrion that is its favorite meal. Its head, a muted red in adult birds, is featherless, bare, and wrinkled, one of Mother Nature's clever design features. When the large bird feasts on the carcasses of deer, cattle, and other animals, it often gets its entire head inside the body cavity. If it were covered with feathers, it would be messy indeed, and the vulture needs clean feathers for proper flight.

So what warrants all this fuss about a bird that considers road kill a gourmet repast? Buzzard boosters (the term buzzard is really a misnomer hung on the birds as a carry-over from when it referred to Buteo hawks). Turkey vultures may be the ultimate environmentalists—the consummate clean-up crew. They go where few other birds choose to venture, and they scavenge what others shun.

They have adapted to their frailties in a number of ways. Whereas the regal eagle can grasp live prey with its powerful talons, the turkey vulture's talons have little strength so it has learned to rely on already-dead prey that can't wiggle away. Its hooked bill enables it to shred food efficiently. Amazingly, the bird's digestive system and overall physiology make it possible to ingest decomposed flesh and gain nutrients from it without becoming ill.

Although sometimes confused with hawks and other raptors, it is relatively easy to identify a turkey vulture in flight. Feathers at the end of its wings appear separated, each individually visible. To differentiate a vulture from a hawk, look for wings held in a shallow V shape when in flight. Hawks' wings are generally flat. Vulture flight looks tippy and off balance, as though they are constantly correcting.

Vultures don't build nests. Females lay eggs on a sheltered ledge, cave, hollow in a tree or even rafters in an abandoned building. They prefer dry, open country with roads that have enough traffic to produce the occasional road kill, yet not enough traffic to frighten. They are shy, quiet, rarely uttering a sound, and are experts at finding the thermals that let them glide effortlessly.

What about the charge that they routinely defecate on their own legs? The bird's bad manners are not without purpose. At least one natural scientist thinks that it's a cooling mechanism the bird employs because it has no sweat glands, and its natural habitat is dry and hot. Moisture in their offal helps keep the turkey vulture cool as it evaporates. Turkey vultures are abundant throughout Arizona.

(Excerpted from Seasonal Guide to the Natural Year: A Month by Month Guide to Natural Events—Southern California, Baja [Fulcrum], by Judy Wade)

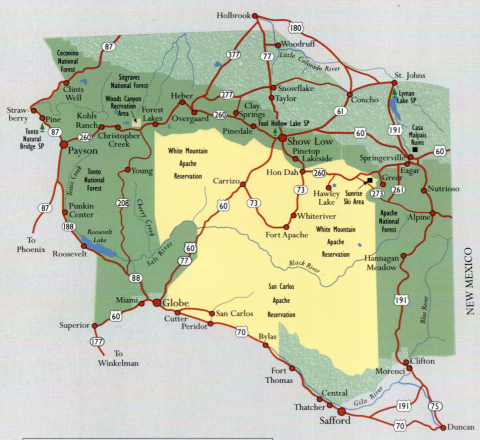

Holbrook

180

Coconino
National
Forest

87

Woodruff

Little Colorado River

377

77

Sitgraves
National
Forest

St. Johns

Clints
Well

Woods Canyon
Recreation
Area

Heber

277

Snowflake

Concho

Lyman
Lake SP

Strawberry

Pine

Kohls
Ranch

Forest
Lakes

Overgaard

260

Taylor

61

191

Casa
Malpais
Ruins

Tonto
Natural
Bridge SP

87

260

Christopher
Creek

Pinedale

Clay
Springs

Fool Hollow Lake SP

60

60

Payson

White Mountain
Apache
Reservation

Show Low

Pinetop
Lakeside

Springerville

Tonto
National
Forest

Young

Carrizo

Hon Dah

260

Eagar

Greer

273

261

Nutrioso

208

60

73

73

Hawley
Lake

Sunrise
Ski Area

Apache
National
Forest

Alpine

Punkin
Center

Cherry Creek

Whiteriver

White Mountain
Apache
Reservation

87

188

Roosevelt
Lake

Fort Apache

Hannagan
Meadow

To
Phoenix

Roosevelt

Salt River

60

Black River

191

77

88

San Carlos
Apache
Reservation

Blue River

Miami

Globe

Superior

60

Cutter

San Carlos

70

Bylas

Clifton

177

Peridot

Morenci

To
Winkelman

Fort
Thomas

Gila River

Central

191

75

Thatcher

Safford

70

Duncan

NEW MEXICO

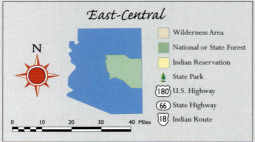

East-Central

N

Wilderness Area

National or State Forest

Indian Reservation

State Park

180 U.S. Highway

66 State Highway

18 Indian Route

0   10   20   30   40 Miles

East-Central—
Above and Below the Rim

An aerial view of the Mogollon Rim shows the
Colorado Plateau and the Gila/Salt River watershed.

East-Central—
Above and
Below the Rim

The unique geologic feature called the Mogollon (pronounced muggy-own) Rim is the most distinctive feature of this part of Arizona. It is named for Don Juan Ignacio Flores Mogollon, from 1712 to 1715 the governor of the Province of New Mexico, which was a portion of New Spain at that time. It forms a natural division between the Colorado Plateau and the Gila–Salt River watersheds, extending from northwestern Arizona into New Mexico and marking a fault line that runs through the state. Massive uplifting during the Paleozoic Era created the sheer walls of horizontally layered sedimentary rock at a time when the area was populated with fishes, sea life, and primitive forms of emerging mammals. Simply put, it is a 200-mile-long escarpment from the edge of the Colorado Plateau that is sheer and steep in some places, more gentle in others, that was created 600 million years ago.

The best-known section, and the most spectacular in terms of scenery, is the portion that begins to the west just beyond Payson below the rim (at Hwys. 260 and 87) and extends east to Pinetop and Lakeside on top of the rim. If you do the Mogollon Rim Interpretive Trail (see Hiking in the Pinetop and Lakeside chapter), the vistas provided by scenic overviews will help you understand how these cliffs were created. You also can see how the storm patterns coming in from the Pacific and Gulf of Mexico are affected by the massive rim. One reason that the area is so lush is that clouds, in their effort to float over the rim, release the heavy rain that they're carrying. Moisture falling on top of the rim flows into the Little Colorado River. Below the rim, rainfall trickles to the Gila, Salt, and Verde Rivers.

Springerville and Eagar

These small sister cities are located on the Little Colorado River in Round Valley, a high mountain bowl at an elevation of 6,969 feet just outside the northern boundary of the Apache–Sitgreaves National Forest. They make a good starting point for recreation opportunities in the entire east-central region. Tourism, agriculture, fishing, and hunting help shape their economy. Springerville is still a center for lumber operations and cattle ranches. Keep your eyes open for pronghorns while in this area. They look like small deer with a fluffy white rump and often sprint across meadows near highways.

History

From its beginnings as a trading post in the late 1800s, run by Henry Springer for whom the town is named, Springerville became a headquarters for lumbering and cattle ranching. Eagar is named for three Mormon pioneer brothers. The first, John T. Eagar, settled 4 miles south of Springerville in 1871. On Main St. across from the post office, an 18-foot statue, *The Madonna of the Trail,* is one of 12 such monuments built across the country in the 1930s as a tribute to the contributions made by pioneer women.

Major Attractions

Casa Malpais Archaeological Park

Ancestors of the Zuni and Hopi, known as the Mogollon people, originally occupied this prehistoric site whose name means "house of the badlands," believed to have been built between A.D. 1250 and 1380. The one-and-a-half-hour guided tour winds past an astronomical observatory, a ceremonial plaza, and a Great Kiva. The site can be windy, and at one point you scramble down a rope ladder and climb up a rocky tunnel, but the view on top is terrific. If you're at all interested in ruins, it is well worth the time. A short interpretive trail has two dozen stopping points with informational signs. Tours originate from the museum in downtown Springerville, 318 E. Main St. Small fee for tours. Tours daily, 11:00 A.M. and 2:30 P.M. Located **2 miles north of Springerville on US 60. P.O. Box 31, Springerville, 85938; 520-333-5375 (museum).**

Festivals and Events

Round Valley Western Celebration and Rodeo
Fourth of July weekend
A parade, 5K and 10K fun runs, food vendors, and more are part of Round Valley's biggest celebration of the year. **520-333-2123.**

Casa Malpais, meaning House of the Badlands, was home to the Mogollon people from about A.D. 1250–1380.

Outdoor Activities

Fishing

Becker Lake, 4 miles west of Springerville on Hwy. 60 regularly produces large rainbows. **Mexican Hay Lake,** 15 miles southwest of Springerville on Hwy. 273 is weedy, small, and not particularly picturesque, but if you want to strap on waders or launch a small boat, it has been known to yield some real lunkers. You also can ice fish at **Luna Lake,** one-half hour south of Springerville on Hwy. 180. For information contact Round Valley Chamber of Commerce, 520-333-2123.

Seeing and Doing

Art Museums and Galleries

Renee Cushman Art Museum

Housed in a special wing of the meeting house for the Springerville and Eagar Third Wards of the Mormon Church, this small but important collection was a gift to the church from Renee Scharf Cushman. It includes an engraving attributed to Rembrandt, three Tiepolo pen drawings, and dozens of other works of European art and furniture that date from the Renaissance to the early 20th century. Open by appointment only, arranged through Round Valley Chamber of Commerce, **520-333-2123.**

Museums

Casa Malpais Museum

Excavated artifacts from Casa Malpais ruins are on display. The museum also serves as the

Getting There

Springerville and Eagar are located near the New Mexico border, where US 191 and US 60 intersect, about 220 miles northeast of Phoenix via roundabout highways.

chamber of commerce office (see Services). Open daily, 9:00 A.M.–4:00 P.M. **318 E. Main St., Springerville, 85938; 520-333-5375.**

Little House Museum

Put together and maintained through the efforts of a local historian, this museum presents life as it was in log cabins during the days of outlaws and ranching. Niched among the crevices of the Little Colorado River canyon, it traces local history with photos, mementos, and lifestyle memorabilia. It is noted for its exceptionally good collection of antique nickelodeons, player pianos, and music boxes that still work. The museum is on X Diamond Ranch property. Tours, the only way to see the museum because much of the contents are quite fragile, are offered May 15–Labor Day, Thur.–Sun., 11:00 A.M. and 1:30 P.M.; Mon., 1:30 P.M. Located **7 miles west of Eagar on South Fork Rd.**, 3.2 miles south of Hwy. 260. **520-333-2286.**

Where to Stay

There's a Super 8 here, and other no-surprises accommodations.

Rode Inn—$$

No-frills 55-room motel is perfectly dandy for a night or two. Rooms have king or queen beds. Rates include continental breakfast. Located **right in Springerville. 520-333-4365 or 877-220-6553.**

Reed's Lodge—$$

Reed's Lodge, in the center of Springerville, is a homey 49-room inn with knotty pine paneling and attractive Native American motif in the lobby. The fifth-generation ranch family and staff are congenial and helpful. 800-814-6451 or 520-333-4323. **Website: www.K5reeds.com.**

Where to Eat

Los Dos Molinos—$$$

The food here is so hot, they sell T-shirts and temporary tattoos attesting to the fact that diners ate here and survived. But you have only to ask for less fiery fare, and it will be served to your liking. Open Tues.–Sat., 11:00 A.M.–3:00 P.M. and 5:00–9:00 P.M. **E. Main St., Springerville; 520-333-4846.**

Mike's Place—$$$

This eatery is noted for its steaks cooked over an open fire. They're huge. Open daily, 4:00 P.M.–9:00 P.M. Located on east edge of town. **65 N. D St. and US 60, Springerville; 520-333-4022.**

Services

Round Valley Chamber of Commerce

Serving Springerville, Eagar, Alpine, and Greer. Located in the same building as Casa Malpais Museum. Open daily, 8:00 A.M.–4:00 P.M. **318 E. Main St., Springerville, 85938; 520-333-2123. Website: www.az-tourist.com.**

Alpine

The town of Alpine looks like an Austrian village, with pine-covered slopes and views at an elevation of 8,050 feet in the Apache–Sitgreaves National Forest. Spring wildflowers and fall color are big attractions.

During summer months, hiking among aspen, oak, and fir, as well as alpine meadows, is a popular sport, and nearby streams with trout draw anglers. During the winter you can rent cross-country ski equipment, ice-fish, sled, and generally get as close as you wish to lots and lots of snow.

History

Alpine was founded in 1876 by Anderson Bush, and named Bush Valley. In 1879 he sold the valley for a brace of horses, a wagon, and a saddle horse. When the name was changed to Alpine is lost in history.

US 191 between Springerville and Morenci to the south is said to be the route taken by Francisco Vasques de Coronado more than 400 years ago as he searched for the fabled Seven Cities of Cibola. The route wiggles along high mountain roads through the Apache–Sitgreaves National Forest and some of the state's most scenic countryside.

Festivals and Events

Working Dog Trials

first weekend in May
A real traffic-stopper, this picturesque event consists of working-breed dogs showing their herding prowess as they guide a group of five sheep through gates and into an enclosure. Held on the outskirts of Alpine in a lovely meadow. 520-339-4330.

Winter Fest

Feb., when there's enough snow
The Alpine Ranger District hosts a snow sculpture competition, ski events, sled races, and a monster bonfire. The exact location shifts, depending on where snowfall is greatest, but it usually is held in Williams Valley, at an elevation 800 feet higher than the town proper; about 3–6 miles west of Alpine. 520-339-4384.

Outdoor Activities

Fishing

Big Lake and Crescent Lake
The attraction at these scenic little lakes is trout fishing, including rainbow, brook, and cutthroat, and good bank fishing from the dam. It's said that more large trout are taken from Big Lake than any other Arizona water, which stands to reason because it is stocked each spring and fall with more than 300,000 fish. But many campers come just to enjoy the cool pine air and peaceful quiet. The season is roughly late Apr.–mid-Nov., depending on weather. At 9,229 feet,

it cools off to jacket weather even at summer's peak. There are a store and boat rental, but no accommodations except camping. **Take Hwy. 273 west 17 miles on a graded dirt road to Big Lake.** The Forest Service has an office near Crescent Lake, which is your best bet for getting maps and information on the area. For more information contact Alpine Chamber of Commerce, 503-339-4330.

Nelson Reservoir

This lake is stocked with trout. It has rest rooms and parking facilities as well as boat launch ramps. Located **on US 191 south of Alpine.** Contact Alpine Chamber of Commerce, 503-339-4330.

Golf

Alpine Country Club

At 8,500 feet above sea level, this course is called the Alps of Arizona. Fairways are surrounded by dense groves of aspen, blue spruce, and ponderosa pine. When Phoenix is sweltering during summer months, this course is guaranteed to be cool. Open seasonally. Located **2 miles east of US 191 and US 180 in Alpine.** 520-339-4944.

Seeing and Doing

Scenic Drives

Coronado Trail Scenic Byway

Exceptional views are the main focus of this spec-

tacular drive that winds for 121 miles through craggy mountains and fragrant pines. From Alpine going south to Morenci, it's pretty desolate, so be sure your gas tank is full and you have emergency road equipment. The good news is that the road is paved and in good condition, unless you cross it in early spring just after winter has taken its toll. The drive is particularly popular mid-Sept.–Oct. when cool fall weather changes the oak, maple, mountain ash, and aspen into brilliant colors. It is not a good idea to attempt the entire trail during winter months because heavy snowfall may make it impassable in spots. However, the sections at either end are reliably open.

Beginning from Springerville, the road descends almost 5,000 feet, passing through life zones similar to those between Canada and Mexico. Along the way, you'll come to Nelson Reservoir. About 22 miles south of Alpine on Forest Rd. 29B there is a small campground at Hannagan Meadow. A 4,000-foot drop at Blue Vista Overlook creates dramatic views of the Blue Range Mountains and the valleys below. A short nature trail begins at the parking lot. The old mining towns of Morenci and Clifton mark the trail's end (see the Morenci and Clifton chapter in the Southeast and South-Central region). For more information contact the Alpine Ranger District, 520-339-4384.

Where to Stay

There are half a dozen laid-back motels and lodges in the Alpine area, most with room rates well under $100 per night.

Resorts

Hannagan Meadow Lodge—$$$–$$$$

This is where you come when you really want to leave the madding crowds behind. Located 22 miles south of Alpine at 9,100 feet, the historic lodge is the highest year-round occupied facility in Arizona. Yet there are a very good dining room, and a country store and gas station that are open from Memorial Day to Nov. 1. The lodge was built in 1926 and completely renovated in 1996. Suites with private baths are located on the second and third floors of the main lodge. Rustic, authentic log cabins are set back from the main road, up a small hill among pine and aspen. During winter months the lodge rents skis and snowmobiles as well as ice skates to try on the lodge's outdoor rink. Dogsled races are a favorite participation event. During summer months, guests usually come for hiking, fishing, mountain biking, and horseback riding. Located **on the Coronado Trail about 22 miles south of Alpine. P.O. Box 335, HC 61, Alpine, 85920; 800-547-1416 or 520-339-4370.**

Sprucedale Guest Ranch—$$$
The road ends at this friendly, family-owned ranch where guests come to spend a week riding in the White Mountains. Rustic, cozy cabins are ideal for families, with activities that include cows to milk and kittens to cuddle. Meals are served family-style. Besides daily rides, there's a gymkhana rodeo each week so guests can show off their newly acquired skills. **P.O. Box 880, Eagar, 85925 (winter); HC 61, Box 10, Alpine, 85920 (summer); 520-333-4984.** Website: www.sprucedaleranch.com.

Sportsman's Lodge—$$-$$$
Knotty pine paneling and rustic atmosphere take this comfortable place out of the usual motel category. You can settle into a kitchen unit for a week or more, or choose a regular room. You're just a two-block walk from restaurants and shops in the village. **42627 US 180, P.O. Box 778, Alpine, 85920; 888-202-1033 or 520-339-4576.** Website: www.alpineaz.com.

Tal-Wi-Wi Lodge—$$-$$$
This cozy lodge meets the criteria of getting away from it all. Some rooms have hot tubs and fireplace stoves, and the restaurant is understated and inviting. The Longhorn Saloon supplies libations. Located **4 miles north of Alpine on US 191. P.O. Box 169, Alpine, 85920; 800-** 476-2695 or 520-339-4319. Website: www.talwiwilodge.com.

Coronado Trail Cabins—$$
Smell the pine trees, catch your breath at the 8,050-foot elevation and enjoy the awesome scenery. One-room housekeeping cabins in the woods have showers and kitchens with pots, pans, silverware, dishes, and linens. Located 0.75 mile south of Alpine on the Coronado Trail. **25302 US 191, P.O. Box 759, Alpine, 85920; 520-339-4772.**

Camping
At Big Lake and Crescent Lake 17 miles west of Alpine on Hwy. 273, there are four campgrounds. **Brookchar and Cutthroat Campgrounds** are for tent camping only. **Rainbow and Grayling** are for RVs and tent camping; the largest campground, Rainbow has 157 full hookups, clean rest rooms, showers, and spaces that allow for privacy. A store and marina are close by. **Winn Campground,** 2 miles from Hwy. 273, has amenities. You may reserve any of these campgrounds by calling **800-280-CAMP.** About 10 miles south of Big Lake, **Buffalo Crossing Campground** is at the east fork of the Black River. There are a number of remote first-come, first-served campgrounds in this area. The Forest Service has an office near Crescent Lake, which is your best bet for getting maps and information on camping in the area.

Services

Alpine Chamber of Commerce
Call well in advance for information because they'll return only local calls, but will send information on request. The phone number is answered by C of C members at their places of business. **Box 410, Alpine, 85920; 520-339-4330.** Website: www.az-tourist.com or www.alpineaz.com.

Greer

A wonderfully remote small town at an elevation of 8,525 feet, Greer sits in Lee Valley, which is most people's idea of what a high alpine valley should be. It has fewer than 100 permanent residents, most of whom run the charming lodges that accommodate winter snow-seekers and summertime guests looking for a heat escape. Greer as a whole is so tiny that you can simply drive along the town's one road and pretty much see it all. North of town, three small lakes are stocked with trout, as are the headwaters of the Little Colorado River nearby.

History

The town is named for Mrs. Ellen Greer, whose cattle-raising family established the town in the late 1800s. It was among the communities established to supply Fort Apache and the White Mountain Apache Nation Reservation with horses, cattle, grain, and other staples. As it became a stopping-off point for travelers between Fort Apache and other areas, lodges were established and eateries opened. These were the forerunners of today's bed-and-breakfasts, lodges, and inns that make Greer an exceptionally popular four-season resort community.

Outdoor Activities

Fishing

The **Greer Lakes,** which include Bunch, River, and Tunnel Reservoirs, are well stocked with large rainbow and brown trout. Those who know say that at River Reservoir, the shallow areas on the south side of the lake are best. The lake has rest rooms and a boat launch. Fly-fishing is the method of choice at Tunnel, which also has a boat launch. Located **about 1 mile north of town just east of Hwy. 373,** across from Rolfe C. Hoyer Campground. For information contact Round Valley Chamber of Commerce, 520-333-2123.

Hiking

Butler Canyon Nature Trail provides a soothing stroll along a path lined with numbered signs that correspond to a brochure that identifies trees and plants, and explains geological features. Look for the marked trailhead off the East Fork Road just before you enter Greer. On the other side of town, a marked forest hiking trail winds along the creek and leads to **Sheep's Crossing.**

Horseback Riding

With so many great places to hop on a horse and explore, in this area horseback riding is big. **Lee Valley Outfitters** does one- and two-hour, half- and all-day rides, as well as hayrides. Located **on Hwy. 373 0.25 mile from Hwy. 260 turnoff; look for Spade Ranch sign. 520-735-7454.**

Skiing

Sunrise Park Resort

About 200 miles from Phoenix or Tucson on the White Mountain Apache Reservation, Sunrise Ski Area, the Southwest's largest, is about 16 miles west of Greer. For a state usually considered a desert, the skiing here is remarkably good, with three 11,000-foot peaks creating terrain that is not so much difficult as it is interesting. The snow-making machine usually assures at least some skiing, no matter what the weather conditions, although an ample supply hasn't been a problem in recent years. Its 800 acres are mostly intermediate and beginner downhill runs, with 20 percent in the expert range. There are 65 trails on the three mountains, with five day-lodges and a hotel (see Where to Stay). All runs are open to snowboarders. Ten lifts, including the high-speed Sunrise Express, serve all three mountains. Also offered are ski lessons, cross-country skiing, snowmobiling, a ski rental facility, a children's "ski-wee" area, and a snow-tube park. In summer Sunrise Lake, within walking distance of the resort's hotel, draws hikers and trout anglers. Scenic chair-lift rides, hiking, and mountain biking are popular in the area. Open for skiing late Nov. or early Dec. **From Hwy. 260 16 miles west of Greer/30 miles east of Pinetop/ Lakeside, take Hwy. 273 southeast to the access road with the resort sign.** 800-772-SNOW snow report, 520-735-7669 general information. Website: sunriseskipark.com.

Seeing and Doing

Museums

The **Butterfly Lodge Museum**, a log cabin built in Greer in 1914, is named for the area's proliferation of the fluttery creatures. It was the home of author James Willard Schultz and later his artist son, Hart Merriam Schultz, also named Lone Wolf to honor his mother's Blackfoot Indian heritage. Listed on the National Register of Historic Places. Small donation. Open Memorial Day–Labor Day, Fri.–Sun., 10:00 A.M.–5:00 P.M. Located **at the junction of Hwy. 373 and County Road 1126;** 520-735-7514.

Getting There

Greer is located at the end of AZ 373, 5 miles south of AZ 260, about 16 miles west of Eagar. The paved road ends at Greer.

Where to Stay

Wonderful guest accommodations that range from basic housekeeping cabins to elegant lodges line narrow Hwy. 373 as it meanders through the pines. Most have minimum stays on weekends and holidays.

Bed-and-Breakfasts

Red Setter Inn—$$$$

This decidedly upscale bed-and-breakfast is a hand-hewn log lodge with rustic but elegant guest rooms on three levels. There are 12 rooms and suites, some with whirlpool tubs, fireplaces, and private balconies overlooking the river. **P.O. Box 133, Greer, 85927;** 520-735-7441, fax 520-735-7425. Website: www.redsetter.com.

Cattle Kate's Dining Hall and Boarding House—$$$–$$$$

Lodgelike feeling here is emphasized by a stuffed grizzly and a wolverine locked in battle on the staircase. Western decor in its eight rooms and one suite is comfortable, not overwhelming. Continental breakfast included. **Box 21, Greer, 85927;** 520-735-7744.

Inns and Resorts

Big Ten Ski Resort—$$$–$$$$

There are nine rustic yet modern cabins set among the pines and completely furnished for housekeeping. The Big Ten pizza and chicken restaurant on-site has carry-out. Open all year. **P.O. Box 124, Greer, 85927;** 520-735-7578. Website: www.wmonline.com/bigten.

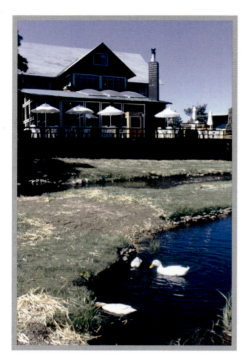

The little town of Greer, snugged into a scenic alpine valley, is filled with charming inns, cabins, and lodges.

Greer Lodge—$$$–$$$$

Overlooking the Little Colorado River, the Greer Lodge has spacious, airy rooms that open onto a main living room from two floors. Housekeeping cabins are scattered around the property. The lodge is open all year; Amberson's and the lounge are open during the summer and on a limited winter schedule. **P.O. Box 244, Greer, 85927; 520-735-7216. Website: www. greerlodge.com**

Greer Mountain Resort—$$$

This resort has rooms, cabins, an RV park with eight full hookups, as well as an on-site restaurant. Located **just north of town. P.O. Box 145, Greer, 85927; 520-735-7560. Website: www.wmonline.com/greermountain.**

Snowy Mountain Inn—$$$

Situated on 100 quiet, off-the-road acres, this inn has main lodge rooms and log cabins. A private pond for guests only is stocked with catch-and-release rainbow trout. **P.O. Box 337, Greer, 85927; 888-SNOWY71 or 520-735-7576.**

Sunrise Park Resort—$$$

The 100-room hotel overlooking Sunrise Lake is on-site at the Sunrise Park ski area west of Greer. It has two restaurants and an indoor pool. During the summer, boat and bike rentals are available. See Skiing. **800-55-HOTEL.**

White Mountain Lodge—$$$

Built in 1892 as a family home, the inviting lodge's rooms include a full breakfast. Housekeeping cabins have fireplaces and a wonderful view of wildlife in the meadow. Open all year. **P.O. Box 143, Greer, 85927; 888-493-7568 or 520-735-7568, fax 520-735-7498.**

Molly Butler Lodge—$$–$$$

This family-focused lodge, built in 1910, has rustic, homey rooms and is the longest continuously operating lodge in Arizona. Open all year. **P.O. Box 134, Greer, 85927; 520-735-7226.**

Camping

Fairly new and set among towering ponderosas, **Rolfe C. Hoyer Campground** has hookups, showers, and toilets; its proximity to town make for easy, civilized camping without sacrificing an in-the-woods feeling. Located **about a mile north of Greer on Hwy. 373. 520- 735-7313.** Overflow camping is available at **Benny Creek Campground,** close to the Greer Lakes that have reliably good trout fishing. Located **2 miles north of Rolfe C. Hoyer Campground.**

Where to Eat

A number of resorts have restaurants, but they may be open seasonally (see Big Ten, Greer Lodge, and Greer Mountain Resort in Where to Stay). **Cattle Kate's Dining Hall and Boarding House** is open year-round daily for three meals; **520-735-7744. Molly Butler Lodge** is open for dinner throughout the year; 520-735-7744. **Snowy Mountain Inn** is open summer, Tues.– Sun., for dinner; rest of the year, weekends and holidays for dinner; 520-735-7576.

Round Valley Chamber of Commerce located in Springerville serves Greer. **318 E. Main St., Springerville, 85938; 520-333-2123.** Website: **www.az-tourist.com** or **www.greer arizona.com.**

Services

Note that there are no gas stations in Greer, so fill up in Eagar or Pinetope/Lakeside. The

Owls

Owls are among the largest and most widely distributed birds of prey. They glide silently, the night air undisturbed by their soft body feathers, with barely a whoosh of wings to betray their presence and scatter their prey. Their inquisitive whoo-hoo-hoo, whoo-hoo is a means of communication. The barn owl, eastern and western screech owl, and great horned owl are abundant in Arizona.

Nature has given owls strong legs, hooked beaks, and sharp claws to catch the rodents, smaller birds, reptiles, fish, and large insects that they seek under cover of darkness. Other unique adaptations essential to their nocturnal prowls are the ability to see well in low light as well as bright sunlight. The owl must turn its head to look up, down, and sideways because its forward-directed eyes are immovable. However, some species can turn their heads so far horizontally that it appears they can look behind themselves.

An owl's ear openings, behind and to the side of the eyes, are not symmetrical in some species. Covered by soft, sound-permeable feathers, these ear openings let the bird compare sound intensity because it is heard differently in each ear, which helps determine the direction from which the sound has come. It also helps them assess the vertical direction of a sound, enabling them to locate prey that may be hiding in grass or bushes.

You'll have to venture out at night to glimpse the large, cat-like great horned owl, the classic tufted owl that adorns Halloween posters and comes to mind whenever the species is mentioned. It likes forests, streams, and open country, and sometimes can be seen silhouetted against the moon as it perches on a power pole or winter-nude branch. It is a fierce and tireless predator, and has been known to attack hikers and birdwatchers who ventured too near its nest.

Pinetop and Lakeside

This lovely little resort community lures residents from other, hotter parts of the state to its cool 7,800-foot altitudes with the slogan "If you're hot, we're not!" It's almost impossible to tell where Pinetop starts and Lakeside leaves off, but if you have to have a defining feature, Lakeside is farther to the northwest and closer to Show Low. Together they make up the hub of the White Mountains resort area. During summer months the traffic on Hwy. 260, the main street for both towns, can be so heavy that you wonder if anyone is left in any other part of the state. The town's year-round population of 8,000 can almost triple. But somehow it all works out by early evening. Summer mornings can be in the brisk 60s, but days heat up to almost 80°F, so if you're hiking be sure to have sunscreen and water. What Phoenicians call monsoons (see Monsoons sidebar in Phoenix chapter) manifest themselves in the White Mountains as cooling showers, briefly sprinkling most afternoons. When the sun sets it can be chilly.

History

As long as a thousand years ago, Native Americans lived in the White Mountains. Coronado, in his quest for gold, marched through the area in 1540. By the late 1800s Mormon settlers arrived. As were many towns in the area, Pinetop was founded by Mormons. Pinetop was first called Penrod after William L. Penrod, one of the early pioneers whose family built a sawmill here before the turn of the century. In 1870 the U.S. Army established an outpost at Camp Mogollon, now called Fort Apache, that was the headquarters for the 1st Cavalry and 21st Infantry. U.S. Army Gen. George C. Crook moved his troops and equipment from Fort Whipple in Prescott to Fort Apache in the White Mountains. Fort Apache's purpose was to protect trade routes, to assure the safety of early settlers, and to train Indian scouts, among whom was Chief Alchesay. Army scout Croydon E. Cooley, one of the participants in the famous card game that gave Show Low its name, did his job well, and through his efforts this region was spared the violent wars that plagued southeastern Arizona around the same time.

Lakeside, another Mormon settlement, was called Fairview and Woodland until Show Low Creek was impounded to form a lake in the 1890s. It became known as Rainbow Lake and, along with other area lakes, now reminds many visitors of northern Minnesota. From early in its history, the area has been recognized as a prime vacation spot. Records from the 1920s show that there already were Boy and Girl Scout camps here more than 70 years ago.

Major Attractions

White Mountain Apache Reservation

Bordering the Pinetop-Lakeside area to the

east, this enormous piece of land covers 1,644,874 acres and is home to some of the area's biggest attractions, including Fort Apache (see Historic Sites), Hon-Dah Casino (see Wagering), and Sunrise Ski Area (see Skiing in Greer chapter). The Salt River Canyon (see Scenic Drives in Superior, Miami, and Globe chapter) is located in the reservation's southern section. The reservation has a population of about 9,000.

Festivals and Events

White Mountain Native American Art Festival

end of July

This popular event, more than a decade old, honors Native Americans through recognition of their cultures. Close to 100 artisans display and sell their creations and demonstrate how their particular crafts are perfected. Carving, weaving, flint knapping, pottery making, and painting are among the skills taught. Native American dancers and storytellers are always popular performers, and visitors can sample fry bread, Navajo tacos, acorn stew, Apache burritos, and other ethnic dishes. Held at **festival site off Woodland Rd., about 1 mile south of traffic light at White Mountain Blvd. (Hwy. 260).** For more information contact the Pinetop-Lakeside Chamber of Commerce, 520-367-4290.

White Mountain Bluegrass Festival

mid-Aug.

Mountain music, cloggers, gospel music, and nightly jam sessions as well as crafts and food booths are part of this annual festival held in the cool pine woods. If you've longed to make this sort of music on your own, workshops are part of the celebration. Entrance fee. Some camping available. Free parking. Held on the grounds of **Blue Ridge High School, 1200 W. White Mountain Blvd.** For more information contact the Pinetop-Lakeside Chamber of Commerce, **520-367-4290.**

Fall Festival

late Sept.

If you don't believe that Arizona has a glorious display of fall colors, just head to the White Mountains anytime late Sept.–mid-Oct. (see Fall Color sidebar in Flagstaff chapter). Yellow and gold aspen, red bigtooth maples, scarlet sumac, and more proudly display their colors. This arts and crafts festival, one of the largest in the state, includes a local talent show, a chili cook-off, and a carnival. One of the most popular events is the Run to the Pines Car Show that draws more than 500 pre-1973 vehicles to compete for awards in the categories of Best Paint, Best Engine, Best Interior, Longest Distance, and more. Games and music from the 1950s and 1960s also are part of the festivities. Held **at various Pinetop-Lakeside sites. 520-367-4290.**

Outdoor Activities

Bicycling

MOUNTAIN BIKING

Springs Trail

Many of the trails in this area, part of the White Mountains TrailSystem, remain underused by mountain bikers. A popular trail heavily used

Getting There

The Pinetop–Lakeside area is about 190 miles north of Phoenix, close to a 4-hour drive, and 90 miles east of Payson, about a 1.5 hour drive. From the East and Southeast Valley areas of Phoenix, take U.S. 60 (Superstition Freeway) through Globe and the Salt River Canyon to Show Low, and proceed south on Hwy. 260. From the Northeast Valley, Scottsdale and Fountain Hills, take Hwy. 87 north, and Hwy. 260 east to the area.

by hikers, equestrians, and mountain bikers, the Springs Trail, a quick 3.8-mile loop, involves smooth and technical riding. It parallels Thompson Creek, crossing it at one point. Connectors to the **Blue Ridge Loop** and **Country Club Loop** (clearly marked) can give you a longer, more challenging ride. To access the Springs Trail **take Hwy. 260 south to Bucksprings Rd. and go 0.6 mile to Forest Rd. 182. Turn left onto Forest Rd. 182 (road to Sky Hi Retreat) and go 1.1 miles to the trailhead on the left.** For information on the TrailSystem, see Hiking.

Fishing

Lakes and streams in the White Mountains are stocked regularly with native Apache trout as well as rainbow, brook, brown, and cutthroat. Other species include walleye, bluegill, large- and smallmouth bass, catfish, northern pike, and arctic grayling. Because many lakes and streams are located near campgrounds, an outing can be a family affair, with hiking and mountain biking trails, boating opportunities, and bird-watching available for nonanglers.

On the White Mountain Apache Reservation, **Big Bonito Creek** is not only a beautifully wooded area with bear and javelina, but also a good place to snag brown and rainbow trout. **Trout Creek** south of Hon-Dah is good for fly-fishing for rainbow, brook, and brown trout. **White River North Fork** is heavily fished because during spring and summer months the tribe stocks it twice weekly. Reports are that Apache trout and brown trout are abundant in the upper areas, while smallmouth bass are best catches in the part below White River and Fort Apache. **Hawley Lake** is one of the few lakes open during the winter, when ice-fishing is offered. To obtain a permit to fish on the streams and lakes in the White Mountain Apache Reservation, write or call **Fort Apache Game and Fish, P.O. Box 220, Whiteriver, 85941; 520-338-4385.**

It's easy fishin' with all the comforts of a well-appointed city park at **Woodland Lake** in Pinetop-Lakeside (see Parks). Go for trout, crappie, bass, and bluegill. For information on specific seasons, license requirements, boating restrictions, campground facilities, exact locations, and what's biting where, contact Pinetop-Lakeside Chamber of Commerce, 520-367-4290.

Rentals and Tours

Troutback Flyfishing Guide Service creates customized lake or stream fishing packages for individuals or groups. Because it holds a special-use permit with the White Mountain Apache tribe, it has access to areas not open to the general public. The company offers full- and half-day trips as well as lessons to introduce novices to the sport. **P.O. Box 864, Show Low, 85902; 520-532-3474. Website: www.troutback.com.**

Hiking

Ice Cave Trail

Listed in the TrailSystem guide, this 3.5-mile route is moderate for hikers and equestrians, but difficult for mountain bikers because it has a steep, rocky descent. It probably is named for the cave it passes, from which a flow of cool air continually rushes. You can't enter the cave because it is protected by a fence, but the trail is scenic, winding along Porter Creek and Scott Reservoir. Elevation goes from 6,700 to 7,200 feet, so if you're not accustomed to high altitudes, take it easy. This trail connects to **Blue Ridge Trail**, an 8.7-mile loop, but to do just the 7-mile round-trip Ice Cave Trail, simply turn around and retrace your steps when you hit Blue Ridge. From Pinetop-Lakeside, travel **south on Hwy. 260 to Porter Mountain Rd. (Forest Rd. 45) and turn left; proceed 1 mile to the trailhead on the right. 520-333-4301.**

Mogollon Rim Interpretive Trail

Easy and fairly level, this trail is extremely popular because it follows the very edge of the Mogollon Rim, providing absolutely amazing views. The 1-mile loop takes a leisurely hour. The first 0.5 mile is paved and wheelchair-accessible. Shaggy ponderosa pine, Douglas fir, piñon pine, and many types of gnarled, wind-twisted juniper and oak grow along with manzanita and mountain mahogany. Interpretive signs explain that in A.D. 1300 there probably were more people living along the rim than there are now. The early residents used the ponderosa for firewood, its gum for healing cuts and scratches, and its needles, when steeped in hot water, for a broth that could cure a cough or cold. You're likely to see Abert squirrels, the ones with light-colored tails, basic gray and ground squirrels, bright blue Steller's jays, and probably huge ravens. The **General Crook Trail** on the Mogollon Rim can also be hiked. An excellent hiking map of the Mogollon Rim, produced by *Arizona Highways* magazine in cooperation with the U.S. Forest Service, shows the trail in good detail and also defines 20 additional hiking trails that branch off from or are near the Rim Trail. It may be ordered from *Arizona Highways* for about $4; 800-543-5432, fax 602-254-4505. From Pinetop-Lakeside, **follow Hwy. 260 west 3 miles, then north of the Lakeside Ranger Station; just past Camp Tatiyee, watch for Mogollon Rim Trail sign; proceed through V-shaped walk-through and follow signs.** 520-367-4290.

White Mountains TrailSystem

This 180-mile network of pathways and tracks extends across the Lakeside Ranger District of the Apache–Sitgreaves National Forest in a series of multiuse loops and trails. Eventually all loops will connect with each other and with neighboring Forest Service districts, providing opportunities for a number of skill levels. The final two trails, 6.5-mile **Los Burros,** whose trailhead is near McNary on the White Mountain Apache Reservation, and the more difficult 16-mile **Ghost of the Coyote** that begins west of Show Low on Burton Rd., were officially opened in June 1997. All trails are designed for hiking, mountain biking, and horseback riding, and range from easy to difficult, with many of the moderate trails suitable for an enthusiastic beginner. Well marked with blue diamond-shaped signs, they range from 4 to 16 miles in length, with trails appropriate for short brisk walks, day

hikes, and overnight backpacking. An excellent TrailSystem guide lists difficulty level for each mode of transportation, highlights, distance, and trailhead access. **Lakeside Ranger Station, Rural Route 3, Box B-50, Lakeside, 85929; 520-368-5111. Or Apache-Sitgreaves National Forest, Supervisor's Office, Box 640, Springerville, 85938; 520-333-4301.** Website: www.wmonline.com.

Horseback Riding

Porter Mountain Stable

The White Mountains TrailSystem is your best bet for riding, as for hiking and mountain biking. This outfitter offers organized one-hour to full-day rides into the Sitgreaves National Forest, including lunch, as well as evening rides with sunset suppers. From Lakeside, **drive 1.5 miles north on Hwy. 260 and turn east at milepost 350 onto Porter Mountain Rd.** 520-368-5306.

Seeing and Doing

Antiquing

The big draws in this area are antiques, collectibles, and high-class junque, purveyed from more than a dozen shops strung along White Mountain Blvd. (Hwy. 260). Just get in your car and hop from place to place. Most shops also are in the business of buying, so if you're looking to cash in on family heirlooms, bring them along. Pick up an antiques map at any of the shops. Sherry's Antiques and Jewelry Mall (**857 E. White Mountain Blvd.; 520-367-5184**) has a good selection of collectible Depression glass as well as an adjacent pawn shop with jewelry and Navajo rugs.

Historic Sites

Fort Apache

Fort Apache includes what is left of General Crook's headquarters, now a small **museum.**

The Pinetop area offers secluded cabins among tall pines as well as luxury lodges.

Officers' quarters and horse barns look like they're about to collapse, but until recently were used as a school that was opened when the fort was abandoned in 1922. Take a short walk along a dirt road up the little hill to the right for a look at the rock-walled **cemetery** where the men from opposing sides now are buried side by side. The **Apache Cultural Center** traces the fort's history with photos and old military gear. It also sells some Apache crafts. Open summers, Mon.–Fri., 7:30 A.M.–4:30 P.M.; winters, Mon.–Fri., 7:30 A.M.–5:00 P.M. **From Pinetop-Lakeside drive Hwy. 260 south 3 miles to Hwy. 73, and drive south 5 miles to Whiteriver; continue 4 miles southwest of Whiteriver. 520-338-4625.**

Parks

Woodland Lake Park

This delightful city park is the hub of the White Mountains TrailSystem and has several trailheads, although its main function is as a day-use area. It has ramadas with picnic tables, some of which are quite isolated in the woods, a large kids' playground, tennis courts, softball fields, a boat dock, and fishing. Llama hikes sometimes are offered during summer months. The Woodland Lake Loop is a 1.25-mile, level, easy walk around the lake. Open daily, 6:00 A.M.–10:00 P.M. **From Hwy. 260 turn west at Frontier State Bank onto Woodland Lake Rd. (watch for green Woodland Lake Park sign) and follow it 0.2 mile to the park.**

Scenic Drives

General Crook Trail

This trail through the Sitgreaves and Coconino National Forests, also called Forest Rd. 300, in many places is a faithful parallel of the trail that U.S. Army Gen. George C. Crook established. It follows the lip of the Mogollon Rim, providing remarkable views. You can hike most any part of the route, or drive along Forest Rd. 300, which has a fairly decent gravel surface in some areas and is simply graded and drained in others. The road is accessible from a number of points along Hwy. 260, including Woods Canyon Lake. It can be bumpy and rough, but the scenery and vistas are well worth it. There are about a dozen campgrounds, and you can camp wherever it isn't posted as not permitted. An excellent map of the Mogollon Rim, produced by *Arizona Highways* magazine in cooperation with the U.S. Forest Service, shows the trail in good detail as well as other trails, plus campgrounds. It may be ordered from *Arizona Highways* for about $5; **800-543-5432, fax 602-254-4505.**

Wagering

Hon-Dah Casino

This large, low, natural wood building with a bright turquoise roof is hard to miss. It is the biggest thing in Hon-Dah. To the Apaches its name means "welcome." If you're a slots aficionado, you're practically guaranteed to feel comfortable in a place that has the greatest number of nickel slots in the state. Unlimited progressive jackpots; video gaming that includes poker, keno, and blackjack; and live gaming in the poker room are all big attractions. On the 1.6-million-acre White Mountain Apache Reservation, it's one of the few Native American casinos in the state that has live, Vegas-style entertainment in the adjacent Timbers Lounge & Showroom. The Indian Pines Restaurant offers truly fine dining with an excellent selection of fish and beef dishes as well as pasta and pizza. The wine list features a lovely Australian chardonnay. A gas station and mini-mart are located **3 miles south of Pinetop on Hwy. 260. 520-369-0299.**

Where to Stay

In the Pinetop–Lakeside area, you'll find a wide range of accommodations that include rustic little housekeeping cabins tucked away in the woods, luxurious lodges, modern condominiums, and basic motels. Chains include Best Western, Comfort Inn, and Holiday Inn Express. Even some of the budget chains have fireplaces and whirlpool tubs. A few of our favorites are listed here, and the very helpful Pinetop-Lakeside Chamber of Commerce is happy to provide you with a complete list (see Services).

Resorts

In the $$–$$$$ range: **Cozy Pine Cabins** (520-367-4558) in Pinetop has six housekeeping cabins. **Hidden Rest Resort** (800-260-REST or 520-368-6336) in Lakeside has 11 housekeeping cabins, some with fireplaces, some with in-room two-person spas. **Mountain Haven Inn** (520-367-2101) in Pinetop has 10 housekeeping cabins. The **Roundhouse Resort** (520-369-4848) in Pinetop has upscale condo units that accommodate up to six. **Whispering Pines Resort** (800-840-3867 or 520-367-4386) in Pinetop has 28 housekeeping cabins.

Northwoods Resort—$$$–$$$$

These charming, blue-and-white wood-frame places could have jumped off the pages of an Austrian Alps brochure. One- and two-bedroom housekeeping cottages, exceptionally well furnished, are scattered over quiet, wooded grounds. For ultimate privacy, request Honeymoon Cottage No. 15. It faces the woods and has a spa tub, fireplace, and wraparound wood deck. Located off Hwy. 260 at milepost 352. P.O. Box 397N, Pinetop, 85935; 800-813-2966 or 520-367-2966. Website: www.northwoodsaz.com.

Lake of the Woods Resort—$$$

Here you'll find log cabins in the trees and on the shores of a beautiful little pine-fringed private lake. One- and two-bedroom housekeeping cabins and two larger chalets have two-night minimums. You can rent fishing boats (people-power only, no motors). Fishing is free (no license) for guests. Open year-round. Located off Hwy. 260 in Lakeside. P.O. Box 777, Lakeside, 85929; 520-368-5353. Website: www.l-o-w.com.

Sierra Springs Ranch—$$$$

For a top-notch, upscale, in-the-woods experience head for Sierra Springs Ranch. Eight well-appointed housekeeping cabins have dishwashers, grills, and full refrigerators. The cozy honeymoon cottage has a clawfoot tub, four-poster bed, and cuddly bathrobes. The four-bedroom four-bath Pueblo accommodates as many as eight guests. In a nose-thumbing gesture at civilization, cabins have no radios, newspapers, or TVs (video players and tapes are available). Catch-and-release fish ponds are stocked regularly. The Country Club Trail, an easy, level 3.5-mile loop through pines and meadows, has its trailhead near the ranch's entrance. The 76-acre ranch has its serenity assured, as it is completely surrounded by the national forest. Located off Hwy. 260, one mile south of Pinetop. 101 Sky High Rd., Pinetop; 800-492-4059 or 520-369-3900. Website: www.sierrasprings ranch.com.

Camping

The White Mountain Apache Reservation's 1.6 million acres have some of the best-maintained, most remote and picturesque sites. Camping permits are required for each family unit, and camping is restricted to designated areas. Sites may have picnic tables, fire rings, trash barrels, toilet facilities, and water, but not all sites have all amenities. Contact the **Whiteriver and Outdoor Recreation Division, P.O. Box 220, Whiteriver, 85941; 520-338-4385 or 520-338-4386, fax 520-338-1712.**

There are 36 campgrounds in the Apache-Sitgreaves National Forest, with amenities that range from full RV hookups to primitive camping with cleared areas only. Area Forest Service offices have camping information. During busy summer months you can make reservations at least five days in advance by calling **800-280-CAMP.**

Hon-Dah RV Park

Across the street from the Hon-Dah Casino (see Wagering) on the White Mountain Apache Reservation, this park's more than 120 full-hookup sites have satellite TV and phone connections. There are showers, laundry facilities, and a recreation room. 520-369-7400.

Where to Eat

Charlie Clark's—$$$–$$$$

This log-sided steak house, filled with taxidermied creatures, has been around since 1938 and features mesquite-broiled chicken and steak as well as huge prime rib and baby back ribs. Open Thurs. and Sun.–Tues., 11:00 A.M.–4:00 P.M. and 5:00 P.M.–9:00 P.M.; Fri.–Sat., 11:00 A.M.–4:00 P.M. and 5:00 P.M.–10:00 P.M.; bar opens at 11:00 A.M. Located on Hwy. 260 in the east end of **Pinetop, at Main and Penrod. 520-367-4900.**

The Christmas Tree—$$$–$$$$

Named for the lighted pine that stands at its entrance, a series of rooms that keep the atmosphere warm and intimate. It is famous for its chicken and dumplings. Open Wed.–Sun., 5:00 P.M.–9:00 P.M. **Woodland Rd. just off Hwy. 260, Lakeside; 520-367-3107.**

Chuck Wagon Steak House and 1890 Saloon—$$$

Those who've eaten here say you'd better have a big appetite or count on asking for a doggie bag. Steaks, burgers, chicken, and pork are grilled western-style over mesquite, then served with cowboy beans, steak fries, sauteed mushrooms, onions, and homemade bread. Hot apple pie is served in big bowls, with a dollop of rich vanilla ice cream. The saloon has a full bar. Open in summer, daily, 4:00 P.M.–9:00 P.M.; in winter, Wed.–Sat., 5:00 p.m.–9:00 P.M. **Located on Porter Mountain Rd. off Hwy. 60; 520-368-5800.**

Coyote Grill—$$$

At the Lakeview Lodge in a log building dating to 1929, when the weather's warm you can eat on a pine-shaded patio. Southwest cuisine with a focus on fresh vegetables is the place's stock in trade. Open Wed.–Thurs., 4:00 P.M.–8:00 P.M.; Fri. and Sun., 11:00 A.M.–9:00 P.M.; Sat., 7:30 A.M.–9:00 P.M.; hours may vary seasonally. **2251 W. White Mountain Blvd., Lakeside; 520-368-5348.**

Baggin' It—$$

For a lunch to tote while hiking or picnicking, stop at Baggin' It. Delicious, healthful sandwiches plus inventive salads are packed to travel in (what else?) a brown paper bag with the menu printed on it. You also can eat in the cheery, garden-like restaurant. Open for lunch. **On Hwy. 260 at Woodland Road in Lakeside; 520-368-8898.**

Pinetop Cafe—$$

Great breakfast cafe with a huge menu; it's also open for lunch and dinner. You can chow down on biscuits and gravy, hotcakes, and all the stuff you don't eat at home. They have a full bar. Hours vary with the seasons. **436 E. White Mountain Blvd., Pinetop; 520-367-2517.**

Services

Pinetop-Lakeside Chamber of Commerce

Located in a line of shops near the post office. **674 E. White Mountain Blvd., Lakeside, 85929; 800-573-4031 or 520-367-4290.** Website: www.pinetoplakesidechamber.com.

Pinetop-Lakeside Parks and Recreation Dept.

1360 N. Neils Hansen Ln., Lakeside, 85929; 520-368-6700.

U.S. Forest Service, Lakeside District

Rural Route 3, Box B-50, Lakeside, 85929; 520-368-5111. Website: www.fs.fed.us.

Show Low

With the Mogollon Rim just to the south and the White Mountains to the southeast, Show Low has become a big outdoor recreation hub. At an elevation of 6,331 feet on the Mogollon Rim, the city is a regional trade and service center for the high country. Although it has taken a back seat in the tourism department to nearby Pinetop-Lakeside, its alpine features and quiet, small-town feel are beginning to draw more visitors. Trout fishing and hiking are major attractions to this town of about 6,000. Population can more than double during summer months.

History

The town is "named after a turn of a card," say its brochures. If you believe a pair of partners homesteaded 100,000 acres around 1870, then had a falling-out and agreed to settle their differences in a poker game, then the town's name makes sense. Marion Clark and Croyden E. Cooley played a game called Seven Up that went into the wee hours. Cooley needed a single point to win. According to accounts, Clark then said, "You show low, and you win." When Cooley cut the deck he turned up an unbeatable card, the two of clubs. The main street, Deuce of Clubs Blvd. (same as US 60), is named for that card.

Festivals and Events

Freedom Fest

Fourth of July
This is a fun, typically small-town celebration with a parade, softball tournament, huge fireworks display, and arts and crafts show. Held **at Main St. Market Place. 520-537-2326 or 888-746-9569.**

Outdoor Activities

Fishing

For fishing information, contact Show Low Chamber of Commerce, 520-537-2326.

Fool Hollow Lake Recreation Area

This 149-acre lake is surrounded by 800 acres of recreation area on Forest Service land. The deep, cool-water lake furnishes natural habitat for rainbow and brown trout, large and small mouth bass, black crappie, green sunfish, channel catfish, and walleye. Catchable-size rainbow trout are stocked mid-May through Sept. Many anglers find their best luck simply casting from shore, although boat motors up to eight horsepower are allowed. Of the two day-use areas, the prettiest for picnics is just east of Cinnamon Teal Loop (pick up a park map as you enter). Along with the whoosh of wind through the tall pines you can appreciate the stunning views of massive wind- and water-eroded cliffs that were sculpted as the creek bed developed. A

Getting There
Show Low is 175 miles northeast of Phoenix, about a three-and-a-half-hour drive, and 195 miles north of Tucson, on US 60 where Hwys. 260 and 77 meet.

stairway leads to the water's edge and to a short path that follows the shoreline. The area has five shower buildings with rest rooms, a dump station, and fish-cleaning station; RV and developed tent sites. Located **on Show Low's northwest edge.** Take Hwy. 260 west 2 miles to Old Linden Rd. Turn right and proceed another 2 miles. Signs direct you to Fool Hollow. Small day-use fee. An on-site manager may be reached at 520-537-3680.

Show Low Lake County Park

Also called Navajo County Park, here the attraction is early spring trout fishing. So say anglers who seem to have equally good luck from the shore or from a boat. It's not surprising because the 100-acre Show Low Lake is stocked weekly with 1,800 of the feisty fish during summer months. With an average depth of about 20 feet, the lake also has catfish, bluegill, walleye, and largemouth bass. It holds the state record for yielding a 12-pound walleye. No live bait is permitted. Facilities at this good family fishing site include a small store, showers and bathrooms, boat rental and launch, dump station, and tent and RV sites with picnic tables. The park is leased from Phelps Dodge Corporation, which built the dam here to provide water for its mining and metallurgical operations at Morenci under a water exchange agreement with the Salt River Project. Located **6 miles south of Show Low on Show Low Lake Rd.,** 1 mile off Hwy. 260. 520-537-4126.

Golf

Show Low Country Club

With grass fairways and bent-grass greens, this par 70 course has distinctively different front and back nines: One meanders through the pines, the other through the meadows. Both are scenic and playable year-round. Call for tee times. Located on west side of Show Low **at Hwy. 260 and Old Linden Rd.** 520-537-4564.

Silver Creek Golf Club

This public 18-hole, par 71 championship course in the White Mountains has lots of undulation in and around the bunkered bent-grass greens, creating challenging play. There are four sets of tees, the longest at 6,813 yards. Although about 35 snow days a year make the course unplayable, it is considered a four-season course. Call for tee times. Located **7 miles north of Show Low and 5 miles east of Hwy.** 77 on **White Mountain Lake Rd.** 520-537-2744.

Seeing and Doing

Museums

Show Low Historical Museum

In an unimposing storefront in what used to be the police department (a jail cell still exists), this collection of local memorabilia includes prehistoric Indian artifacts, a Silver Creek Railroaders display, an old-time kitchen, and photos of Show Low as it once was. Open May 1–Oct. 25, Tues.–Sat., 1:00 P.M.–5:00 P.M. **542 E. Deuce of Clubs Blvd., Show Low, 85901;** 520-532-7115.

Wildlife Viewing

Pintail Lake Wild Game Observation Area

This preservation area was built in the late 1970s by a young biologist named Allen Severson, and immediately attracted capacity numbers of birds. Migratory geese, ducks, and other waterbirds rest here among unique grasses and reeds. The lake's slender, white-breasted namesake likes the preserve so well it has become a permanent resident. The fences keep free-range cattle out, not to confine creatures in the

The dramatic Mogollon Rim, a 200-mile-long escarpment, was uplifted during the Paleozoic era.

preserve. You can get close-up looks at various species (depending on the time of year) from observation platforms and an enclosed blind. Informative signs along the 0.25-mile paved, wheelchair-accessible entrance trail, which leads to the blind, point out local vegetation. Try to get there in the early morning or at dusk for best sightings. From Show Low **take Hwy. 77 north about 3.5 miles, turn east on Pintail Lakes Rd., and proceed 0.5 mile.** 520-537-3236.

Where to Stay

Bed-and-Breakfasts

Fool Hollow Bed & Breakfast— $$$–$$$$
Two suites and one room are part of a 4,100-square-foot home with wide decks that overlook Fool Hollow Lake. Just sit back with your binoculars for good wildlife viewing. Homemade apple butter is part of the full breakfast. 2351 N. 22nd Ave., Show Low, 85901; 888-339-

1144 or 520-537-1924. Website: www.fool hollow.com.

Hotels, Motels, and Inns
On Deuce of Clubs Blvd. there are a Best Western, Days Inn, Holiday Inn Express, Sleep Inn, and Motel 6, most in the $$–$$$ range. For more resorts, head south to Pinetop and Lakeside.

The Pines Resort—$$$–$$$$
This totally civilized, cozy, and comfortable place offers 46 luxury one-, two-, and three-bedroom condominiums with fireplaces and full kitchens. 2700 S. White Mountain Rd., Show Low, 85901; 800-537-4632 or 520-537-1888.

Camping

Fool Hollow Recreation Area
Though the campground at Fool Hollow Lake serves mainly RVs, there is a picturesque area for tenters. There are 92 RV hookups and 31

developed tent sites, each with picnic table, water, and fire ring. Spaces are wooded and well planned so that each has maximum privacy. Developed campsites for tent camping in Bald Eagle Loop have wonderful views of the lake through fairly heavy woods. During summer months, a campground host is in residence in a marked space. **Take Hwy. 260 west 2 miles to Old Linden Rd., turn right, and proceed another 2 miles.** On-site manager, 520-537-3680.

Pine Shadows Mobile Home & RV Park

The upscale adult park has 129 spaces with hookups, telephone lines, and cable TV. Open May 1–Nov. 1. 4951 S. White Mountain Rd., Show Low, 85901; 520-537-2895.

Where to Eat

All you have to do is cruise Deuce of Clubs Blvd. and take your pick. Most restaurants are in the $$ price range.

Branding Iron Steak House—$$

As the name implies, they serve up great steaks. Open Mon.–Fri., 11:00 A.M.–2:00 P.M. and 5:00 P.M.–9:00 P.M.; Sat.–Sun., 5:00 P.M.–9:00 P.M. 1231 E. Deuce of Clubs Blvd.; 520-537-5151.

JB's Restaurant—$$

Great baked goods and a buffet. Upstairs is One Eyed Jacks Bar & Grill, the place to go to watch sports on big-screen TV. Open daily, 6:00 A.M.–10:00 P.M. **480 W. Deuce of Clubs Blvd.; 520-532-1266 restaurant, 520-537-7460 bar and grill.**

La Casita—$$

This is part of a group of 11 top-notch Mexican restaurants operated by the Esparza family. They've been local favorites for almost 20 years. Open Tues.–Thurs. and Sun., 11:00 A.M.–8:00 P.M.; Fri.–Sat., 11:00 A.M.–9:00 P.M. **Located on Hwy. 260 4 miles south of Show Low; 520-537-5179.**

Pat's Place—$$

Pizza, burgers, sandwiches, and spaghetti. Open Sun.–Thurs., 7:00 A.M.–8:30 P.M.; Fri.–Sat., 7:00 A.M.–9:00 P.M. **981 E. Deuce of Clubs Blvd.; 520-537-2337.**

Services

Show Low Chamber of Commerce

The Chamber is tucked away in the corner of a little retail center next to Northland Pioneer College but is scheduled to move. The phone number should remain the same, so call first. **915 W. Deuce of Clubs Blvd., P.O. Box 1083, Show Low, 85901; 888-SHOW-LOW, 520-537-2326 phone and fax. Website: www. showlow.com.**

Snowflake and Taylor

The neatly tended fields and farms of this gently rolling countryside look much like those of Minnesota and Wisconsin. This pair of small towns are located 16 miles north of Show Low in the valley formed by Silver Creek. The largest industry is Abitibi Consolidated Corp., a pulp and paper mill about 15 miles west of Snowflake. It's the largest such mill in the state. Products are made from recycled fiber, not live trees. The towns have more than 100 historical homes, half a dozen of which are listed on the National Register of Historic Buildings. Among them are good examples of Victorian, Georgian, Greek Revival, Gothic, Colonial, and Neoclassical architecture, all part of Brigham Young's master plan for a utopian community. Today the towns still serve as a center for Mormon experience in the Southwest.

History

In 1846 the Mormon Battalion's 400 ill-equipped and underfed men walked more than 2,000 miles at the behest of President James K. Polk, who hoped to rid the Midwest of Mormonism. In 1878 Erastus Snow and William J. Flake arrived, Mormon pioneers in hopes of colonizing the area for the church; Snowflake is named for them. Taylor is named for John Taylor, a president of the Church of Jesus Christ of Latter-Day Saints who was on the same mission. Together they purchased the 5,640-foot-high town site, then known as Stinson's Ranch, for 500 head of cattle. Snow, Flake, and Taylor still are prominent family names in the area.

Getting There
Snowflake and Taylor are located on Hwy. 77 about 19 miles north of Show Low/US 60, 30 miles south of Holbrook/I-40.

Festivals and Events

Pioneer Days Celebration
July
The community's builders are honored with a rodeo, ball games, dances, crafts demonstrations, a parade, and more. 520-536-5450.

Outdoor Activities

Golf

Snowflake Golf Course
The course is lush and green, playable year-round—even in winter, when the rye and blue-grass fairways and bent-grass greens are dormant.

Named for Mormon pioneers Mr. Snow and Mr. Flake, Snowflake looks like it belongs in the Midwest.

Located next door to the Putter's Paradise RV Park, which offers packages that allow two to play 18 holes a day for a week, for $45. On Hwy. 77 about 3 miles west of Snowflake. **Heber Rd. and Country Club Dr.; 520-536-7233.**

Seeing and Doing

Museums

Stinson Pioneer Museum
Part of the historic homes tour, the Stinson House built in 1873 is now the Stinson Pioneer Museum. It contains memorabilia donated by local residents, including an Edison phonograph, a replica of an early kitchen, and a photograph of William Jordan Flake in prison stripes, jailed for polygamy. A display traces the long, cruel 1846 route of the Mormon Battalion. Donations accepted. Open Mon.–Fri., 9:00 A.M.–3:00 P.M. **102 N. First E., Snowflake, 85937; 520-536-4331.**

Tours

Historic Walking Tour
A map, available from the chamber of commerce, directs visitors to 26 buildings that include the 1889 Greek Revival home of Charles L. Flake,

the 1893 Gothic Revival home of John A. Freeman, and the impressive Victorian mansion of James M. Flake, built in 1895. **520-536-4331.**

Where to Stay

Camping

Putter's Paradise RV Park
With 90 full hookups and generous spaces, this may be one of the area's best-kept secrets, so far as RVers are concerned. The RV park is almost entirely populated with golfers who come for the package deal with the golf course next door. Packages may be arranged through the RV park or the course. Summer reservations are essential. Located **on Hwy. 77 about 3 miles west of Snowflake. P.O. Box 336, Snowflake, 85937; 520-536-2127.**

Where to Eat

Katy's Kountry Kitchen—$–$$
Located on the main drag of Snowflake, this low-key restaurant has earned a local reputation for its barbecue ribs, chicken-fried steak, and homemade baked beans. Hearty breakfast omelets with homemade biscuits fill a 12-inch oval platter, and lunch burgers with a mountain of fries are huge. The rough-cut knotty pine walls, open-beam ceiling, and western relics hung on the walls set the tone. Open daily, 6:00 A.M.–9:00 P.M. **205 N. Main St., Snowflake; 520-536-5450. Website: www.wmonline.com/services/katys.**

Services

Snowflake–Taylor Chamber of Commerce
Located in the same building as the Stinson Pioneer Museum, with public rest rooms. Open Mon.–Fri., 9:00 A.M.–3:00 P.M. **P.O. Box 776, Snowflake, 85937; 520-536-4331. Website: www.wmonline.com/cities/snof.**

Heber and Overgaard

These twin towns at elevations of 6,435 and 6,520 feet, respectively, are north of the Mogollon Rim in the Sitgreaves National Forest on Hwy. 260. The sparsely populated area is gaining popularity as a destination for fishing and camping. Christopher Creek and Kohl's Ranch, about 28 to 32 miles west of Heber and Overgaard, are two little communities that have become summer getaway destinations for heat-suffocated Phoenicians (see Where to Stay).

Snugged under the Rim, Christopher Creek is a delightful little mountain community at 5,900 feet in the Tonto National Forest. Streams run year-round. There are several restaurants, cabins, and a gas station. Tonto Creek runs close to the ranch, and the Tonto Fish Hatchery is just up the road. North of the hatchery is the area in which Zane Grey had his cabin and penned many of his Western novels.

History

In about 1880 Heber, a Mormon settlement, was established and named for Heber C. Kimball, a chief justice of the State of Deseret, in 1883. In 1927 the Kohl family bought grazing land in the area, and the ranch became a community center for parties and get-togethers. Native Americans lived along the banks of Tonto Creek before settlers arrived.

Outdoor Activities

Horseback Riding

Kohl's Stables
At Kohl's Ranch you can pop in and do a one-hour, two-hour, or half-day ride along easy trails, with a guide who knows the area and its history and is more than willing to talk about it. This isn't a Wild West experience, where you charge off into parts unknown, clinging to the back of a barely broken steed. Rather, these are enjoyable family rides taken only with a guide. Rides are moderately priced, and horses are in good shape. Located **27 miles west of Heber on Hwy. 260. 520-478-4211;** ask for the stables.

Fragrant pine forests are ideal for a summer stroll.

Skiing

CROSS-COUNTRY

Forest Lakes Touring Center and Cabins

Sufficient snow keeps this cross-country ski facility active about Jan. 1–mid-Mar. There are 27 miles of groomed double-set trails, with additional ungroomed trails on the other side of Hwy. 260. They rent skis, poles, and boots, and sell trail day-passes. Snowshoeing here is fun, and instructors say it is a good way for parents to move alongside a very young child just learning to ski. Open during ski season, 8:00 A.M.–5:00 P.M. Located **in village of Forest Lakes, 35 miles east of Payson** and 14 miles west of Heber. 520-535-4047.

Seeing and Doing

Parks

Navajo County Tall Timbers Park

At this pleasant day-use site, groups who live in the surrounding area reserve the pavilion, then use the racquetball, softball, basketball, volleyball, horseshoes, and shuffleboard courts. If you're just passing through, it is a good place to relax with a picnic or get out and stretch your legs. From the park, a 12-mile dirt road accesses Forest Rd. 300, the Rim Trail Rd. Snow covers the park and closes it during the winter; during summer months a ranger is on-site. Located **1 mile east of Overgaard.** 520-535-3404.

Where to Stay

Reasonably priced accommodations can be found at the 43-room **Best Western Sawmill Inn.** Rates include a continental breakfast, and there is a restaurant next door. 520-535-5053.

Resorts

Kohl's Ranch Lodge—$$$–$$$$

People have been coming to this cool creek-side location for more than 75 years. The lodge, built in the 1940s, has 41 comfortable rooms decorated in a western theme. Some of the rooms have fireplaces, refrigerators, and coffeemakers. There also are eight one- and two-bedroom cabins on the creek that have individual decks, outdoor spas, and fireplaces. When booking, be sure to ask for a room on the creek side. You won't be directly on the creek (that's where the cabins are), but you will be on the side away from the road. Since this is Zane Grey country, movies made from the famous author's books are shown in the lodge loft Fri.–Sun., and on request. There is a small market with gifts, supplies, and books about the area, including Zane Grey novels and Tony Hillerman's current favorites revolving around the ambitious antics of Sgt. Jim Chee of the Navajo Tribal Police. The Zane Grey Dining Room is on-site (see Where to Eat). Open year-round. Located 17 miles northeast of Payson. **E. Hwy. 60, Payson, 85541; 800-331-5645 or 520-478-4211.** Website: **www.ilxresorts.com.**

Christopher Creek Lodge—$$–$$$

You really can be right on the creek in these rustic log and stone cottages. Although they look as if they were built years ago, they have modern facilities. Most have fireplaces and can accommodate a family or two couples. There also are motel-type rooms that are not nearly as charming as the cottages, but if you're just looking for a place to headquarter while you tour the area, they can be a good home base. Firewood provided. Located **21 miles east of Payson on Hwy. 260 in Christopher Creek. Star Route, Box 119, Payson, 85541; 520-478-4300.**

Forest Lakes Touring Center and Cabins—$$–$$$

The cross-country ski-touring center has six rental cabins with kitchenettes open year-round. In summer, guests can rent canoes for day trips to nearby Black Canyon Lake and Willow Springs Lake. Located **just past milepost 288 on south side of Hwy. 260, 14 miles west of Heber. 520-535-4047.**

Camping

One of the most beautiful, **Ponderosa Campground,** is in a huge stand of its namesake pines that truly "whisper" in the wind. There are 60 spaces with water, a dump station, and rest rooms. Open May–Sept. Located along **Hwy. 260 about 15 miles east of Payson; 520-474-2269.** Others in the area, such as **Christopher Creek Campground,** fill up so quickly that it's almost pure luck if you manage to snag a space there; 520-474-2269.

Webwood Acres RV Park and Campground

Between Overgaard and Show Lowis a well-kept, off-the-beaten-track park in the tall pines. There are 21 large RV sites with sewer, water, and electric hookups, and a separate tent and group-camping area. There are flush toilets, exceptionally clean showers, and a laundry room with curtains in the windows. Kids and teens can hike and toss horseshoes, but some have discovered they can take their computers to the laundry room and plug them in to play games. Open mid-Apr.–mid-Oct. From **Hwy. 260 between mileposts 320–321,** take Forest Rd. 139 north about 3 miles to Webwood Acres sign and turn right. P.O. Box 914, Clay Springs, 85923; 520-587-4517. Website: webwoodrv.com.

Where to Eat

Zane Grey Dining Room (Kohl's Ranch)—$$$

People staying in Payson often make a late-afternoon drive out to Kohl's Ranch to look around, have a drink at the Cowboy Bar, and stay for dinner at the dining room. Low-key and casual, it has comfortable booths and good, hearty food. A readers says this is "a beautiful, tranquil place for a delicious breakfast." Thurs. is all-you-can-eat barbecue beef rib night, and prime rib is always available. Open Mon.–Thurs., 7:30 A.M.–2:00 P.M. and 5:00 P.M.–8:00 P.M.; Fri.–Sat., 7:30 A.M.–9:00 P.M.; Sun., 7:30 A.M.–8:00 P.M.; hours vary. Located **17 miles east of Payson and 27 miles west of Heber on Hwy. 260. 800-331-5645.**

Creekside Steakhouse & Tavern—$$–$$$

This rustic tavern has been a stopping-off point for 25 years for people driving down off the Mogollon Rim. Portions are huge, so the kitchen will fix many sandwiches by the half. On the menu for years, the Mad Jack with chiles, cheese, and bacon was one of our favorites. Half a dozen steak selections range from petite to enormous. Stop in the bar to see generations of initials carved in its rugged top. Service is friendly and down-home, and there's live bar entertainment on weekends. Open in summer, daily, 6:00 A.M.–10:00 P.M., in winter, daily, 7:00 A.M.–10:00 P.M. Located **about 22 miles northeast of Payson on Hwy. 260, in Christopher Creek. 520-478-4557 or 520-478-4389.**

Tom's Cabin Saloon & Restaurant—$$–$$$

This place recently has begun serving full meals in the piney woods. Open daily, 10:00 A.M.–1:00 A.M. 2763 Hwy. 260, Overgaard; 520-535-4117.

Services

Heber–Overgaard Chamber of Commerce

P.O. Box 550, Heber, 85928; 520-535-4406. Website: www.wmonline.

Roosevelt Lake and Dam

This impressive construction feat corralled the Salt River and Tonto Creek, which are fed by snow runoff from the White Mountains. The result created central Arizona's largest lake. At an elevation of 2,100 feet, with an area of more than 17,000 surface acres, the lake is 23 miles long and as wide as two miles in some places. It has 89 miles of shoreline and is a maximum of 234 feet deep.

Construction of the Theodore Roosevelt Dam began in 1903. When it was dedicated in 1911, the year before Arizona became a state, it was the largest masonry dam in the world. It was part of President Roosevelt's plan to grow the West by constructing a system of irrigation works that would store, divert, and develop available water sources. In 1996 modifications were completed using steel-reinforced concrete that heightened the dam by 77 feet. The lake's surface area was expanded by 1,862 acres, immediately increasing recreational opportunities.

History

The Salado people lived in this area for about 300 years, between A.D. 1400 and 1450 abandoning what must have been a comfortable living site. Archaeologists have found decorated earthenware, probably made by the Salado, as well as seashells from the Gulf of California and Mexican macaw feathers that affirm an established system of trade. This primarily agrarian culture built canals to irrigate corn, beans, cotton, and pumpkins, supplemented by the deer, quail, rabbit, and other game that flourish in the area. Native plants such as the saguaro cactus that grow here today supplied moist, tender fruit.

Major Attractions

Tonto National Monument

This Salado cliff dwelling was relatively undiscovered until construction began on the dam. In 1907 it was declared a national monument. The **Lower Ruin**, a small village, consists of 16 ground-floor rooms plus a 12-room annex. Interesting features are saguaro cactus ribs covered with clay and used as beams to create a roof. A *mano* and *metate* (grinding stone and basin) remain in a room that probably was used for communal food preparation. The larger **Upper Ruin** had 32 rooms on a first floor, with eight additional rooms forming a second story.

A self-guided tour winds upward 350 feet to the Lower Ruin for a close-up look. It also affords sweeping views of the Tonto Basin, which helps place the site in context as a desirable dwelling place. The path is paved and easy to negotiate, but the rapid elevation gain may dictate frequent stops to catch your breath. The Upper Ruin is accessible only with a park guide, with tours scheduled as interest warrants. Be sure to take water, especially in summer. As in many parts of the desert, Mar. and Apr. are wildflower months when clouds of yellow brittlebush, little Mexican gold poppies, blue lupine,

Getting There

The lake is 76 miles northeast of Phoenix on Hwy. 88. From Phoenix, take Hwy. 87 north 60 miles to the junction of Hwys. 87 and 188. Turn right and follow Hwy. 188 south to the lake. From the Miami-Globe area, take Hwy. 88 northwest 32 miles to its junction with Hwy. 188. Take Hwy. 188 north to the lake.

and an occasional firecracker penstemon line the hiking path.

The visitor center, which is wheelchair-accessible, has a good video that explains the park's history and geology. Displays on the culture and crafts of the Salado further detail their lives at this site. There is no camping here, but a picnic area about 0.5 mile from the ruins has tables and shade. Open daily, 8:00 A.M.–5:00 P.M., except Christmas Day. Located **4 miles east of Roosevelt Dam and 1 mile off Hwy. 88.** From Globe, take Hwy. 88 west or from Jake's Corner and Punkin Center, take Hwy. 188 south. From Phoenix and Apache Junction, for an interesting but slower and rougher route, take the Apache Trail, Hwy. 88 (see Scenic Drives in Apache Junction chapter). **520-467-2241.**

Outdoor Activities

Boating/Fishing

Visitors come to fish, launching small car-top boats as well as large trailered craft. Water skiing is generally good on the lake's calm surface. **Roosevelt Marina** has some boat rentals; **about 2 miles south of the dam; 520-467-2245.**

Where to Stay

Spring Creek RV Park & Motel—$$

As you approach Roosevelt Lake, there is a clus-

Roosevelt Dam, built between 1905–1911, has created 23-mile-long Roosevelt Lake.

ter of services that include **Spring Creek Store** (520- 467-2468) and a gas station. The RV park here has pull-through spaces and full hookups, including cable TV. The motel has standard rooms and kitchenettes with all cooking and eating utensils. Although the site itself is not particularly picturesque, its obvious attraction is that it is within minutes of the lake. A golf course is schedule to open late in 2000. Located **on Hwy. 88. 520-467-2888.**

Camping

Facilities for camping at Roosevelt Lake are widely considered the best of any desert lake in the state. All sites are on a first-come, first-served basis. Three great campgrounds, developed by Tonto National Forest, offer a variety of choices. Cholla and Windy Hill are available for individuals; **Grapevine** is for groups of 15 and more, and may be reserved; **520-467-3200, fax 520-467-3239.** Volunteer camp hosts usually are on-site. Sites have shelters, drinking water, fire pits, picnic tables, showers, flush toilets, and fish-cleaning stations. In addition to campgrounds below, there is **primitive shoreline camping** at Bermuda Flat, Cholla Bay, and Bachelor Cove.

Cholla Campground

The nation's largest all-solar-powered campground, Cholla is covered with thick brush for privacy, yet has refreshing lake views. A number of short walking trails branch off, leading through brush and along the lake. It has about 200 sites on six loops, one of which is reserved for tent camping. Loops are named for various types of cholla cactus and include Teddy Bear and Jumping. There are four shower buildings and 10 restroom facilities. It is wheelchair-accessible. Located **5 miles northwest of Roosevelt Dam on Hwy. 188. 520-467-3200, fax 520-467-3239.**

Windy Hill Recreation Site

This larger 347-site campground is on the opposite end of the lake from Cholla, on a peninsula jutting out into the lake. The nine loops (one just for tents) are named for local creatures like Jack Rabbit and Coyote. It has two high-water and two low-water boat ramps. Vegetation is sparse here, but the campground is fairly new, and with enough rain it will grow. There are several barrier-free, wheelchair-accessible camp units. **From Hwy. 88 either 4 miles east of its junction with Hwy. 188 or 25 miles north of the Globe-Miami area, turn left on Forest Rd. 82A and proceed 2 miles to the site. 520-467-3200, fax 520-467-3239.**

Services

Roosevelt Lake Visitor Center

This is also the headquarters for the Tonto Basin Ranger District. It has exhibits, videos, and an interactive computer system to let you test your knowledge of how water affects this arid environment. For a true Kodak moment, step out to the back patio. Open daily, 7:45 A.M.–4:30 P.M.; closed Thanksgiving and Christmas Day. Located **1.5 miles east of dam. 520-467-3200. Website: www.fs.fed.us.**

Roadrunners

This amusing bird inhabits Arizona's chaparral, desert scrub, and other arid brush year-round. If the bird's behavior seems a little cuckoo, it's because the roadrunner, geococcyx californianus, belongs to the cuckoo family. It's between 20 and 24 inches long, much of it tail, with a proud, bushy crest and streaky brown plumage.

When startled, it will sprint across a road at speeds that have been documented at up to 12 miles an hour. His amazing ground speed allows him to handily nab the little lizards that are a staple of his diet. He also enjoys small snakes, and has been known to entice a predatory rattler to strike. At the last moment the bird hops out of harm's way, returning to grab the hapless snake by its head and fling it into the air. As the snake lies stunned, the bird grabs it again, securing its grip, and beats the dazed reptile to death.

Roadrunners are devoted mates. During courtship, the male often brings the female a gift of a lizard, caterpillar, small snake, or insect. If she accepts it, she is willing to mate. The female lays three to six eggs that hatch at intervals. Both parents forage for food, mincing lizards and small prey with their long bills before stuffing the morsels into the chicks' bills.

When watching for roadrunners, remember they can flatten themselves against the ground, scuttling like a rat or mouse. Watch for their tracks, easily identifiable with two toes pointing forward and two pointing backward. Although sightings will be brief, they are reliably rewarding and seldom fail to invoke a smile.

Superior, Miami, and Globe

Approaching these interesting small towns from Phoenix, you travel through beautiful saguaro-studded landscape. As you gain elevation, the mountains at varying distances appear in shades of gray, as in an uncomplicated watercolor painting. The road follows the bases of massive rock formations. Out of Superior, it climbs to picturesque Mountain Pass, through a tunnel where Queen Creek has carved a steep canyon in the craggy Pinal Mountains. From the bridge you get a good look at uplifted layers that provide a framework for understanding area geology. The vegetation changes dramatically over the 2,000-foot elevation gain.

Between Superior and Globe–Miami, US 60 is designated as the Gila Pinal Scenic Rd. Although it is two lanes, there are frequent pull-outs for passing. Everywhere there is evidence, in tailings and scars on the landscape, of the industry that gave Arizona one of its nicknames, the Copper State. Globe and Miami, 5 miles apart, are linked by their mining history as well as US 60.

In the last few years copper prices have re-bounded from their 1982 low, and the Carlota Copper Company has reopened a mine in Globe. Boards have been removed from businesses along Broad St. and new restaurants welcome eager customers. Globe's history is a major draw. Many buildings, solidly constructed in the first place, have endured for decades with enough vitality to give them second lives. Old hillside homes are being bought up and restored. Globe is picturesque in a quirky sort of way, with skeletons of mining equipment creating sculptures against a skyline of old open-pit mine tailings. You'll feel especially welcome here because locals have

learned the importance of promoting tourism and the pitfalls of an economy that is dependent on copper mining alone.

History

It is thought that the Hohokam were the earliest residents of this area, leaving around A.D. 1100. A century later they were replaced by the Salado, who constructed the pueblo that stands today at Besh-Ba-Gowah (see Museums and Historic Sites). They, too, abandoned the site, sometime after 1400, and it became home to the Apaches in the 1600s.

As did most of the towns in this area, Superior grew up around a mine, the Silver King, opened in 1875. The rubble piles along the road north of town are mine tailings from the Magma Copper Mine, earlier called the Silver Queen, and the abandoned smelter is another remnant. Exit US 60 to see what remains of this town. Along Main St. the Magma Hotel is boarded up, and the only businesses that seem to be functioning are the bars.

Apache Tears

A beautiful Apache legend, centuries old, centers on Picket Post Mountain near the city of Superior. A group of warriors were once cornered by Spaniards. If captured, the braves would become lifelong slaves in Spanish gold mines. But to flee meant tumbling over a precipitous cliff and certain death. Since slavery was an impossible concept for them, the braves chose death. Later, as the women of the tribe prepared the bodies for burial, they heard a whisper on the wind: "Thy bitter tears shall be turned into beautiful stones, for I should not have made those cliffs so high." The Apaches say the breeze still carries the message of the women's broken hearts. As you walk near Picket Post Mountain, don't be surprised to hear the whispers, then look down to see glossy black Apache tears scattered among the rocks and vegetation. The satiny stones are nodules of obsidian, a glass formed by rapidly cooling lava. The stones are common around Picket Post Mountain, which has volcanic origins.

Native Americans discovered that because obsidian is brittle and heat-sensitive, it fractures sharply, making it ideal for arrowheads, knives, and other pointed tools and weapons. Such tools are relatively rare, and each source of obsidian has slightly different characteristics, so archaeologists use them to trace ancient trade routes. Occasionally nodules are red or brown if iron oxide dust is present. Sometimes they are naturally faceted. A type known as snowflake obsidian is dotted with flecks of translucent quartz crystals called cristobalite. Another type, rainbow obsidian, gleams with multicolored iridescence. The semiprecious gemstones are used in jewelry, but most often they are simply carried as a token of good luck to encourage the watchful eye of the spirits.

At one time it was possible to prowl a site on the eastern slopes of Picket Post to search for Apache tears, but it is now closed for safety reasons. The stones are inexpensive and widely available at souvenir and mineral shops throughout Arizona. The world's largest Apache tear, a baseball-sized, gem-quality piece of obsidian, is on display at the **World's Smallest Museum** *in Superior at Buckboard City. Smaller Apache tears also are for sale.* **Located on US 60 on west side of Superior. 520-689-5800.**

Miami and Globe first flourished during gold and silver days. The discovery of high-grade copper ore in the surrounding mountains forever established their identity as mining towns.

Getting There

These towns are about an hour's drive from Roosevelt Lake along Hwy. 88; you can approach from the Phoenix area along US 60, a distance of about 87 miles.

The Old Dominion Copper Company, one of Globe's first, is among the most famous mining names in the world. During the area's salad days, mining created an affluent upper class of managers and executives, as well as a solid, prosperous middle class. Cattle ranching flourished as well, nourished by grasslands kept green by a stable water supply. But by 1931 the Old Dominion closed down. Copper ore was playing out and the Great Depression was taking its toll. Miami continued to function as a center for ore processing, but on a diminishing basis. In 1982 a final blow was dealt to the area when copper prices tumbled from more than a

Boyce Thompson Southwestern Arboretum is filled with more than 300 species of desert plants.

dollar a pound to less than 60 cents. Businesses foundered and workers moved to other areas. Lately copper prices have recovered; mining is still the biggest industry, but tourism is fast gaining a toehold in the local economy.

Major Attractions

San Carlos Apache Reservation

This 1.8-million-acre reservation straddles Graham, Gila, and Pinal Counties and includes mountains, waterways, and Sonoran Desert. It was created in 1871 to convert the Apaches to farmers, an enterprise doomed to failure by the very nature of its residents. Over the years the reservation was reduced five times to accommodate the mining industry. In the fall, well into Nov., miles of golden cottonwoods and salt cedar, also called tamarisk, enrich the Gila River banks in bright contrast to shadowy hills and blue skies. Bird-watchers come to view wintering bald eagles as well as migratory water-fowl on San Carlos Lake, on Talkalai Lake (named for a turn-of-the-century San Carlos Apache policeman), and on many stock ponds. Mountain-biking devotees can cruise around San Carlos Lake, down the 700 Rd. (maps are available; see below) or up the 900 Rd. Apache Route 8, 50 miles of paved road, leads to the beautifully wooded Point of Pines area. Be sure to bring water because there is none available on this route.

On the reservation about 20 miles east of Globe, the San Carlos Apache Recreation and Wildlife Office issues hunting, fishing, and camping permits for the reservation, and can provide trail maps and recreation advice. It is worth the stop for its display of taxidermy-preserved creatures that inhabit the area. Black bear, desert bighorn sheep, puma, deer, fox, birds, and fish all are on display here. The office is open Mon.–Sat., 8:00 A.M.– 4:30 P.M.; Sun., 8 A.M.–noon. Located **on US 70, 20 miles east of Globe, just past milepost 272. P.O. Box 97, San Carlos, 85550; 888-475-2344, 520-475-2343, 520-475-2344.**

Festivals and Events

For information on any of these events, contact the Globe-Miami Chamber of Commerce, 1360 N. Broad St., P.O. Box 2539, Globe, 85502; 800-804-5623 or 520-425-4495. Website: www.globe-miami-chamber.org.

Historic Home & Building Tour

weekend in late Feb.
Globe's Golden Age is the basis for this celebration highlighting the historic homes and buildings that date to the turn of the century and before. Local antiques dealers get together for a show, and quilters participate in a display and sale of their handiwork at the Cobre Valley Center for the Arts.

Boomtown Spree

mid-Apr.
True mine aficionados come to Miami for this three-day event, which features the Arizona State Mining Championships. The strenuous daylong competition of individual events includes hand mucking, spike driving, individual and team machine drilling, and hand drilling. These skills, essential to the miner's trade, have become much admired, competitive talents. The event, held off and on since 1939, includes a parade, barbecue, and fun run.

Copper Dust Stampede Pro-Rodeo

mid-Apr.
This Fri.–Sat. celebration in Globe has everything a rodeo should have—an Old West dress-up competition, three rodeo performances with all the classic rodeo events, including PRCA-sanctioned bull-riding and calf-roping, and a parade with rodeo queens. Team riders thundering through historic downtown Globe, a little buckaroo rodeo for kids ages three to eight, and a traditional country western dance cap it off. Held at Gila County Fairgrounds.

Annual Apache Jii Day

late Oct.
Jii, the Apache word for "day," is an Indian celebration held in downtown Globe that features talented dancers, singers, and storytellers from around the Southwest. It's definitely worth going, if only to see the beautiful ceremonial costumes. The Hoop, Jingle, and Eagle Dances usually are part of the schedule. The famed Apache Crown Dancers are among the day's highlights. This is an excellent opportunity to see and purchase Native American arts and crafts, worked on all year for this event. Traditional food is available. This one-day event is a good day trip from Phoenix because accommodations in Globe often are booked months in advance.

Outdoor Activities

Boating

San Carlos Lake

The 19,900-acre lake has excellent bluegill, black crappie, flathead catfish, and largemouth bass fishing. **San Carlos Lake Marina,** a fairly new facility, has picnic ramadas, rest rooms, and a large boat ramp. Groceries, beer, wine, fishing licenses, bait, and camping permits are available at the marina store, behind which is a small RV park with hookups. The setting is quite pretty, with red cliffs and vistas looking east across the lake. Located **about 7 miles off US 70 on Reservation Rd. 3.** For information and RV spaces call the store at **520-475-2756.**

You can drive around the lake by taking Reservation Rd. 3 from US 70 at Peridot, about 15 miles east of Globe. The road crosses Coolidge Dam and continues around the lake, rejoining US 70 near Calva. The drive has pretty views of flat-topped mesas and rock formations. In spring elegant, torchlike yuccas dot the desert. There are small campgrounds at points around the lake, including **Soda Canyon Point.**

RIVER RAFTING

Despite the ongoing controversies about water, or lack of it, rafting and floating are popular sports in Arizona. Rafting a river gives you a look at scenery you may see no other way, and if done properly, has low impact on the environment. The state of Arizona requires that rafting guides have first-aid training. Many have Advanced Wilderness First Aid and Wilderness First Responder training as well.

Salt River

Salt River rafting depends on snowmelt from the White Mountains, which most years provides enough runoff to guarantee a brisk-running river in spring, Mar.–May. It's the basis for a good time that ranges from mellow to real high-class abuse. Everything that happens on the Upper Salt River is regulated by the White Mountain Apache Tribe, which owns the land. Private rafting companies pay fees to obtain permits to operate on the Salt. You are not permitted to launch your own raft, and many areas are closed even to hiking. The portion of the Salt River within the Tonto National Forest may be rafted noncommercially by applying for a permit. Request an application packet from **River Permit Coordinator, Tonto National Forest, 2324 E. McDowell, Phoenix, 85006; 602-225-5200.**

The rafted part of this wild river, whose chilly water requires wet suits, is located above the dam systems, so melted snow for white water makes it the earliest spring-running river in the country. The unregulated flow creates some spectacular rapids. You may glimpse an American bald eagle soaring on thermals. Many trips put in at the US 60 bridge, where guests get suited up and receive paddling instructions, then load into rafts. Rapids are rated on a scale of difficulty from Class 1 to 6, as established by the American Whitewater Affiliation, with a Class 1 defined as "easy, with riffles and small waves, few obstructions," and a Class 3 as "intermediate, with moderate, irregular waves which may be difficult to avoid."

Among the rapids on this stretch is a **Class 2** called **Kiss and Tell,** named for the way the water rushes at a solid rock wall. If inept paddlers allow the raft to bump the rock sideways (the kiss), the raft will tip, bouncing passengers into the chilly flow. On sunny weekends when the river is awash with paddlers, dozens of other rafters can watch smugly (the tell), hoping they aren't next into the drink. The challenging swirl of **Maytag Rapids** leaves no doubt about the origins of its name. **Mescale,** which has been as tough as a **Class 4,** catapults even an occasional guide into the rushing water. At this time of year, most rapids are Class 1–2, but if conditions are right, you'll hit an occasional more challenging rapid.

Lunch is set up at a convenient stop, after which rafts continue on to cover a total of about 15 miles of quirky river, arriving at the takeout point at Salt Banks. Returning to the put-in point requires a conveyance vehicle that's able to negotiate a primitive, single-lane gravel road, roughly carved from the sheer canyon wall. The transport of choice usually is a bright orange school bus that drivers understatedly dub "a durable vehicle." Rafters may rate the toughest rapids a Class 3, but we feel the bus ride back is a definite Class 5.

Far Flung Adventures offers one-, three-, and five-day trips in self-bailing rafts with all necessary equipment and comfortable campsites. Camping trips cover a 50- to 60-mile scenic stretch, and one-day trips go from Horseshoe Bend to Salt Banks. **Box 2804, Globe, 85502; 800-359-2627 or 520-425-7272. Website: www.farflung.com.**

Blue Sky Whitewater does one- and two-day trips that include gear, wet suits, booties, paddle, jackets, food, and beverages. Two-day trips include waterproof bags as well. The one-day trip covers 10 miles and 12 rapids. Add another 18 miles downstream for the two-day trip. **143 N. High St., Globe, 85501; 800-425-5253 or 520-425-5252. Website: www.gobluesky.com.**

Sun Country Rafting has one-day tours that cover 10 river miles; two-day tours that cover 20 miles; and 32-mile, 3-day tours. **800-272-3353.**

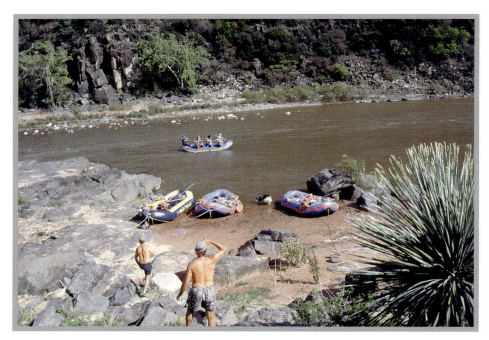

On the Salt River, early spring rafting involves calm stretches as well as white water.

Gila River

You can float an 8-mile stretch of the mellow Gila River in comfortable six-person, self-bailing rafts piloted by expert guides. Inflatable kayaks also are an option. You'll see graceful great blue herons, flycatchers, circling vultures, and possibly deer. On BLM land, the Gila flows from San Carlos Lake at Coolidge Dam. The lake belongs to farmers who use it for downstream irrigation. The summer rafting season, June–Aug., basically coincides with the growing season. Water is shut off around the first week of Sept. because the growing season is over, effectively terminating summer rafting within a week. With never more than a couple of small rapids, there are opportunities to swim in the cool, clean water. The day includes a picnic lunch on sandy shores. Wear your swimsuit but bring a coverup and plenty of sunscreen. Tubing is not recommended because of the large number of submerged logs and clogs of brush. The trip meets at Winkelman City Park in Winkelman, about 90 minutes from Phoenix. Take US 60 east to Superior, then go south from Superior on Hwy. 177. For information and reservations contact **Blue Sky Whitewater, 143 N. High St., Globe, 85501; 800-425-5253 or 520-425-5252. Website: www.gobluesky.com.**

Hiking

The Pinal Mountain Recreation Area is within the Globe Ranger District of the Tonto National Forest, about 25 miles from Phoenix and due south of Globe. Summer hiking is popular at these higher elevations because of cool temperatures, but winter with its snow and cold is only for the most intrepid souls. Picnic sites are scattered throughout the area.

For shorter hikes that you can combine with lunch and sight-seeing, head for Globe's **Round Mountain Park,** where there are four trails and three routes, ranging from a little over 1.5 miles to 3 miles. At the mountain's top, a ramada invites picnicking. Located **on Globe's east side, north of U.S. 60.**

Your best bet is to stop at the **Globe Ranger District Office** of the National Forest

Service in Six Shooter Canyon. You can pick up trail guides and get reliable directions. Once there, you're within less than 1 mile of many of the trailheads. **From US 60, go left on Oak St., continue two blocks to Broad St., and bear right at the Y; follow signs to the office. Route 1, Box 33, Globe, 88501; 520-425-7189.**

Pioneer Pass Toll Road Trail

This flat, gentle trail for hikers and equestrians was built originally as a toll road to the Pioneer Mine. About 3.2 miles one way, there are scenic views of Upper Pinal Creek and thick stands of pine. The **trailhead is at the junction of Icehouse Canyon Rd. and Six Shooter Canyon Rd., near the Globe ranger station. Route 1, Box 33, Globe, 88501; 520-425-7189.**

Sierra Ancha Wilderness

This difficult-to-access wilderness area is rough, rugged, primeval, and one of the most scenic areas of the state. The effort is worth it. Filled with high vertical cliffs protecting prehistoric Indian ruins, the wilderness's elevations vary from 4,000 to 7,400 feet. Trails are open for hiking and horseback riding. Located south of the town of Young, but most often accessed from Claypool, between Miami and Globe. From **Claypool on US 60, take Hwy. 88 north to Hwy. 288 and continue north;** you will be within striking distance of a number of trailheads, beyond which a four-wheel-drive vehicle usually is required. For the most up-to-date and reliable information, before heading into this area contact the **Pleasant Valley Ranger District, P.O. Box 450, Young, 85554; 520-462-4300,** or the main office of **Tonto National Forest, 2324 E. McDowell, Phoenix, 85006; 602-225-5200.** A booklet will be mailed to you on request.

Seeing and Doing

Art Museums and Galleries

Cobre Valley Center for the Arts

In downtown Globe, the 1906 Gila County

Cobre Valley Center for the Arts, in Globe, was built in 1906 as the Gila County Courthouse.

Courthouse has been recycled into the Cobre Valley Center for the Arts. In use for 70 years, it was placed on the National Register of Historic places in 1975 and vacated in 1976. Although its bright, airy rooms are now filled with contemporary art, the old building's many traces of grandeur remain. Banisters along the staircase to the third floor are covered with copper from the Old Dominion Mine. The courtroom has become a theater. Excellent local art in stained glass, ceramics, painting, sculpture, photography, jewelry, prints, and more is on display and for sale. Open Mon.–Sat., 10:00 A.M.–5:00 P.M.; Sun., 12:00 P.M.–5:00 P.M. **101 N. Broad St., Globe, 85502; 520-425-0884.**

Gardens and Arboreta

Boyce Thompson Southwestern Arboretum

The 350-acre haven for desert plants, surrounded by the Tonto National Forest, was endowed by William Boyce Thompson in the 1920s. He wanted to establish a place where plants from the world's arid and semiarid regions could be studied, a goal admirably fulfilled in this living laboratory. Many of the drought-resistant plants developed here have become part of Arizona's general landscaping designs. The remarkably lovely place near Superior, in the shadow of Picketpost Mountain and straddling Queen Creek Canyon, creates a number of life zones in which low-desert, high-desert, and even higher-altitude plants flourish. More than 3,000 water-efficient species from all continents grow here. Sales held in early Apr. and in the fall offer Arizona-appropriate plants to visitors. Each Sept. the Arboretum holds a fun event called Bye Bye Buzzards, at which lovers of the unlovely creatures gather to say *"arrivederci,* vultures" (the correct avian term for buzzards) and send the birds on their migratory way.

Pick up a guide at the visitor center and set out on the **Main Loop Trail** for a 1.5-mile, two-hour walk. You'll pass plants typical of the Arizona desert as well as cactuses that represent different geographic areas of the United States. Farther along grows an oddity called a boojum tree, named for the mythical creature in Lewis Carroll's poem "The Hunting of the Snark." **Ayer Lake,** from which the arboretum draws its water, shelters two endangered fish species—the Gila topminnow and the desert pupfish. Don't miss the fragrant **herb garden** or the **demonstration garden** that explains how to use water-efficient plants in residential landscaping. On other self-guided trails, tour an area with landscape trees suitable for south-central Arizona and an extensive **cactus garden.** Interpretive ramadas along the way afford opportunities for "seeing and smelling."

Because any stream or water hole in the desert draws animals, more than 300 species live at the arboretum. Snakes, tortoises, and toads are dawn and dusk creatures, while lizards enjoy midday sun. The presence of night-roaming javelina, deer, coyote, raccoons, and ringtails is verified by their droppings, often found near trails. Pack rats have become so abundant that the resident tortoiseshell cat, Miss Kitty, has "ratting" as her primary job description.

The arboretum is a favorite rendezvous for birders because of its 200-plus resident, wintering, and migratory avian species. Expect to see pine siskins, a number of goldfinches, evening grosbeaks, flickers, phoebes, shrikes, and vireos. Stop at the platform at Ayer Lake to see mallards, redheads, ring-necked ducks, buffleheads, mergansers, and other waterbirds. Bald eagles and northern harriers pass through, and several hawk species are seen less frequently.

The gift shop carries an excellent selection of nature books as well as the expected T-shirts and trinkets. Rest rooms are at the visitor center and the **Smith Interpretive Center.** The shady picnic area, beside Silver King Wash, has water, tables, and barbecue pits. Pets are welcome but must be kept leashed. Open daily, 8:00 A.M.–5:00 P.M., except Christmas Day. Located 3 miles west of Superior and 60 miles east of Phoenix on US 60. **37615 E. US 60, Superior, 85273; 520-689-2632. Website: www.arboretum.ag.arizona.edu.**

Museums and Historic Sites

Besh-Ba-Gowah Archaeological Park

There's no hands-off attitude at this 700-year-old pre-Columbian pueblo, whose name comes from the Apache language and means "place of metal" or "metal camp." It has been restored so that visitors can walk into rooms, climb ladders, and see the pottery, utensils, and furnishings that belonged to the ancient Salado culture. It's easy to spend an hour exploring the ceremonial chamber and household rooms where all that's missing are cooking smells and snoozing dogs. The visitor center has the world's largest single collection of Salado pottery, which includes basic utilitarian vessels as well as intricately decorated pots and jars. A small **ethnobotanical garden** demonstrates the relationships between people and their environment, and illustrates how native plants were used by the Salado. At the bottom of the hill as you approach the park are several sheltered picnic tables. Most portions of the pueblo are wheelchair-accessible. Open daily, 9:00 A.M.–5:00 P.M., except Thanksgiving, Christmas Day, and New Year's Day. **Take Broad St. to Jesse Hayes St. and follow signs to park's turnoff. 150 N. Pine St., Globe, 85501 (mailing address only); 520-425-0320.**

Gila County Historical Society Museum

This 1914 building used to be the Old Dominion Mine Rescue Station and now houses relics and artifacts from mining days. Mining equipment sits outside, while inside rooms have been re-created to include a mine superintendent's office, a lady's boudoir, and other scenarios typical of the era. Open Mon.–Fri., 10:00 A.M.–4:00 P.M. Located next to Chamber of Commerce office on US 60. **1330 N. Broad St., Globe, 85502; 520-425-7385.**

San Carlos Apache Cultural Center

This small museum and crafts center on the San Carlos Apache Reservation merits a look-see for the way it details the tribe's history in well-designed tableaus and old photographs. One display shows the Changing Woman ceremony that celebrates the transformation of a girl into adulthood. Old photos show the reservation land being ravaged by an 1874 order of President U. S. Grant to allow copper mining and grazing. In an 1886 photo, the Army recruits Apaches as scouts. Paintings by Native American artists depict tribal scenes, spirits, and Apache daily life. The center also is an excellent place to purchase Apache burden baskets, conical receptacles woven of willow and other fibers, often accented with buckskin fringe and metal cones. You're likely to hear Apache spoken here, even though English is the first language on the reservation. Manager Herb Stevens will happily show you (and sell you) jewelry made by local artists from peridot, a light green semiprecious stone that is mined on a nearby mesa, one of only three places in the world where the gem is found. Darker stones are of higher quality. Tribal members free, small charge for others. Open Mon.–Fri.; hours vary, so call first. Located **in the village of Peridot on US 70 approximately 20 miles east of Globe. As you go east it's just at the top of a little rise at milepost 272.** You have to watch carefully or you'll miss it. If you come to the Recreation and Wildlife Office, turn around, you've gone too far. **P.O. Box 760, San Carlos, 85550; 520-475-2894 phone and fax.**

San Carlos Lake

Created by Coolidge Dam in 1930, this lake became a watery cemetery as it covered an Apache graveyard dating to the 1800s. The U.S. government offered to move the graves before the lake was filled, but Apache leaders felt that disturbing their sleeping brothers would be a desecration, so they accepted the offer to cover the graves with a cement slab. Also at the bottom of the lake are the remains of Camp San Carlos, the original Indian agency station abandoned in 1900. Located **near US 70 at Peridot, about 15 miles east of Globe.**

Scenic Drives

Highway Mine Tour

This drive may be somewhat questionable as scenic, but if you're interested in the mines that made Miami and Globe famous, and if you see beauty in piles of slag, tailings, and oddly shaped equipment, this is for you. The chamber of commerce (see Services) has a brochure with map that directs you to six mines, or their former sites, along US 60. The drive begins 6 miles west of Miami between mileposts 238 and 239, at the **Pinto Valley Mine,** and proceeds east toward Miami-Globe. Other stops are at milepost 242 at the **Blue Bird Mine,** at **Miami Town Park,** at the **Cyprus Miami Mining Corp.** across from the Copper Hills Inn (look for the FLOSBEs—see sidebar), at the **Sleeping Beauty Mine** that now produces turquoise, and at what is left of the **Old Dominion Mine.**

Salt River Canyon

This wild and beautiful gorge, a rafter's favorite, exists because the melting snow in the White Mountains flows into the Black and White Rivers, which in turn converge west of the town of Fort Apache to create the Salt River. Over millions of years it has carved out Salt River Canyon, sort of a Grand Canyon that you can drive into. The Pima Indians named the river for the water's brackish taste that comes from several large salt springs near the western edge of the White Mountain Apache Reservation. The river is a natural border between the San Carlos Apache Reservation on the south and the White Mountain Apache Reservation on the north. As you leave Globe heading northeast on US 60/Hwy. 77, you'll notice that there are no more saguaros at this 5,000-foot altitude. They've been replaced by scrub oak, piñon pine, and manzanita spread over gently rolling hillsides, as well as a stand of cottonwoods along Seven Mile Wash. About 40 miles north of Globe at Seneca, which is not much more than a boarded-up store, you begin a 6 percent grade down to the bottom of the canyon and the bridge, built in 1934, that crosses the Salt River. The scenery is spectacular, but stay alert. The 2,000-foot descent is 9 miles of wide, well-paved switchbacks that create white knuckles in some but that others find exhilarating.

About a third of the way into the canyon you can pull out at an overlook called Hieroglyphic Point, where there are excellent views and petroglyphs carved into black boulders lining the slope below the road. If you're an intrepid hiker, you can scramble up the rocky trail that leads to an even higher vantage point. Back on the highway heading north, just before crossing the bridge there is a small slump-block building with ornamental grating that looks like an office, but it's actually a rest room with composting toilets. Outside, interpretive signs explain how the bridge was built and tell you that the canyon is inhabited by black bear, javelina, raccoons, mule deer, and other mammals. Bald and golden eagles and osprey are frequently seen. Smallmouth bass, bluegill, channel catfish, and squawfish live in the river. If you need to gather your nerve before proceeding up the other side of the canyon, break out a picnic and enjoy the views, stroll across the footbridge for a great photo opportunity, and follow paved paths to the river's edge. A gas station and small market are just north of the bridge.

Those who have a high-clearance four-wheel-drive vehicle and are in the mood to explore can take the turnoff just north of the bridge and follow the dirt road that parallels the river as it heads west. The left fork doubles back under the bridge and heads toward Apache Falls. The right fork takes you past a few primitive campsites along the river to Cibecue Creek, the end of the road for passenger vehicles. On the way out of the canyon,

Shopping for antiques and collectibles is a big pastime in the small mining town of Globe.

Beckers Butte Overlook is a worthwhile vantage point for a stop and a few photos looking back at the colorful bridge. The overlook faces its namesake on the canyon's far side.

Because this is Indian-owned land, you must have a permit to get off Hwy. 77 at any point. Permits are available at the Salt River Canyon store at the bridge. 520-367-8547.

Shopping

Bacon's Boots and Saddles

This fascinating store might seem to belong more appropriately in a Museums or History section. In the Keegan Building, built from adobe in 1895 and partially rebuilt with brick, a father-son pair turn out exquisite handmade saddles. Edwin Bacon, 70, has been making saddles for more than 50 years. His son Earl, 48, works with him. The saddles begin at about $1,700 and can go as high as $4,000, but they last forever, says Ed. On the day we visited, Ed was repairing a saddle he made in 1979. The cowboy-owner had given it so much use that his rope had burned the leather off the horn, and Ed was replacing it. Besides the workmanship that involves hand sewing with flaxen linen threads, the aesthetics of each saddle make it a work of art. Elaborately drawn-in floral designs are hand-tooled to create intricate tapestries in leather. The father and son make about 20 saddles a year, putting more than 80 hours of work into a plain saddle, and upward of 100 into the fancy models. There is a wait of almost a year from the time orders are placed, which pour in from all over the world.

If you don't have time to wait for a saddle, drop by this friendly place anyway and pick out a new set of western duds. The store stocks great boots, hats, jeans, shirts, pants, and all the accouterments to make you look like you belong in a saddle whether you do or not. Open Mon.–Sat., 8:30 A.M.–5:30 P.M. **290 N. Broad St., Globe, 85501; 520-425-2681.**

Wagering

Apache Gold Casino & Resort

One of the many low-key casinos that flourish on Arizona's Indian reservations, this one is filled with a sea of quarter slots. It also has bingo, video and progressive poker, as well as live poker, keno, and a well-priced buffet. The impressive sculpture that greets visitors, the Apache Games Warrior, holding a hoop and stick, represents traditional games of chance played by the Apaches. The casino is appropriately named for a legend that says the Apache Indians buried a cache of gold deep in a mountainside, which was eventually unearthed by the Mexican Peralta clan. They disappeared, and with them the gold, which occasionally surfaces in myths and legends. On the site are a Best Western—ask about well-priced Stay and Play packages (see Where to Stay), a convenience store, and a 60-space RV park with full hookups. An 18-hole golf course is now open; call for tee times. Located **on US 70, 5 miles east of Globe, just inside boundary of San Carlos Apache Reservation. 520-425-7800 or 800-APACHE3.**

Where to Stay

Hotels, Motels, and Inns

Chain hostelries in the Globe-Miami area include Comfort Inn, Days Inn, Holiday Inn Express, and Motel 8.

Best Western Apache Gold Hotel—$$$

This is a good bet if you plan to spend time at the casino. A covered walkway joins the motel with gaming areas as well as the Wickiup Buffet and Apache Grill that serve reliably good, well-priced meals. Rooms are spacious, comfortable, and quiet. Located **on US 70, 5 miles east of Globe. P.O. Box 1210, San Carlos, 85550; 800-APACHE-8 or 520-492-5600.**

TraveLodge Copper Hills Inn—$$$

We list this comfortable, reliable chain motel here because it is conveniently located and it has refrigerators and coffeemakers in the rooms. Even though it is on a fairly busy highway, rooms are well insulated and noise doesn't seem to be a problem. The restaurant is open for three meals a day. Located **at US 60 and US 70. Route 1, Box 506, Miami, 85539; 800-825-7151 or 520-425-7151.**

Noftsger Hill Inn—$$–$$$

If you had a crush on perky Miss Blanders in third grade, here's your chance to relive school days on your terms. This stately inn, built in 1907 as the North Globe Schoolhouse and later renamed the Noftsger Hill School, sits atop a hill overlooking Globe. Front rooms offer a view of the rugged Pinal Mountains, while those in the rear face the Old Dominion Mine. Arizona luminaries including former governor Rose Mofford were educated here. So much of the school's personality remains that it even has the warm, furniture-polish smell of a schoolhouse. As you stand in the main hallway, it's not difficult to imagine the sound of running feet on the hardwood floors and the cheerful chatter of kids released from their studies. Classrooms, now guest rooms, have high ceilings and original blackboards on which visitors have recorded their comments. Onetime coat closets contain bathrooms with claw-foot tubs and pedestal sinks. Owners Frank and Pam Hulme have furnished the inn with mining-era antiques and art, complemented by mission-style furniture. Rooms with private baths have king or queen beds. A full breakfast is included. 425 North St., Globe, 85501; 520-425-2260.

El Rey Motel—$-$$

You'd almost expect to see a little 1930s Chevrolet coupe parked outside this vintage motor court. It looks much like it did in the 1930s and 1940s. However, the Southwestern ranch style, so popular at a time when motoring was the means of choice to explore the country, has been updated with modern comforts. 1201 E. Ash St., Globe, 85501; 520-425-4427, fax 520-402-9147.

Camping

There are a number of campgrounds in the Pinal Mountain Recreation Area. At **Pioneer Pass** along the banks of Upper Pinal Creek, at 6,100 feet, there are about two dozen tent sites, rest rooms, and fire grills. Water is available May–Oct. At **Pinal Recreation Site,** among tall stands of ponderosa pine and white fir, there are 22 tent sites, picnic tables, rest rooms, fire grills, and water in summer. With just six tent sites, **Upper Pinal Recreation Site** on the north side of Pinal Peak remains quiet and lovely. It has picnic tables, rest rooms, fire grills, two wind shelters, and water in summer. For more information on these sites contact the **Globe Ranger Station** (see Hiking for how to get there), 520-425-7189.

Where to Eat

For its size, Globe has an unusually large number of excellent Mexican restaurants, almost all of them family-run. A number of small, individually owned eateries, without a trace of chain-food mentality, also offer food truthfully labeled "genuine home cooking." Along US 60 on the city outskirts, there's no shortage of pizza and burger chains.

TraveLodge Copper Hills Inn, Dining Room and Coffee Shop—$$-$$$

In the coffee shop, where coffee is free if you're a motel guest, chatty waitresses fill you in on local happenings and tell tales of foreign tourists who expect tomahawk-wielding Indians and tobacco-chewing cowboys to pop out from behind every saguaro. Food is basic and good and comes in large portions. The cocktail lounge, adjacent to a larger dining room, is friendly and casual, as are most eateries in Globe. Yes, that is an original DeGrazia mural on the wall behind the bar. There is live entertainment Tue. and Thu. evenings. Open daily, 5:00 A.M.–9:00 P.M. Located on US 60/70 between Miami and Globe; 520-425-7151.

Guayo's—$$

Run by the third generation of the Esparza family, with a fourth on the way up, at Guayo's the food is flawless Mexican at its best. The place opened in January 1970. Owner Eddie Esparza jokes that in those early days, customers were asked if they'd like their food "with or without [mine] tailings," so fierce were the winds that blew dust from the nearby mines against the little prefab building. Over the years Guayo's was enlarged and improved to today's casually comfortable dining room. Eddie's grandfather, also an Eddie, was nicknamed Guayo, and the name stuck to the restaurant he founded. The family says their grandparents figured that if they owned a restaurant, they'd never starve. It's one of 11 Esparza-owned restaurants in the state. Specialties like green-chile enchiladas and superb beef tamales are served on cheerful Fiestaware, topped with an unusual, slightly sweet salsa or a variation with a bit more authority, but still not killer. The restaurant uses fresh, not powdered, chiles, and the appetizer bowl of mixed corn and flour tortilla chips is decidedly not prepackaged. Open daily, 10:30 A.M.–9:00 P.M. Located on Hwy. 88 about 1 mile north of junction with US 60, at the east end of the Apache Trail, between Miami and Globe. 520-425-9969.

Guayo's El Rey—$$

This Guayo's El Rey is run by Greg Esparza, brother of Eddie Esparza (who owns the other Guayo's, above). The smoke-free atmosphere alone attracts many diners to this low-key place in the town of Miami. Everything is fresh daily and made from scratch. You won't find enchilada sauce from a can here! Specialties are beef and chicken tacos and outstanding chiles rellenos. The real draw is the homemade salsa, a family tradition since 1938, when Greg's grandparents had the place. Can you get the recipe? "Sorry, my grandpa would hate me if I gave it out," says Greg. On Sun., when they're open for breakfast, they'll sell as many as 60 gallons of menudo, the classic hangover remedy. Also on the Sunday menu are chorizo and eggs, huevos rancheros, and the traditional American ham or steak and eggs. The decor is authentic Mexican, with wrought iron, cheerful colors, and comfortable booths and tables, Open Thurs.–Tues. 10:30 A.M.–9:00 P.M. Located one block from US 60 in downtown Miami. 716 Sullivan St., Miami; 520-473-9960.

La Luz del Dia Bakery—$

Rib-sticking breakfasts are served all day at this little Mexican cafe, where a steaming pot of menudo is always ready and huevos rancheros come with warm, fresh tortillas just right to wrap around the accompanying pinto beans. Sit at the yellow formica counter, the three booths, or genuine 1950s-style tube-leg table and chairs and try to decide between the short stack of pancakes, or chorizo and eggs (hot Mexican sausage with eggs any style). Look up to see the painted tin ceiling where a second floor once existed. The aroma of fresh empanadas, Mexican baked bread, and cookies wafts through the cafe from the bakery in the back, where bread and hamburger buns are baked daily. The specialty of the house is a fried tortilla with green chile and beans, lettuce, tomato, and cheese. Everything here is good and gets even better when you realize it's almost impossible to order anything over $4. Owners Ernie and Carmen Vasquez are almost always there. Open Mon–Fri., 7:00 A.M.–4:30 P.M.; Sat., 7:00 A.M.–3:00 P.M. 304 N. Broad St., Globe; 520-425-8400.

FLOSBEs

Miami takes an interesting, creative approach to reclaiming the hills of dusty mine tailings that have existed for decades. Four-Legged Organic-Soil-Building Engineers—FLOSBEs (pronounced FLOSS-bies)—known as cattle to most people, rise to the task. Though cattle are usually thought of as eaters and destroyers of grass, an expert in range management, Terry Wheeler, has devised a way to employ the beasts to restore the grasslands. He began thinking of the chemically depleted, pulverized rock mine tailing as soil, rendered sterile and potentially unproductive by mining operations. He noticed that deer and cattle left manure on the fringes of some of the tailing deposits, and in these places, things were growing. So he tried spreading hay over the dead hills, then penning cattle in selected areas. The small herd slowly stomped the hay into the tailings and ate their way across the hills, doing what cattle do best, making manure. This accomplished the first step in making the mounds fertile and productive. Now cattle droppings fertilize the vegetation, which in turn flourishes so the FLOSBEs have more food.

Services

Globe–Miami Chamber of Commerce

1360 N. Broad St., P.O. Box 2539, Globe, 85502; 800-804-5623 or 520-425-4495. Website: www.communitylink.com/globe miami.

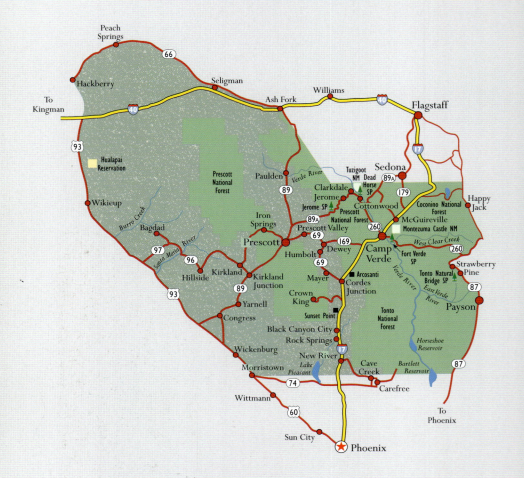

Peach Springs
66
Hackberry
Seligman
Williams
Flagstaff
Ash Fork
40
40
To Kingman
93
17
Hualapai Reservation
Prescott National Forest
Verde River
Tuzigoot NM
Dead Horse SP
Sedona
89A
Paulden
89
Clarkdale
Jerome
179
Wikieup
Iron Springs
Jerome SP
Cottonwood
Coconino National Forest
Happy Jack
Burro Creek
Bagdad
89A
Prescott National Forest
McGuireville
Montezuma Castle NM
260
West Clear Creek
260
97
Prescott
169
Camp Verde
Fort Verde SP
Strawberry
Santa Maria River
96
Humbolt
69
Dewey
Tonto Natural Bridge SP
Pine
Hillside
Kirkland
69
Verde River
87
Kirkland Junction
Mayer
Arcosanti
East Verde River
Payson
89
Yarnell
Cordes Junction
Congress
Crown King
Sunset Point
Tonto National Forest
Wickenburg
Black Canyon City
Rock Springs
Horseshoe Reservoir
Morristown
New River
17
Cave Creek
Bartlett Reservoir
87
74
Lake Pleasant
Carefree
Wittmann
60
To Phoenix
Sun City
Phoenix

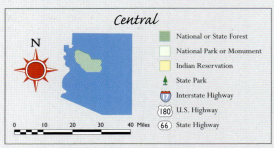

Central

N

National or State Forest
National Park or Monument
Indian Reservation
State Park
17 Interstate Highway
180 U.S. Highway
66 State Highway

0   10   20   30   40 Miles

Central Region

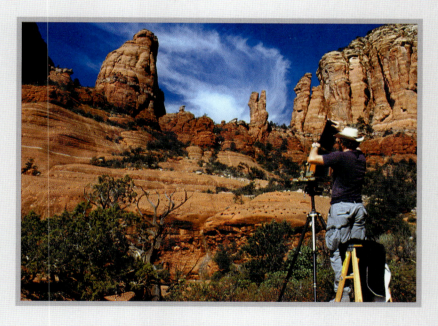

*Photographer captures the beauty of the red rock formations
in Sedona.*

Central Region

Arizona's solar plexus has a low-key character. Main cities—Prescott, Sedona, Camp Verde— are blissfully free of big-city mentality, preferring to work at maintaining a small-town aura that appeals to residents who promote it as well as to visitors who come for respite from multi-story living and frenetic paces. From a river valley that supported ancient farmers to elevations that draw the occasional snowfall, Central Arizona has its own distinct appeal.

Payson, Pine, and Strawberry

Completely encircled by the 2.9-million-acre Tonto National Forest, these woodland mountain towns are among Arizona's oldest communities. At an elevation of 5,000 feet and located in the state's geographic center, Payson is "The Heart of Arizona" to the locals. Never a rich town, its pine-covered slopes have come into their own in terms of real estate value in recent years. The craggy, tree-studded hills, favored sites for upscale vacation homes, attract residents of the steamy-in-summer Valley of the Sun in droves.

The area takes its animals seriously. Coming down off the Mogollon Rim from the Heber area, countless roadside signs caution drivers to watch for elk. One of the cleverest, a four-parter, says "You Speed … You Choose … Hit an Elk … You Both Lose." All that's missing are the words "Burma Shave" at the end.

The two little towns of Pine and Strawberry have a great deal of appeal because they're out of the mainstream, and because they've retained a genuine small-town feel. Strawberry, about 20 miles north of Payson (3 miles north of Pine) at a cool 6,000-foot elevation, lies in the shadow of the Mogollon Rim. Strawberry has become something of a retirement destination as well as a favorite place for summer visitors. An annual June celebration remembers the wild strawberries for which the town is named.

History

Payson got its name from an Illinois senator who never even saw the place. It was christened in Senator Payson's honor because, in 1884, he was instrumental in getting a post office for the town, then called Union City. Early residents, mostly miners, were lured by tales of mineral wealth in the surrounding mountains. When the stories didn't pan out, they stayed anyway, enticed by the mild four-season climate and the fact that all of them were basically in the same boat. Zane Grey was drawn to Arizona in general and the Mogollon Rim area near Payson in particular by the wild and untamed mountains. He penned many novels in a small two-bedroom cabin at 6,500 feet just beneath the Rim. A 1990 forest fire destroyed the cabin, but plans to reconstruct a replica are in the works.

Pine's first white settlers arrived around 1866, to run cattle and raise corn to feed the hogs that supplied food for the army stationed at Camp Verde. Pine was established in 1879 by Mormon pioneers. By the late 1880s Pine was a thriving religious and social center for the Tonto Basin.

Strawberry, which lies along a small creek of the same name that flows southwest into Fossil Creek, is said to have been named by settler Isaac Lowthian in 1868. The rich riparian area was perfect for the large quantities of wild strawberries that the settlers found.

Payson Municipal Airport offers charter service and is open to private aircraft. There is a fly-in campground adjacent to the runway. **Payson Express** provides shuttle service to and from Payson and the Greater Phoenix area, with door-to-door service, or daily service from Phoenix Sky Harbor International Airport Mon.–Sat. **P.O. Box 2601, Payson, 85547; 520-474-5254 in Payson or 602-256-6464 in Phoenix, fax 520-474-1368.**

Major Attractions

Tonto Natural Bridge State Park

This unusual state park is home to a wonder that has taken thousands of years to create. Hidden in a pine-studded valley, the world's largest natural travertine bridge spans a 400-foot tunnel 183 feet above little Pine Creek. It was so well concealed, it took a prospector being chased by Apaches in 1877 to stumble on it. Over the centuries, water seeping from the creek undermined a portion of travertine to create a tube that eventually became a natural bridge.

First view the bridge from above, then clomp down **Gowan Loop Trail,** a narrow 0.5-mile path to a series of boardwalks, where you can stand in a shadowy fern-draped grotto practically underneath the bridge. The springs that created the bridge are still at work today. If you opt for the short way back to the top, you'll hand-over-hand your way up cables on either side of an extremely steep trail; be sure you're in good shape, or return the way you came. The **Pine Creek Trail** extends for 0.5 mile to the Pine Creek natural area. A quaint **old lodge,** once used by Zane Grey and Al Capone, is settled comfortably in an orchard of apple, pear, plum, and apricot trees in a pretty meadow above the bridge. Built in 1927 by Beryl Goodfellow and Andy Ogilvie, it accommodated travelers who came to see the unusual attraction. Purchased by the state of Arizona in 1991, the three-story

The enormous Tonto Natural Bridge spans a small creek that has cut through the travertine.

lodge furnished with antiques and original fixtures, is open for tours. A Victrola scratches out tunes in the foyer, and the Goodfellow Room has its original porcelain tub and wicker bed. Tours are Fri.–Sat. if a volunteer is available. A small herd of javelina has migrated into the area, there is a resident deer population, and birdwatching is excellent. No pets. Small fee per vehicle. Open Apr.–Oct., daily, 8:00 A.M.–6:00 P.M.; Nov.–Mar., daily, 9:00 A.M.–5:00 P.M. except Christmas Day. Park office is **0.5 mile off Hwy. 87, 13 miles northwest of Payson. 520-476-4202. Website: www.pr.state.az.us.**

Festivals and Events

World's Oldest Continuous Rodeo

mid-Aug.

Celebrated for more than 100 years, this PRCA-sanctioned event in Payson draws entrants and

Getting There

Payson is about 75 miles northeast of Phoenix via Hwy. 87, known as the Beeline Highway. The highway has four lanes most of the way, with additional lanes under construction, scheduled for completion sometime in 2001. Hwy. 260 links the three towns to the East-Central region to the east and to the Verde Valley and I-17 to the west.

spectators from all over the country. It's a fun, colorful competition, held among the tall pines in a place that's cool when temperatures in the most heavily populated portions of the state are in triple digits. Events include barrel racing, bull riding, team roping, bareback riding, calf roping, saddle bronc riding, and steer wrestling, with participation by both cowboys and cowgirls. The four-day event also includes an elaborate parade, dances, and queen and junior queen coronation. On Sun. morning there's even a cowboy church service at the arena. Held **at Payson Rodeo Grounds, on Hwy. 87 approximately 0.5 mile south of town. 520-474-4515.**

State Championship Fiddlers Contest

late Sept.

During this thoroughly enjoyable weekend, Arizona fiddlers and musicians gather in Payson to compete for state championship titles. They play a very specific type of music that has its roots in mountain and rural areas and is preserved by a dedicated group. Fiddlers range from youngsters just learning to old-timers who have mastered the art of "fiddlin'," which has little to do with playing the violin. There also are storytellers, a fiddle-making demonstration, folk dancers, and arts and crafts booths. The event usually begins with a "21-fiddle salute." Held

at rodeo grounds on Hwy. 87 approximately 0.5 mile south of Payson. 520-474-4515.

Outdoor Activities

Hiking

Fossil Springs Wilderness

This 12,000-acre protected area has a wonderful hike from near the town of Strawberry to Fossil Springs. This reliable water source produces a pleasant 72°F gush that creates a little environmental oasis populated with lush trees and plants, and more than 100 bird species. In canyon walls near the spring, there are small fossilized shells, remnants of a vast sea that covered this area 350 million years ago. You can swim in the pools that have formed along the creek, but the water is not reliably safe for drinking. The wood flume directs water to the turbines of the Irving and Childs Power Plants that depend on it for power generation. The **Upper Trail** is a dusty, 2.5-mile trek that descends about 1,300 feet from the trailhead to the springs. The **Flume Trail** also leads to the springs, covering about 4 miles. It is longer but easier, because the grade is gentler. To do both trails, leave one car at the Upper Trail trailhead and another at the beginning of the Flume Trail, where you'll end your hike. Motorized and mechanical equipment, including mountain bikes, are not allowed on the trail. **From Hwy. 87 in Strawberry, turn west on Fossil Creek Rd. (Forest Service Rd. 708—Strawberry Lodge is on this corner) and go past the schoolhouse 4 miles on the dirt road. Turn right to the marked trailhead parking lot. The Flume Trail is accessed about 5 miles farther along Fossil Creek Rd.** For information contact the Pine-Strawberry Chamber of Commerce, 520-476-3547.

Woods Canyon Lake

Between Heber and Payson, this pretty little 52-acre lake is stocked with trout and largemouth bass. This is probably one of the most scenic stretches in the state. Every few hundred yards there is a vista point with a parking lot from which you can get unparalleled views of the Mogollon Rim. From this area, you may pick up several trailheads, including the **Willow Creek Trail** and **Crook Trail.** Memorial Day–Labor Day, you can join in Fri. nature walks, Sat. hikes to a nearby sinkhole, and assorted organized Sun. hikes. In addition to Aspen and Spillway Campgrounds, there is a well-stocked store at the lake. A day-use picnic area has tables and fire pits. **Take Hwy. 260 approximately 26 miles east to the Forest Rd. 300 exit,** marked with a green sign that says Woods Canyon Lake, and **follow it about 5 miles.** Make camping reservations by calling **800-280-CAMP.**

Seeing and Doing

Museums and Historic Sites

Rim Country Museum
Formerly called the Museum of the Forest, these three green wood-frame buildings on the shore of a small lake in Green Valley Park house artifacts and photos that show the history and lifestyle of Payson pioneers, including the cavalry that came to secure the area under General Crook. Displays trace local Arizona culture and ecology. The statue in front of the museum, a firefighter in full gear, honors the forest firefighters who died protecting lives and trees. A tour starts in the original 1930s forest ranger's residence, now the museum store. You can pick up good reference material here on Payson's history. The center building is a re-creation of the Herron, Payson's finest hotel at the turn of the century, which burned to the ground in 1918. Behind the hotel, the tower with the little house on top is the original Forest Ranger's Station. In the last building you can see how the first forest ranger, Fletcher Beard, conducted business from his office from 1908 to 1913. The museum's hours are short because it's staffed by volunteers, but it's well worth planning around them. Open Wed.–Sun., noon–4:00 P.M. From Hwy. 87 in Payson, take Main St. west

about 1 mile to Green Valley Parkway (just before the lake) and turn right. **700 Green Valley Parkway, Payson, 85544; 520-474-3483.**

Shoofly Village
You really have to use your imagination to picture what this onetime village must have been like when occupied. All that's left are the outlines of more than 80 rooms and courtyards, with remnants of a perimeter wall that encloses about 4 acres. A ring of trees identifies the location of the wall. At an elevation of 5,240 feet, on top of Houston Mesa just under the Mogollon Rim, the area is covered with low scrub and junipers and was active between A.D. 1000 and 1250. The people who lived here had close ties to the Hohokam and Salado prehistoric cultures. A small reconstruction shows how dwelling walls were built of wood, adobe, and stone. A 0.25-mile interpretive trail, some of it paved and wheelchair-accessible, has excellent signs that help visualize how the site once looked. There are rest rooms and picnic ramadas. **Take Hwy. 87 north from Payson 5 miles to Houston Mesa Rd. and turn east. At the fork in the road,** with the sign for Mesa del Caballo subdivision, **take the right fork.** The parking lot is just beyond the fork. 520-474-4515.

Strawberry Schoolhouse
Its claim to fame is Arizona's oldest school. Built in 1885, this one-room log building's interior has been restored to its pre-1900 status. It has wainscoting as well as wallpaper, and was considered quite elegant in its day, especially for a student population that totaled just 22 during the 1889–90 school year. Open summer, Sat.–Sun., whenever volunteer staff are available, and by appointment. From **Hwy. 87 in Strawberry, take Fossil Creek Rd. about 2 miles to the schoolhouse.** Call the Pine–Strawberry Historical Society, **520-476-4324.**

Tours

WALKING TOURS
A number of early rock and log cabins remain

The Rim Country Museum in Payson commemorates firefighters killed in the line of duty.

in present-day Pine as reminders of its Mormon pioneers. Most places have been updated to become cafes and gift shops, but enough structure remains to capture the original character. Stop in at the chamber of commerce (see Services) to pick up a self-guided walking tour map. There is a very small charge.

Wagering

Mazatzal Casino

Run by the Tonto Apache Tribe and named for the Mazatzal (pronounced MA-ta-zal) Wilderness, this casino is typical of Indian gaming sites in the state. It offers a "Hot Time in the Cool Pines," with 318 player-friendly slot machines, $25,000 keno, high-stakes bingo, and a card room. The Cedar Ridge Restaurant serves above-average casino food, and you can take a break in the Apache Spirits Sports Bar. Open 24 hours daily. Located on Payson's south edge **on the Beeline Hwy. (Hwy. 87) at milepost 251,** the first light as you enter from the south. Turn right into the casino. **800-777-PLAY.**

Where to Stay

Many visitors head east on Hwy. 260 toward Heber and Overgaard (see East-Central region) to stay in the cool mountain areas around Christopher Creek and Kohl's Ranch.

Hotels, Motels, and Inns

Inn of Payson—$$$

This newish motel is pleasant and quiet, with patio rooms facing the pool or a grassy garden area. Large, comfortable rooms have coffeemakers and mini-refrigerators. A full-service restaurant, Michael's at the Inn, serves continental breakfast, lunch, and dinner. **801 N. Beeline Hwy., Payson, 85541; 800-247-9477 or 520-474-3241.**

Majestic Mountain Inn—$$$

This classy inn has deluxe rooms with fireplaces and in-room, two-person spas. All rooms have coffeemakers, wet bars, and refrigerators, and most look out over an uninterrupted expanse of pine forest. It can be a quiet, romantic getaway as well as a comfortable home base for exploring the area. 602 E. Hwy. 260, Payson, 85541; 800-408-2442 or 520-474-0185.

Pueblo Inn—$$$

You can't miss this adobe-style building on the south side of Hwy. 260 as you come into Payson from the east. It looks just like its name. Rooms are well furnished and exceptionally comfortable. For a real treat, book yourself into one of the luxury rooms that has a two-person spa, coffeemaker, refrigerator, fireplace, and wet bar. Winter prices are slightly lower than in summer. 809 E. Hwy. 260, Payson, 85541; 800-888-9828. Website: www.puebloinn.com.

Resorts and Lodges

Happy Jack Lodge & RV Park—$$$

This remote, quiet resort on top of the Mogollon Rim is a haven for the goshawk and spotted owl in an area of fragrant ponderosa that has survived the logging industry. The onetime logging camp has been renovated to accommodate today's guests and has a lodge, RV park with 74 full hookups (may be open summer months, only so check first), and kitchenette cabins. There are five major fishing lakes and streams within a 25-mile radius, and a network of old logging roads to explore on foot or with a mountain bike. Located **39 miles north of Payson.** Stay on Hwy. 87 north from Payson to Forest Rd. 3 (if you're coming south from Flagstaff, it's also called Lake Mary Rd.), and continue north 2 miles to the lodge. **P.O. Box 19569, Happy Jack, 86024; 520-477-2805, fax 520-477-2806.**

Strawberry Lodge—$$–$$$

This is one of those delightful little gems that you can't help but love. The Turner family bought it more than 35 years ago when it was a hunting lodge, and now Jean Turner, born in 1918, runs it with cheerful hospitality. Small, rustic rooms, some with fireplaces, have no

Shoofly Village in Payson, once a bustling city, now has only a quarter-mile walking trail.

phones or TVs. The dining room is famous for its well-priced family specials that include fried chicken, meat loaf, prime rib, ribs, and more. Don't miss their fabulous fruit pies and outstanding buttermilk pie. Jean says that a group of locals, once named the Spit 'n' Whittle Club, meet about 6:30 A.M. to discuss the problems of the world. "Then they come back around 3:00 P.M. to see if anything has changed," she laughs. Summers are busy, with winter snow days also popular, so call for reservations. Located **on Hwy. 87 in downtown Strawberry. HCR 1, Box 331, Strawberry, 85544; 520-476-3333.**

Camping

Campgrounds in the area are located north and east of Payson, mostly along the Rim. Call the Rim Country Regional Chamber of Commerce (see Services) for an up-to-date list before you set out. See the Heber and Overgaard chapter in the East-Central region for camping options there.

Where to Eat

Many fast-food chains are strung along the major highways that intersect in Payson. People staying in Payson often make a late-afternoon drive out to Kohl's Ranch to have dinner in the Zane Grey Dining Room, 17 miles northeast on Hwy. 260 (see Heber and Overgaard chapter in East-Central region).

The Oaks—$$$

One of the area's fine-dining restaurants, it occupies a classic frame building set back from the road, and has a reputation for attentive but unpretentious service. The dinner menu changes every month, and a nightly special is offered. Prime rib always is on the menu, as is an excellent, generous Caesar salad. It's a popular place among the locals for its expansive Sun. brunch. A reader says, "We had a superb meal and excellent service. What a delightful find!" Reservations are recommended. Open Wed.–Thu. and Sun., 11:00 A.M.–2:00 P.M. and 5:00 P.M.–8:00 P.M.; Fri.–Sat., 11:00 A.M.–2:00 P.M. and 5:00 P.M.–9:00 P.M. **302 W. Main St., Payson; 520-474-1929.**

Mario's—$$–$$$

Besides being a great place to watch sports, Mario's has outstanding hand-tossed (we took their word for it) pizza, subs, a good selection of pastas, and some truly tasty vegetarian specialties that include spinach ravioli and vegetarian pizza. It's worth a stop just for their homemade bread. They'll package up food for takeout, too. Open Sun.–Thu., 10:30 A.M.–9:00 P.M.; Fri.–Sat., 10:30 A.M.–10:00 P.M. Happy hour, Mon.–Fri., 5:00 P.M.–7:00 P.M., really gets happy. Located adjacent to Majestic Mountain Inn. **600 E. Hwy. 260, Payson; 520-474-5429.**

Services

As you approach Payson on Hwy. 87 from Phoenix, the new **Mazatzal rest area** is open at the Hwy. 188 junction, the turnoff to Roosevelt Lake. The location is scenic as well as practical, so it's a good place to stretch your legs.

Pine–Strawberry Chamber of Commerce

Staffed by volunteers, it may be open just a few hours a day. Located **on west side of Hwy. 87 in Pine, at Old County Rd. P.O. Box 196, Pine, 85544; 520-476-3547.**

Rim Country Regional Chamber of Commerce

There is a large parking lot behind the small building at the corner of W. Main and Hwy. 87/260. Open Mon.–Fri., 8:00 A.M.–5:00 P.M.; Sat.–Sun., 10:00 A.M.–2:00 P.M. **100 W. Main, P.O. Box 1380, Payson, 85547; 800-672-9766 or 520-474-4515. Website: www.rim country.com.**

Verde Valley

Arizona's midsection is a cummerbund of green forests and flowing streams, Indian ruins and historic sites, preserved (one hopes) forever as part of the state park system. A string of small towns follows along the central part of the Verde River. This mellow waterway begins in the Chino Valley near the town of Seligman, flows through the Verde Valley, briefly becomes part of Horseshoe Lake, and finally ends up joining the Salt River above Granite Reef Dam. The part most commonly called the Verde Valley extends from the Clarkdale area in the north to past Camp Verde in the south. The town of Camp Verde marks the valley's southern entrance.

Northwest of Camp Verde, off Hwy. 89A, the ghost town of Jerome clings to the side of Cleopatra Hill. Part of Mingus Mountain, which once yielded copper in great abundance, the little town has expansive views of the Verde Valley. If you think you're feeling an earthquake, you probably aren't. The hill on which Jerome is built is honeycombed with old mine tunnels that shift constantly, creating earth movements that frequently cause small but definite tremors on the surface. About half of today's population of 403 are full-time working artists, their wares available in a number of shops along Hull Ave. and Main St. Not all mining memories are visual. A shrill noon whistle still blows as it did during mining days. You can walk just about anywhere you want to go in Jerome, so park in

one of the small city lots, if you can find a place, and set out on foot to explore.

Five miles from Jerome, at the upper end of the Verde Valley, a onetime smelter town called Clarkdale dates to 1912. The last smelter smokestack in Clarkdale came down in 1966. Small, tidy frame houses that date to 1913 still line the historic district. Today's Main St. is clearly recognizable in photos from the 1920s. The original town, next to Clarkdale, was first named Verde, then later Clemenceau for the French premier Georges Clemenceau. The school-cum-museum still bears his name.

Cottonwood, named for the graceful trees that flourish in this rich riparian area, lies 8 miles southeast of Clarkdale. Today Cottonwood is something of a retirement destination, favored for its reasonable cost of living and slower pace. Retirees make up more than half the residents of a new Del Webb community called Cottonwood Ranch, although it's not age-restricted. Old Town Cottonwood has a developing community of artisans with a working stained-glass studio and a couple of good, browsable antiques shops.

Getting There

The Verde Valley is crossed by I-17 about an hour and a half north of Phoenix. If you exit I-17 and follow Hwy. 260 in either direction you will be in the Verde Valley. It is 80 to 100 miles from Phoenix, depending on where you exit.

Reinactments at Fort Verde State Historic Park help bring this old Army post back to life.

History

Camp Verde originally was populated by miners who poured into the area to seek their fortune. These new residents severely hindered the hunting and gathering economy of the Native Americans, so the Tonto Apaches and Yavapais raided Verde Valley fields for corn. In 1865 the military secured the area from Apache raids to protect settlers, who farmed the rich river valley. As late as the 1930s, Apaches lived along the Verde River in wickiups made of willows lashed together with bear grass.

Eugene Jerome, an early financier and a well-known New York City attorney, agreed to underwrite a speculative mining venture on the condition that the town carry his name. In 1882, Territorial Governor Frederick Tritle connected with Jerome while casting about for financing for a mining operation in the Black Hills that form one side of the Verde Valley. During the 1920s, this hillside town's salad days, 15,000 people had homes on the mountainside. Ore from Jerome was processed in Clarkdale, then cast and shipped as ingots to alleviate the expense of transporting ore

across the country. Cottonwood began as a trading center, purveying supplies and the necessities of life to those attracted by the mines.

First settled around A.D. 700, Tuzigoot (the name means "crooked water" to the Apache) grew over a 400-year period. The Verde Valley was a living grocery store, with antelope, deer, and small game. The meadow above the river produced grains and beans. The river itself was filled with fish and turtles, and attracted migratory Canada geese, white-wing doves, and a variety of ducks. These life-sustaining features made it a natural settling place. Long after the Sinagua left, around 1400, miners discovered that the area produced some of the richest copper deposits in the world.

Festivals and Events

Sizzling Salsa Sunday

first Sun. of May
The Verde Valley's Mexican heritage is remembered on Cinco de Mayo with a salsa contest among Verde Valley restaurants. Mariachis, a street dance, food and craft booths, and piñatas for kids to swing at are part of the celebration. Various cities in the valley host different events, but you can be sure that Cinco de Mayo will be celebrated in some way in all of them. **Throughout Verde Valley.**

Jerome Home Tour

mid-May
The buildings on this tour once served as apartments or rooming- and boardinghouses for miners, grand Victorian homes for mine executives, or sturdy frame dwellings for mine middle management. Today they are part of an annual home tour that also may include shops, businesses, and restaurants essential to a thriving community. Among the buildings usually open to visitors, the Surgeon's House is poised on a lofty knoll with a commanding view of the hillside (see Where to Stay). **520-634-2900.**

Verde River Day

last Sat. of Sept.

At Dead Horse Ranch State Park, State Forest Service and public land exhibits help raise awareness of this special riparian area. Located in Cottonwood just off 10th St. 520-634-5283. Website: www.pr.state.az.us.

Fort Verde Days

second weekend in Oct.

For more than 25 years, Camp Verde has celebrated its history with precision cavalry displays, a small rodeo, and an art show that attracts craftspeople from around the state. People dress up in period costume and really get in the spirit of the event. 520-567-9294.

Outdoor Activities

Hiking

Northeast of Camp Verde, West Clear Creek surges across more than 40 miles of wilderness. Twenty of these follow the Mogollon Rim and make up the West Clear Creek Wilderness. A rewarding hiking area, trails here are generally challenging, scenery is spectacular, and nature is at its best. Soaring red-tailed hawks, icy pools, and stands of cottonwoods and willows make this seem more like a rain forest than an area surrounded by desert. Easiest of the hikes include the **Bull Pen,** at the creek's western end, and the **Calloway and Maxwell Trails,** near the creek's upper end. Summer hiking is best because the creek is flowing, yet not unmanageable. However, it's also the time when annoying gnats and poison ivy flourish. For more information contact **Beaver Creek Ranger Station, H.C. 64, Box 24, Rimrock, 86335; 520-567-4501.**

Dead Horse Ranch State Park

This pretty 325-acre park (one of our personal favorites) is filled with great wildlife. Easy hikes of just a few hours wind along the Verde River

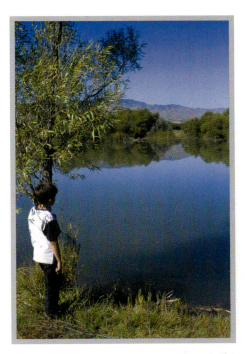

Dead Horse Ranch State Park near Cottonwood offers great fishing in a well-stocked lake.

riparian area and near a large fishing lagoon. Hiking trails begin at picnic areas and follow the banks of the river. At an elevation of 3,300 feet, it's far enough above the Phoenix area to attract campers escaping summer heat, but its best months are spring and fall, when days are cool and nights are crisp. More than 150 bird species have been identified here. Around the river and lagoon we have seen great blue herons, bitterns, mallards, cinnamon teal, gadwall, and other waterbirds. The small footprints in the wet sand are likely those of beavers and raccoons, and the larger canine ones belong to coyotes, distinguishable from domestic dog prints because coyotes walk in a straight line, their slow, loping gait leaving sets of four aligned prints. Dogs leave side-by-side tracks like humans. A number of types of hawks, bald eagles, and turkey vultures soar overhead, and at least three hummingbird species frequent the park.

Each Oct. the 4-acre lagoon is stocked with catfish for Verde River Days (see Festivals and

Events). Enough bass from previous stockings survive that at least one grew to 10 pounds before recently succumbing to an angler's lure. In winter, catfish and trout are stocked as well. We have visited this lovely riparian area on a weekday morning and found ourselves blissfully alone on some of the longer trails. Two first-come, first-served campgrounds have pull-through and back-in sites with rest rooms and showers, and several day-use sites have rest rooms. The park is wheelchair-accessible. Open daily, 8:00 A.M.–sunset. The ranger station is staffed various hours, depending on season and day of week. Located in Cottonwood just off 10th St. **675 Dead Horse Ranch Rd., Cottonwood, 86326; 520-634-5283. Website: www.pr.state.az.us.**

Horseback Riding

Horseback Adventures

Look for these stables at Cowboys and Outlaws Wild West Town. Owner Bill Jones says that he offers "horses matched to your skills and adventures matched to your imagination." The company's trail rides cover some of the best the Verde Valley has to offer. One parallels Beaver Creek near Montezuma Castle, and another follows the General Crook Trail in Copper Canyon. An all-day ride covers piñon-covered Pine Mountain. Overnight rides also are available. Located **at I-17 and Middle Verde Rd. off exit 289. P.O. Box 593, Camp Verde, 86322; 520-567-5502.**

Seeing and Doing

Museums and Historic Sites

Clemenceau Heritage Museum

It began life in 1926 in Cottonwood as Clemenceau Public School, providing kindergarten through ninth-grade education for mostly the children of mine workers. The smelter closed in 1937, but the school remained open until the last classes were taught in 1986. Shortly thereafter local volunteers requested a portion of the building to use as a small museum, then filled it with artifacts and photographs of the Verde Valley from years gone by. There is an operational model railroad of the 1895–1953 era, with little well-crafted ore cars and a steam locomotive, and a replica classroom. Other parts of the building still are used as district administrative offices. Open Wed., 9:00 A.M.–noon; Fri.–Sun., 11:00 A.M.–3:00 P.M. **11 N. Willard, Cottonwood, 86326; 520-634-2868.**

Fort Verde State Historic Park

The 1870s are preserved here with four fort buildings that demonstrate just how tough life could be 100 years ago. On most weekends, "reenactors" in period costume play the roles of soldiers, wives, doctors, and cavalry officers. In summer it's so hot that "the only shade's a swarm of flies," says one "soldier," authentically (and not too happily) clad in a wool uniform over wool underwear. The fort "doctor" will tell you he got the job for being able to "take off a leg in one minute or less without killing the patient through blood loss or shock." Very small fee. Open daily, 8:00 A.M.–5:00 P.M., except Christmas Day. Located one block east of Main St. (Hwy. 260) in downtown Camp Verde. **125 E. Hollamon, Campe Verde, 86331; 520-567-3275. Website: www.pr.state.az.us.**

Jerome State Historic Park

As you enter Jerome, you'll have great views of the Verde Valley and a look at the adobe Douglas Mansion. Never meant to be a family home, it was built by the owner of the Little Daisy Mine as a place to wine, dine, and lodge mining officials and investors. The 8,700-square-foot mansion, constructed in 1916 for $150,000, now houses artifacts and exhibits that tell of the town's heyday and the mining industry that supported it. Guides point out the central vacuum cleaning system, an innovation for its day. A picnic area has tables, and rest rooms are in the park museum. Small fee. Open daily, 8:00 A.M.–5:00 P.M., except Christmas Day. Located **off Hwy. 89A at milepost 345. P.O. Box D, Jerome, 83331; 520-634-5381. Website: www. pr.state.az.us.**

Montezuma Castle National Monument

Just north of Camp Verde, Montezuma Castle is one of the best-preserved examples of cliff dwellings in the country, even though Montezuma was never there and it is definitely not a castle. Settlers named it, believing it was built by Aztec refugees fleeing from the Spanish conquistadors in Central Mexico. More than 800 years ago, it housed Sinagua Indians (the name means "without water" in Spanish), who found a cool, shady home beneath overhanging cliffs and a ready water supply in Beaver Creek. The five-story dwelling was constructed around 1150. By the 1300s the civilization here was at its peak with as many as 50 people making their home in 20 different rooms. But a century later the site was abandoned for reasons unknown, and the Sinagua left the Verde Valley completely. Because of their sheltered position, the ruins are well preserved, but visitors have not been allowed to climb up to them since 1951.

Remnants of another larger pueblo that stood six stories high and had about 45 rooms remain in low rock walls that outline portions of the bottom floor. It is believed that wood ladders connected various levels. Its unprotected position allowed the elements to erode it to what you see today. The level, hard-surface walking trail is wheelchair-accessible. Near Montezuma Castle and part of the monument, **Montezuma Well** is a limestone sink that was formed by the collapse of a huge underground cavern that was then filled by continuously flowing springs. At the same time that 50 Sinagua lived at Montezuma Castle, more than 100 lived here, building irrigation channels from the well to feed their crops. Remains of their ditches are here, as well as a Hohokam pit house built about 1100.

Bring a picnic lunch to eat at tables beneath sycamores along the creek. Even in midsummer the shade and (usually) a breeze keep temperatures tolerable. Benches and drinking fountains are scattered along the walkway. The visitor center has excellent displays that explain area history and contain artifacts from the castle. Small admission. Open Memorial Day–Labor Day, daily, 8:00 A.M.–7:00 P.M. or sundown; winter, daily, 8:00 A.M.–5:00 P.M. Located about 5 miles north of Camp Verde, off I-17 at exit 289. 520-567-3322. Website: www.nps.gov.

Old Town Cottonwood

The area around the Sundial Inn in Cottonwood is considered Old Town. At one time the big cottonwood trees in the wash just north of what is now the visitor center provided a protected site for wagons that belonged to ranchers and cattlemen. They stopped overnight, sitting around their campfires swapping stories and sharing camaraderie that happened all too infrequently among those who lived on far-apart ranches. Most of the buildings in Old Town were built before 1925 and are clearly recognizable as belonging to that era. They now house shops, art galleries and antiques stores, a vintage clothing boutique, cafes, and delis. Movies are shown nightly at the Old Town Palace Theater. Mount Hope Foods on Main St. has been the area's natural-foods center for 30 years. It stocks a good supply of organically grown fruits and vegetables, dried nuts, and fruits as well as teas and homeopathic remedies. Local pine nuts usually are available at reasonable prices. The **Old Town Association Visitor Center** was once the old town jail. The original cells are there, and a 1950s mural by local artist Randolph Pyne recently was uncovered and restored. It shows red rocks and the San Francisco Peaks as well as residents and workers of the area. **1101 N. Main St.; 520-634-9468.**

Tuzigoot National Monument

Another Sinagua village of the same era as Montezuma Castle, this restored site once sheltered more than 450 people. Pick up a booklet at the visitor center for a self-guided tour along the 0.25-mile trail through the ruins. The original two-story pueblo, rising 120 feet above the valley, had 77 ground-floor rooms with ladders leading to the upper floor. A second-story viewpoint, with the same panoramas that attracted the Sinaguans, looks out over Mingus Mountain. The mining city of Jerome is visible on the mountain's upper slopes. The adjacent visitor center is particularly interesting for its display of pottery, turquoise and shell jewelry, and stone axes and tools that were discovered while the site was being excavated in 1933–34. Tuzigoot became a national monument in 1939. Small fee. Open Memorial Day–mid-Sept., daily, 8:00 A.M.–7:00 P.M.; rest of year, daily, 8:00 A.M.–5:00 P.M. Located between Clarkdale and Cottonwood off Hwy. 89A at Broadway Rd. 520-634-5564.

Nightlife

Blazin' M Ranch Chuckwagon Suppers and Western Stage Show

This family-oriented place is a combination amusement area, dinner venue, and cowboy show. Times and days vary with the season, so call ahead for schedules, then arrive at least an hour early to browse through the Old West town and shops. The Blazin' M has always been a dairy farm and cattle ranch, its roots evident in the yard full of friendly farm animals and small ponies ready to give young wranglers a thrill. For dinner you sit at family-style picnic tables, drinking sarsparilla, then watch a show that includes a medley of cowboy songs and comedy routines filled with good times and simple humor. For example, servers will tell you they put your cowboy beans on your plate upside-down "so they'll give you only the hiccups." One of the cowboy entertainers talks about his girl named Bureau—"a big wide thing with drawers." You get the idea. Cost is in the $$–$$$ range. In Cottonwood, adjacent to Dead Horse Ranch State Park. P.O. Box 160, Cottonwood, 86326; 800-WEST643 or 520-634-0334.

Scenic Drives

FOUR-WHEEL-DRIVE TRIPS

Copper Canyon Tours

Tours from one hour to half a day are available along mountain trails, led by owner Clay Miller, who's been leading them for years. The Iron Horse Expedition goes to 6,000 feet, following the narrow-gauge railroad bed built for what was billed as the "crookedest railroad in the world" because of the mountain switchbacks it had to maneuver. The railroad was built in 1895 for the train that hauled the occasional passenger as well as ore from Jerome's mines. Other tours cover area geology, Native American heritage, and myths and legends. P.O. Box 591, Jerome, 86331; 520-634-3497. Website: www.arizonahealingtours.com.

Tours

Verde Canyon Railroad

The Sycamore Wilderness Area and North Verde River Canyon, known as the "other" Grand Canyon, are among the state's most beautiful untouched places. The only way to see this carefully protected region is on the Verde Canyon Railroad, an excursion train that does a four-hour, 40-mile round trip into otherwise inaccessible wilderness. Mar.–June, the high desert canyon is abloom with Indian paintbrush, daisies, ocotillo and other cactuses, and wildflowers. Cottonwood and aspen create a blaze of color in the fall. The railroad dates to 1911 when it hauled copper along the river. Today it transports passengers on the Clarkdale-Perkinsville round trip in Pullman Standard coach cars built in 1946–47. Cowboy balladeers entertain as guests look out at giant cottonwoods, hovering eagles, 700-foot sandstone walls, and great blue herons. The old depot and water tower still stand along the tracks. Vintage FP7 engines pull the train along at a sedate, rattly 12 miles per hour, allowing occasional sightings of mountain lions, wild turkeys, and javelinas. The engines (it takes two to pull the train with its maximum of 340 passengers) were built in 1953 for the Alaskan Railroad by the Electro-Motive Division of General Motors. The impressive eagle paintings on the engines were done by wildlife artist Doug Allen.

Each passenger has an inside seat, but open gondola cars are ideal for snapping photos. Each coach has a snack bar and rest rooms. The train leaves from the new depot in Clarkdale, which has a gift shop, reservation offices, minimuseum, and snack bar with patio dining. Take a few minutes to browse the historic photographic display. Trains run year-round, but the schedule

Verde Canyon Railroad takes passengers on rides back into history in the Sycamore Wilderness.

is subject to change, so call first. Moonlight excursions are sometimes available. Advance reservations are required. **300 N. Broadway, Clarkdale, 86324; 800-293-7245 or 520-639-0010.** Website: www.verdecanyonrr.com.

WALKING TOURS

Jerome

Local historian and author Nancy Rayne Smith takes individuals and groups on walking tours of Jerome, covering the town's history, building by building. If you have a particular interest, such as architecture, a tour can be tailored to your needs. Tours are by reservation only, primarily during summer months because it's pretty cold to walk around Jerome in winter. **520-634-8654.** Website: nrsmith@verdenet.com.

Wagering

Cliff Castle Casino

Typical Native American low-key gaming venue with lots of slots, keno, and video poker. Run by the Yavapai Apaches. Located **at I-17 and Middle Verde Rd., 3 miles north of Camp Verde on Montezuma Castle Rd. 800-524-6343.**

Where to Stay

Hotels, Motels, and Inns

Jerome Grand Hotel—$$$–$$$$

Opened in July 1996, this superhotel is an example of recycling at its best, and now is a national historic landmark. Built in 1926 as the United Verde Hospital, it was one of the most modern hospitals of its day. It closed in 1950 but its owner, Phelps Dodge Mining Company, kept it in medical readiness until the 1970s in case it was needed. After it was purchased in 1994 and underwent three years of renovation, guests here no longer feel like they should strip for surgery. The original Otis elevator is in service, and the Kewanee boiler system that heated the hospital still warms guest rooms. At 5,260 feet (just up the road from the Surgeon's House) it has 180-degree valley views, extending to the San Francisco Peaks. Relax in a 1920s-style lounge or dine in the Grand View Restaurant, open for three meals a day. Don't let the narrow cobblestone street put you off. Go slowly and follow it to the top. It's worth it. The hotel is in walking distance (mostly uphill) from downtown Jerome. 200 Hill St., P.O. Drawer H, Jerome, 86331; 888-817-5788 or 520-634-8200. Website: jeromegrandhotel.net.

The Surgeon's House—$$$–$$$$

Built in 1917 for the man charged with keeping mine workers healthy, this lovely home is poised above the main town of Jerome and has what can be described only as breathtaking views of the Verde Valley that reach all the way to the red rocks of Sedona. Andrea Prince furnished the home, which is on the National Register of Historic Places, with charming personal antiques and mementos. A cool, shady garden adjacent to the dining room is a quiet place to relax. The master suite has a private balcony. Rates include a full breakfast, homemade snacks, and complimentary beverages. Take the cobblestone driveway off Clark St. past the Episcopal Church that now houses the Jerome Historical Society. **P.O. Box 998, Jerome, 86331; 800-639-1452 or 520-639-1452.**

Cliff Castle Lodge—$$$

This Best Western is also notable as a gaming place, with the Cliff Castle Casino run by the Yavapai Apaches a part of its complex. Rooms with balconies have king or queen beds. There are a large pool and a restaurant. Surprisingly, when you stay at the hotel you won't hear noise from the casino. Because it has so many rooms you often can get a room here at the last minute when all else is full. Located **at I-17 and Middle Verde Rd., 3 miles north of Camp Verde on Montezuma Castle Rd. P.O. Box 3430, Camp Verde, 86322; 800-524-6343 or 520-567-6611.**

Little Daisy Motel—$$–$$$

The motel is named for the Little Daisy Mine, properly known as the United Verde Extension Mine, and for the original Little Daisy Hotel, built in 1918 and still standing in Jerome but not open. This tidy, light blue frame motel has kitchenettes and rooms that accommodate a family. Kitchen utensils are available on request. It's an affordable alternative to Sedona's pricey digs just 16 miles north. 34 S. Main St., Cottonwood, 86326; 520-634-7865, fax 520-639-3447.

Sundial Motel—$$

This unpretentious little place, built in 1921 in a sort of Indian-Spanish style in Cottonwood's Old Town, is a budget gem. The outside is faced with natural river rock, and an interior courtyard welcomes with tables and umbrellas. Rooms have TV, a microwave, and a small refrigerator, so you can tuck in for several days or a week (rates are lower by the week) to explore the area. Some rooms have kitchenettes. Don't expect the Ritz, but you'll be comfortable, and the price definitely is right. 1034 N. Main St., Cottonwood, 86326; 520-634-8031.

Camping

The two RV Parks mentioned below are notable for being cool and pleasant in the summer, but they also fill up very fast.

Dead Horse Ranch State Park

Two first-come, first-served campgrounds have pull-through and back-in sites with rest rooms and showers. Located in Cottonwood just off 10th St. 675 Dead Horse Ranch Rd., Cottonwood, 86326; 520-634-5283. Website: www.pr.state.az.us.

Rio Verde RV Park

Large, shady spaces with full hookups. Located on Hwy. 89A just north of Cottonwood, right on the Verde River, next door to the White Horse Inn. 520-634-5990.

Turquoise Triangle RV Park

On the Verde River, this RV park has 60 full hookups. Spaces lined with huge cottonwood trees keep it cool, even in summer. Located on Hwy. 89A just south of the river. 520-634-5294.

Where to Eat

At the I-17 exit for the Verde Valley you'll find a Denny's, Dairy Queen, Burger King, and McDonald's. It's a mile or so east from the freeway to Camp Verde for other eateries, or head in the other direction to Clarkdale, Cottonwood, or Jerome.

The Ranch House—$$–$$$
The setting, on Beaver Creek Golf Course at Lake Montezuma, makes this a good place to relax and enjoy a well-prepared meal. Casual and low-key. Open Sun.–Thu., 6:00 A.M.–8:00 P.M.; Fri.–Sat., 6:00 A.M.–9:00 P.M. From I-17 take Lake Montezuma Rd. about 5 miles to Lake Montezuma. 520-567-4492.

Clarkdale Antique Emporium & Soda Fountain—$–$$
Browse through remnants of yesteryear, then hop on a stool at the old-fashioned fountain for a further taste of the past. Sodas, sundaes, and pies with a giant scoop of ice cream are among the present-day crowd pleasers. Open Tues.–Sun., 10:00 A.M.–6:00 P.M. 907 Main St., Clarkdale; 520-634-2828.

Haunted Hamburger—$–$$
Voted by Jerome businesses as the town's best restaurant, it's known for its half-pound creation for which the place is named. It's big, juicy, and smothered with a ton of toppings. Located at one of Jerome's highest points, across from the Surgeon's House and down the street from the Jerome Grand Hotel (see Where to Stay), the building was built in 1908 as a boardinghouse. The small outdoor balcony has views to rival the burgers. Open daily, 11:00 A.M.–9:00 P.M. 410 Clark St., Jerome; 520-634-0554.

Services

On I-17, 53 miles north of Phoenix, **Sunset Point Rest Area** is large and busy, with covered ramadas, bathrooms, and drinking water. Good interpretive signs explain the valley you're overlooking.

Camp Verde Chamber of Commerce
It occupies an old painted adobe school built in 1911. The original red oak floor creaks in friendly fashion as you come in. Open Mon.–Fri., 9:00 A.M.–5:00 P.M. Located **downtown near First and Main Sts.** across the parking lot from the town hall, where there are public rest rooms. **P.O. Box 3520, Camp Verde, 86322; 520-567-9294.** Website: www.insightable.com/cvcc.

Camp Verde Historical Society
In the same building as the Chamber of Commerce, this is a good source of information to help put the Verde Valley in historical perspective. Open by appointment only. 520-567-4324.

Cottonwood–Verde Valley Chamber of Commerce
A separate room with tables and chairs is lined with brochures, so you can take the time to figure out what you want to do and ask questions before you leave. Open daily, 9:00 A.M.–5:00 P.M. Located at Hwys. 89A and 260. **1010 S. Main St., Cottonwood, 86326; 520-634-7593.** Website: chamber.verdevalley.com.

Jerome Chamber of Commerce
Located inside a gift shop. Open daily, 11 A.M.–3:00 P.M. 136 Main St., Jerome, 86331; 520-634-2900. Website: www.jeromechamber.com.

Sedona and Oak Creek Canyon

Considered by many to be one of the state's loveliest areas, Sedona also is known as a place of healing and emotional rejuvenation. Within five minutes of leaving I-17 and heading west on Hwy. 179, you catch glimpses of breathtaking red rocks. The road-flanking, just-minted shops and businesses do nothing to diminish the beauty of the sandstone spires and buttes. Brilliantly colored by the minerals in the rocks, they then were sculpted by the waters of ancient oceans and the forces of desert winds. Fortunately this strip of road has many pullouts.

In the mid-1970s a group of spiritualists declared that Sedona has four electromagnetic energy sources called vortexes. Consequently there are a number of practitioners of alternative healing who regularly schedule seminars and events here. You can pick up a vortex map at the chamber of commerce. Sedona also is an arts center with more than 40 galleries. Everyone comes to Sedona during the summer, when its elevation makes it cooler than Phoenix and the Valley of the Sun to the south. Dec., Jan., and Feb. are considered low season but are preferred by many visitors for the crisp, cool weather, occasional snow, and dearth of tourists.

History

In prehistory, the Anasazi fished Oak Creek and farmed and hunted in the area, which at one time was a major trade-route crossroads. More recently, Sedona's namesake, Sedona Schnebly, moved here with her husband, Carl, from Missouri in the early 1900s. Because they owned the only home large enough to accommodate paying guests, the pair soon became known for their hospitality to travelers making the exhausting journey between Flagstaff and Jerome. When Carl applied for the area's post office, his first choices of names were Oak Creek Crossing and Schnebly Station. The Postmaster General rejected them because the cancellation stamp didn't have room for so many letters. So Carl named the town for his wife, Sedona, whose six-letter name not only fit the stamp but had a melodious ring that appealed to everyone.

Festivals and Events

Jazz on the Rocks

mid-Sept.

This is one of the most celebrated jazz and blues festivals anywhere, partially because of its scenic setting in red-rock country, but also because it attracts top performers. Louis Bellson, Count Basie's Orchestra, Gerry Mulligan, and other jazz notables have appeared in the past. Local groups perform in area restaurants during the festival, giving everyone a chance to join in the fun.

Held at new Sedona Cultural Park, a natural amphitheater backgrounded by the Mogollon Rim and Capital Dome, at Cultural Park Place and Hwy. 89A in west Sedona. 520-282-1985.

Sedona Sculpture Walk

first weekend in Oct.

The three-day event attracts more than 100 artists and sculptors from across the country. Artistic themes range from Native American to western, contemporary to abstract. Held **at Los Abrigados Resort & Spa.** For information call the Sedona Arts Center, **520-282-3809.**

Red Rock Fantasy

late Nov.–mid-Jan.

More than 100,000 people come annually to this spectacular holiday light display that gets its glow from more than a million lights. Fifty families from around Arizona are chosen to create unique light displays that they set up on the 22 acres of Los Abrigados Resort, competing for the votes of visitors, who choose the best display. An ongoing crowd-pleaser called Dancing Lights, located creekside in the Sycamore Grove, involves tiny twinklers performing a synchronized dance to holiday and classical music. Tickets are available at the admission booth at Los Abrigados. **160 Portal Ln., Sedona, 86336; 520-282-1777. Website: www.sedona.net/fun/fantasy.**

Outdoor Activities

Bicycling

There are lots of outstanding trails in the area, including more than 100 miles of single-track, and bike shops with rentals to help you get out on them. Sedona Red Rock Pathways project aims to connect most of the area with a series of bicycling trails. At present a good, **fairly easy one-way route** begins on Hwy. 89A, along Lower Red Rock Loop, and winds through Red Rock State Park, ending up on Verde Valley

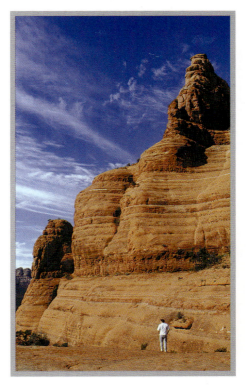

The famous red rock formations of Sedona.

School Rd. Don't try to continue to the Upper Loop Rd. because it is narrow with no room for bikes. Hard-core cyclists bike the steep **Schnebly Hill Rd.,** which can be rocky and dusty. Try it if a great view is enough reward for you. Forest Service roads offer good riding, but remember that in the Coconino National Forest, designated Wilderness Areas are not open to cyclists. **Dry Creek Rd.** is not too difficult and connects with Boynton Pass Rd., also marked. Pick up Dry Creek Road in west Sedona off Hwy. 89A. Riders also use Hwy. 89A where it is four-lane, but many cyclists are not comfortable with the amount of traffic, especially during summer. It's well worth $4.95 to pick up the Experience Sedona Recreation and Activity map at the Sedona Chamber of Commerce. It details hiking and biking trails all over the area.

Rentals and Tours

Mountain Bike Heaven has double-suspension

Getting There

Sedona is a two-hour drive north of Phoenix. From I-17 take exit 298 onto Hwy. 179 and proceed 15 miles north to Sedona.

bike rentals and gets you on your way with maps and suggested rides. Open Mon.–Fri., 9:00 A.M.–6:00 P.M.; Sat.–Sun., 9:00 A.M.–5:00 P.M. **1695 W. Hwy. 89A, Sedona, 86336; 520-282-1323.**

Desert Jeep & Bike Rentals has bikes, technical assistance, and dual full-suspension bikes. Jeep® Wranglers and Harleys, too. **75 Bell Rock Plaza, Sedona, 86351; 888-GO-4-JEEP or 520-284-1099. Website: www.rentajeep andbike.com.**

Sedona Bike & Bean Shop dispenses cappuccino and espresso along with its bike rentals. They'll show you a 3-D topographic map that helps you plan your ride. If you're looking for a riding companion, ask about the group rides that run daily. Located off Hwy. 89A in uptown Sedona. **6020 Hwy. 179, Sedona, 86351; 520-284-0210. Websites: www.bike-bean.com and www.epicmap.com.**

Golf

Oakcreek Country Club

This 6,800-yard, par 72 championship course, designed by Robert Trent Jones, is a challenge to golfers for its tree-lined layout. Thirty years old, it's been around long enough to be well settled, and is open year-round. The signature 187-yard, par 3 fourth hole is tucked cleverly into a red-rock formation. **690 Bell Rock Blvd., Sedona, 86351; 520-284-1660 or 888-703-9489.**

Sedona Golf Resort

They call it Golf on the Rocks, which pretty well describes this 18-hole championship course designed by Gary Panks. The 6,640-yard lay-

out plays to a par 71, and winds through the red rocks that have made Sedona famous. Its famous par 3 11th hole begins at the course's highest point and shoots 200 yards to a right-sloping green. It may be one of the few courses in the country with bunkers of red sand. A dining room opens for breakfast and lunch. Located on Hwy. 179, 7 miles from I-17. **7260 Hwy. 179, Sedona, 86351; 520-284-9355.**

Hiking

Red Rock and Slide Rock State Parks (see Parks in Seeing and Doing) have many great trails, including the easy, almost-level **Pendley Homestead Trail** at Slide Rock that meanders through the apple orchard. Another beautiful hike follows a narrow side canyon off Oak Creek called **West Fork**. It is particularly lovely in fall when the giant cottonwoods along the canyon floor burst into color. The fairly level trail crosses the creek at several points and is cool and shady. Pick up the **trailhead 3.2 miles north of Slide Rock State Park on Hwy. 89A.** As you head north, on your left is a parking area with a path leading down to the creek. Just on the other side of the creek are the ruins of an old cabin and trail markers. Everyone seems to hike **Red Rock Crossing** because it is easy, doable even by fairly young children and the definitely unfit. From the parking lot a cement walkway ends at Oak Creek, continuing on as a dirt trail to Cathedral Rock. The **trailhead is off Upper Red Rock Loop Rd.** Once you're on it, just follow the signs. **Long Canyon Trail,** an easy 4.5 miles, leads to some lovely petroglyphs. **From Dry Creek Rd. follow signs to Boynton and Long Canyon, turn right at Long Canyon Rd., and the trailhead is 0.5 mile ahead.**

Seeing and Doing

Nature Centers

Red Rock State Park

This extensive park and center for environmental

education preserves one of the loveliest parts of Oak Creek. It is crosshatched with easy hiking trails of 1 to 2 miles. In the nature center you'll learn about what you'll see out in the park. The wheelchair-accessible ramp leading to the center is imprinted with tracks of bear, bobcat, great blue heron, raccoon, and other creatures of the area. The park, at one time slated to become a housing development, was part of the Smoke Trail Ranch, originally purchased by TWA owner Jack Frye, who bought it in 1941 as a vacation retreat. Migrating birds in Apr. and Nov. share the forest with resident ravens, jays, Gila woodpeckers, and Say's phoebes. Alders, cottonwoods, and sycamores create fall color. The park's 286 acres once sheltered the Sinagua and Yavapai Indians, drawn to the Oak Creek area by its life-sustaining natural resources. Solar-powered toilets with circulating fans are placed along trails. A nature walk is held daily at 10:00 A.M. to acquaint visitors with the park's ecology. A spectacular overlook called Eagles Nest is the destination of a guided hike held May–Sept., Sat., 8:00 A.M., and Oct.–Apr., Sat., 9:00 A.M. Small per-vehicle entrance fee. Open during summer, 8:00 A.M.–6:00 P.M.; in winter, 8:00 A.M.–5:00 P.M. Located on Red Rock Loop Rd. off Hwy. 89A about 5 miles south of Sedona. **4050 Red Rock Loop Rd., Sedona, 86336; 520-282-6907. Website: www.pr.state.az.us.**

Other Sights

Chapel of the Holy Cross

As you drive the picturesque route into Sedona, your eye is drawn up to the right to the pristine, modern Chapel of the Holy Cross snugged among the rich red crags. Completed in 1956, it is the vision of Marguerite Brunswig Staude, a noted sculptor and painter who saw spirituality in art. Inside, the Stations of the Cross are fashioned from antique nails in a modern design. There are magnificent views from the patio, and a gift shop offers souvenirs. The chapel doors are open year-round, daily, 9:00 A.M.–6:00 P.M. Located 1 **mile off Hwy. 179 on Chapel**

Rd., about 3 miles south of the "Y"—intersection of Hwys. 179 and 89A. **520-282-4069.**

Parks

Slide Rock State Park

Nature has worn a 30-foot water slide between steep, extremely slippery red rock walls along Oak Creek in this 43-acre natural recreation area. For the summertime activity of water sliding, wear old heavy-duty denim shorts and tennis shoes, but be forewarned: The water temperature is a chilly 65°F, or less. For current water-quality conditions, call **602-542-0202.** From the parking lot to the slide it's an easy stroll through an apple orchard, in full fragrant bloom by mid-Apr., that dates to 1912. Thirteen apple varieties, including red delicious, Arkansas black, and Jonathan, are grown here and sold at the refreshment center as cider, caramel apples, and just plain apples for eating out of hand. Harvesting takes place in Sept.–Oct. You can join a ranger-narrated history program that focuses on the Pendley homestead, owned by the family that planted the original apple trees; in spring and fall, Sat., 1:00 P.M.; in summer, Sat., 9 A.M. There are bird walks Apr.–Nov., Sun., 8:00 A.M. You'll find picnic tables, grills, a snack bar, hiking trails, and rest rooms at the site. Small per-vehicle entry fee. Open summer, 8:00 A.M.–7:00 P.M.; fall and spring, 8:00 A.M.–6:00 P.M.; winter, 8:00 A.M.–5:00 P.M. Located 7 **miles north of Sedona on Hwy. 89A. P.O. Box 10358, Sedona, 86339; 520-282-3034. Website: www.pr.state.az.us.**

Scenic Drives

This whole area is so scenic, it's difficult to drive anywhere without coming upon a view. But here are a few of our favorites.

Oak Creek Canyon

Head north from Sedona (already you're in some of the state's most scenic territory) along Hwy. 89A, which follows Oak Creek and passes Slide Rock State Park. As you proceed north, glimpses

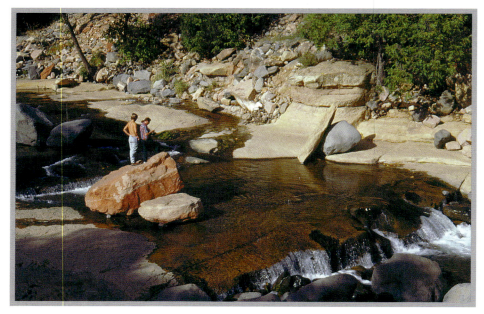

Anglers enjoy Slide Rock State Park, where nature has worn a 30-foot water slide.

of the creek through thick, lush forest tell you you're in the heart of the Coconino National Forest. A 2-mile climb of tight switchbacks as the road winds out of the canyon ends at a scenic viewpoint that's worth the uneasiness. It is about a 25-mile drive. You can retrace your steps back to Sedona, or continue on to Flagstaff. For more information see the **Sedona Chamber of Commerce's website: www.sedonachamber.com.**

Loop Trail

Loop Trail is less than a half hour's drive, so go slowly and savor the scenery. From Hwy. 89A at the edge of Sedona, heading for Cottonwood, turn left onto Upper Red Rock Loop Rd. After a few miles the pavement ends, but the dirt road is graded and fine for regular automobiles. You pass distant red rocks, rolling farmland, and, in the fall, trees in full color. The pavement resumes at just about the point where you pass the entrance to Red Rock State Park. Continue on 3 miles to Hwy. 89A. You're now off the Loop Trail, but since you're in the area, you might as well continue on for another short segment. Turn right (back toward Sedona) and continue about

a mile to Dry Creek Rd. (Forest Rd. 152) and turn left (north). Follow it another mile to Forest Rd. 152C and turn right. You can park and hike to Devil's Bridge, a spectacular natural arch in the red rocks.

Red Rock Scenic Rd.

This is the classic route taken by many visitors to Sedona, and offers much of the scenery that everyone looks for. From I-17 turn left onto Hwy. 179 and follow it about 14 miles into Sedona. It passes some of the area's famous rock formations, including Cathedral Rock on the left and Bell Rock on the right, easy to recognize from their descriptively named outlines. Don't miss the Chapel of the Holy Cross (see Other Sights in Seeing and Doing). Your view of it from the highway is the best, but once you reach the red cliffs among which it is set, you'll be treated to even better views of the spectacular red rocks.

FOUR-WHEEL-DRIVE TRIPS

A number of area operators go out to the red rocks, with varying focuses for their tours. Your best bet is to study the brochures, find out exactly how many guests go at one time, and ask where the tour stops for photo opportunities. Most companies will pick you up from and return you to your hotel. Some will rent you a jeep, but unless you know the area well, you may miss the best parts. Also, licensed companies have permits to go where private vehicles aren't allowed. Most can get you to a point where you can see the history of the area layered in the rocks.

Pink Jeep Tours

For years this company has taken guests right up rock walls and out onto trails that bear no resemblance to roads. Choices include winding among spires and pinnacles (which guides point out are different from mountains), looking at rock art and ancient ruins, checking out canyonlands and ancient geologic formations, and viewing areas that are sacred to Native Americans. Guides are among the most knowledgeable in the area. 240 N. Hwy. 89A, P.O. Box 1447, Sedona, 86339; 800-873-3662 or 520-282-5000. Website: www.pinkjeep.com.

Sedona Red Rock Jeep Tours

Sedona's original cowboy tour company takes you among the red rocks on jaunts that include the rugged Soldier Pass and Legends of Sedona. The ancient wisdom of Native Americans is revealed on The Medicine Wheel and Sedona's Original Vortex tour. Petroglyphs and cave dwellings are explored on more adventurous tours. The vortex tour visits two main vortices, allowing time for meditation and exploration. Located in Uptown Sedona. 270 N. Hwy. 89A. P.O. Box 10305, Sedona 86339; 800-848-7728 or 520-282-6826. Website: www.redrockjeep.com.

Shopping

Tlaquepaque

Pronounced "T-laca-POCKy," it looks like a cool, charming Spanish colonial village, and it is indeed named for the town in Guadalajara.

The shopping village of Tlaquepaque in Sedona is named for its Mexico counterpart and features great shops in shady courtyards.

But this town is an upscale arts and crafts center near Oak Creek, with boutiques, galleries, and restaurants. Although you'll find a few, there's no T-shirt-and-ashtray mentality here. It's been planned so that no shop competes with another, thus you won't see endless rows of the same merchandise. The series of small pathways and graceful arches, with individual courtyards shaded by huge sycamores, create a village feeling. Seasonal vendors and farmers offer fruits, baked goods, fresh flowers, organic vegetables, and even homemade dog biscuits; mid-July–Oct., Sat., 7:00 A.M.–noon. Most shops are open daily, 10:00 A.M.–5:00 P.M. Located adjacent to Los Abrigados Resort just south of the "Y" on Hwy. 179 in Sedona. P.O. Box 1868, Sedona, 86339; 520-282-4838, fax 520-282-4805.

Tours

AERIAL TOURS

Skydance Helicopter Tours

Swoop into canyons, past Indian ruins and near

formations like Bell Rock and Kachina Woman. Or, venture further into the shadowy depths of the Grand Canyon. Bell Jet Ranger helicopters allow maximum viewing. Passengers can communicate with headsets and microphones. Want to impress someone big time? The 'copter gently sets you on a private mesa for a romantic meal with white linens, crystal, and silver. Adventures are recorded on video that you can purchase (complete with your spoken comments) at the end of the trip. **1225 Airport Rd., Sedona 86336; 800-882-1651 or 520-282-1651. Website: www.sedona.net/fun/skydance.**

Northern Light Balloon Expeditions

Seeing the red rocks from above may be even more spectacular than from ground level. Colors take on a different dimension, and formations have new shapes. Best of all, the ride is quiet, the stillness interrupted only by the occasional blast of the propane burner. Hotel pickup and return. **P.O. Box 1695, Sedona, 86339; 800-230-6222 or 520-282-2274.**

Where to Stay

Resorts and Inns

Enchantment Resort—$$$$

Breakfast on your patio as you gaze up at magnificent red rock formations, hiking secluded trails, and spotting brightly colored birds among the pines are part of the Enchantment experience. Luxury accommodations range from casita guestrooms to two-bedroom haciendas at this 4-star, 4-diamond property. Our favorite is the casita parlor, with a beehive fireplace in a small living room and a huge bath with deep-soaking tub. By the end of 2000, the new Mii Amo spa will be complete. Separate from the resort, with its own guest accommodations, restaurants, and activities, the spa will offer many unusual treatments incorporating healing rituals of Native Americans. The Southwest-inspired cuisine of chef Kevin

Maguire is a perfect complement to the setting. Located in Boynton Canyon, a spectacular, lovely niche among the red rocks, about 15 minutes from downtown Sedona. **515 Boynton Canyon Rd., Sedona 86336; 800-826-4180 or 520-282-9249. Website: www.enchantment resort.com.**

L'Auberge de Sedona—$$$$

This classic country French inn is in the center of downtown, but fronts on Oak Creek so that you feel secluded and in a most romantic setting. Creekside cottages are the ultimate in privacy. Lodge rooms have king canopy beds, and orchard rooms have panoramic views of Oak Creek Canyon. You need to come here more than once to figure out which accommodation is your favorite. Ask about packages that combine a stay with dining at L'Auberge (see Where to Eat). **301 L'Auberge Ln., Sedona 86339; 520-282-1661 or 800-272-6777. Website: www.lauberge.com.**

Los Abrigados Resort & Spa—$$$$

Part of the charm of this timeshare, which also welcomes overnight guests, is that everything is right here—spa facilities; fine restaurants (see Where to Eat); comfortable rooms with microwaves, small refrigerators, and coffeemakers; and shopping next door at Tlaquepaque. Some rooms have patio spa tubs for bubbling under the stars. If it has a fault, it's that a few rooms are a bit claustrophobic because the patio looks out onto an enclosed area. When booking, ask about the view. Located just south of the "Y" on Hwy. 179. **160 Portal Ln., Sedona, 86336; 520-282-1777 or 800-521-3131.**

Southwest Inn at Sedona—$$$$

The Santa Fe-style inn offers a picturesque red-rock setting and all the civilized accouterments you'd expect—fireplaces, phones, modem jacks, refrigerators, coffeemakers, hair dryers, decks, and patios. Plus a pool and continental breakfast. The inn partners with the Verde Canyon Railway on accommodations and train packages. **3250 W. Hwy. 89A, Sedona, 86336;**

800-483-7422 or 520-282-3344. Website: www.swinn.com.

Apple Orchard Inn—$$$–$$$$

If b-and-bs sometimes have more togetherness than you're looking for, Sedona's newest certainly fixes the problem. The Apple Orchard Inn, located a few blocks off Sedona's main street, is like a tiny resort. A small plunge pool sits on a deck with gorgeous mountain views. All seven luxury rooms have private patios, refrigerators, jacuzzi tubs, phones, and TV/VCRs. Three-course breakfasts, prepared by a professional chef, often include eggs Benedict with Canadian bacon, freshly baked rolls, and lighter fare on request. **656 Jordan Rd., Sedona 86336; 520-282-5328 or 800-663-6968.** Website: www.appleorchardbb.com.

Doubletree Sedona Resort—$$$–$$$$

This new hostelry sits in desert-colored splendor along Hwy. 179 before you get into the heart of the village of Sedona. All rooms are suites, with minibars, microwaves, fireplaces, and coffee facilities. The decidedly upscale Grill at ShadowRock features a healthful, light California menu that includes a fabulous grilled ancho chile honey-glazed salmon. **90 Ridge Trail Dr., Sedona, 86351; 520-284-4040 or 800-222-TREE.** Website: www.doubletree hotels.com.

Hostels

Hostel Sedona—$

Just behind Los Abrigados Resort, you'll find Hostel Sedona. It offers 12 bunks, two private rooms, a communal kitchen, a chore list, and storage for gear. Wheelchair-accessible. Conveniently located less than a mile from downtown Sedona. From Hwy. 179 south of the "Y," take Ranger Rd. to Brewer Rd., go left, then take another immediate left into the hostel. From Hwy. 89A west of uptown Sedona, take Brewer Rd. south past Ranger Rd; take the next left into the hostel. **5 Soldiers Wash Dr., Sedona, 86336; 520-282-2772.**

Camping

Lo Lo Mai Springs Outdoor Resort

This pleasant 26-acre park hugs Oak Creek for almost a mile, with shaded RV sites that have patios and full hookups. Tenters can set up camp in secluded sites at the edge of the creek. There are rest rooms, swimming pool and spa, showers and laundry, a convenience store, and a clubhouse. Hiking trails radiate out from the park in a number of directions. Located 9 miles southwest of Sedona. Take Hwy. 89A southwest from Sedona toward Cottonwood. Approximately 8 miles from Sedona, go left on the Page Springs–McGuireville turnoff (Hwy. 50). Continue approximately 1 mile to the entrance. **11505 Lo Lo Mai Rd., Page Springs, 86325; 520-634-4700.**

Rancho Sedona Mobilodge

Along Oak Creek, this luxury 10-acre park has 82 full hookups, large shade trees, access to the creek, rest rooms, showers, and laundry facilities. The park is close enough to downtown Sedona and Tlaquepaque that you can walk, and a free shuttle runs 8:00 A.M.–10:00 P.M. For a premium price you can have a large executive site on the creek. Exit Hwy. 179 at Schnebly Hill Rd. and turn left onto Rancho Sedona. **135 Bear Wallow Ln., Sedona, 86336; 520-282-7255 or 888-641-4261.**

Where to Eat

Yavapai Restaurant (at Enchantment)— $$$–$$$$

It's worth a drive from Phoenix to explore the area, then linger over lunch at this spectacular resort. Outdoor tables in the shadow of Boynton Canyon showcase the Southwest-style cuisine of chef Kevin Maguire. A jazz brunch on Sunday is a local favorite. Reservations strongly suggested. Located **at Enchantment Resort in Boynton Canyon,** about 15 minutes from downtown Sedona. **800-826-4180 or 520-282-2900.** Website: www.enchantmentresort.com.

L'Auberge Restaurant—$$$$

Some folks don't consider a visit to Sedona complete unless they eat at this fine restaurant, whose reputation is no exaggeration. The six-course prix fixe menu is created weekly, and there also is an a la carte menu. Open Mon.–Sat. 7:30 A.M.–10:00 P.M.; Sun. 7:00 A.M.–3:00 P.M. and 6:00–10:00 P.M. **301 L'Auberge Ln.; 520-282-1661.** Website: www.lauberge.com.

Rene at Tlaquepaaque—$$$–$$$$

Exceptionally charming restaurant with lace curtains and plush banquettes provides outstanding dining in a casual atmosphere. Continental cuisine and American favorites are admirably created by chef Walter Paulson. Try the crusted salmon salad or crepes pompadour for a memorable lunch. Open daily, 11:30 A.M.–2:30 P.M. and 5:30 P.M.–8:30 P.M. Located **in Tlaquepaque arts and crafts village. 520-282-9225.**

Joey Bistro—$$$

You might not immediately catch on to the significance of this friendly Italian place's name until you realize that the huge photos on the walls are all famous Joeys—Joe DiMaggio, Joe Bonano, Josef Stalin. The menu is definitely a notch or two above your average Italian fare, featuring interesting pastas combined with vegetables, fish, and meat in pleasing blends. Open daily, 5:00 P.M.–varying closing times. Located at Los Abrigados Resort. **160 Portal Ln.; 520-204-JOEY.**

Robert's Creekside Cafe & Grill—$$–$$$

This is a delightful lunch or dinner stop. As you munch your aubergine and goat cheese, spicy Ruben or veggie wrap, keep in mind that the fruit cobbler has won awards. From the shady patio or a window table, take time to find the supine Snoopy, outlined in the red rocks directly in your line of sight. Robert's is just below the "Y" on the right as you enter Sedona on Hwy. 179. Open Sun.–Thurs., 8:00 A.M.–9:00 P.M.; Fri.–Sat., 8:00 A.M.–10:00 P.M. **251 Hwy. 179; 520-282-3671.**

WenDeli's Delicatessen—$$

They'll pack a picnic to take to the red rocks. Specialties are fruit salad and generous sub sandwiches with all the trimmings. Open daily, 8:00 A.M.–4:00 P.M. Located in uptown Sedona. **276 N. Hwy. 89A, No. B.; 520-282-7313.**

Services

Innhouse Video & Cybercafe

Computer rentals at $9 per hour. **160 A Coffee Pot Dr., Sedona, 86336; 520-282-7368.** Website: www.innhousevideo.com.

Sedona–Oak Creek Canyon Chamber of Commerce

This large tourism office is well staffed and well stocked with just about all the information you need to enjoy the area. Open Mon.–Sat., 8:30 A.M.–5:00 P.M.; Sun., 9:00 A.M.–3:00 P.M. Located **on the town's main drag. P.O. Box 478, Sedona, 86639; 800-288-7336 or 520-282-7722.** Websites: www.arizonaguide. com/sedona or www.sedona chamber. com.

Prescott

Pine-scented air and Arizona history characterize this mile-high city. At 5,374 feet above sea level, it sits comfortably in one of the largest stands of ponderosa pine in the world, on the craggy slopes and in the gentle foothills of the Bradshaw Mountains. Thumb Butte, the town landmark, stands sentrylike in the background. Surrounded by more than a million acres of national forest and the 1,400-acre Yavapai Indian Reservation, Prescott is a cool retreat from Arizona's low-desert heat. During summer months, it fills with folks from Phoenix in an escape mode.

Prescott adopted the slogan "Everybody's Hometown," and it definitely has that feeling. Transplanted Midwesterners, many of whom have arrived via California, especially identify with the town square and Victorian homes. More relics of earlier times are found in the antiques and collectibles shops, most of which are located on Cortez between Gurley St. and Sheldon. Prescott is in a growth pattern, partially because of an influx of retirees over the last decade, but three institutions of higher learning—Yavapai College, Prescott College, and Embry Riddle Aeronautical University—attract young people as well.

History

The country's attention was turned to Prescott when gold was discovered in 1838, followed by another big strike in 1861. Then-president Abraham Lincoln saw it as a source of funding for the North during the Civil War, and in 1864 created the Arizona Territory. Prescott is named for historian William Hickling Prescott. Believing the area's Indian ruins were of Aztec origin, the founding fathers named the city streets—Montezuma, Cortez, Alarcon—after figures chronicled in Prescott's book on Mexico. It was the state capital until November 1, 1867, when that honor shifted to Tucson. The capital moved briefly back to Prescott before Phoenix permanently garnered the title in January 1899. At one time Prescott was named Granite for the large deposits of this attractive building stone just north of the city. In 1900 much of Prescott, mainly wood-frame buildings, went up in smoke when an inebriated miner knocked over a kerosene lamp in a lodging house. So what you see now are mostly post-turn-of-the-century buildings.

Prescott Transit Authority (520-778-7978) provides transportation to Sky Harbor International Airport in Phoenix, 102 miles south. From Prescott Municipal Airport there is scheduled passenger service to Phoenix on America West Express.

Major Attractions

Arcosanti

This unusual "city" is located at Cordes Junction, about 23 miles east of Prescott. "An Urban Laboratory," says the large brown sign at the property entrance. Off to the right, over rolling prairie, a group of unimpressive buildings snugs

To get to the complex, **take Hwy. 69 east from Prescott to Cordes Junction (exit 252 from I-17).** Skip the McDonald's and the Subway at this exit in favor of the bakery and cafeteria at Arcosanti, which have more interesting fare. **Following the Arcosanti signs, you'll reach a 2.5-mile stretch of dirt road that takes 15 minutes to cover** because of its washboarded condition. Proceed slowly and you'll be okay. You can browse the gift shop at no charge, but there is a charge for tours. Tours daily, on the hour, 10:00 A.M.–4:00 P.M. Cafeteria open daily, noon–3:00 P.M.; bakery open daily, 9:00 A.M.–4:00 P.M. Arcosanti is closed Thanksgiving and Christmas Day. **HC 74, Box 4136, Mayer, 86333 (mailing address); 520-632-7135, 520-254-5309 from Phoenix. Website: www.arcosanti.org/.**

Festivals and Events

Frontier Days

Fourth of July weekend
Home of the oldest continuous rodeo in the United States, going strong since July 4, 1888, and now held at the Yavapai County Fairgrounds, Prescott pulls out all the stops for this celebration. It begins with a parade that attracts entries from around the state. Another big draw is the arts and crafts show, along with food booths, in Courthouse Plaza. There's also a carnival with typical rides and a truly fine fireworks display on the Fourth. As many as 100,000 people attend this annual event, so if you're even thinking of going, get campground or hotel reservations early. If you can't find a place, call the **Prescott Chamber of Commerce (520-445-2000)** for a list of available options.

Arizona Cowboy Poets Gathering

mid-Aug.
Cowboys have a tradition of writing, reciting, and singing about the lives they lead. Held annually for more than a decade, the event promotes that tradition and gets bigger every year as more and

into the desert landscape. But appearances are deceiving, and it soon becomes apparent that this futuristic site, as planned by Italian architect Paolo Soleri, is truly a combination of architecture and ecology. "Arcology," as he calls it, purposes to create new urban habitats. It was begun in 1970 and so far is less than 5 percent complete. When finished, this prototype will house 6,000 residents in compact structures on 25 acres of a 4,000-acre preserve. You approach Arcosanti from the back, so it is only when you take the one-hour tour (the only way you're allowed to walk around the grounds) that you get a sense of Soleri's vision. Many of the multi-function buildings are apses (quarter-circles), allowing them to be warmed by the sun in winter but shielded in summer. Tours begin at the visitor center, which presents artwork and an explanation of Arcosanti. The lower tier houses a cafeteria and bakery. The tour takes visitors past a ceramics studio and a foundry where Soleri wind-bells are forged to help fund the project. At any given time about 100 students and workshop participants are in residence. A limited number of rather spartan rooms and one apartment may be rented for overnight stays. They're popular with guests who come for the musical events scheduled May–Oct. Among the most popular, the light and sound show is projected onto a natural mesa that faces Arcosanti.

more poets come together to share their music, stories, and love of the West. If you've ever wanted to pen an ode, you can attend free workshops that help you get in the spirit of writing while you pick up tips from established, acclaimed poets. In the evening, top-name western entertainers perform. Held at **Sharlot Hall Museum, 415 W. Gurley St., Prescott, 86301; 520-445-3122.**

Faire on the Square

Labor Day weekend
Close to 200 of the best handcrafters in the Southwest show up for this event. It is Prescott's premier arts and crafts show, and is juried so you know that the best of the best are represented. Many people come up from Phoenix for the day, not only to enjoy cooler weather but also to buy Christmas gifts. Held **in Courthouse Plaza. 800-266-7534.**

Outdoor Activities

Prescott National Forest is the area's biggest recreational draw. Lakes, hiking trails, campsites, and an equestrian facility are all within minutes of Prescott. The forest covers more than 1.25 million acres, most of which is accessible to varying degrees year-round.

Golf

Even though Prescott gets a light dusting of snow most winters, courses usually are playable all year.

Antelope Hills

It has two 18-hole municipal golf courses, one ranked fifth in the state among public courses. The 6,778-yard North course has challenged golfers since 1956 with its unforgiving par 72 fairways that wind through stands of cottonwoods, elms, spruce, and poplars. The South course, 7,014 yards playing to a par 72, is a putter's trial, giving anyone's short game a real workout. A full-service restaurant and bar, driving range, and complete pro shop are on-site.

1 **Perkins Dr., Prescott, 86301; 800-972-6818 or 520-776-7888.**

Hiking

Fall and spring are the recommended seasons for hiking because they tend to be cool and dry. Keep in mind that you're in the mountains, and on any given hike the elevation change can make a huge difference in temperatures. Some trails have elevational changes of more than 3,000 feet, and temperatures can vary from the mid-50s to below freezing with a foot of snow, all in the same day. For all trails listed below except the Ackerman, contact the **Bradshaw Ranger District (520-445-7253)** for maps and more information.

Ackerman Memorial Park Trail

This easy loop trail takes about an hour, covers about 3 miles, and passes through rolling hillside with a few great views. At the start you have the choice of going to the picnic area to your right, from where you can follow a rough, rocky creek bed, or taking the main trail on the left that winds up Old Water Tank Hill, elevation 5,605 feet, for a good view. When you return to your car, if you're into old cemeteries, drive down the dirt road another 0.3 mile, and you'll end up at the International Order of Odd Fellows cemetery, where graves date to the late 1800s. To reach the trailhead, **from Gurley St. take Virginia St. east about 0.4 mile. The road dead-ends at the trailhead,** where there is limited parking.

Aspen Creek Trail

Rated easy and offering scenic Prescott-area views, this 2.2-mile trail begins about 30 minutes out of Prescott and takes about one and a half hours one way. It overlooks Spruce Mountain, Mount Union, and the Wilhoit area. Climbing sharply from Copper Basin Rd., it is used most frequently by hikers, but is open to mountain bikes and equestrians as well. If you hike it in summer, expect extreme heat and come prepared with adequate water. **From Prescott take Montezuma St. (Hwy. 89) south 1.1** miles to Copper Basin Rd. Turn right on Copper Basin Rd. and continue for approximately 4.7 miles to the trailhead on the left.

Thumb Butte Trail

This heavily used hikers-only trail, just 10 minutes/2.5 miles from downtown Prescott, is a good way to get acquainted with hiking in the area. Interpretive signs identify plant life, and directional signs keep you on the right path. Rated moderate for the steep climb to a ridge below Thumb Butte, it is 1.4 miles long and takes about 45 minutes one way. The trailhead is at the Thumb Butte recreation site. **Take Gurley St. west for 2.5 miles to Thumb Butte Rd. and continue for 1.5 miles to the site.** Toilets and picnic tables are just across the road from the trailhead.

Horseback Riding

Groom Creek Loop Trail

This 9-mile loop is a good day ride, passing through one of the most impressive stands of ponderosa pine in the forest. A horsecamp exclusively for mounted campers is located just south of Groom Creek, where most riders access the trail. The trail follows forested areas almost entirely, climbing to the top of Spruce Mountain, then returning via a 4-mile downhill back to the Groom Creek area and the camp. It is approximately **6.5 miles south of Prescott on Senator Hwy., which becomes Forest Rd. 52.**

Woodchute Trail

In the Chino Valley Ranger District, bulldozers making way for cattle watering tanks on Woodchute Mountain built this trail, now open only to hikers and equestrians. In the late 1800s miners from the town of Jerome got their shoring timbers for the mines from Woodchute Mountain, cutting all the ponderosa pine, so that the trees you see growing here now all are second growth. The trail, not recommended for winter use because it often is clogged with snow, climbs 2.75 miles from the south trailhead to the top of Woodchute Mountain and continues an additional 3.5 miles down on

the north side. It can be accessed from the **Potato Patch Campground just east of the summit on Hwy. 89A.**

Seeing and Doing

Art Museums and Galleries

Phippen Museum

A bonus to visiting this picturesquely sited museum is driving through landscape that is rough with massive boulders that make up the Granite Dells. This rambling, rustic ranchhouse-like gallery features art of the American West. Historic western paintings as well as those by contemporary artists are featured. The permanent collection features the bronzes and paintings of George Phippen, who founded the Cowboy Artists of America. Changing exhibits touch on historical themes, as did a recent show on early transportation in Arizona, and on specific artists and their work. It also houses historic artifacts. Small fee. Open Wed.–Sat. and Mon., 10:00 A.M.–4:00 P.M.; Sun., 1:00 P.M.–4:00 P.M. Located 6 miles from downtown Prescott. **4701 Hwy. 89 N., Prescott, 86301; 520-778-1385.**

Museums and Historic Sites

Courthouse Plaza

Prescott's white granite courthouse, surrounded by shady elm trees, statues, and thoughtfully placed benches, is the centerpiece of a true town square, reflecting the Midwestern and New England heritage of many of Prescott's first residents. At one entrance, a statue of local hero Rough Rider Buckey O'Neill greets visitors. O'Neill served as sheriff of Yavapai County, then mayor of Prescott, a position he resigned to enlist for the Spanish-American War. On July 2, 1898, he was fatally wounded on San Juan Hill. A statue called "Cowboy at Rest" reminds guests of the area's western heritage. A plaque tells of Prescott's founding in 1864 on Granite Creek, a source of placer gold. The original courthouse was erected in the plaza during Prescott's days as the state's territorial capital. When it burned in the early 1900s, the present white-columned capitol was built to serve as the seat of government for Yavapai County.

Mount Vernon St.

Along this elegant street, locust trees shade carefully restored Victorian homes that tell of a time when bright entrepreneurs saw money to be made in farming and sheep herding. Many homes were built as badges of their success. They are part of Prescott's Last Territorial Period, which began in 1900 immediately after the fire of 1900 destroyed 11 blocks in the center of the city. The last homes of this period were built about 1912. Many now are charming bed-and-breakfast inns. You can see a number of them along Mount Vernon St. as well as on S. Pleasant.

Sharlot Hall

At this skillfully re-created living-history museum, docents relate tales of early Prescott as they point out artifacts from settler days. The museum is actually a group of historic buildings clustered together in a gardenlike setting. Spread across 3 acres, exhibits explore the Arizona Territory in the 1860s. The 1877 William C. Bashford House serves as the gift shop. An 1864 governor's mansion, built of ponderosa pine logs, and the 1875 John C. Fremont House show how the fifth territorial governor lived. Central to the grounds is an unusual windmill, built in the 1870s in Springfield, Ohio, and freighted via train to Prescott.

The grounds are planted with old-time flowers that include hollyhocks, columbine, and daisies. The Territorial Women's Memorial Rose Garden is filled with a fragrant collection of "antique" as well as newly developed rose varieties. It is dedicated to women born before 1900, who lived in Arizona before 1912, and who were part of the state's development. Near Fort Misery, the oldest log building associated with the territory of Arizona, a kitchen garden flourishes with beans, tomatoes, beets, and other vegetables that were summer staples more than 100 years ago. The museum is named for its founder, Sharlot

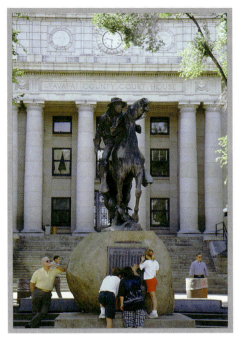

In Prescott's Courthouse Plaza, a statue of Rough Rider Buckey O'Neill greets visitors.

Mabridth Hall, a poet and historian with a passion for preserving Arizona history. Her efforts to save the territorial Governor's Mansion grew into the movement created in the museum campus that exists today. Small donation requested. Open Apr.–Oct., Mon.–Sat., 10:00 A.M.–5:00 P.M., and Sun., 1:00 P.M.–5:00 P.M.; Nov.–Mar., Tue.–Sat., 10:00 A.M.–4:00 P.M., and Sun., 1:00 P.M.–5:00 P.M. Archives open Tue.–Fri., 10:00 A.M.–5:00 P.M.; Sat., 10:00 A.M.–2:00 P.M. Closed Thanksgiving, Christmas, and New Year's Day. 415 **Gurley St., Prescott, 86301; 520-445-3122. Website: www.sharlot.org.**

Smoki Museum

This worthwhile museum looks like an Indian pueblo. Since its opening in 1935, it has preserved collections of pre-Columbian and contemporary pottery, as well as jewelry of shell, stone, and turquoise. Its most unusual feature, its construction of native stone and wood, includes pine logs used for columns, vigas, and *latillas* and for door and window enclosures. On your right as you enter is a display showing how a piece of pottery, found in shards, is reconstructed to remain authentic. A Hopi-style kiva is the museum's centerpiece. Even the reception desk is sandstone, built in place after the museum opened. Don't bother trying to identify the Smoki tribe. The word was created in the 1930s by a group of non–Native American professionals who set out to preserve Native American culture, dances, and artifacts. They considered themselves much like the Moose, Elks, or any other philanthropic group. Open May–Sept., Mon.–Tue. and Thu.–Sat., 10:00 A.M.–4:00 P.M.; Sun., 1:00 P.M.–4:00 P.M. **147 N. Arizona St., P.O. Box 10224, Prescott, 86304; 520-445-1230.**

Whiskey Row

During the late 1800s, the block facing Courthouse Plaza on the west included 20 saloons and restaurants where hard-driving miners and cowboys came to enjoy booze, food, and ladies of the evening. If you stand near the courthouse and look across Montezuma St. to face this once-notorious block, you can easily see the remnants of those days. The **Palace Hotel (120 S. Montezuma)** was destroyed except for its ornate back bar, which had come to San Francisco by ship and was then laboriously transported overland by wagon. When fire broke out, reverent patrons picked up the bar and carried it across the street to Courthouse Plaza. The **St. Michael Hotel,** built in the Second Renaissance Revival style, replaced a smaller hotel built in 1890. The **chamber of commerce (520-445-2000)** has an excellent brochure for $1 that outlines a walking tour of historic downtown buildings. It has detailed pen-and-ink sketches of many, and paragraphs about their architectural style and history.

Seasonal Favorites

Young's Farm

In Dewey just east of Prescott, this working farm has something going on all year. The produce barn opens the first weekend in July. Just-picked sweet corn is available through Sept. You choose your own ears from large wagons, loaded in the fields and brought to the barn. Melons start in early July, and by late that month green beans are in. Home canners come here to stock up. In the fall the farm is a pumpkin center, and around the holidays fresh turkey and ham are the attraction. Produce prices are not much less than at supermarkets, but you always are assured of absolute freshness. A general store stocks kitchen gadgets, canned jams and jellies, handcrafted items, and more. Kids like the petting zoo with its gentle cows, goats, and other farm animals. The farm restaurant serves up basic fare in generous portions. Craft barn and critter corral open daily, 9:00 A.M.–4:00 P.M. Restaurant and store open daily, 7:00 A.M.–6:00 P.M. **Located at Hwys. 69 and 169 east of Prescott. Watch for the sign. P.O. Box 147, Dewey, 86327; 520-632-7272. Website: www.youngsfarminc.com.**

Scenic Drives

Prescott to Crown King

The 40 miles from Prescott to Crown King wind from Mount Vernon St. to Senator Hwy.—a lovely drive if you have a high-clearance vehicle. It's difficult to believe that this primitive road, carved out among the piñon and ponderosa, once was a main stagecoach route. About 7 miles from Prescott, the pavement ends near campgrounds and an equestrian camp. You then pass the ruins of the old Senator Mine on the north side of Mount Union, one of the richest sources of gold ore in the 1860s. At Palace Station you'll find a log cabin stage stop, now on the National Register of Historic Places. You should be able to get a historical brochure here if you get out to stretch your legs. In 22 miles from Palace Station is Crown King, with a small cafe, general store, and gas station. You might want to stop for a rest here, 40 miles from Prescott. After Crown King you go through the ghost town of Bumble Bee. From here graded dirt and paved county roads follow a winding route out of the mountains, heading to I-17. From the interstate you can loop back to Prescott, or follow it south to Phoenix. As you travel south along I-17, you're following one of the earlier major highways in Arizona, still called the Black Canyon Freeway by many. It is the main north-south thoroughfare for the central part of the state. The scenery includes flat-topped mesas and low, craggy mountains, all of which were mined in one way or another.

FOUR-WHEEL-DRIVE TRIPS

Bradshaw Backcountry Tours

If time is limited and you want to see some of the Prescott National Forest and surrounding territory, a four-wheel-drive tour can be the best way to do it. Bradshaw has jaunts from two hours to all day, taking in pine forests, great views, and history. Guides are well versed in local lore. Operates during summer only, usually Apr.–Oct. 520-445-3032.

Shopping

Bashford Court

This three-level atrium mall is filled with interesting shops and boutiques. A favorite, **The Raven (on first floor)** purveys Poe memorabilia and writing paraphernalia, including cards, pens, stationery, and other fun stuff. If you collect Christmas tree ornaments, don't miss the **Mountain Christmas shop (just across from Prescott Brewing Company). Across Gurley St. from the courthouse.**

Wagering

On the Yavapai Indian Reservation within the Prescott Resort, unintimidating **Bucky's Casino (520-776-5695)** offers 5-cent, 25-cent, and $1 slots as well as video poker machines; permitted because the resort is on the reservation. Open 24 hours. Located **at Hwy. 69 and Heather Heights.** For even more slots (175, to be precise), head to the **Yavapai Gaming Center (520-445-5767)** and its 150-seat bingo hall. Located **across Hwy. 69.**

Where to Stay

Because Prescott is such a popular vacation destination, you'll find ample lodging in all price ranges.

Bed-and-Breakfasts

Pleasant Street Inn—$$$–$$$$

Built in 1906, this sleek blue Victorian was moved to its present site in 1990, just a swing ahead of the wrecking ball that would have demolished it to make room for a new police station. It has four rooms, two of which are suites that can accommodate up to four guests. A full or continental breakfast is served in the dining room or on the covered porch. 142 S. Pleasant St., Prescott, 86303; 520-445-4774 or 877-226-7128. Website: www.cwdesigners.com/pleasantstreet.

Prescott Pines Inn—$$$–$$$$

Out a way from most of the other b-and-bs, this inn includes a 1902 two-story main house and five guest houses for a total of 12 rooms, some with gas fireplaces. Some rooms have small refrigerators and microwaves, some have complete kitchens. This is not a true b-and-b because breakfast is not included (for a small charge, a huge breakfast is available by reservation), but coffee, tea, juice, and an endless jar of chocolate chip cookies always are at hand. Kitchen rooms open onto a flagstone patio with a barbecue grill, shade trees, and an abundance of songbirds. A large chalet also is available. Located 1.3 miles south of Courthouse Plaza on Hwy. 89 S., on the east side of town at the edge of the Prescott National Forest. 901 White Spar Rd. (Hwy. 89 S.), Prescott, 86303; 520-445-7270 or 800-541-5374. Website: www.prescottpinesinn.com.

Rocamadour—$$$–$$$$

In the scenic Granite Dells 4 miles north of Prescott, this b-and-b has some of the elements of Chenonceau as well as a decidedly Southwest ambiance. Rocamadour, meaning "rock lover"

From the Phippen Museum visitors are treated to a dramatic view of the Granite Dells near Prescott.

in French, reflects the background of owners Mike and Twila Coffey who operated the Chateau de Trucy in Burgundy. Rocamadour is decorated with gorgeous antiques and offers four guest rooms that cater to adults who are looking for privacy in scenic surroundings. One room has an onyx whirlpool tub, a cottage has a hot tub and deck, and a suite has a fireplace, full kitchen, and patio so you can settle in for extended periods. Full breakfasts are served in a French country-style dining room. An elegant crystal chandelier hangs over the table, and a baby grand piano occupies one corner. It's definitely classy, without a trace of snobbery. A favorite early-morning guest activity is a challenging 15-minute hike up the rock trail that faces the inn. The reward at the top is an expansive view of Willow Lake. The Coffeys say they do not typically accept kids or pets, but you could ask; it may depend on who the other guests are at the time. This is a place best savored as a twosome. **3386 N. Hwy. 89, Prescott, 86301; 888-771-1933 or 520-771-1933. Website: www. arizona-bandbs.com.**

Hotels and Resorts

Hassayampa Inn—$$$–$$$$

The state's hot weather gave this inn its beginnings. In the pre-air-conditioned 1920s, as Phoenix developed into a metropolis, its most affluent citizens sought relief from the soaring summer temperatures in the Valley of the Sun. Mile-high Prescott, an easy day's drive north, was the destination for many. City fathers soon saw the need for a luxury hotel to accommodate these visitors, and in 1927 the Hassayampa Inn became a reality. Named for the nearby Hassayampa River, the new four-story building immediately lived up to its purpose, delighting guests with its elegant lobby and porte cochere. But by the mid-1950s the hotel had become run-down as it competed with newer inns with more modern amenities. In 1986 the Hassayampa underwent a complete renovation, with air-conditioning and new furnishings added. Today 68 refurbished rooms and a restored lobby return it to its status as Prescott's grand dame of hotels. The lobby is decorated in the original art deco style, and an old-fashioned elevator takes guests to upper floors. For a possible taste of the supernatural, ask for balcony suite No. 428. Past guests and housekeepers swear they've seen the ghost of Faith, a young woman who was spending her honeymoon at the hotel the first year it opened. Her new groom dashed out to get a pack of cigarettes and never returned. The distraught Faith hanged herself, and some say her spirit lingers there today. **122 E. Gurley, Prescott, 86301; 800-322-1927 or 520-778-9434. Website: www.hassayampainn.com**

Hotel Vendome—$$$–$$$$

Small and elegant, its two stories hold 17 rooms and four suites. Built in 1917 and renovated in 1994, the hotel retains its yesteryear charm with a wide white-railed front porch and tales of a resident ghost. Rooms all have cable TV and private baths, some with claw-foot tubs. Guests can order wine and beer at the hand-carved cherry-wood bar, where a large continental breakfast also is served. **320 S. Cortez, Prescott, 86303; 520-776-0900. Website: www.vendomehotel.com.**

Prescott Resort—$$$–$$$$

On a bluff overlooking forests and granite mountains, the resort contains Bucky's Casino (see Wagering). Paintings and sculptures by nationally recognized local artists give a gallery feel to the resort's public areas. It has a pool and workout facilities. Rooms have refrigerators and coffeemakers, and some have balconies with great views. The 180-degree vistas looking out over the city from the hotel restaurant, the Thumb Butte Room, make it a favorite local dining spot. **1500 Hwy. 69, Prescott, 86304; 800-967-4637 or 520-776-1666. Website: www.prescottresort.com.**

Forest Villas—$$$

This lovely hotel looks far more expensive than it is. The elegant lobby has a grand staircase that's truly worthy of the name, yet somehow you don't feel out of place shouldering your backpack and treading up to the second floor in your Reboks (there is an elevator). Rooms are large and comfortable with small balconies just big enough to enjoy the morning coffee you brewed with your in-room coffeemaker. Most rooms have gorgeous mountain views. The expansive continental breakfast includes Danish, bagels, muffins, toast, cereal, fruit, coffee and juice, and more. The lobby champagne bar offers favorite vintages and top-notch bubbly, as well as mixed drinks. From the heated pool you look up at the mountains. One of the hotel's most convenient features is an underground parking garage from which an elevator takes you to your floor. Located 4 miles east of Courthouse Plaza on Hwy. 69 at the Lee Blvd. stoplight—convenient if you're coming from Phoenix. At the light at Lee Circle, look up to your right and you'll see the hotel. The entrance is another 200 yards ahead on your right. **3645 Lee Cir., Prescott, 86301; 800-223-3449 or 520-717-1200. Website: www.forestvillas.com.**

Hotel St. Michael—$$–$$$

Built in 1900 on old Whiskey Row and now on the National Register of Historic Places, this turn-of-the-century hotel's gargoyles are said to be purposely ugly. Each was named after one of the county commissioners at the time, who refused to allow the hotel's builder to erect a structure higher than three stories, the height restriction imposed by building codes then in effect. Although never quite achieving the luxury that its builder aspired to, it is comfortable and up-to-date, thanks to a number of restorations. Located directly across from Courthouse Plaza, within walking distance of museums, shops, and restaurants. The hotel lobby opens onto a series of shops themed to the 1900s. To be sure your room looks out at the square and not at a brick wall, request a courthouse view when booking. A continental breakfast is included. **205 W. Gurley, Prescott, 86301; 800-678-3757 or 520-776-1999, fax 520-776-7318.**

Camping

There is camping at **Lynx Lake** Apr. 1–Nov. 15 and at **White Spar** year-round, although there is no water in winter. For reservations, call the **National Forest Reservation Center (800-280-2267)** at least 10 days in advance. **Granite Basin Campground,** open year-round, sits on the edge of a very small lake that usually has plenty of crappies and sunfish. The setting, amid a forest of boulders, makes it seem private and protected. **Take Iron Springs Rd. about 4 miles north of Prescott, and turn north on Forest Rd. 374.** At **Indian Creek,** open May 15–Sept. 30, and Granite Basin, camping is first-come, first-served.

Orchard RV Ranch

One of you must be 55 or older to stay in this attractive mobile home and RV park, formerly called Rafter Eleven. It has ample spaces with picnic tables shaded by cottonwood trees. It's okay if you have your grandkids with you, but not permanently. It attracts a lot of full-timers, with longer stays the norm, but during the off-season it often is possible to get in for just a night or two. Located in Dewey, 12 miles east of Prescott (78 miles north of Phoenix) on Hwy. 69. **11250 E. Hwy. 69, Dewey, 86327; 520-772-8266.**

Point of Rocks RV Park

Spaces with full hookups for 96 RVs dot the pleasant grounds in the Granite Dells, shaded by cottonwoods and piñon pines. Located about a block from Watson Lake, the park has a laundry room and showers. The lake itself is much different from the steep-walled canyon lakes, and intrigues with its softly eroded rocks and explorable inlets. Located about 4 miles north of Prescott, just off Hwy. 89 about 0.25 mile north of Willow Lake Rd. **3025 N. Hwy. 89, Prescott, 86301; 520-445-9018. Website: www.northlink.com/~rhorsley.**

Willow Lake RV & Camping Park

This scenic park is located in the Granite Dells in the Heritage Park area north of Prescott. Willow Lake, dry for years, received a recent infusion of snowmelt that has filled it to its banks. Two hundred tree-shaded spaces are available with full hookups. Separate areas are set aside for tent camping and for guests with kids. A laundry room, showers, pool, and convenience store are on-site. From the junction of Hwys. 69 and 89, go 3.5 miles north on Hwy. 89, turn left onto Willow Lake Rd., and proceed 2.25 miles to Willow Creek Rd. Turn right and proceed 1.25 miles to Heritage Park Rd., turn right, and go 0.5 mile. **1617 Heritage Park Rd., Prescott, 86301-6010; 520-445-6311 or 800-940-2845.**

Where to Eat

Peacock Room—$$$–$$$$

Three-diamond cuisine in this lovely old dining room at the Hassayampa Inn is always a special occasion. Rich mahogany and flowered upholstery are restorations of its art deco beginnings in 1927. As you enter, just before the maitre d' station on the right, there's an old photo of how the dining room originally looked, with a lunch counter and solid wall where etched-glass panels now create an artistic focal point. The menu, a changing melange of continental and American styles, consistently wins awards. Open Mon.–Sat., 7:00 A.M.–2 P.M. and 5 P.M.–9:00 P.M.; Sun. 7:00 A.M.–1:00 P.M. and 5 P.M.–9:00 P.M. **122 E. Gurley St.; 520-778-9434.**

The Palace—$$–$$$

On Whiskey Row, this historic bar and one-time hotel specializes in steaks and seafood in very large quantities. The original establishment opened in 1877, then burned in the 1900 fire, but the ornately carved 1880s Brunswick bar survived and is used today in the Palace, rebuilt in 1901. Recently extensively remodeled, it traces history in framed photos and clippings that line the walls. Fare ranges from grilled roast beef and cheddar sandwiches for lunch, to barbecued ribs, T-bone steaks, salmon, and trout for dinner. It's worth a stop here just for a beer, to chat with friendly bartenders, and to take a leisurely look at the back bar that so narrowly escaped destruction. Open Sun.–Thurs., 11:00 A.M.–9:30 P.M.; Fri.–Sat., 11:00 A.M.–10:30 P.M. **120 S. Montezuma St.; 520-541-1996. Website: www.historicpalace.com.**

Prescott Brewing Company—$$

In Bashford Court, this award-winning micro-brewery turns out beers that have garnered honors at the Great American Beer Festival for a number of years. The staff will let you "journey down the path of production," if time allows and they're not in a brewing cycle. Before ordering from the menu, decide on your beer by ordering a selection of 4-ounce samples for under a buck each. At any given time they'll have their Lodgepole Light, Liquid Amber (our favorite), Prescott Pale Ale, and Petrified Porter, as well as a number of specialty beers. Kids love old-fashioned cream soda by the pitcher. The menu features exceptionally hearty burgers, sandwiches, pizzas, and inventive appetizers like stuffed mushrooms and artichoke hearts with beer mustard. The beer bread is decidedly not to be missed. Parking on the street may be hard to find, but there's a large parking lot behind the building, off Montezuma St. Open Sun.–Thurs., 11:00 A.M.–midnight (menu served until 10:00 P.M.); Fri.–Sat., 11:00 A.M.–1:00 A.M. (menu served until 11:00 P.M.). 130 W. Gurley St.; 520-771-2795. Website: www.prescottbrewingcompany.com.

Zuma's Woodfire Cafe—$$

As soon as you walk into this terra-cotta-colored Mediterranean-style building, you smell the fragrance of the pecan logs firing the ovens. If you sit in the lower dining room, you can watch the chefs shoveling pizzas in and out of the ovens, preparing salads, and cooking pasta. The copper-walled display kitchen is as much a part of Zuma's as its well-prepared food. Pizza, salad, and pasta make up the menu and might sound a bit humble. But clever items like Thai peanut and chicken pasta, penne vodka pasta, Peking duck pizza, and grilled albacore salad (ask for the albacore rare—it's delicious) take dishes well beyond the ordinary. The wine list has a good variety and is well priced. You can dine alfresco on either of two patios, which are warmed by fire pits on chilly evenings. Open Sun.–Thurs., 11:00 A.M.–10:30 P.M.; Fri.–Sat., 11:00 A.M.–11:00 P.M. 124 N. Montezuma St.; 520-541-1400. Website: www.prescottinfo.com.

Kendall's Famous Burgers and Ice Cream—$

This 1950s-style diner makes a convenient stop for light fare while you're exploring Prescott's downtown area. Order your burger (quarter pounders are good) at the back counter, then hit the ice-cream bar where your malt or shake is mixed fresh while you wait. Open Mon.–Sat., 11:00 A.M.–8:00 P.M.; Sun., 11:00 A.M.–6:00 P.M. Across from Courthouse Plaza. 113 S. Cortez St.; 520-778-3658.

Services

Prescott Chamber of Commerce

The helpful volunteers at the chamber office can supply you with everything from hiking trail maps to pamphlets on the town's history. 117 W. Goodwin, P.O. Box 1147, Prescott, 86302; 520-445-2000. Website: www.prescott.org.

Fire

Travelers in Arizona may occasionally find that certain areas are closed to recreation because of high fire danger. Trails may be posted as inadmissible, and some National Forests may not allow visitors past a certain point. Besides extreme drought, human-induced fire suppression has contributed to these conditions. Accumulated dry brush and debris can turn forests into tinderboxes. Controlled burns are helping to alleviate the danger.

When you see posted areas, please do not enter. Not only the safety of the forest is at stake, but also your own. Hikers in a narrow canyon can be cut off from escape within a very short time, should a fire start at the canyon mouth.

Ash Fork and Seligman

Three forks of Ash Creek converge here, hence the town's name. Today its claim to fame is its flagstone quarries that ship the Arizona building-stone to all parts of the globe. Ash Fork has markets, motels, service stations, a KOA, and several restaurants.

By the time you reach Seligman (east of Ash Fork) from Williams, you've made a gradual 40-mile, 2,000-foot descent, leaving ponderosa pines behind as you enter juniper territory. Seligman is a must for Route 66 fans (see sidebar). Today it is a pleasant, touristy place of about 900. Between Williams and Kingman, to the west, the vast open country that surrounds the friendly little town of Seligman provides ideal habitat for the pronghorn, so numerous they were chosen as the mascot for Seligman High School athletics. As you drive along, watch for these light buff-colored creatures streaking across the landscape at speeds of up to 75 miles per hour.

History

One of Ash Creek's forks was followed by the railroad that brought copper ore from the now-ghost-town of Jerome. At one time Ash Fork's jewel was the elegant Escalante, one of the West's Harvey Houses. You can visit an Old West Settler's Cemetery with cross-marked graves and etched sandstone tombstones.

Seligman was founded in 1886 at an Atchison, Topeka and Santa Fe main junction that had repair facilities, so train traffic was heavy. Seligman takes its name from a pair of East Coast investment banker brothers who helped finance the railroad's southern route.

Seeing and Doing

Museums and Historic Sites

Pick up a walking tour guide at the visitor center for detailed information on what to see on foot.

Angel & Vilma Delgadillo's Route 66 Gift Shop & Visitor Center

Angel Delgadillo, a native and semiretired town barber, keeps his memento-filled shop, really more of a museum, open to tourists. Look for the "Route 66 Memorabilia" sign on the left as you enter Seligman from the east. Angel won't take regular appointments, but if you catch him at the shop and can convince him you're a true Route 66 aficionado, he'll snip away as he answers your questions. Open daily, 8:00 A.M.–6:00 P.M. 217 E. Route 66, P.O. Box 426, Seligman, 86337-0426; 520-422-3352. Website: www.route66giftshop.com and angelsbarbershop.com.

Getting There

Ash Fork sits on Route 66, just barely bypassed by I-40, near the junction with Hwy. 89 that leads south to Prescott. Seligman is on Route 66 midway between Flagstaff and Kingman.

Vintage cars and an old gas pump help keep Route 66 alive at The Snow Cap in the small town of Seligman.

Where to Stay

There are seven motels in the budget category including the Stagecoach 66 Motel, on Route 66, with adjacent restaurant. **888-511-1237 or 520-422-3470.**

Camping

Seligman KOA
The KOA, on the west side of Seligman right on Route 66, has a pool, volleyball court, and two playgrounds as well as showers, bathrooms, grocery store, and laundry room. Tent sites are available. **P.O. Box 156, Seligman, 86337; 520-422-3358 or 800-562-4017.**

Where to Eat

The Copper Cart—$–$$
For more than 40 years this family-owned eatery has served, it says, "the best coffee on Route 66." The building remains little changed from its construction in the early 1950s, next to the main Atchison, Topeka and Santa Fe rail line. Railroaders have always frequented the place, as have Grand Canyon visitors and the intrepid rafters who challenge the Colorado River. The specialty is a half-pound of grilled ground beef with gravy, salad, and all the trimmings. Open daily, 6:00 A.M.–9:00 P.M. **Located on Route 66 on west side of Seligman. 520-422-3241.**

The Snow Cap—$
Angel Delgadillo's brother, Juan, runs this unforgettable walk-up stand a few doors down from the barber shop. It may be the last of what once was a national chain. Today it is Juan's alone. "Do you want yesterday's coffee or tomorrow's?" he'll query with a grin as he "squirts" you with a string of plastic mustard. "Eat here and get gas," says the Snow Cap's business card. Despite the humor, burgers are juicy and shakes are thick and rich. Pick one up for your nostalgic drive along Route 66. Open May–Sept., daily, 9:00 A.M.–

Route 66: Niched Forever in Northern Arizona History

Why has a simple ribbon of tarmac created such a surge of nostalgia? It existed just 47 years, from 1937, when the final piece was paved between Chicago and Santa Monica, to 1984, when its last active section was bypassed by the new four-lane I-40 at Williams. Martin Milner, who starred as Tod Stiles along with George Maharis as Buzz Murdock in the Route 66 television series of the 1960s, has no explanation for its resurgence of popularity, but he looks back on the show with a great deal of fondness. "We made 116 episodes, and no more than half a dozen actually were filmed on the real Route 66. But that didn't seem to matter. It was the sense of adventure and escape that kept viewers coming back," he says.

Called America's Mother Road, the route was the pathway west during the dust-bowl days of the 1930s for Depression-era workers looking for a better way of life. In the post-war 1950s, it was traveled by vacationing American families enjoying the new prosperity. Today its nostalgia value is what attracts travelers. Angel Delgadillo, president of the Arizona Chapter of the Historic Route 66 Association, says that people want to go back to a slower era. "We're such a young nation. We've destroyed so much of ourselves. We've plowed it under. People want to return to the America of yesteryear before it is completely gone."

Route 66 enters Arizona on the east, at Lupton on the New Mexico border (see Northeast region), and roughly parallels I-40 to Holbrook. Mostly the historic route now is the main drag through small towns left isolated by the interstate superhighway bypass. A few notable stretches of Route 66 remain. A piece swoops north from Seligman through Peach Springs, where many decades ago Mormons planted the flowery fruit trees for which the town is named, and continues through Truxton to Hackberry, where an old general store has been converted to a particularly wonderful Route 66 visitor center by folks who obviously love the old road, before it finally wanders on to Kingman.

The most spectacular, however, is the stretch from Kingman to Oatman, where switchbacks and narrow pavement press a driver to choose between watching the road and enjoying the see-for-days vistas. The old route continues along a particularly desolate stretch to Topock on the California border. (See Arizona's West Coast region.)

The Historic Route 66 Association, with chapters in all eight of the states through which the road crosses, is dedicated to preserving the old route and the memorabilia that surrounds it. Each year the organization sponsors an Annual Fun Run, a three-day event held the last weekend of Apr. in which cars travel the entire continuous 160 miles of Route 66 from Seligman to Topock. You can "Run What Ya Brung," as flyers say, or show up in a historic vehicle, which is what most participants do. Classic Thunderbirds, Ford Fairlanes, Chevys, Pontiacs, Buicks, and other cars from past decades are spiffed and shined to brand-new elegance. Women don pink poodle skirts, put their hair in ponytails, and slide into saddle shoes, while men Bryl Cream their hair and roll packs of cigarettes into T-shirt sleeves. Towns along the route come alive as the caravan leaves Seligman for Kingman, where bed races, slow drags, and a barbecue in the park are main events. The next day the cars arrive in Oatman, practically overwhelming this funky little mountain town with their shiny magnificence. Topock hosts an awards ceremony and closing reception. For more information on the Fun Run, contact the **Historic Route 66 Association of Arizona, P.O. Box 66, Kingman, 86402; 520-753-5001.**

9:00 P.M.; Oct.–Apr., daily, 9:00 A.M.–4:30 P.M.—or whenever they feel like it. Located in Seligman's town center on Route 66. 520-422-3291.

Services

Ash Fork Chamber of Commerce & Tourism Center
Located under the big Santa Fe Railroad water tower. Open Mon.–Fri., 9:00 A.M.–5:00 P.M. 793 Hwy. 66, P.O. Box 494, Ash Fork, 86320-0494; 520-637-0204.

Seligman Chamber of Commerce
P.O. Box 65, Seligman, 86337; 520-422-3939.

Recommended Reading
An excellent little reference for anyone thinking about traveling Route 66 is the book written by Tom Snyder, founder and director of the US Route 66 Association. Called *Route 66 Traveler's Guide and Roadside Companion,* it has maps showing driveable portions of the old highway, with recommendations for stops along the way. It is published by St. Martin's Press and is available in most bookstores.

A glossy *Route 66* magazine, published quarterly for $3.95 per issue, is available at 326 W. Route 66, Williams, 86046; 520-635-4322. Website: www.route66.com.

Yarnell and Wickenburg

About 25 miles southwest of Prescott lies Peeples Valley, a lush pastureland named for prospector A. H. Peeples, who led other adventurers into the area in 1863. Looking down into the valley from the east side of Weavers Mountain is Yarnell, a pleasant little town 28 miles north of Wickenburg that shares a common history with many of Arizona's small towns: gold. Never a boomtown, Yarnell was content to stay small, serving the ranchers and miners who called it home. At 4,800 feet its mild climate attracted permanent residents, including retirees, artists, and those involved in local service industries.

Today Yarnell has several antiques shops and galleries, as well as a gas station and a bank. Many residents work at nearby ranches or in Prescott or Wickenburg.

Even when Wickenburg was a boomtown celebrating its glory holes and copper mines, it has had a sense of humor about itself. It's hard not to like a town that erects a "No Fishing From Bridge" sign over a river that's perpetually dry, flowing 20 feet below the surface at this point and for most of its 100-mile course through the desert. From the late 1800s, tales of its wealth were so exaggerated that any raconteur of overstated stories became known as a "Hassayamper" in honor of the dry Hassayampa River. To local Native Americans, its name means "river that flows upside down." Legend says that if you drank from it, you'd be unable to tell the truth.

Today the small Sonoran Desert town 60 miles northwest of Phoenix doesn't have to try hard to retain its Old West ambiance. Surrounding ranches, both dude and working, lend credibility to the cowboy at the local sandwich saloon decked out in spurs and chaps. Three western apparel and tack shops reinforce the

image that helps sustain the charm that makes tourism Wickenburg's most important economic staple. Its population of around 5,000 more than doubles during winter months.

History

On a mesa near present-day Yarnell, Peeples' prospecting venture unearthed gold that turned out to be the richest placer gold discovery ever made in the state. Small claims were staked and the area slowly grew, until 1889 when prospector Harrison Yarnell struck gold near Antelope Peak, east of what now is Yarnell, and gave the town its name. When it was no longer profitable to extract gold from underground, sometime in the early 1940s, the mines were abandoned.

The Yavapai Indians were the sole inhabitants of the Wickenburg area until the late 1500s, when the first Spaniard, Antonio de Espejo, took a look at the area. He claimed to have discovered gold, but it wasn't until 1863, when German immigrant Henry Wickenburg began working the famous Vulture gold mine on the Hassayampa River's banks, that its

Getting There

Wickenburg is 60 miles northwest of Phoenix. Take I-17 north to Hwy. 74 (the Carefree Highway), and follow it west to US 60. Follow US 60 north to Wickenburg. Or you can take US 60 all the way from Phoenix. This diagonal road faithfully follows the Atchison, Topeka and Santa Fe Railroad line that was Wickenburg's original link to Phoenix. However, it is absolutely ablaze with traffic lights and can move at a month a mile during morning and evening rush hours. Yarnell is 28 miles north of Wickenburg on Hwy. 89.

A poignant statue "Thanks for the Rain" by Joe Beeler is at the Desert Caballeros Museum in Wickenburg.

reputation as a mining center was validated. No one is sure if the mine is named for the birds that circle in this desert environment or the manner in which so many hopefuls fell prey to the allure of gold, only to find the Vulture Mine too stubborn to release its riches. The Vulture had checkered success, sometimes yielding its booty with barely a whimper, other times bankrupting the company that owned it. It's one of the reasons that the mine changed hands so many times. Wickenburg sold it after just two years and turned to farming. Fortunately the Hassayampa River channel supported agriculture.

As more and more people moved into the area, confrontations over water became frequent until six passengers were killed in a stagecoach ambush just outside of town. Blame was placed on Mexican bandits, Yavapai, and even Americans masquerading as Native Americans. But the truth of the 1871 Wickenburg Massacre was never fully revealed. In 1891 the railroad came to town, linking Wickenburg to Phoenix, and by the 1920s a tourism trade was well established. Cattle ranches became dude ranches and well-heeled tourists became repeat visitors.

Festivals and Events

Gold Rush Days

early Feb.

Celebrating Wickenburg's mining and ranching heritage, this three-day weekend begins with a shoot-out on Frontier St. and includes a parade with more than 1,000 horses, more than 200 arts and crafts exhibits, a gem and mineral show, a family carnival, and stage entertainment. Highlight is the Senior Professional Cowboy's Rodeo Sat.–Sun. afternoons. **520-684-5479.**

Bluegrass Festival & Fiddle Championship

second weekend in Nov.

This spirited event, going on for almost 20 years, features at least three prominent bands plus fiddle competition in more than a dozen categories.

Competitors vie for some serious prize money here. An arts and crafts fair, food, and kids' activities round out the weekend. Held at Constellation Park in Wickenburg. 520-684-5479.

Seeing and Doing

Museums and Historic Sites

Desert Caballeros Western Museum

This truly nifty museum details Wickenburg's history from prehistoric times through its mining days, using miniature dioramas and a full-size reproduction of a turn-of-the-century town. The two-level building also has an outstanding collection of western art, including works by Russell, Remington, Catlin Phippen, and others. The poignant life-sized bronze statue out front, of a cowboy kneeling in gratitude beside his tired horse, is called "Thanks for the Rain," created by famed cowboy artist Joe Beeler. The country store, Las Señoras Museum Store, is so well stocked you'll want to shop; 520-684-7075. Small fee. Open Mon.–Sat, 10:00 A.M.–5:00 P.M.; Sun.,noon–4:00 P.M. 121 N. Frontier St., Wickenburg, 85390; 520-684-2272. Website: www.westernmuseum.org.

Robson's Arizona Mining World

This re-creation of a rough-and-tumble mining town brings together machinery, artifacts, and antiques from the days when gold was king. Located in the Harcuvar Mountains at the site of the once-flourishing Nella-Meda gold mine about 26 miles west of Wickenburg, 14 original buildings date to the mine's active days. A barber shop doubling as a surgery, a mercantile, a print shop, a saloon, and more invite exploration. Small fee. Open Oct. 1–May 31, Mon.–Fri., 10:00 A.M.–4:00 P.M.; Sat.–Sun., 8:00 A.M.–6:00 P.M. Take US 60 west from Wickenburg, then turn right (north) on Hwy. 71. Watch for the signs. 520-685-2609.

Vulture Mine

Looming on the horizon like a roughed-up thumb, Vulture Peak, at the east end of the Vulture Mountains, defines an area once rich in ore. A great self-guided tour directs you among tumbledown structures, once an assay office, bunkhouse, store, and more. You can easily spend a couple of hours here, reading the interpretive signs and trekking up to the Glory Hole. For a more in-depth study of the mine, guided tours for 10 or more are offered by the on-site caretakers. Small fee. Tours Oct.–Mar., Thurs.–Mon., 8:00 A.M.–4:00 P.M.; Apr.–Sept., Fri.–Sun, 8:00 A.M.–4:00 P.M. From Wickenburg take US 60 west 2.5 miles and turn south on Vulture Mine Rd. Follow it 12 miles to the mine entrance. 602-859-2743 (this is a cellular phone number, so you must dial the 602 area code even if you're calling from the 602 area).

Nature Centers

The Nature Conservancy Hassayampa River Preserve

The Hassayampa River, which rarely makes an appearance in its sandy bed south of town, bubbles to the surface 3 miles to the southeast, where it supports one of Arizona's finest Sonoran Desert streamside habitats. The Nature Conservancy manages a 5-mile stretch that flows year-round. Its grassy banks, lined with cottonwoods and willows, form a ribbon of green, a favorite spot for picnickers and hikers. It preserves a cottonwood-willow forest (especially lovely in the fall) inhabited by Harris and zone-tailed hawks, vermilion flycatchers, Abert's towhees, and more than 200 other bird species that are drawn to this area by reliable water and food sources. Visitors come to spot mule deer, mountain lion, bobcat, javelina, and ringtailed cats that come to the river's edge to drink, their presence verified more by their tracks than by actual sightings. The visitor center is an 1860s adobe built by Frederick Brill, an early rancher. An easy hike through the preserve follows a trail from the visitor center along the river. A loop around Palm Lake leads to an area alive with ducks, other waterfowl, and shorebirds. Open May 15–

Sept. 15, Wed.–Sun., 6:00 A.M.–noon; Sept. 16– May 14, Wed.–Sun., 8:00 A.M.–5:00 P.M. Located about 8 miles south of Wickenburg on west side of US 60 near milepost 114. Box 3290, Wickenburg, 85385; 520-684-2772. Website: www.tnc.org.

Scenic Drives

Joshua Forest Parkway

North of Wickenburg just as you cross the county line from Maricopa into Yavapai County, this stretch of US 93 is either stunningly beautiful or depressingly desolate, depending on your point of view. Those voting for beautiful find the Joshua trees (see sidebar) fascinating and the rolling, rocky countryside a treasure to explore. The two-lane road has occasional passing areas, and there is a roadside picnic table with a ramada about 8 miles into the drive. Just before the Burro Creek Bridge, which spans an impressive chasm that surpasses its "creek" denomination, there is a pullout with good views of the Juniper Mountains to the west. By the time you cross the attractive trickle called the Big Sandy River and reach the wide spot in the road known as Wickieup, the scenery becomes pretty ordinary. But you might want to stop at the Subway for a snack or for gas, or to look at the Indian jewelry there. The historical marker just north of Wickieup tells you that you're looking at the Big Sandy Valley, first explored by the Spanish in 1582. It became an important agricultural, mining, milling, and smelting area in its early days.

Either return the way you came, or continue north to I-40 and head east to Seligman and Ash Fork, for a tour of the northern part of the Central region.

FOUR-WHEEL-DRIVE TRIPS

Wickenburg Jeep Tours

For some basic desert four-wheeling, this outfit will take you to the old San Domingo Mines, to the Box Canyon riparian area, past petroglyphs, and through desert brush and scrub. A little humor and history are mixed with educational

information about desert plants and animals. Tours are two and a half to four hours long. 295 E. Wickenburg Way, Wickenburg, 85385; 800-596-JEEP or 520-684-0438. Website: www.wickenburgjeep.com.

Seasonal Favorites

Apple and Peach Picking at Date Creek Ranch

On weekends July 4–Oct., you pick your own peaches and apples at this rustic ranch. You'll be given a bag (or you can bring your own), and wire mesh pickers are also available to reach those high-up prizes. You can also buy grass-fed beef. Located in foothills of Date Creek Mountains north of Wickenburg. Take US 93 past Wickenburg to milepost 177 and turn right. Follow signs to the ranch. Be sure to call first to see what's available; 520-776-8877.

Where to Stay

Guest Ranches

Good information is available from the Dude Ranchers' Association websites: www.duderanch.org and www.arizonaguide.com/azduderanch.

Merv Griffin's Wickenburg Inn—$$$$

This inn has been around since 1974 and recently was purchased by entrepreneur and entertainer Merv Griffin. One of its many charms is that it sort of snuggles into the desert at the end of a winding dirt road. Buildings are gently tucked into hillsides and sheltered by a rolling landscape, becoming a true part of the desert in the midst of a 4,700-acre preserve. Because it was planned as a time-share, the casita accommodations have small stoves, refrigerators, and coffeemakers. Some casitas have private rooftop decks with fireplaces. It has tennis courts, a new swimming pool and spa, including a children's pool with sandy "beach," an arts and crafts room, and nature trails. Remarkably

A trail ride heads out from Rancho de los Caballeros, one of several dude ranches near Wickenburg.

pristine acreage is crossed by trails for accompanied, open trail, or sunset horseback rides. During the cattle drive, steers are driven into the open range for guests to help round up and herd back to the arena, a real guest-pleaser. The object is not to lose any along the way. Located 8 miles north of Wickenburg on Hwy. 89, about a 90-minute drive from Phoenix. 34801 N. Hwy. 89, Wickenburg, 85358; 800-942-5362 or 520-684-7811. Website: www.merv.com.

Rancho de los Caballeros—$$$$

This resort-style ranch was named for the grand tradition of the Spanish caballeros, the "gentlemen on horseback," who explored and settled the Southwest. At the ranch your attention is divided about equally between dude activities and the 18-hole private golf course that winds among upscale homes. Various rides accommodate equestrians of all abilities. There's even a pony named Shorty who's good with children. There are four tennis courts, trap and skeet shooting, hayrides, cookouts, and a swimming pool. Tile-floor guest rooms and suites have

handcrafted furnishings brought from Mexico and Santa Fe, so the overall look is rustic but the comfort level is high. Some rooms have kitchenettes and wet bars. Open Oct.–May. Take US 60 for 3.5 miles west of Wickenburg and turn south on Vulture Mine Rd. 1551 S. Vulture Mine Rd., Wickenburg, 85390; 520-684-5484. Website: www. sunC.com.

Motels

None of these are standouts, but if you're not staying at one of the dude ranches, they are your only choice for good, basic accommodations.

Americinn—$$–$$$

This 29-room motel is the closest motel to the Hassayampa Preserve, and has a pool and spa. Its restaurant, The Willows, is open for three meals a day, closed Sun. eve. and Mon. Located on US 60 just south of Wickenburg. 850 E. Wickenburg Way, Wickenburg, 85390; 800-634-3444 or 520-684-5461. Website: www. americinn.com.

Best Western Rancho Grande Motel— $$-$$$

Refrigerators, coffee makers and some rooms with kitchenettes make a longer stay possible here. In downtown Wickenburg. 293 E. Wickenburg Way, Wickenburg, 85390; 800-528-1234 or 520-684-5445. Website: www. bestwestern. com.

Los Viajeros—$$-$$$

This newer motel has a pool, with continental breakfast included in the room rate. On US 93 at Wickenburg's north edge; 800-915-9795. Website: www.wick-web.com/viajeros.

Oak Park Motel—$$

In Yarnell, this small 7-room motel and RV park is clean and tidy, if not fancy, with cable TV and air conditioning. One unit has a kitchenette. The adjacent RV park has mostly long-term guests, but at any given time it should be possible to find a spot there with full hookups. A pizza place called Sundance is two doors down, and the Ranch House Restaurant is about 0.5 mile. For a breakfast treat, the Millstone Bakery opens at 7:30 A.M. 22658 Hwy. 89 in Yarnell; 520-427-6383.

Camping

Burro Creek Recreation Site

Always-flowing Burro Creek cuts a rugged, picturesque swath through miles of basalt, providing riparian habitat for birds, bighorn sheep, and fish. Except for trammeling by cattle, the area is one of the loveliest little-trafficked places in the state, an ideal winter site at an elevation of about 2,000 feet. The campground has 25 sites, seven day-use picnic sites, and rest rooms. Located 60 miles north of Wickenburg. For information contact the Bureau of Land Management, 520-692-4400.

Where to Eat

The expected chains like McDonald's, Denny's, and Taco Bell are part of Wickenburg's dining-out scene, as are two pizza parlors, a couple of steak houses, and a deli.

Homestead Restaurant—$$-$$$

Appealing restaurant serves the best of American fare, specializing in Yankee pot roast. A reader says, "The food was very good and the ambiance lovely, decorated in turn-of-the-century style." Open daily, 6:00 A.M.–9:00 P.M. Located on US 60. 222 E. Wickenburg Way, Wickenburg; 520-684-0648.

Anita's Cocina—$-$$

This unpretentious two-room place isn't fancy, but service is friendly and the food's great. The giant taco salad and superduper tostada (order it only if you're starving) are delicious, and remarkably well priced. Open daily, 11:00 A.M.–9:00 P.M. Located just a block off Wickenburg Way, the main drag. 57 N. Valentine, Wickenburg; 520-684-5777.

Custer Cowboy Cafe—$-$$

"We pride ourselves on the size of our portions. If for any reason you feel you did not get enuf food for the money you paid, you just let us know and we will give you more, guaranteed," signed, Jim Bob and Tina Custer. This little sign on the tables pretty much expresses the character of this genuine-cowboy-owned cafe. Walls are covered with framed belt buckles won in rodeo events and photos of bronc- and bull-riding contests. Come here for a breakfast steak that'll keep you busy for awhile plus home fries—boiled, diced, and crispy-browned without being greasy. It's not unusual to see a grizzled cowboy pause when his meal is served, remove his hat, and bow his head for a brief grace before diggin' in. Open daily, 6:00 A.M.–8:00 P.M. Located on US 93 just north of town. 666 N. Tegner St., Wickenburg; 520-684-2807.

Services

Wickenburg Chamber of Commerce

Open Mon.–Fri., 9:00 A.M.–5:00 P.M.; Sat., 9:00

A.M.–4:00 P.M.; Sun., noon–4:00 P.M.; summer hours may vary. 216 N. Frontier St., P.O. Drawer CC, Wickenburg, 85358; 800-942-5242 or 520-684-5479. Website: www.wick enburgchamber.com.

Yarnell–Peeples Valley Chamber of Commerce

P.O. Box 275, Yarnell, 85362; 520-427-3301.

Trees Shaped Like Joshua

The Joshua tree is one of many plants and animals with a Biblical connection. It was named by Mormon pioneers following the call of Brigham Young to journey to Salt Lake City, who thought the tree branches resembled the arms of Joshua motioning them even farther westward to the Promised Land. When one is silhouetted against a red desert sunset, a lively imagination and inventive eye can surely discern "arms," wispy "hair," and perhaps a scraggly beard. This is truly a living thing whose beauty is unquestionably subjective. Some see the tree as a fascinating example of nature's sense of humor. Others view its contorted configurations as grotesque, or eerily beautiful. It is impossible to remain neutral about its attractiveness, or lack of same.

Found in the desert from California to Utah and in parts of Arizona and Nevada at elevations between 2,000 and 6,000 feet, the 20- to 30-foot Joshua tree bristles with dagger-shaped, spine-tipped leaves and greenish-white flowers in long clusters, which bloom from Feb. to late Apr., generally at their best in Mar. Blossoms open quite unspectacularly for just one night, then close to remain on the tree for two to three weeks.

Without a tiny creature called the yucca moth to pollinate the blossoms, the Joshua tree wouldn't be able to flower. One cannot exist without the other. The female moth col-

Joshua trees flourish near Wickenburg.

lects the tree's pollen in a ball and carefully spreads it within the flower, fertilizing the seeds. She's not an altruistic conservationist. She's just assuring her offspring a food source when they hatch from her eggs. The hungry larvae eat only a few seeds, however, leaving more than enough for the wind to scatter across the desert. Although the tree may propagate via its root system, it must have the seeds it produces in pollinated flowers to establish itself in new areas.

cont.

The Joshua tree's shallow root system and top-heavy growth pattern cause it to cling tenaciously to sandy desert soil. It may not bloom every year, choosing to display its blossoms based on nature's distribution of rainfall and warm weather. It grows slowly, taking its time to develop new branches and blooms, adding just one-third to one-half inch each year. Because a Joshua tree doesn't have rings like a conventional tree, it is difficult to determine the age of one. But if the harsh desert environment allows, the many-armed elders can survive for several hundred years.

Besides its interesting architectural appearance, the Joshua tree provides a focal point for a complex wildlife community. Oftentimes a graceful red-tailed hawk or canny sparrow hawk uses the tree's topmost reaches as a lookout point for its next meal.

Noisy cactus wrens flit and chatter among its branches as they nibble away at insects. Woodpeckers sometimes work their rapid-fire techniques on the fibrous trunk in a search for bugs.

Creamy, waxy, podlike Joshua tree flowers supply food for more than two dozen bird species. The fleshy fruits, and later the dry seeds, are an important food source for ground squirrels.

The shaggy trunks provide fibers that augment the nest-building materials of desert birds. Fallen trees are a safe haven for the seldom-seen desert night lizard. Termites find protection from heat and cold in the decaying fiber, and convert plant energy to animal energy. Stinkbugs munch on the tree's fibrous trunk, helping transform its nutrients into another living form. So even as it dies the Joshua gives life.

To Flagstaff · Lake Pleasant · Bartlett Reservoir · Tonto National Forest · Theodore Roosevelt Lake

74 · Cave Creek · Carefree · 188 · Four Peaks · Apache Lake

60 · Wittmann · aqueduct · Salt River Reservation · Verde River · 87 · Saguaro Lake · Canyon Lake

Sun City · Peoria · Glendale · Scottsdale · 88

Litchfield Park · Goodyear · Phoenix · Mesa · Tempe · 60 · Chandler · Central Arizona Project · Superior · 60 · 177

Buckeye · Gila River · Gila River Reservation · 347 · 87 · 79 · Gila River · Kearny · Hayden · Winkelman

85 · Maricopa · 10 · Florence · 387

238 · Ak-Chin Reservation · Casa Grande Ruins NM · Coolidge

Gila Bend · 8 · 84 · Casa Grande · 287 · 87 · 79

To Tucson

The Valley of the Sun

N

OVERALL MAP SCALE
0 · 10 · 20 · 30 · 40 Miles

DETAIL MAP SCALE
0 · 1 · 2 · 3 · 4 Miles

■ National or State Forest
□ National Park or Monument
□ Indian Reservation
▲ State Park
🛡 17 Interstate Highway
◯ 180 U.S. Highway
◯ 66 State Highway

Scottsdale Municipal Airport · Taliesin West · aqueduct · Cactus Road · Shea Blvd · 104th St

51 · Squaw Peak Park · Paradise Valley · Tatum · McDonald Dr · Pima St · SALT RIVER RESERVATION

60 · Black Canyon Freeway · Camelback Road · Camelback Mountain · Scottsdale · Scottsdale Road

Indian School Road · 44th St · Civic Plaza · 101 · Beeline Hwy · 87

17 · 19th Ave · Grand Ave · Encanto Park · Heard Museum · Phoenix Art Museum · PHOENIX · Scottsdale Road

McDowell Road · Desert Botanical Garden

10 · 60 · Arizona Center · 202 · Van Buren · Papago Park · Phoenix Zoo · Salt River

43rd Ave · 35th Ave · State Capitol · Civic Plaza · Washington · Sky Harbor International Airport · 202 · Country Club Dr

17 · 60 · Jefferson · Pueblo Grande · 143 · Old Town · Arizona State University · Apache Boulevard · 87

10 · Central Ave · 7th St · 24th St · 48th St · Tempe · Mill Ave · Rural Road · Superstition Freeway

Baseline Road · 60 · Baseline Blvd

Dobbins Road · Guadalupe · Guadalpe Road · Chandler

Laveen · Summit Lookout · 10 · Arizona Ave

South Mountain Park · Ahwatukee Foothills

The Valley of the Sun

The saguaro cactus has come to be the symbol of the Sonoran Desert area and the Valley of the Sun.

The Valley of the Sun

Although they maintain very distinct images, Phoenix, Scottsdale, Mesa, and Tempe blend into one geographically indistinguishable urban area in a smooth segue of suburbanism, with distinctions marked by little more than a difference in street signs. Rapid growth has created panoramas of red tile roofs as subdivisions eat up the desert at what some clock as an acre an hour. An astonishing 22 incorporated cities cover more than 9,000 square miles in Maricopa County. Economically the distinctions are clear. Scottsdale's upmarket persona is a decided contrast to the lower-key lifestyle of Mesa.

Yet all are part of the Valley of the Sun, an apt appellation considering that it averages 300 sun-filled days each year. It helps keep the 150-plus golf courses green and grassy, no doubt part of what attracts the 12 million people that visit the Valley each year. It's a term falling into disuse, however, as city officials have determined that references to the sun often conjure up images of heat, not always an attractive prospect to tourists. Nonetheless, Old Sol is around for 86 percent of daylight hours, creating a pleasant average yearly temperature of 72°F with almost no humidity. With everything air-conditioned, the terms of Phoenix life are no longer set by the desert. And despite Phoenix's desert location, there are six lakes within a 75-minute drive of the city. They create an eclectic mix that makes this one of the fastest-growing areas of the country. It doesn't seem destined to stop anytime soon.

The flip side of all this sunny news is that during the Valley's hottest months—June, July, and Aug.—records put the average high at 102–105°F. Days that top 110°F are common, and recorded 120°F days have been verified. The 72°F average mentioned above kicks in Nov.–Apr., when days are absolutely lovely and temperatures rarely rise above 82°F.

Phoenix

In 1997 Phoenix became the nation's sixth-largest city, nudging out San Diego for what many residents consider a dubious honor. Population is about 1.3 million, with 2.8 million people currently calling Maricopa County home. The median resident age is 31.1 years, more than 25 percent of whom are under the age of 18. Despite its reputation as a retirement city, Phoenix has a decidedly youthful orientation. Less than 10 percent of the population is over the age of 65.

At an elevation of 1,113 feet, and geographically larger than Los Angeles, Phoenix spreads over more than 100 square miles, which so far has made any extensive public transportation system unfeasible. So people depend on their cars, often creating serious air-pollution problems. Traffic on I-10 entering Phoenix from the south or coming in from the west on any given business day can be bumper to bumper. Yet new residents continue to arrive. Cost of living remains just a hair above the national average, due in part to reasonable housing costs. Many homes are in tightly packed subdivisions where only a wall assures any privacy. The good news is that Phoenix is one of the few cities where you can still buy a home with a pool, albeit small, in some areas for around $100,000.

First-time visitors sometimes are intrigued by the fact that in front of homes often there is desert landscaping rather than lawns. Others are amazed that in the middle of a desert there are so many lush, green golf courses. Ever since the web of canals called the Central Arizona Project guaranteed a continuing water supply from the Colorado River, Phoenix has figured its water needs were taken care of. Yet water is at the center of a never-ending controversy, with some saying there is enough for decades to come, while others assert that with nonstop development, quirky weather, and greater-than-anticipated water use, nothing but a cough of dust will emerge from city faucets within just a few years.

Water in the Valley of the Sun is distributed in approximately these proportions: about 50 percent to crop irrigation, about 30 percent to home use, about 6 percent to Native American water rights, and the remaining 14 percent to industry and other uses. Despite its difficulties, Phoenix remains the Southwest's premier winter vacation destination.

History

Most of the world's great cities have grown up along the banks of rivers; Phoenix falls right in line. A visit to the ruins at Pueblo Grande, just east of downtown Phoenix, clearly shows how the Hohokam depended on the Salt River. One of the city's present-day canals follows the route of a canal constructed prior to 1400 to irrigate crops.

Not much was happening in the Phoenix area once the Hohokam mysteriously left around 1450. Coronado, Cardenas, Alarcon, and Diaz explored some of the state in the name of Spain, and Spanish padres established the Mission San Xavier del Bac south of Tucson in 1797. In 1821 Arizona became a Spanish province. In 1850 the

Getting There

Phoenix Sky Harbor International Airport is served by 18 major carriers. The airport is 15 minutes from downtown, and within 15–30 minutes of major area hotels and resorts. British Airways has daily nonstop service from Gatwick Airport, and Air Canada offers daily nonstop flights to Toronto. This number of airlines coming into a single city helps create a competitive atmosphere that tends to keep fares down, even during prime winter months.

Greyhound (800-231-2222) *provides bus service. The main terminal is located at **2115 E. Buckeye Rd.** in Phoenix, with suburban stations in Apache Junction, Chandler, Mesa, and Tempe.*

There is no train service to Phoenix; Amtrak discontinued service to Phoenix in 1996.

Arizona–New Mexico Territory was created, by 1860 a small settlement was thriving on the banks of the Salt River, and in 1870 a group of local residents formally laid out a town site. Suggested names were Stonewall, after Stonewall Jackson, and Salina. But one of those first entrepreneurs saw the new city as rising from the ashes of a previous civilization, evidenced by the canals, and the name Phoenix was approved.

Settlers followed the Pima and Maricopa Indian tradition of growing cotton and other crops, and in 1879 the first factory was built for producing artificial ice. In 1887, with the tracks for the railroad completed, the first train roared into the depot. In 1889 the city received recognition when Prescott reluctantly relinquished the title of territorial capital to Phoenix. By the time Arizona became the 48th state, on Feb. 14, 1912, Phoenix was a true city, with regal Victorian homes not far from what became a busy railroad-centered downtown.

Yet in the eyes of the world, Phoenix is a young city. In 1940 its population was just 65,000. By the early 1960s it was still under a half million. And then the widespread availability of air-conditioning, in addition to evaporative cooling, made the desert a much more attractive place to live.

Festivals and Events

Spring Training

month of Mar.

Major league baseball's spring training has been a tradition in Arizona and Florida since 1909 when the Chicago White Sox started playing their first exhibition games in Yuma and Tucson. By 1947 the New York Giants and the Cleveland Indians had become part of the athletic migration. The Arizona Diamondbacks, the state's own new major league team, play at Bank One Ballpark in downtown Phoenix (see Sports in Seeing and Doing). All together, 10 ball clubs comprise the Arizona Cactus League, whose teams train in the state each spring. More than 125 games begin in late Feb. or early Mar. and continue for approximately a month. Ticket prices depend on venue, but generally cost under $5 for lawn seating where offered, to $12–$19 for preferred seating. Tickets are available at game time, but the surefire way to nab choice seats is to order tickets by mail. A number of area hostelries have Spring Training Hotel Packages that guarantee premium Cubs box seats with a hotel room. Most games begin at 1:00 P.M. For information on schedules (usually available by early Nov.), times, and advance ticketing, contact the **Mesa Convention & Visitors Bureau, 120 N. Center St., Mesa, 85201; 800-283-6372 or 480-827-4700.** Website: www. mesacvb.com.

Arizona State Fair

late Oct.–early Nov.

The 13-day event runs the gamut from nontraditional, space-themed attractions including a

UFO encounter to more fairlike barnyard animals, fast rides, and artery-clogging foods. One year may feature rhythm and blues performers, with mainstream music the next. Grandstand events usually include an all-Indian rodeo, horse shows, boxing, monster trucks, a demolition derby, and more. Presently events are held at the **Arizona State Fairground at 19th Ave. and McDowell,** but call 602-252-6771 to check because the venue may change.

Fiesta Bowl Parade

Dec. 30

A highlight of the overall Fiesta Bowl celebration, the parade generally features two dozen bands, more than a dozen elaborate floats, and equestrian, honorary, and specialty groups that can include folkloric dancers and jump-rope teams. Usually starting at 11:00 A.M., the parade begins at **Bethany Home Rd. and proceeds south on Central Ave. to Thomas Rd.** You can rent bleacher and chair seats along N. Central, but most parade-goers simply line the avenue on foot.

Fiesta Bowl

Dec. 31

It's billed as Arizona's Biggest Party. Considering that festivities begin in Sept. for this end-of-year event, it may be true. The Tostitos Fiesta Bowl Football Classic, played at Sun Devil Stadium in Tempe, during the months preceding the game includes golf and tennis tournaments, soccer and running events, parties, a formal ball, and tours.

On New Year's Eve, 4:00 P.M.–midnight the night before the game, the Fiesta Bowl Block Party is held in downtown Tempe. It's easy to understand why more than 150,000 guests attend annually, with big-name bands, fireworks, carnival rides, plus souvenir and food booths. For ticket information call **480-350-0900. Website: www.tostitosfiesta bowl.com.**

Home Team	Stadium Site
Anaheim Angels	Tempe
Arizona Diamondbacks (spring training only)	Tucson
Chicago Cubs	Mesa
Chicago White Sox	Tucson
Colorado Rockies	Tucson
Milwaukee Brewers	Phoenix
Oakland A's	Phoenix
San Diego Padres	Peoria
San Francisco Giants	Scottsdale
Seattle Mariners	Peoria

Outdoor Activities

For more opportunities for urban hiking, mountain biking, and scenic drives, see South Mountain Park under Parks in Seeing and Doing, as well as chapters for individual Valley of the Sun cities.

Bicycling

MOUNTAIN BIKING

South Mountain Park

You see mountain bikes on trails throughout South Mountain Park, but the favorite, and biggest challenge, is the 14.3-mile **National Trail** (nonmotorized use only) that runs along the park's middle. You have to allow the better part of a day to bike it. You'll probably spend four to five hours on the trail and several more recuperating. If the elevation gain of more than 1,000 feet doesn't get you, carrying your bike over rock outcroppings and picking yourself up from sliding through loose gravel probably will take their toll. The rewards are great views and seeing Indian petroglyphs. Do this ride in winter months, because there aren't enough cool morning hours in summer (even if you start at dawn) to keep you comfortable for the whole

Landmark Camelback Mountain defines the Phoenix skyline looking north.

ride. You can access the trail from the park's **48th St. entrance.** Leave your car in the lot and follow a busy dirt road (on weekends there are lots of hikers, walkers, and families with kids) about 0.25 mile to a sign that says "National Trail."

A 17-mile round-trip ride begins with an almost-flat trail, the **Desert Classic,** that starts from the east ramada in Pima Canyon and follows the southern base of the mountains to **Telegraph Pass Trail,** where you start to gain elevation. Turn right onto **National Trail,** then to the **dirt road,** and return. It's a good trail for beginners to hone skills and also is easy enough to get your heart rate up.

Golf

With close to 200 golf courses dotting the Phoenix area, you're never more than a chip shot away from the links. There are more courses per capita here than in any state west of the Mississippi, creating available tee times even during the practically ideal golf months of Jan.–Apr., when average high temperatures range from 65° to 83°F. It helps account for the 11 million rounds of golf played annually in the state. The Phoenix Open (PGA) is played at the Tournament Players Club of Scottsdale in late Jan., and the Tradition (Senior PGA) is played at Desert Mountain in Scottsdale in late Mar. The **Arizona Central website has a Course Surfer** that lets you find courses by location, by course name, by city name, and by your preference of price and difficulty: **azcentral.com;** click on "Sports" and then "Golf."

Raven Golf Club

This club has large greens and forgiving fairways. Formerly agricultural land, the course is flanked by mature pine trees, framing mountain views. Expensive. Near South Mountain in central Phoenix. **3636 E. Baseline Rd.; 602-243-3636.**

Hiking

Camelback Mountain

This Phoenix landmark, a subterranean uplifting of granite, is widely used for recreation, particularly the Echo Canyon area with a steep and challenging 1-mile hike to the top of the camel's head. Although once thought to be preserved in its natural state, the camel's flanks are now dotted with pricey homes. Stay on the trail, bring plenty of water, and enjoy the city view from the top. You may spot a peregrine falcon, now off the endangered list, slicing through the sky. Access is from **Echo Canyon Parkway on McDonald Dr. in Paradise Valley.** To be assured of a parking place, arrive very early in the morning.

North Mountain Park

Part of the Phoenix Mountain Preserve, the same system that protects South Mountain but in a different geographical area, this 10,000-acre preserve has one central 7,000-acre section and several other chunks of parkland. All are webbed with hiking trails, with easy access to trail-heads from many points in the residential area that surrounds it. The 10-mile-plus **Charles Christiansen Trail** is the most popular with hikers, equestrians, and mountain bikers. It basically traverses the whole preserve. Located **at Seventh St. and Peoria Ave. in Phoenix.** From I-17 take the Seventh St. exit and proceed north to Peoria Ave.

Papago Park

If you like the kind of hike that has a destination, the **Hole-in-the-Rock** trek can fill the bill. There really is a hole, at the top of a 1-mile marked trail that is rated advanced beginner or low-moderate in difficulty. Once at the top, you can see most of the park, including the Phoenix Zoo. **Take Galvin Parkway to the park entrance.**

South Mountain Park

One of our favorite, easy strolls in this popular park begins at the East Gate off 48th St. and simply follows the dirt road in **Pima Canyon.** It parallels a wash on one side where we often spot coyote tracks, and on the other are cliffs where we've watched a pair of red-tailed hawks build a nest and produce a pair of chicks. For a longer hike, still just over 2 miles, take the **Pima West Loop** north from the North Ramada and circle around to connect with the Pima East Loop. The 5.5-mile **Mormon Loop Trail** branches off from the National Trail, gains a bit of elevation, and presents more of a challenge. A large sign at the 48th St. entrance details all the trails, so you can pick and choose before you set out.

All trails in the park are clearly marked. Be sure to carry water. Cell phones do work in the park. There is a staffed office at the main entrance at the south end of Central Ave. For more information and for trail maps, contact the **Phoenix Department of Parks and Recreation, 10919 S. Central Ave., Phoenix, 85040-8302; 602-495-0222, fax 602-495-0212.**

For general information on South Mountain Park, stop at the **Environmental Education Center,** the first building on the left as you enter the park from Central Ave. The center sponsors hikes and programs year-round, so call first to see what you might be able to join. Open Mon.–Sat., 9:00 A.M.–5:00 P.M.; Sun., noon–5:00 P.M. **10419 S. Central Ave., Phoenix, 85040; 602-534-6324.**

Squaw Peak Park

When you see helicopters hovering over this peak north of town, also in the Phoenix Mountain Preserve, it's a pretty safe bet they're extricating someone who's gotten in trouble on the **Squaw Peak Summit Trail.** This 1.2-mile route has an elevation gain of more than 1,200 feet and is favored by true exercise enthusiasts. For a much easier and safer trail, take the **Squaw Peak Nature Trail,** a complacent stroll that gets you away from the city in minutes. Wildlife is similar to that found at South Mountain. We take out-of-town guests here to get a feel for the Sonoran Desert without a lot of strenuous hiking. The 1.5-mile loop takes well under an hour, even moving at a snail's pace. 602-262-7901.

Horseback Riding

Trailhorse Adventures

This outfitter offers scheduled rides at varying times and days of the week, depending on the season. Rides leave from the stables on Pointe Parkway, winding first through suburbia but quickly getting into the park's Pima Canyon area. The scenery keeps the ride at a comfortable pace. Located at **the Pointe Hilton Resort near South Mountain Park. 800-723-3538. Website: www.trailhorse adventures.com.**

Seeing and Doing

Art Museums and Galleries

Heard Museum

This unforgettable museum was founded in 1929 by Dwight B. and Maie Bartlett Heard to house their personal collection of primarily Native American art. It is internationally acclaimed for its artifacts documenting the history of native cultures, as well as the ongoing special events that include Native American hoop dancers and artists demonstrating ancient crafts. It promotes appreciation and respect for native people and the products of their cultural heritage, which include pottery, baskets, jewelry, weavings, and an extensive kachina doll collection donated by former Arizona senator Barry Goldwater. A recent $16.2 million expansion added galleries and a studio for artists in residence. Sat. usually features Native American music and dance performances or artists' demonstrations. Be sure to allow time to browse the museum shop and bookstore for top-quality authentic Native American baskets, pottery, textiles, jewelry, and other crafts. The museum's premier event, the Heard Museum Guild Indian Fair and Market, held in early Mar., draws visitors from all over the country. Moderate admission. Open daily, 9:30 A.M.–5 P.M., except major holidays. Located one block east of Central Ave. and three blocks north of McDowell Rd. **2301 N. Central Ave., Phoenix, 85004; 602-252-8848. Website: www.heard.org.**

Phoenix Art Museum

A recent $25-million renovation and expansion more than doubled the size of this respected museum. Unique architectural details give it an unusual quality of liveliness not often seen in museums. Those details include imaginatively placed openings in walls and windows that create visual cues to help visitors orient themselves. Permanent collections cover three areas of emphasis: Art of Asia, Art of the Americas and Europe to 1900, and Art of Our Times: 1900 to the Present. A child-friendly gallery called ArtWorks offers youngsters a creative way to look at art. The Throne collection of miniature rooms appeals to children and adults. Fans of Phoenix artist Philip Curtis appreciate the newly opened gallery that features his distinctive work. Half-hour gallery talks, called "ArtBreaks," are offered Tues.–Sun., noon. Family programs and performances are offered on third Sun. of each month, free with general admission. Don't miss the gallery store, where the merchandise reflects the collections and exhibits currently in progress. Open Tues.–Wed. and Sun., 10:00 A.M.–5:00 P.M.; Thurs.–Fri., 10:00 A.M.–9:00 P.M.; except major holidays. Located at corner of Central Ave. and McDowell Rd. **1625 N. Central Ave., Phoenix, 85004; 602-257-1222. Website: www. phxart.org.**

Children and Families

Arizona Science Center

This is one of our very favorite places to bring out-of-town guests, especially those with children. From the time you get a look at its sweeping exterior curves and angles, you have a pretty good idea that what's inside will be terrific. The $47-million center, opened in 1997, is filled with more than 350 interactive exhibits geared for everyone from toddlers to grandparents. Don't miss the giant nose, with "cilia" that can be irritated by "dust particles." Kids throw nerf balls up a pair of giant nostrils, and when the nose has had enough, it erupts in a startling sneeze. Another display features a field of shaggy little creatures that shake and shudder in an electromagnetic field in time to music that you select. Upstairs you can "fly" a Cessna in a wind tunnel. An Iwerks theater, a 203-seat planetarium, hosts a variety of shows and simulated heavenly events. Admission varies, beginning with a base price for exhibits only, with the Iwerks and planetarium additional. You can park in a garage at Monroe and Second Sts. Open daily, 10:00 A.M.–5:00 P.M., except Thanksgiving and Christmas. Call for a schedule of special exhibits, planetarium shows, and events. **600 E. Washington St., Phoenix, 85004; 602-716-2000. Website: www.azscience.org.**

Hall of Flame

Trucks, horse-drawn and mechanized, and hand-to-hand implements used between 1725 and 1955 are part of the world's largest collection of fire-fighting equipment. Children may explore a tyke-friendly area with a small replica fire truck and a large, real 1951 vehicle. They can try on turnout gear, helmets, and coats worn by firefighters. A Safety House helps them pick out fire hazards, then use a bedroom window as an escape route. Special kids' story hours and workshops are scheduled regularly; contact the museum for times and dates. Small fee. Open Mon.–Sat., 9:00 A.M.–5:00 P.M.; Sun., noon–4:00 P.M. Located in Papago Park. **6101 E. Van Buren, Phoenix, 85008; 602-275-3473. Website: www.hallofflame.org.**

Gardens and Arboreta

Desert Botanical Garden

The nationally acclaimed 150-acre Desert Botanical Garden provides an excellent starting place to become acquainted with the desert. It exhibits, conserves, and studies the world's arid-land plants, with special emphasis on the ones native to the southwestern United States. Nature trails run through the garden, with interpretive signs and helpful docents to introduce guests to the mysteries of the many-armed saguaro cactus and the secrets of the colorful Gila woodpecker.

Feb.–Apr., Mother Nature schedules her own very special event. The wildflower season bursts into bloom in the desert in general, and in a concentrated way at the garden. It's possible to see a range of flowers and cactuses in bloom that would take weeks to track down in the open desert. For desert plants to take home, including those not widely available elsewhere, check the Mar. and Oct. Landscape Plant Sales. Helpful attendants advise you on which ones will flourish in other parts of the country. One purchaser is successfully growing prickly pear cactus in Wisconsin. At the gift shop, look for treasures with a Southwest flavor to take home, as well as books about the desert and its inhabitants, lovely pottery, and T-shirts with creative designs that take them out of the "souvenir" category. Open May–Sept., daily, 7:00 A.M.–8:00 P.M.; Oct.–Apr., daily, 8:00 A.M.–8:00 P.M., except Christmas Day. Located in Papago Park at 64th St. and McDowell Rd. **1201 N. Galvin Parkway, Phoenix, 85008; 480-941-1225 or 480-481-8134 events hotline. Website: www.dbg.org.**

Museums and Historic Sites

Arizona Mining & Mineral Museum

One of the Southwest's largest mineral museums, it features extensive ore and minerals from Arizona, including those associated with copper, such as turquoise, malachite, azurite, chrysocolla, and bornite. A favorite with kids is the "hamburger" made of jaspar sitting on a quartzite "bun," garnished with obsidian "olives," "french fries" that are splinters of rhyolite, and iron oxide "ketchup." Free parking west of the museum. Free. Open Mon.–Fri., 8:00 A.M.–5:00 P.M.; Sat., 11:00 A.M.–4:00 P.M. **1502 W. Washington, Phoenix, 85007; 602-255-3791. Website: www.admmr.state.az.us.**

Arizona State Capitol Museum

Once the capitol of the Arizona Territory and then the State Capitol, this honorable edifice now holds interesting records of Arizona's past. It was built in 1899 of native malapai, granite, and tuff stone; in 1976 the state's copper industry gave 15 tons of copper to cover the dome. Restored House and Senate chambers, offices of

The front door of the Heard Museum faces Central Avenue, giving it an impressive presence.

Governor and Secretary of State, and an exhibit tracing the life of the USS *Arizona* are among the displays on the building's four floors. Free parking west of the building. Free. Open year-round, Mon.–Fri., 8:00 A.M.–5:00 P.M.; second Sat. of Jan.–end May, Sat., 10:00 A.M.–3:00 P.M. **1700 W. Washington, Phoenix, 85007; 602-542-4675 information or 602-542-4581 tours. Website: dlapr.lib.az.us.**

Orpheum Theater

Built in 1929 at a cost of $750,000 in the Spanish Baroque Revival style so popular at that time, this beautifully restored theater was considered the most luxurious playhouse west of the Mississippi. It hosted the best of vaudeville, including W. C. Fields and Mae West. In 1984 the City of Phoenix purchased the theater, placed it on the National Register of Historic Places, and re-opened it in 1997. Intricately carved and restored sandstone gargoyles leer from lofty perches and an elegant interior again welcomes theatergoers. Free tours by appointment. Located **at Third Ave. and Adams St. 602-252-9678.**

Pueblo Grande Museum and Cultural Park

Located close to downtown Phoenix, this pre-historic Hohokam village site along the Salt River was home for more than 1,000 years to people who engineered hundreds of miles of canals; cultivated corn, beans, and squash; and constructed towns of adobe. Flourishing from A.D. 450 to 1450, they disappeared sometime during the 15th century. The crumbling walls and outlines of buildings that now remain are not spectacular as ruins go, but as you stand on the platform mound ruin, possibly the homesites of Hohokam elite, the roar of jets shakes your thoughts—Sky Harbor International Airport is just a few miles away. In three out of four directions, your line of sight encounters traffic-clogged freeways. The centuries superimposed give many observers cause to reflect. There is a brief orientation video, a hands-on room for youngsters, and a main gallery used as a repository for items of interest unearthed during excavation anywhere in Phoenix.

The 0.3-mile-long ruin trail, accessible to wheelchairs, wanders up and over a 30-foot mound about the size of a football field. In the middle foreground an active canal, lined with paloverde trees, follows the route of an original Hohokam canal. Many Phoenix canals are so sited, testifying to the wisdom of ancient peoples as they used the water from the then-mighty Salt River to create a green and fertile valley. The gift shop stocks a good selection of native crafts and reference materials. The park is the only National Historic Landmark in Phoenix. Call ahead for a schedule of events and workshops. Small admission fee; free on Sun. Open Mon.–Sat., 9:00 A.M.–4:45 P.M.; Sun., 1:00 P.M.–4:45 P.M. **4619 E. Washington St., Phoenix, 85034-1909; 602-495-0901. Website: www.pueblogrande.com.**

Nightlife

A decade ago, Phoenix's downtown streets were practically deserted after about 6:00 P.M. on weekdays. Office workers scurried to the suburbs and home. But now a re-energized downtown entices people to linger for evening events, and to return to downtown for dinner and entertainment.

Arizona Center

This $515-million complex consists of eight blocks of restaurants, shops, and nightclubs. Its boutiques and vendor carts, spaced among palm trees and fountains, draw visitors in search of take-home gifts and items distinctively Arizona. A new 24-screen movie complex has just opened. It's the place to come for dinner before the theater, a sporting event, or a presentation at the symphony hall, and is always a good bet for a meal on a cool patio at an interesting restaurant. **Lombardi's** at the Arizona Center, **Mi Amigo's Mexican Restaurant,** and **Sam's Cafe** (Southwestern food) all are good choices (see Where to Eat).

Parks

Phoenix Zoo

This medium-size zoo is the nation's largest privately owned, self-supporting zoo. You can meander on four separate trails that represent Arizona, Africa, and the tropics, plus a children's trail. The zoo is home to 1,300 animals that live in environmental settings, including 200 endangered species from around the world. Among new arrivals are four cheetah cubs. Moderate fee. Open May 1–Labor Day, daily 7:30 A.M.–4:00 P.M.; Labor Day–Apr., daily 9:00 A.M.–5:00 P.M. **455 N. Galvin Parkway, Phoenix, 85008; 602-273-1341. Website: www.phoenix zoo.org.**

South Mountain Park

The mound of mountains that border the city's southern edge make up the largest municipal park in the world, truly a treasure that so far has managed to stave off encroaching development. Within almost 17,000 acres there are picnic areas, five lookout points, trails that range from mellow mile-long strolls to challenging hikes of a dozen miles and more (see

The Arizona Science Center in downtown Phoenix delights children and adults with hands-on activities.

Hiking), well-preserved petroglyph sites, and, on weekends, lots of people. Because the park is a preserve, everything within its boundaries is protected by law. It provides a home for coyotes, javelinas, cactus wrens, gilded flickers, Gila woodpeckers, Gambel's quail, tiny yellow-headed verdin, and dozens of other species. It is a favorite of mountain bikers and equestrians as well. At its 2,692-foot summit, a series of radio towers, capped with flashing red beacons, both orient and warn away planes headed for nearby Sky Harbor International Airport.

Remnants of civilizations that have used the area date to prehistoric times, with the ephemeral Hohokams among the more recent residents. They lived all over the Valley of the Sun (see Pueblo Grande under Museums and Historic Sites), leaving their mark in hundreds of petroglyphs. Although many sites are remote and difficult to reach, some are easily accessible on nonchallenging trails. From the 48th St. parking lot, take the Desert Classic Trail just five minutes around the base of the mountain to the west, and you'll be standing in front of a group of vivid petroglyphs, centuries old.

For general information on South Mountain Park, stop at the **Environmental Education Center,** the first building on the left as you enter the park from Central Ave. Replicas of Hohokam pottery, information on mining, and a relief map of the area help you understand what you'll find. Open Mon.–Sat., 9:00 A.M.–

5:00 P.M.; Sun., noon–5:00 P.M. **10419 S. Central Ave., Phoenix. 85040; 602-534-6324 or 602-261-8457 South Mountain Park.**

Performing Arts

THEATER

Herberger Theater Center

This lovely live theater venue has two small stages for intimate productions that include children's theater, ballet, performances by the Arizona Theatre Company, and others. Check to see what's playing. Located in the heart of downtown across from Civic Plaza. **222 E. Monroe St., Phoenix, 85004; 602-254-7399.**

Scenic Drives

The best vantage point from which to put Phoenix in perspective is Dobbins Lookout in South Mountain Park. The 180-degree view of the Valley of the Sun encompasses the misty Superstition Mountains to the east, unmistakable Camelback Mountain, a cluster of high rises marking downtown Phoenix, and the Bradshaw and Estrella Mountains to the west. On a clear day you can see Phoenix, Mesa, Tempe, Scottsdale, and a half dozen other Valley of the Sun towns. The memorable panorama reveals the area's multifaceted personality—as well as the brown cloud that has earned the city a number of wrist slaps from the Environmental Protection Agency in recent years. From the Central Ave. entrance to South Mountain Park, follow paved Summit Rd. to the north-facing lookout, about 3 miles.

Shopping

Phoenix Park 'n Swap

The area's biggest flea market, swap mart, whatever you want to call it, is the place to come for tools, stereo stuff, clothes, antiques, and assorted garage-sale cleanouts. It's been going on for decades, and is a regular weekend stop for many bargain hunters. Haggling is part of the fun. "Get real, we've got the deal," they say. And they usu-

ally do. Nominal admission fee. Open Wed., 4:00 P.M–10:00 P.M.; Fri., 6:00 A.M–2:00 P.M.; and Sat.–Sun., 6:00 A.M–4:00 P.M. Held in parking lot near Greyhound Park. **3801 E. Washington St., Phoenix, 85242; 602-273-1250. Website: www.americanparknswap.com.**

Sports

Professional Sports Teams

Phoenix's major league **baseball** team, the **Arizona Diamondbacks,** got their own stadium in 1998. Changing the downtown Phoenix skyline forever, the dramatic 48,500-seat Bank One Ballpark, nicknamed BOB, is designed with a retractable roof and natural grass playing surface that's replanted twice a year. The clubhouse has vintage and current major league uniforms and memorabilia. Six private party suites, full-service restaurants, a food court, swimming pool, and picnic area make the park a multiuse venue (see Major Attractions). **At 7th St. and Jefferson in downtown Phoenix. 602-462-6799 tours, 602-514-8400 or 888-777-4664 tickets.**

Next door to BOB, the 19,000-seat **America West Arena** is the home of the **Phoenix Suns,** the city's **National Basketball Association** team. The **Phoenix Coyotes,** the **National Hockey League** team, also plays at America West Arena. **At 2nd St. and Jefferson. 602-379-7800.**

Car Racing

West of Phoenix, cars have been zooming around **Phoenix International Raceway,** which promoters call the world's fastest 1-mile paved oval, since 1964. During a season that runs Nov.–Apr., NASCAR events, sports cars, Indy cars, midgets, and more provide motorized excitement. The NASCAR Winston Cup in early Nov. draws an international audience. Located at **115th Ave. and Baseline Rd. 602-252-2227. Website: www.phoenixintlraceway.com.**

Horse Racing

For decades **Turf Paradise** has occupied this

location. Horse racing is exciting, but the place itself is understated. You can sit and watch from the grandstand, clubhouse, or Turf Club, or just hang out at the rail where you can actually get dirt in your face. The club features parimutuel wagering with a minimum bet of $2. Season generally runs end of Sept.–beginning of May; post time 12:30 P.M. Located **at 19th Ave. and Bell Rd.** 602-942-1101. Website: www.turf paradise.com.

Tours

Coronado Historic District
We often take visitors on a drive through this area to prove to them that Phoenix really does have a quite interesting recent history. The area bounded by **Virginia Ave., McDowell Rd., Seventh St., and 16th St.** at one time marked the northernmost edge of Phoenix's prime residential area. When a trolley line was established along Brill St. in 1910, the area became more accessible. Homes here were generally built between 1910 and 1940, and represent the diversity of the city's population at that time. There are some magnificent mansions, many restored to a comfort level that satisfies present-day owners. Other, humbler dwellings were built in the Craftsman style so popular in California at that time. Also represented are mission style, charming English cottages, and basic bungalows. While some have been subjected to anachronistic additions and expansion, many others have been beautifully restored, so you get a definite feeling for the streets of decades past.

AERIAL TOURS

Hot-Air Ballooning
There may be no better place to enjoy this sport than the Sonoran Desert at dawn. Tethered to a multistriped orb of ripstop nylon, you skim the tops of saguaros and paloverdes, and few sounds mar the silence. As the balloon gains altitude, multiarmed saguaro cactuses grow small, and the sun turns the mountains warm shades of yellow and red. Settling back to earth can be a tricky maneuver because air is layered, affect-

ing the top of the balloon differently from the basket. But bumps usually are mild, and with a ground crew to steady the gondola, landings are uneventful. The traditional bottle of champagne is at the ready, along with orange juice in concession to the early hour. Most companies pick you up from and return you to your hotel. Among the Phoenix-area companies that soar: **Unicorn Balloon Company of Arizona, Inc., 800-468-2478 or 480-468-2478; Hot Air Expeditions, 800-831-7610 or 602-788-5555; Rainbow Balloon Flights, 602-258-2812 or 800-378-0470.**

WALKING TOURS

Heritage Square
It may not seem particularly exciting to visitors from the East and Midwest, where vintage homes are fairly common, but to Phoenicians, whose city is comparatively young, this collection of historic buildings dating to the late 1800s is an essential link to the past. They were part of the city's original development and have been restored and decorated to reflect a period in history when elegance was an anomaly in the Old West. The Eastlake Victorian **Rosson House,** built in 1895, is a classic example of the architecture of the time. The **Carriage House,** once a mule barn, is now a sandwich and gift shop. Lunch, tea, and pastries are offered at the **Teeter House** Victorian Tea Room, and the Arizona Doll & Toy Museum is in the **Stevens bungalow.** Homes are open varying hours for tours, some with a small admission charge. Heritage Square is located **between Sixth and Seventh Sts., between Monroe and Adams,** near the Science Center. You can get a self-guiding brochure by stopping at Heritage Square offices at Seventh and Monroe in **The Duplex, 115 N. Sixth St., Phoenix, 85004;** 602-262-5029.

Where to Stay

Because it is such a popular winter travel destination, the Valley of the Sun has places to stay

A palm-lined entrance welcomes guests to the Royal Palms, once a private mansion.

that range from the most basic digs to chain motels to off-the-charts luxury and elegance. Room rates can fluctuate wildly, depending on season and capacity.

Bed-and-Breakfasts

Maricopa Manor—$$$$

This delightful b-and-b once sat on the far north edge of Phoenix. When city growth encompassed the small Spanish-style bungalow by the 1970s, it was purchased and expanded to become a family home. Today there are six rooms and suites with private baths. Decades-old citrus trees shade a walled courtyard. Each room has a refrigerator and microwave, and some have fireplaces. Breakfast in bed is assured, because muffins, fruit, and juice are delivered to your room in a wicker basket. **15 W. Pasadena Ave., Phoenix, 85013; 602-274-6302 or 800-292-6403. Website: www.maricopamanor.com.**

Hotels and Inns

Arizona Biltmore—$$$$

Opened on Feb. 23, 1929, this hotel blended with the saguaros and chaparral then 8 miles northeast of Phoenix as though it had been there for ages. Today luxury homes and golf links surround it. The Biltmore was the dream of architect-builder Albert Chase McArthur and his two brothers, who set out to create a grand and lovely resort hotel to present the desert and romantic West to the rest of the country's social elite.

McArthur, once an apprentice draftsman to Frank Lloyd Wright, employed Wright's principles of using indigenous materials in harmony with surrounding landscape. A copper roof, a tribute to the state's flourishing mining industry, is still a distinctive feature. Concrete blocks were designed by a prominent Southwestern sculptor and cast in a small factory on-site. Imprinted with a geometric palm-tree pattern, they have come to be known as "Biltmore Block" and provide a striking element in the hotel's exterior appearance. Rooms have gone through many updates to include minibars and voice mail, but the Wright direction prevails in mission-style furnishings and western-design lamps à la the 1930s. The two-story lobby remains almost unchanged and the original pool is still lined with famed Catalina tile, manufactured on Wrigley-owned Catalina Island, California, and brought by the family to the Biltmore. Ask for a room in the main building to stay in the hotel's oldest part. **24th St. and Missouri, Phoenix, 85016; 800-950-2575 or 602-955-6600. Website: www.arizonabiltmore.com.**

Royal Palms—$$$$

This absolutely wonderful place, once great, turned tacky and then re-emerged to outdo even its former self. In 1928 the Royal Palms was the winter home of Cunard Steamship executive and entrepreneur Delos Cooke, who died in 1931. By 1948 investors bought and opened it for guests, naming it for the palms that line its driveway. Longtime Phoenicians remember it as one of several inns—Jokake, which was torn down to make room for the Phoenician, Smoketree, and Hermosa—that became functionally obsolete. During its first incarnation, the inn featured entertainment by Carmen Cavallero, Hildegard, Frank Sinatra, Tony Martin, and other idols of the era. Today, luxury casitas, plus villas with private patios and outdoor showers, are each individually decorated. No question it's pricey, but for a big splurge it's definitely the place to go, especially July–Aug. when rates on casitas are less than half of the winter high-season tariff. The rate includes two full breakfasts at T. Cook's (see Where to Eat) and a minibar stocked with soft drinks and fresh fruit. **5200 E. Camelback Rd., Phoenix, 85018; 602-840-3610 or 800-672-6011. Website: www.royal palmshotel.com.**

Wigwam Resort—$$$$

In Litchfield Park west of Phoenix, this venerable resort owes its existence to the motorcar. When Goodyear Tire & Rubber discovered that cotton extended the life of automobile tires, the company required a dependable local supply of the high-quality fiber. World War I had closed off Egypt as a source, and boll weevils had ravaged Georgia's cotton. So Arizona became the site. A 13-room guest lodge was built to house visiting Goodyear executives. By 1929 the "wigwam," as it was affectionately dubbed, had become so popular that it opened to the public

as a resort. A year later a nine-hole golf course was added, and today it is the only Valley of the Sun resort with three championship courses. It includes 300 guest casitas, four fine restaurants, two pools, and nine lighted tennis courts. The original 1919 main lodge, now the Fireplace Room, displays photographs of guests in cool white 1920s resort wear and ranch dress of the 1940s and 1950s. It has gained a national reputation for its exceptional selection of wines and spirits. **Litchfield Park, 85340; 800-327-0396 or 623-935-3811. Website: www.wig wamresort.com.**

Hotel San Carlos—$$$–$$$$

Things here have been so ideally restored and refurbished, you'd swear it's 1928 and the hotel has just opened. The Italian Renaissance downtown hotel was the first high-rise, fully air-conditioned hotel with an elevator in Phoenix. Hollywood stars including Spencer Tracy and Clark Gable stayed in rooms with spigots that dispensed circulating ice water. The original glazed terra-cotta tiles decorate the entryway, and one of the two attendant-operated elevators still functions. Rooms, with coffeemakers, are comfortable and low-key elegant. From the rooftop pool you look up at recent skyscrapers that bring you back to the present. Privately owned and operated. **202 N. Central Ave., Phoenix, 85004; 602-253-4121. Website: www.hotel sancarlos.com**

Resorts

The Pointe Hilton South Mountain—$$$$
The Pointe Hilton at Squaw Peak—$$$$
The Pointe Hilton at Tapatio Cliffs—$$$$

These three resort properties are located in different parts of Phoenix and have diverse personalities, yet all have the unmistakable Hilton mark of luxury. The South Mountain property is adjacent to a highly acclaimed desert-target/ links golf course. Focal point of Tapatio Cliffs is The Falls, a 3-acre oasis of pools, terraces, and outdoor dining . At Squaw Peak there are seven pools, four lighted tennis courts, and an extensive spa and salon. The "River Ranch" at Squaw Peak has a lagoon pool. **The Pointe Hilton on South Mountain, 7777 S. Pointe Parkway, Phoenix, 85044; The Pointe Hilton at Squaw Peak, 7677 N. 16th St., Phoenix, 85020; The Pointe Hilton at Tapatio Cliffs, 11111 N. Seventh St., Phoenix, 85020; 800-876-4683.** Website: www.pointehilton.com.

Hostels

The Metcalf House Hostel—$

This is the only hostel in Phoenix that we know of, and it's a good one. It has 35 beds and a large common room, all part of a great old home built in a sort of Craftsman-cottage style. They prefer to receive reservations by mail, so jot your dates on a postcard as early as you can. Call the hostel for the phone number of the local taxi, which charges a small fixed rate to transport you from the airport or bus station. Located on Ninth St. between Portland and Roosevelt, two blocks east of Seventh St. **1026 N. Ninth St., Phoenix, 85006; 602-254-9803.**

Where to Eat

Planet Hollywood, Hooters, Hard Rock Cafe, Houston's—most of the successful upscale chains you'd expect to find in a big city are here. The Phoenix dining scene is casual, even in the most upscale restaurants.

Durant's—$$$$

A Phoenix legend for decades. You can't go wrong with a huge steak or fresh seafood. A throwback to an era when flocked wallpaper was cutting edge, here waiters still wear tuxes and martinis are made as they were in the '40s. Your dad would love this place, and so will you. Open Mon.–Fri., 11:00 A.M.–4:00 P.M. and 4:30 P.M.–10:00 P.M.; Sat., 5:00 P.M.–10:00 P.M.; Sun., 4:30 P.M.–10:00 P.M. **2611 N. Central Ave.; 602-264-5967.**

LON's at the Hermosa—$$$$

This very popular place (reservations essential) combines historic Arizona ambiance with award-winning regional cuisine. The 1930s hacienda-style adobe is filled with Southwestern furnishings and cowboy artwork. Portions are not overwhelming so you can order an appetizer, salad, entree, and dessert without feeling like you've overindulged. One of the best entrees is the sesame seared *ahi* tuna with mango relish. Open Mon.–Fri., 11:30 A.M.–2:00 P.M. and 6:00 P.M.–10:00 P.M.; Sat., 6:00 P.M.–10:00 P.M.; Sun., 10:00 A.M.–2:00 P.M. and 6:00 P.M.–10:00 P.M. **5532 N. Palo Cristi Rd., Paradise Valley; 602-955-7878.**

T. Cook's at the Royal Palms—$$$$

The best strategy here is to go for breakfast so you can experience the ambiance and skills of the chef without paying dinner prices. Don't miss the grilled date nut French toast with homemade sausages. "Rustic Mediterranean" best describes its atmosphere, and food is beautifully prepared without undue froufrou. The dining room has a tree growing in its center. Open Mon.–Sat., 11:00 A.M.–2:00 P.M. and 5:30 P.M.–10:00 P.M.; Sun., 10:00 A.M.–2:00 P.M. and 5:30 P.M.–10:00 P.M. **5200 E. Camelback Rd.; 602-808-0766.** Website: www.royalpalms hotel.com.

Bistro 24—$$–$$$

At the Ritz-Carlton, yet casual and unpretentious, this true bistro opens daily at 6 A.M. for cappuccino, croissants, and full breakfasts, and goes strong into the late evening hours. Big, bolt artwork plus European and American antiques surround comfortable sofa-style banquettes. Classic French bistro cuisine includes seared rare tuna loin, filet mignon, and smoked salmon pizza. **At the corner of 24th Street and Camelback; 602-952-2424.**

Vincent's on Camelback—$$$$

For years the quintessential place to see and be seen, Vincent's award-winning American Southwestern cuisine is the same high quality as ever, served in a charming country French setting.

Duck tamales and checkerboard cake are classics. Open daily, 11:00 A.M.–2:30 P.M. and 6:00 P.M.–10:00 P.M. **3930 E. Camelback Rd.; 602-224-0225.**

Eddie Matney's—$$$–$$$$

In the heart of Phoenix's trendiest area, on the corner of 24th St. and E. Camelback Rd., chef Eddie Matney's signature New American cuisine reflects the techniques he says he learned at the knee of his Lebanese mother. Big food with lots of flavors, he calls it. You can sink into a black leather booth and choose from inventive pastas and sandwiches, plus half a dozen salads that incorporate fresh fish. Valet parking off 24th St. Open Mon.–Fri., 11:30 A.M.–10:00 P.M.; Sat.–Sun., 5:00 P.M.–10:00 P.M. **2398 E. Camelback; 602-957-3214.**

Lombardi's—$$$–$$$$

In the Arizona Center in downtown Phoenix, Lombardi's serves upscale Northern Italian food that's not an overgross in the calorie department. Outstanding focaccia bread comes warm and fragrant from wood-burning ovens. Ask about nightly seafood specials, always fresh, sometimes served with an inventive pasta. With an early 5:30 dinner reservation, you still have time to make opening curtain at the Herberger Theater, or slip into your seat at a sporting event. Afterward, stop in for a creme brulee, Tuscan bread pudding, or icy gelato. Open Mon.–Fri., 11:00 A.M.–10:00 P.M.; Sat.–Sun., 11:00 A.M.–11:00 P.M. **455 N. Third St.; 602-257-8323.**

RoxSand—$$$–$$$$

The freshest of the fresh reigns here, in an inventive fusion of flavors from Asia, Europe, and the Middle East. The stunning, dual-level dining room is filled with contemporary art. At Biltmore Fashion Park. Open Mon.–Thurs., 11:00 A.M.–3:00 P.M. and 5:00 P.M.–9:00 P.M.; Fri., 5:30 P.M.–10:30 P.M.; Sat., 11:00 A.M.–3:00 P.M. and 5:00 P.M.–10:30 P.M.; Sun., noon–3:00 P.M. **2594 E. Camelback Rd.; 602-381-0444.**

Stockyards Restaurant and 1889 Bar—$$$–$$$$

Until the 1960s, when the breeze wafted less-than-lovely aromas from E. Washington St. near the railroad tracks, Phoenicians shut their windows. The Livestock Exchange, overlooking the world's largest feedlot with 200 acres of pens, accommodated up to 40,000 head of cattle. A small coffee shop served cattlemen. When it burned in 1954 it was replaced by today's building. The decor is 1890s, with old photographs chronicling the restaurant's history. The smelly stockyards are long gone, but the tradition of serving great beef lives on. Open Mon.–Sat., 11:00 A.M.–10:00 P.M. **5001 E. Washington St.; 602-273-7378.**

Sam's Cafe—$$$

At Biltmore Fashion Park, 24th St. and Camelback in a super trendy area, this is the place to lunch after a tough morning's shopping. The outstanding Southwestern menu has great fish tacos and black bean soup. Their signature is a white chocolate tamale, a skinny shaft of sweetness wrapped in a corn husk and presented frozen at the end of your meal. Open Mon.–Thurs., 11:00 A.M.–9:00 P.M.; Fri.–Sat., 11:30 A.M.–11:00 P.M. **2566 E. Camelback Rd.; 602-954-7100.**

The Farm at South Mountain—$$

One of our favorite pleasant-weather places to eat, here you order a salad, sandwich, scones, or other equally delicious fare, then take it to a patio under pecan trees, or to picnic tables scattered throughout this 10-acre grove. Everything here is wholesome and delicious, made from scratch. Open Tues.–Sun., 8:00 A.M.–3:00 P.M., "weather permitting," they say; call first if the sky looks iffy. Located just south of Southern on 32nd St. **6106 S. 32nd St.; 602-276-6360.**

Services

Local Visitor Information

The Arizona Republic and the *Arizona Business*

The Frank Lloyd Wright–inspired Arizona Biltmore, recently renovated, is one of Phoenix's oldest luxury hotels.

Gazette have a wonderfully helpful website: www.azcentral.com; it hosts other websites for various organizations. The site also offers ever-changing news topics from the *Republic.* In the fine print you'll find a guide to more than 200 Arizona golf courses, Arizona sports information, a travel and lodging guide, and more. Another good statewide website: access arizona.com; click on Travel for destination information. Accessarizona.com also has lots of Phoenix information.

Arizona Office of Tourism

Call the 800 number to receive a large packet of information on visiting the state. 2702 N. Third St., No. 4015, Phoenix, 85004; 800-842-8257. Website: www.arizonaguide.com.

Bureau of Land Management Office

Open Mon.–Fri., 7:30 A.M.–4:30 P.M.; public room open 9:00 A.M.–4:00 P.M. 222 N. Central Ave., Phoenix, 85004-2203; 602-417-9200, fax 602-417-9399.

Greater Phoenix Convention & Visitors Bureau

One Arizona Center, 400 E. Van Buren St., Phoenix, 85004-2290; 602-252-5588. Website: www.phoenixcvb.com. Call for a complementary copy of the magazine *PHXplorer,* the city's official 122-page visitor guide.

Gypsy Java

At this cybercafe, you'll find coffee, board games, a friendly atmosphere, and three computers on cable modem at $9 per hour. Open Mon.–Thurs., 7:00 A.M.–8:00 P.M.; Fri.–Sat., 7:00 A.M.–11:00 P.M.; Sun., 1:00 P.M.–8:00 P.M. 3321 E. Bell Rd.; 602-404-9779. Website: www.gypsyjava.com.

Transportation

In Phoenix bus service is sketchy at best. In 2000, Phoenix voters approved a light-rail system, which won't be in place for at least five years. There is no big, reliable mass transit system such as BART in San Francisco. 602-253-5000.

Monsoons

For many, the word "monsoon" creates images from an aged, grainy black-and-white film set in a jungle, with turban-wrapped, white-skirted servants scurrying to batten shutters against an onslaught of wind, rain, and other nasty surprises from the elements. In Arizona, "monsoon" means the season between sometime in early July and the middle of Sept., when the southern part of the state gets most of its rain. The word "monsoon" refers to a wind pattern that affects a large climatic region and reverses direction seasonally, but in common usage it covers the entire process. Moisture from the Gulf of Mexico and the Gulf of California flows into the state when hot summer desert air rises and moist air replaces it. It doesn't have to rain to be a "monsoon day." As defined by meteorologists, a monsoon day is officially any day when the dew point, an indicator of the amount of moisture in the air, reaches 55 degrees or higher. The monsoon season begins officially when the dew point, as recorded at Sky Harbor International Airport, hits 55 for three consecutive days.

Arizonans have a sort of love-hate relationship with the monsoons. Combined with the most intense solar heat of the year, monsoons create undesertlike humidity that makes evaporative coolers ineffective and requires air conditioners to work even harder. Thunderstorms build quickly, creating flash floods, dust storms, and winds that have been known to uproot manufactured homes, take roofs off buildings, and strew branches and debris across city streets. On the other hand, for the brief time it actually rains, the desert can be blessedly cool. And these rains, which account for 40–50 percent of Arizona's annual precipitation, bring the spectacular desert bloom that occurs in Apr.

Recently it has been debated whether the cement and asphalt city center, referred to in local news accounts as an "urban heat island," chases away the monsoons. Because the paved city holds heat and remains up to 15°F warmer than the surrounding desert, which cools naturally at night, some theorize that storms are deterred from passing over Phoenix. So far no statistics bear out that theory, but unquestionably downtown Phoenix, and ever-expanding areas in Scottsdale, Tempe, Mesa, and other surrounding cities, are heat capsules.

If you're caught in an Arizona monsoon, stay in your car and wait the storm out. If it becomes so dusty or rainy that you can't see to drive, pull as far off the road as possible, turn off your lights, and keep your foot off the brake pedal so other cars won't think you're moving in traffic and possibly rear-end you. If you can continue driving, remember that the road will be slick. There isn't enough rain in Arizona to keep the roads washed clean. Don't cross flooded washes. If you stall and the rain continues, you easily could be swept away. If you're on foot, don't stand under a tree, especially a palm tree, which acts as a lightning rod. Get out of a canyon or wash immediately.

Scottsdale

On Phoenix's northwest side, this pleasant resort town with humble beginnings now has such big-city badges as a Nieman-Marcus, countless luxury resorts, and a population of more than 200,000. In keeping with its now-sophisticated image, Scottsdale has abandoned the slogan "The West's Most Western Town" in favor of promoting itself as the Spirit of the American Southwest. Despite the rush of development to the city's deserts, and proliferation of luxury hostelries, you still can find the horses-and-cowboys experience. The almost 7 million tourists who visit Scottsdale yearly just have to look a little harder for it.

Adjacent to Scottsdale but very much its own city, Paradise Valley could be considered the area's Beverly Hills. Single-family homes are the only structures allowed, except for historic properties like the Hermosa Inn (see Where to Stay) and golf courses. Most homes are set on very large plots, some also protected by walls. A drive through this tony enclave of about 16,000 reveals glimpses of how the likes of Dan Quayle and Alice Cooper live.

retired to a little farm on a plot of land northeast of Phoenix. Others arrived to farm and to run cattle and sheep. As recently as the 1940s, sheepherding along Scottsdale Rd. was a spectator sport. And as recently as 1951, Scottsdale was so small that the entire town budget was operated from a cigar box at the fire station. Today Scottsdale is well out of the small-town category.

History

Scottsdale had its beginnings in the 1880s when the Rev. Winfield Scott, a Civil War veteran,

Getting There

Scottsdale is northeast of downtown Phoenix, centered at Scottsdale Rd. and Camelback Rd. The distance between the northernmost and southernmost points is 31 miles. Landmark Camelback Mountain parallels the road that bears its name, defining some of Scottsdale's most upscale areas, and on its north side is Paradise Valley, along McDonald Dr.

Festivals and Events

Thursday ArtWalks

year-round

Scottsdale's art district hosts walks to its famed galleries. Oftentimes walks are themed, such as the Fall Cowboy Artists of America event that coincides with the sale and show at the Phoenix Art Museum. Visiting artists usually are on hand to chat about their works. At any given time at least 40 galleries participate. The city of Scottsdale helps create a market for the work of local artists because, by city ordinance, 1 percent of all capital improvement funds is allocated to public art. Thurs., 7:00 P.M.–9:00 P.M. Galleries are primarily located **along Main St., on Marshall Way, on Fifth Ave., and in Old Town near the Civic Center.** 480-990-3939.

Celebration of Fine Art

Jan.–Mar.

You don't even have to like art to enjoy this informal event that's actually one of the biggest art markets in the West. More than 100 artists present their wares to buyers and browsers who come from around the world. Located **on Scottsdale Rd. 1 mile north of Bell at Mayo Dr.** 480-443-7695. Website: www. celebrateart.com.

Scottsdale Arabian Horse Show

mid-Feb.

The largest Arabian horse show in the world, it features more than 2,000 Arabians, half-Arabians, and national show horses in competition. Held at **Westworld, 16601 N. Pima Rd., Scottsdale, 85259;** 480-515-1500.

Festival of the West

mid-Mar.

It's four days of hootin', hollerin', western-style fun that includes western film celebs, music, cowboy poetry, costume contests, arena events, chuck-wagon cookin' competition, and a huge trade show with western art and cowboy collectibles. Held at Rawhide Western Town. **2302 N. Scottsdale Rd., Scottsdale, 85251;** 602-996-4387. Website: www.festivalofthe west.com.

Thunderbird Balloon Classic

early Nov.

A spectacularly colorful event going on for 25 years, it's a favorite among spectators because you can walk among the balloons as they're laid out on the ground before launching, and chat with pilots and ground crew. In the past, special-shape hot-air balloons have included the Korbel "Champagne Bottle," the Burger King "Whopper," Planter's "Mr. Peanut," Sea World–Busch Gardens' "Air Shamu," and Famous Footwear's "Big Foot." In all, more than 100 of the hot-air classics fill the skies over the McDowell Mountains and the Sonoran Desert. In addition to balloon races and evening balloon glows, events include exhibits, arts and crafts displays, interactive games, food, rides, and entertainment at the Polo Field at Westworld. **16601 N. Pima Rd., Scottsdale, 85258;** 602-978-7790.

Outdoor Activities

Golf

Grayhawk Golf Club

The Raptor course, considered one of Scottsdale's most picturesque, is backdropped by the McDowell Mountains. Famed golf architect Tom Fazio designed the 7,000-yard, par 71 layout. A second course, par 72 Talon, recently was selected as one of *Golf* magazine's "Top 10 You Can Play." **8620 E. Thompson Peak Parkway, Scottsdale, 85259;** 480-502-1800.

Sanctuary Golf Course at Westworld

Newest addition to the roster of Scottsdale courses is Sanctuary at Westworld, an 18-hole daily-fee golf club. So-called because it is the first Audubon International Signature course in the area, it gives new meaning to the term "birdie." Sensitively integrated with the environment, it is designed to enhance wildlife habitat while providing excellent risk-reward golf. The 6,650-yard par 71 course features wetlands and cattails in a desert oasis setting. **16601 N. Pima Rd., Scottsdale, 85259;** 480-502-8200.

Talking Stick Golf Club

On the Salt River Pima-Maricopa Indian Community, this truly spectacular 36-hole facility was designed by two-time U.S. Masters Champion Ben Crenshaw and partner Bill Coore. The North course is a low-profile desert grasslands setting, while the South course is elevated, with scalloped bunkers and more treed areas. Talking Stick is the Southwest headquarters for the *Golf Digest* Instructional Schools. Located at **Alma School and Indian Bend Rds.** 480-860-2221.

Troon North Golf Club

Mature cactus and rock outcroppings that were part of the landscape decades ago dramatically enhance the two upscale courses here. Each, over 7,000 yards, plays to a par 72. Recently they were ranked the number-one and number-two public access courses in the state by *Golf Digest.* Although pricey, its reputation assures that it is always busy. **10320 E. Dynamite Blvd., Scottsdale, 85255; 480-585-5300.**

Seeing and Doing

Art Museums and Galleries

Fleischer Museum

Dedicated to artists of American Impressionism, California School, this charming small museum is filled with *plein air* canvases depicting the abundance of sunlight and brilliantly colored landscapes. Open daily, 10:00 A.M.–4:00 P.M. Go north on Pima Rd. past Frank Lloyd Wright Blvd, then left on Bell to Perimeter. **17207 N. Perimeter Dr., Scottsdale, 85258; 480-585-3108.** Website: **www.fleischermuseum.org.**

Scottsdale Museum of Contemporary Art

Among featured artists in this lovely new museum's seven galleries are glass sculptor Dale Chihuly and William Wegman, famed for whimsical depictions of his sleek, gray weimaraners. Changing exhibits assure a fresh experience each time you visit. Moderate fee; Tues. free. Open Tues.–Wed. and Fri.–Sat., 10:00 A.M.–5:00 P.M.; Thurs., 10:00 A.M.–9:00 P.M.; Sun., noon–5:00 P.M. Located **at northwest corner of Second St. and Civic Center Blvd.** in Scottsdale. 480-994-2787.

Balloon festivals are held throughout Arizona. The largest is the November Thunderbird Balloon Classic held in Scottsdale for more than 25 years.

Children and Families

McCormick-Stillman Railroad Park

This park, an absolute must for younger kids and railroad buffs, features a five-twelfths-scale steam locomotive that chugs a 1.25-mile route around the 30-acre park. It leaves from Stillman Station, a 5,200-square-foot replica of a historic depot in Clifton, named for Guy Stillman who donated the train. The park opened in 1975 on land donated by Anne and Fowler McCormick, on the edge of the onetime McCormick Ranch. Extensively renovated, the park includes a 1950s aluminum carousel, railroad museum, four model railroad clubs, and an area for birthday parties and celebrations. At holiday time the station and train are covered with lights. Open Oct.–May, 10:00 A.M.–6:00 P.M.; call for June–Sept. schedule. Located at southeastern corner of Scottsdale and Indian Bend Rds. **7301 E. Indian Bend Rd., Scottsdale, 85250; 480-312-2312.**

Rawhide

Come to this fun, rowdy 1880s western town for a full day of family fun. The largest western-themed attraction in Arizona, it has two dozen shops to keep adults happy while young ones hang out in Kids' Territory. Visit the petting ranch, museum, and interesting Native American village. The obligatory cowboy gunfights are staged regularly. Special events include the Haunted Express, safe trick or treating, and in the fall a sundown cookout and western show. If you've never tried rattlesnake, you'll have your chance at the Rawhide Steakhouse and Saloon, which also serves great ribs and huge steaks; open daily for dinner, seasonally for lunch. The park is open 11:00 A.M.–10:00 P.M. **23023 N. Scottsdale Rd., Scottsdale, 85250; 480-502-1880. Website: www.rawhide.com.**

Museums and Historic Sites

Arizona Cowboy College

Want to find out how the West was once? Eschewing resort-style cookouts and dude-type horses, the weeklong course includes two rigorous days of horsemanship and learning about cattle, and four days of on-the-range lessons in cutting, branding, inoculating, dehorning, and driving. You eat and sleep under the starry skies. **480-767-7640. Website: www.cowboy college.com.**

Hoo-hoogam-Ki Museum

Home of the Salt River Pima-Maricopa Indian Community, the Salt River Indian Reservation is the most urbanized of any Arizona reservation. On the south it shares a border with the city of Mesa, and parallels Scottsdale on the west. Despite its proximity to dense population areas, here tribal members cultivate about 12,000 of the reservation's 52,600 acres, producing cotton, melons, potatoes, onions, and carrots. For general information about the reservation, call the **Community Relations Office (480-874-8056).** On the reservation, the Hoo-hoogam-Ki Museum displays baskets, pottery, and artifacts typical of the Maricopa and Pima tribes.

Frank Lloyd Wright's famous architectural campus, Taliesin West, has tours of his home and classrooms.

Token fee. Open year-round, Mon.–Fri., 10:00 A.M.–4:30 P.M.; Oct.–May, Sat., 10:00 A.M.–2:00 P.M. Follow Longmore Rd. north from McDowell Rd. The museum is at the southeast corner of Longmore and Osborn. **10000 E. Osborn Rd., Scottsdale; 85250; 480-874-8190.**

Taliesin West

If you've seen Taliesin East, you'll be absolutely stunned at how different it is from this Frank Lloyd Wright enclave. The curiosity is not so much in the structures themselves, but in how the same principles of design can successfully apply in two such diverse areas. The architect built his studio, home, and architectural campus here in 1937, and occupied it until his death in 1959. Recognized as an architectural masterpiece and declared a National Historic Landmark, it began when Wright sought a winter home for himself and for his architectural school located in Wisconsin. He found the desert climate appealing and its rocks, boulders, and subtle colorations irresistible. He linked the elements of his school with walkways and terraces, adding fountains as a contrast to the surrounding Sonoran Desert.

Taliesin West remains much as it was in Wright's day, with revered portions such as the **Garden Room** practically untouched. Visitors enter through a low-ceilinged, stone-walled vestibule typical of his technique of compression of space, which bursts into a large, well-lighted area covered with a translucent roof that makes it seem even more expansive. Wright-designed furniture and the famous **Music Room** are much in use today. You can walk around most of the exterior, but the only way to see interiors is by guided tour because Taliesin West is still a working educational facility. A variety of **tours** (480-860-8810) are offered seasonally, ranging from one to three hours. Located at Cactus Rd. and Frank Lloyd Wright Blvd. (about 114th St.) in North Scottsdale. **12621 N. Frank Lloyd Wright Blvd., Scottsdale, 85259; 480-860-2700. Website: www.franklloydwright.org.**

Other Sights

Fountain Hills

This mostly residential bedroom community's claim to fame is the 560-foot fountain that spurts higher than the Washington Monument, every hour on the hour, daily, 10:00 A.M.–9:00 P.M. **Take Scottsdale Rd. north to Shea Blvd., turn right, and proceed 12 miles to Fountain Hills. Fountain Hills Chamber of Commerce, 480-837-1654. Website: www.fhchamberofcommerce.org.**

Scenic Drives

FOUR-WHEEL-DRIVE TRIPS

Desert Storm Hummer Tours

Those low, wide, flat 4x4s are among the most powerful vehicles on earth. They hug the terrain as they crawl over rocks and washes, and can be your vehicle of choice for exploring. Desert Storm Hummer Tours' experienced guides, trained in desert survival, take you on half-day or longer adventures into the Sonoran Desert to places including Tonto National Forest in the Four Peaks area. Those with back conditions, heart problems, or recent surgeries, or who are pregnant, should take another tour, as these vehicles are noted not so much for comfort as for being able to go just about anywhere. The company motto is "There are no dead ends." Located **in Scottsdale. 480-922-0020. Website: www.dshummer.com.**

Wagering

For games of chance on the Salt River Indian Reservation, visit **Casino Arizona** (480-850-7777). **Fort McDowell Casino** (602-843-3678) is operated by the Yavapai Indians.

Where to Stay

Scottsdale has everything from over-the-top luxurious to basic and simple accommodations, plus most of the chains. We've listed some of our favorites, but your best bet is to get the "Destination Guide" from the Scottsdale Convention and Visitors Bureau (see Services).

Resorts

Most upscale resorts have on-site spas.

Camelback Inn—$$$$

The only Arizona resort to hold the Mobil Five Star & AAA Five Diamond awards for 24 consecutive years, this Southwestern hacienda situated on 125 acres has been welcoming guests for more than 60 years. Owned by Marriott, it features 453 rooms, 36 holes of championship golf, tennis, and fine dining in The Chaparral, a longtime favorite of locals as well as guests. The uniquely Southwestern spa features an adobe clay purification treatment inspired by the ancient healing rituals of Native American cultures. Hopalong College is one of the resort industry's longest-running children's programs. **5402 E. Lincoln Dr., Scottsdale, 85253; 800-24-CAMEL or 480-948-1700. Website: www.camelbackinn.com.**

Fairmont Scottsdale Princess—$$$$

Many guests settle into a room or casita at this sprawling hotel and never leave. Nine tennis courts and two championship 18-hole golf courses, three swimming pools, plus walking trails and a spa can keep most people occupied. Located about 20 minutes north of downtown Scottsdale. **7575 E. Princess Dr., Scottsdale,**

85255; 480-585-4848 or 800-344-4758. Website: www.fairmont.com.

Four Seasons—$$$$

Located at Troon North and just opened, it's the first Four Seasons property in Arizona. It lives up to the luxury Four Seasons image in every way. Appropriately, it's of Southwest-territorial design with rooms and suites arranged in Southwestern casitas. Guests have priority use of the Pinnacle and Monument golf courses at Troon North (see Golf). **10600 E. Crescent Moon Dr., Scottsdale, 85255; 800-332-3442 or 480-515-5700. Website: www.four seasons.com.**

The Phoenician—$$$$

For sheer opulence, this palacelike resort has it all. To many, it symbolizes luxury. Even if you aren't staying here, you can stroll through the Italian marble lobby (guest rooms have marble baths and berber carpet), have lunch at Windows on the Green, take a look at the cabana-flanked pools and waterfalls, and have a drink at the bar. One of the best spas in the area, The Centre for Well-Being at the Phoenician offers extensive treatments and programs, including personal training and nutrition for couples, as well as a meditation atrium and aerobics studio that overlooks the golf course. Southwestern body treatments use desert plants and minerals such as aloe vera, jojoba, and sage that are native to the area. **6000 E. Camelback Rd., Scottsdale, 85251; 480-941-8200, 800-888-8234, or 480-423-2452 (spa direct). Website: www.thephoenician.com.**

Hyatt Regency Scottsdale Resort at Gainey Ranch—$$$$

This is a classy resort in every way, with all the amenities you'd expect. Making it even better is the Hopi Learning Center at the resort, a sort of mini-museum with Hopi kachina dolls, pottery, jewelry, baskets, and more. Learning stations let guests try the Hopi way of grinding corn in stone bowls as a way to understand the culture. **7500 E. Doubletree Ranch Rd.,** Scottsdale, 85258; 480-991-3388 or 800-233-1234. Website: www.hyatt.com.

SunBurst—$$$–$$$$

If you visited Scottsdale in the 1960s, you'll remember the Executive House, just north of Camelback on Scottsdale Rd. After slipping into a decline, it was purchased by Noble House, and is now a little gem of a boutique resort. SunBurst's edge is that it is in the heart of downtown Scottsdale, within blocks of Fashion Square, less than a mile from Old Town, and in the midst of great restaurants. Southwest-decor rooms have mini-refrigerators, in-room coffee, and French doors that open onto wonderful gardens with flowing streams. The Rancho Saguaro restaurant serves contemporary cuisine in an indoor-outdoor setting. **4925 N. Scottsdale Rd., Scottsdale, 85251; 480-945-7666; 800-528-7867. Website: www.sun burstresort.com.**

Where to Eat

El Chorro Lodge—$$$$

Even though it's been around for six decades, El Chorro does not rest on its laurels. If you ate here 20 years ago, you would still find many of the same things on the menu today, such as breaded chicken livers sauteed with bacon, eggs Benedict, chicken-fried steak with mashed potatoes and gravy, or shad roe on toast. Additions like mesquite-broiled chicken and blackened swordfish are a concession to a new generation of heart-healthy diners. Take the time to appreciate the John W. Hampton cowboy sculpture at the entrance, and the photos of countless celebs who have enjoyed El Chorro over the years. Open Mon.–Fri., 11:00 A.M.–3:00 P.M. and 5:30 P.M.–11:00 P.M.; Sat.–Sun., 5:30 P.M.–11:00 P.M. **5550 E. Lincoln Dr.; 480-948-5170.**

Marquesa—$$$$

At the Fairmont Scottsdale Princess, this five-diamond restaurant creates Catalan cuisine that

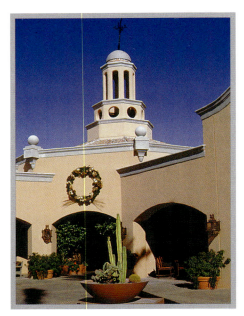

The Fairmont Scottsdale Princess offers luxury rooms and casitas in a natural desert setting.

uniquely blends Italian, French, and Spanish influences. This is where you come to celebrate a special occasion, or to create a real impression. We love to bring guests to the Spanish market-style Sun. brunch. With dozens of food stations, including outdoor grills on which fresh fish, chops, and vegetables are freshly cooked, it is truly spectacular. Open Tues.–Thurs., 6:00 P.M.–10:00 P.M.; Fri.–Sat., 6:00 P.M.–11:00 P.M.; Sun., 10:00 A.M.–2:30 P.M. **7575 E. Princess Dr.; 480-585-4848.**

Medizona—$$$$

A Mediterranian-inspired Southwestern menu is featured at this new, charming, small restaurant in Old Town Scottsdale that takes its name from its cuisine. Chef/owner Lenard Rubin deftly uses unusual combinations to create flavors that keep diners coming back. The eggplant tacos with lamb appetizer, and achiote-rubbed pan-fried salmon are favorites. Open Tues.–Sat., 6:00 P.M.–10:00 P.M. **7217 E. 4th Ave.; 480-947-9500**

Michael's at the Citadel—$$$–$$$$

Airy, comfortable surroundings with three pa-

tios in a small shopping area complement exquisitely prepared food from the kitchen of chef/owner Michael DeMaria. Be sure to start with the arugula and endive salad with apples, walnuts, and Gorgonzola in Chianti vinaigrette. For entrees, you can't go wrong with pan-seared Chilean sea bass, osso bucco, or orange duck. Open Mon.–Sat., 11:00 A.M.–2:00 P.M.; daily, 6:00 P.M.–10:00 P.M.; Sun. brunch from 10:00 A.M.–2:00 P.M. **8700 E. Pinnacle Peak Rd.; 480-515-2575.**

Old Town Tortilla Factory—$$$–$$$$

In historic Old Town Scottsdale, with a 50-foot pecan tree sheltering a patio, this restaurant beautifully prepares and serves regional Mexican cuisine. Hand-made tortillas are served with matched herb butters. Have an award-winning margarita with your meal, then linger over a tequila from their collection of more than a hundred different brands. Open daily 4:00 P.M.–9 P.M., 10:00 P.M. on weekends. **6910 E. Main, Scottsdale, 85251; 480-945-4567. Website: www.amdest.com.**

Rancho Saguaro—$$$–$$$$

About as pleasant a place to dine as you'll find in Scottsdale, this rustic Southwest-style restaurant in the Sunburst Hotel features American cuisine with decidedly southwest influences. Everything is prepared over a wood fire using Mexican red oak and Arizona pecan. The fragrance scents the dining room. When the weather's comfortable, ask to be seated on the patio overlooking waterfalls and a lagoon. Open Mon.–Sun., 6:30 A.M.–11 A.M. and 11:30 A.M.–2:30 P.M.; Sun.–Thurs., 5:00 P.M.–10:00 P.M.; Fri.–Sat., 5 P.M.–10:30 P.M.; **4925 N. Scottsdale Rd.; 480-945-7666. Website: www.sunburst resort.com.**

Los Olivos Mexican Patio—$$$

Since 1948, this casual place has served hand-made tortillas along with some of the best enchiladas anywhere. Owned by the Corral family since it opened, it has a staunchly loyal local following. The adobe-walled building dates to 1928 when it was a chapel. Reasonably priced and low-key, this is our favorite place to go for Mexican food. Open Mon.–Thurs., 10:00 A.M.–10:00 P.M.; Fri.–Sat., 10:00 A.M.–1:00 A.M. 7328 E. Second St.; 480-946-2256.

Pinnacle Peak Patio—$$$

A longtime local favorite since it opened in 1957, Pinnacle Peak Patio delivers the cowboy experience with gusto. At one time practically isolated on a tiny dirt road, it is now surrounded by housing developments. In the 1960s, driving "all the way to Pinnacle Peak" for dinner was a real journey. Although homes have crept near and the dirt road is now paved, its character remains. It still serves platter-sized steaks and mesquite-grilled chicken along with cowboy beans and crispy salads. If you wear a necktie, be prepared to have it snipped off to become a ceiling decoration. And if you order your steak well done, you can count on finding an old leather boot, neatly garnished, on your plate. A country western band plays nightly. Open Mon.–Thurs., 4:00 P.M.–10:00 P.M.; Fri.–Sat., 4:00 P.M.–11:00 P.M.; Sun., noon–10:00 P.M. Located a 25-minute drive north of Scottsdale's center. 10426 E. Jomax Rd.; 480-585-1559. Website: www.pppatio.com.

Roaring Fork—$$$

This open, airy cafe's specialties include (what else with a name like Roaring Fork?) American western cuisine; don't miss the rainbow trout that comes in a sizzling skillet. Far from pretentious, the uncomplicated menu features good beef items a tad more substantial than Southwest fare. The patio cooled by misters is a good alternative to indoor dining except during July and Aug. monsoons. Open Mon.–Thurs., 11:30 A.M.–2:00 P.M. and 5:00 P.M.–10:00 P.M.; Fri., 11:30 A.M.–2:00 P.M. and 5:00 P.M.–11:00 P.M.; Sat., 5:00 P.M.–11:00 P.M.; Sun., 5:00 P.M.–10:00 P.M. 7243 E. Camelback Rd.; 480-947-0795.

Terra Cotta—$$$

The aroma of fare from the wood grill wafts through this casual place, named for the predominant color on floors, walls, and tablecloths, accented with soft Southwest greens and blues. The attraction is great contemporary Southwestern cuisine with signature dishes that include garlic custard, tortilla soup, and grilled-chicken pizza. Open Sun.–Thurs., 11:00 A.M.–10:00 P.M.; Fri.–Sat., 11:00 A.M.–11:00 P.M. Located in the Borgata of Scottsdale shopping village. 6166 N. Scottsdale Rd.; 480-948-8100.

Sugar Bowl Ice Cream Parlor—$$

When you want to toss caution and calories to the winds, plan a stop here for a frozen extravaganza. A Scottsdale landmark, it's been around since the 1950s when real cowboys tied their horses to hitching rails when they came into town. Don't miss the Camelback soda. They also have a good sandwich and salad menu. Open Mon.–Thurs. and Sun., 11:00 A.M.–10:00 P.M.; Fri.–Sat., 11:00 A.M.–midnight. 4005 N. Scottsdale Rd.; 480-946-0051.

Services

Scottsdale Convention and Visitors Bureau

7343 Scottsdale Mall, Scottsdale, 85251; 800-877-1117, 888-936-7786, or 480-945-8481. Website: www.scottsdalecvb.com.

Tempe

With a population of close to 165,000 in about 40 square miles, Tempe is Arizona's fifth-largest city. More transplanted Midwesterners live here than in any other region of the United States. Historic Mill Ave., around which the city grew up, is alive with shops, hotels, restaurants, and art festivals. At first you may think you'll never find a parking space in downtown Tempe. Look for green parking signs directing you to parking lots off the main drag.

History

Tempe's founder in 1871, Charles Trumbull Hayden, ran Hayden's Ferry across the Salt River, which flowed vigorously at that time. He also built a flour mill, still in operation today. The name Hayden figured prominently in Arizona history, as Charles Trumbull Hayden's son, Carl, was a U.S. congressman from 1912, the year Arizona became a state, until 1937, when he became a U.S. senator, an office he held until 1969. Tempe, originally called Hayden's Ferry, was renamed Tempe by an English tourist who thought it looked like Greece's Vale of Tempe.

A diverse group of farmers, Hispanic homesteaders, gold prospectors, and hopeful entrepreneurs made up Tempe's early population. By the turn of the century, Victorian homes, Hayden's mill, and a lumber yard verified that Tempe was a real city. When the price of cotton bottomed out in the early 1920s, the city, by this time surrounded with huge cotton fields, went into an economic slump that didn't get any better with the countrywide Depression of the 1930s.

But things were looking up by the 1940s, when Tempe Normal School became a four-year liberal arts college, welcoming returning servicemen from World War II. It later became Arizona State University. For years the city prospered. Then, as shopping malls drew consumers away from the city's center in the 1970s, Mill Ave. became a sort of hippy-dippy hangout for the bearded and long-haired. Today it is revitalized, with coffeehouses, boutiques, restaurants, and shops housed in newly constructed buildings designed à la the past.

Festivals and Events

Way Out West Oktoberfest

first weekend of Oct.

Held in Tempe, this beer-and-bratwurst fest began in 1973 as a salute to Tempe's sister city in Bavaria, Regensburg. This event is now the main fund-raiser for the Tempe Sister City organization, and includes a polka band from Germany, burritos along with bratwurst, mimes, magicians, organ-grinders, 200 storybook characters in costume, and 25 different beers. The West meets the wurst in Hayden Square in downtown Tempe. 480-894-8158.

Tempe Fall Festival of the Arts

early Dec.

For a refreshing alternative to mushing through the malls, many area shoppers wait for this event to stock up on holiday gifts. At the third-largest arts festival in the country, artists are at work, musical groups are playing and caroling, and usually the days are sunny and warm. Arts and crafts, pottery, hand-blown glass, clothing, jewelry, and other gift items are generally part of the mix. Everything is handmade, nothing is premanufactured, and a "jury" decides which craftspeople will be allowed to sell, so quality of merchandise is consistently high. Held Fri.–Sun., 10:00 A.M.–6:00 P.M., **in a five-block area in downtown Tempe.** Plentiful parking is scattered throughout surrounding lots, so be prepared for a bit of a walk. **480-894-8158.**

Seeing and Doing

Art Museums and Galleries

Nelson Fine Arts Center

ASU's outstanding art museum houses five galleries and outdoor sculpture courtyards. The collections include paintings, sculpture, and crafts of the 19th and 20th centuries as well as an interesting selection of Latin American art. Open Tues., 10:00 A.M.–9:00 P.M.; Wed.–Sat., 10:00 A.M.–5:00 P.M.; Sun., 1:00 P.M.–5:00 P.M. Located **on ASU campus just south of downtown Tempe.** 480-965-2787.

Museums and Historic Sites

Arizona Historical Society Museum

This excellent contemporary-history museum provides an introduction to the personalities and entities that helped develop Central Arizona. Two floors of exhibits include one that explains agricultural history and a World War II exhibit detailing the role played by Central Arizona. Open Mon.–Sat., 10:00 A.M.–4:00 P.M.; Sun., noon–4:00 P.M.; closed major holidays. **1300 N. College Ave., Tempe, 85281; 480-929-0292.**

Arizona State University

Tempe is obviously a college town. Just walk along Mill Ave. to see throngs of students on

Getting There

Tempe Old Town is centered around Mill Ave. and Apache Blvd., near the junction of I-10 and US 60. Hwys. 101, 202, and 143 surround it.

bikes, toting books, and just hanging out. The 650-acre campus, landscaped with citrus trees, palms, and assorted cactuses, opened in a single one-story building as the Territorial Normal School in 1885, became Tempe State Teachers College in 1925, and in 1958 attained university status. The 43,000-student institution is one of Arizona's three state universities, along with University of Arizona in Tucson and Northern Arizona University in Flagstaff. The three-story red brick building built in 1898 when it was called the Arizona Normal School is now **Old Main,** the oldest building on campus. **Gammage Auditorium,** a community center for the performing arts and the last public building to be designed by Frank Lloyd Wright, regularly hosts symphony concerts and Broadway shows. Both the Sun Devils and the NFL's Arizona Cardinals play their games at ASU's **Sun Devil Stadium** (see Sports). For more about the ASU campus, see Tours. Located just south of downtown Tempe. **ASU Visitor Information Center** open Mon.–Fri., 8:15 A.M.–4:45 P.M. **826 E. Apache Blvd., Tempe, 85282; 480-965-0100. Website: www.asu.edu.**

Petersen House Museum

This Queen Anne Victorian, built in 1892 by pioneer farmer Niels Petersen, once was one of the most elegant homes in the Salt River Valley. Its furnishings reflect Arizona's territorial days as well as the 1920s. Interior detailing includes hand-stenciled wallpaper, ornate moldings, and intricate curlicues typical of the era. The tour is self-guided. Small donation. Open Tue.–Thurs. and Sat., 10:00 A.M.–2:00 P.M.

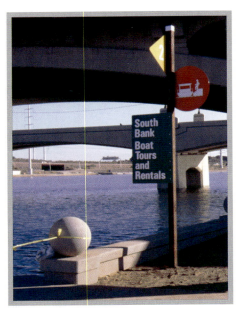

Tempe Town Lake creates water-based fun.

Located about a mile west of the Tempe Historical Museum. **1414 W. Southern Ave., Tempe, 85282; 480-350-5151.**

Tempe Historical Museum

This hands-on museum lets you play rain god on a large model by diverting water from the Salt River into agricultural fields. It's one of the exhibits that helps detail Tempe's past through an understanding of what goes on today. An "archaeological dig" replicates the way artifacts are unearthed. On the walls, old photos establish a time line of Tempe's development. Serious historians can spend time in the library, where files, microfilm, and tapes preserve Tempe's history. Microfilm copies of newspapers from the 1890s to 1950s provide one of the most accurate accountings of what life was like as the city developed. Changing exhibits recently have included Victorian Secrets, a lingerie retrospective, and a history of the Cactus League. A staffed tourism satellite office in the museum foyer stocks brochures and maps. Small fee. Open Mon.–Thurs. and Sat., 10:00 A.M.–5:00 P.M.; Sun., 1:00 P.M.–5:00 P.M.; closed major holidays. Located at Rural Rd. and Southern Ave. **809 E.** Southern Ave., Tempe, 85282; 480-350-5100. Website: www.tempe.gov/museum.

Parks

Tempe Town Lake

Tempe's new recreational centerpiece, this 2.5-mile-long lake is formed by inflatable dams stopping up the Salt River (Rio Salado). Additional water has been brought from the Colorado River through the Central Arizona Project (canals). Controversial for its extravagant use of water in an arid land, its boosters point to the recreational opportunities it affords. **Rio Lago Cruise** rents kayaks, paddleboats, and canoes at a landing on the south bank, and excursion boats do regularly scheduled tours. Both banks have concrete pathways for bicycling, walking, and in-line skating, as well as grassy picnic areas and rest rooms. Still on the drawing board are a major hotel and designated riparian habitat. Located **at Rio Salado Parkway and Mill Ave.** Parking available on Rio Salado Parkway and Ash. 480-517-4050.

Shopping

Arizona Mills

This 1,480,000-square-foot outlet-style mall's racetrack layout allows you to enter at one point, hit all the stores, and end up back where you started. Its art gives it more charm than most such malls. "Red Rock Towers," a stone and ceramic collage, sits at the main entrance; "Copper Mine Two," a series of asymmetrical panels framed in turquoise, and a stylized cactus called "Saguaro Totem" decorate other entrances. Inside, six "neighborhoods" divide the mall and are identified by specially themed works of art. You'll see a mural of the ruins at Montezuma's Castle (see Verde Valley chapter in the Central region), petroglyphs, indigenous trees, and more incorporated into the overall design. American Wilderness, JCPenney Outlet, Marshall's, Ross, Burlington Coat Factory, an IMAX theater, and a 24-plex theater are part of the retail mix. The parking lot has two recharging stations for electric vehicles. Located off US 60 and I-10. 480-491-9700.

Sports

Arizona Cardinals

The NFL football team plays a full season at **Sun Devil Stadium,** part of Arizona State University's campus. **Ticket office is located at Warner and Hardy in south Tempe.** 602-379-0102. Website: azcardinals.com.

Tours

WALKING TOURS

Arizona State University Campus

Seeing the ASU campus on foot provides an overview and allows you to stop at some of the highlights. During the school year, you can linger at the **Galvin Playhouse** in the Nelson Fine Arts Center complex for breakfast or lunch, served 7:00 A.M.–1:30 P.M. The **Moeur Building,** a WPA project built during the Depression, stands out as the only adobe building on campus. It houses the Mars Global Surveyor Space Flight Facility, which supports the Thermal Emission Spectrometer (TES) experiment. The Mars Global Surveyor spacecraft, launched in 1996 with TES aboard, will send back data from Mars into the year 2000. NASA TV is part of the viewing area, open to the public Mon.–Fri., 8:00 A.M.–5:00 P.M. The **Law Library** is designed to look like an open book. Noble trees, some of them more than 80 years old and over 90 feet tall, line **Palm Walk.** At the **Bateman Physical Sciences Center,** there are regularly scheduled planetarium shows (480-727-6234). At the **Meteorite Center,** specimens of what look like pretty dull rocks are actively used for space research; open Mon.–Fri., 8:30 A.M.–4:00 P.M. The small **Geology Museum** houses gemstones, fossils, minerals, and more, but the show-stopper, the six-story Foucault Pendulum, demonstrates the rotation of the earth; open Mon.–Fri., 9:00 A.M.–12:30 P.M. The **State Arboretum** weaves among campus buildings with color-coded plant markers that help identify the 10 vegetation categories represented. **ASU Visitor Information Center** has brochures for the self-guided tour; open Mon.–Fri., 8:15 A.M.–4:45 P.M. **826 E. Apache Blvd., Tempe, 85287; 480-965-0100. Website: www.asu.edu.**

Where to Stay

Tempe Mission Palms—$$$

Recently renovated around a charming central courtyard, this lovely hotel is a handy place to stay for Tempe sporting events and for access to ASU. Don't miss the romantic rooftop pool. Harry's Place is a non-intimidating lounge, and the food at the bistro-style Mission Grille is excellent. **60 E. Fifth St., Tempe, 85281; 800-547-8705 or 480-894-1400. Website: www.missionpalms.com.**

Where to Eat

Monti's La Casa Vieja—$$–$$$

Leonard Monti Sr. opened his restaurant, a favorite family eatery since 1956, on the home-site of Tempe's founder, Charles Trumbull Hayden. The 1872 building marks the city's birthplace, and has welcomed generations of eager steak-eaters with its garlicky, juicy steaks and prime rib. Local athletes like it, they say, for the huge top sirloins. Open Sun.–Thu., 11:00 A.M.–10:00 P.M.; Fri.–Sat., 11:00 A.M.–midnight. **3 W. First St.; 480-967-7594. Website: www.montis.com.**

Rainforest Cafe—$$–$$$

You come to this restaurant for the theme-park atmosphere as much as for sustenance. Waiters are "safari guides," the hostess is a "tour guide," and lunch is a "rainforest adventure." It really does look and smell like someplace in the heart of Costa Rica, with mist rising from jungle plants, splashing waterfalls, and "rain" dripping from greenery that covers walls and pillars. Every 20 minutes or so, you can expect a "thunderstorm" complete with lightning and unsettled elephants trumpeting in the background. It's noisy, fun, and totally visual—and the food's not bad either. The full bar is smoke-free, as is the restaurant. The cafe donates money tossed into the Atlas fountain to organizations that support environmental causes. Open Mon.–Thurs. and Sun., 11:00 A.M.–9:00 P.M.; Fri., 11:00 A.M.–10:00 P.M.; Sat., 10:30 A.M.–10:00 P.M. Located in Arizona Mills megamall at I-10 and US 60. 480-752-9100. Website: www.rainforestcafe.com.

Gordon Biersch Brewing Company—$$

Four flagship German-style lagers brewed on-site make this casual microbrewery and restaurant a new favorite. Pilsner, Blonde Bock, Marzen, and Dunkles are complemented by seasonal beers all brewed with yeast and hops from Germany. An eclectic menu and friendly setting make it as popular with the college crowd as it is with the professorial set. Open daily, 10:00 A.M.–1:00 A.M. 420 S. Mill Ave.; 480-736-0033. Website: www.gordonbiersch.com.

Beeloe's Cafe and Underground Bar— $$–$$$

On Mill Avenue, this trendy place attracts a younger crowd, with its resident artists and live jazz in the evenings. The eclectic menu has a southwestern flair. Open Sun.–Wed., 4:00 P.M.– 1:00 A.M. 501 S. Mill Ave.; 480-894-1230.

Aunt Chilada's—$$$

Located on Baseline Road just off the I-10 freeway at the Pointe Hilton South Mountain, this longtime area favorite has pleased locals as well as Hilton guests for years. Have a margarita on the patio, then chow down on tamales, fajitas, and regional specialties. Open Sun.–Thurs., 11:00 A.M.–10:00 P.M.; Fri.–Sat., 11:00 A.M.– 11:00 P.M. 2021 W. Baseline Rd.; 602-431-6470.

House of Tricks—$$$

Named for the current owner, this delightful 1920s cottage has a tree-shaded patio and is pleasant enough for outdoor dining most of the year. The new American menu features seasonally fresh fruits and vegetables, inventively prepared. Great lunch spot to linger and chat. Open Mon.–Sat., 11:00 A.M.–10:00 P.M. for lunch and dinner. 114 E. Seventh St.; 480-968-1114.

Services

Tempe Convention and Visitors Bureau

Here you'll find brochures on the city and on area attractions. Open Mon.–Fri. 8:30 A.M.–5:00 P.M. 51 W. Third St., No. 105, Tempe, 85281; 800-283-6734 or 480-894-8158. Website: www.tempe.cvb.com.

Mesa

With a population of 350,000, Mesa is the second-largest city in the Valley of the Sun, larger than Minneapolis or St. Louis. Mesa enthusiastically welcomes snowbirds to dozens of RV parks. It hosts the Chicago Cubs for Spring Training (see Major Attractions in Phoenix chapter).

History

Mesa was established in Feb. 1878 by 80 Mormon pioneers from Salt Lake who figured that the location was good for agriculture. Mesa, which means "table" in Spanish, was founded on a flat-topped tableland about 3 miles above the Salt River.

Outdoor Activities

Boating

RIVER TUBING

Salt River Recreation

Tubing on the Salt River has become a revered summer pastime in the Phoenix area. May–Sept., the river (usually) provides cool mountain-stream waters for a mellow float that gets you away from the heat of the Valley of the Sun. Salt River Recreation supplies tubes and shuttles. Rent a tube where you put in. Rent an extra for your ice chest so your drinks and food can float right along with you. Everyone gets on the river at a central point, then leaves the river at designated points to catch a shuttle bus back to their cars. The usual technique is to gather tubes in a circle and link them together with a center tube to hold the cooler. On a hot summer weekend, the river is almost choked with boom boxes, rafts, tubes, and the ubiquitous Styrofoam cooler. Trips of one and a half to four hours, five hours on weekends, are offered. Rest rooms, soft drinks, popcorn, ice cream, hats and visors, T-shirts, ice chests, and more are available at tubing headquarters. Caution: Arizona's summer sun can be devastating to unprepared skin. Be sure to wear a hat, slather yourself with sunscreen of at least SPF 15, and, even though you'll be wearing a swimsuit, cover up with a long-sleeve shirt. Tube rentals are about $9. Children should be age eight or older. From I-60 in Mesa take Power Rd. northeast for 15 miles to the well-marked Salt River Recreation headquarters. **P.O. Box 6568, Mesa, 85216; 480-984-3305, fax 480-984-0875.**

Golf

Mesa offers golf packages for those who come to play the 13 courses that participate. Golfers call one of 11 hotels to select the course or courses they prefer to play, and the hotel handles the rest. Tee times may be guaranteed up to 90 days prior to arrival. (Similar packages are available

---

Getting There
Mesa is adjacent to Tempe, on the east, on US 60.

The Arizona Temple of the Church of Jesus Christ of Latter-Day Saints in Mesa.

for Chicago Cubs and Arizona Cardinals games.) The Best Western Superstition Springs is one hotel that offers the packages. Call 480-641-1164.

Seeing and Doing

Museums and Historic Sites

Arizona Temple of the Church of Jesus Christ of Latter-Day Saints

Mesa's Mormon beginnings are abundantly evident in this impressive monument. The groundbreaking took place in 1922, and the temple was completed in 1927 at a cost of $800,000. Built of crushed rock from nearby Tempe Butte quarry, its concrete frame is reinforced with 130 tons of steel that make it practically indestructible, said the builders at the time. The exterior finish, faced with a terra-cotta glaze, repels dust so well that elders say it has never been cleaned. More than 72,000 square feet and 193 rooms are used for marriages and other ceremonies. Non-Mormons are not allowed inside the temple. Most interesting to visitors are the beautifully maintained gardens and rich architectural details. In Dec., more than 400,000 lights decorate the grounds and building, and the largest Easter pageant in the world dramatizes the resurrection of Christ. The visitor center has replicas of rare religious art, and invites visitors to view a video explaining the basic doctrines of the Mormon Church. Open Jan.–Thanksgiving, daily, 9:00 A.M.–9:00 P.M.; day after Thanksgiving–New Year's Eve, 10:00 A.M.–10:00 P.M. **525 E. Main, Mesa, 85211; 480-964-7164.**

Champlin Fighter Aircraft Museum

Considered by some the Smithsonian of fighter aircraft, this museum has three hangars that house 34 flyable vintage fighter planes, the world's largest private collection of these beauties. You can see fragile wood and fabric planes from World War I, like the Fokker Triplane and Sopwith Camel; the heavy iron Goodyear F2G-1 Corsair and P-38 from World War II; and U.S.- and Soviet-built jets that flew in Korea and Vietnam, including the McDonnell-Douglas F4 Phantom. In May, on Barnstormers and Bi-Plane Day, you can catch a ride with a pilot in one of these open-cockpit machines. The American Fighter Aces Association headquarters is at the museum; to be an "ace," a pilot must have five verified downings of enemy aircraft in aerial combat. Guided tours are conducted at 10:30 A.M., 1:30 P.M., and 3:00 P.M. Moderate admission. Open Apr. 15–Sept. 15, daily, 8:30 A.M.–3:30 P.M.; Sept. 16–Apr. 14, daily, 10:00 A.M.–5:00 P.M. Located at Falcon Field off McKellips Rd. **4636 Fighter Aces Dr., Mesa, 85215; 480-830-4540.**

Mesa Southwest Museum

More of an experiential visit than a simple museum stop, this place is filled with re-creations of Hohokam Indian dwellings and a real jail. The museum traces the area's development from prehistory to the present. The new natural history wing features Dinosaur Mountain, which includes three animated dinosaurs, an aquarium with descendants of prehistoric creatures, swampy water pools, and a "flash flood" every 15 minutes. Small fee. Open Tue.–Sat., 10:00 A.M.–5:00 P.M.; Sun., 1:00 P.M.–5:00 P.M. 53 N. MacDonald St., Mesa, 85215; 480-644-2230.

Where to Stay

Mesa, which caters to conventions, has hotel accommodations at a number of resort-style hotels, mostly of the large-chain variety. Hotel/motels include Holiday Inn, Budget Inn, Courtyards by Marriott, Days Inn, Hampton Inn, Motel 6, Quality Inn, Ramada, Sleep Inn, Super 8, and Travelodge.

Superstition Springs Inn & Suites—$$$
This Best Western is almost in the resort category, with heated pool, spa, and workout room. Rooms have microwaves and refrigerators. Located on Mesa's east edge, it is close to the Superstition Mountains. 1342 South Power Rd., Mesa, 85206; 800-528-1234 or 480-641-1164. Website: www.bestwestern.com.

Sheraton Mesa Hotel—$$–$$$
Located in the middle of Mesa just off Main Street, this 273-room hotel has a large resort-style pool complex with whirlpool and fitness center, and a concierge to help with planning local sightseeing. The Quail Run Restaurant and Lobos Cantina are good options for dining in.

200 North Centennial Way, Mesa, 85201; 480-898-8300. Website: www.sheraton mesa.com.

Where to Eat

Michael Monti's Mesa Grill—$$$–$$$$
Following in the tradition of Monti's La Casa Vieja in Tempe, this new eatery across from Fiesta Mall serves Monti's classic steaks and the restaurant's trademark Roman bread. Open Sun.–Thurs., 11:00 A.M.–10:00 P.M.; Fri.–Sat., 11:00 A.M–11:00 P.M. Happy Hour daily from 3:00 P.M.–6:00 P.M. 1233 S. Alma School Rd.; 480-844-1918. Website: www.montis.com.

The @ Cafe—$$
Adjacent to Monti's Mesa Grill, it serves breakfast burritos, fresh-baked pastries, espresso, and cappuccino. Two computers with free Internet connections let diners surf the net and check e-mail. Open Mon.–Fri., 6:30 A.M.–3:00 P.M. 1223 S. Alma School Rd.; 480-844-1918. Website: www.theatcafe.com.

Services

Mesa Convention and Visitors Bureau
120 N. Center, Mesa, 85201; 800-283-MESA or 480-827-4700. Website: www.arizona guide.com/mesa or www.mesa.az.us.

Around Phoenix

West: Glendale

This town of about 200,000 is Arizona's fourth-largest city. Between 1980 and 1990 it doubled in size as newcomers discovered affordable housing and a good school system. It capitalized on its past to turn itself into an antiques hub and it is still surrounded by producing cotton fields. Original 100-year-old brick storefronts like the Old Towne shopping area line Glendale Ave., downtown's main street. Restored Craftsman bungalows, a general store, soda fountain, teahouse, and other remnants from a gentler era give the place an almost-Midwest feeling. In 1995 Glendale annexed Luke Air Force Base, the largest jet-fighter training center in the world.

History

Glendale, established in 1892, was a cotton and farming center early on, fed by a canal that brought water to a barren land from the New River to the west. Established by the New England Land Company in 1892 for the Church of the Brethren of Illinois, it was incorporated in 1910.

GETTING THERE

Glendale is northwest of Phoenix on US 60. Between Glendale and The Sun Cities is Peoria.

Seeing and Doing

Antiquing

Glendale's **Catlin Court** is one of its main shopping districts. **Murphy Park,** Glendale's town square, is the center of a charming four-block area close to 100 antique stores, shops, and restaurants that create fertile fodder for a day of browsing. Most stores have complimentary maps

to guide you on a downtown walking tour. Located **at Glendale and 58th Ave.**

Museums and Historic Sites

Recently moved to Glendale from Prescott, the 7,000-sqare-foot **Bead Museum** houses what may be the largest collection of beads in the country. Among its treasures are centuries-old beads carved from coral, glass beads designed by master artists, beads of amber, and more. A gift shop, research library, and workshops are part of the museum. Small admission to museum; no admission to bead store. Open Mon–Wed. and Fri. –Sat., 10:00 A.M.–5:00 P.M.; Thur., 10:00 A.M.–8:00 P.M.; Sun., 11:00 A.M.–4:00 P.M. **5754 W. Glenn Dr., Glendale, 85301; 623-931-2737. Website: www.The BeadMuseum.com.**

Sahuaro Ranch Park, listed on the National Register of Historic Places, preserves an early 20-acre Glendale homestead. Visitors come for its citrus groves, turn-of-the-century buildings, rose garden, and noisy and beautiful peacocks. Open Thurs.–Fri., 10:00 A.M.–2:00 P.M.; Sat., 10:00 A.M.–4:00 P.M.; Sun., noon–4:00 P.M. Located **at 59th Ave. and Mountain View Rd. 623-939-5782.**

Tours

Tues.–Sat., a **free trolley** loops through Glendale's Old Towne and Catlin Court, one of the main shopping districts. 623-435-0556.

Since 1930 the family-run **Cerreta Candy Factory** has been turning out creamy fudge truffles, chocolate-dipped cherries, walnut caramels, and more in its 35,000-square-foot factory. The aroma alone encourages you to indulge. For a free sample and tour, show up Mon.–Sat., 8:00 A.M.–6:00 P.M. Located five minutes from Old Towne Glendale **at Glendale and 54th Ave.** 623-930-1000. Website: www.cerreta.com.

Where to Stay

Gaslight Park Hotel—$$$

Right in the middle of Glendale's historic district, walking distance to antiques shops and the Bead Museum, this little nine-room find has all the charm of its 1926 beginnings. The large lobby has the original tin ceiling, along with an art gallery, candy shop, and bakery/cafe, so a snack is readily at hand. Rooms, updated for the 21st century, have full private baths, TV/VCR, refrigerator, microwave, and coffeemaker. Enter from the rear, where there is free parking. **5747 W. Glendale Ave., Glendale, 85301; 623-939-1998.** Website: www.historic-glendale.net.

Where to Eat

Jacka's Alley—$$–$$$$

When you need a break from antiquing, this hideaway with an open patio beckons. In a breezeway planted with trees and vines, Belgian waffles and frittatas highlight the breakfast menu, with salads and burgers big for lunch. If you can round up five friends for dinner, order the Cioppino Feast, prepared for six or more. Open Mon.–Wed., 11:00 A.M.–5:00 P.M.; Thurs., 11:00 A.M.–8:00 P.M.; Fri.–Sat., 9:00 A.M.–5:00 P.M.; Sun., 9:00 A.M.–4:00 P.M. The Back Alley Grill is open Fri.–Sat., 5:00 P.M.–9:00 P.M. **5739 Glendale Ave.; 602-274-1998.**

Services

Glendale Marketing/Communications Dept., Tourism Division, 5850 W. Glendale Ave., Glendale, 85301; 623-930-2957. Websites: www.arizona-guide.com/glendale and www.tour.glendaleaz.org.

West: The Sun Cities

For a look at a first-class way to spend retirement years, drive through any of The Sun Cities, master-planned active retirement communities that welcome residents age 55 and better. The original Sun City, with a population of 38,000, sold out years ago but now attracts a second generation of retirees, drawn to well-kept resale homes in tidy neighborhoods. Sun City West has more than 25,000 retirees enjoying an active lifestyle. The 7,000-seat outdoor amphitheater is the venue for a continuing stream of nationally known performing artists. The original Sun City was established in 1960; followed by Sun City West in 1978 and Sun City Grand in 1996 by the Del Webb Corporation.

The Sun Cities are northwest of Phoenix on US 60 past Glendale and Peoria.

Seeing and Doing

Art Museums and Galleries

The **West Valley Art Museum,** a lovely small gallery between Sun City and Sun City Grand, features the work of local and visiting artists. Small admission. Open Tues.–Sat., 10:00 A.M.–4:00 P.M.; Sun., 1:00 P.M.–4:00 P.M. **17420 Ave. of the Arts, Surprise, 85060; 623-972-0635.**

Services

For information on any Del Webb community, call **888-932-2639.** Website: www.suncity.com.

Goldfield Ghost Town in the Superstition Mountains near Apache Junction has mine tours, gold panning, live rattlers, and a museum.

North: Carefree and Cave Creek

Unique mineral outcroppings and boulders, flanked with majestic saguaro cactuses and a background of craggy little mountains, become focal points in a fascinating high-desert landscape that forms the background of these two towns. Carefree lies in the lee of Black Mountain, an extinct volcano covered with huge boulders. Along with larger Continental Mountain, it creates a rugged natural skyline. Two adjacent but very different communities, Carefree is a planned enclave where multimillion-dollar homes are so well situated they seem part of the landscape. A good afternoon's trip from Phoenix can include a leisurely drive among magnificent homes, with a stop to eat at the Sundial Center. The exclusive, discreet, gorgeous, and very expensive Boulders Resort is tucked into giant rock formations here.

In Cave Creek, which is typically high desert, homes have views of Elephant Butte, so-named because its outline resembles that of a kneeling pachyderm. A onetime mining town that dates to an 1874 gold strike, it has a pleasant small-town atmosphere. These two towns are about 22 miles east of Lake Pleasant, a favorite recreation area north of Phoenix.

GETTING THERE

Drive north on Scottsdale Rd. 8 miles, past Carefree Hwy., and you're in Carefree. The two towns are adjacent.

Major Attractions

Lake Pleasant Regional Park

Lake Pleasant was created in 1926 when Waddell Dam stopped the flow of water along the Agua Fria River, which is fed by the Colorado River as well as runoff. The lake is named for Carl Pleasant, an engineer involved in the 1926 construction. Frequently spotted wild burros are descendants of those used in the late 1800s by miners trying their best to wrest, with minimal results, something valuable from the hills around the lake.

Within a 25,000-acre park, Arizona's second-largest lake is part of the Maricopa Water District, intended to develop arid lands into agricultural opportunities. The 1926 dam was replaced by the current structure, completed in 1993 and named for Donald C. Waddell, who helped garner financing for the first dam. The earth-filled dam is 4,700 feet long and 300 feet high, holding back a lake that can fluctuate almost 200 feet. The lake's long sweep makes it good for sailing, and it's also favored for fishing. A nesting pair of bald eagles are part of the wildlife that surrounds the park, as are gray fox, javelina, mountain lions, bobcats, and mule deer. The saguaro-studded shores and the general aridness can make things crushingly hot, but for those who are summer-starved by asphalt and concrete, this expanse of blue water is a true oasis. About two dozen picnic sites with tables and grills border the lake, and you also can use vacant RV sites at Desert Tortoise Campground (see Where to Stay). From Phoenix, **take I-17 north to the Carefree Hwy./Hwy. 74 (exit 223), turn left, and continue 7 miles to the park entrance.** Facilities are clearly marked. **520-501-1710.**

An 1800s village provides interesting exploring at the Pioneer Living History Museum north of Phoenix.

Outdoor Activities

Boating
Fishing boats, ski boats, and power skis may be rented at **Lake Pleasant Regional Park.** Houseboats also are available. **623-566-3100.**

The Desert Princess, a comfortable launch-type boat, does sightseeing, lunch, and dinner cruises. **623-566-3100.**

Pleasant Harbor Marina has boats for rent and places for you to trailer your own craft. A general store and deli purvey necessities, including sandwiches, beer, anchors, and lures, for a fun day at the lake. Store and deli open daily, 7:30:00 A.M.–5:00 P.M. **623-566-3100.**

Fishing
Anglers say that largemouth bass fishing can be outstanding at **Lake Pleasant.** You need an Arizona license, and there is a limit of six large-

mouth per day. Crappie, bluegill, carp, and channel catfish also are plentiful. **520-501-1710.**

In the Air
The friendly skies are particularly welcoming near Lake Pleasant, where thermals off the desert give new meaning to the phrase "up, up, and away." At **Turf Soaring School,** you take off in a tandem-seating glider, with you in front and the pilot behind you, towed by a powered plane. Once you are airborne, cars on the ground become ants and fields turn into patchwork quilts. Then the pilot tells you to pull the red knob. This detaches your sailplane from the tow plane, and you soar and climb, catching thermals in exactly the same way that hawks and eagles do. The company has eight sailplanes and three tow planes, and flies every day that the weather permits. Take I-17 north to the Carefree Hwy. exit (exit 223) and continue west to 99th Ave. The school is located at Carefree Hwy. and Lake Pleasant Rd. **8700 W. Carefree Hwy., Peoria, 85382; 602-439-3621. Website: www.turfsoaring.com.**

Seeing and Doing

Museums and Historic Sites

If you attended grade school in Phoenix, you probably went on a field trip to **Pioneer Arizona Living History Museum**. It's still there, with a real blacksmith plying his trade, a furnished Victorian house, miners' cabins, a reconstruction of the 1884 Valley Bank in Phoenix, and a print shop. On Sun. the Spur Cross Cowboy Church holds services in a reconstructed 1879 wood-frame church. Most weekends you can expect shoot-'em-ups and costumed interpreters at this 93-acre museum, which emphasizes authenticity. The reconstructed Whiskey, Road-to-Ruin Saloon features an 1861 cherry-wood bar and specializes in "pulled pork," smoked for two days until it's so tender you just pull it apart. Saloon open Wed.–Thurs. and Sun., 8:00 A.M.–5:00 P.M. Small admission to museum. Museum open Wed.–Sun., 9:00 A.M.–5:00 P.M. Located about 30 minutes from downtown Phoenix. Take I-17 north to exit 225 and follow signs. **3901 W. Pioneer Rd., Phoenix, 85086; 623-465-1052.**

Hundreds of petroglyphs are carved on the dark basalt rocks at **Deer Valley Rock Art Center,** a site that spans centuries. A research center for Arizona State University, the sleek, modern visitor center has interpretive displays and a Glyph Shop stocked with rock-art items that include books, clothing, and gifts. An easy 0.25-mile trail, with ramadas along the way, leads through the Sonoran Desert to the petroglyphs. Small admission. Open Tues.–Fri., 9:00 A.M.–2:00 P.M.; Sat., 9:00 A.M.–5:00 P.M.; Sun., noon–5:00 P.M. Take I-17 about 15 miles north of Phoenix, exit on Deer Valley Rd., and follow it 2.5 miles west until it dead-ends. **3711 W. Deer Valley Rd., Phoenix, 85080; 602-582-8007. Website: www.asu.edu/clas/anthropology/dvrac.**

Where to Stay

Camping

Two campgrounds on Lake Pleasant's west side, **Desert Tortoise** with 151 semi-improved sites with grills and shade, and **Road Runner** with 74 full hookups, are open year-round. For information on camping at Lake Pleasant and on the RV park below, call the port of entry to the RV park, 520-501-1035.

Although **Pleasant Harbor RV Resort** looks like it was built yesterday, it's been here long enough for trees to create shade for its 200 spic-and-span sites. Most are claimed during winter months by snowbirds anchored here until the flakes back home melt away, but overnighters are welcome if space is available. It has large circular rosette spaces with tables, a heated pool with plenty of loungers, a clubhouse with big-screen TV, a game room, shower facilities, a laundry, and a small store. It's okay to bring your boat because a parking lot accommodates trailers. The park is close to Pleasant Harbor Marina, overlooking Lake Pleasant. **8708 W. Harbor Blvd., Peoria, 85382; 800-475-3272 or 602-269-0077. Website: www.pleasantharbor.com.**

Where to Eat

Harold's Cave Creek Corral—$$$

This wild-west saloon adventure offers a fun, down-home sort of evening, complete with dancing. You can watch your favorite team over a 25-ounce mug of draft beer, then tear into some hefty steaks, ribs, and more. Open daily, 8:00 A.M.–1:00 A.M.; dinner served until 11:00 P.M. **6895 E. Cave Creek Rd., Cave Creek; 480-488-1906.**

Wild Horse—$$

A favorite sustenance stop on the way to or from Lake Pleasant, the Wild Horse is not known for its extensive menu (burgers, grilled ham, hot dogs, and chips are about it), but it bases its widespread reputation on its sumptuous, well-priced cheeseburgers. Open Mon.–Thurs., 7:00 A.M.–9:00 P.M.; Fri.–Sun., 7:00 A.M.–10:00 P.M. Located on Carefree Hwy., 6 miles west of I-17. **8415 W. Carefree Hwy./Hwy. 74; 623-566-0740.**

Services

Carefree/Cave Creek Chamber of Commerce

6710 E. Cave Creek Rd., Cave Creek, 85331; 480-488-3381.

East: Apache Junction

Because it is so close to lakes and the Superstition Mountains, this little town of 26,000, for years a sort of suburban trailer park to Phoenix, is on a definite economic upswing. Retirees, lured by low housing costs, are pouring in as year-round residents. Apache Junction is a new town, incorporated in 1978 in Pinal County.

History

Apache Junction is in an area left untouched by early miners because it was the homestead of hostile Apaches. Early legends say that the Aztecs buried gold in the Superstition Mountains, north of Apache Junction, after the 1519 Spanish invasion of the Mexican mainland. The conquistadors and later the Jesuits supposedly hid their treasures in the Superstitions. The Peralta family from Arispe, Sonora, owned (so goes the tale) a dozen extremely rich mines in the area. As the Mexican-American war wound down in 1848, the Spanish hurried to wrest whatever gold they could from the mountains before the Southwest came under the flag of the United States. Apaches protected "their" gold by sending anyone who came searching on a quick trip to the hereafter. And then German prospector Jacob Waltz showed up, evaded the Apaches, and is said to have discovered the mines' whereabouts. When he died, a bag of extremely rich gold ore was discovered under his bed. Now known as the Lost Dutchman (the German word for German, *Deutsch,* sounded like "Dutch"), Waltz's gold was never found. One theory, which supports the mine's obscurity, is that in the 1880s an earthquake rocked this area, shifting sight lines and moving landmarks that Waltz had used to pinpoint the mine's location.

What put Apache Junction on the maps was the discovery of gold at Goldfield in 1893. Once a booming mining town as a result of the gold strike, Goldfield existed for just five years, 1893–1897. Tortilla Flat began in 1904 as a stagecoach stop on the Apache Trail, which was built around the turn of the century as a construction road to get materials through the Superstition Mountains to the site of the new Roosevelt Dam. Tortilla Flat was the first of two stops between Phoenix and the Roosevelt Dam construction site; the second stop was at Fish Creek Hill.

Building Roosevelt Dam gave Apache Junction a real boost because the Tonto Wagon Rd. (Apache Trail) was built to access the construction site, and telephone and telegraph lines were strung from Mesa, through Apache Junction, to the dam. The construction of both Mormon Flat Dam, which formed Canyon Lake in 1925, and Horse Mesa Dam, which created Apache Lake in 1927, helped further establish the town. By 1922, US 60 to Globe had been completed, creating a circle route that Americans, made newly mobile by the automobile, found fascinating.

GETTING THERE

Apache Junction is on US 60 at its intersection with Hwy. 88, 35 miles east of Phoenix. Goldfield is 3.5 miles north of Apache Junction on Hwy. 88, the famous Apache Trail. Tortilla Flat lies 15 miles beyond Goldfield.

Major Attractions

Superstition Mountains

The Superstition Wilderness Area east of Apache Junction appears in a number of places in this section. Its general background revolves almost entirely around gold. For decades the tales of gold have fired the imagination of moviemakers. Parts of *Lust for Gold,* produced in 1949 by Columbia Pictures and starring Glenn Ford and Ida Lupino, were filmed in the Superstitions. The construction of Apacheland, an 1880s western movie town, drew more

The first resting point on the Apache Trail is Tortilla Flat, a onetime stagecoach stop beyond Goldfield.

production companies and became home base for *Arizona Raiders,* starring Audie Murphy; *Charro,* filmed in 1968 with Elvis Presley; Marty Robbins in the 1972 film *The Drifter; The Gambler,* starring Kenny Rogers; and the epic *How the West Was Won.* One of the classic landmarks of the Superstitions, Weaver's Needle, a volcanic spire, juts 4,535 feet into the sky. The spire was probably named for scout and guide Pauline Weaver (a man), one of Arizona's first white settlers.

Goldfield

Once a boomtown as a result of the 1892 gold strike in the Superstitions, today Goldfield has been rebuilt into more of a theme park than a town. The present-day version includes a museum, a railroad tour, a live rattlesnake exhibit, a mine tour, and an Indian jewelry shop. There is no charge to park and walk around. Goldfield is open daily, 10:00 A.M.–5:00 P.M. Located **3.5 miles north of Apache Junction on Hwy. 88.** 480-983-0333.

Tortilla Flat, population 6, was pretty much leveled by a 1987 fire, which destroyed many of the wood-frame buildings that had been

part of a restoration. The rebuilt version features an ice cream and candy store. Try the prickly pear ice cream to curb the fire of the chili served next door at the Superstition Saloon, where an estimated $15,000 in dollar bills hang on every available inch of wall space. Local lore says that early travelers left change at the tavern to help the next sojourner through this remote place. The wooden Indian that guards the saloon door, and bar stools worn smooth by countless derrieres, are examples of chainsaw art. Saddles serve as other stools, letting you ride into the sunset as you sip your beer. There are public rest rooms in the saloon. The town is generally alive daily, 9:00 A.M.–6:00 P.M. Located **15 miles beyond Goldfield.** 480-984-1776.

Festivals and Events

Lost Dutchman Days
end of Feb.
This fun, down-home event features a Senior Pro-Rodeo, marching band competition as part of one of the area's biggest parades, an art show, a carnival, and entertainment. Of course the Lost Dutch-

Dollar bills line the walls of the Superstition Saloon, a custom that once helped down-and-out travelers.

man and his burro play a prominent part in the festivities. In Apache Junction. **280-982-3141.**

Outdoor Activities

Boating and Fishing

Saguaro, Canyon, and Apache Lakes form a chain below Roosevelt Lake along the Salt River. Canyon and Apache can be reached from Apache Junction, but Saguaro must be reached by Hwy. 87, which is between Mesa and Tempe west of Apache Junction.

It's difficult to place **Saguaro Lake** in sensible reading order. If you look at a map, the lake is obviously the third and last in the chain of lakes that eventually return to the Salt River. But the lake can't be accessed from the Apache Trail, as can Canyon and Apache Lakes. The usual route is to **take Hwy. 87 north from Phoenix, and exit at the marked sign.** Saguaro Lake Marina, **480-986-5546.**

The *Desert Belle,* a comfortable pontoon boat, offers 90-minute Saguaro Lake tours year-round. It's a smooth glide enjoyed in the open air or under cover in the boat's midsection. The tour goes to Stewart Mountain Dam, which created the lake, accompanied by narration that fixes the lake's time in history and explains the vegetation on its sandy shores. **480-984-5311.**

Located 14 miles northeast of Apache Junction on Hwy. 88, **Canyon Lake** is the middle of the three lakes below Roosevelt Lake along the Salt River. Held back by the Mormon Flat Dam built in 1925, it was known as Mormon Lake until the 1940s. Anglers say that depending on water level and stocking schedules, bass, crappie, bluegill, and walleye are catchable. You can rent kayaks, runabouts, and pontoon boats, and get fishing supplies, at the **Canyon Lake**

The Dolly *steamboat takes Canyon Lake tours.*

Marina. For a good day trip, rent a slow-moving pontoon boat, basically a floating porch, and watch the passing scenery. Pack a picnic and a cooler full of cold drinks, slather on the sunscreen SPF 15, and you're set. There are a number of picnic grounds where you can tie up, and lots of canyons to explore. From Apache Junction **take Hwy. 88/ Apache Trail north 15.2 miles. 480-944-6504.**

A replica paddle-wheel steamboat, the *Dolly,* does 90-minute narrated cruises on Canyon Lake, some of which include lunch or dinner. Passengers sit on shaded upper and lower decks as the boat glides past steep canyon walls and spectacular scenery. You may glimpse desert bighorn sheep and bald eagles. **480-827-9144.**

The only way to reach **Apache Lake,** midway between Roosevelt Dam and Tortilla Flat, is via the Apache Trail, one of the reasons why you often encounter boats being trailered along this twisty route. The 18-mile-long, skinny body of water has a **marina** with boat rentals, launch ramp, fishing and camping supplies, and a grocery store. From Apache Junction **take Hwy. 88/Apache Trail north 32 miles to the turnoff** for Apache Lake Recreation Area. 520-467-2511.

Golf

Gold Canyon Golf Resort recently took nine of its existing 18 holes, built an additional nine, and created the spectacular new Mountain course that plays to 6,008 yards from the blue tees. The remaining nine are now the Resort course. In an area where most courses are relatively flat, the variances in topography and elevation changes in the Superstition foothills make it not only interesting but also scenic. (See Where to Stay for directions.) **480-982-9449.**

Hiking

Many marvelous hiking trails cross the 160,000 acres that make up the Superstition Wilderness Area of the Tonto National Forest. You'll see easy-to-access trailheads marked all along Hwy. 88. Motorized vehicles and mechanized equipment are prohibited unless specifically authorized.

The 18.2-mile **Dutchman's Trail** crosses a number of other trails, some heavily used, in the Superstition Wilderness. Access it at First Water trailhead by driving east on US 60. At exit 196 take Idaho Rd. and proceed north 1 mile to Hwy. 88. Turn right and continue approximately 3.5 miles to Forest Rd. 78, near milepost 200. Turn right and follow Forest Rd. 78 approximately 3 miles. You can access the 3.3-mile **Second Water Trail** at this point, for a shorter hike that passes through Garden Valley. For maps and trail guides, contact the **Tonto Basin Ranger District, Hwy. 88, HCO 2, Box 4800, Roosevelt, 85545; 520-467-3200, fax 520-467-3239.**

Lost Dutchman Moonlight Hike is very special, not to be missed if you can work it into your schedule. Rangers lead a 2.5-mile hike along the base of the Superstition Mountains in Lost Dutchman State Park during the full moon. The two-hour hike is eerily lovely. You'll see saguaros silhouetted against the moon, hear coyotes yip in the distance, and thrashers and night birds call as they flit among creosote and manzanita. At one point the ranger stops to tell the tale of Indian Canyons, inhabited by the Thunder Gods, now turned to stone and visible in the silvery light as stolid rock formations. As the ranger talks, Native American chants issue from a tape player. Before the hike, the bearded Lost Dutchman himself puts in an appearance, telling his tale and explaining why his gold will never be found—at least not so far. Some of the trail covers rocky and uneven ground, so you should be in pretty good condition and have no problems with night vision. Bring a flashlight and meet at the Cholla group ramada after checking in at the ranger station. Small per-vehicle fee. Held once a month Nov.–Apr., Sat. night as close to full moon as possible. See Parks for directions to the park. **480-982-4485.**

Heavily used and readily accessible, the 6.2-mile **Peralta Trail** is not recommended for horses because it can have uncertain footing. From the trailhead to Fremont Saddle, the elevation gain is more than 1,000 feet, but scenery and desert vegetation are interesting. From

US 60, 8.5 miles past Apache Junction, take the Peralta Rd. 77 turnoff and proceed about 8 miles north to the trailhead. You may also access the shorter, but steep and rocky, 3.4-mile **Bluff Spring Trail** at this point.

Horseback Riding

Many visitors to Arizona look for a real Old West experience, like riding off into the sunset. **Don Donnelly Horseback Vacations and Stables** takes would-be cowpokes on dude-friendly horses into the fabled Superstition Mountains on rides that last an hour and a half or overnight. You also can arrange three- to seven-day horseback vacations, Feb.–Nov., riding for six to eight hours every day. But at the end of the day you have tents, hot showers, and entertainment. Open all year. **6010 S. Kings Ranch Rd., Gold Canyon, 85219; 800-346-4403 or 480-982-7822.**

Rockhounding

For treasure hunting and prospecting, go to Pro-Mack South, home of **Superstition Mountain Treasure Hunters** in Apache Junction. Mining supplies, metal detectors, even free panning lessons and training videos are available. **940 W. Apache Trail, Apache Junction, 85217; 800-722-6463 or 480-983-3484. Website: www.promackminingsupsouth.com.**

Seeing and Doing

Museums

At **Lost Dutchman Museum** you can explore the geologic history of the Superstition Mountains, which yielded all that gold. You may join the countless visitors who have pored over the 23 maps, all purporting to lead to the Dutchman's gold. Located **in Goldfield** (see Major Attractions). 480-983-4888.

Parks

Lost Dutchman State Park's location, at the base of the Superstitions close to Phoenix, creates heavy use. Still one of the loveliest parks in the state system, its magnificent saguaro cac-

tuses and ocotillo thrive in this part of the Sonoran Desert. For years the legend of the Lost Dutchman mine has lured adventurers to look for the golden treasure supposedly hidden there by miner Jacob Waltz. Rangers lead a leisurely nature hike along park trails, averaging 2–3 miles and lasting about one and a half to three hours; Sat., 10:00 a.m. There are campsites here, but no hookups. Located 5 miles northeast of Apache Junction on Hwy. 88. **6109 N. Apache Trail, Apache Junction, 85219; 480-982-4485. Website: www.pr.state.az.us.**

Scenic Drives

The Apache Trail, a National Scenic Byway, is a rugged route that follows Hwy. 88. It was built around the turn of the century as a construction road to the site of the new Roosevelt Dam. Once the dam was complete, the road was forgotten, except by intrepid souls looking for adventure. But by the 1950s, it was rediscovered for its scenery, and also for the challenges it posed. On a map it looks like a benign 48-mile stretch of some paved, some gravel road, giving no hint of the beautifully dramatic volcanic fields and buttes it crosses. It can take a couple of hours, or much longer, depending on your tolerance for jouncing around and how many times you stop. When you drive it (you can do it in a passenger car), be aware of trail etiquette: The vehicle coming uphill has the right of way, and if you are a slower-moving vehicle, use pullouts to let the traffic behind you pass.

From Apache Junction, in 4.5 miles you come to the first place of note, on the right: Goldfield (see Major Attractions). At 5.5 miles you come to Lost Dutchman State Park (see Parks). A sign lets you know that you're entering Tonto National Forest, unusual because the "trees" are cactus and scrub, but spectacularly beautiful and blissfully free of commercial signs or billboards. The terrain was created more than 29 million years ago during the Tertiary Period. The road follows the shores of Canyon Lake (see Boating/Fishing), about 15 miles from Apache Junction. About 2 miles past Canyon Lake and 15 miles from Goldfield, you come to the town of Tortilla Flat (see Goldfield under Major Attractions).

Five miles beyond Tortilla Flat there is a new rest area at Fish Creek Hill Scenic Vista. Here the pavement ends, and so do most signs of civilization. But this is why you're on the trail in the first place. After an ascent, drivers have to be alert for the steep downhill along Fish Creek Hill, a real misnomer because the creek is almost always dry and certainly hasn't supported fish for decades. The downhill, however, really gets your attention as it descends sharply along a sheer cliff. As you leave Fish Creek Canyon, one of the trail's most famous landmarks, Geronimo Head, lies in front of you. Try to relax and enjoy the scenery until you come to the next civilized sign, the turnoff to Apache Lake (see Boating/Fishing). Stunning views overlook the massive cliffs of Goat Mountain and Four Peaks. If you scan the ridge lines, you could spot a desert bighorn sheep. At this point you are about 14 miles from Roosevelt Dam (see East-Central region), where you again pick up the paved road, and from where you can continue on into Globe on Hwy. 88.

Beginning in Apache Junction and ending in Lordsburg, New Mexico, the **Old West Hwy.** drifts for 203 miles, passing through pieces of history that span more than 600 years. It follows US 60 and US 70, with plenty of side trips, from the area haunted by Jacob Waltz, the Lost Dutchman, and the Superstition Mountains to the Tonto National Monument Cliff Dwellings, to the copper mines of Globe-Miami, through the Apache San Carlos Reservation, and on to Safford. An excellent booklet, written by Arizona journalist Sam Lowe, takes you mile by mile across this intriguing route. The booklet is available for $4.95 from **The Old West Hwy. Committee, P.O. Box 2539, Globe, 85502; 800-804-5623.**

Tours

One of the best ways not to miss any of the great stuff (like bighorn sheep, old mines, running streams, and waterfalls) is to hook up with an experienced guide who has a vehicle that can take an off-road beating. **Apache Trail Tours** uses genuine Jeep® Scramblers to bounce along desert roads, or simply to follow the Apache Trail. Tours of four hours to all day can be arranged, some incorporating hiking, with a driver-guide who really knows the area. Before setting out, owner Jodi Akers carefully explains the "leaverite" concept to all clients. "If you find something that interests you, take a look, take photos, even pick it up. But then, you leaverite there," she says. Their office is **in Goldfield Ghost Town. 480-982-7661. Website: www. arizonaadventures.com/apachetrail.**

Walk Softly Tours, ecologically sensitive tours in the Superstition Mountains of varying levels of difficulty, are among the best for introducing newcomers to the Sonoran Desert flora and fauna, and to indigenous cultures. A tour called Mile in their Moccasins is a half-day odyssey to an Indian reservation led by a native guide. Another, A Walk on the Wild Side, is an all-day hike through backcountry into a desert canyon filled with unusual rock formations and desert oases. The company partners with the Arizona American Indian Tourism Association, the Forest Service, and the BLM. **P.O. Box 5510, Scottsdale, 85261-5510; 480-473-1148. Website: www.walksoftlytours.com.**

The **Superstition Scenic Narrow Gauge Railroad** leaves from Goldfield on a 25-minute tour through the Superstition foothills, past old mining claims in the Goldfield district. **480-983-0333.**

Where to Stay

Gold Canyon Golf Resort—$$$$

This is a very special place, snugged into the Superstition foothills, made up of large casitas with patios that have great desert views. Once called Gold Canyon Ranch, the name was changed to call attention to the 18-hole golf course (see Golf). New casitas have fireplaces and wet bars, and some have a private spa. If you don't care about tee times and handicaps, there are tennis courts, a pool, and riding stables. For one of the most enjoyable times in the desert, sit on your patio in the early morning while aggressive cactus wrens visit in search of a handout. During a full moon, the silhouettes of saguaros are spectacular. Located 7 miles east of Apache Junction off US 60. Signs on the highway point you in the right direction. **6100 S. Kings Ranch Rd., Gold Canyon, 85219; 800-624-6445 or 480-982-9090.**

Apache Lake Resort—$$–$$$

For something more civilized than camping, this 58-unit motel has kitchenettes, a new restaurant, and lounge. A new general store offers snacks, basic canned goods, beer, and sodas. Call for reservations, essential most weekends and almost always during the summer. Located **at Apache Lake. 520-467-2511.**

Camping

At **Canyon Lake,** there are 10 RV spaces with electric and water hookups and 17 spaces with no hookups, as well as tent camping right on the lakeshore, at **Laguna Beach Campground** (480-944-6504). The campground has tables for day use and its own private beach with swimming area. In **Lost Dutchman State Park,** there are campsites, but no hookups. Located 5 miles northeast of Apache Junction on Hwy. 88. **6109 N. Apache Trail, Apache Junction, 85219; 480-982-4485.**

Where to Eat

Mammoth Steak House & Saloon—$$$

This is a truly funky place with stuffed elk, mountain lion, and other Arizona critters watching you eat. A hundred feet of hitching post out front accommodates cowboy guests. There's live entertainment along with char-broiled steaks. Open Sun.–Thurs., 7:00 A.M.–8:00 P.M.; Fri.–Sat., 7:00 A.M.–9:00 P.M. **In Goldfield. 480-983-6402.**

Mining Camp Restaurant—$$$

This good-fun eatery is built of ponderosa logs and surrounded by buildings that replicate an old mining camp. Meals are served family style from big bowls and platters, with "all you can

The Church of Our Lady of Guadalupe serves the Yaqui and Latino population of Guadalupe, next to Tempe.

eat" a mandate rather than an option. The specialty is barbecued ribs accompanied by coleslaw, baked beans, homemade raisin bread, and prospector cookies for dessert. If you're looking for continental cuisine, this is not the place. Open Oct.–June, Mon.–Sat., 4:00 P.M.–9:00 P.M.; Sun. and holidays, noon–9 P.M. Located north of Apache Junction **on Hwy. 88 about a mile south of Goldfield. 480-982-3181.**

The Lakeshore Restaurant—$$–$$$

On the shores of Saguaro Lake, meals are served indoors or out, overlooking the sparkling waters. Open daily for three meals; hours vary by day and season, breakfast Sat.–Sun. year-round. 480-984-5311.

Services

Apache Junction Chamber of Commerce

They have lots of good pamphlets, plus a knowledgeable staff. Open summer, Mon.–Fri., 8:00 A.M.–5:00 P.M.; winter, Mon.–Sat., 8:00 A.M.–5:00 P.M. **112 E. Second Ave., P.O. Box 1747, Apache Junction, 85219; 800-252-3141 or 480-982-3141.** Website: www.apachejunction coc.com.

South: Guadalupe

Thirty years ago, Guadalupe was way south of Phoenix, just a little village that you zipped by on I-10 on your way to Tucson. Now, as the boundaries of Phoenix have expanded, it is surrounded by the homes and businesses of Tempe on three sides, and the I-10 freeway that marks the Phoenix boundary on the west. As it was then, its population of about 6,000 is Yaqui Indian, with Mexicans the more recent arrivals. When the area called Ahwatukee began to develop in the late 1970s on the Tempe-Phoenix border and Tempe found itself in an accelerating growth spiral, Guadalupe felt the squeeze. Yet it manages to hang on despite the fact that its 450 acres are being eyed by developers. Shoppers come to browse curio corners and pottery shops.

History

Until recently the Yaquis lived in what is now Guadalupe much as they had for decades. In the 1800s they cultivated sustenance crops along the Salt River, with enough left over to sell to early Phoenix residents. A 40-acre parcel, given to the Yaquis by President Woodrow Wilson in the early part of the century, was formally named Guadalupe in honor of Nuestra Señora de Guadalupe, the Mexican Virgin Mary.

GETTING THERE
Guadalupe is off I-10 at Guadalupe Rd.

Seeing and Doing

Historic Sites
The Church of Our Lady of Guadalupe is the site of elaborate Christmas and Easter celebrations, but most days it is a quiet, cool refuge for simply sitting and thinking. Located in the center of town off Ave. del Yaqui.

Seasonal Favorites
At the Guadalupe Farmers Market you'll find a fragrant selection of absolutely fresh, delicious vegetables, with hot roasted chiles always available. Depending on the season, locally grown tomatoes, squash, melons, and more are in stock.

Located at Calle Guadalupe and Ave. del Yaqui (Priest Rd.).

Where to Eat

San Diego Bay—$$–$$$
One of Guadalupe's big draws is this marvelous Mexican seafood restaurant. Formica-topped tables, plastic booths, and fluorescent lights do not exactly make for great atmosphere, but that's not why you come here. All fish is absolutely fresh. The ceviche appetizer served on a crisp corn tortilla is flavorful and moderately spicy, and red snapper Veracruz, with mounds of fresh chopped vegetables, is unsurpassed. If you're there for dinner, see if they have a pot of clam soup brewing. This clear, fragrant broth with pieces of chewy clam is delightful. Wash it all down with a frosty Negra Modelo and you're in heaven in this unobtrusive little restaurant. Open Mon.–Fri., 10:00 A.M.–9:00 P.M.; Sat., 8:00 A.M.–10:00 P.M.; Sun., 8:00 A.M.–9:00 P.M. Located across from Guadalupe Farmers Market in a big blue mercado. 9201 Ave. del Yaqui; 480-839-2991.

South: Ahwatukee Foothills

Really part of Phoenix, this burgeoning community of close to 100,000 represents a good share of Phoenix's growth. Today, below Ray Ave., half a dozen subdivisions merge in a sea of red tile roofs. Proximity to the hiking and biking trails in South Mountain Park and five golf courses are among the area's draws.

History

At one time Phoenix reached no farther than South Mountain, but in the 1970s far-sighted developers saw the beauty in the mountain's southern slopes and began building what is now Ahwatukee.

GETTING THERE
The Ahwatukee Foothills area is off I-10 beginning at Elliott.

Golf

The Ahwatukee Country Club's 18 semi-private holes wind through interesting upscale homes, along fairways flanked with mature eucalyptus. A good restaurant is open Mon.–Sat., 6:00 A.M.–10:00 P.M.; Sun., 6:00 A.M.–7:00 P.M. **Located at the corner of 48th Street and Warner. 480-893-9772.**

The Lakes at Ahwatukee is an outstanding executive 18-hole 4,000-yard course that's widely considered one of the best public courses in the state. It has water on 11 holes, 44 bunkers, and flawless greens. Located on **44th Street between Warner and Knox; 480-893-3004.** (See also Sheraton San Marcos Golf Resort in Chandler.)

Where to Stay

In Ahwatukee you can stay at the **South Mountain Quality Inn (480-893-3900)** or the **Grace Inn Best Western (480-893-3000),** both at the Elliott Rd. exit off I-10, as well as a dozen other reliable chains strung along the freeway at exits farther south.

Where to Eat

In Ahwatukee, **Matthews** restaurant **(480-893-3000)** in the Grace Inn has a good lunch buffet; open daily, 6:00 A.M.–10:00 P.M. A sleeper is the **Seafood Market &Grill (480-496-0066),** tucked unobtrusively into a corner mall at Elliott and 48th St. beside a Safeway. It has the largest selection of absolutely fresh seafood in the area, wonderfully prepared. Open Sun.–Thurs., 8:00 A.M.–9:00 P.M.; Fri.–Sat., 8:00 A.M.–10:00 P.M.

Services

Ahwatukee Foothills Chamber of Commerce

12020 S. Warner-Elliott Loop, No. 111, Phoenix, 85044; 480-753-7676. Website: www.ahwatukeechamber.com.

South: Chandler

This onetime agricultural town southeast of Phoenix wanted to be the Salt River Valley's answer to Pasadena, California. But it eventually grew to become a place of lovely homes, hotels, and resorts. It has continued to grow to its present population of about 170,000. Adjacent to Chandler in the community of Sun Lakes, almost 15,000 moderately affluent seniors enjoy the amenities of a resort retirement development.

History

Chandler was founded in 1912 by Canadian immigrant Dr. Alexander John Chandler, a veterinary surgeon, who purchased 80 acres of land from the federal government in 1891. He became a farmer and an expert in irrigation, a process essential to the success of farming in this arid land. Settlers soon discovered that water was at a premium, and the newly formed Salt River Project limited each landowner to 160 acres that could be irrigated. This put a decided crimp in Chandler's ability to farm his land, which had by that time increased to 18,000 acres. So he became one of the first land developers, advertising plots to Easterners. Three hundred eager buyers were brought by train to a "town" that consisted of the subdivision office, a place to eat, and a small grocery store.

The town got a boost with the opening of the San Marcos Resort on Nov. 22, 1913. The gala was attended by Governor W. P. Hunt and Vice President Thomas Marshall. It became the first Arizona hotel to offer guests the complete resort experience, with golf, tennis, horseback riding, and polo among its attractions. Fred Astaire, Joan Crawford, and Clark Gable were on its glittering guest list. The dining room, awash in crystal and silver, featured ostrich from local farms. By this time, ostrich farming had become a thriving industry with the increasing demand for the big birds' plumes, which had become a trendy women's fashion accessory. Chan-

Raising sheep in Chandler, south of Phoenix, is a lifestyle that is fast disappearing.

dler incorporated in 1920, building a high school, jail, and other trappings of an established community. It received a population boost in 1941 with the opening of Williams Air Force Base.

GETTING THERE
Chandler is on Hwy. 87 (also known as Arizona Ave.) south of Guadalupe Rd.

Seeing and Doing

Museums
The small nonprofit **Arizona Railway Museum** is dedicated to the preservation and restoration of Arizona's railroad history. The outdoor display features a number of railroad cars, including a tank, refrigerator, dome, and flat car as well as the staple boxcars and cabooses. Those who aren't captivated by cabooses appreciate the collection of railroad china that includes the most common of all Southern Pacific china, "Prairie Mountain Wild Flower," first used in the 1930s. Open Labor Day–Memorial Day, Sat.–Sun., noon–4:00 P.M., or by arrangement. **399 N. Delaware St., Chandler, 85224; 480-821-1108. Website: www.siege.net/~arm.**

The **Chandler Museum** contains a replica of a tent house used by early settlers, Southwest Indian artifacts, and a good representation of implements and furnishings from early Chandler days. Old black-and-white photos are especially appealing. Open Mon.–Sat., 11:00 A.M.–4:00 P.M. Located in a small facility in downtown Chandler behind the library. **178 E. Commonwealth Ave., Chandler, 85244; 480-782-2717.**

Where to Stay

Sheraton San Marcos Resort—$$$$
Calling itself Arizona's Original Golf Resort, this lovely old hotel, on the National Register of Historic Places, is a good example of how updating can be accomplished to accommodate a present-day desire for amenities without losing a sense of the past. Built in 1913 adjacent to Chandler's central square, it is the focal point of the downtown area. The town's founder, Dr. Alexander John Chandler, saw the hotel as an anchor in a master-planned community. It has had it ups and downs, closing its guest accommodations in 1979 and reopening seven

Rattlesnakes

Although their danger is somewhat exaggerated, quite a few rattlesnakes live in the Valley of the Sun, as in most desert climates. You rarely find them in residential areas, but they sometimes linger in places with new construction. Baby rattlers are born in Aug.–Sept.—and arrive with fangs. They give no warning because their rattles have not yet developed. They're born with a little budlike tip on their tail, and a second one develops in about a month.

Well over half of the baby rattlers, at less than a foot in length, fall prey to hawks and other raptors. Survivors seek shelter under shady rocks and bushes, where you're most likely to encounter them. So be careful where you put your hands, don't lean against a rock or canyon wall if there is a ledge just above or next to you, and wear high-top shoes or boots with pants that flop over the tops. If you do hear a hiss or rattle, stand still until the snake moves away. For snakebite information in the Valley of the Sun, call the **Samaritan Regional Poison Center (800-362-0101)**. In the unlikely event that you are bitten, call 911.

years later after a complete renovation. Today its 295 rooms are lovely and welcoming. Even if you don't stay here, stop by for lunch to see the classic architecture. The 18-hole PGA championship golf course has challenged players for more than half a century. Many package deals bring somewhat pricey winter rates into a more affordable range; mid-May–early Sept., room prices are less than half of those Dec.–Apr. **One San Marcos Place, Chandler, 85224; 800-325-3535 or 480-963-6655. Website: www.sheraton.com.**

Where to Eat

The Original Jake's—$

Authentic Chicago fare, featuring red hots boiled in Lake Michigan water, include Pucker Dogs (sauerkraut) and char-broiled Italian sausage sandwiches. Remember White Castles? The Jake Burger is about as close as you can get to this moist, square onion-smothered patty without trademark infringement. At 69 cents apiece, buy them by the bagful. Pick up the wall phone and dial any of a dozen numbers that connect to phone booths in Chicago. Read the Chicago Sun Times, pick up a Windy City tourism brochure, you'll think you're in Chicago. Open Mon.–Thurs., 11:00 A.M.–9:00 P.M.; Fri. and Sat., 11:00 A.M.–10:00 P.M.; Sun., 11:00 A.M.–8:00 P.M. On **Rural Road just south of Ray Road; 480-592-0114. Website www.theoriginaljakes.com.**

Buca di Beppo Restaurant—$$–$$$

The atmosphere is lively and unpretentious in this southern Italian restaurant that feels like you're in one of the Italian-American supper clubs of the 1940s and '50s but is part of a dozen-state chain. The marinara, spaghetti, and ravioli are reliably good, served in huge quantities that overflow from family platters. You'll try to clean your plate, but it will be almost impossible. Vintage family photos and images of Sophia Loren, Joe DiMaggio, and other famous Italians make up the decor. Open Mon.–Thurs., 5:00 P.M.–10:00 P.M.; Sat., 4:00 P.M.–11:00 P.M.; Sun., noon–10:00 P.M. **7111 W. Ray Rd.; 480-785-7272.**

Services

Chandler Chamber of Commerce

218 N. Arizona Ave., Chandler, 85225; 480-963-4571. Website: www.chandlerchamber.com.

Between Phoenix and Tucson

Florence

The county seat for Pinal County, this homey little town is often overlooked as a destination, which is too bad because it has interesting things to see. Main St. has retained its original architectural integrity, with many store facades dating to the turn of the century. Positioned away from an interstate, it remains small-town, even though the name "Florence" and "prisons" have become synonymous in Arizona. Florence has five places of incarceration: two private prisons that contract to import prisoners from other states, one Immigration and Naturalization Service detention center, one county prison, and the state prison, which moved here from Yuma in 1909 and is the largest of the five. The population of Florence, around 7,000, swells to 17,000 when you add the prison population—not all bad, considering that state revenue sharing is based on the larger population.

History

The Florence after whom the town was named remains elusive. Some say it was named by Territorial Governor Richard McCormick for his sister, and other sources claim that Governor Anson Safford named it for his sister. Both could be true, as Florence was a popular name in 1866 when the town was established. In the late 1800s it became a stagecoach hub and the agricultural center of the upper Gila River. That it is a true Arizona territorial town is immediately evident in the architectural styles of the 139 structures that make up its nationally registered historic district. Current badges of memorabilia include a water tower bearing the town name, a True-Value Hardware, and Rexall Drug complete with the old orange and blue sign.

GETTING THERE

Florence is located at the junction of Hwys. 79 and 87/287, about an hour's drive from either Phoenix or Tucson. From Phoenix take I-10 south to exit 185 and follow signs to the east. From Tucson take Hwy. 77/79 (Oracle Rd.) through Oracle Junction north to Florence.

Major Attractions

Gila River Reservation

Bordering the south end of the East Valley, this 584-square-mile reservation in Maricopa and Pinal Counties, with a population of 12,000, is much publicized for its Indian **gambling casinos,** convenient to Phoenix players.

The **Gila River Arts & Crafts Center** offers more than just arts and crafts. You may browse through a **museum and replicated villages** of various Indian cultures. We spent more than an hour in the exhibit that uses the words of indigenous peoples to explain how their ancestors lived during the past 2,000 years. A 10,000- to 20,000-year-old mammoth tusk, discovered on the reservation in 1987, verifies the presence of ancient creatures. Photos are all that exist of extensive ruins called Snaketown. They were excavated, then covered up again to preserve what the Indians consider sacred ground. Other old photos tell the story of 110,000 Japanese who were forcibly evacuated and confined at the Gila River Internment Center on the reservation at FDR's 1942 decree.

The shop area sells authentic silver and turquoise jewelry, baskets, pottery, and more. Basketry from the Tarahumara Indians in Mexico's Copper Canyon, very different in material and design from the Pima baskets, also is sold here. Outdoors in **Heritage Park,** recreations represent villages of the Papago, Pima, Maricopa, Hohokam, and Apache Indians. The heat is killer at midday during the summer, but other times of the year it's a pleasant, level walk.

You can get full meals and cool drinks in the **restaurant.** The **Native American Dance Festival** includes spectacularly costumed performers from eight different tribes, as well as arts and crafts demonstrations; held on Thanksgiving weekend. The center is open daily, 9:00 A.M.–5:00 P.M. Located southeast of Phoenix off I-10 at exit 175. **P.O. Box 457, Sacaton, 85247; 480-963-3981.**

Seeing and Doing

Museums and Historic Sites

Named for the U.S. senator, governor, and supreme court justice who founded the Arizona State Parks system in 1957, **McFarland State Historic Park,** a low wood ranch-style building, was the first Pinal County Courthouse, built in 1878. You can see its adobe construction through a "window" carved in the plaster that now covers the exterior. The building's incarnation as the county hospital for almost 50 years is traced in exhibits of enameled basins and bedpans, a cruel-looking tonsil guillotine and gynecological instruments, and a vacuum-pressure pump used by eye, ear, nose, and throat doctors in the days before Dristan. The most compelling exhibit may be that of the World War II Prisoner of War Camp in Florence. From 1942 to 1946 it held 13,000 prisoners, mostly Italian and German soldiers captured in North Africa and Europe and shipped to the United States to relieve England's overcrowded prisons. Prisoner documents, records, and photos verify that soldiers were much the same the world over. In

back, the Ernest W. McFarland Library and Archives houses personal McFarland family memorabilia. Small fee. Open Thu.–Mon., 8:00 A.M.–5:00 P.M. Located **at Main and Ruggles. P.O. Box 109, Florence, 85232; 520-868-5216 phone and fax. Website: www.pr.state.az.us.**

Pinal County Courthouse, an impressive brick and gingerbread building with mansard roof and dormers, is Florence's best example of Victorian architecture. Built in 1891 at a cost of $29,000 and an additional $5,765 spent on jail cells, it is the oldest public building in daily use in the state. No one seems to know why the painted wood tower clock has shown 11:46 since the day it was built. Inside, tall narrow doors with transoms are anachronistically flanked by glowing soda machines. Years of paint clog the intricacies of a sweeping carved-wood staircase, which historians say is made of redwood. But the beauty is still there in a building that has good bones, so take the time to admire its flamboyant exterior, then stroll the quiet hallways inside. Located **at Pinal and 11th St.**

When we picked up a battered geography text at **Pinal County Historical Museum,** among its pages we found a sheet of child-drawn doodles scratched on the back of a yellowed application form for a 1920s Ohio automobile registration. The youngster who learned from that book would be hard pressed to recognize the geographic world as it exists today. Morbidly fascinating museums exhibits include the hangman's nooses and wood gas-chamber chairs that actually saw active duty. Displays of electrical insulators and barbed wire, farm and mining machinery, sun-colored amethyst and carnival glass, and huge tomes of prison records tell of Florence's early days. Donations welcome. Open Apr.–July 15 and Aug. 31–Nov., Wed.–Sun., noon–4:00 P.M.; Dec.–Mar., Wed.–Sat., 11:00 A.M.–4:00 P.M., and Sun., noon–4:00 P.M. **715 S. Main St., Florence, 85232; 520-868-4382.**

Parks

Main Street Park has picnic tables and ramadas. Located **just across from Pinal County Historical Museum.**

The Pinal County Historical Museum in Florence has a monument to Tom Mix and his horse Tony, Jr..

Tours

For a **walking tour of historic Florence,** pick up a map at the chamber of commerce, which is headquartered in an 1890 building, once Brunenkant's Bakery. Other historic structures include the Church of the Assumption, its original part dating to 1870; the brick-on-adobe Cosgrove House on Baily St., built in 1878; and the 1879 Elena Llescas House, constructed in the Sonoran style. A **Tour of Historic Florence** is held, with trolleys taking visitors among the various sites, first Sat. in Feb., 11:00 A.M.–3:00 P.M. **520-868-9433.**

Where to Eat

Among half a dozen good family-owned restaurants, there is only one fast-food outlet in town, which city officials dub "a mistake," although it is on the outskirts so it does not intrude on historic downtown. For fast food you can go 10 miles west and south on Hwys. 287/87 to much newer Coolidge, founded in 1926.

Murphy's—$–$$

This low-key soup and salad restaurant may look familiar to movie buffs. It doubled as the drugstore in the 1985 motion picture *Murphy's Romance* starring Sally Field and James Garner. Walls are lined with movie memorabilia, and the classic May–Dec. romance flick runs on video as you eat. Food in this self-serve place is health-conscious and delicious. The sandwiches on the menu are a concession to the men in town, whom owner Sandy Tyus says "took awhile to learn that you really can fill up on soup and salad." Open Mon.–Fri., 11:00 A.M.–2:00 P.M. **310 N. Main St.; 520-868-0027.**

Services

The visitor center at the **Greater Florence Chamber of Commerce** is extensive, and is staffed with helpful folks. Clean public rest rooms are across the street. Open winter, Mon.–Fri., 10:00 A.M.–4:00 P.M.; summer, 10:00 A.M.–2:00 P.M. **291 N. Bailey, P.O. Box 929, Florence, 85232; 800-437-9433 or 520-868-9433. Website: www.florenceaz.org.**

Casa Grande

Casa Grande's borders, marked by vast fields of green bushes with fluffy bolls as well as feed lots, confirm that two of Arizona's Five "Cs," cotton and cattle, are alive and well here. A number of RV parks with signs declaring they cater to "Over 55" show that the area has been discovered by snowbird retirees who swell its population of 24,000 to 35,000. Many see it as a lower-priced alternative to Phoenix or Tucson, yet it is close enough to both to benefit from their shopping and cultural opportunities.

History

Although it has had a post office since 1880, Casa Grande began as just a stop on the Southern Pacific Railroad. Mining and agricultural implements were dropped off here. Before the

Casa Grande Ruins National Monument protects a Hohokam farming village dating to before 1350.

turn of the century, mining went into a decline, and agriculture became the economic backbone.

GETTING THERE

Casa Grande is on US 10 at Hwy. 84, 45 miles south of Phoenix, near the junction of I-8 and I-10.

Major Attractions

Casa Grande Ruins National Monument

These impressive ruins, the remains of an ancient Hohokam farming village that surrounded a Great House, have puzzled observers since Father Eusebio Kino and his group of missionaries came upon the deserted village. Over the centuries the elements and looters took their toll, until President Benjamin Harrison declared Casa Grande the country's first archaeological preserve in 1892. Today a shelter protects the ancient four-story building, which archaeologists believe dates to before 1350 and is the tallest, most massive of any Hohokam structure known to exist.

The building's walls face the four compass points. Various openings align with heavenly bodies, perhaps to reveal the best times for planting and harvesting. On a gravel path, vegetation placards point out creosote, prickly pear, saguaro, and other desert plants. Pick up a pamphlet for a self-guided tour through the ruins. Guided tours are sometimes scheduled, so call ahead. It's not a good idea to visit at high noon in the middle of summer, because the monument is hot, and desert winds may make it truly uncomfortable. Early mornings are best during summer months. You can bring a lunch and picnic at shaded tables on the grounds. Small fee. Open daily, 8:00 A.M.–5:00 P.M.; closed Christmas. From I-10 take the Coolidge exit (Hwy. 387) and follow the signs about 15 miles east to the monument entrance off Hwy. 87. **1100 Ruins Dr., Coolidge, 85228; 520-723-3172.**

Outdoor Activities

In the Air

Jumping from an airplane may not be everyone's cup of tea, but at **Skydive Arizona** you can see what it's like and decide if you want to try it. The little town of Eloy, just south of Casa

Grande, is home to the largest skydive training facility in the world. Professional jumpers, those who compete internationally, come here to train. But so do average folks who just want to see what the sport is all about, and "get their knees in the breeze," as school instructors say. No one dives solo the first time. Students are harnessed to instructors. If that's all you want to do, you can stop there. But after a few tandem jumps and hours of training, you may choose to jump solo. Located midway between Phoenix and Tucson 4 miles off I-10 near Eloy. **4900 N. Taylor Rd., Eloy, 85231; 800-858-5867 or 520-466-4777. E-mail: SkyAZ@aol.com. Website: www.skydive-az.com.**

Seeing and Doing

Museums and Historic Sites

If you're into old stone buildings, stop at **Heritage Hall Museum** just to see its remarkable architecture. Built in 1927 as the First Presbyterian Church of Casa Grande, the natural fieldstone structure now belongs to the Casa Grande Valley Historical Society, which uses the former social hall for its museum. It traces the area's rural life with photos of early farming equipment and relics from the late-19th-century mining boom. Small donation requested. Open Sept. 15–Memorial Day, Mon.–Sat., 1:00 P.M.–5:00 P.M. Located two blocks east of Pinal Ave. and Florence Blvd. **110 W. Florence Blvd., Casa Grande, 85222; 520-836-2223.**

Scenic Drives

A pleasant alternative to I-10 between Phoenix and Tucson, **Pinal Pioneer Parkway** (Hwy. 79) branches south from US 60 near Florence Junction. You may also access it from Hwys. 87/287 through Coolidge and Florence. The parkway opens a window on the Sonoran Desert scenery before the days of billboards and red-tile roofs. If you're not speeding, you'll glimpse, on small placards, the names of some of the cactuses you're seeing. Near the start of the drive you can turn west on Hwy. 87 for a visit to the Casa Grande Ruins National Monument (see Major Attractions).

Shopping

Casa Grande's biggest current claim to fame may be its two outlet malls, located about halfway between Phoenix and Tucson. **Factory Stores of America (800-SHOP-USA or 520-986-7616),** on I-10 at exit 194 (Florence Blvd.), features about 30 stores including Farberware, VanHeuseun, Westport, and Adidas. Just a few exits farther south, **Tanger Factory Outlet Center (520-836-0897 or 800-4TANGER),** on I-10 at exit 198, has more than 50 stores including Barbizon Lingerie, Big Dog, Guess?, Koret, Levi's, Liz Claiborne, Springmaid-Wamsutta, Reebok, and more.

Where to Stay

Francisco Grande Resort and Golf Club—$$$

This 160-room luxury resort, one of the area's few multistory buildings, is visible on the flat desert for miles. Its roots as the spring training home of the San Francisco Giants in the 1960s are evident in the bat-shaped pool, and wading pool in the shape of a ball; the parking lot is diamond-shaped. Palms mark fairways along an 18-hole PGA championship golf course, open to the public. It offers some real golf package bargains and excellent off-season rates. **26000 Gila Bend Hwy. (Hwy. 84), Casa Grande, 85222; 520-836-6444 or 800-237-4238.** Website: www.franciscogrande.com.

Services

Greater Casa Grande Chamber of Commerce

Area information and public rest rooms. Open Mon.–Fri., 9:00 A.M.–5:00 P.M.; Sat., 10:00 A.M.–4:00 P.M.; Sun., noon–4:00 P.M. **575 N. Marshall St., Casa Grande, 85222; 800-916-1515 or 520-836-2125.** Website: www.chamber@casagrande.com.

Bloomin' Cactuses

Desert sands support one of the richest collections of plants in the world. If summer monsoons have done their job, they'll burst into exuberant bloom the following spring. Cactus flowers, from pale translucent white to vibrant magenta, are among the loveliest blossoms in the desert.

Perhaps the world's best example of water conservation, cactuses have evolved to have no leaves. Their spines protect fat green stems that store water between rains. Pinched places on an "armed" cactus, such as a saguaro, indicate a drought year, during which the plant pulled in its fleshy stem as it used its store of water. The "pleats" that make up its arms expand as it stores water during years of abundant rainfall.

Arizona is one of two states, along with California, where saguaros grow naturally. Arizona has by far the greatest number. At maturity, the saguaro can be massive and many-armed, reaching a height of more than 30 feet. Its first arms don't develop until it is 50 to 100 years old. Spectacular, pale waxy flowers appear on arms that are a year or two old, last just a few hours, then die.

Similar to the saguaro, the senita has arms that grow from a central base. It blooms at night, producing huge, 6-inch blossoms that are observable in early morning, then close by noon, never to reopen. If bees, bats, and moths have done their pollinating job, fruit will appear. When it begins to blush (birds will tell you when it's ripe), inside you'll find white fruit dotted with tiny black crunchy seeds similar to kiwi. Its flavor is bland and mild like figs.

Short, fat, and close to the ground, barrel cactuses come in many varieties. Common in Arizona is the compass barrel, so-called because of its tendency to lean to the south or southwest. This behavior is thought to create shade for the cactus as it leans into the sun, that its angle exposes its growing tip to the sun, and that the north side grows faster, thus making it lean. In August or September, later than other cactuses, yellow or orange blossoms appear.

Flat, broad-leafed beavertail prickly pear is easy to identify for its lack of spines and blue-gray color. Their blossoms are reddish, with large petals and yellow hearts. Prickly pear fruit is considered so desirable that it is sold in some southwestern food stores.

A cactus with a cuddly name, teddy-bear cholla, is anything but huggable. Its gray, fuzzy covering is really spines that are much sharper than any needle. A relative, the jumping cholla, doesn't actually jump, although many hikers beg to differ. Its spines are so loosely attached that when it is touched, no matter how lightly, spines immediately attach themselves to whatever has brushed by. This allows it to be propagated by the wind. If you happen to brush against a cholla accidentally, take a fine pocket comb and gently comb your leg (where the spines most often get you) or your clothing. Don't try to pick them off or you'll end up with fingers and legs both in an aggravated condition.

Summerhaven Mt. Lemon

Coronado National Forest

Santa Catalina Mountains

Oro Valley

Ina Road

Skyline Drive

Sabino Canyon

Hitchcock Highway

Mt. Lemon Highway

Sunrise Drive

Sabino Canyon Road

Oracle Road

Fort Lowell Park Museum

Craycroft Road

Swan Road

Arizona Historical Society

Grant Rd

Tanque Verde Road

Santa Catalina Highway

Speedway Boulevard

Saguaro National Park West

Silverbell Road

U of A

Broadway

Arizona–Sonora Desert Museum

Gates Pass Road

Old Tucson Studios

TUCSON

Randolph Park

Alvernon Way

Wilmot Road

Kolb Road

Old Spanish Trail

Freeman Road

Saguaro National Park East

Kinney Road

Davis-Monthan Air Force Base

Ajo Way

Mission Road

Colossal Cave

86

Pascua Yaqui Reservation

Tucson International Airport

BUS 19

Old Spanish Trail

Vail

San Xavier Reservation

San Xavier del Bac Mission

Exit 279

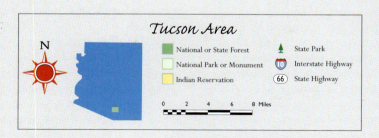

Tucson Area

N

National or State Forest	State Park
National Park or Monument	10 Interstate Highway
Indian Reservation	66 State Highway

0   2   4   6   8 Miles

Tucson Area

Prickly pear cactus blossom is a common sight in the Sonoran Desert in spring.

Tucson

In 1869 J. Ross Browne's book *Adventures in the Apache Country: A Tour Through Arizona and Sonora* described Tucson as "a city of mud boxes, dingy and dilapidated, cracked and baked into a composite of dust and filth littered about with broken corrals, carcasses of dead animals, and broken pottery."

Today's Tucson is a sophisticated city of about 850,000, a pleasant blend of metropolis and small town that mixes the best of the West with trendy resorts, velvety golf courses, outstanding restaurants, and an active arts scene. At an elevation of 2,389 feet, almost 1,300 feet higher than Phoenix, it stays a bit cooler than its neighbor to the north. More than 350 days each year are sunny and fair, according to the Tucson Bureau of the U.S. Weather Service. With a metropolitan area covering nearly 500 square miles, the city sprawls north, from a re-emerging downtown, toward the picturesque Santa Catalina Mountains, one of five ranges that surround the city. It sits in the eastern portion of the high Sonoran Desert, the only place in the world where saguaro cactuses grow naturally. Tucson is flanked by Saguaro National Park East and West, where you can see the largest concentration of these "giants with arms" anywhere.

Tucson is a civilized city, one of just 14 in the country with a resident symphony, as well as opera, theater, and ballet companies. An event called Downtown Sat. Night, on the first Sat. of each month, features gallery open houses (there are more than 35 in the downtown area), musical performances, and street dancing. Thurs. Night Artwalks, held the first and third Thurs. of each month, have become a choice way to get acquainted with the Tucson arts scene. Led by docents, visitors move among galleries that welcome guests with coffee and cookies. Oftentimes displaying artists are on hand to talk about their work.

It's difficult to get lost in this well-laid-out city if you remember that the biggest mountain range, the Santa Catalinas, are always to the northeast. If you're trying to go north, remember that main east-west streets usually end up feeding into I-10, and main north-south streets usually feed into I-10, as it skirts the south of the city, or I-19, another north-south thoroughfare. You do have to watch street signs because they can be misleading. Street names frequently change and you can drive for miles before you realize you're on the wrong one. For example, where Kolb/Grant crosses Tanque Verde, the sign facing westbound says Kolb, but it says Grant for eastbound drivers. You have to look behind you to realize you've just missed your turn. Just stay alert and you'll be okay.

Tucson's website (see Services) suggests that you get your bearings by going up Sentinel Peak, the large hill with the white "A" emblazoned on it. You can see it from I-10 as you head south through Tucson. The annual whitewashing it receives from the University of Arizona freshman class keeps it sparkling clean. From here you'll see the ring of mountains that surrounds the city. It's easy to identify the 9,000-foot-high Santa Catalinas on the north and northeast, Rincon Mountains to the east, Santa Rita Mountains to the south and southeast, Tucson Mountains on the west, and the Tortolita Mountains on the northwest.

History

Tucson is the oldest continually inhabited settlement in the country. As early as A.D. 100, the Hohokam people raised crops along the soil-rich Santa Cruz River and charted their activities in petroglyphs, visible today in Saguaro National Park West at Signal Hill. The Spanish arrived in the late 1600s to find the peaceful Pima Indians living near what is now downtown. In 1775 Irishman Hugh O'Connor, in his explorations for Spain, founded the walled presidio of San Agustin del Tucson as protection against the Apaches. Almost a century before, the area had been called Chuk Shon by the Pima Indians. An interpretive translation is "spring at the foot of a black mountain," referring to the Santa Cruz River that follows an uneven above- and below-ground flow. The word became anglicized as Tucson.

The city, briefly part of Mexico in 1821 when it became independent from Spain, returned to U.S. jurisdiction when it was sold as part of the Gadsden Purchase in 1854. The Butterfield Stage clattered through Cochise territory and on to Tucson in the 1860s. Remnants of Tucson's unruly frontier origins live on in lively country western bars. Ethnic Indian, Mexican, and Spanish roots are evident in the no-high-rise architecture and popular Southwest-style decor. And the Wild West thrives at places like Old Tucson Studios (see Major Attractions). Nicknamed "Old Pueblo" for its original walled presidio, Tucson once was the capital of the Arizona Territory, a title it lost to Phoenix even before Arizona became a state in 1912.

Major Attractions

Kitt Peak

Even if you're not a Trekkie and stars are something you prefer to see on the silver screen, Kitt Peak is worth a visit just for the sheer beauty of the stark white domes poised on various crests, blending with cumulus clouds against a sheer blue sky. A steep paved road kinked with switchbacks begins a 12-mile upward spiral that sometimes is closed during the winter because of snow buildup.

Kitt Peak was chosen for the location of one of seven national observatories because of the dry atmosphere that guarantees an average of 260 clear days a year. Winter months are driest, and therefore most reliable. The observatory closes during Aug., when Arizona experiences what it calls its "monsoon" season (see sidebar in Phoenix chapter). Kitt Peak also is relatively isolated from light pollution.

Kitt Peak is located on the country's second-largest Indian reservation. A 1958 lease for the lofty 6,875-foot-high site, negotiated with the Tohono O'odham Tribal Council, is in effect "until the end of time," say its terms. The Tohono O'odham, also called Papago, have stipulated that the observatory cannot be used for military purposes, which means no Star Wars or spy satellites. The observatory shop helps perpetuate the Tohono O'odham's culture by offering beautifully designed woven baskets for sale, with all proceeds going to Native American artisans. Prices for these lovely works of art are kept low because the shop charges no sales tax and the baskets are purchased directly from the artists.

Here displays demystify the working of telescopes. A huge cylinder of fused quartz, the core removed from the Mayall 4-meter telescope mirror, helps explain how light-gathering (rather than magnification) works. Exhibits demonstrate why no one ever "looks through a telescope" anymore. There is nothing to look through. Charge-coupled devices (CCDs) now convert light into digital form for computer storage so that astronomers work at video screens

Getting There

Tucson is about two hours south of Phoenix on I-10. Because a number of other highways extend out from it like spokes, the city is a convenient hub for exploring all of southern and eastern Arizona.
*Tucson International Airport is served by AeroCalifornia, Aerolitoral, Aeromexico, America West, American, Continental, Delta, Northwest, Southwest, and United Airlines. The airport is located about 20 minutes west of downtown. Call individual airlines or the **Tucson Airport Authority, 520-573-8100.** You can also fly into Phoenix and use surface transportation for the remaining two hours to Tucson. A number of companies offer sedan service from Phoenix Sky Harbor International Airport to many Tucson destinations. One of them is the **Arizona Shuttle 800-888-2749.***
Greyhound** serves Tucson from a terminal at **2 S. Fourth Ave., Tucson, 85701; 520-624-6651 or 800-231-2222. Website: www.greyhound.com.

rather than eyepieces. LTOs, large telescope operators, adjust and position the telescopes to accomplish specific tasks.

The National Optical Astronomy Observatories, under contract with the National Science Foundation, oversees site operations on Kitt Peak. Responsible for the world's largest collection of telescopes, which includes 22 optical and a radio telescope, the observatory provides major telescope facilities for the world's astronomers and has ongoing research programs in observational astronomy. Telescopes are accessible to professionals as well as students through an application process. Once an application is accepted, the astronomer comes to the observa-

tory on the specified dates and hopes that viewing conditions are optimal. If they aren't, he or she must reapply for new dates.

A **guided tour,** free because the observatory is funded with taxpayer dollars, begins with an overview of the observatory's operations. Of the 24 operational telescopes on Kitt Peak, visitors can visit three on the tour. The 2.1-meter telescope is closest to the visitor center, up a short hill, then up four flights of stairs inside the dome. The dome turns noisily while a viewing slit accordions open to aim the scope heavenward. The telescope is tilted at the same angle as the earth's axis, which simplifies the job of accurately tracking the stars. It is used to view very distant stars and galaxies. Moons and planets are too close for this scope.

You also can look at the world's largest solar telescope, the McMath-Pierce, installed here in 1974. Its 500-foot length, 300 feet of which are underground, houses mirrors that produce a 30-inch image of the sun displayed on a TV monitor. The scope looks like a giant grasshopper poised for a leap. You may also visit the 4-meter Mayall telescope, the fourth-largest optical telescope in the world.

Temperatures on Kitt Peak are as much as 20°F cooler than on the valley floor. Those with cardiac and respiratory concerns should remember the 6,000-foot-plus altitude and be aware that there are steps and steep hills to some of the telescopes. There are no food or gas facilities, but public rest rooms are adjacent to the parking lot. There is a picnic area with tables, a ramada, drinking water, and rest rooms about a mile down the hill from the visitor center. One-hour guided tours begin at the visitor center, daily, 10:00 A.M., 11:30 A.M., and 1:30 P.M. Most visitors take an additional hour to visit the telescopes not covered on the tour. You also can do a self-guided tour. Open daily, 9:00 A.M.–4:00 P.M., except Thanksgiving, Christmas Day, and New Year's Day. Located **56 miles southeast of Tucson via Hwy. 86. National Optical Astronomy Observatories, P.O. Box 26732, Tucson, 85726; 520-318-8726 Kitt Peak Visitor Center or**

Telescopes at Kitt Peak National Observatory, near Tucson, create a sculptural skyline.

520-318-8200 recorded information. Website: www.noao.edu.

Arizona-Sonora Desert Museum

One of Tucson's jewels and not to be missed, this ever-changing attraction set away from the city, on almost 100 acres of desert that is still truly wild (only 30 acres are under exhibit), is part zoo, part museum, and part botanical garden. More than 300 species of animals and 1,300 kinds of plants of the Sonoran Desert region exist happily in natural settings. The concept of featuring **communities of plants and animals** rather than individual species makes a visit here similar to a journey through a succession of habitats. From a mountain canyon with pine trees, you stroll into grasslands, for example, leaving behind black bears, wolves, Steller's jays, and other woodland creatures. It's as if you were walking down a mountain slope into high-desert grasslands where the vegetation becomes clumps of bear grass, yucca, and ocotillo. This is where the prairie-dog colony frolics. If you come in the morning, you'll see the clownish creatures sunbathing on mounds above their burrows. Other

habitats are home to mountain lions, white-tailed deer, Mexican wolves, and desert bighorn sheep. The hummingbird aviary is filled with dozens of the iridescent winged creatures that often perch within feet of observers as if posing for the camera. New exhibits feature coatimundis (long-tailed, monkeylike creatures native to Arizona) and Sonorasaunus dinosaur bones.

At the Arizona-Sonora Desert Museum in Tucson, a prairie dog colony is always an entertaining sight.

A **cactus garden** displays more than 140 species of Sonoran Desert plants, a half dozen of which are endangered. A cool, dim, walk-through underground replica of a limestone cave has sleeping bats clinging to walls and ceilings. Other exhibits explore cave development, fossils, and a packrat midden.

Two gift shops stock an outstanding selection of nature products and books, including educational items perfect to take home for the grandkids. The **Ocotillo Cafe** serves brunch Sun., 10:30 A.M.–2:00 P.M., with a fixed-price menu that includes museum admission. There is a picnic area just down the road from the museum entrance. While enjoying a quiet picnic lunch, we were approached by a pair of shy, hopeful coyotes banking on a hand-out. The parking lot is wheelchair-accessible, as are most areas of the museum. During the summer, try to get there first thing in the morning, when animals are at their most active and temperatures haven't yet started to soar. When you call the museum, if you're put on hold, you won't get elevator music; you'll hear the sounds of desert birds, flowing water, and gentle breezes. Open Mar.–Sept., daily, 7:30 A.M.–6:00 P.M.; Oct.–Feb., daily, 8:30 A.M.–5:00 P.M. From Tucson take Gates Pass Rd. to Kinney Rd., or simply follow Kinney Rd. to the entrance. **2021 N. Kinney Rd., Tucson, 85743; 520-883-2702. Website: www.desertmuseum.org.**

University of Arizona

Tucson almost didn't get the University of Arizona, even though the 13th Territorial Legislature approved $25,000 for its founding, 27 years before Arizona was a state. Oddly enough, the money was there but the land wasn't. Lawmakers assumed that Tucson could come up with a place to put the institute of higher learning, once funding was available. This miffed local citizens, especially since the state capital site had gone to Phoenix, and neither the state prison nor the asylum for the insane were offered to Tucson. At the last minute, just before the Leg-

islature reclaimed the funds, a saloon keeper and two gamblers donated 40 acres of land, deemed almost useless because they were "way out east of town." By 1891 classes were in session with 32 students and six teachers, and what was to become one of the top research universities in the nation had its beginnings.

You can easily spend very little exploring the campus because most of its museums charge no admission; the **Flandrau Science Center** has minimum charges for some events. Stop by the visitor center for a fistful of brochures and a campus map. One of the brochures available at the visitor center directs you to a **campus walking tour** that identifies plants of the Sonoran Desert as well as "imports," brought by people from the East and Midwest as they migrated west. A grove of olive trees, west of Park Ave. in front of Gila, Maricopa and Yuma Halls, dates to 1889 when they were planted to test their adaptation to Arizona's arid conditions. Today they're thriving.

You'll find public parking directly behind the **visitor center** (bring quarters to feed the meter). Open during the school year, Mon.–Sat., 7:30 A.M.–5:00 P.M.; Sat., 9:00 A.M.–1:00 P.M.; call for summer hours. Located **at Cherry Ave. and University. 520-621-5130.**

Picacho Peak State Park

That large, looming pinnacle to the west of I-10 about midway between Phoenix and Tucson has served as a travelers' landmark for centuries. The 3,382-foot eroded lava flow, distinctively shaped and formed by wind and weather, is the site of Arizona's largest Civil War battle. The Butterfield Overland Stage once used the pass it guards. More than 100 campsites with hook-ups are available (the higher ones have wonderful nighttime views of lights below) on a first-come, first-served basis, and picnic areas with shade ramadas are scattered throughout the park. In the spring, if winter rains have cooperated, wildflowers absolutely explode along the roads and on the slopes. In Mar. more than 100 "soldiers" stage a reenactment of the famous

Civil War battle, blasting away on foot and horseback with black powder rifles. Take the **Picacho exit off I-10,** about 35 miles north of Tucson. 520-466-3183 phone and fax. Website: pr.state.az.us.

Festivals and Events

Tucson Gem & Mineral Shows

Feb.

The world's largest shows of their kind, they attracts an international assemblage of buyers and dealers in gems, minerals, fossils, jewelry, and other lapidary-related items. The wholesale and retail shows are held separately. Some participants come simply to exhibit fabulous finds and collections. The Tucson Gem Society show offers special displays from museums and private collectors as well as seminars to help educate both novices and seasoned lapidary enthusiasts. Held **at the Tucson Convention Center** and other locations citywide. For information contact **Tucson Gem and Mineral Society (520-322-5773),** or **Metropolitan Tucson Convention and Visitors Bureau (800-638-8350)** for a show guide and map.

La Fiesta de Los Vaqueros

mid-Feb.

Tucson's biggest rodeo and the largest outdoor midwinter rodeo in America has thrilled crowds for more than 70 years. The celebration features a parade around the rodeo grounds, the world's largest such nonmotorized event. Tickets are required. 520-741-2233.

Pima County Fair

mid-Apr.

If you're accustomed to Midwest fairs, usually held in the fall of the year and filled with farm equipment, Arizona's fairs will seem quite different. The emphasis is more on fun and games.

This 10-day event always begins the second Thurs. of Apr. and has competitions in home arts, fine arts, and hobby categories. Four-H and Future Farmers of America (FFA) kids proudly display their projects, and you can stroll down a huge carnival midway. Located **south of Tucson off I-10 at exit 275.** 520-762-9100.

Outdoor Activities

Bicycling

Bicycling Magazine recently rated Tucson one of the top three cities for two-wheel pursuits, because of its myriad trails and great scenery. See also Hiking for trails open to both bikers and hikers.

MOUNTAIN BIKING

Saguaro National Park

In the east unit of this park, a 2.5-mile segment of single-track trail runs through the middle of Paved Loop Dr. and is open to mountain bikes. It is the first single-track, shared-use trail to allow mountain bikes in the U.S. national parks. The **Cactus Forest Trail,** just 2.5 miles long but spectacularly beautiful, can be made into a longer ride by continuing on to Cactus Forest Dr., a paved road that loops through more gorgeous Sonoran Desert. **Go east on Broadway to Freeman Rd., turn right to Old Spanish Trail, turn left, and look for park signs.** 520-733-5153.

In the west unit, at this time there is no mountain biking except on dirt roads shared with cars. **Go west on Speedway, which becomes Gates Pass Rd.; the road ends at Kinney Rd. Turn right, into the park entrance.** 520-733-5158.

Tucson Mountain Park

Mountain bikers are the largest users of this county natural-resource park. Its 26 miles of protected and preserved trails are open to all nonmotorized users, including hikers and equestrians. Located **14 miles west of Tucson. Take**

Speedway Blvd. west through Gates Pass Rd. to the park. 520-733-5153.

Golf

Tucson truly is a golf-oriented city, mainly because the weather allows for year-round play. Three new courses—Raven at Sabino Springs, Rancho Vistoso, and Torres Blancas—each have 18 holes of challenging desert terrain as well as stunning views of the Sonoran Desert. Some are very expensive, but greens fees drop as much as 70 percent during summer months. If playing in 100°F-plus heat isn't appealing, do what the locals do: get the earliest possible tee time so you're off the course by midmorning. The day's most extreme heat doesn't hit until mid-afternoon.

RESORT, PRIVATE, AND SEMIPRIVATE COURSES

El Conquistador Country Club

The 18-hole Sunrise and Sunset courses flow along the desert's natural contours, with rabbits and roadrunners common visitors. For more variety in landscape, the Sunrise course has a greater number of elevated tees and greens. The slightly more challenging Sunset course follows shallow ravines that make it much easier to get into trouble. **10555 N. La Canada Dr., Tucson, 85737; 520-544-1800.**

La Paloma Country Club

The 27 holes here, on three nine-hole courses, are uniquely designed to blend with rather than dominate the desert. Dotted with stately saguaros, the dramatic landscape makes it difficult to keep an eye on the ball. Jack Nicklaus designed these courses in the foothills along Sunrise Dr. in an area once thought unsuitable for a golf course. You must be a La Paloma guest or member to play the course. Other occasional reservations are sometimes accepted 48 hours before tee time. **3660 E. Sunrise Dr., Tucson, 85718; 520-299-1500. Website: www. troongolf.com.**

The Lodge at Ventana Canyon

The Canyon course and the Mountain course, both Tom Fazio-designed championship 18-hole PGA courses, wind through the natural rock features of the Catalina Mountain foothills. Guests at Loews Ventana Canyon Resort (see Where to Stay) have playing privileges on the Canyon course on odd-numbered days and the Mountain course on even-numbered days. **6200 N. Clubhouse Ln., Tucson, 85750; 520-577-4015 or 520-577-4061.**

Tucson National Golf Resort

This semiprivate course hosts the Tucson Chrysler Classic each Feb., in which 156 top pros compete for a million-dollar-plus purse. The 3,470-yard orange course, 3,638-yard gold course, and 3,222-yard green course make up 27 challenging holes. **2727 W. Club Dr., Tucson, 85742; 520-297-2271. Website: www. omnihotel.com**

PUBLIC COURSES

The city has a good choice of municipal courses that can become crowded during winter months. Call individual courses for tee times.

Dell Urich

You might remember this as the old Randolph South course if you've been here before. Completely reconstructed, it reopened in spring of 1996. **600 S. Alvernon Way, Tucson, 85711; 520-325-2811.**

El Rio

For those whose long game isn't their strongest, this older course provides a good challenge. Measuring 6,013 yards from the regular tees, it is relatively flat with few trouble spots. It was the original site for the Tucson Open, and before the city of Tucson bought it, it was the city's first country club. **1400 W. Speedway, Tucson, 85711; 520-623-6783.**

Fred Enke

If you've never played a real desert course, here's your opportunity. On this limited-turf course, prickly pear, saguaros, cholla, and other cactuses are found where other courses might have lakes and sand traps. Greens (exceptionally large), tees, and ball landing areas are planted with grass, but most of the rest is pretty much natural desert. Just navigating the hilly course can be a challenge. Unless you have lots of stamina, opt for a cart here. 8251 E. Irvington Rd., Tucson, 85742; 520-296-8607.

Randolph North

This longish course has hosted PGA tournaments, and welcomes top female professional golfers in Mar. for the Welch's/Circle K Championship LPGA. The mature eucalyptus and pines verify that the course, a traditional country-club layout, has been around for awhile. 600 S. Alvernon Way, Tucson, 85711; 520-325-2811.

Raven Golf Club at Sabino Springs

On this outstanding public (but not municipal) course, desert creatures still come to drink at the lateral-hazard pond on number 12. The natural spring once provided water for the native Hohokam. Designed by Robert Trent Jones Jr., the course's construction seems to have done little violence to the rocky outcroppings and huge stands of cactuses that give it its personality. It follows the natural contours of the Santa Catalinas' lower slopes, and in doing so creates sweeping views of the city below. 9777 E. Sabino Greens Dr., Tucson, 85749; 520-749-3636.

Hiking

The Tucson area is filled with outstanding hiking opportunities for all fitness levels throughout the front range of the Catalinas. The Santa Catalina Ranger District of the Coronado National Forest encompasses about 262,000 acres directly around Tucson, and the 300,000-plus Nogales Ranger District includes most of the Santa Rita Mountains south of the city. Both are loaded with miles of backcountry roads and trails, with opportunities for everybody, including motorized users.

Aspen Draw Trail

This 1.5-mile trail on Mount Lemmon is all uphill one way and all downhill the other if you make it a 3-mile round trip. It leaves from Ski Valley, the region's premier ski area, 30 miles northeast of Tucson. See Skiing.

Catalina State Park

This beautiful 5,511-acre park is set at the foot of the west face of the Santa Catalina Mountains, which form a background for the entire city of Tucson. Within the Coronado National Forest, just 12 miles north of the city, the park feels wild and remote. The geological formations on the north side of Pusch Ridge are spectacular from the park. The **Romero Ruin Interpretive Trail,** a popular, short (0.33-mile), easy hiking route, winds through typical desert vegetation to the site of an ancient Hohokam village. For a challenge, try the **Romero Canyon Trail,** a 14.4-mile round trip that goes from 2,700 to 6,000 feet. Though not a true technical climb, in several places it becomes a scramble. The **Sutherland Trail,** a real killer, eventually ends up at the top of the Catalinas and Mount Lemmon. You can backpack in and spend the night before returning. The two trails roughly parallel each other, and are tied together by the **Mount Lemmon Trail,** so for some real high-class abuse, you can do them as a loop. The rewards include coming across cool ponds that support a variety of wildlife and, in some cases, being entirely isolated.

Don't hike alone, though. There are no rescue services along the way. The park rangers are very helpful, and will provide you with a trail map and latest trail information. There is an equestrian center in the park, and many trails are ideal for riding. Less strenuous pursuits include picnicking (there are tables and grills) and bird-watching. The Audubon Society holds a Fri.-morning bird walk that begins between 7:00 and 8:30 A.M., depending on time of year. Call the ranger station to verify. There are 48 campsites in the park with water, rest rooms, showers, and a dump station, open all year. Small fee. Located **on Hwy. 77 north of Tucson,**

Mount Lemmon Highway

Milepost: Hiking, Picnicking, Camping

0–2: Trailhead for Soldier Trail.

2–5: Trailhead 706 for Babat Duag Trail.

5–6: Entrance to Molina Basin picnic area and campground, open during winter months. Solar compost toilets.

10–12: Bear Canyon picnic area.

12: Entrance to General Hitchcock Camp-ground.

12–14: Trailhead 21 for Green Mountain Trail.

17.2: Rose Canyon Recreational Area entrance. Picnicking, trout fishing, and camping at Rose Canyon Lake. No boating or swimming. Fee.

18.6: Primitive camping and picnicking area with no facilities. Helicopter pad for emergency and Forest Service use.

19.7: Turnoffs for half a dozen children's camps.

19.8: Palisades Visitor Center.

21.6: Spencer Canyon Campground, open May 1–Oct. 1. Fee.

21.8: Trailhead 22 for Box Camp Trail.

22.2: Trailhead 16 for Butterfly Trail.

23.4: Sykes Nob picnic area, 0.25 mile off main road to left.

23.4–23.5: Inspiration Rock picnic area; three picnic sites.

24: Loma Linda picnic area.

24.6: Trailhead for Oracle Trail 0.25 mile down Old Mount Lemmon Control Rd.

25: Summerhaven.

with aspen, Douglas fir, and ponderosa pine, becomes a favored destination when the desert floor heats up to 100°F-plus during summer months. The mountain is named for botanist Sara Lemmon, who identified and named many new plant species on a horseback expedition with her husband in 1881.

The Mount Lemmon Hwy. leading to Summerhaven and the summit was completed in 1951 and recently reconstructed with wider and more frequent turnouts, new overlooks, and better parking areas. During construction, cuts were left uneven and craggy rather than sheer, to blend with the cliffs sculpted by nature. As you climb the 25 miles to the summit, you leave the saguaros of the Lower Sonoran Life Zone, pass through riparian areas, an oak woodland community, the Upper Sonoran Life Zone, a transition zone with juniper and piñon pine, on through evergreen woodland vegetation to lush pine forest. There are 15 picnic and camping areas and **more than 140 miles of hiking trails** on Mount Lemmon (see sidebar), all maintained by the Forest Service. The little village of Summerhaven grew up around summer cabins that started appearing in 1916. There are restaurants, gift shops, and a picnic area on the other side of Summerhaven. From here it is 1.5 miles to Mount Lemmon Ski Valley, the southernmost ski area in the country (see Skiing). There is no gas here, so fill up before you leave the valley floor. **Take Tanque Verde Rd. to Catalina Hwy., which becomes Mount Lemmon Hwy. at milepost 1. Follow it north to Mount Lemmon** (see sidebar).

Picacho Peak

The **Calloway Trail** offers an easy 1.5-mile round trip. Or you can tackle **Hunter Trail,** where you go up hand-over-hand by gripping steel cables. You can stop halfway, admire the valley and Santa Cruz River, then go back. Or if you're feeling particularly robust, continue another mile to the peak for a total of 2 miles round trip. **Sunset Vista Trail** is 3.1 miles one way and another toughie, also takes you to the summit. This close to I-10, you'll find civiliza-

about 6 miles north of Ina Rd. on the right. P.O. Box 36986, Tucson, 85740; 520-628-5798. Website: www.pr.state.az.us.

Mount Lemmon

This is Tucson's premier playground. The cool, conifer forest at its 9,157-foot summit, fragrant

tion within minutes in the form of restaurants and gas stations. Take the **Picacho exit off I-10**, about 35 miles north of Tucson. 520- 466-3183 phone and fax. Website: pr.state.az.us.

Sabino Canyon

You don't have to hike or bicycle to enjoy this exquisitely lovely canyon that winds up the slopes of Mount Lemmon in the Santa Catalina foothills, but they are the most popular options for exploring. The canyon was closed to private motor vehicles in 1981. You can bird-watch, picnic, even swim when the natural pools along Sabino Creek are full enough. You don't even have to leave the visitor center to see white-wing doves, little ground doves, roadrunners, cardinals, round Gambel's quail, and half a dozen other native birds.

Sabino Canyon is in Coronado National Forest, which covers Southern Arizona like a patchwork quilt with more than a dozen detached areas designated as national forest. The canyon was home to the Clovis people 12,000–15,000 years ago, who sustained themselves by hunting abundant bison and mammoths. More recent residents, the Hohokam farmers knew how to get the most from the desert with sophisticated irrigation systems. When Europeans arrived in the 1500s, the Pima and Papago Indians were hunting game in the canyon and depended on Sabino Creek for water.

Today's visitors find tranquility along the creek, which flows all but a month or two out of the year. Hiking and biking trails are so extensive it is possible to feel quite alone. The creek's whiskey color comes from tannin found in oak tree roots and pine needles. Its waters support crayfish and sunfish, and are an essential source for rock squirrels and other small mammals that live in the canyon. If time is short, your best bet is to hop on the **tram** for the 50-minute, 3.8-mile round-trip ride to the end of the paved road and back. You can get off and on as often as you like, reboarding any passing tram at designated points to get to the next stop, or to return to the visitor center. Stops 1 and 6 have picnic tables, stops 1 and 2 have water, and all stops except 2 and 7 have rest rooms.

Some visitors ride the tram to stop 9 and do the easy downhill hike back. Others use the tram to get to trailheads that lead into other parts of the canyon. From stop 9, you can access **more than 300 miles of hiking trails** in the Catalinas. The round-trip fare is moderate, with no charge for toddlers. Trams leave from the visitor center June–Dec., daily, every half-hour, 9:00 A.M.–4:30 P.M.; Jan.–May, Sat.–Sun. and holidays, every half-hour, 9:00 A.M.–4:00 P.M.; Mon.–Fri., hourly on the hour, 9:00 A.M.–4:00 P.M.

Cyclists can ride the canyon before 9 A.M. and after 5 P.M. daily, except Wed. and Sat. They must observe a 15-mile-per-hour speed limit.

Hikers headed for the **Bear Canyon Trail** and Seven Falls, a particularly lovely destination in the Pusch Ridge Wilderness, can catch a shuttle to the trailhead (small fee) daily, every hour on the hour, 9:00 A.M.–4:00 P.M. The moderate hike is about 4.5 miles round trip and takes about three hours on a wilderness hiking trail.

Evening moonlight rides take guests into the canyon at a slower pace than daytime rides, and without narration. The trip takes about 75 minutes and stops at the top. Apr.–June and Sept.–Dec., 9:00 P.M.; call for schedule. Prepaid nonrefundable reservations only. 520-749-2327.

The canyon is always open, and the visitor center is open daily, 8:00 A.M.–4:30 P.M. The visitor center and canyon entrance are about 13 miles from downtown Tucson. **From Tanque Verde Rd., go north on Sabino Canyon Rd. about 4.5 miles to the canyon entrance,** which is clearly marked. 520-749-8700 Santa Catalina Ranger District office, 520-749-2861 recorded information. Website: www.fs.fed.us/R3/Coronado/SERD.

Saguaro National Park

The east unit of this national park consists of 65,000-acre near the Rincon Mountains; it has **more than 75 miles of top recreational trails for hikers** and equestrians. There is a small fee to use the east side of the park. **Go east on Broadway to Freeman Rd., turn right to Old Spanish Trail, turn left, and look for signs.** 520-733-5153.

Saguaro National Park West, just next door to Tucson Mountain Park, is a saguaro forest that covers 25,000 acres, 13,700 of which are federally designated wilderness. More than 50 miles of trails are open to hikers and equestrians. One favorite, **Sweetwater Trail,** offers tremendous views. This 6.4-mile round trip starts at a Pima County trailhead at the end of El Camino del Serro at the far west side of the park. It's the formal access into the west unit of the park from the east side (Tucson metro) of the range. The trail provides great vistas of the Tucson basin and the saguaro forests. It connects to other trails in the system, including a short spur that takes you up to Wasson Peak, at an elevation of 4,687 feet the highest point in the Tucson mountains (ee Madera Canyon in Green Valley and Tubac chapter for additional hiking in this area). **Go west on Speedway, which becomes Gates Pass Rd. and ends at Kinney Rd.; turn right, into the park. 520-733-5158.**

Ventana Canyon Trail

This breathtakingly beautiful canyon has a trailhead just next door to Loews Ventana Canyon Resort (see Where to Stay). Craggy and rugged, decorated with a stand of mature saguaros, it is often used by hotel guests. Begin the clearly marked access trail, owned by Pima County, at the trailhead at the back of the resort's employee parking lot, where there are spaces for about two dozen trail-user cars. Dogs are not allowed on the access trail. The route meanders in and out of a dry wash bed following the path cut in 1902 by a mining exploration party. At about 0.5 mile, on your left, the cactus that looks like it has a gnarly growth at the top is actually a crested saguaro. Cardinals appear as bright flashes of red among cactus and scrub. Cactus wrens, quail, dove, Gila woodpeckers, thrashers, and hummingbirds make up a rich bird population here.

For a short hike, many visitors proceed the 2 miles to Maiden Pools, a point along the creek where water collects, then turn around. The ventana (which means "window" in Spanish) for which the trail is named is a picturesque hole in a rock about 6 miles up the trail. The grade is fairly level, with one long, moderately steep climb onto a plateau. Pick your way carefully and you'll be fine. If you start out on a short hike about 6:00 A.M., even on a hot July–Aug. day, rugged granite cliffs and scrub will shade much of the trail. You should be cool until about 7:30 A.M.

Recommended Reading

The *Southern Arizona Trails Resource Guide* by John Dell and Steve Anderson is an excellent primer of basic information for anyone wanting to access the best trails in southern Arizona. It has the nitty-gritty information that hikers, mountain bicyclists, equestrians, and OHV/ORV enthusiasts really need. It tells where the trails are, what they're open for, and what special precautions to take when using Arizona trails. A special section covers current trail projects, programs, and events. Available at outdoor stores and through the nonprofit **Pima Trails Association, P.O. Box 41358, Tucson, 85717.**

Horseback Riding

Along with the variety of guest ranches in the Tucson area (see Where to Stay), there are many local stables that offer trail rides covering interesting terrain. They are not as active in summer as in winter, and in fact some of the stables send their steeds north to cooler climes during hot months. Call first to find out where their rides go. Reservations usually are necessary.

Big Sky Rides at Desert Trails

Rides into the Tucson Mountains and other pretty areas with lots of saguaros furnish an experience much different from mountain riding. Choose this stable if you're a photographer or want great sight-seeing along with the ride. **6501 W. Ina Rd., Tucson, 85704; 520-744-3789. Website: www.montanaweb.com/horse/.**

Pusch Ridge Equestrian Center at the Sheraton El Conquistador Resort

Their main barn is at the address below, but

they have a beautiful equestrian center at the resort, as well as offering rides into the Catalinas. The center has riding rings and English and western riding instruction. This is especially good for riders who haven't been on a horse for awhile and just need a few pointers in the ring, so they can go out on the trail with confidence. Kids and family rides are a specialty. **10000 N. Oracle Rd., Tucson, 85739; 520-825-1664.**

Pusch Ridge Stables

They offer rides into the Catalinas with mounts for riders of all levels, from definite dudes to accomplished equestrians. You can do a one-hour ride or set up a two- or three-night pack trip into the mountains. Specialty, dawn, and sunset rides are available. **13700 N. Oracle Rd., Tucson, 85739; 520-825-1664.**

Walking Winds/El Conquistador Stables

Located 0.5 mile south of the entrance to Catalina State Park, this outfitter will take you into the Catalina Mountains on well-mannered horses. The ride through the state park follows ancient Indian trails, while another goes into the Coronado National Forest wilderness area. "No riding past housing developments," they say. One-, one-and-a-half-, and two-hour rides leave daily. Ask about cookout rides, often available during winter. **10811 N. Oracle Rd., Tucson, 85739; 520-742-4200.**

Skiing

Tucson is one of the few areas where you can ski in the morning, then play golf in your shirtsleeves in the afternoon. **Mount Lemmon Ski Valley** is the southernmost ski area in the country. At 9,100 feet in the Santa Catalina Mountains, a one-hour, 35-mile drive northeast of Tucson, the area gets about 200 inches of snow that keeps slopes covered about mid-Dec.–Apr. It has 15 trails, a chair lift, and two rope tows. You'll find a snack bar, cafe, and rental shop on the mountain. Private cabin rentals usually are available in nearby Summerhaven. During summer months, take the chair lift for a scenic "sky ride." Forest Service trails all over the mountain are especially popular in summer because the area is a reliable 30°F cooler than Tucson. **520-576-1321 information/snow report, 520-576-1400 recorded information.**

Seeing and Doing

Art Museums and Galleries

Center for Creative Photography

Across from the University of Arizona art museum, the Center for Creative Photography, a combination museum and research institution, houses a collection of more than 70,000 fine prints. Photographers come to use the extensive archives and library, and everyone enjoys the changing exhibits in the main gallery. Look here for postcards to send home; dozens of racks have interesting, off-beat, lovely, and funny cards that you probably won't find elsewhere. You can park for the center, as well as the art museum, in the Visitor Section of the Park Ave. Garage, on the northwest corner of Park and Speedway, then walk through a tunnel under Speedway to the center's front door. Free. Building open Mon.– Fri., 8:00 A.M.–5:00 P.M.; library open Mon.–Fri., 10:00 A.M.–5:00 P.M.; gallery open Mon.–Fri., 11:00 A.M.–5:00 P.M.; all three open Sun., noon– 5:00 P.M. Located **at Park and Speedway. 520-621-7968. Website: www.ccp.arizona.edu/ccp.html.**

DeGrazia Gallery in the Sun

If you think this famous Southwest artist did little more than paint appealing, big-eyed children, you're in for a revealing treat. DeGrazia was born in 1909 in Morenci, a Phelps Dodge mining town near the state's eastern border. His subject matter, the Southwest and Mexico, was not widely known. So when his subtle desert colors and the Indian way of life he depicted made their way into mainstream art circles, the artist drew national attention. Considered foremost among American Impressionists, Ettore "Ted" DeGrazia produced an enormous body of work in his lifetime. The gallery itself, actually more a museum built to the artist's design, houses his most famous collections that focus on subjects of deep interest to DeGrazia. Permanent themed exhibits include Padre Kino, Papago Legends, Yaqui Easter, Bull Fight, and Retrospective collections. The renowned Cabeza de Vaca collection illustrates the journey of the dauntless adventurer, the first non-Indian to travel in Arizona, New Mexico, and Texas. The Retrospective collection includes paintings from 1925 to 1972, clearly tracing DeGrazia's artistic evolution, embodying the free, unrestrained style that characterizes his work. DeGrazia's ceramics, bronzes, and enamels also are on display. Next door in the charming little Mission in the Sun, hand-built by DeGrazia and his Indian friends some years before the museum, interior walls are alive with whimsical angels, children, deities, and other appealing figures. Donations appreciated. Open daily, 10:00 A.M.– 4:00 P.M. Located in north Tucson. Take Swan Rd. north of Sunrise Rd. and turn right at the gallery sign. **6300 N. Swan Rd., Tucson, 85718; 800-545-2185 or 520-299-9191. Website: arizonaguide.com/degrazia.**

Tucson Museum of Art

Part of the city's Historic Block downtown, this respected establishment has been thoughtfully constructed with low-rise sensibilities to blend with its revered surroundings. Yet inside, it is classically contemporary with linear sight lines creating spatial dividers. It neighbors with five distinctive homes built between 1850 and 1907 and a sculpture garden. The Plaza of the Pioneers is a pleasant, shady place for a rest. The museum's permanent 4,000-work-plus collection focuses on art of the Americas, including pre-Columbian, Spanish colonial, and contemporary American. The Campbell Collection of Western Art, a group of paintings and sculptures that reflect the imaginative spirit of the Southwest in days past, is displayed in the renovated Edward Nye Fish House for 10 months of the year. Called the Goodman Pavilion of Western Art, the historic home also displays other

western collections. In the museum proper, rotating exhibits include work in all media. Stop by the museum shop to see interesting jewelry, handcrafts, and art. A scale model of the Historic Block (see Museums and Historic Sites) gives you a sense of your location in the downtown milieu. Docent-led tours held daily. Small charge for adults; children 12 and under admitted free; admission free on Tue. Open Sept.–May, Mon.–Sat., 10:00 A.M.–4:00 P.M., and Sun., noon–4:00 P.M.; June–Aug. and major holidays, Tues.–Sat., 10:00 A.M.–4:00 P.M. and Sun., noon– 4:00 P.M. **140 N. Main Ave., Tucson, 85701; 520-624-2333.**

University of Arizona Museum of Art

This museum houses a permanent collection of more than 4,500 works. A single large room holds the Retablo of Ciudad Rodrigo that dates to the late 15th century and consists of 26 separate panels, depicting scenes from the New Testament. Works by Rodin, Tintoretto, Picasso, Matisse, Kandinsky, Dürer, Rembrandt van Rijn, Goya, Daumier, Manet, Whistler, and others round out a truly impressive collection. Open Labor Day–mid-May, Mon.–Fri., 9:00 A.M.–5:00 P.M., and Sun., noon–4:00 P.M.; mid-May–Labor Day, Mon.–Fri., 10:00 A.M.–3:30 P.M., and Sun., noon–4:00 P.M. Located **at Speedway Blvd. and Park Ave. in northwest corner of campus. 520-621-7567.**

Historic Sites

El Presidio Historic District

This is quite literally Tucson's birthplace. Pit houses and pottery shards left by the Hohokam date the site to A.D. 800. In the 18th century, the Spanish built the walled fort called San Agustin del Tucson, a presidio used as a safe haven from Indian attack. Today the neighborhood is on the National Register of Historic Places. Its boundaries are roughly St. Mary's/ Sixth St. on the north, Granada on the west, W. Alameda on the south, and Court on the east; within this area are examples of architecture dating to the 1800s, when walls were made of adobe and mesquite wood was used to frame doors and windows. The arrival of the railroad in 1880 created an architectural revolution. Previously unavailable building materials now were priced within the budget of many residents, who brought their own notions of design, reflected today in the interesting mix of architecture within the area. Among the most notable structures is the **Stork's Nest,** so-called because it was a lying-in home from 1922 to 1946. At 182 N. Court Ave., it now houses the office for Southwest Parks and Monuments Association. For an interesting blend of Mexican and Anglo, see the **McCleary House** at 241 W. Franklin. Walls 22 inches thick attest to the home's Mexican heritage, with a wide porch decorating the front, heralding the Victorian era. For the Spanish Colonial Revival style, as interpreted by noted architect Henry Trost, explore the design of **The Owls Club** at 378 N. Main Ave. Built in 1902, it was occupied by the last of a group of wealthy bachelors, Leo Goldschmidt, who made it his home until 1944. Other interesting buildings in the community are in the California Mission Revival style, and there even are a few California and Craftsman bungalows to see. A self-guided walking tour brochure with detailed descriptions of 14 historic properties is available at Old Town Artisans (see below) and at the Tucson Museum of Art (see Art Museums and Galleries).

Historic Block

Actually part of the Tucson Museum of Art, which maintains and preserves these historic homes, this city block was once bounded on the south and north by the wall of the original presidio. Three feet thick and almost 12 feet high, it was built over a seven-year period by the Spanish military to enclose their enclave, and was completed in 1783. **La Casa Cordova,** thought to be the oldest remaining residence in Tucson, was built in 1848. Open to the public, it features two period rooms that show the lifestyle of the late 1800s. The **Romero House,** part of the Tucson Museum of Art School, is now a pottery studio. Next door is the 1855

adobe **Stevens house.** And the youngest of the historic properties, the **J. Knox Corbett house,** was used as a law office until 1970. Docents lead guided tours of the Historic Block at no charge, Oct. 1–May 1, Wed.–Thurs., 11:00 A.M.; meet in front of art museum on Main St. (see Art Museums and Galleries). Open Labor Day–Memorial Day, Mon.–Sat., 10:00 A.M.–4:00 P.M., and Sun., noon–4:00 P.M.; Memorial Day–Labor Day, Tues.–Sat., 10:00 A.M.–4:00 P.M., and Sun., noon–4:00 P.M. **520-624-2333.**

Mission San Xavier del Bac

It took 14 years of off-and-on labor, 1783–1797, to build this lovely church on the southwest side of Tucson. Even before that, in 1692 Father Eusebio Kino visited the site and named it San Xavier in honor of St. Francis Xavier, the illustrious Jesuit Apostle of the Indies. The mission was built for the Tohono O'odham Indian community, which it serves today. Called the White Dove of the Desert because of its striking appearance from afar, it is a beautifully balanced blend of Byzantine, Moorish, and Mexican Renaissance architecture. An interior renovation completed by Italian craftspeople in mid-1997 revealed detailed frescoes and colorful murals that were cleaned and restored, giving it new status as the Sistine Chapel of North America. Carved wood figures and the ornate altar are treasured examples of Mexican baroque art. On the left as you enter is a reclining statue of St. Francis Xavier.

As you face the mission outside, note that the tower on the right is missing. One legend says Apaches destroyed it in the late 19th century. But records have shown it simply was never completed, because of lack of funds. A new legend says that if ever the tower is completed, the mission will be destroyed. During winter months, especially on weekends, visitors crowd the mission. But if you can go on a weekday, you may have the place to yourself, if just for a few moments. It is not difficult to imagine the murmur of prayerful voices responding in Spanish as an 18th-century priest raises a golden chalice.

Works at the Tucson Museum of Art focus on arts of the Americas.

A new museum opens onto a cool courtyard, creating much more of a feeling of what the mission must have been like at one time. The museum features old vestments and religious artifacts as well as books and crafts. Across from the mission, small shops purvey jewelry, dream catchers, and pottery friendship bowls with linked figures. This is a good place to find reasonable prices on lovely Tohono O'odham baskets. Mass is said Mon.–Sat., 8:30 A.M.; Sun., 8:00 A.M., 9:30 A.M., 11:00 A.M., and 12:30 P.M. Tours are self-guided; admission free. Open daily, 8:00 A.M.–6:00 P.M. You can see the mission as you drive south from Tucson on I-19 about 8 miles; exit at Mission Rd. **Franciscan Friars, 1950 W. San Xavier Rd., Tucson, 85746; 520-294-2624.**

Old Town Artisans

This little gem of an area, within the El Presidio Historic District, hides in downtown Tucson among a forest of office buildings with few signs to point you in the right direction. It is a bit difficult to find, but ultimately worth it. Visit the blocklong restored 1850s adobe marketplace, filled with the works of hundreds of artists and craftspeople, as well as imports from Latin American cultures.

The building once protected the Mexican settlement of Tucson from Indian attacks. As with traditional Spanish structures, the walls are built right on the lot line, with all activity focused on a center courtyard. If you enter through the door on the corner of Telles and Meyer, you'll be in SoWest Territories, Inc. Look up to your right where the wall joins the ceiling, and you'll see traces of the original wallpaper. On the opposite wall, a saguaro skeleton has been used as a lintel. As you stroll through the Pot Shop, you can see the original saguaro-skeleton beams supporting the ceiling. Next door, charcoal-stained staves from old whiskey barrels create a ceiling, while the original red oak floor creaks pleasantly underfoot. High on the wall, original wallpaper is printed with swagged ropes, a remnant of more elegant days.

The building doesn't look like much from the outside, but its interior has witnessed a lively past. It once afforded office space to assayers who measured miners' gold, and shelves for Yuen Lee to sell groceries to the miners for their return trips. Early records show a "ladies' nurse" tenant, an essential caregiver in an era when ladies of the evening were an accepted part of a community's nightlife. In 1888 Julius Goldbaum turned the building into a residence and distillery. The family sold the building in the mid-1920s. Over the decades, incarnations continued until a developer purchased it in 1978 and began the restoration to create its present persona. La Cocina Restaurant (See Where to Eat) is always open for lunch. Shops are open Mon.–Sat., 9:30 A.M.–5:30 P.M.; Sun., noon–5:00 P.M. Exit I-10 at St. Mary's and proceed on St. Mary's past Main, until you pass the Tucson Electric Power building on the left. Turn right on Meyer Ave. and go three blocks to the Old Town Artisans Complex on the left. You can park in the lot straight ahead. **201 N. Court Ave., Tucson,**

DeGrazia Studio has works from the artist's life including his famous big-eyed children.

85701; 520-623-6024 or 800-782-8072. Website: www.oldtown artisans.com.

Old Tucson Studios

Old Tucson studios began in 1939 as a set for the motion-picture epic *Arizona*, starring William Holden and Jean Arthur. Since then, more than 300 productions have been filmed here, and it continues as a sought-after venue for motion picture and television productions. Destroyed by fire in 1995, this family-oriented theme-park-cum-studio was back in operation less than two years later. You can stroll the streets walked by John Wayne and other greats of western movie history, spending an entire day reliving how the West was once. At the Grand Palace, saloon girls draped in feathers and sequins show off their garters in a high-kicking revue, and a sultry chanteuse ends up on the lap of at least one gent in the audience. "Cecil Bee DeVille" demonstrates how movies are made, with clever bad guys outsmarting an inept deputy. Toddlers can visit the Petting Zoo where burros, sounding like squeaky doors, nudge pockets for handouts. Five different shows are presented at intervals throughout the day. Always a crowd-pleaser, the live gunfight features high falls and lots of shooting. The studio remains open during filming, so it's possible to get a behind-the-scenes look at how Hollywood really works if you're lucky enough to be there on a shooting day. For filming information call the main studio number and a menu selection will give you a schedule. Children three and under are admitted free. Open daily, 10:00 A.M.– 6:00 P.M. except Thanksgiving and Christmas Day. Located in Tucson Mountain Park 12 miles west of Tucson. Take Speedway or Ajo Way west and follow the signs. **201 S. Kinney Rd., Tucson, 85735; 520-883-0100. Website: www. oldtucson.com.**

Museums

Arizona Historical Society Museum

Just a two-block walk south on Park from the Center for Creative Photography (see Art Museums and Galleries), this museum holds a replicated underground mine tunnel and fashions since the Spaniards came to the state in 1539.

Authentically furnished period rooms and a transportation hall with wagons, buggies, and buckboards give a realistic sense of the past. Recent changing displays have included an interactive exhibit that invited visitors into the lobby of a territorial hotel, and a photographic exhibit of the restoration of Mission San Xavier south of Tucson. The Society's archives often are used by scholars researching Arizona history. Free. Open Mon.–Sat., 10:00 A.M.–4:00 P.M.; Sun., noon–4:00 P.M. Located at Second Street and Park Ave. **949 E. Second St., Tucson, 85719; 520-628-5774, fax 520-629-5695.**

History of Pharmacy Museum

This isn't just your basic one-room small museum. It's part of all four floors of the University of Arizona Pharmacy Building, and contains more than 60,000 bottles, books, drug containers, sales sample kits, and more. When you get off the elevator on the first floor, you're in a territorial pharmacy, surrounded by polished mahogany and etched stained glass. It dates to the 1870s. Grab a self-guided tour brochure from racks in the lobby of most floors and look at pre-Advil remedies that include a fertility drug called Syrup of Figs that cost $1 and guaranteed "A Baby in Every Bottle." A Materia Medica cabinet, with 300 numbered samples of herbs and remedies in hinged-lid metal boxes with glass windows, helped yesterday's pharmacy students learn their drugs. Free. Open Mon.–Fri., 8:00 A.M.–5:00 P.M. Located at Mabel and Warren. **1703 E. Mabel, Tucson, 85721; 520-626-1427.**

Mineral Museum

This quiet, well-lighted place is filled with specimens that range from meteor fragments to precious gems. Special emphasis on Arizona's rich mineral history includes its status as the copper state. As you walk down the stairs to the museum, notice the murals. Painted walls mimic the geologic layers that you would pass through if you were descending into the Grand Canyon. Open daily, 9:00 A.M.–5:00 P.M. Located on **lower level of Flandrau Science Center** (see Observatories and Planetariums). **520-621-4227.**

Pima Air and Space Museum

This extensive indoor-outdoor museum features more aircraft of more different types than you'd ever figure to see in one place. Almost 200 vintage and present-day aircraft are displayed in hangers and tie-downs. You enter under a huge Sikorsky Skycrane helicopter used for transporting heavy loads, and proceed into a cool gallery with planes parked and hanging everywhere. Straight ahead, the exhibit "Women Aloft" has photos of early stewardesses, called flight attendants now. Directly outside of this first building is the last prop-driven Air Force One, used by John F. Kennedy as well as Lyndon B. Johnson. It went into service in 1961 and, although jets were available then, this Douglas DC-6 was preferred, for its ability to land at smaller airports. Pre-transistor equipment includes an old Hallicrafter radio with vacuum tubes. Three separate cabins—for the president and his aides, the press (with a wireless teletype), and the Secret Service (with pull-down berths)—lead to a complete galley. A separate seat was designated for an extra pilot, always carried when the president was aboard. Although this aircraft usually had a crew of three, it always held a crew of five on presidential flights. Volunteers take visitors on scheduled 15-minute guided tours of Air Force One.

The plane that everyone comes to see is the Lockheed SR-71 Blackbird, the strategic reconnaissance aircraft, operational 1966–1990. It flies at Mach 3–plus, three times the speed of sound. As a onetime Blackbird pilot put it, "It flies real high, at 80,000 feet, where you see black above you, blue below you, and the only identifiable thing is the curve of the earth." The sleek black aircraft, poised like a pointy-nosed insect, once flew coast to coast in 68 minutes, 17 seconds.

The museum includes four hangers plus a World War II barracks with additional aviation exhibits. A separate section is devoted to the famous 390th Bomb Group and 390th Strategic Missile Wing. Here you'll find the famous B-17 Flying Fortress. Because many exhibits are outdoors, plan your visit as early in the day as possible during hot summer months. A snack bar and ramada with picnic tables are on-site. The gift shop has flight-related items, including "flight suits" for youngsters. Moderate fee. Open June 1–Aug. 31, 7:00 A.M.–3:00 P.M.; Sept. 1–May 31, except Christmas Day, 9:00 A.M.–5:00 P.M. From I-10 take the Valencia Rd. exit, and continue east 2 miles to the museum entrance. **6000 E. Valencia, Tucson, 85706; 520-574-9658.**

World Team Pro-Yo Center and International Museum of YoYo History

This hands-on museum, devoted solely to the yo-yo and its place in history, really has its ups and downs (somebody had to say it). Since the yo-yo was first marketed by Donald Duncan in 1929, there's hardly a kid alive who hasn't tried Walkin' the Dog or Around the World. But it's not just kids who come here. Adults seem the most fascinated by the collection of more than 2,000 yoyos, including a 14-karat gold yo-yo used as a party favor by the Vanderbilt family in the 1930s. There is a sterling silver version, as well as one marketed by Tiffany. Some yo-yos are smaller than a penny, one giant is 6 feet across. Among the most popular are the promotional yo-yos, marked with names of sports teams and events, companies and corporations, and even the White House, which appears in gold on a yo-yo, presented as a gift at an official dinner. Free yo-yo lessons given. Admission free. Open Mon.–Fri., 10:00 A.M.–6:00 P.M.; Sat., 10:00 A.M.–4:00 P.M.; Sun., noon–3:00 P.M. Located at Decorator Square. **2947 E. Grant Rd., Tucson, 85730; 520-322-0100. Website: www.proyo.com.**

Observatories and Planetariums

Flandrau Science Center

If you park behind the University of Arizona visitor center and stuff enough quarters in the meter, you'll have plenty of time to walk across the street to Flandrau Science Center. It's filled with hands-on exhibits designed to engage and educate people of all ages. If you arrive on a summer afternoon, don't be surprised to find the Planetarium Theater filled with five-year-olds enthralled as they encourage "Hector Vector Star Projector" to make simulated heavenly bodies appear in a pseudo sky. The theater also features laser light shows set to music. A public observatory has a 16-inch professional telescope available to visitors on clear nights throughout the year. Viewing is free. Call **520-621-4310** for current astronomy information. Pick up star charts, science kits, and other educational toys at the science and astronomy store. Parking is free evenings and weekends. The building is open daily, 9:00 A.M.–5:00 P.M.; weather permitting, it also is open Wed.–Sat., 7:00 P.M.–10:00 P.M., for telescope viewing. For program information and telescope hours, call **520-621-4515** during weekday business hours or **520-621-STAR** for recorded information. **Website: www.flandrau.org.**

Other Sights

Biosphere 2

In 1991 in a valley north of Tucson, eight researchers and more than 3,800 plant and animal species entered an experimental self-contained enclosure that was to be their home for two years. Intended as the first step toward colonizing Mars, with "biospherians" living off the land, it didn't work out that way for the eight who lived there 1991–93. Oxygen had to be pumped in from the outside, and crop production could not support the residents. Birds and animals died, except for cockroaches and ants. The 3-acre glass-and-steel complex, covering an area larger than three football fields, contains a rain forest, savanna, marsh, ocean, desert, farm, and microcity. Today no one lives in Biosphere 2 (our planet Earth is Biosphere 1), but the Biosphere received a new lease on life, and renewed prestige, when in 1996 Columbia University's Lamont-Doherty Earth Observatory took over management and helped restore the facility's credibility as a serious research center.

You can visit the complex and take a tour that reveals the conditions under which the biospherians lived. Detailed tours show living quarters, the communal dining room, library, and kitchen. An "ocean," complete with simulated waves, and neatly tended gardens demonstrate how it was hoped the biospherians would remain self-sustaining. From the parking lot, a shuttle takes you to the main entrance, where you're directed to the visitor center. Here, a half-hour video fills in the Biosphere's background. A half-hour tour then leaves for the greenhouses, which hooks up with a tour to the Biosphere, on the hour. The tour involves lots of walking, but everything is wheelchair-accessible, including the Biosphere itself, which has a lift that goes to the living quarters.

Guided tours offered daily, 9:00 A.M.–4:30 P.M. Discounts are offered to Arizona residents. You can make a day or a weekend trip to Biosphere 2, staying at the **Biosphere 2 Hotel,** a 27-room property poised on a small hill overlooking the Biosphere itself. Large rooms have view terraces and well-stocked wet bars; a pool, tennis court, and exercise facilities are on-site. Cost-effective packages for two include an overnight in the Biosphere 2 Hotel, admission to Biosphere 2, dinner, and breakfast. The Biosphere's **Canada del Oro restaurant** is open daily, 11:00 A.M.–7:00 P.M.; **520-896-6220.** Located 35 miles northeast of Tucson, just **off Hwy. 77 and Biosphere Rd. near the town of Oracle.** Columbia University/Biosphere 2, P.O. Box 689, Oracle, 85623; 800-828-2462 or 520-896-6222. Website: www.bio2.edu.

Parks

Saguaro National Park
This two-unit park (half is to the east of Tucson, the other is to the west) was recently upgraded from a national monument to a national park, much to the delight of desert lovers, who welcome the additional protection for its fascinating 91,327 acres. In **Saguaro Park East,** a paved 8-mile drive through a thick saguaro cactus forest introduces you to Sonoran Desert life in general. There are two picnic areas along Cactus Forest Dr. At the visitor center, a 15-minute slide presentation helps you identify what you'll see in the park. Displays include skeletons of desert creatures, a saguaro cross section, and books to help identify plants and animals. Located **on Freeman Rd. south of Old Spanish Trail. 520-733-5153.** Also see Biking and Hiking. **Saguaro Park West's** popular Bajada Loop Dr. winds through a saguaro forest along a dirt road. There are four picnic areas along park roads. The Red Hills Visitor Center is at the park entrance **off Mile Wide Rd. 520-733-5158.**

Tohono Chul Park
Tohono Chul, which means "desert corner" to the Tohono O'odham Indians, is a 49-acre nonprofit desert preserve that has been donated, over time, by several generous philanthropists. Although it is very close to a busy intersection, traffic sounds all but disappear once you begin your walk. As you stroll the trails of this lovely park, you'll see much the same flora and fauna that you'd see in the desert, except here they're labeled with informative signs. You're likely to see little top-knotted Gambel's quail scurrying under low-hanging branches, and cardinals creating a splash of red against the green branches of paloverde trees. Hummingbirds are permanent residents. If you're lucky, you'll spot a phainopepla, which looks like a black cardinal. It's the bird responsible for the spread of desert mistletoe, winding among host tree branches throughout the Southwest. The birds consider the mistletoe berries a delicacy, and often nest in mistletoe-infested trees to be close to a food source. You also see cactus wrens, easily spotted if you follow the sounds of their strident *chirrups.* The wren's messy nest, usually composed of randomly placed sticks and twigs, can become exceptionally creative.

The **Geology Wall** represents the structure of the Catalina Mountains, the range that you see when you're standing at the wall and looking straight ahead. Eight illustrated panels explain 2 billion years of the mountains' geologic history, and give a sense of Tucson's place in time. The **Children's Garden** is planted with thorn-free, kid-friendly plants. Older children can follow a map to locate the vine-covered topiary coyote and the enchanted throne room. Youngsters are invited to dabble in flowing water and pools. Crops grown locally by indigenous peoples, as well as those introduced by the Spanish, flourish in the **Ethnobotanical Garden.** Area residents often visit the **Demonstration Garden** to get ideas on how to xeriscape their yards using water-conserving fountains and arid-adapted plants. The **Exhibit House,** a 1937 restored adobe, has changing art and cultural exhibits, and the park's two gift shops have an unusually interesting variety of items from local artists and craftspeople. Don't miss the pool of bright blue desert pupfish. This endangered species was named 50 years ago by ichthyologist Carl L. Hubbs, who thought their animated antics looked playful like those of puppies.

There are docent-led tours, or you can pick up a self-guiding booklet for 25 cents at coin boxes and at the visitor center. Docent walks are offered regularly, but less frequently during the hotter months June–Sept. Park open daily, 7:00 A.M.–sunset; Gift Gallery open daily, 9:30 A.M.–5:00 P.M. **7366 N. Paseo del Norte, Tucson, 85704; 520-742-6455, 520-575-8468** recorded information, **520-297-4999** exhibit house gift shop. Website: **www.tohono chulpark.org.**

Shopping

In Tucson, you can uniquely satisfy the urge to acquire with high-quality Native American pieces that include jewelry, baskets, kachinas, fetishes, and more. In Tucson's city center, more than 35 art galleries, antiques shops, and crafts stores line **Congress St.** and the **Downtown Arts District** (get a map from the Convention and Visitors Bureau). For more artsy finds, search out one-of-a-kind items on **Fourth Ave.** between downtown and the University of Ari-

A welcome wall greets children in their special area of the garden at Tohono Chul desert preserve in Tucson.

zona. The **Old Town Artisans** complex, near downtown's Museum of Art, brings together a fine group of purveyors of Southwestern wares (see Historic Sites). For things truly Tucson, you can bring home locally bottled salsas and *ristras* (dried chile pepper strings).

Tours

Davis–Monthan Air Force Base

In 1927 Col. Charles Lindbergh dedicated Tucson's second landing field, readied for military operations, to two Tucson residents who had died in separate aerial accidents while serving the U.S. Army. Second Lt. Samuel H. Davis and Oscar Monthan became the new field's namesakes. Early on, the base was used to service transient aircraft bound for California. It wasn't until 1941 that the Army stationed units at the base, just in time to go on 24-hour alert after the Japanese attack on Pearl Harbor. Subsequently Davis–Monthan was used to train and prepare bomber crews for battle, and after the war became a separation center to process soldiers returning to civilian life. The Air Force inherited the installation in 1948, and personnel became involved in strategic missions with the Titan II missiles and U-2 reconnaissance forces. In 1964 an additional wing began training crews for the F-4 Phantom, and training continues as its main function today. In 1989–1990, D–M personnel helped secure and defend Panama's main airport, and later supported Operations Desert Shield and Desert Storm. You can take a guided bus tour among the rows of stored planes, all of which can be made ready to fly again. The Aerospace Maintenance and Regeneration Center (AMARC) tour, also called the "Boneyard Tour," is given several times a day. Moderate fee. Tours leave from the Pima Air & Space Museum, **6000 E. Valencia Road, 5 miles east of the airport and 2 miles west of Kolb Road; 520-618-4806. Website: www.pimaair.org.**

Desert Archaeology Tours

Tucson's dry, mild climate has had the fortuitous effect of preserving its ancient past, giving present-day adventurers the opportunity to tour back in time. An archaeologist from the **Center for Desert Archaeology** will take you on a half-day tour to petroglyph sites to view ancient works of art pecked out long ago in rock outcroppings and canyon walls by prehistoric artists. Another tour option is to examine the remnants of four great cultures beginning with the Archaic hunters, all within the boundaries of Catalina State Park. The company picks up from and drops off at all hotels. **3975 N. Tucson Blvd., Tucson, 85716; 520-885-6283. Website: www.cdarc.org.**

Wagering

Casino of the Sun

This unintimidating casino on the Yaqui Reservation has more than 500 slot machines plus keno, bingo, and pull tabs. It has an inexpensive buffet and snack bar. Open 24 hours daily. Located five minutes west of I-19 off Valencia Rd. **7406 S. Camino de Oeste, Tucson, 85746; 800-344-9435 or 520-883-1700.**

Desert Diamond Casino

A new card room with live poker recently opened at the casino located on the San Xavier Tohono O'odham Reservation. Otherwise you'll find the expected keno, slots, and high-stakes bingo beginning at 11:00 A.M., with the last late-night session starting at 9:45 P.M. Open 24 hours daily. Near Tucson International Airport 1 mile south of Valencia Rd. **7350 S. Nogales Hwy., Tucson, 86706; 520-294-7777.**

Where to Stay

Tucson is blessed with a goodly number of luxury resorts, historic hotels, middle-of-the-road chains, and budget hostelries. We've listed a range of accommodations, with various prices and types of experiences. During summer months, even the priciest digs lower tariffs to a very reasonable level, so don't just assume that a place is out of reach price-wise. Call the hotel directly (they'll usually give a better deal than the reservation center's toll-free number) and ask for their lowest-price room, then ask if there are any discounts on top of that, such as AAA, corporate, or senior discounts.

Mi Casa Su Casa/ Old Pueblo Home Stays

A service that's been offered in Europe for years is now available in Arizona. You typically are lodged in a private home where accommodations can range from modest to luxurious. The home-stay service matches guests with homes, based on information given by the guests. For example, in one home Greek and English are spoken. In another, pets are welcome. If you're coming from a two-story typically Midwest farm home, or a Manhattan high-rise, staying in a low-profile ranch home that sprawls among cactuses and coyotes could be a real cross-cultural experience. The service has many listings in the Tucson area, as well as more than 200 in other parts of the state. Prices vary widely, depending on type of accommodation and season. The service also lists bed-and-breakfast inns in Phoenix and statewide. 800-333-9776, 800- 456-0682, or 480-990-0682. Website: www. azres.com.

Guest Ranches

These modern-day versions of the Old West provide rough and ready experiences tempered by well-behaved horses and 20th-century amenities. A stay gives you access to the once-rowdy world of wranglers and rustlers while maintaining firm footing in the present. Horses called Diablo and Lightning may be misnomers. Most establishments are family-friendly (some prefer children older than 11) and laid-back, generating an unusually high percentage of repeat guests, some of whom return for generations. Many ranches have no TV, no phones in rooms, and no newspapers. It's part of the experience of getting away from it all and establishing a closeness with nature and the outdoors. Some ranches close for the summer. (See also Where to Stay in Yarnell and Wickenburg chapter, and Grapevine Canyon Ranch in Benson and Willcox chapter.) For centralized information about Arizona guest ranch vacations, call **800-444-DUDE**. Website: www.gorp.com/oldwest.

Bellota Ranch—$$$$

About as realistic a taste of the Old West as you'll get, this working ranch runs 700 head of cattle in the Rincon Mountains is just behind the Tanque Verde Ranch, owned by the same people. Eight rooms with private baths can accommodate 24 guests (children must be at least 12). You should have intermediate riding skills and be ready for roundups and cattle drives. You'll catch and saddle your own horse every morning, learn to rope and brand, and spend hours on the open range. **14301 E. Speedway, Tucson, 85748; 800-234-DUDE or 520-296-6275.** Website: www.tanqueverderanch.com.

La Tierra Linda Guest Ranch—$$$$

At the base of scenic Sombrero Peak, the family-run 30-acre ranch offers riding, haywagon rides, tennis, swimming, horseshoes, and volleyball. Hiking and bird-watching are good options for non-riders. All skill levels are welcome on trail rides of one, two, and three hours. Casitas and one-, two-, or three-room suites have cable TV, phones, refrigerators, and bathtubs. There's even room service from the Ranch House Grill, one of Tucson's best new eateries. It's open to the public, featuring indigenous ingredients to create uniquely Arizona dishes served in a casually elegant desert setting. **7501 N. Wade Rd., Tucson, 85743; 888-872-6241 or 520-744-7700.** Website: www.latierra linda.com.

Tanque Verde Ranch—$$$$

This picturesque, century-old slice of real Arizona history considers itself one of the last luxurious outposts of the Old West, and apparently guests do too, because they return by the dozen year after year. Sixty-five lodge rooms and desert-view patio casitas, some with fireplaces, include three meals a day in the rate. The ranch has more than 120 well-trained ranch horses, some for walking rides with beginners and others for loping with more experienced riders. Since 1957, Tanque Verde has been owned by the Cote family, a name Minnesotans will recognize because the family also owns Grand View Lodge near Brainerd. Rides often wind through the spectacular Saguaro National Park East that borders the ranch, where saguaro cactus form a stately forest. In addition to trail rides, guests make use of indoor and outdoor pools, tennis courts, and nature and exercise hiking trails. A series of evening programs include line dance instruction, talks on astronomy and star gazing, and wildlife lectures. Located 35 minutes due east of downtown Tucson, in the foothills of the Rincon Mountains. **14301 E. Speedway, Tucson, 85748; 800-234-DUDE or 520-296-6275.** Website: www.tanqueverderanch.com.

White Stallion Ranch Guest Ranch—$$$$

Within 10 minutes of Tucson shopping and city amenities, this warm and friendly ranch sits on the other side of the hills, so there is a feeling of remoteness. The small (29 guest rooms) ranch has been run by the True family since 1965. It encompasses 5 square miles of desert, two of which are adjacent to Saguaro National Park on the west side. Wood-paneled rooms have comfortable, rustic pine furnishings. The Happy Hour Saloon stocks healthful fruit juices as well as stiffer stuff. Meals are set at long wood tables, so getting to know fellow guests happens naturally. Those who would rather pet a horse than ride one can use the pool, play tennis, soak in the hot tub, hike in the desert, or get involved in a volleyball game. **9251 W. Twin Peaks Rd., Tucson, 85743; 888-977-2624 or 520-297-0252.** Website: www.wsranch.com.

Hotels and Inns

Arizona Inn—$$$-$$$$

This small, lovely 86-room Tucson resort has matured as gracefully as any well-bred 65-year-old. Within its brick and adobe walls, 14 acres of low haciendas and lush gardens are quiet, serene, and welcoming. The civilized custom of afternoon tea is carried out unhurriedly in the teak-floored library. Guests relax into high-backed chairs to be warmed, if the season is right, by a grand fireplace. The inn's founder, Isabella Greenway, set out to create a homelike retreat in the 1930s, filling it with furnishings made by disabled doughboys from World War I, who came to Tucson for medical care at the Veterans Hospital. She accented the rustic decor with 19th-century Audubon prints and African art acquired on safari. It remains civil and understated, as if it belongs to a quieter era, because Mrs. Greenway's granddaughter looks after the inn with the same practiced eye as her predecessor. Come here for a quiet sojourn, to enjoy the flower-scented grounds and a leisurely dinner in the inn's award-winning restaurant (see Where to Eat). **2200 E. Elm St., Tucson, 85719; 800-933-1093 or 520-325-1541.** Website: www.arizonainn.com.

Hacienda del Sol—$$$-$$$$

Strolling the grounds of this adobe onetime girls' school, it's not hard to imagine primly frocked young ladies gathered in the shady courtyard to do their sums. Today's guests stay in updated courtyard rooms with a Southwest decor, in newly built suites, and in spacious casitas. In 1941 when it shifted gears to accommodate guests, it became a favorite hideaway for Spencer Tracy and Katherine Hepburn and served as home base for Joseph Cotten while he filmed the 1946 film *Duel in the Sun.* The resort maintains a strong sense of the past without sacrificing comfort. The overstuffed leather sofa in the pine-beamed living room clearly belongs to the 1940s, and the library includes early school yearbooks. Stables, a pool, tennis courts, and hiking trails are scattered over 34 peaceful acres. Low-season rates July 1–Aug. 31 are a real bargain. The Grill at Hacienda del Sol (see Where to Eat) is a true dining experience. **5601 N. Hacienda del Sol Rd., Tucson, 85718; 800-728-6514 or 520-299-1501.** Website: www.haciendadelsol.com.

The Lodge on the Desert—$$$

Built in the 1930s, this charming hotel with just 40 rooms in the middle of a quiet residential district has been owned by the same family since it opened. The grounds, naturally desert landscaped, help create the feeling that you're miles away from civilization. Only the occasional intrusion of aircraft noise from nearby Davis-Monthan Air Force Base verifies that the real world is just around the corner. Rooms are large and inviting, some with fireplaces that are welcome during winter. **306 N. Alvernon Way, Tucson, 85711; 800-456-5634 or 520-325-3366.** Website: www.lodgeonthedesert.com.

Hotel Congress—$$

This downtown Tucson landmark was built in 1919 to serve passengers of the Southern Pacific Railroad as they journeyed to and from what was then a little desert cow town. The classic brick and marble structure, once the height of elegance, had a guest register with the signature of the infamous John Dillinger. In the 1930s a fire devastated the third floor, which was never rebuilt. Although the hotel was refurbished, the Depression years precluded the Congress being as grand as it once was. Today, thanks to a 1985 purchase that led to its restoration, the hotel has piloted the development of the Tucson Downtown Arts District, and is once again a charming place to stay. Its Old West personality is preserved in the deco-style Native American lobby designs painted by artist Larry Boyce, and in guest rooms furnished with the original mirrored vanities and metal bedsteads. Residents say it has the liveliest nightclub in town, and in fact the rooms directly over the **Club Congress** have a discount rate because "the nightclub and its patrons may generate a great deal of noise during peak hours," says hotel literature. Earplugs are available free at the front desk (no joke). **Youth Hostel** rooms also are available. Don't miss the great breakfast pancakes in the little coffee shop. 311 E. Congress, Tucson, 85701; 520-622-8848. Website: www.hotcong.com/congo/.

Resorts

Loews Ventana Canyon Resort—$$$$

In the Big Splurge category, but definitely worth every penny. You might not need the three phones in your room, but you'll love the spalike tub big enough for two. The resort, settled comfortably on 93 acres of plateau, provides impressive views of the city below. Behind the resort (take a look at the huge fish in the koi pond) a short nature path leads to an 80-foot waterfall that is fed by springs in the Catalinas, then flows into a small lake near the Flying V Restaurant (see Where to Eat). You don't have to leave your workout regimen at home, because at the **Spa and Tennis Center** there are eight lighted tennis courts, a weight and exercise room, a mirrored aerobics studio, water aerobics and outdoor lap pool, two championship golf courses (see Golf), and a par course. Leave time for a relaxing massage. Although winter months are pricey, room rates during summer are less than half of winter rates. 7000 N. Resort Dr., Tucson, 85750; 800-234-5117 or 520-299-2020. Website: www.loewsventanacanyon.com.

As the moon rises over Sheraton El Conquistador resort, lights twinkle the evening alive.

Sheraton El Conquistador—$$$$

You can relax for a week or more here and never miss the outside world. With 31 lighted tennis courts and two pro shops, it is the largest tennis resort in the West, as well as the largest golf facility, with one nine-hole and two 18-hole courses (see Golf). Its own equestrian center offers organized rides, including breakfast rides and sunset champagne rides. 1000 N. Oracle Rd., Tucson, 85737; 800-325-7832 or 520-544-5000. Website: www.sheraton.com.

Westward Look Resort—$$$–$$$$

An all-time favorite because of its absolutely civilized approach to guests, this is the only Arizona resort to receive AAA's Four Diamond Award for 15 consecutive years, but it is far from the most expensive. Built as a private residence in 1912, its guest rooms are discreetly scattered throughout shady grounds, home to rabbits and a variety of colorful birds, including brilliant cardinals and soft gray doves. Exceptionally large rooms have a seating area with couch, refrigerator, coffeemaker with coffee, and a balcony or patio. It is a great tennis retreat, with eight courts and a USPTA instructor available. Three pools, basketball and sand volleyball courts, and a nature/jogging trail encourage you to stay and enjoy the property. Be sure to book a massage or facial at the **Wellness Center.** You can tuck in here for days, just enjoying the property and its amenities. Golfers who stay here have special privileges at the Raven Golf Club at Sabino Springs (see

The Miraval, Life in Balance Resort near Tucson combines desert landscaping with lush flower gardens.

Golf). For a special occasion, try dinner in the **Gold Room** with its fantastic sunset views; highly recommended. If you've never tried ostrich, it's on the menu here. **245 E. Ina Rd., Tucson, 85704; 800-722-2500 or 520-297-1151. Website: www.westwardlook.com.**

Spas

In addition to the spas that are part of most large resort hotels, Tucson has two award-winning destination spas that attract a worldwide clientele.

Canyon Ranch—$$$$

One of the most respected and most expensive spas, here accommodations are in lovely casitas with patios that open onto desert-landscaped grounds. Tennis courts, gyms for aerobics and other classes, a spa complex, health and healing center, and life enhancement center cover just about any issue that needs addressing. Meals are served in an elegant restaurant-style dining room. An ever-changing menu offers "real food,"

healthfully prepared, but carefully marked according to calories, fat, and cholesterol content. Although there are hiking trails adjacent to the ranch, vans take guests to trailheads for scheduled hikes to Saguaro National Park, Sabino Canyon, the Catalina Mountains, and other local venues. **8600 E. Rockcliff Rd., Tucson 85750; 800-742-9000 or 520-749-9000. Website: www.canyonranch.com.**

The Miraval, Life in Balance Resort—$$$$

This classy, contemplative spa says it's the place to come to get your "life in balance." The picturesque location, in the shadow of 10,000-foot-high Mount Lemmon, is in itself enough to render you boneless. Public rooms are exquisitely decorated with Navajo rugs, Saltillo tile floors, and subtle Southwest colors. Constructed streams trickle among rooms grouped in "neighborhoods." The average stay here is three days (although you can do just an overnight or even a Day Spa program), tailored to your goals—weight loss, de-stressing, hiking and riding, or just getting away from it all. One of the most unusual programs is Miraval's Equine Experience. Its proponents say you have to try it to understand it, sort of like hanging wallpaper or having a baby. Through working with horses (no riding is involved), you learn how you create your own personal stress, how body language contributes to and conveys that stress, and how you can unlearn the behavior by communicating at a most basic level. Unlike many spas, it has a full bar. Located **in Catalina, north of Tucson. 800-232-3969 or 520-825-4000. Website: www.miraval resort.com.**

Where to Eat

Tucson's dining scene includes the sophistication you'd expect to find in a well-bred city. On the other hand, roisterous cowboy steak houses, trendy cafes and bistros, basic coffee shops, and fast food are readily available. The city has too many great Mexican restaurants to make an accurate count; many of the best lie in the city's southern part, where its deep Hispanic-Latino roots began. Because Tucson was once part of Sonora across the border in Mexico, mainstays of that area—such as burritos, tamales, and enchiladas—are a part of many menus. The greatest concentration of Mexican restaurants in the area is in the district along S. Fourth Ave. in south Tucson. **El Dorado Bar & Restaurant, La Indita** (Mexican-Indian), and others cluster there, although there are several out on Oracle Rd. as well. Don't make the mistake of thinking that Mexican food is just hot stuff folded in tortillas. Some of its best is seafood, which includes shrimp, sea bass (sometimes on a menu as *cabrillo*), and other sea creatures that became part of the Mexican diet because they were readily available in surrounding waters. The Native American culture is apparent in menu items like blue corn tortillas and fry bread. Just look around, read posted menus, and you'll find you could easily eat your way through Tucson and never duplicate your order.

Dining Room at the Arizona Inn—$$$$

This is one of our favorite romantic dinner places. In one of Tucson's loveliest historic hostelries (see Where to Stay), the dining room is noted for continental gourmet food served in a quiet, gracious atmosphere. At various times of year, meals are served on patios, in the courtyard, or on the terrace. This is an inspired place to linger over lunch. Be sure to stroll through the comfortable library and around the inn's flower-banked grounds for a look at elegance that dates back to the 1930s. Open daily, 7:00 A.M.–10:00 A.M., 11:30 A.M.–2:00 P.M., and 6:00 P.M.–10:00 P.M.; Sun. brunch. **2200 E. Elm St.; 800-933-1093 or 520-325-1541. Website: www.arizonainn.com.**

Janos—$$$$

After 15 years downtown, this Four Star, Four Diamond restaurant has moved to the foothills on the grounds of the Westin La Paloma. The decor is a stunning blend of French and Southwestern custom and antique furnishings. Panoramic views, elegant service, and a carefully chosen wine list, with several Arizona wines, are keeping newcomers and longtime fans happy. The name of owner-chef Janos Wilder has become synonymous with French-inspired Southwest cuisine. Come here for a big splurge and know it will be more than a meal—it will be an event. Or try the less-expensive, more casual bar menu next door. Open Mon.–Sat., 5:30 P.M.–varying closing hours. **3770 E. Sunrise Dr.; 520-615-6100. Website: janos.com.**

Ventana Room—$$$$

More marriage proposals have been made at table No. 21 of this fine restaurant than they can count, say the staff. One look and we knew why. The candlelit table is hidden behind a two-way fireplace, so that couples look over the flames to a panoramic city view beyond. A harp plays softly in the background. Service here is impeccable. The menu includes lightly seared fois gras as a starter, and fresh fish, usually grilled then embellished with an authoritative sauce. Reservations suggested. Open Sun.–Thu., 6:00 P.M.–9:00 P.M.; Fri.–Sat., 6:00 P.M.–10:00 P.M. Located in Loews Ventana Canyon Resort (see Where to Stay). **7000 N. Resort Dr.; 520-299-2020. Website: www.loewsventanacanyon.com.**

Daniel's—$$$–$$$$

This fashionably understated eatery is a study in deco. Fresh fish and pasta done in the Northern Italian style are always outstanding. Scotch connoisseurs have something to chat over with the bartender, because the place offers a selection of close to 100 single-malt scotches. Misters and heaters make it possible to eat on the outdoor patio year-round. Open daily, 5:00 P.M.–8:00 or 9:00 P.M. **4340 N. Campbell Ave.; 520-742-3200. Website: www.ibs-net.com/daniels/.**

Flying V Bar & Grill—$$$–$$$$

It's worth a stop here just to read the menu, but be sure not to miss the gorgeous view of the 18th green. Strong Latin and Southwest influences have helped shape the menu. Tues. is rib night, and Wed. is lobster/seafood night. A spa menu, with nutrition information, is available on request. Open Tues.–Sun., 11:00 A.M.– 10:00 P.M. At Loews Ventana Canyon Resort (see Where to Stay). **7000 N. Resort Dr.; 520-299-2020.** Website: **www.loewsventanacanyon.com.**

The Grill at Hacienda del Sol—$$$–$$$$

Furnishings custom-made in Mexico, wrought-iron chandeliers, and a personality that feels old but is up to the minute in terms of cuisine characterize this fine restaurant. The roasted pork loin represents the scope of the chef's expertise. An in-depth wine list includes a few local Arizona vintages. **5601 N. Hacienda del Sol Rd.; 520-529-3500.**

Cafe Poca Cosa—$$$

This colorful, lively place has furnishings from Guatemala and works by local artists on the walls. Hip servers dressed in black present the daily menu on a chalkboard. Don't look for your typical cheese-smothered border food; the outstanding menu features a selection of cuisines that represent various regions in Mexico. Mole sauces and traditional dishes with new twists are specialties. Open Mon.–Sat., 11:00 A.M.–10:00 P.M. **88 E. Broadway; 520-622-6400.**

La Cocina—$$$

We love this casual place after a day of sightseeing. In the courtyard at Old Town Artisans (see Historic Sites), it is set in a shady patio, further cooled on warm days by micromisters. Air-conditioned indoor rooms are decorated with art objects from next-door shops. Display shelves show off cloudy, iridescent "dug" bottles that were unearthed when the courtyard was excavated. Morphine, opium, ladies leg ale bottles, and other vessels attest to an era when fun was free-wheeling and unregulated. At La Cocina's Court St. entrance, the base of old gasoline pumps and a front facade at a 45-degree angle to the street tell of the days when the restaurant was a corner gas station. Don't miss the *camarones* de Tucson, shrimp sauteed

in roasted red pepper butter with penne pasta. Open Tues.–Thurs., 11:00 A.M.–3:00 P.M. and 5:00 P.M.–9:00 P.M.; Fri.–Sat., 11:00 A.M.–3:00 P.M. and 5:00 P.M.–10:00 P.M.; Sun., 11:00 A.M.–3:00 P.M. and 4:30 P.M.–8:00 P.M. **201 N. Court; 520-622-0351.**

Pinnacle Peak Steakhouse—$$$

This cowboy steak house is the centerpiece of Trail Dust Town, a 40-year-old landmark originally a movie set. Wood boardwalks and red brick-paved streets lead to a railroad and mine tunnel tour, horse soldier museum, opera house, plus shops and galleries. Mesquite-broiled steaks, chicken, fish, and ribs. Open daily, 5:00 P.M.–10:00 P.M. **6541 E. Tanque Verde Rd., 520-886-5012.**

Li'l Abner's—$$$

This is where you come for the urban cowboy experience, to have your tie snipped off if you're wearing one and to tear into a steak that weighs upward of a pound. In this old Butterfield Stage stop, the atmosphere is rustic and down to earth. Steaks are broiled over open mesquite fires, and ribs, chicken, and seafood are also on the menu. If you've never tried the two-step, come on a Fri. or Sat. night when a western band encourages diners to give it a try. Open daily, 5:00 P.M.–10:00 P.M. **8500 N. Silverbell Rd.; 520-744-2800.**

Two Micks Grill & Cantina—$$$

This place has been voted Tucson's best for Happy Hour food. Try it yourself Mon.-Fri., 4:00 P.M.–7:00 P.M. Same lunch and dinner menu as La Cocina. Open Tues.–Thurs., 11:00 A.M.–3:00 P.M. and 5:00 P.M.–9:00 P.M.; Fri.–Sat., 11:00 A.M.–3:00 P.M. and 5:00 P.M.–10:00 P.M.; Sun., 11:00 A.M.–3:00 P.M. and 5:00 P.M.–8:30 P.M. Located **at Old Town Artisans** across the courtyard from La Cocina. **520-622-0351.**

El Charro Mexican Cafe, Gift Shop & Bar—$$–$$$

Run by the Flores family since 1922, this downtown favorite is said to be the oldest Mexican restaurant in the country. Its food will tell you why it has endured. They bill their fare as "Tucson-style Mexican food," which means it has grown up pleasing the palates of the locals, who swear by it. The restaurant is on the walking tour of the historic El Presidio neighborhood (see Historic Sites), and was built by Jules le Vlein, a French master stoneworker. Go early or linger afterward to spend time in the gift shop, which is open late. Open Sun.–Thurs., 11:00 A.M.–9:00 P.M.; Fri.–Sat., 11:00 A.M.–10:00 P.M. Located in the Santa Rita Clarion. (Other locations at El Mercado on Broadway and at Tucson International Airport.) 311 N. Court Ave.; 520-622-1922.

Guillermo's Double L Restaurant—$$–$$$

This place gets consistently high ratings when inspected by the health department, always a good sign for any restaurant. It's been in the same family since 1948, remaining popular because of an extensive menu of Sonoran-style Mexican food. Be sure to order at least one margarita; they're hand-mixed, not mangled into slush by a blender. Open Mon.–Sat., 11:00 A.M.–10:00 P.M. Located at 29th St. 1830 S. Fourth Ave.; 520-792-1585, fax 520-622-1660.

Tea Room at Tohono Chul Park—$$

Combine breakfast, brunch, or lunch at this pleasant courtyard tearoom with a visit to Tohono Chul (see Parks). That's what we did one June morning, and we loved their muffins and scones hot from the oven. Tea is served 2:30 P.M.–5:00 P.M., featuring finger sandwiches, scones, pastries, and jam. Beer and wine are available. Open daily, 8:00 A.M.–5:00 P.M. 7366 N. Paseo de Norte; 520-797-1222. Website: www.tohonochulpark.org.

Eegee's—$

Something of a Tucson tradition, Eegee's are slushy, slurpy desserts sold at take-out stands throughout the city. You eat them with a spoon from Styrofoam cups until they start to melt, then finish with a straw. Standard flavors are lemon, strawberry, and piña colada plus a flavor of the

month. They also have Teegees, which are basically iced tea with lemon, and deli-style sandwiches and subs on home-baked breads. Fifteen Tucson locations. There are Eegee's at the Tucson Mall on Oracle Road, and 7102 E. Broadway; 520-885-8502. Website: www.eegees@azstarnet.com.

Services

Local Visitor Information

Metropolitan Tucson Convention & Visitors Bureau

Their numbers operate 24 hours and connect you to a visitor information specialist, or give you an automated choice to order brochures. Their entertaining website provides instant information on attractions, accommodations, and activities, and links to an e-mail address. Located at Broadway and Church Sts. in a brightly colored center called La Placita. Open Mon.–Fri., 8:00 A.M.–5:00 P.M.; Sat.–Sun., 9:00 A.M.–4:00 P.M. 130 S. Scott Ave., Tucson, 85701; 800-638-8350 or 520-624-1817. Website: www.visittucson.org.

Transportation

Old Pueblo Trolley, Inc.

Historic electric streetcars follow a track between the University of Arizona and the Fourth Ave. business district. Call for fares, days, and hours of operation. 360 E. Eighth St., Tucson, 85705; 520-792-1802.

Sun Tran

Tucson has public service citywide for just 75 cents a ride. It may take a bit of planning to get from place to place if you rely on this service alone, but it can be done. Call for help in trip planning. Tucson Transit Management, P.O. Box 26765, Tucson, 85726; 520-792-9222, fax 520-791-2285.

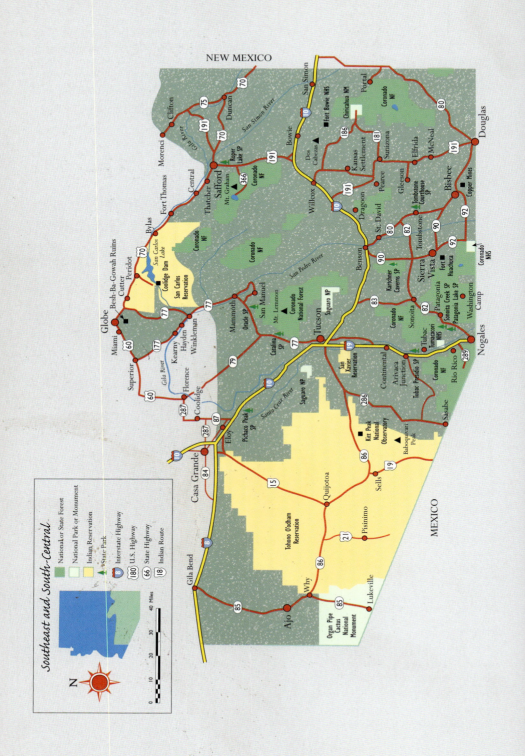

NEW MEXICO

MEXICO

Southeast and South-Central

National or State Forest
National Park or Monument
Indian Reservation
State Park
Interstate Highway
U.S. Highway
State Highway
Indian Route

Miles
0 10 20 30 40

N

Southeast and South-Central— Old West Country

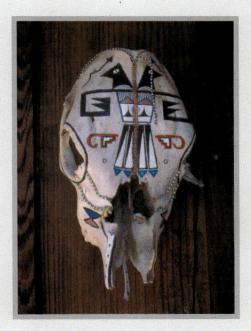

A decorated cow skull is part of the ranch decor of the Wickenburg Inn.

Southeast and South-Central— Old West Country

This area embraces everything from lofty, snow-crowned mountain peaks to saguaros to Douglas fir, and is enriched by a history colored with Indian lore that tells of tribes coming to an uneasy peace with encroaching white settlers. The Butterfield Stage rattled along dusty, rocky routes, and Cochise holed up here in his legendary stronghold. This region is dotted with separate parcels of the Coronado National Forest, appearing as scattered patches of green on area maps. It also has an enormous diversity of wildlife, including the greatest concentration of hummingbirds in the country, in Ramsey Canyon.

Benson and Willcox

Benson, a quiet little town of about 4,500 on the San Pedro River, has received an economic boost with the recent opening of Kartchner Caverns State Park, as well as a number of new motels and attractions. Just down the road is **Willcox,** fast gaining favor with retirees for its inexpensive land and housing, mild high desert climate, and rural lifestyle. Willcox, population 3,600 at an elevation of 4,167 feet, is a one-stoplight town, best known as an agricultural and ranching center. Where other areas have ecotourism, Willcox says it has agritourism because so many people come to do their own picking (see Seasonal Favorites). Birders find good viewing at Cochise Lake.

History

As early as the 1500s, the Chiricahua Apaches supplemented their hunter-gatherer culture in the area that later became Willcox, with frequent raids against neighboring peoples. The county is named for their leader, Cochise, who besieged settlers and the U.S. military, but was widely respected for the commanding authority he held over his tribe. In 1872 Cochise made peace with the military for an exchange of land, a reservation where the Indian leader eventually died. As years went by, clashes often escalated because the government broke faith with the Indians and reappropriated reservation land. Geronimo took over where Cochise left off, but to no avail. He surrendered in 1886, and the remaining Chiricahua were moved to forts in Oklahoma, Florida, and Alabama. It closed another chapter on the existence of the American Indians in their longtime homeland.

Benson was an 1880s railroad center on the Southern Pacific line, sending mining supplies south to Bisbee and Douglas. Its position in the San Pedro Valley made it a shipping center in the early 1900s as copper and silver were mined in the surrounding hills and sent from Benson for smelting. Although somewhat apocryphal, early records show it was named for a peddler who had the town on his route. An 1880 list of stage stations called it Benson City.

First a base camp for construction workers building the railroad's southern route, Willcox then became a central spot for local cattle ranchers to receive supplies and ship their steers. At one time it was known as the Cattle Capital of the nation. In the 1880s, army personnel stopped here on their way to Fort Grant, and in fact it is named for Gen. Orlando B. Willcox. The Southern Pacific Depot, the oldest original railroad station still standing on the line's southern route, was built in 1881. During the town's real boom years, 1914–1920, ranchers ran cattle on huge spreads and nearby mines were rich.

Major Attractions

Kartchner Caverns State Park

The newest of Arizona's state parks, opened at the end of 1999, this spectacular cave is destined to put the little city of Benson on the map. The mandate to do the job right, without disrupting the natural process that created this spectacular cave, necessitated a $28.4 million total budget. A pair of spelunkers discovered the caverns in 1974. They kept it a secret until they were sure protective measures were in place. Arizona State Parks acquired it in 1988, naming it for the family on whose land the cave was discovered. It has two enormous 1,200-foot rooms connected by 2.75 miles of tunnel. Brilliant colors, the result of natural chemical reactions, plus stalactites, stalagmites, and whimsical geologic formations have been created from hollowed-out limestone rock. The "live" cave has more than 0.5 mile of trails inside. Despite the surrounding desert heat, it has a constant 68°F temperature and a humidity of almost 100 percent. Services at the cave site include a 16,000-square-foot discovery center and a "cavatorium" that re-creates the experience of going beneath the earth's surface. Hiking trails invite exploration of the surrounding area, which has excellent birding. Hour-long tours offered 8:30 A.M.–5:30 P.M.; reservations strongly recommended. Admission fee per car, plus additional fee for cave tours. Open year-round, daily, 8:00 A.M.–6:00 P.M., except holidays. Located **off Hwy. 90, 8 miles south of Benson.** 520-586-2283. **Website: www.pr.state.az.us.**

The Magic Circle of Cochise

On a map it's easy to see this "magic circle," bounded by Hwys. 186 and 181 on the east and south, US 191 on the west, and I-10 on the north, with the city of Willcox at its northernmost point. While the magic may be mostly in the mind of the beholder, the area's history contains a definite mystique. Travelers usually begin the 100-mile route in Willcox, heading south 15 miles on Hwy. 186 to the ghost town of **Dos Cabezas,** which means "two heads" in Spanish.

Massive rock formations in the Chiricahua National Monument dwarf a fascinated hiker.

Take a look at the mountains to the east to understand the name. Seven miles farther south on Hwy. 186 is the turn off to **Fort Bowie National Historic Site** in Apache Pass (see Museums and Historic Sites). "Remember boys, nothing on God's earth must stop the United States mail," said John Butterfield to his drivers when he began his 24-day mail service from St. Louis to San Francisco in 1858. The stage used Apache Pass as a water stop, even though it took travelers and the mail through dangerous Indian territory. A brief halt to hostilities, which for two years had allowed stages to proceed unhindered, ended in 1861 with the Bascom Affair, in which an army officer wrongly accused Cochise of raiding stock from a local rancher. Cochise retaliated with more than two decades of attacks. The fort, which played an essential role in the wars against the Chiricahua Apaches, was abandoned in 1894. Today Apache Pass Rd., a graded dirt thoroughfare that can be in various states of repair depending on the season, leads to the crumbling fort (and continues on to I-10 at Bowie). Hwy. 186 then heads south to Hwy. 181 and the turnoff to **Chiricahua National Monument** (see below). From Chiricahua National Monument, continuing the

Getting There

Benson is on I-10 (use exit 304) 45 miles southeast of Tucson. Willcox is about 35 miles east of Benson on I-10 about 200 miles southeast of Phoenix and 85 miles from Tucson. Use exit 340 to get onto Rex Allen Dr. and turn right onto Haskell, the town's main street. **Amtrak***'s Sunset Limited stops in Benson, providing service between Los Angeles and Orlando, through San Antonio and New Orleans.* **800-USA-RAIL. Website: www.amtrak.com.**

circle south leads to the junction of Hwy. 181 and US 191 and heads back north again. US 191 travels to Pearce, then north to I-10 near **Willcox Playa** (see Birding); traveling east on I-10 to Willcox closes the circle.

Chiricahua National Monument

Geologists believe that 27 million years of violent volcanic activity created these mountains, which were then shaped and formed by the elements into the twisted formations that exist today. With a name that means "big mountain" to the Apaches, this area presents a wonderland of monumental spires, colossal columns, and precariously balanced boulders that seem about to teeter at any moment. The monument once was the stomping grounds of Cochise, Geronimo, and his successor Massai, and the Chiricahua Apaches. They used its protective forest and rocks as a hideaway from which they launched attacks on encroaching settlers. In 1924 President Coolidge established the area as a national monument, and footpaths were built in 1933.

Its position 50 miles north of Mexico, and the cool, damp forest, provide habitat for a number of unusual birds, including elegant trogons and hepatic tanagers. Coatimundis, fox squirrels, and peccaries live among the oaks, cypress, man-

zanita, and juniper. Huge ponderosa pine and Douglas fir are found at the high elevations. For a superquick overview, take the scenic drive along Bonita Canyon Dr. that winds 8 miles up to Massai Point and a sweeping view. Roadside pullouts allow access to exhibits and rock formations.

The best way to explore, however, is on foot, a pursuit made easy by the availability of detailed trail maps. Stop at the park visitor center first to see a well-produced video about the park. All of the park, except the road, is designated as wilderness, so ask about regulations and be forewarned that nature can be unpredictable, weather may be harsh, and altitudes that range from 5,400 feet at the visitor center to 7,010 feet near Inspiration Point can trigger unexpected physical reactions. Spring and fall are best times for amiable temperatures; it often snows in winter, but the white stuff melts quickly. Trails range from easy 0.25-mile strolls to challenging treks of up to 9 miles. A park shuttle leaves the visitor center daily at 8:30 A.M. and will drop you at trailheads. An easy hike of just over a mile from the visitor center leads to historic Faraway Ranch and the Stafford cabin, or you can drive to the cabin for a .25-mile stroll to the site. Tour guides explain that this was a farm and cattle ranch in the early 1900s, and by the 1920s it had become a guest ranch where visitors came to ride horseback and explore the rocks. By moving slowly and quietly you are practically guaranteed great bird sightings. The raucous call and flash of blue may be a Mexican or gray-breasted jay, one of the jays without a crest. The rufous-sided towhee, a robinlike bird with black back and rusty-red sides, is also a common resident. A pleasant picnic area at Massai Point provides a posthike resting spot. See Hiking.

Open daily, 8:00 A.M.–5:00 P.M. except Christmas Day. Located 36 miles southeast of Willcox **at Hwys. 186 and 181.** An extensive telephone menu answers many questions about the park. For more information call **Chiricahua National Monument Visitor Center, 520-824-3560. Website: www.nps.gov.**

Cochise Stronghold

As you head into the Dragoon Mountains, the elevation gain is apparent as the vegetation changes from desert scrub to madrones, walnut, and cypress. It's easy to see why Cochise chose this beautiful canyon, wooded with twisted oak and whispery cottonwood, for his hideaway. It is believed that his bones are still here. One account says his braves buried him in a deep crevasse along with his horse, dog, and rifle. Another says that Cochise was buried on a verdant mesa, his grave site then ridden over by men on horseback to hide the burial site from desecration. It doesn't seem to matter which version is true, because many visitors say that among the boulders, manzanita, and cottonwoods the spirit of Cochise is abundantly present.

On the temporal plane, keep an eye out for coatimundis, monkeylike creatures that forage for grubs, roots, lizards, and fallen berries in the underbrush. You may also spot them in trees, swinging from branch to branch, usually in groups. Along the Cochise Trail is Cochise Spring, sometimes dry, but the area is green and pleasant. Just beyond is Half Moon Tank, built so local ranchers could water their cattle. In summer months it is usually alive with frogs among the cattails. At the Stronghold's apex is a boulder-strewn vantage point with spirits in every shadowy crevice and behind each looming pinnacle. It's easy to understand how the 40-mile view of the high-desert floor below gave the resident Apaches an unsurpassed advantage over approaching enemies, whose dust clouds could be seen while they were still a day away. There is a Forest Service campground in the West Stronghold that has water during summer months. To reach Cochise Stronghold, turn off US 191 a mile north of the small town of Sunsites (restaurants and services), onto Ironwood Rd. Don't let the paved road fool you. It turns to gravel in less than a mile, but is passable in a regular passenger car. A number of dirt Forest Service roads in the Stronghold require four-wheel-drive vehicles.

For information call the **National Forest Service, 520-826-3593.**

Festivals and Events

Wings over Willcox Sandhill Crane Celebration

mid-Jan.

Visitors come from all over the world to witness more than 12,000 regal sandhill cranes overwintering in the Willcox Playa lakebed and surrounding fields. The three-day weekend event includes guided tours of best places to view, seminars on cranes and other wildlife, and an art auction and banquet. Birders stay overnight to get an early jump on the day, which means accommodations fill up quickly. 520-384-2272.

Rex Allen Days

first weekend in Oct.

The famed cowboy star was born in Willcox in 1920 and stayed until lured to the West Coast by performing opportunities in music, movies, and television. Over a 35-year span, his Decca Records hit songs included "Crying in the Chapel" and "Streets of Laredo." Since 1951 Willcox has honored its famous son in an annual celebration that includes parades, rodeos, stage shows, and dances. Until his accidental death in 1999, Allen lived on a ranch near Sonoita, 75 miles southwest of Willcox. 520-384-2272.

Livestock Auctions

throughout the year

Every Thurs. morning, ranchers bring cattle to Willcox for auction. You're welcome to watch while Herefords, Angus, Charolais, and many other breeds go to the highest bidder. Don't raise your hand unless you want to go home with a heifer. You'll see a gaggle of trucks and trailers **just off I-10 0.5 mile north of Rex Allen Dr.**

Outdoor Activities

Birding

Birders find good viewing at Cochise Lake, a small gray-water pond where as many as 42 species have been identified in a single day. Nov.–Feb. are best birding months. **Adjacent to golf course off Hwy. 186 southeast of Willcox at end of Rex Allen Dr.**

Willcox Playa and Sandhill Cranes

From US 191 just south of I-10, look toward the east to see a huge lakebed called Willcox Playa that's usually dry, but if it's been raining it may be filled with shallow water. The 60-square-mile, 37,000-acre lakebed was once the bottom of a Pleistocene sea. Visitors sometimes find unexploded shells and casings left over from World War II, when the Army used the surrounding area as a gunnery range. Despite the barren, desolate appearance of the playa, magnificent sandhill cranes have come here for decades to winter. They actually roost with their feet in the water, so they can hear coyotes and other predators coming through the water. Their numbers, once around 800, increased dramatically in the 1970s when agriculture took hold, providing bountiful grain and water for the wintering birds. Today an estimated 8,000–12,000 cranes come each year. In mid-July great thunderstorms drench the playa, bringing to life the tiny crustaceans that have been dormant under the parched surface. The cranes feed on the little shrimps, which also attract avocets, sandpipers, and killdeers. One of nature's largest birds, the greater sandhill crane can be as tall as 5 feet and weigh up to 12 pounds. Once widely hunted for their spectacular feathers, today they live protected in the Willcox area mid-Oct.–late Feb. or early Mar. For more information contact **Willcox Chamber of Commerce, 800-200-2272 or 520-384-2272.**

Hiking

Chiricahua National Monument

The best way to explore the monument is on foot. Stop at the park visitor center to pick up trail and topographical maps. Spring and fall are best, although you can hike any time of year. A park shuttle leaves the visitor center daily at 8:30 A.M. and will drop you at trailheads at Sugar Loaf, Echo Canyon, Massai Point, and "wherever you want to go that the shuttle can take you," say park rangers. Trails range from easy 0.25-mile strolls to challenging treks of up to 9 miles. The 7-mile **Heart of Rocks Trail** begins at Massai Point and appeals to the whimsical as it winds past formations called Punch and Judy, Duck on a Rock, and others. **Echo Canyon Trail** is a photographer's dream, with massive rock columns, pillars, and boulders along a 3.5-mile loop. To verify how the canyon got its name, just let out a whoop if you can bear to interrupt the stillness. See Major Attractions. Open daily, 8:00 A.M.–5:00 P.M. Located at **Hwys. 186 and 181. Chiricahua National Monument Visitor Center, 520-824-3560. Website: www.nps.gov.**

Seeing and Doing

Museums and Historic Sites

The Amerind Foundation

Between Willcox and Benson, 64 miles east of Tucson in rugged, rocky Texas Canyon, the Amerind Foundation has a **museum, art gallery,** and museum store in a series of clean-lined Spanish Colonial Revival buildings. Founded by archaeologist William Fulton in 1937, its name is a combination of the words "American" and "Indian," which describes its diverse contents. It houses one of the most respected privately maintained archaeological and ethnological collections in the country, including artifacts found during excavations in the Southwest and Mexico. Included are examples of crafts, weapons, and household items used by various Indian cultures. The art gallery has paintings and sculptures fashioned around western themes. This serene, tranquil place is an authoritative source for information on Native American culture and history. Small fee. Open Sept.–May, daily, 10:00 A.M.–4:00 P.M.; June–Aug., Wed.–Sun., 10:00 A.M.–4:00 P.M.; closed major holidays. Located 1 mile off I-10 at Dragoon exit (exit 318). P.O. Box 400, Dragoon, 85609; 520-586-3666. Website: www.amerind.org.

Dos Cabezas

From 1854 to 1859, this ghost town on the Magic Circle of Cochise was the base for members of the commission that established the boundary between the United States and Mexico. Although all public buildings are closed, you can see remnants of the stage station built by the National Mail & Transportation Co. in 1884. You can still identify the old stage depot, one block off the main road, as well as the main-street post office with its fading Dos Cabezas sign. A well-preserved cemetery lies north of town. See Major Attractions. Located **on Hwy. 186 15 miles south of Willcox.**

Chiricahua Regional Museum and Research Center

Formerly located in the Willcox Chamber of Commerce building, this expanding museum contains historically significant artifacts from Native Americans and cavalry, minerals and rocks of the area, and maps tracing the route of the Butterfield Stage Line that once stopped nearby. A beautifully crafted bronze of Cochise is a highlight. Free. Open daily, 1:00 P.M.–4:00 P.M. 127 E. Maley, Willcox, 85643; 800-200-2272 or 520-384-2272.

Colossal Cave Mountain Park

The first thing you notice once you're inside this hollowed-out mountain is the cool 70°F temperature, a welcome relief from summer surface highs that can top 100°. This is a dry cave, which means there is no moving or dripping water inside to make the limestone formations "grow." It has a rich history of use dating to prehistoric times, but more recently served as a hideout for gold-rustling outlaws. One of its areas is called Bandits Escape Route. In 1923, when the cave was first explored, visitors were

roped to guides and to metal pins embedded in cavern walls. They wore miners' hats with built-in lights or carried lanterns. Since then, lights and flagstone steps have been added, which makes exploration much easier, but still involves more than 350 steps, up and down, covering a height of six and a half stories. It's OK to take flash photos and videos inside. You can bring a picnic lunch to eat at tables in an adjacent wooded area. The cave is operated by the Pima County Parklands Foundation and is on the National Register of Historic Places. Moderate fee. Open mid-Mar.–mid-Sept., Mon.–Sat., 8:00 A.M.–6:00 P.M., and Sun. and holidays, 8:00 A.M.–7:00 P.M.; mid-Sept.–mid-Mar., Mon.–Sat., 9:00 A.M.–5:00 P.M., and Sun. and holidays, 9:00 A.M.–6:00 P.M. Located 22 miles east of Tucson and about 23 miles west of Benson. **From I-10 take exit 279 and follow signs for about 6 miles** to entrance and gift shop. 520-647-7275. Website: www.collosalcave.com.

Fort Bowie National Historic Site

Fort Bowie played an essential role in the wars against the Chiricahua Apaches. The fort, established in 1862, consisted of tents surrounded by stone breastworks that were replaced six years later by adobe brick barracks, officers quarters, a hospital, and other buildings. Despite the fort's growth to a total of 38 buildings, its isolation, crude quarters, and constant threat of Indian attacks made it tough duty for early military men. From a small National Park Service office, it is a moderate 3-mile round-trip hike into the ruins of the fort, a trek that can be beastly hot in summer. Open daily, 8:00 A.M.–5:00 P.M., except Christmas. Located **on Apache Pass Rd., 22 miles southeast of Willcox off Hwy. 186.** Or, from the town of Bowie on I-10, drive south 12 miles on the partly paved road that leads directly to Apache Pass. **520-847-2500. Website:** www.nps.gov.

Gammons Gulch

This ghost-town movie set is actually in the town of Pomerene, which is, appropriately, a ghost town. Jay Gammons has constructed

17 buildings over 10 acres that mirror the Old West of the late 1800s. Vehicles from the early 1900s still run, and the saloon serves cold sarsaparilla. Everything's authentic, including the working telegraph and the outhouses, although more modern facilities are also available. Moderate admission. Open Wed.–Sun., 9:00 A.M.–5:00 P.M. Located 12 miles north of Benson. **Take Pomerene Rd. to Cascabel Rd., continue to milepost 7, then to E. Rockspring Rd. Turn left and take first gate on left. P.O. Box 76, Pomerene, 85627; 520-212-2831.**

Holy Trinity Monastery

The monastery in the small town of St. David is marked by a huge Celtic cross on the right as you approach from Benson. This community of monks, nuns, and laity follows the covenants of the Catholic Benedictine order. Mass is said daily at Our Lady of Guadalupe Church. The 130-acre property has a 1.3-mile **bird sanctuary trail** bordering the San Pedro River that visitors (no pets) are welcome to stroll. Just remember it is a monastery, so no shorts or beachwear. A small RV park with some hookups offers sites on a first-come, first-served basis. The farm has grazing cattle, but commercial beef is used for the **barbecue dinners** held in spring and fall, that draw up to 12,000 people in a weekend. Browse the bookstore and gift shop, small **art gallery,** and **museum,** with Civil War artifacts and an antique Bible collection. Benedict's Closet, their thrift shop, gives the word "bargain" real meaning. This tranquil place offers retreats of one day and longer. For more information contact the guest coordinator. Located **7 miles south of Benson on Hwy. 80. P.O. Box 298, St. David, 85630; 520-720-4016. Website: www.trinitymonastery.org.**

Rex Allen Arizona Cowboy Museum and Willcox Cowboy Hall of Fame

Early photos, elaborate costumes, and posters from some of the 19 movies he made for Republic Pictures between 1950 and 1954 trace this singing cowboy's career. The Willcox Cowboy Hall of Fame in the same building contrasts

working cowboys with their celluloid counterparts. Across from the museum, a larger-than-life Rex strums away in bronze permanence beside the grave of his horse, KoKo, whose epitaph says "Belly high in the green grass of horse heaven." The museum occupies an 1890s adobe structure that was the Schley Saloon until 1919. Next door, the 1935 art deco Willcox-Rex Theater shows weekend movies. Between the two structures, a new little park has an open-air stage for concerts. Small fee. Open daily, 10:00 A.M.–4:00 P.M. **155 N. Railroad Ave., Willcox, 85643; 520-384-4583.**

Scenic Drives

Sunsites, Pearce, Courtland, and Gleeson

Three little towns in the Sulphur Springs Valley formed by the Dragoon Mountains can make an interesting side trip for serious aficionados of towns of the past. **Sunsites,** which was developed a number of years ago as a retirement destination 28 miles southwest of Willcox on US 191, is very much alive, with two golf courses and a community rec center. But 0.5 mile south, a turnoff called Ghost Town Trail leads to **Pearce,** about 1 mile down the road. Miner and rancher James Pearce, whom it is believed to be named for, discovered gold near the town and inspired an influx of fortune hunters from nearby Tombstone. The Commonwealth Mine opened and findings were rich. But when water began to fill the shafts faster than was economically feasible to pump it out, the mine closed. Today the general store and church are closed. If you follow the sign that says "Pearce Cemetery" for 0.5 mile, on your right you'll see the entrance and a large rock full of symmetrical holes, created by Commonwealth Mine workers testing their drills. Inside the cemetery are the graves of Abraham Lincoln's bodyguard and General Sherman's adjutant, as well as a number of Union and Confederate soldiers. For information contact **Pearce-Sunsites Chamber of Commerce, P.O. Box 308, 133 Frontage Rd., Pearce, 85625; 520-826-3535.**

Courtland, named for miner Courtland Young and established in 1909, lies 10 miles south of Pearce on a graded dirt road. All that remains are a few concrete slabs, with the exception of the sturdiest building, the jail. The leaching tanks of the Mame Mine are still standing. Follow the road south for another 10 miles and you'll come to Gleeson, named for an early rancher, where mines and buildings are posted as off-limits because their ramshackle condition makes them dangerous. But the crumbling adobe post office and the Gleeson Saloon remain picturesque in a quirky way. From Gleeson you can head east 8 miles to Elfrida on US 191 and head north to close the loop. (To make this drive coming from the south, turn left off US 191 a mile north of Elfrida, at the sign that says Gleeson. The first 6 miles are paved, and Gleeson is 2 miles beyond the marked turnoff to Courtland. You'll have to backtrack those 2 miles to continue north to Courtland and Pearce.)

Seasonal Favorites

From the Fourth of July through Halloween, peaking in early Sept., an amazing variety of produce comes from the fields around Willcox. Southeastern Arizona has the largest variety of direct-sales farms in the state, attracting more than 120,000 fruit and vegetable lovers who come to pick each season. Most of the farms, about 20 miles northwest and southwest of town, offer big plastic buckets, inform you of a few simple picking rules, and then you're on your own. When finished, you pay for your fruit and vegetables by weight. Available at varying times, you'll find more than 40 varieties of squash, sweet corn, pears, apples, peaches, tomatoes, peas, green beans, hot chiles, bell peppers, okra, pumpkins, cucumbers, and at least five varieties of apples. Wear old shoes that can get muddy, pick in cool morning hours, wear gloves, and bring a cooler for toting your pickings home.

The farms listed here all are off I-10 at exit 340, left on Fort Grant Rd. Watch for signs for various farms. Because they're so close

together, you can visit several in a day. It is essential that you call first to see what's available, because a late frost easily can wipe out all of a particular crop, and previous pickers may have depleted a field.

Apple Annie's Orchard

The Holcomb family grows freestone peaches, Asian pears, and many apple varieties. An on-site bakery has apple pies in dozens of varieties, dumplings, bread, and other baked goods. Lunch is offered mid-July–Oct. 520-384-2084 or 800-840-2084.

Briggs Orchard

Pears, peaches, and apple varieties include Granny Smith, red and golden delicious, criterion, Jonathan, gala, fuji, and winesap. Some are organically grown. Bring your own containers. 520-384-2539.

Country Treasures

If you don't want to do the picking and preserving yourself, visit this charming shop. Myrna, the proprietor, who has pickled and canned regional produce since 1987, offers vegetables and fruits, jams, jellies, fruit and nut syrups, honey, candies, brittles, and more. Items can be packaged to ship just about anywhere. There's also an on-site bakery and snack bar, so you can get a fresh sandwich to eat at a shady picnic table or park bench. 800-577-6496 or 520-384-3675.

Hunsdon Farms

Crops include sweet corn, summer squash, bell peppers, and eggplant. A special watermelon festival is held Labor Day weekend, and a pumpkin festival is held weekends in Oct. Open July–Oct. 520-384-4362 or 800-351-6698.

Stout's Cider Mill

The fragrance of apples and spices is overwhelming as soon as you set foot into Stout's Cider Mill. Cider, of course, but also apple butter, apple nut cake, and fabulous apple pie are their stock-in-trade. You can have a single warm slice

Native son Rex Allen of Willcox yodels on in bronze permanence in front of the Rex Allen Arizona Cowboy Museum, which traces his singing-cowboy movie career.

to eat there, or take home a whole pie. In nearby orchards, Stout's grows its own tart green Granny Smiths, as well as red delicious and other varieties for use in cider blends. The tourist information center is next door. Open daily, 8:00 A.M.–6:00 P.M. **1510 N. Circle 1 Rd., Willcox, 85643; 800-871-7437 or 520-384-3696. Website: www.cidermill.com.**

Where to Stay

Near Benson, the Holiday Inn Express and Motel 6 are at the junction of I-10 and Hwy. 90. Days Inn, Super 8, and the Best Western Quail Hollow are right in Benson. Many basic chain motels, including Days Inn, Super 8, and Best Western, cluster around Exit 340 off I-10 in Willcox. By far the more interesting accommodations, the bed-and-breakfasts in town and the ranches some miles out of town get you close to nature and give a sense of the area's history.

Bed-and-Breakfasts and Inns

Heritage Manor Bed & Breakfast—$$$
Set in quiet countryside surrounded by green agricultural fields, it looks like a lovely transplant from the South or Midwest. The white frame inn with second-story dormers, shuttered windows, and wide front porch is warm and welcoming. It has a suite with kitchenette, veranda, and private bath, and two rooms with shared bath. Located 10 miles from Willcox. From I-10 exit at Fort Grant Rd. and follow it past the Country General Store to the inn. **HCR 1, Box 93, Willcox, 85643; 520- 384-2953.**

Skywatcher's Inn, Arizona Astronomy and Nature Retreat—$$$
One of the state's neatest, most interesting, and unique bed-and-breakfast inns and part of Vega–Bray Observatory, the inn comes fully equipped with seven major telescopes, ranging from 6 to 20 inches. One is completely computerized. You can arrange an astronomy session with an amateur astronomer or professor and be almost guaranteed of seeing one major planet, and certainly the Milky Way. Because it is 47 miles from a major city, light pollution is negligible. There are two main bedrooms, each with private bath, and a smaller bedroom and bath in the adjacent observatory. A living room and kitchenette are communal. Even if heavenly bodies aren't your thing, the observatory's location, on top of a small hill overlooking the San Pedro River Valley, is filled with birds, wildlife, and hiking trails. Located 47 miles from Tucson and 4 miles south of Benson. Take Pomerene exit (exit 306) off I-10, and go east on Frontage Rd. to Airport Rd. Turn south for 1.9 miles to Serenity Ranch, then go past the lake on your right to the inn. **420 S. Essex Ln., Tucson, 85711; 520-615-3886 reservations or 520-586-7906 inn. Website: www.communiverse.com/skywatcher.**

Cochise Hotel—$$
Opened in 1882, this adobe inn was built at the junction of the Southern Pacific and old

Arizona Eastern Railways. Trains still rumble by, lending validity to the old Wells Fargo freight office filled with antiques of the era. Rooms are small, sunny, and pleasant, with touches like patchwork quilts, oak dressers, brass headboards, and lace curtains. All rooms have private updated baths. Reservations essential. Located **5 miles south of I-10 (exit 331) on US 191.** Watch for Cochise signs. **P.O. Box 27, Cochise, 85606; 520-384-4314.**

Willcox Historic Inn—$$

This lovely 1882 adobe home is surrounded by mesquite trees, flowers, and cactus. The wrap-around veranda is a pleasant vantage point for watching hummingbirds, roadrunners, and quail. High-ceilinged rooms have fireplaces and great views. Private and shared baths are available. **213 N. Historic Railroad, Willcox, 85644; 520-384-3597.**

Guest Ranches

Grapevine Canyon Ranch—$$$$

This popular ranch, niched in a secluded canyon about 35 miles southwest of Willcox, has an exceptional number of options for all riding abilities. Adventure rides take guests to abandoned mining camps, Apache lookout points, ghost towns, and burial grounds. Special weeks each month are devoted to learning the techniques of cutting, how to be a cowhand, and how to buy and enjoy a horse. During history week, guests ride to the Cochise Stronghold, along the Butterfield Stage Trail, and to Apache hideouts. Rates include three meals a day, all horseback riding, and accommodations in casitas or large cabins. **From I-10 near Willcox, take Dragoon Rd. exit (exit 318) that dead-ends on US 191 south. Turn south to Sunsites and at south end of Sunsites, take Treasure Rd. west and follow ranch signs. P.O. Box 302, Pearce, 85625; 520-826-3185 or 800-245-9202.** Website: www.grapevinecanyonranch.com.

Sunglow Guest Ranch—$$$–$$$$

With peace and quiet guaranteed by the sur-rounding national forest and wilderness, Sun-glow provides an almost spiritual getaway. Owners Bob and Sue Paral say it's so quiet you can hear the stars twinkle. The ranch was once a town built to serve the sawmill teamsters. Although it has everything you'd expect in a ranch—trail rides, hayrides, bird-watching, hik-ing—there is a sense of remoteness. Spanish mission-style casitas have fireplaces, courtyards, and kitchens so you can cook for yourself, or let the dining room know and they'll do the cook-ing. You also can stay in a rustic tepee on the shores of Sunglow Lake. Hiking, horse rentals, and fishing are available on the property. They'll arrange a ranch-to-ranch ride that takes you to Price Canyon Ranch, a working cattle ranch a day's ride away. Located 15 miles south of Chiricahua National Monument. **From Will-cox, take Hwy. 186 south to Hwy. 181, then to Turkey Creek Rd. HC 1, Box 385, Pearce, 85625; 520-824-3334. Website: www.sun glowranch.com.**

Muleshoe Ranch/The Nature Conservancy—$$$

Owned and managed by The Nature Conser-vancy in conjunction with the U.S. Forest Serv-ice and the Bureau of Land Management, this ranch is where to come when you really want to get away from civilization. The quiet, secluded area encompasses 48,120 acres of rugged beauty on a Nature Conservancy preserve in the foot-hills of the Galiuro Mountains. The preserve has hiking trails and excellent bird-watching. In Jan.–Feb., you're likely to see troops of coa-timundis in the canyons, and in July–Aug. white-tailed deer are plentiful in the mesquite bosques. Hummingbirds practically storm the feeders set out at headquarters. The headquar-ters is staffed Thu.–Mon., 9:00 A.M.–4:00 P.M.

Within this vast backcountry area, Pride Ranch lies within Muleshoe about 6 miles from Conservancy headquarters and may be rented overnight. Jackson Cabin, about 14 miles away, can be used for basic shelter, but there are no furnishings, water, or even much of a roof. Both are accessible with a four-wheel-drive vehicle.

Camp overnight or stay in refurbished ranch buildings and casitas with bathrooms, kitchens, or kitchenettes, some with fireplaces. One of the bonuses, available to overnight guests only, is use of the natural hot springs. Reservations are a must. Located 30 miles northwest of Willcox. **From Willcox, follow Bisbee Ave. past the high school to Airport Rd. Turn right and proceed 15 miles, bearing right at the fork just past mailboxes. Follow the road another 14 miles to Muleshoe Ranch Headquarters at the end of the road. Rural Route 1, Box 1542, Willcox, 85643; 520-586-7072.**

Camping

There are overnight campgrounds without hookups or showers in Bonita Canyon and a few RV parks scattered throughout the Chiricahua National Monument area. For campgrounds with amenities, head north 36 miles to Willcox.

Butterfield RV Resort

Upscale park with 173 landscaped lots, full hookups, and free cable TV. Large clubhouse with meeting room, library/computer room with computer, and two free phone connections to e-mail and the Internet. Workout room, billiards room, laundry, heated pool, and spa. Walled for privacy, and within walking distance of grocery shopping and restaurants. Use exit 304 off I-10 and go south 0.3 mile. **251 S. Ocotillo Ave., Benson, 85602; 800-863-8160 or 520-586-4400. Website: www.rv-resort.com.**

LifeStyle RV Resort

Full hookups plus fitness center, indoor pool and spa, and laundry facilities. On-site restaurant and pizza parlor. **622 N. Haskell Ave., Willcox, 85642; 520-384-3303.**

Magic Circle RV Park

Full hookups, tent area, shower and laundry facilities, swimming pool, shade trees, and picnic tables under redwood shelters. You can see it from the freeway. **From I-10, take exit 340; located in Willcox. 520-384-3212 or 800-333-4720.**

Where to Eat

For food without the chain mentality, bypass the eateries on the highway and drive into Benson or Willcox.

Rodney's—$-$$

The best burgers, ribs, and catfish for miles around are served up in Willcox by Rodney Brown, whose reputation has reached as far as Wisconsin. From a tiny kitchen, meals are brought out to a pleasant patio shaded by a giant fig tree. Be prepared to chow down big-time. The food is fabulous. Open daily, except Mon., 11:00 A.M.–10:00 P.M. Located two doors down from the Rex Allen Museum. **118 N. Railroad Ave.; 520-384-5180.**

Horseshoe Cafe Restaurant & Lounge— $$-$$$

A Benson landmark for more than 60 years (look for the 1940s horseshoe-shaped neon sign), this low-key place serves up biscuits and gravy for breakfast, and chicken fried steak just about any time, as well as Southwestern dishes plus plates such as liver and onions and prime rib. The present building dates to the mid-1940s, with the murals of stately steeds by noted cowboy artist Vern Parker added in 1952. Famous Southern Arizona ranch brands are burned into the cafe's center posts. Open daily, 6:00 A.M.–9:00 P.M. **154 E. Fourth, Benson; 520-586-3303.**

Solarium Dining Room—$$

At the Best Western in Willcox, this pleasant restaurant is probably the closest thing to fine dining in town. Each night the chef whips up something special, like stir-fry, in addition to standard seafood and steaks. **1100 W. Rex Allen Dr., Willcox; 520-384-3556.**

Regal Restaurant and Lounge—$-$$

Retirees and ranchers congregate over coffee in a homey atmosphere as comfortable as mom's kitchen. Everyone seems to know everyone else. Expect a minute of silence when you walk in as the regulars try to figure out who you are. Open daily, 6:00 A.M.-9:00 P.M. **301 N. Haskell Ave., Willcox; 520-384-4780 or 520-384-9959.**

Ruiz's Family Restaurant—$–$$

Since 1971 this family-run Benson restaurant has offered homemade everything, including their own taco shells, tortillas, and chips. Famous for chiles rellenos and steak ranchero, they also have 15 different combination plates. The special includes a taco, beef tamale, cheese enchilada, tostada, cup of soup, chips, and salsa, for under $6. Margaritas for $2, 14 kinds of tequilas, and beers that include Negra Modelo, Tecate, Bohemia, Corona, and others can really slake a desert thirst. Open daily, 11:00 A.M.–9:00 P.M. **687 W. Fourth, Benson; 520-586-2707.**

Services

A comfortable **rest area** sits among picturesque boulders in Texas Canyon on I-10 between Willcox and Benson, just past "The Thing" (you'll have to see it for yourself; admission 75 cents).

Benson/San Pedro Valley Chamber of Commerce

249 E. Fourth St., Benson, 85602; 520-586-2842. Website: www.BensonChamberAz.com.

Benson Visitor Center

249 E. Fourth St., Benson, 85602; 520-586-4293.

Willcox Chamber of Commerce

They have a good selection of pamphlets and books on the area and exceptionally friendly personnel. Stout's Cider Mill is just across the parking lot. **1500 N. Circle 1 Rd., Willcox, 85643; 520-384-2272 or 800-200-2272.** Website: www.willcoxchamber.com.

Sky Islands

Rising above grassland and low scrub, high on the slopes of various mountains are what have become known as "sky islands." These ecosystems, where plant and animal life develop independently from the flora and fauna on lower slopes, are distinct mountaintop habitats. The arid distances between them, the "seas" that make them "islands," have allowed their biotic communities to evolve without outside influence. Darwin credited the same principle with creating the ecosystems on the isolated Galapagos Islands. There are sky islands in the Huachuca Mountains, the Chiricahuas, and the Santa Rita Mountains near Tucson. San Jose Peak, which pokes up from the Mexican desert, is a sky island. The greatest concentration of these lofty ecoregions lies in the area where Arizona, New Mexico, and Mexico meet. To explore one of them, you ascend from the grasslands of the desert, pass through low oak woodlands, and finally emerge among elegant pine and fir at the summit.

An easy-to-get-to sky island is accessible from Chiricahua National Monument off Hwys. 186 and 181 south of Willcox (see Major Attractions). It takes a high-clearance vehicle and two or more hours. At the national park visitor center, you can get a map (essential) that shows Pinery Canyon Rd. By following it, and road signs, you will get to Onion Saddle and Rustler Park Campground, and eventually to the mountain village of Portal. From here you can head east on a paved road leading to Hwy. 80, which you can take north to I-10 just over the New Mexico border, or south to Douglas.

Safford

The largest city in Graham County and also the county seat, Safford's *raison d'etre* today is agriculture, with 22,000 of its 35,000 irrigated acres planted in cotton. In the town of Pima just west of Thatcher (named for Mormon apostle Moses Thatcher), Glenbar Gin processes more than 20,000 bales annually. You have only to drive a few miles in any direction to see flourishing cotton fields and, depending on season, tomatoes, grain crops, apples, and pecans.

The Graham County Courthouse, an imposing brick building with white Greek columns at the end of Main St., built in 1916 and still in use today, tells you that Safford is a town with history.

Along roads and highways near Safford, signs warning not to pick up hitchhikers reflect the presence of three correctional facilities in the area. Arizona State Prison Complex currently houses about 715 minimum-security inmates and 40 medium-security inmates. Fort Grant, at varying times a cavalry post, army post, and juvenile industrial school, now is a minimum-security state prison. "Club Fed," the Federal Correctional Institution, is the building with circular razor wire ringing it that you pass on your way up Mount Graham. It houses about 700 low-security prisoners.

History

Safford was founded in 1874 by four farmers looking for arable land near a water source, which

they found in the Gila River. It is named for Anson B.K. Safford, territorial governor at the time. Safford was influenced by Mormon settlement early on, as missionaries obeyed the edict of leader Joseph Smith to colonize the West.

Outdoor Activities

Birding

Roper Lake State Park

This attractive park at the foot of Mount Graham surrounds 30-acre Roper Lake, which is large enough to attract a good variety of water- and shorebirds, and other avian species that depend on water. Within about 100 feet of each other, you may see a grebe on the lake diving for dinner, a spindly-legged killdeer searching the shore, and in the brush around the lake a strutting roadrunner with a trophy lizard. Picnic tables are thoughtfully placed for privacy; some are within feet of the water, so you can settle in for the day, get in some fishing (the lake is stocked with rainbow trout, bass, crappie, and a few other varieties), and take short local hikes. Very few local lakes offer good swimming, but here you'll find a beach and large ramada in the Island area. About 1 mile away,

---

Getting There

Safford is at the junction of US 70 and US 191, 46 miles north of Willcox.

the park's Dankworth Ponds section has a smaller lake with picnic ramadas. No gasoline-powered boats allowed. The park has three campgrounds (see Where to Stay). Located 6 **miles south of Safford, 0.5 mile off US 191. Route 2, Box 712, Safford, 85546; 520-428-6760. Website: www.pr.state.az.us.**

Hiking

Gila Box Riparian Area

Named for a canyon, this specially designated area includes 15 miles of Bonita Creek and 23 miles of the Gila River, popular spots for bird-watching, hiking, and picnicking. Hiking here is excellent Oct.–mid-Dec. when fall colors are magnificent and the weather is comfortable. You can get to cliff dwellings and historic home-steads from graded dirt roads with a high-clearance vehicle; major access points are usually passable in a passenger car. From Safford **take Eighth Ave. north to the airport and continue 2 miles beyond to Sanchez Rd.; turn left (pavement ends) and follow Bonita Creek signs to the creek and river.** From the north, from US 191 at milepost 160, 4 miles south of Clifton, the dirt road is marked with a large, colorful Black Hills Backcountry Byway sign; follow it 4 miles to the Old Safford Bridge and you'll be in the Riparian Area. For information contact the **BLM, 711 14th Ave., Safford, 85546; 520-348-4400.**

Rockhounding

Near the south end of the Safford-Clifton Scenic Byway (see Scenic Drives), the Black Hills Rockhound Area regularly yields fire agates. Formed by volcanic activity, the agates are a variety of silica in which mineral impurities have created vibrant colors. You can bring a pick and shovel and dig, because most agates are found within 2 feet of the surface, but ardent rock-hounders say you'll be just as successful scouring the surface near washes and other areas where the soil has been disturbed. Primitive camping is allowed. Located about 20 miles east of

Discovery Park offers glimpses into other universes.

Safford. Proceed **east on US 70 for 10 miles, then follow US 191 toward Clifton to milepost 141. Just beyond is an entry sign on the left. Follow a dirt road for 2 miles to the rockhound area.** For more information contact the **BLM, 711 14th Ave., Safford, 85546; 520-348-4400. Website: safford.az.blm.gov.**

Seeing and Doing

Museums

Graham County Historical Society Museum

In Thatcher, 2 miles west of Safford, this relocated museum occupies the 1917 red brick Thatcher High School. Classrooms with creaky oak floors are filled with area memorabilia. The one called Main Street has signs, implements, and artifacts representing doctors, dentists, the local newspaper, the fire department, and shoe and barber shops from the 1890s to the 1940s. In the vintage clothing room you can see a beaded handbag that was carried to Lincoln's inauguration, as well as christening dresses and sleeping bonnets. No admission fee. Open Mon., 1:00 P.M.–8:00 P.M.; Tues. and Sat., 10:00 A.M.–5:00 P.M. Located in Thatcher on the corner of 4th Street and Hwy. 70; 520-348-0470.

Eastern Arizona Museum and Historical Society

This interesting museum building, once the Bank of Pima, was constructed in 1916 and still has the original ornate tin ceiling. It houses collections of Southwest artifacts found locally, as well as memorabilia donated by local residents. A large barbed wire collection and a number of old quilts are among the highlights. The adjacent "pioneer rooms," housed in the old tufa stone Cluff Hall built in 1882, include a sitting room, bedroom, music room, and kitchen of the past. Open Wed.–Fri., 2:00 P.M.–4:00 P.M.; Sat., 1:00 P.M.–4:00 P.M. Located on northwest corner of Main and Center (US 70) in Pima. P.O. Box 274, Pima, 85543; no phone.

Nature Centers

Discovery Park

At this unusual science center, interactive galleries let you measure radio emissions from the sun with the 0.5-meter radio telescope, and hear sounds from distant galaxies. An especially well-planned Origins Room displays varying cultural theories on how the world began. On clear nights you can look at the planets through a 20-inch reflecting telescope. Jupiter and its moons and ringed Saturn are reliably visible. The Polaris Shuttlecraft, a full-motion flight simulator, blasts you at warp speed to the surface of the moon, then to planets beyond during a 13-minute journey.

On the park's 200-plus acres, 65 of which are wildlife habitat, a small train chugs along a 2-mile track through a riparian area, past ponds and a marsh, and eventually will circle a planned 1860s ranch house. A self-guided nature walk helps you identify common desert plants, including variations of prickly pear, night blooming cereus, yucca, ocotillo, and desert lavender. A large stand of cottonwoods shades a picnic area. Open Tues.–Wed., 1:00 P.M.–4:00 P.M.; Thurs.–Sat., 1:00 P.M.–9:00 P.M. In Safford, from US 70 turn south onto 20th Ave. and follow it to the park. Or, from US 191 just south of Safford, turn west onto Discovery Park Blvd. and follow it to 20th Ave. Turn south on 20th Ave. to the park. Signs clearly mark the way. 1651 Discovery Park Blvd., Safford, 85546; 520-428-6260. Websites: www.discovery park.com and discovery @discoverypark.com.

Observatories and Planetariums

Mount Graham International Observatory

Safford is a favored region for astronomy because big-city light pollution is far distant, air stability is unaffected by thermals from city heat, and skies are consistently clear. At the 10,720-foot summit of Mount Graham, considered a sky island (see sidebar in Benson and Willcox chapter), you may arrange a tour to the Vatican Advanced Technology Telescope and the Heinrich Hertz Submillimeter Telescope during summer months. You are not allowed to go to the observatory on your own; you must book a tour and travel in the observatory van. Once there, you can see how the telescopes work and learn a bit about the projects under way, which currently include galactic and extragalactic research. Not much planetary work is being conducted. No one "looks through a telescope" anymore because video screens provide the viewing area; everything is controlled by computer. Tours are conducted approximately Apr. 15–Nov. 1, ceasing when winter ice and snow make the road unsafe for van travel. The last unpaved 9 miles to the observatory creates such tricky driving conditions in freezing weather that observatory workers who must travel it nicknamed it the "luge run." For information on observatory tours, arranged through Discovery Park (see Nature Centers), call 520-428-6260.

Scenic Drives

Swift Trail

Take Hwy. 366, the road that goes up to the top of Mount Graham, for an experience in ecology. As you follow its switchbacks and twists through the Pinaleno Mountains, you pass through five life zones in 30 miles. The scenery from so high up is nothing short of amazing. The road was built in the 1930s along the route of a turn-of-the century logging road, and paved in the 1960s. A number of campgrounds are along the way, as are private cabins used mostly during summer months. The mountain to the right is Heliograph Peak, where in 1886 Col. William A. Glassford constructed a heliograph station for the U.S. Army Signal Corps that was used for troop communication. One of a system of such mountaintop stations across southern Arizona and southwestern New Mexico, it functioned with a system of movable mirrors that reflected sunlight. Called the Swift Trail for T. T. Swift, the first supervisor of the Coronado National Forest, it is open year-round except when closed for snow removal. Though paved and well maintained, the road is not recommended for overlong trailers and motor homes. If there is any chance at all of snow, be sure to check the phone number below before setting out. This road eventually leads to the other side of the mountain and Riggs Lake, a popular summer vacation site. Pick up a guide, which includes mileage for points of interest along the drive, from the **Safford Ranger District Office** in the Post Office Building, **504 Fifth Ave., third floor, Safford, 85546; P.O. Box 709, Safford 85548-0709 (mailing address); 520-428-4150.**

Safford-Clifton Scenic Byway

As part of the BLM Backcountry Byway Program, the old Safford-Clifton road was graded a few years ago to make its bumpy 21 miles passable by many conventional cars, although high-clearance and four-wheel-drive vehicles do it in more comfort. It also is popular with mountain

A submillimeter telescope reaches skyward at the Mount Graham International Observatory.

bikers and hikers. Once a wagon trail through the canyons, it was built by prisoners incarcerated nearby. Near the kiosk at the trail's south end, you can see the grave of a prisoner who tried to escape. The rugged Black Hills, formed by volcanic uplifting more than 20 million years ago, today provide habitat for deer, javelina, eagles, red-tailed hawks, deer, and other creatures. The road passes through five working ranches that lease 65,000 BLM acres for grazing and support close to 700 head of cattle. A number of scenic overlooks create sweeping views of the Gila River on its way to San Carlos Lake. At milepost 7, the Black Hills Overlook, you can see Mount Graham in the distance, the Gila Mountains to the west, and to the north the enormous Phelps Dodge open-pit copper mine in Morenci. The picturesque old rock bridge, built by prisoners in 1918, spans the Gila River and is still structurally sound. This is a popular put-in point for rafters and kayakers, and for picnickers who seek the cool shade near the river. There are kiosks with maps and current road information at either end of the trail, but no services on the road, so be sure to bring water. A cell phone works in most places. An audiocassette with cowboy narrative is available at the Graham County Chamber of Commerce in Safford. For more information contact the **BLM Safford Field Office, 520-348-4400.** Website: azwww.blm.gov.

Where to Stay

A Comfort Inn, Days Inn, and Ramada Inn Spa Resort are among Safford's chain accommodations.

Olney House Bed & Breakfast—$$$
On the National Register of Historic Places, this 1890 mansion, built in the Western Colonial Revival style, once belonged to George A. Olney, the sheriff of Graham County. Today it offers rooms and cottages in a quiet residential area. There are three rooms with shared bath in the main house, behind which two cottages with kitchens and cable TV open onto a rose garden. **1104 Central Ave., Safford, 85546; 800-814-5118 or 520-428-5118.** Website: www.zekes.com/~olney/.

Camping

At Roper Lake State Park (see Birding), the **Hacienda Campground** has 20 hookup sites with electricity and water. At **Cottonwood Campground** there are 26 campsites with water and a ramada at each site. Hacienda and Cottonwood have showers, rest rooms, and vending machines. Lesser-developed sites at **Gila Campground** are in a more natural setting. Along the Swift Trail (see Scenic Drives) there are a number of campgrounds, including **Hospital Flat,** for tents only. 520-428-6760. Website: www.pr.state.az.us.

Services

Graham County Chamber of Commerce
A good assortment of literature, as well as displays that explain the county's agricultural personality. Dioramas with mammoths and condors show the area in ancient times. There are clean public rest rooms next door. Open Mon.–Fri., 8:30 A.M.–5:30 P.M. 1111 **Thatcher Blvd., Safford, 85546; 888-837-1841 or 520-428-2511.** Website: www.chamber.safford.az.org.

Clifton and Morenci

Northeast of Safford, in Greenlee County, Clifton and Morenci are mining towns in every sense of the word. They lie at the base of the Mogollon Rim in a craggy canyon carved by the San Francisco River.

For well over a century copper mining has driven their economy. Those who happened through the area early on, including Mace Greenlee, for whom the county is named, were interested in more valuable metals. Phelps Dodge, however, realized a bonanza when it saw one, and soon moved in. Remnants of a rowdy mining town remain along Chase Creek Street (see Historic Sites).

An anomaly in Clifton are the city's floodwalls, enormous slabs of concrete along the roadway that follow the San Francisco River. These movable gates can seal off the south part of the city, something not usually a concern in arid Arizona. But the San Francisco has a history of flooding. A devastating 1891 flood washed away the Wells Fargo Depot, whose safe functioned as the local bank. It was filled with gold and personal valuables. Despite years of digging through silt and rubble, the safe has not been found. The last big flood happened in 1983, and in 1995 the Army Corps of Engineers built the flood gates. So far, no flood.

History

In about 1865, while chasing Indians, Union cavalry discovered minerals in the area. The news immediately brought prospectors looking for gold. They found outcroppings of blue and green copper oxides, hardly worth much of a risk in this wild country rampant with Apaches. But claims were staked, and by 1881 Phelps Dodge bought half interest in what would become the Morenci Mine (see Historic Sites).

Morenci was named after a town about 75 miles from Detroit, Michigan, which had ties to the Detroit Copper Mining Company that later became one of the entities making up Phelps Dodge. Though Morenci is proclaimed the official birthplace of Geronimo, accuracy is questionable.

Depending on whom you believe, Clifton was named either for the cliffs surrounding the site where copper was discovered along Chase Creek, or for Henry Clifton, an early prospector.

Seeing and Doing

Historic Sites

Historic Chase Creek St.
Currently Clifton is restoring this narrow byway that once was the town's rough-and-tumble

Getting There
Clifton and Morenci are on US 191 about 30 miles northeast of Safford. The town of Morenci quite literally sits inside Phelps Dodge mine. US 191 winds through the mine and climbs to the Sitgreaves National Forest and the Colorado Trail, leading to Alpine (see East-Central region).

Huge 21-ton ore trucks look like toys at the bottom of the immense Morenci Mine.

A "baby gauge" railroad with tracks only 20 inches apart was built in 1879, with mules pulling cars down the mountain to the smelter in Clifton. An 1888 locomotive that replaced the mules stands spiffed and shiny at the Morenci Plaza. At first, all mining was underground, and during the Depression copper was priced so low that mining ceased entirely. In 1937 Phelps Dodge reopened the Morenci Mine as an open pit, and when World War II broke out two years later, copper prices soared. Since then the operation has become a computerized behemoth that has removed more than 3 billion tons of material from the mine. Mine tours (no charge) run Mon.–Fri., at 8:00 A.M. and 1:00 P.M. Tours leave from **Morenci Motel, across from Phelps Dodge Mercantile,** the present-day version of the company store. For information and reservations call **520-865-4521, ext. 1-6435.**

main drag. Highlights include the **Catholic Church** built in 1917 of local rocks, and the 1913 **Eagle Hall** that currently houses the Greenlee County Historical Society. You can pick up a walking tour brochure at the Greenlee County Chamber of Commerce located **in the Clifton Passenger Railroad Station,** built in 1913, where there are public rest rooms. The chamber is open Mon.–Fri., 8:30 A.M.–4:00 P.M. **P.O. Box 1237, Clifton, 85533; 520-865-3313.**

Morenci Mine

Owned by Phelps Dodge, this enormous amphitheaterlike open-pit mine relinquishes more copper than any other mine in North America. About 2 miles long and nearly as wide, it covers 32,000 acres and is about 0.5 mile deep. A 180-degree mine lookout reveals layers, terraces, water, tailings, and equipment chewing away at the earth far below. Depending on your point of view, you are looking at either one of humankind's greatest examples of doing violence to the earth, or one of our greatest achievements.

Where to Stay

Rode Inn Motel—$$–$$$

In Clifton, basic accommodations in a clean and fairly quiet 33-room motel. Food is just a block away at P.J.'s. **186 S. Coronado Blvd.; 520-865-4536.**

Morenci Motel—$$

A 5-minute walk from the mine, and a 2-mile drive to the lookout point, this is where mine tours gather. It has an adjacent restaurant and lounge. **In Morenci on Burro Alley; 520-865-4111.**

Services

Greenlee County Chamber of Commerce

Open Mon.–Fri., 9:00 A.M.–4:00 P.M. Located **in Clifton Passenger Railroad Station,** where there are public rest rooms. **P.O. Box 1237, Clifton, 85533; 520-865-3313.**

Douglas and Agua Prieta, Sonora

Douglas, a typical small mining town, has a population of about 17,200. The Phelps Dodge company closed its smelter there in January 1987, but the town continues to grow with agricultural interests and trade with Mexico. During peak production, more than 375,000 tons of ore per day were brought north from Mexican mines to be processed in Douglas. Now the town attracts retirees who like its slow pace and low living cost. It also ships 125,000 head of beef cattle each year.

Douglas and Agua Prieta, its sister city across the border in Sonora, Mexico, have become economically bonded in the last few years because of the *maquiladoras,* factories that draw on Mexico's cheaper labor pool to assemble products made in the United States. Thirty-two such businesses exist in Agua Prieta, employing more than 10,000 workers. Agua Prieta itself has a population of nearly 100,000. The factories, and the ancillary services they generate, have swelled Agua Prieta's population to more than 100,000, most of them family folks who venture across the border by the thousands to shop.

History

In 1902 two large-capacity smelters, the Calumet and Arizona and the Copper Queen, were built in Douglas, named after Dr. James Douglas,

a Phelps Dodge executive at that time. The Calumet and Arizona companies merged in 1931, and the Copper Queen was closed. Today all that remains of the smelters is a black slag pile about 1 mile west of town.

Outdoor Activities

Golf

Douglas Golf and Social Club
Recently expanded to 18 holes, this public course has inexpensive greens fees and offers year-round play. The swimming pool and playground are for member use only. There is also a small RV park at the club with 28 full hookups. Located **on N. Leslie Canyon Rd. 0.75 mile north of Hwy. 80 junction. P.O. Box 1220, Douglas, 85608; 520-364-3722.**

Seeing and Doing

Museums and Historic Sites

Gadsden Hotel
One of Douglas's biggest attractions is also its

Getting There
Douglas is 118 miles southeast of Tucson, on US 191 at its junction with Hwy. 80; it is right on the Mexico border.

premier hostelry (see Where to Stay). Built in 1907 and rebuilt in 1929 after a devastating fire, the Gadsden Hotel is named for James Gadsden, who negotiated the 1853 purchase of $10 million worth of land that later became Arizona and New Mexico. Once the hub of Douglas's cattle and mining interests, it thrived for years as a grand social and economic center. But as so many hotels do, it became the victim of neglect. In 1988 it was reprieved, and today the 150-room Gadsden, listed in the National Register of Historic Places, retains its original grand staircase, Italian marble columns, manned elevator, and 42-foot span of Tiffany murals depicting Sonoran Desert scenes. More than 200 cattle brands decorate the bar. A chip in the marble of the grand staircase supposedly was gouged by Pancho Villa's horse in 1911 when he rode the animal into the lobby during a clash between his forces and Mexican *federales*. Display cases on the balcony hold photos from the hotel's past. 1046 G Ave., Douglas, 85607; 520-364-4481. Website: www.theriver.com/gadsdenhotel.

Slaughter Ranch Museum

Adjacent to the San Bernardino Wildlife Refuge, this 19th-century cattle ranch has been restored to show what rural life was like at the turn of the century. The old adobe ranch house, ice house, wash house, granary, and commissary built by John Slaughter, Texas Ranger and sheriff of Cochise County, are on the tour offered Wed.–Sun., 10:00 A.M.–3:00 P.M. Take **15th St. east out of Douglas and follow it (name changes to Geronimo Trail) 15 miles to a large white gate marked with a "Z"**—the Slaughter family cattle brand. **P.O. Box 438, Douglas, 85608; 520-558-2474.**

Shopping

Agua Prieta, Sonora

Brief visits across the Mexican border do not require visas or documentation, but you should carry personal identification. You can lock your car and leave it in the city-owned vacant lot on the Douglas side and walk across into Mexico. Head south on Pan American Ave. (Ave. 3) and in the third block you'll find a saddle shop, **La Azteca Curio Store,** and a second curio shop around the corner on Calle 3. Turn right at Calle 6, a one-way eastbound street, right again at Ave. 4, and you'll be headed back to the border. For a pleasant lunch, try the modern, clean **La Hacienda Hotel** at the corner of Calle 1 (First St.) and Ave. 6, one block south and three blocks east of the border. There are fewer than half a dozen curio shops, but their merchandise is a notch above that offered in other border towns. Prices are equitable and bargaining is not a part of the experience.

Tours

WALKING TOURS

Historic Douglas

Pick up a map at the Douglas Visitor Center (see Services) and set out to enjoy representations of Sonoran row houses, Queen Anne cottages, and period revivals that include Gothic, Spanish, Colonial, and mission architecture. The town has 335 buildings listed in the National Historic Register dating to 1905–1920 when copper mining was at its peak. You also can see the **El Paso and Southwestern Depot** (it later served Southern Pacific passengers), built in 1913; it is impossible to miss as you enter town heading south on Pan American Ave. As many as eight trains stopped here daily during the 1920s, releasing passengers under the impressive beaux arts porticos. Rail passenger service ended in 1961. The station was rehabilitated using asset sharing money, Douglas's portion of cash and property seized from arrested drug lords, and in the spirit of meting out just desserts, the building now houses the Douglas Police Department.

A few blocks south on the right, the distinctive mission revival building once was the **YMCA,** built in 1906 with a bowling alley, basketball court, and indoor pool. It gave up

Coyotes

Sleek, gray-brown, friendly-faced, bushy-tailed coyotes have become a romanticized symbol of the Southwest. Experts at survival, they are bold, cautious, pragmatic opportunists. You may spot one on a golf course in the early morning, lurking around desert picnic areas hoping for leftovers, or simply strolling in the wilds, unfazed by the approach of hikers because they know they can run far faster than you.

Coyote tracks let you know they're in the area. They differ from those of a domestic canine because their slow, loping gait leaves sets of four aligned prints. Dogs leave side-by-side tracks like humans.

The legends of Native Americans of the Southwest are filled with coyotes. Says one, if a coyote crosses your path, it is calling attention to your obligations and responsibilities in the natural world. The coyote, says another, brings rain, prevents death, places the North Star, and guides humans into being.

Adult coyotes weigh 20–50 pounds, similar to a medium-size dog. Their diet consists mainly of rodents, rabbits, the eggs of ground-nesting birds, and occasionally carrion. Swift and sure runners, they are extremely vocal. Throughout still nights their barks, howls, and yelps are both mournful and encouraging. Although coyotes are accused of killing defenseless young livestock, large healthy animals have little to fear because at an average of 30 pounds, the coyote is too small to be much of a threat. Hungry coyotes quickly learn to bring down slower-moving sheep, easy prey because domestication has bred out defensive instincts.

Innately clever, coyotes play dead in order to trick birds into pouncing range. A keen sense of hearing and quick reflexes allow their catlike pounce to swiftly dispatch mice. Where coyotes have been controlled, the rodent population often explodes, bearing out the coyote's importance as a predator.

Coyotes are loving parents, behaving in a much more civilized manner than do domestic dogs, which immediately rely on humans to aid in the puppy-rearing process. When pups are three weeks old, the father coyote brings home small prey animals. Ground squirrels, stunned but alive, are presented to the pups to become a learning experience as well as a food source. As the pups acquire eating skills, they must learn to be predators. At this stage, they themselves are prey for bobcats, owls, and other large birds. But soon they venture out as a family.

Those who make a study of nature observe that coyotes are victims of their own success. Humans have allowed the coyote population to expand because we have upset the balance of predator and prey. So now we try to manage the coyote's existence, oftentimes making it the blameless enemy.

athletic purposes in 1958 and is now a recreational center under the Douglas Parks Dept. The elaborate classic revival **Grand Theater** on G Ave., built around 1917 by the Lyric Amusement Company for $175,000, hosted luminaries including Edgar Bergen and Charlie McCarthy. It closed in 1962. Four churches on four corners in the same block make **Church Square** unique. It is bounded by D and E Aves. and 10th and 11th Sts.

Where to Stay

There is a Motel 6 in Douglas, plus several small family-owned motels.

A pair of cowboys relax in the historically elegant Gadsden Hotel in Douglas.

Gadsden Hotel—$$–$$$

The 150-room Gadsden Hotel was rescued from neglect in 1988, and today the Gadsden is Douglas's premier hostelry as well a big attraction (see Museums and Historic Sites). The hotel, listed in the National Register of Historic Places, is currently undergoing a refurbishment. If you're looking for a ghostly encounter, ask for Rm. 333. A number of guests, and hotel housekeepers, have reported spirit sightings. 1046 G Ave., Douglas, 85607; 520-364-4481. Website: www.theriver.com/gadsdenhotel.

Where to Eat

El Conquistador Lounge & Dining Room—$$–$$$$

White-tablecloth dining in a pleasant room with a spectacular tile mural on one wall is quite remarkable for a very small town. Located in the Gadsden Hotel, the El Conquistador pulls it off with style. The menu is typically American, with a good selection of Mexican specialties. Open daily, 6:00 A.M.–9:00 P.M. 1046 G. Ave., Douglas; 520-364-4481.

The Grand Cafe—$$–$$$

Gourmet magazine reviewed this unexpected little place for its top-notch Mexican food and unusual ambiance. One of the owners is a Marilyn Monroe fan, attested to by hundreds of photos of the blonde goddess papering the walls. The other owner, a native of the state of Chihuahua, is the chef responsible for the cafe's good reputation. Open Sun.–Thurs., 10:00 A.M.–10:00 P.M.; Fri.–Sat., 10:00 A.M.–11:00 P.M. Located across the street and one block north of the Gadsden Hotel. 1119 G Ave., Douglas; 520-364-2344.

Services

Douglas Visitor Center

Open Mon.–Fri., 8:00 A.M.–5:00 P.M.; Sat. and Sun., 8:00 A.M.–2:00 P.M. 1125 Pan American Ave., Douglas, 85607; 520-364-2478 or 888-315-9999. Website: www.discoverdouglas.com.

Bisbee

Drive along Hwy. 80, through the Mule Pass Tunnel, around a curve, and you're in the walls of Mule Canyon that shelter Bisbee. The surrounding Mule Mountains, which put Bisbee at a 5,300-foot elevation, are the cradle for some of the richest copper ore ever taken from the state. Old Bisbee has become a popular weekend destination for antiques and collectibles shoppers, where browsers search for local arts and crafts, and travelers seek a fun and funky getaway. Its streets, a warren of slim alleys, nooks, and crannies filled with shops, invite exploration. Old miners' cottages and larger edifices that once were brothels are stacked up steep hillsides. Some have been converted to cafes and bed-and-breakfasts. Shops are eclectic and interesting, including a number purveying fine Bisbee turquoise in handmade silver settings.

The resident philosophy of Bisbee, which has a present population of about 6,500, is a mix of humor and an acceptance of reality. "The only way to make a small fortune in Bisbee is to come with a large one," jokes one cafe owner. Or, as another resident puts it, "change your notion of what constitutes a fortune."

History

Before the turn of the century, an emerging electrical industry, spurred by Thomas Edison's invention in 1879 of the first widely marketed incandescent lamp, created an increased demand for the copper wire that conducted this new energy source. By 1880 the Copper Queen Mine Company was flourishing, and Bisbee was on its way to becoming a sophisticated urban center. It once was the largest city between San Francisco and St. Louis. The elegant Copper Queen Hotel, built in 1902, welcomed noted guests including Black Jack Pershing and young Teddy Roosevelt. By 1910 Bisbee's streets were lined with aristocratic Victorian mansions, miners' cabins, and ornate buildings of commerce. For decades the town prospered, at one time boasting a population of close to 20,000. Miners, saloon girls, bankers, restaurant and hotel operators, and families coexisted happily (except for some labor disputes between workers and mine owners) on a number of economic levels.

But inevitably the rich ore that fed the open-pit and underground mines ran out, and in 1974 the huge Lavender Pit Mine was closed, marking the end of an era. The area is left with more than 2,000 miles of underground tunnels that channel through the surrounding mountains. Today the town laps at the edge of the open pit, its boundaries shaped by the huge hole, its personality cast in the rubble that came from the mine. Bisbee was named for Judge DeWitt Bisbee, an early stockholder.

Festivals and Events

Brewery Gulch Daze

Labor Day weekend
Held on this long weekend for more than a decade, the celebration includes a sale of photographic

reproductions from the Bisbee Mining & Historical Museum (see Museums and Historic Sites) and craft vendors in Brewery Gulch selling pottery, jewelry, prints, and posters by local artists. A hard-rock drilling contest and mucking contest, where contestants shovel dirt into an ore car against the clock, tell of the town's history. A highlight is the Sun. chili cook-off, the products of which are offered to interested spectators for tasting. Held on Sat. and Sun. 520-432-5421.

Home Tour

Sat.–Sun. after Thanksgiving

For close to two decades, owners and residents of Bisbee's best turn-of-the century homes open their doors to the public on this special weekend. Many of these houses have been beautifully restored. 520-432-5421.

Outdoor Activities

Birding

Sulphur Springs Valley

This remote area, west of the Chiricahua Mountains between Bisbee and Douglas on the south and Willcox on the north, is wonderful for winter birding, especially for raptors that include ferruginous hawk, prairie falcons, bald and golden eagles, and others. For more information on birding in this area, contact the Southeastern Arizona Bird Observatory, **P.O. Box 5521, Bisbee, 85603-5521; 520-432-1388.** Website: **www.sabo.org.**

Seeing and Doing

Museums and Historic Sites

Bisbee Mining & Historical Museum

It is the only small-town museum to be a Smithsonian affiliate, and houses an excellent collection of gems and minerals from early mining days. An award-winning exhibit includes a mural-sized photo, taken in 1908, that shows throngs of residents celebrating the arrival of the trolley. The town's population, about 9,000 then, peaked out at about 25,000 in 1910 when the mine was in full swing. Between 1881 and 1975, more than 7.7 billion pounds of copper were removed from the Bisbee district. The museum's second floor houses an outstanding cowboy retrospective, with recollective quotes and grainy black-and-white photos paying tribute to the most important things in a ranch hand's life—horses, chuck-wagon food, roping, and women. A separate room, Shattuck Memorial Archival Library, is filled with reference tomes. Bisbee's daily newspaper, dating back to 1902, is available on microfilm. Small fee. Open daily, 10:00 A.M.–4:00 P.M. Located in old Phelps Dodge General Office Building that dates to 1897, **at Brewery and Howell Aves.** in Copper Queen Plaza, an excellent place to begin a walking tour of Bisbee (see Tours). **520-432-7071.** Website: **www.azstarnet.com/non profit/bisbeemuseum.**

Lavender Open-Pit Mine

The consequences of this type of mining (380 million tons of ore and the soil that surrounds it were taken from the chasm) are eerie and unsettling. You can park and look into the gaping hole through a chain-link fence with viewing ports. The mine was named not for the vivid colors that paint its walls, but for an early mining official. Located **1 mile south of downtown Bisbee off Hwy. 80.**

Nightlife

Once an infamous street that roared with gunplay,

rowdy saloons, sporting houses, and alluring ladies of the evening, Brewery Gulch remains a toned-down version in a number of establishments.

Stock Exchange Bar has the original stock board from Bisbee's heyday. Located in the Muheim Block in a 1905 building that housed offices, a restaurant, and a stock exchange. Open daily, 12:00 P.M.–1:00 A.M. **15 Brewery Gulch; 520-432-9924.**

St. Elmo Bar, just down the street from the Stock Exchange, is said to be the oldest continuously operating bar in Arizona. Bartenders cheerfully point out bullet holes from contentious days gone by. Take time to check out the multitude of memorabilia that decorates the walls. On weekends, blues groups usually perform. Open daily, 10:00 A.M.–1:00 A.M. **36 Brewery Gulch; 520-432-5578.**

Tours

Queen Mine Tours

The Copper Queen Mine is such an icon that in 1997 it became one of the mining regions represented at the Smithsonian Institution's new Gem and Mineral Hall at the National Museum of Natural History. You can see the real things in Bisbee on an organized tour. After outfitting guests with hard hats, slickers, and 5-pound battery packs, former miners take guests underground into a once-active copper mine, closed since 1943. You'll learn how drilling and blasting dislodged the copper ore from the rock, to be loaded into carts and brought to the surface for smelting. The 75-minute tour, in open cars with guests straddling padded seats, goes 1,500 feet into the 4-level mine. The train runs on level three. The 8-foot-by-6-foot tunnel is just big enough for the train. Chilly 47°F mine temperatures might deter a few. A "claustrophobia stop" as the tour begins enables the faint of heart to change their minds. Moderate fee. Tours leaves Queen Mine Building daily, 9:00 A.M., 10:30 A.M., noon, 2:00 P.M., and 3:30 P.M. Reservations suggested. Take **Hwy. 80 interchange when entering Old Bisbee. 520-432-2071.**

The old mining town of Bisbee is niched in a hillside between steep canyon walls.

WALKING TOURS

Bisbee Self-Guided Walking Tour

Pick up a free map from the visitor center on Main St. (see Services) and set off on your own. You'll see the **Copper Queen Library,** built in 1907 and still in service with the post office on the ground floor; the 1904 **Pythian Castle,** whose gas-lighted tower served as the city timepiece; and the **Bisbee Convention Center,** built in 1939 by Del Webb. It's easy to spend an entire day wandering, with stops for cappuccino, lunch, and a frosty brew. Take a look at the architecture. It seems that very little is newly built in Bisbee, and that almost every building was once something else.

Where to Stay

Winter months are high season here, when accommodations fill up quickly. Reservations, especially on weekends, are recommended. Bed-and-breakfast inns have been restored to varying degrees of comfort, and small hotels are plentiful.

Bed-and-Breakfasts

School House Inn—$$$

Bisbee children once attended classes in this 1918 structure, but kids now must be 14 and older to spend the night. Rooms have names like The Principal's Office, private baths, and great town views. A full breakfast is included. **818 Tombstone Canyon, Bisbee, 85603; 800-537-4333 or 520-432-2996.**

The Inn at Castle Rock—$$–$$$

Lovely Victorian-style rooms in an 1890s miners' boardinghouse all have private baths. Set on an acre of hillside gardens with fish ponds and an old silver mine shaft, it's a unique escape, comfortable and homey. Room rates include full breakfast. **112 Tombstone Canyon, Bisbee, 85603; 800-566-4449 or 520-432-4449. Website: www.theinn.org.**

Main Street Inn—$$–$$$

In the middle of the historic district, this 1888 hotel was formerly called The Mann, and then became a boardinghouse for miners. Present furnishings give a Southwestern flavor, which works unexpectedly well with its bay windows. There are two suites with private bath, plus nine rooms with shared baths. Continental breakfast is served. **26 Main St., P.O. Box 433, Bisbee, 85603; 800-467-5237 or 520-432-1202. Website: www.admass.com/Bisbee/msi.**

Hotels and Inns

There are no chain lodgings in old Bisbee. **San Jose Lodge (520-432-5761)** on Naco Hwy. is a full-service motel.

OK Street Jailhouse Inn—$$$$

Built in 1904, this former jail was in use until 1915 when it became too small, then sat empty until 1989 when it was renovated. Where big-time crooks once languished, upstairs there is a bedroom with shower and whirlpool tub. It also has a full kitchen, living room, and half bath. More of an apartment than an inn, it is very unjail-like now. Two large metal doors are the only reminders of its first incarnation. Accommodates four. 9 OK St., Bisbee, 85603; 520-432-7435.

Copper Queen Hotel—$$$

In 1902, a decade before Arizona became a state, when Bisbee was the largest mining town in the world, the Copper Queen Mining Company (later Phelps Dodge Corporation) built the elegant Copper Queen Hotel. The four-story hostelry hosted mining executives, traveling men, territorial governors, and well-heeled cowboys in an atmosphere of grace and elegance. Those who were not so flush went around the corner to Brewery Gulch where Muheim's Brewery and an array of shady ladies guaranteed an exciting evening. When the ore played out, the Copper Queen Hotel went into a temporary decline, but because it was built to last, its architectural integrity allowed it to undergo restoration that returned it to its former level of luxury. The Queen's 45 rooms, updated to today's comfort level, retain their historic ambiance with period draperies and wallpaper as well as genuine antiques. 11 Howell St., P.O. Drawer CQ, Bisbee, 85603; 800-247-5829 or 520-432-2216. Website: www.copperqueen.com.

Shady Dell RV Park—$$

Not to be missed for its collection of vintage trailers that you can rent for an overnight or a whole season, this is one of Bisbee's true treasures. It is a living museum of travel's bygone days and the era of the tin-can tourist. Stay in a 1957 El Rey, a 1954 Crown, or even a 1950 Royal Mansion made by Spartan Aircraft Co., complete with pink plastic flamingos on the lawn. Magazine racks hold decades-old issues of *Arizona Highways,* aluminum coffeepots have the characteristic curvy designs of the 1950s, art-deco radios play swing music, beds are covered with chenille spreads, and nostalgic cookie jars are filled with treats. White picket fences surround the hitches. Newest addition is a 1947 CrisCraft boat that sleeps two. Dot's Diner (see Where to Eat), a gleaming stainless-steel monument to the 1950s, is on-site. Nightly stays in a vintage trailer include central bathrooms and showers nearby. Located just off the traffic circle. 1 Douglas Rd., P.O. Box 1432, Bisbee, 85603; 520-432-3567.

Camping

Shady Dell RV Park (see above) also has 12 full hookups with cable TV and laundry facilities for present-day RVers. 1 Douglas Rd., P.O. Box 1432, Bisbee, 85603; 520-432-3567.

Queen Mine RV Park

This is possibly the only park in the world that practically hangs on the edge of an open-pit mine, and the only RV park in historic downtown Bisbee. Located on the upper terrace of the mine, it has amazing views. From here you can walk to the historic district. Has 25 full hookups, showers, laundry, and cable TV. P.O. Box 488, Bisbee, 85603; 520-432-5006.

Where to Eat

There are many restaurants here, at least half of them in Old Bisbee, ranging from basic home cooking to what borders on haute cuisine.

Copper Queen Hotel Dining Room and Saloon—$$$$

A sophisticated menu and impeccable continental service at first seem incongruous in this little mining town. But as you settle into the mood created by lace curtains, candlelight, and fresh flowers, the seared rare ahi seems appropriate. The chef's European background is evident in the very thin, crispy-crust pizza, suggested as an appetizer, and in menu offerings that include pheasant confit with Belgian endive salad and grilled mallard duck breast. If you feel that someone is looking over your shoulder, it could be the ghosts of diners past, who included governors, gamblers, and presidents. Open daily, 7:00 A.M.–10:30 A.M.; 11:00 A.M.–2:30 P.M.; 5:30 P.M.–9:00 P.M.

Located in Copper Queen Hotel. 11 Howell St.; 520-432-2216.

Cafe Roka—$$$

This trendy place, a onetime department store in the 1907 Costello building, still has the huge metal doors through which stock was received. The original tin ceilings and maple flooring keep it connected to the past. Its two most-requested dishes are white corn and pine nut risotto cakes with jalapeño cream sauce, and roasted half duck with cranberry, honey, and merlot sauce. It is often fully booked during winter months, so make reservations early. Listed in *100 Best Restaurants in Arizona,* it has built a reputation for its contemporary Italian food. Open Wed.–Sat., 5:00–9:00 P.M. 35 Main St.; 520-432-5153.

Dot's Diner—$

This place is a mandatory stop. The classic 1957 deco-style eatery has all the great memories of diner days, including the food. Ten swiveling stools with magenta metal-flake tops, shiny stainless-steel interior, a green malt machine, and hand-lettered signs with features and specials are unchanged from Sputnik days. Silver and red with glowing neon, the diner was transported from the Los Angeles area. Bisbee berry pie, a luscious melange of raspberries and blackberries, is the specialty of chef Charles Lewis. Along with traditional diner fare, there's a vegetarian burger and good salads. Open Mon.–Tues., 7:00 A.M.–2:00 P.M.; Wed.–Sun., 7:00 A.M.–2:00 P.M. and 5:00 P.M.–8:00 P.M. Located at Shady Dell RV Park (see Where to Stay). 1 Douglas Rd.; 520-432-2046.

Services

The Bisbee Chamber of Commerce and Visitor Center

Open Mon.–Fri., 9:00 A.M.–5:00 P.M.; Sat. and Sun., 10:00 A.M.–4:00 P.M. 31 Subway St.; Bisbee, 85603; 520-432-5421. Website: www.arizonaguide.com/bisbee or www.bisbeearizona.com.

Tombstone

This little town has done a good job of reinventing itself. Part history, part entertainment, it has all the elements for a wholesome good time. Considered high desert at an elevation of 4,600 feet and surrounded by mountains, it is probably the most glamorized mining town in America. Today its population includes about 1,400 hardy souls, some of whom are employed in nearby Sierra Vista and Fort Huachuca.

Much of the fun of Tombstone is simply exploring. Start by picking up a map and list of sites and sights at the visitor center, plan your route, and set out. Stagecoaches and buckboards drawn by mules, Clydesdales, and other steeds clatter through the streets, providing local color and offering narrated tours.

History

Because prospector Ed Schieffelin was told he

Famed Boot Hill in Tombstone is filled with graves marked by humorous epitaphs.

would find only his tombstone in the Apache-infested San Pedro Valley, he named his first silver claim Tombstone. The surrounding hills, rich in silver ore, created a booming economy in the 1880s. The town became notorious for saloons, gambling houses, and the famous Earp-Clanton shoot-out at the OK Corral. More than 10,000 folks called Tombstone home. But by 1886, collapsing silver prices and a huge increase in groundwater in the mines contributed to the town's decline.

Yet it survived, pulling through the Depression and the indignity of Bisbee taking over as the county seat, earning the title "The Town Too Tough to Die." It built on its reputation to re-create itself as a Registered Historical Landmark that rapidly became a tourist attraction.

Festivals and Events

Vigilante Days

early Aug.
Western reenactments, fashion shows, and a chili

Tombstone, "The Town Too Tough to Die," has reinvented itself as a prime Old West tourist attraction.

cook-off are part of this three-day event. Tombstone Vigilantes, identified by their six-sided badges, belong to an organization that promotes a western atmosphere locally and statewide. Proceeds from this event go to the Vigilantes Charity Fund. The fashion show features originals and copies of clothes worn in Tombstone from the early 1880s through 1915. Other events are a 10K run, a 2K fun run, and street entertainment that goes on throughout the event. 520-457-9317.

Rendezvous of Gunfighters

late Aug.

If you're into shooting and the craft of guns, you'll love this event that draws gunfighter groups from across the country to participate in demonstrations and activities. An authentic costume parade features great gunfighter gear as worn by the men who blasted their way through the West. **520-457-9317.**

Seeing and Doing

Museums and Historic Sites

Bird Cage Theatre

A registered national monument, the theatre was more famous for "private performances" than for stage productions. The 14 "bird cage" crib compartments that hang from the ceiling were really small rooms used by ladies of the evening to entertain their clients. Opened in 1881, the saloon and dance hall were dominated by turmoil and rowdiness. It was the site of more than a dozen gunfights, remnants of which are obvious in the bullet holes that riddle the walls and floor. An 1889 showbill advertises the "Human Fly," a troop of lady gymnasts, and a painting of a rosy, rotund Fatima smiles down onto a bar pierced with a massive bullet hole. The Bird Cage closed in 1889 and through fortuitous farsighted thinking, the owner boarded it up completely intact so when it was reopened in 1934 its contents were close to their original state. Although its heydays lasted just eight years, 1881–1889, it was referred to by the distant *New York Times* as the "wildest, wickedest night spot between Basin St. and the Barbary Coast." Open daily, 8:00 A.M.–6:00 P.M., for self-guided tours. Sixth and Allen Sts., Tombstone, 85638; 520-457-3421. Website: www.tombstoneaz.net.

Boot Hill

The famous final resting place covers a sunny little hill reached via a gift and curio shop. Used from 1879 to 1884, when it was considered full, Boot Hill's more than 250 graves trace a rough-and-tumble history. "Here lies Lester Moore, Four slugs from a 44, No Les, No More," and "John Heath, taken from County Jail & lynched by Bisbee Mob in Tombstone Feb. 22, 1884" are among the eloquent epitaphs. The one above Les, say historians, is not authentic. Les never was. He's a figment of a filmmaker's imagination. Open daily, 7:30 A.M.–6:00 P.M. Located on Hwy. 80 as you enter Tombstone from the north. 520-457-3421.

OK Corral, Tombstone's Historama, *Tombstone Epitaph*

You can visit the site of the famous Earp-Clanton gunfight, then get a reprint of the edition of the *Tombstone Epitaph* that reported the shoot-out. The

Epitaph was started in 1880 and is still going strong, with the original presses still in place, if not in use. The Historama, a half-hour audiovisual presentation narrated by Vincent Price, details Tombstone's history. The OK Corral and Historama are next to each other on Allen St., located at Fifth and Fremont, near the city park.

The Rose Tree Inn Museum

This delightful museum owes its existence to a Lady Banksia rosebush shoot brought from Scotland in 1885 and lovingly tended. Millions of white blossoms appear each year, the sheer size of the bush earning it a place in the *Guinness Book of World Records*. Rooms at the inn are furnished with 1880s antiques brought by a young bride and her husband who hoped to prosper from the rich silver mines. Open daily, 9:00 A.M.–5:00 P.M. Located at Fourth and Toughnut. 520-457-3326.

Tombstone Courthouse State Historic Park

The brick courthouse, Cochise County's first, was built in 1882 at a cost of nearly $50,000, a princely sum for a public building in those days. To assure that justice was swift, a gallows was built in the adjacent courtyard. When the county seat was moved to Bisbee in 1931, the courthouse had no real use, so it stood vacant until 1955 when restoration began. It opened as a state park in 1959 and now contains photos and memorabilia from Tombstone's salad days. Small fee. Open daily, 8:00 A.M.–5:00 P.M. Located at Third and Toughnut; 520-457-3311. Website: www.pr.state.az.us.

Where to Stay

You'll find a number of bed-and-breakfasts and a few smaller motels right in town. Go about a mile north on Hwy. 80 to the Best Western Lookout Lodge to find a conventional large chain motel. Rates may go up at all Tombstone accommodations on special event weekends, and generally are higher Jan.–May.

Bed-and-Breakfasts

Tombstone Bordello—$$–$$$

Built in the 1800s in Tombstone's red-light district, the Bordello's rooms are spacious, with TVs, queen size beds, and private baths. A full breakfast is served in the dining room. 101 W. Allen St., Tombstone, 85638; 520-457-2394.

Marie's Bed and Breakfast—$$

Four rooms are furnished to Tombstone's glory days in a 1906 adobe home with original floors, windows, and woodwork that show generations of good care. A player piano provides entertainment, as does sittin' and rockin' on the front porch. Includes continental breakfast, or a voucher for breakfast next door at Don Teodoro's, at Fourth and Safford. P.O. Box 744, Tombstone, 85638; 520-457-3831. Website: www.theriver.com/maries.

Victoria's Bed and Breakfast—$$

Next to the courthouse, this 1880 stucco-adobe home is cottagelike and comfortable. Rooms have queen beds, cable TVs, and private baths. 211 Toughnut St., Tombstone, 85638; 520-457-3677 or 800-952-8216.

Motels

Trail Riders Inn and Mini RV Park—$$–$$$

In town, two blocks from Allen St., the 14-room motel has rooms with queen beds, TV, and phones. There are also RV spaces adjacent to the motel (see Camping). Located at Seventh and Fremont. 520-457-3573 or 800-574-0417. Website: www.tombstone1880.com/trailriders.

Tombstone Motel—$$

This small wood-frame single-story place in downtown is a member of AAA and has cozy, comfortable rooms. All have TV, some have refrigerators. They accept small, quiet pets. 502 E. Fremont St., Tombstone, 85638; 520-457-3478 or 888-455-3478. Website: www.tombstonemotel.com.

Camping

There are 10 RV spaces with hookups adjacent to the Trail Riders Inn and Mini RV Park (see above).

Wells Fargo RV Park

What it lacks in charm it makes up for in convenience. You can walk to everything. Full hookups with cable TV, showers, and laundry facilities. Located right in the middle of Tombstone a block from the courthouse and half a block from the OK Corral on Hwy. 80. P.O. Box 1076, Tombstone, 85638; 800-269-8266 or 520-457-3966. E-mail: wellsfargorv@si-systems.com. Website: www.si-systems.com/wellsfargorv.

Where to Eat

There are lots of fun, old-style places like Big Nose Kate's 1880 Saloon, the Longhorn, and Nellie Cashman's Restaurant. Since you don't come to Tombstone for an epicurean experience, it's no surprise that none particularly stands out, but most serve good, basic steak-and-potatoes fare.

Services

Public rest rooms are located in the city park at Third and Allen, and on Allen across Sixth St. from the Bird Cage Theatre.

Tombstone Visitor Center

Open daily, 10:00 A.M.–4:00 P.M. Located at Fourth and Fremont. P.O. Box 1314, Tombstone, 85638; 520-457-3929. Website: www.tombstone.org.

Sierra Vista

Once dependent on U. S. Army Fort Huachuca for its economic sustenance, Sierra Vista has become a substantial city of its own, mainly through efforts by city directors to publicize its amiable climate and great diversity of area activities. Somewhat of a retirement mecca, its cost of living is low and it has a small-town atmosphere, yet Tucson is just 70 miles to the northwest. Military retirees come here to use base privileges. Situated on the eastern slope of the Huachuca Mountains overlooking the San Pedro River Valley, Sierra Vista's name means "mountain view" in Spanish. You can look in any direction and see the Mule, Dragoon, Whetstone, or Huachuca Mountains.

Its main claim to fame, besides reliably good weather averaging 75°F in summer and 50°F in winter, is its position at the hub of one of the country's finest birding areas. A variety of habitats attract more than 100 species. These habitats include desert mesquite shrubland, grassland, brushland, riparian, oak woodland, and pine forest with Douglas fir and aspen at higher elevations. In this part of the state, elevations range from 2,389 feet in Tucson to 9,324 feet at the top of Mount Wrightson, with Sierra Vista at a comfortable 4,623 feet. The town itself, population 41,000, is low-key but lively, with 75 restaurants ranging from basic fast food to truly fine dining.

Fort Huachuca (located within Sierra Vista's city limits) is headquarters for the U.S. Army Information Systems Command, the Intelligence Center and School, the Electronic Proving Ground, the Department of Defense Joint Test Element of the Joint Tactical Command, the 11th Signal Brigade, and the U.S. Army Communications Security Logistic Activity. Currently about 11,700 military and civilian employees work there. An additional 11,200 military family members live in Sierra Vista.

History

Established in 1877 as a cavalry post to safeguard settlers, Fort Huachuca (say "wah-CHOO-cah") was the center of operations for thwarting the marauding Geronimo. Ramsey Canyon's history includes a period in the 1880s when miners from Bisbee and soldiers from Fort Huachuca flocked to the saloons and hotels that were built among the shady sycamores that line its walls. A few old cabins and foundations remain. Fort Huachuca, deactivated at the end of World War II and reactivated during the Korean conflict, became part of Sierra Vista in 1972.

Festivals and Events

For information on current events, call the Events Hotline, 520-459-3868.

Southwest Wings Birding Festival
mid-Aug.
One of the biggest birding festivals in the state,

it includes field trips to the San Pedro Riparian Area, Ramsey Canyon, Coronado National Historic Site, and Patagonia/Sonoita; lectures by nationally recognized Audubon authorities; plus owl prowls and bat stalks. Thousands of local and international visitors come to this highly respected event. It is based at a local hotel, where vendors and exhibitors set up tables and booths. Oftentimes live birds and animals are on display in connection with rehabilitative programs. Bird-banding classes, beginning birding workshops, identification skills, habitat recognition, and choosing and using binoculars are activities that also appeal to outdoor lovers. If you're thinking of going, book a hotel room early. If you're too late, try surrounding towns like Bisbee, one-half hour away.

Festival of Color Balloon Rally

mid-Oct.

Calm desert air makes this countywide event an ever-increasing success as more and more balloonists participate. Although not as dramatic as the Nov. balloon spectacular held in Phoenix, this event is a photographic delight because of the assurance of clean, blue skies as a background for their colorful display.

Outdoor Activities

Birding

Ramsey Canyon
Nature Conservancy Preserve

The best-known of Arizona's Nature Conservancy preserves, Ramsey Canyon is a shady, green 300-acre arroyo in the Huachuca Mountains that is practically a shrine to hummingbirds. From spring until early autumn, this unique biological crossroads hosts more than 14 species, attracted by an all-season stream that also appeals to other wildlife. Apr.–May are prime months (see Where to Stay for birders' packages if you plan to stay several nights). You'll see hummers hovering and darting, gorg-

The "Eyes of the Army" at Fort Huachuca commemorates the Indian Scouts who helped the white man.

ing themselves at feeders set up near the visitor center. Conveniently placed benches are best for quiet viewing. Among the 230 bird species that reportedly spend at least part of the year in the canyon, elegant trogons sometimes nest in the sycamores, and sulphur-bellied flycatchers are easy to spot. Golden eagles nest high in the

The Nature Conservancy's Ramsey Canyon is considered the hummingbird capital of the world.

Getting There

*Sierra Vista is about 70 miles southeast of Tucson just off Hwy. 90, 30 miles south of I-10. From Fort Huachuca, continue straight ahead from the main gate and you will be on Fry Blvd., Sierra Vista's main drag. The **municipal airport** has daily flights to Phoenix and other area cities via **Mesa Airlines.***

canyon and can sometimes be seen floating against an early morning sky.

You're likely to see a troop of coatimundis frolicking in the trees. The long-tailed critters, much like monkeys, are friendly and mischievous but can bite, so don't get close. White-tailed deer, in groups of three and four, will watch placidly if you stroll by quietly. An irrigation pond has become a home for the Ramsey Canyon leopard frog, found only in the Huachuca Mountains, and one of only two frog species in the United States known to call under water. They depend on the preserve for their future.

Ramsey Canyon Inn, adjacent to the preserve (see Where to Stay) has bed-and-breakfast accommodations for May and Aug., prime birding months. Parking in just 21 spaces is on a first-come first-served basis. Pets are not allowed in the preserve. About 6 miles south of Sierra Vista on Hwy. 92, take Ramsey Canyon Rd. and follow it 4 miles to the preserve. **27 Ramsey Canyon Rd., Hereford, 85615; 520-378-2785. Website: www.tnc.org.**

Bicycling

In 1997 *Bicycling* magazine rated Sierra Vista one of "America's 10 Best Bike Towns," lauding it for its "endless mountain biking and lightly trafficked, beautiful road loops." The town's moderate elevation and year-round climate that allows riding in any month also were

mentioned as pluses. To qualify for this honor, a city must have both on- and off-road rides suitable for many abilities.

MOUNTAIN BIKING

Brown Canyon

This ride, above the tree line, is a single track through the tall pines with a little bit of everything, incorporating almost every type of riding. The 5-mile loop crosses a creek, then comes back to Ramsey Canyon. It takes one-half to one hour, depending on riders' strength and ability, and is doable by riders at all levels. From Sierra Vista, go **south on Hwy. 92 for 6 miles, turn right onto Ramsey Canyon Rd., and proceed 1.5 miles to Brown** Canyon, which is marked, and turn right.

San Pedro River

This easy, flat, 14-mile, one-way ride extends from Sierra Vista to the Mexican border, following the river along a riparian area filled with large cottonwoods. Stop and dangle your feet in the river, bring a picnic, and enjoy the cool shade. Park at the bird sanctuary on Charleston Rd., east of Sierra Vista, and follow the riverside trail past Hereford Rd. to the Mexican Border.

ROAD BIKING

One of the reasons Sierra Vista is so cycling-friendly is that roads have wide shoulders, and motorists and other riders are generally courteous. These on-road routes require caution, but generally are not heavily trafficked. For more information on cycling in the Sierra Vista area, stop in at **Sun 'N Spokes Inc.** Friendly folks will provide you with a detailed trail map of Cochise County that has virtually all the county's best cycling trails on one map. A ride calendar lists 30–40 rides per month, rated by difficulty, that are fun and free. "It's about who has the biggest smile at the end of the trip," say the folks at Sun 'N Spokes. Open Mon.–Fri., 9:00 A.M.–6:00 P.M.; Sat., 9:00 A.M.–5:00 P.M. **164 E. Fry Blvd.; 520-458-0685. The Dawn to Dust Mountain Bike Club** has a helpful **website: www.primenet.com/~tom held/ddtrails.html.**

Bisbee Loop

This challenging 60-mile loop is part of the annual La Vuelta de Bisbee Stage Race, the oldest continuous road race in the United States. It follows **Hwy. 90 east to Hwy. 80 up over Mule Mountain, through the tunnel, then descends into Bisbee. It returns to Sierra Vista via Hwy. 92.**

Charleston Rd. to Tombstone

Named for the ghost town it passes through along the San Pedro River, this easy-to-moderate 17-mile ride starts in Sierra Vista **at Charleston Rd. and Hwy. 90** (there's a Wal-Mart on that corner) **and follows Charleston.** At the point where a small bridge crosses the San Pedro, a town named Charleston once flourished, in the 1880s when mines were working overtime. But when the mines died, so did Charleston, and today adobe walls and sheets of tin are all that remain. The ride **ends on Allen St. in Tombstone.**

West Gate Ride

On Fort Huachuca Army Post, this up-and-downer keeps you shifting gears for 17 miles. A dozen trails on the post include **Stampede Trails,** mainly a horse trail that begins across from Wren Arena, and **Arena Loop,** which begins at the post cemetery and loops around Wren Arena with some steep, rocky climbs. Enter the post through the **main gate at Fry Blvd. and Buffalo Soldier Trail.** You will be asked for drivers license, registration, and proof of insurance, then issued a temporary base pass and a map.

Golf

Retirees lament that there are just two golf courses in the immediate Sierra Vista area. Fortunately, they're both good ones.

Mountain View Golf Course

On Fort Huachuca property, this course with 18 high-desert holes is open to civilians. Following the base of the pretty Huachuca Mountains, the course has water on five holes. Come through the fort's **main gate at Fry Blvd. and Buffalo Soldier Trail** for directions. 520-533-7092.

Pueblo del Sol Golf Course

Part of Sierra Vista's Country Club community, this course has Kentucky bluegrass fairways and bent-grass greens that wind through lovely homes with mountains all around. It's been around for 25 years, and so has the comfortable look and feel of a truly mature course. The 6,600-yard, par 72 layout is PGA rated and open to the public. Located off Hwy. 92 in Country Club Estates. **2770 St. Andrews Dr., Sierra Vista, 85650; 520-378-6444.**

Hiking

To join a group hike, inquire with the Huachuca Hiking Club, which has regular local hikes Nov.–Apr., Tues., 7:30 A.M.; and May–Oct., Tues., 7:00 A.M. They usually begin at the east side of the grocery store parking lot **at Fry Blvd. and Seventh St.** Write to the club at **P.O. Box 3555, Sierra Vista, 85636-3555; 520-459-8959. Website: www.primenet.-com/~tom held/hhc.html.**

Coronado National Historic Site

The 600-foot Coronado Cave was formed more than 250 million years ago when southern Arizona was a sea. Inside are stalagmites, helectites, and flowstones, identified by numbers on the map provided by the visitor center. Occasionally bats inhabit the cave and should not be disturbed. A 1.5-mile, round-trip **hike to Coronado Cave** requires map and free permit from the visitor center, and two flashlights per person. **Joe's Canyon Trail** is tougher, climbing about 1,000 feet in the first mile, but levels out for the remainder of its 3-mile length. Only the fittest of the fit should tackle the **Crest Trail,** which climbs for 2 miles, then follows the crest of the Huachuca Mountains to

Despite Arizona's desert reputation, golf courses are lush and green, often with mountain views.

Miller Peak, the highest point in the mountains. Open daily, 8:00 A.M.–5:00 P.M. Located 5 **miles south of Hereford and 21 miles south of Sierra Vista off Hwy. 92.** The turnoff to the memorial is clearly posted. 520-366-5515. Website: www.nps.gov.

Hamburg Trail in Ramsey Canyon

Follow the main canyon's rough dirt road 0.5 mile from The Nature Conservancy visitor center. A sign on the left marks the Hamburg Trail, which heads uphill. You'll immediately realize the wisdom of the trail builders who placed benches to encourage hikers to rest. If you move steadily for about 45 minutes, you'll come to an overlook with a spectacular view of the forests, grasslands, and the town of Sierra Vista. Watch for golden eagles floating on thermals.

From the canyon you can go directly into the surrounding national forest where there are more than **120 miles of trail.** Violent thunderstorms often pelt the area July–Aug., so be prepared. Ramsey Canyon is the first canyon south of Sierra Vista on Hwy. 92. Turn right at Ramsey Canyon Rd. and follow it approximately 4 miles to The Nature Conservancy preserve. 27 **Ramsey Canyon Rd., Hereford, 85615; 520-378-2785. Website: www.tnc.org.**

Seeing and Doing

Museums and Historic Sites

Arizona Folklore Preserve

In addition to its hummingbirds and coatimundis, Ramsey Canyon holds another treasure. The Arizona Folklore Preserve, part of the University of Arizona South Campus, is open now, with additional facilities scheduled for a mid-2001 completion date. The project is spearheaded by Dolan Ellis, Arizona's Official State Balladeer for more than three decades. His goal is to provide a place that protects the songs, legends, myths, and stories of Arizona. Ellis, an original member of the New Christy Minstrels in the 1960s, earned a number of gold records and a Grammy during those years. Longtime Arizona residents and visitors to Scottsdale in the 1960s remember Ellis as the talented proprietor of Dolan's, a folk-music nightspot on the corner of Camelback and Scottsdale Rds.

in Scottsdale. The not-for-profit preserve will have a 44-seat theater to showcase presentations and performances highlighting Arizona legends. In an audiovisual recording facility, visiting folk artists produce tapes and compact disks, offered for sale in the preserve's bookstore. Performances are held Sat.–Sun., 2:00 P.M. Take Hwy. 92 south from Sierra Vista about 6 miles. Turn west on Ramsey Canyon Rd. for about 3 miles to the preserve. 44 **Ramsey Canyon Rd., Hereford, 85615; 520-378-6165.** Website: www.arizonafolklore.com.

Hikers explore the river and cottonwoods in the San Pedro Riparian National Conservation Area.

Coronado National Historic Site

Here, at the southernmost end of the gently folded Huachuca Mountains, almost 5,000 acres commemorate the first major exploration of the American Southwest by Europeans. The memorial follows the route traveled by Don Francisco Vasquez de Coronado and his men in the 1500s in search of riches. White-tailed deer, coatimundi, gray fox, and javelina are frequently seen residents. A paved road winds through colorful oaks to the visitor center. From the visitor center you can drive to Montezuma Pass over a mostly dirt and gravel road for a spectacular view. Hiking trails include one to Coronado Cave (see Hiking).

The visitor center has displays tracing the explorations of Coronado and the Spanish conquistadors in 1540. Authentic 450-year-old armor including a chain-mail helmet, dagger, and spurs are displayed under glass. You're invited to touch replicas of these to see how Spanish soldiers must have felt under their protective weight. A small gallery of nature photographs shows the area's wildlife. Adjacent to the visitor center, a 50-yard nature trail introduces some of the area's plants. No camping. Open daily, 8:00 A.M.–5:00 P.M. Located 5 miles south of Hereford and 21 **miles south of Sierra Vista off Hwy. 92.** The turnoff to the memorial is clearly posted. 520-366-5515. Website: www.nps.gov.

Fort Huachuca Museum

This thoughtfully planned series of museum buildings, located on the post, are outstanding places to get a sense of U.S. Army history on

the Southwestern frontier. The main building, complete with creaky wood floors, at various times served as bachelor officers quarters, a chapel, home to the base chaplain, and finally in 1960 the museum. The series of rooms has displays on the last Indian scout, who retired in 1947, and on types of horse- and mule-drawn wagons used for freight, as ambulances, and for personnel transportation. The base's earliest residents, the Hohokam Indians, are represented with pre-Columbian artifacts.

Don't miss the area dedicated to the Buffalo Soldiers. At one time the post was home to all four famous black regiments, the Army's 24th and 25th Infantry, and the 9th and 10th Cavalry. These men, former slaves, were commanded by white officers to help control the Indians, an irony that received little attention at the time but has been remarked on recently in books and motion pictures. Buffalo Soldiers got their name from the Plains Indians, who thought their hair had an appearance similar to the curly buffalo.

Open Mon.–Fri., 9:00 A.M.–4:00 P.M.; Sat.–Sun., 1:00 P.M.–4:00 P.M.; closed Thanksgiving, Christmas, and New Year's Day. Enter the post through the **main gate at Fry Blvd. and Buffalo Soldier Trail.** You will be asked for drivers license, registration, and proof of insurance, then issued a temporary base pass and a map directing you to the museum area, **Fort Huachuca Museum 520-533-3898, Gift Shop 520-458-4716. Website: huachuca-www. army.mil.**

Nature Centers

San Pedro Riparian National Conservation Area

Forming the eastern edge of the town of Sierra Vista, this lovely area along the San Pedro River is so environmentally important that it has been designated one of the "Last Great Places" by The Nature Conservancy, one of just a dozen such places in the Western Hemisphere. The river flows north from Mexico, joining the Gila River near Winkelman. Segments of the river flow all year long, providing a reliable water supply for 80 species of mammals. Huge cottonwoods and willows, among the most water-dependent trees, line the river, providing bird and insect habitat.

Almost 400 bird species, two-thirds of all North American species, including grey and red-tailed hawks, green kingfishers, coots, and grebes, have been observed on the river. The slender, rust-capped green-tailed towhee breeds in northern Arizona, then comes to the San Pedro for the winter. The area shelters more than three dozen species of amphibians and reptiles, including the Gila monster. You may spot a giant bullfrog hiding among the bulrushes, or you may just hear the splash as it plops into the water, scattering the tiny mosquito fish that dart in the shallows. Bullfrogs were introduced for food as froglegs that are delicious delicacies, but the downside is that they are voracious and will eat anything. At one time beavers were plentiful along the river, were trapped out decades ago, and recently have been reintroduced to the ecosystem. They're doing well, building dams, which helps restore reparian habitat. An excellent bookstore and gift shop, in a historic adobe house, are open daily, 9:30 A.M.–4:30 P.M. The area is managed by the Bureau of Land Management. Located 7 **miles east of Sierra Vista just off Hwy. 90. 520-458-3559. Website: www.blm.gov.**

Scenic Drives

Most travelers going south to Sierra Vista leave I-10 at Hwy. 90 and head on into town. But there's another route, on Hwy. 83, that exits I-10 and continues south 29 miles to Sonoita. If you are coming from the south, you can stop at the Sierra Vista Chamber of Commerce (see Services) and pick up (for $10) a driving tape called "How the West Was Fun," narrated by Willcox native son Rex Allen. It points out landmarks and fills you in on historical notes. Part of the drive, marked by colorful Scenic Route signs, crosses the Coronado National Forest, which covers most of southern Arizona in a patchwork of preserved areas and was named for the famous Spanish explorer who came through here in 1540. Unless you're accustomed to the Arizona notion of forest, you may wonder where the trees are. In this state, a forest may consist of cactuses, scrub, low vegetation, and just about any living thing that covers the surface of the earth. To the west are the Santa Rita Mountains, stretching almost to the Mexican border; on the right are the Empire Mountains, behind which are the Whetstones. The mountains catch the moist air that creates rainfall, essential to keep the desert flourishing. The road passes through primitive areas where hunting, fishing, and bird-watching are popular pastimes. The town of Sonoita was a railhead for the cattle industry in the 1920s and 1930s, understandable when you consider the open grasslands and prairie that you've just passed through. It now lies on the edge of Arizona's emerging wine industry around Elgin. From Sonoita you can hook up with Hwy. 82 and proceed east to Hwy. 90. The tape narrates the trip to Sierra Vista, continuing on to Tombstone and Bisbee.

Where to Stay

Accommodations range from basic motels to multiroom resorts, many with housekeeping units. Some have birders' packages if you plan to stay several nights. The ones mentioned here offer something other than a traditional motel stay.

Bed-and-Breakfasts

Ramsey Canyon Inn, Bed & Breakfast—$$$–$$$$

Adjacent to the Ramsey Canyon Preserve and leased by The Nature Conservancy for visitors to the preserve, this delightful inn has six rooms with private baths in a main building, and two one-bedroom housekeeping units that accommodate four and overlook Ramsey Creek. Duplex units appropriate for four (breakfast not included) are equipped with cooking utensils. **31 Ramsey Canyon Rd., Hereford, 85615; 520-378-3010. Website: www.tnc.org.**

Casa de San Pedro Bed & Breakfast—$$$

This upscale territorial-style inn with hand-carved furniture from Mexico, has 10 guest rooms around a central courtyard, where a fountain creates a gracious oasis. Rooms have private baths and a king or two double beds. It's adjacent to the southern end of the San Pedro Riparian National Conservation Area, so birding and hiking are just out the door. It includes full breakfast. Located 20 miles southeast of Sierra Vista. Take Hwy. 92 south to Palominas, and go north (left) onto Palominos Rd. Continue 2 miles, turn east (right) onto Waters Rd., and proceed 1 mile to Yell Ln. **8933 S. Yell Ln., Hereford, 85615; 520-366-1300. Website: www.naturesinn.com.**

Hotels

Windemere—$$$

What takes this large, comfortable hotel out of the ordinary is that the double room rate includes a happy hour with table service and a good spread of hors d'oeuvres, and a complete buffet breakfast with all kinds of hot entrees. Rooms have microwaves and coffeemakers. For total comfort in the center of Sierra Vista, this place can't be beat. **2047 S. Hwy. 92, Sierra Vista, 85635; 800-825-4656 or 520-459-5900. Website: windemere-hotel.com.**

Camping

Lakeview Campground

Centered around Parker Canyon Lake, one of the few sizable bodies of water in the area, this campground has rest rooms and drinking water, but no hookups at its 64 sites. The lake gets a fair amount of day use by anglers pursuing channel catfish, sunfish, rainbow trout, and largemouth bass. Open all year, at an elevation of 5,422 feet, it's a cool respite from summer's heat in other parts of the state. **Take Hwy. 83 south from Sonoita about 25 miles** to the lake.

Sierra Vista Mobile Home Village

It has 30 spaces and full hookups in a mountain setting. Coyotes call at night, and it's not unusual to see javelina and quail near the park. Fairly upscale, with indoor and outdoor pools, spa, minigolf, a weight room, a lending library, a barber, and a beauty salon. Located on Hwy. 90, 2 miles east of Sierra Vista. **733 S. Deer Creek Ln., Sierra Vista, 85635; 520-459-1690 or 800-955-7606.**

Where to Eat

As you come into town, there are any number of fast-food restaurants and coffee shops along Fry Blvd. that cater particularly to dashboard diners. This proliferation has led locals to dub the street "French Fry Blvd." There also are steak houses; Vietnamese, Chinese, and Mexican restaurants; and informal cafes and buffets.

The Grille at Pueblo del Sol Country Club—$$$–$$$$

This attractive dining room has an eclectic menu and overlooks a lovely golf course. The upscale setting doesn't require getting dressed up; clean jeans and a shirt are perfectly appropriate. Try to get there at sunset and watch the sky change colors behind the mountains. Truly gourmet fare is presented in the evening, while breakfast and lunch feature inventive, well-priced choices. Even though it's in the desert, count on at least one flown-in fresh-fish selection each evening. Open Wed.–Sun., 7:00 A.M.–9:00 P.M. Located in Country Club Estates. **2770 St. Andrews Dr.; 520-378-2476.**

Mesquite Tree—$$$

Entertainment comes from a number of sources in this friendly place. A model train chugs overhead as it travels around the perimeter of the ceiling of the Arizona room, and the patio is filled with vintage stoves along with the hundred-year-old mesquite tree that gives the place its name. During most months, meals are served outdoors to take advantage of the view of the Huachuca Mountains. Count on good steaks and ribs in large portions. Hikers often pop in after a day in the canyons, so you're assured that the atmosphere is casual and comfortable, and you can come as you are. Open Tues.–Sat., 5:00 P.M.–9:00 P.M.; Sun., 5:00 P.M.–8:00 P.M. Located at **Hwy. 92 at Carr Canyon Rd. 520-378-2758.**

Daisy Mae's Stronghold—$$–$$$

A casual, easygoing steak house, it has won awards for mesquite-barbecued steaks done on indoor and outdoor grills. A generous 32-ounce porterhouse can daunt all but hard-core beef fans, and a full rack of baby back pork ribs almost guarantees you'll need a doggy bag. The building started as an 1870s trading post, became a post office, then a general store and a stagecoach stop. Existing bedrooms are remnants of the late 1800s when soldiers at Fort Huachuca used them to rendezvous with ladies of the evening. Open Mon.–Thurs., 4:00 P.M.–9:30 P.M.; Fri.–Sat., 4:00 P.M.–10:30 P.M.; Sun., 4:00 P.M.–9:00 P.M. Lounge opens daily, 3:00 P.M. **332 N. Garden Ave.; 520-452-8099.**

Outside Inn—$$–$$$

We like the casual, personal atmosphere of this smaller inn. The floor is covered with Saltillo tile, and furnishings are attractive natural wood. Try the outstanding veggie club sandwich, and if you happen in on a Fri., don't miss the clam chowder. During appropriate weather, meals are served on an umbrella-shaded patio that doubles as an herb garden, providing fresh mint to complement iced tea. Open Mon.–Fri., 11:00 A.M.–1:30 P.M. and 5:00 P.M.–9:00 P.M.; Sat., 5:00 P.M.–9:00 P.M. Watch for it on your left as you drive south on Hwy. 92, because it is set back a bit from the highway. **4907 S. Hwy. 92; 520-378-4645.**

The Bright Spot—$$–$$$

Highly recommended by locals, this unobtrusive little gem is located in the town of Hereford about 20 miles south of Sierra Vista. There's practically a cult following for Wednesday night rib specials. Other menu items are prime rib, steaks, burgers, and seafood. Three separate dining rooms have a rustic western decor that's comfortable no matter how you're dressed. Open Mon.–Sat., 4:00 P.M.–9:00 P.M.; Sun., noon–9:00 P.M. **10989 Hwy. 92, Hereford; 520-366-5203.**

Popeyes—$

Part of the famous franchised chain, but with a personality all its own, this friendly Popeyes specializes in spicy fried chicken. It shows its Cajun roots in menu items that include red beans and rice, Cajun battered fries, and sometimes shrimp or chicken étouffée and jambalaya. Great grub that does little violence to the budget. Open Mon.–Sat., 10:30 A.M.–8:00 P.M. Located on **Fort Huachuca army base, in Bldg. 82301 at Bissell and Allen. 520-459-4275.**

Services

Sierra Vista Chamber of Commerce

Knowledgeable volunteers, cheerfully enthusiastic about their community, will patiently take as much time as you wish to answer questions. Open Tues.–Sat., 8:00 A.M.–5:00 P.M. **21 E. Wilcox Dr., Sierra Vista, 85635; 800-288-3861 or 520-458-6940. Website: www.sierra vistachamber.org.**

Arizona Hummingbirds

Their movements are so swift and precise, they look computerized. Their colors are as brilliant as precious gems, displaying jewel-like iridescence that seems to come and go. They'll attack a bird many times their size, and can beat their wings more than 870 times per minute. They can fly sideways and backward, hover in place, and execute amazing aerobatic displays that are the envy of pilots everywhere.

During Victorian times, hundreds of thousands of the tiny birds were killed and stuffed to adorn women's hats. Fortunately, fashion's whims changed and legislation protected future hummingbirds from such devastating indignities.

Hummers, so called because of the sound produced by their wings, have a special job in nature. They aid bees, moths, and bats in the process of pollination. While drawing nectar from blossoms, their heads and long slender bills become dusted with pollen that they brush on the next blossom they visit.

Of the 14 species of hummers found in Ramsey Canyon (the state as a whole claims 17 species), five are common and the ones you will most likely be able to identify.

Blue-throated—Its broad tail, with big white patches, and overall larger size make this hummer identifiable, rather than its light blue throat, which sometimes is difficult to see.

Magnificent—Almost as large as the blue-throated, it has a bright green throat. From a distance it looks all black, but has white streaks around the eye.

Black-chinned—It has a white collar under a black throat that is fairly easy to identify. It is difficult to distinguish this little guy from a Costa's or a ruby-throated, common in the east.

Anna's—At about 4 inches long, it's medium-sized by hummer standards, and the only U.S. hummingbird with a red crown. Its metallic green back is absolutely dazzling when it catches the sun.

Costa's—Smaller than Anna's and not as common in Ramsey Canyon, it has a brilliant purple or amethyst throat and long side feathers. Its high whistling song sounds like a zinging bullet. An identifying behavior is soaring between flower clusters rather than zeroing in on a straight line.

Even if you never identify a single hummer, you'll be mesmerized by their collective beauty.

Wine Country

The word "wine" usually brings to mind California's hospitable Napa and Sonoma Valleys and the rich French countryside. But it has been established by viticulturists that the soil and climate at 5,000 feet in parts of southern Arizona mirror those of Burgundy and Bordeaux so faithfully that producing fine wine is not only possible but happening regularly.

Covering just 300 acres, the state's vineyard acreage is less than 0.1 percent of the vineyard acreage of California, yet many vintners supply restaurants and beverage stores around the state with award-winning vintages. Vineyards in southern Arizona are clustered around Willcox, Vail, near Sonoita, and in small areas east and west of Nogales, in a small wine belt that parallels the Mexican border. If you visit in Aug.–early Sept., you should be able to see grapes on the vines about to be harvested. Most wineries welcome visitors and offer tastings for a small charge, but because circumstances change seasonally, call ahead to verify hours.

History

Arizona and wine have been compatible as far back as the 1600s when the Spanish padres brought vine cuttings from Europe and gave wine-producing a fling. By the late 1800s the cattle industry was flourishing near Elgin and Sonoita, and Elgin was a railroad station on the Calabasas-Fairbanks branch, from which steers were shipped to market.

More recent history records that the present-day award-winning Sonoita Vineyards were developed by Dr. Gordon Dutt, professor emeritus of soil and water science at the University of Arizona. The winery began production in 1982, with the first public release in 1984. In 1989 its cabernet sauvignon was selected for President Bush's Inaugural Food and Wine Gala.

Seeing and Doing

Museums and Historic Sites

La Capilla de Santa Maria Consoladora des Afligadoros

The name of this charming little shrine means Chapel of St. Mary, Consoler of the Afflicted. Overseen by the Monks of the Vine, a group of area vintners, it is the site of the Apr. Blessing of the Grapes ceremony and the Aug. Harvest Festival. The little Santa Fe-style chapel is nondenominational and welcomes all for quiet, contemplative moments. **In the tiny village of Elgin near Sonoita.**

Wineries

In addition to the wineries in this region, **Arizona Vineyards (520-287-7972)** is located 2 miles east of Nogales on Hwy. 82 (see Nogales, Arizona, and Nogales, Sonora, chapter).

Callaghan Vineyards

The outstanding wines produced by this small company are available at restaurants including Karen's Wine Country Cafe in Sonoita (see Where to Eat), Janos in Tucson (see Where to Eat in Tucson chapter), and AJs Markets in Phoenix and

Tucson. It's worth seeking out their Callaghan, Cochise County fume blanc and their Callaghan, Sonoita, Buena Suerte Cuvee. Tastings at the vineyards Sun., 11:00 A.M.–4:00 P.M. Call for information and directions. 520-455-5322.

Dark Mountain Winery and Brewery

This beautiful Spanish-style building at the base of the Rincon Mountains has a cool patio with a fountain and a graceful olive tree. Among its award winners are a cabernet sauvignon, a Johannesburg Riesling, and an Arizona gold sherry that is truly spectacular. Warm, sunny days; cool, dry nights; and cold winters, plus the slightly acidic, sandy loam soils of the Sulphur Springs Valley produce the grapes necessary for these wines. It also is the site of the Dark Mountain Brewery, making it the only winery and brewery combo in the state. Informal guided tours and tastings are offered Mon.–Sat., 10:00 A.M.–6:00 P.M.; Sun., noon–6:00 P.M. Located 20 miles south of Tucson in Vail. **13605 E. Benson Hwy., P.O. Box 130, Vail, 85641; 520-762-5777.** Website: www.darkmountainbrewery.com.

Domaines Ellam

This new winery is owned by His Noble Lord, The Right Honourable, The Earl of Ellam, a hereditary Lord of Scotland, and produces Ultra-Premium wines. They include two Grand Reserves, three Clarets, and a Reserve Blanc, all produced in small quantities in the European style. Grapes are stomped for crush. Tastings daily, 10:00 A.M.–5:00 P.M. **471 Elgin Rd., HC1, Box 46, Elgin, 85611; 520-455-4734.** Website: www.earl-of-ellam.com.

Sonoita Vineyards

Pack a picnic lunch and come for tasting at this recently expanded vineyard. The red, sandy loam soil here and a longer growing season than in France produce award-winning cabernet sauvignons. Other favorites include a fume blanc and a Sonora rossa, a spicy red Chianti-style wine. Open daily, 10:00 A.M.–4:00 P.M. Located **12.5 miles southeast of Sonoita. HCR 1, Box 33, Elgin, 85611; 520-455-5893.**

> ### *Getting There*
> *Most of the places in this chapter are near Sonoita, which is 26 miles south of I-10 on Hwy. 83 at its junction with Hwy. 82. Elgin is about 14 miles east of Sonoita.*

Village of Elgin Winery

This winery stomps its grapes and uses new wood casks for aging. Winemaker/owners Gary and Kathy Reeves welcome visitors. Outstanding pinot noir, cabernet sauvignon, and Colombard. Tastings daily, 10:00 A.M.–5:00 P.M. Next door to the chapel in downtown Elgin. **HC 1, Box 47, Elgin, 85611; 520-455-9309.** Website: www.concentric.net/~elgnwine.

Where to Stay

Bed-and-Breakfasts

Rainbow's End Bed & Breakfast—$$$$

Not only you, but you *and* your horse, are welcome at this equine-friendly bed-and-breakfast. It's a 64-acre working ranch where Rocky Mountain, Mountain Pleasure, and Kentucky Mountain saddle horses are bred and raised. The owners have completed a renovation of the original ranch manager's home, which now is a four bedroom/four bath inn with a living/dining/kitchen, great room, and two patios. Equine guests are put up in an 18-stall barn. Each 12-foot-by-12-foot stall has an automatic waterer and a 100-foot run. Located on Hwy. 83 in Sonoita, 1 mile south of the crossroads of Hwys. 82 and 83. **3088 Hwy. 83, P.O. Box 717, Sonoita, 85637; 520-455-0202.** Website: www.gaitedmountainhorses.com.

The Vineyards Bed & Breakfast—$$$

Set on a knoll overlooking tidy rows of vines, the Hacienda Los Encinos dates to 1916 when

The Village of Elgin Winery relies on a bit of heavenly help for a good grape harvest.

the original ranch was built. Today, Ron and Sue DeCosmo have completely refurbished the place to provide three guest rooms plus a separate casita with sitting room and bath. Here at 5,100 feet elevation, summers are warm, but there is snow in the winter. You'll be greeted by Molly and Rosie, a pair of black labs, as well as Pepperoni and Cocoa, classic Jerusalem burros with their crosslike marking on backs and withers. Ron cooks a full breakfast. From The Vineyards it's an easy drive to wineries and birding territory. **92 S. Los Encinos Rd., P.O. Box 1227, Sonoita, 85637; 520-455-4749. Website: www.virtualcities.com.**

Inns and Guest Ranches

Crown C Ranch—$$$–$$$$

This ranch is truly unique because you are completely on your own. Chances are you'll never see the staff, except maybe on your arrival. The rambling 60-year-old adobe ranch house has individual rooms with baths that can be con-

nected in a number of configurations to accommodate groups or couples, and a separate guest house that's ideal for a family. There are two complete kitchens (no meals are served unless you arrange for them), barbecues, firewood for fireplaces, a swimming pool, and a tennis court. Horses for riding are available from nearby stables. You come here for total privacy, to enjoy the absolutely serene surroundings, watch the birds, read a book, appreciate that there is this much open land and peace and quiet left in the world. **Take Hwy. 82 west of Sonoita 2.7 miles and look for the Crown C brand sign. Turn right and drive 1 mile** to the ranch. **P.O. Box 984, Sonoita, 85637; 520-455-5739.**

Sonoita Inn—$$$–$$$$

Common areas in this 18-room western country lodge are galleries of local history, filled with photos and artifacts. Large guest rooms, named after local ranches, have private baths, TVs, VCRs, and telephones. Room rates include a substantial continental breakfast. Located **at Hwys. 82 and 83 in Sonoita. P.O. Box 99, Sonoita, 85637; 520-455-5935. Website: www.sonoitainn.com.**

Where to Eat

The Grasslands Restaurant, Bakery, Bar—$$–$$$

A fabulous place to eat in this out-of-the-way little town, Grasslands offers just-baked breads, muffins, Danish, breakfast breads, filled croissants, quiches, and more. The family-owned place draws clientele from Tucson as well as surrounding ranches. The light wood decor, airy and bright, adds to its upbeat atmosphere. Local and organic wines, German beers, and cocktails are available. Don't miss the feta and spinach-stuffed croissant, always freshly baked. On Sat. there are authentic German entrees along with mellow guitar, mandolin, or fiddle music. Open Wed.–Sun., 8:00 A.M.–3:00 P.M. **3119 S. Hwy. 83, Sonoita; 520-455-4770.**

Karen's Wine Country Cafe—$$–$$$

Southern Arizona's flourishing wine industry has created enough cachet to support upscale fine-food restaurants. In Sonoita, this unexpected little gem, along with Grasslands (see above), is a good example. Karen's is a cheery mix of press-back chairs and blue mixed-print tablecloths. Many Arizona wines are stocked, so you can try them with a meal after you've been to the vineyards for tastings. The menu includes truly inventive salads (the soy ginger dressing is outstanding) served with Karen's fresh-baked bread, excellent steaks, always a grilled fish, and desserts (like Mexican spice cake) to die for. Open Sun.–Wed., 11:00 A.M.–6:00 P.M.; Thu.–Sat., 11:00 A.M.–4:00 P.M. and 5:00 P.M.–9:00 P.M. **3266 Hwy. 82, Sonoita; 520-455-5282, fax 520-455-0075.**

The Steak Out Restaurant and Saloon—$$–$$$$

This typically cowboy eatery was a fixture in Sonoita for years, suffered a devastating fire, and has reopened to serve diners its famous mesquite pit–broiled steaks, chicken, ribs, and more. Prime and choice cuts include a huge porterhouse that's a carnivore's fantasy. Everything comes with beans, bread, and a big family-style salad. Open Mon.–Thurs., 5:00 P.M.–9:00 P.M.; Fri.–Sun., 11:00 A.M.–10:00 P.M. Located next to the Sonoita Inn **at Hwys. 82 and 83. 520-455-5205.**

Services

Arizona Wine Commission

For more information on the Arizona wine industry and a map showing vineyard locations, call the commission **(Dept. of Agriculture),** 602-542-0877.

Patagonia

This unassuming little town is a good place to headquarter for exploring the Patagonia–Sonoita Creek Preserve (see Birding), or as a jumping-off point for visiting Nogales (see the next chapter). Located about 18 miles north of the Mexican border at an elevation of 4,044 feet, it is in a pretty little valley with the Santa Rita Mountains to the north and the Patagonias to the south. A charming feature is a butterfly garden in the center of town, planted with desert senna, lantana, and other blooming plants that attract pipevine swallowtails, queen butterflies, fritillaries, and more. Picnic tables nearby provide shady sites for lunch alfresco.

History

Patagonia takes its name, as do the mountains, from the Patagonia Mine, later called the Mowry Mine, that produced substantial quantities of silver and lead ore in the mid-1800s. The Patagonia post office was established in 1866, when the Southern Pacific Railroad reached the town. The old station, now the town hall, still stands in the center of town. Surrounding grasslands have supported ranching for decades.

Festivals and Events

Celebration of Arts & Music

second weekend in Oct.

For more than a decade, this two-day event has drawn crowds from as far away as Phoenix for its juried arts and crafts displays and music that usually includes mariachi bands, country western and bluegrass music, Native American musicians, and other performers. Sun. festivities begin with an old-fashioned pancake breakfast. Held **at Patagonia Town Park in center of downtown Patagonia. 520-394-0060.**

Outdoor Activities

Birding

Patagonia–Sonoita Creek Preserve

The Nature Conservancy's first preserve in Arizona, its 770 acres include an exceptionally rich cottonwood-willow riparian habitat with 100-year-old trees that provide homes for more than 260 bird species. The greatest diversity of birds appears Apr.–June, before summer's heat sets in and chiggers become voracious. But because of the large number of migrants that pass through, any season has good birding.

The ever-running stream supports four native fish species that are critically endangered in the Southwest. The Gila topminnow, among the most imperiled, recently has been found to contain cells that divide in ways to mimic cancer, making it an invaluable tool in the study of the disease. You can expect to see white-tailed deer and perhaps a coatimundi, with plenty of fluffy-tailed Arizona gray squirrels to keep you entertained. A new visitor center has rest rooms, water, and interpretive displays. A number of

Getting There

Patagonia is about 18 miles north of Nogales on the Mexican border on Hwy. 82, and 12 miles south of Sonoita. From Phoenix, take I-10 south through Tucson to AZ 83. Turn south and follow AZ 83 for 26 miles to AZ 82. Follow AZ 82 for 11 miles to Patagonia.

The wood-frame Patagonia town hall once was a busy railroad station.

trails provide easy walking. A guided walk is held Sat., 9:00 A.M. Open Wed.–Sun., 7:30 A.M.–4:00 P.M. Located about 60 miles southeast of Tucson. From Patagonia, turn **west on Fourth Ave.**, then south on Pennsylvania. Cross the creek and go about 1.5 miles to entrance on Blue Haven Rd. P.O. Box 815, Patagonia, 85624; 520-394-2400 phone and fax. Website: www.tnc.org.

Sonoita Creek State Natural Area

Located adjacent to Patagonia Lake State Park (see Fishing) on state trust land, this interesting area encompasses 5,000 acres just below the dam on Sonoita Creek. Arizona's first major state natural area, it supports an abundance of bird life that includes nesting black hawks and several endangered species. Hiking trails along the creek wind among giant cottonwoods, willows, sycamores and mesquites. A new Visitor and Boating Safety Center offers area information and guided tours. Located **5 miles southeast of Patagonia just off Hwy. 82. 520-287-2791.** Website: www. pr.state.az.us.

Fishing

Patagonia Lake State Park

More than 640 acres of wooded desert make this a comfortable place to camp or picnic. During many months it is underutilized, possibly because of its comparatively remote location. The 265-acre lake, created by damming Sonoita Creek, regularly produces crappie, bass, bluegill, and catfish. Oct.–Feb., it is stocked every three weeks with trout. Expect to see white-tailed deer, great blue herons, vermilion flycatchers, and a number of hummingbird species. Try the easy Sonoita Creek Trail for a mellow stroll. Picnic areas have ramadas, tables, and grills; there is also a campground. There are boat ramps, a marina, and a camper supply store. Small day-use fee. Located **5 miles southeast of Patagonia just off Hwy. 82. P.O. Box 274, Patagonia, 85624; 520-287-6965, fax 520-287-5618. Website: www. pr.state.az.us.**

Seeing and Doing

Shopping

Along Naugle Ave. (Hwy. 82), shops include **Red Mountain Foods (520-394-2786)**, a natural foods place with fresh organic produce. **Kazzam Nature Center** is a gift, book, and garden store, and has information and supplies for birders. Open Tues.–Sun., 9:30 A.M.–5:00 P.M. **348 Naugle Ave.; 520-394-2823 or 877-627-9482. Website: www. kazzam.com.**

Where to Stay

The Duquesne House—$$$

Built by the owner of the Duquesne Mine as housing for his workers when Patagonia was a copper and silver center, this turn-of-the-century adobe has been renovated so that each suite has its own bedroom, bath, sitting room, and private entrance. Breakfast is served in the dining room or on a screened porch, where guests also can gather to socialize. One efficiency unit with kitchenette and three suites are available. Located 60 miles south of Tucson and 20 miles east of Nogales. **357 Duquesne St., P.O. Box 772, Patagonia, 85624; 520-394-2732.**

Stage Stop Inn—$$$

Located in downtown Patagonia, this is the largest hotel in the area, with 43 rooms. It has a heated pool and some kitchenettes. A restaurant and saloon are next door. **303 W. McKeown, P.O. Box 777, Patagonia, 85624; 800-923-2211 or 520-394-2211.**

Camping

Patagonia Lake State Park (see Fishing) has 106 sites with showers, hookups, rest rooms, and dump station. **P.O. Box 274, Patagonia, 85624; 520-287-6965, fax 520-287-5618. Website: www. pr.state.az.us. Patagonia RV Park** has full hookups with cable TV. **Located on Harshaw Rd. P.O. Box 768, Patagonia, 85624; 520-394-2491.**

Where to Eat

Gathering Ground—$$

Gathering Ground is a deli-cafe that packs picnic lunches with things like quirky turkey sandwiches on cranberry bread, southwestern grilled vegetables on rosemary bread, and chicken tarragon walnut salad. Open Thurs.–Mon., 7:30 A.M.–5:00 P.M. **319 McKeown; 520-394-2097.**

Wagon Wheel Saloon & Restaurant—$$

"We don't have a town drunk. We take turns." The declaration on the wall pretty much characterizes this fun cowboy bar, where everyone looks up when you enter, then includes you in the conversation. There are booths, a pool table, and hearty chow. An order of pork ribs, slaw, and beans is a frequent special, along with chicken and burgers. Open daily, 11:00 A.M.–1:00 A.M. **400 W. Naugle; 520-394-2433.**

Services

Patagonia Visitor Information Center

Located between the lobby and the dining room of the Stage Stop Inn (see Where to Stay), in the Mariposa Book Store. Open Wed.–Mon., 10:00 A.M.–5:00 P.M. **305 McKeown Ave., Patagonia, 85624; 888-794-0060 or 520-394-0060.**

Nogales, Arizona, and Nogales, Sonora

The state's best-known border town, Nogales, is joined with Nogales, Sonora, in Mexico to form a pair that consider themselves one community. Arizona's Nogales has just 25,000 people, whereas the one in Mexico has a population of 250,000, but there is an active industrial and trade exchange between the two. Sonora, an agricultural state, together with Sinaloa, another agricultural state on its southern border, make Nogales the largest port of entry for produce into the United States. During winter months, Mexican farms fill U.S. produce departments with 80 percent of the cucumbers and zucchini and 66 percent of the tomatoes they sell. More than 65 *maquiladoras* employ close to 20,000 workers here. Working under a two-nation agreement, these plants assemble and manufacture computer parts, electronic components, medical products, typewriter ribbons, welders, battery chargers, sunglasses, auto parts, and more.

Nogales (which means "walnut" in Spanish), Sonora, has niched itself as a tourist destination, and is fun to explore for the better part of a day. Note that street signs are at intersections on the corners of buildings. Since a self-imposed spruce-up a few years ago, there are clean rest rooms located in most restaurants and at the border crossing. Opinions differ about where to change money, but it really doesn't matter unless you're changing thousands of dollars, because the rate of exchange varies by just pennies from place to place. In fact it really isn't necessary to change money at all if you'll be across the border just for the day. U.S. dollars are accepted everywhere, as are credit cards. If you'd like a peso coin or note for a souvenir, just ask when you make a purchase.

If you're not a seasoned Mexico traveler, note that a day's foray into Nogales, Sonora, is not "going to Mexico." This is a border town, with little of the charm of Mexico's marvelous beaches, spectacular canyons, or sophisticated tourist resorts farther south. But it has a low-key, naive appeal all its own that certainly has kept Arizona residents, and generations of tourists, coming back for decades.

History

Early on, Native Americans used Nogales Pass to move between what now is Arizona and the Sea of Cortez, traffic verified by seashells found in ancient Arizona ruins. With the signing of the Gadsden Purchase in 1854, the present-day boundary was established. Nogales itself was founded in 1880 as a center of customs control between the two countries. By 1910 it had become the most important city in the state of Sonora. During subsequent turbulent years, it often was the target of forceful takeovers by various Mexican factions.

In 1976 then-President Gerald Ford visited to meet with Mexican President Luis Echeverria

Nogales, Sonora, Mexico, just across the border from Nogales, Arizona, has great shopping opportunities.

Alvarez to reaffirm an informal good-neighbor policy. By then a stream of U.S. tourists heading over the border and a steady flow of Mexico-grown produce into the United States had created a strong economic bond between the two Nogales.

Festivals and Events

Fiestas de Mayo

Apr.–May

In Nogales, Sonora, from the last few days in Apr. until May 5, the traditional Battle of Puebla is remembered with a celebration that involves bullfights, *palenque* (cockfights), horse races, arts and crafts exhibits, and industrial expositions. Whatever your feeling about bull- and cock-fights, keep them to yourself when you're across the border. They are part of a tradition that residents are not ready to forfeit, and their merits generally are not a favored topic of debate.

Seeing and Doing

Museums

Pimeria Alta Historical Society

On the Arizona side of the border, this combination museum and archives traces the history of southern Arizona and northern Sonora, and gives a sense of how the two states relate. At varying times the 1914 building served as the firehouse, jail, courthouse, customs house, and city hall. The old firehouse pole and a gleaming 1900s engine, a particularly grim jail cell, and a rolltop customs house desk are remnants of the building's past lives. Free. Open Fri., 10:00 A.M.–5:00 P.M.; Sat., 10:00 A.M.–4:00 P.M.; Sun., 1:00 P.M.–4:00 P.M. These odd hours serve the visitors that cross the border on weekends. Located at Crawford St. **136 N. Grand Ave., Nogales, 85628; 520-287-4621.**

Shopping

From the border crossing, turn right on Campillo St. and walk about three short blocks to downtown Obregon St., which is lined with shops. From there, just explore. **Little Mexico on Campillo St.** has a good selection of arts and crafts from all over the country. **El Cid Mall on Obregon St.,** the main shopping thoroughfare, is a collection of shops with higher-quality leather goods, clothing, and art. Haggling and bargaining become an art form here and are part of the fun of making purchases. Even in what appear to be fixed-price shops, don't hesitate to try.

Especially interesting is **Pasaje Morelos,** an alleyway parallel to Obregon that you can enter through some of the Obregon shops. It's chock-a-block with genuine kitsch as well as lovely decorator items like tin-framed mirrors, large pottery pieces and decorative papier-mâché. When wearied, stop and have a Corona in the cool patio of **Hotel Pasaje,** from where you can watch the interaction of shoppers and vendors on the adjacent walkway.

You're allowed to bring back $400 in duty-free merchandise monthly that can include a quart of liquor and a carton of cigarettes. Most shoppers generally consider Kahlua, the rich coffee-flavored liqueur made in Mexico, the most reliable buy. Heavy blue-rimmed Mexican glassware is a popular item, available at about half of what it sells for in trendy U.S. decorator shops. Wood and wrought-iron furniture, ceramics, leather goods, and colorful knickknacks of all sorts are plentiful and well priced. Floaty, lightweight cotton dresses, often with intricate embroidery, are popular as nightgowns. On Sats. that correspond with big holidays, such as Memorial Day, Fourth of July, Labor Day, and Thanksgiving, merchants tend to take advantage of bigger crowds by reducing prices.

It is no secret that large numbers of U.S. citizens cross the border to buy prescriptions that, while available in the United States, are often a fraction of the cost in Mexico. Also, many drugs that require a doctor's prescription in the United States are available without a prescription in Mexico. The danger is that there is no Food and Drug Administration that eagle-eyes these drugs. While many ill people, dependent on very expensive prescriptions, say they must use the Mexican versions or do without, others have had less pleasant experiences. A number of Mexican pharmacies are within blocks of the border. As with any unknown quantity, caveat emptor.

Wineries

Arizona Vineyards
This kitschy spot is as much showplace as winemaking establishment. They say they sell more wine than any other winery, due to their position on a well-traveled road to Nogales. They specialize in sweet wines and proudly offer an award-winning Rattlesnake Red. Their bestseller, a sweet, fruity mountain Rhine, combines French Colombard and muscat grapes grown in Chandler near Phoenix. A motion-picture prop-rental service also is centered here, hence the Roman chariot, oak icebox, crank phone, ancient

Getting There
Nogales, Arizona, is on I-19 about 65 miles directly south of Tucson, at the junction with Hwy. 82 at the Mexico border. To get to Nogales, Sonora, take I-19 south until it practically dead-ends into parking lots within blocks of the border. Park in one of them (there's a good one just behind McDonald's that charges about $5 for the whole day) and walk across at Garita A, the place with the big double humps, which is the main 24-hour walking entrance. Just ahead is the Flag Island of the Americas, aflutter with banners from Mexican states.

license plates, and other collectibles that line the walls. The owner, Tino Ocheltree, whose oil paintings are part of the decor, is a world traveler and seldom in residence, but the accommodating manager is more than happy to pour samples. On crowded winter weekends, tasters are on their own to take a "wine barrel tour," with printed information directing them from bottle to bottle. Open daily, 10:00 A.M.–5:00 P.M. Located 2 miles east of Nogales on Hwy. 82. **1830 Patagonia Hwy., Nogales, 85621; 520-287-7972.**

Where to Stay

Many visitors prefer to stay in Tucson or nearby, then drive the 65 miles to Nogales for the day. But there are a number of reliable, if not luxurious, hotels on the U.S. side right at the border.

NOGALES, ARIZONA
All of these middle-of-the-road places are in the $$–$$$ range.

Americana Motor Hotel, 639 Grand Ave., Nogales, 85621; 520-287-7211 or 800-874-8079.

Best Western Siesta, 673 Grand Ave., Nogales, 85621; 520-287-4671 or 800-528-1234.

Best Western Time, 921 Grand Ave., Nogales, 85621; 520-287-4627 or 800-528-1234.

Super 8 Motel, 537 W. Mariposa Rd., Nogales, 85621; 520-281-2242 or 800-800-8000.

NOGALES, SONORA

Fray Marcos de Niza Hotel—$$

This tall pink building in the center of town has clean, comfortable, air-conditioned rooms with phones and TVs, and is convenient to shopping. You'll find purified water and ice in the restaurant and bar. This is about as luxurious as it gets in Nogales, Sonora, but then, that's not why you come here. Anyplace you stay right in town is noisy until the early morning hours, so it's a good idea to stay in an air-conditioned place so you can close the windows. Located at Obregon and Campillo; phone 2-16-51.

Camping

Mi Casa RV Travel Park

This place has 48 spaces with full hookups. About 4.5 miles north of the border. 2901 Grand Ave., Nogales, 85621; 520-281-1150.

Where to Eat

NOGALES, ARIZONA

On the U.S. side, you'll find Arby's, Kentucky Fried Chicken, Pizza Hut, and Shakey's Pizza conveniently positioned so that you could purchase a lunch before crossing the border and eat it later. Zula's Restaurant and Sweets 'N Subs bakery and deli, both on Grand Ave., are convenient eateries.

San Cayetano—$$$

The menu is typically upscale Southwest, with interesting salads and sauces, as well as some Mexican dishes. Choose this resort if you're look-

ing to linger over a well-prepared meal, share some wine, and perhaps snug into one of the resort's rooms, from where you can peacefully memorize the mountains. Open daily, 6:30 A.M.–2:00 P.M. and 5:00 P.M.–9:30 P.M. Located off I-19 at exit 17, at Rio Rico Resort and Country Club about 12 miles north of the border. 520-281-1901.

Molina's Pete Kitchen Outpost—$$

On the historic Pete Kitchen Ranch established in 1854, in an old ranch building, you'll find the last remnant of a memorable pioneer. The thick-walled adobe building has a foundation laid of rock from a nearby canyon and door posts fashioned from oaks that grew on the property. Ranch artifacts and memorabilia decorate the dining room. The specialty is Mexican food with many flavorful fish dishes prepared in the Santa Cruz style. Open daily, 11:00 A.M.–9:00 P.M. Located 3 miles north of Nogales on Frontage Rd. off I-19. 520-281-9946.

NOGALES, SONORA

If you are genuinely terrified of contracting Montezuma's revenge, don't put a thing in your mouth while in Nogales, Sonora. However, big hotels and the major restaurants have purified water, even in ice cubes. By all means, ask before you order. Most regular border-crossers report no problems with food in Nogales. Of course, it isn't wise to lap up a colorful ice from a street vendor, or buy homemade tortillas from adorable, big-eyed children. But don't be afraid to try the truly wonderful restaurant food available in Sonora. Stick to bottled beer and sodas if you really are concerned.

El Cid—$$–$$$

On the Mexico side, lunch at El Cid is a tradition for many visitors. This airy, spacious second-floor restaurant has balcony views of rooftops, small houses on a steep hillside, and busy Calle Obregon below. Guaymas shrimp and beef from Hermosillo are specialties, and the Mexican combination plate is a surefire pleaser, as is any dish with thick, rich mole. Wash it all down with a couple of Negra Modelos for the full South-of-the-Border effect. Arrive early for lunch, before noon, to get a window table. **Ave. Obregon No. 124.**

El Greco—$$–$$$

Although you're in a border town and probably dressed in shorts and a T-shirt, you're treated like royalty. The waiters here are career waiters, and the service reflects it. The menu features steaks and seafood, with a number of excellent Sonoran dishes. The dining room is upstairs from a boutique shopping mall. You can't miss it, as there often is a friendly soul on the avenue giving out coupons for free margaritas. **Ave. Obregon No. 152.**

Services

To make a phone call to Nogales, Sonora, dial 011-52-631 and the five-digit telephone number; 011 is the international code, 52 is the country code, and 631 is the city code.

Nogales–Santa Cruz Chamber of Commerce

This is a good place to stop for information about where to park and walk across the border. Located in **Kino Park, Nogales, 85621; 520-287-3685. Website: www.nogaleschamber.com.**

Sonora, Mexico

The city maintains a visitor information hot line, **800- 4-Sonora,** where you can leave your name and number and get a return call.

Tourist Delegate Center

This office in Mexico functions like tourism offices in the United States. 011-52-631-206-66.

Green Valley and Tubac

This part of the Santa Cruz River Valley south of Tucson is an especially lovely riparian area (once you get off the freeway) in the spots where the Santa Cruz River chooses to flow aboveground. Green Valley and Tubac, each with a distinct personality, cluster along the ribbon of I-19.

The 5,000-acre community of Green Valley, in essence a retirement community with a few family subdivisions mixed in, has an appealing desert beauty. The pretty Santa Rita Mountains provide views to the east, and the huge open-pit copper mine, known historically as the Duval Copper Mine and run by Cypress Amax Minerals Company of Colorado, is to the west. From the freeway you'll see it as a distant large berm, kept watered and covered to hold down dust and minimize eyesore potential. The big attraction in Green Valley is golf. Two of the town's seven courses are private, with the remaining five open to public play (see Golf).

Tubac is a hub of artistic activity reminiscent of Santa Fe, billing itself as the place "where art and history meet" and it does have plenty of both. The entire little town is quite literally an arts and crafts center, now so trendy that decorators and designers from Phoenix and Tucson regularly trek south in search of accent pieces and accouterments to please clients. Much of the fun is in discovering small interesting restaurants, many accessed by little alleyways that open onto sunny patios. See Art Museums and Galleries below.

History

Green Valley was once part of the original San Ignacio de las Canoa land grant conveyed to the Spanish monarchy more than 400 years ago.

Once a small Pima Indian village, Tubac became a mission farm and ranch when Jesuit priest Eusebio Francisco Kino established the mission at Tumacacori in 1691, just a few miles to the south. A bloody battle in 1751 between the Pima Indians and the Spanish led to the construction of the Presidio San Ignacio de Tubac the following year. Tubac was founded in 1752 as the first European settlement in what would later become Arizona. When the Tucson Presidio was established 45 miles to the north in 1775, the colonists and garrison were moved there. Juan Bautista de Anza, the commander of the Tubac Presidio, Fray Francisco Garces, and 240 immigrants who had dreams of finding an overland route to California used what is now called the de Anza trail in 1775 to travel from Nogales to San Francisco, California. During the ensuing years, the little settlement of Tubac was plundered by Apaches. The mission was abandoned in 1828 when a Mexican decree forced all Spanish priests to leave. It was resettled, abandoned once again, then repopulated until in 1860 it was the largest town in Arizona. But the Civil War demanded that the troops protecting Tubac be deployed elsewhere, and once again it was abandoned.

Festivals and Events

Annual Tubac Festival of the Arts

Feb.

The premier arts festival of southern Arizona, it usually begins the first weekend of Feb. and runs for nine days. It consists of more than 100 crafts and merchandise booths, a juried fine-arts show, and tons of food. Merchants and artists who have permanent shops in Tubac are joined by area craftspeople who set up outdoor booths and stands. For information call the Tubac Center of the Arts, 520-398-2371.

Anza Days

third weekend in Oct.

In Tubac, this cultural celebration commemorates the trek of Spanish explorer Juan Bautista de Anza from Sonora to California with re-enactments by costumed volunteers. Riders in Spanish military garb brandishing shields and lances make a colorful appearance, and foot and mounted soldiers perform precision drills. Native American music and dances from the Apache, Tohono O'odham, and Mexican cultures are presented. Much of the fun of this festival is getting into the spirit of the old days, imagining how things must have been. Tubac's shops and galleries are open for browsing when you tire of historical pursuits. 520-398-2252.

Outdoor Activities

Birding

Buenos Aires National Wildlife Refuge

Once a vibrant grasslands that supported pronghorn, falcons, Mexican wolves, bear, and jaguar, the range was decimated in the mid-1800s by overgrazing and fire suppression. When a non-native grass called Lehmann lovegrass was planted, it became a monoculture inhospitable

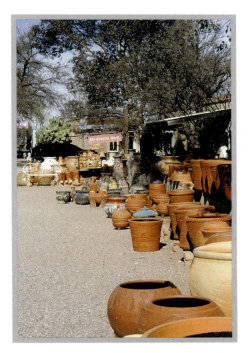

Mexican pottery is among the interesting arts and crafts found in the town of Tubac.

to most species. In 1985 the U.S. Fish and Wildlife Service bought Buenos Aires ranch to preserve habitat for the masked bobwhite, whose breeding population is gaining a foothold in the refuge. Although it's a long process, restoring native plants is in progress. Hwy. 286 follows the refuge's western border, and is lined with giant sunflowers in early Oct. Paved Arivaca Rd. bisects the refuge about midway. You can explore more than 100 miles of back roads, taking care to stay directly on the roads, except to camp at any of 100-plus primitive campsites scattered in the backcountry. In the southeast portion of the refuge, there are challenging mountain-bike trails. In the refuge's far northwest corner, Brown Canyon provides an excellent birding spot, lined with sycamore and live oak. A guided hike (the only way at present to enter the canyon) leads to a 47-foot natural bridge. A good map showing back roads and campsites is available at the visitor centers.

There are two entry points with information.

Refuge Headquarters/visitor center is open Mon.–Fri., 7:00 A.M.–4:00 P.M. Located **at milepost 7 on Hwy. 286. P.O. Box 109, Sasabe, 85633; 520-823-4252.** The Arivaca Information Office is open Mon.–Fri., 9:00 A.M.–3:00 P.M., or as volunteers are available. Located **in Arivaca, 2 miles west of I-19. Take Amado-Arivaca exit and follow Arivaca Rd. west.**

Madera Canyon

East of Green Valley in the north and middle of the Santa Rita Mountains in the Coronado National Forest, Madera Canyon is a very special place for outdoor lovers. North-flowing Madera Creek trickles along its bottom, eventually joining the Santa Cruz River to create the riparian habitat that supports more than 220 bird species. Serious birders are attracted by the great number of rare species, including the elegant trogon and magnificent hummingbird, as well as elf and whiskered screech owls. Although Mar. is considered the beginning of birding season because hummers and owls arrive then, migrating species make the canyon a rich birding area all year long. July–early Sept. are prime hummingbird months. See Santa Rita Lodge Nature Resort in Where to Stay. **From I-19 take exit 63, which winds about 15 miles to the canyon.** Or, from Hwy. 83 via Greaterville Rd., there is a lovely scenic drive over about 23 miles of dirt road.

Golf

As courses in Phoenix and the Valley of the Sun to the north become ever more crowded and expensive, the great unsung links between Tucson and the Mexico border are often relatively open and less pricey.

Haven Golf Course

This par 72, 6,829-yard public course is the oldest in Green Valley. Pretty fairways are wide enough so that even real duffers can stay out of trouble. Mature trees and attractive ponds backgrounded by the Santa Rita Mountains make it scenic, with a cool feeling even when temperatures soar. It has a pro shop, practice range, lounge, and food service. **110 N. Abrego Dr., Green Valley, 85614; 520-625-4281.**

Rio Rico Resort & Country Club

Also part of a resort complex (the resort is on the other side of the freeway) at 4,000 feet, Rio Rico is ruggedly beautiful and can be quite a challenge. It hosts the Arizona PGA Tour and Senior PGA Tour qualifying tournaments each year. Designed by Robert Trent Jones Sr., it has bent-grass greens and Bermuda grass on tees and fairways, overseeded with rye in winter. The front nine follows the base of a small mesa, with the back nine leveling out along the Santa Cruz riverbed. The demanding, close-to-nature 18 holes total 7,119 yards. Deluxe room and golf packages are available. East side of I-19 at exit 17, south of Tubac. **1069 Camino Caralampi, Rio Rico, 85621; 800-288-4746 or 520-287-1901.**

San Ignacio Golf Club

This championship desert course, designed by Arthur Hills, meanders through groves of mesquite and around water. Because it is at 3,000 feet, it tends to stay cool. Bent-grass greens are well kept. It has a pro shop, practice range, restaurant, and lounge. Well-priced golf packages that include accommodations in nearby condos can make this a pleasant vacation for families and non-golfing spouses. John Jacobs Golf Schools are offered throughout the year. **4201 S. Camino del Sol, Green Valley, 85614; 520-648-3468.**

Torres Blancas Golf Club at Santa Rita Springs

Green Valley's newest 18-hole championship course opened in winter 1995 and is doing its best to be one of the most attractive. Roughs hydro-seeded with brilliant red Mexican hats, golden marigolds, and other wildflowers form a colorful contrast to Bermuda fairways and greens. A National Archaeological Society Hohokam Indian burial ground is on the first fairway. The club recently was given Audubon Society sanctioning as a course that provides habitat for migrating birds. Four sets of tees per hole are reportedly user friendly from the forward tees and a definite challenge from the rear tees. A new clubhouse was completed in 1997. **3233 S. Abrego Dr., Green Valley, 85614; 520-625-5200.**

Tubac Golf Resort

At an elevation of 3,400 feet, this well-designed 18-hole course 40 minutes south of Tucson is considerably cooler than city courses. Traditionally designed with bent-grass greens and wide Bermuda grass fairways flanked by cottonwood trees, it is kept green by the nearby Santa Cruz River. The course's 16th hole was featured in the movie *Tin Cup.* The Spanish-style resort offers comfortable rooms that can be a good home base for exploring the area. At La Montura restaurant, inventive cuisine is served in an 1800s building, once the stables for the Otero Ranch that became Tubac. Located 40 miles south of Tucson at exit 40 off I-19. **One Otero Rd., Tubac, 85646; 520-398-2211.**

Hiking

See also Hiking in the Tucson chapter for more outdoor opportunities in the area south of Tucson.

De Anza Trail

Extending 4.5 miles along the Santa Cruz River from Tubac to Tumacacori National Historic Site, this trail is part of the National Historic Trail that follows the 1775 route between Nogales, Arizona, and San Francisco, California. Plans are underway to include the 600 miles of the route that lie in Mexico, beginning in Culiacan, Sinaloa, which would make it the first International Historic Trail. The portion between Tubac and Tumacacori is open to hikers and equestrians, with plans in the works for a bike route along back roads between Nogales and Tubac. The trail crosses the Santa Cruz River several times, following a pleasant riparian area lined with cottonwoods. The river may be dangerous if it's been raining and the water level is high. It's best to hike early in the morning and carry lots of water, because the trail gets hot during the day. Do not drink the river water. The Tubac trailhead is at south side of picnic grounds south of State Historic Park **where Tubac Rd. deadends into Burruel St. 520-398-2252.**

Madera Canyon

The area has many trails for hiking and mountain biking, including one that's wheelchair-accessible. Major trails off the canyon range from 2.5 miles to 8.1 miles and longer. Some are easy and well graded (**Bog Springs** and **Nature Trail** are easy, short hikes if time is limited), while others can be steep and difficult, but all offer the kind of mountain scenery and fresh, clean air that clears your mind. The **Super Trail** is a favorite of many hikers. This exceptionally scenic trail meanders 4.5 miles to Josephine Saddle, but you can go all the way to Mount Wrightson for a 16.4-mile round trip. Shady picnic areas with tables and barbecues are scattered throughout the canyon.

Stop at Santa Rita Lodge (see Where to Stay) about a mile from the end of Madera Canyon Rd. for books, trail guides, and information about the canyon. The lodge has a register to sign before you hike that lets others know where you're planning to go and when you expect to return. Drive to upper end of Madera Canyon, where a sign indicates parking for trails; trailhead is in north corner of parking lot. **From I-19 take exit 63, which winds about 15 miles to the canyon. Or, from Hwy. 83 via Greaterville Rd., there is a lovely scenic drive over about 23 miles of dirt road.**

Seeing and Doing

Art Museums and Galleries

Tubac has more than 80 galleries and studios, shops, and restaurants gathered in a four-block area that you can't miss in this tiny town. It flourishes with exhibitions and performing-arts presentations Sept.–May, and tends to slumber during the heat of summer. You easily can spend half a day poking into interesting shops, studios, and galleries, many with truly wonderful locally produced art. Styles and influences include western, Arizona, Mexican Impressionist, and contemporary. Pick up a visitor's guide at any of the shops when you arrive, open it to the large center map, and you can choose your route.

Tubac Center of the Arts

This tile-roofed center has changing fine-arts exhibits as well as music and cultural events. In the Gallery Shop, the work of more than 100 local craftspeople is for sale. Events scheduled Sept.–June, Tues.–Sat., 10:00 A.M.–4:30 P.M.; Sun., 1:00 P.M.–4:30 P.M. Located **at Calle Baca and Plaza Rd. 520-398-2371.**

Museums and Historic Sites

Old Tumacacori Bar

This wonderfully kitschy place, owned and run by Abe T. Trujillo for 47 years, is in an adobe building that dates to the 1930s, and Abe, who always seems to be there, says he holds the oldest liquor license in the same family in the state of Arizona. The barroom has a huge pool table surrounded by walls lined with gifts from customers, steins and figural bottles, his great-grandmother's coffee grinder, and more. Bum checks hang alongside signed $1 bills that span four generations. At one time the place did a land-office business, bolstered by the Tucson-Nogales bus that stopped at the bar to use the bathrooms. But the freeway passed Abe by, and he now stays solvent with local trade and the visitors who straggle over from the mission.

Open Tues.–Sun., 2:00 P.M.–1:00 A.M. Located **across from Tumacacori National Historic Site** (see below). No phone.

Titan Missile Museum

When you drive up to this desolate spot, there is no indication that something as impressive as a Titan II missile lurks underground. A huge antenna looking like a denuded Christmas tree, a chain-link fence, and a small building are the only aboveground structures. That's just the way the designers wanted it when this once-deadly projectile was installed here as part of the chain of 54 such defense mechanisms that guarded the nation during the Cold War. While it was active, few people in the surrounding area even knew the site was here. Missiles were kept at the ready in underground silos, complete with nuclear warheads, since removed. Within a minute of receiving the word, they could be launched by a specially trained team, on duty 24 hours a day. By 1987 the country was deemed safe and all Titan II missiles were dismantled except for this one, now available for public viewing. A one-hour guided tour takes you 35 feet underground to see the missile and the control center that fortunately never received the order to launch. Simulated countdowns and a walk through the 200-foot cableway to the silo are part of the tour. Moderate admission. Guided tours offered May 1–Oct. 31, Wed.–Sun., 9:00 A.M.–4:00 P.M.; Nov. 1–Apr. 30, daily, 9:00 A.M.–4:00 P.M.; closed Thanksgiving and Christmas Day. From **I-19 in Green Valley, take exit 69, Duval Mine Rd., then continue west a few blocks to museum entrance. 520-625-4759 or 520-625-7736. Website: www.pimaair.org.**

Tubac Presidio State Historic Park

In 1974 archaeological explorations unearthed portions of the walls, foundation, and plaza floor of the Presidio San Ignacio de Tubac, which was built in 1752. The remains now are open to the public as part of an underground display. The State Historic Park has a new visitor center where a nine-minute video gives a good history of what can be seen on the walking tour. The

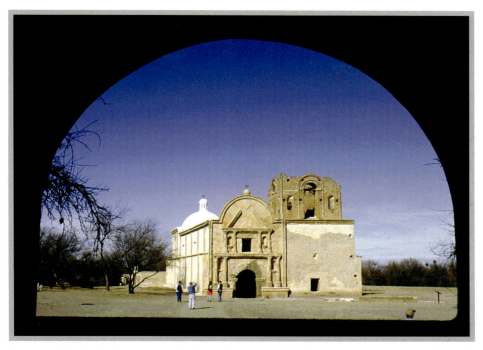

Tumacacori Mission sits in a rich agricultural area that once served settlers and Indians.

1885 Tubac schoolhouse and artifacts from the town's history are part of the park, as is the press used by Charles Poston to print the state's first newspaper, *The Weekly Arizonian.* Volunteers in the park's living-history program authentically portray Tubac life between 1752 and 1776; Oct.–Mar., Sun., 1:00–4:00 P.M. Small admission. Open daily, 8:00 A.M.–5:00 P.M.; closed Christmas Day. Located **where Tubac Rd. dead-ends into Burruel St. P.O. Box 1296, Tubac, 85646; 520-398-2252. Website: www. pr.state.az.us.**

Tumacacori National Historic Site

This lovely mission was the centerpiece of a thriving community terrified of Apache raids in the early 1700s, when a small adobe church was built. Construction on the existing larger church wasn't begun until the 1800s, with the final phase still in progress in 1823. The mission was abandoned in 1828 and the bell tower dome was never built. In 1908 it was declared a national monument, halting its rapid deterio-

ration. The present visitor center was built in 1937, and in 1990 the mission received national historic site status and added protection. A self-guided walking tour takes you into the mission and around the grounds. It's easy to imagine what a pleasant community this must have been, with orchards and gardens flourishing along the banks of the Santa Cruz River. The mission's thick adobe walls keep its interior consistently cooler than the outdoors. Remnants of once-colorful paintings cover inside walls, and a few of the original wood statues remain. Graves in the courtyard are marked with wood crosses. Adjacent to the visitor center is a lovely little patio garden where neatly tended mission-period plants surround a trickling fountain. The small visitor center has books and videos about the mission. Small admission. Open daily, 8:00 A.M.–5:00 P.M.; closed Thanksgiving and Christmas Day. **Take exit 29 off I-19. From Tubac, take east frontage road 3 miles south. 520-398-2341. Website: www.nps.gov.**

Observatories and Planetariums

Smithsonian Institution
Whipple Observatory

Appearing as a white dot on top of Mount Hopkins, the observatory interests mostly serious amateur astronomers, although everyone can enjoy the scenic ride into the mountains. Here, the Smithsonian uses one of the world's largest telescopes, the Multiple Mirror, to gain knowledge of the stars and planets. Six-hour public guided tours begin with a half-hour video presentation at the observatory visitor center in Amado, then a bus takes you to the observatory; tours conducted Mar.–Nov., Mon., Wed., and Fri., 9:00 A.M. Reservations required. Open Mon.–Fri., 8:30 A.M.–4:30 P.M. Located **east of I-19 near Amado, off I-19 at exit 48. 520-670-5707.**

Shopping

Santa Cruz Chili & Spice Company

The fragrance alone is enough to make you linger in this interesting shop and museum. Across the street and a few hundred yards south of the mission at Tumacacori, it's the place to stock up on spices at less than half of supermarket prices. Professional chefs make regular runs here to find the unique, gourmet seasonings not readily available in local markets. Most also are available by mail, including its famous chile paste. A small table is filled with bowls of chips and products to sample. Jean England Neubauer and her husband are the second generation to run the spice company, which began in 1943, along with the adjacent Rock Corral Ranch. The museum here is filled with artifacts from El Alamo, a stronghold on the Sonoran Desert. It eventually became a guest ranch. Open Mon.–Wed. and Fri.–Sat., 8:00 A.M.–5:00 P.M. **1868 E. Frontage Rd., Tumacacori, 85640; 520-398-2591. Website: www.santacruzchili.com.**

Where to Stay

Because this area is widespread and sparsely populated, there aren't many places to stay. The two chain motels in Green Valley are Best Western and Holiday Inn Express. To find lots of luxury resorts, simply go north to Tucson. To the east, Sierra Vista has many seasonal rentals available for just a week or for months. Most realtors can find one for you. The accommodations we list here are our picks for the unusual and memorable. For more accommodations, see Golf.

Rex Ranch—$$$$

Secluded in the Sonoran Desert 30 miles south of Tucson, this lovely Territorial-Colonial ranch has gone from a beans-and-potatoes, dusty dude ranch to a rustic retreat with a spa. The attraction is the unspoiled outdoors. You can spend days hiking the 50-plus acres of mesquite and chaparral, riding a spirited horse with no nose-to-tail mentality, or tracking feisty cactus wrens and Gila woodpeckers as they flit from saguaro to prickly pear. Then return to the ranch for a massage. Cielo, the ranch spa, features a treatment called La Stone, in which the therapist quickly moves smooth heated basalt river rocks over the body. The stones are placed strategically under the body and on pressure points in a combination that results in ultimate relaxation. Accommodations are in adobe casitas, some with kitchens, some with fireplaces and patios that offer desert views. Three meals a day, with fitness-friendly choices, are prepared by a chef who truly understands how to combine European style with the flavors of the Southwest. Rather than the 10 o'clock news, evening entertainment can mean hot-tubbing under the stars that seem particularly bright in the clear desert air. Room-only and packages with meals are available. Because summers can be very hot, horses are at the ranch only Oct.–May. Located about 12 miles south of Green Valley. **From I-19 take exit 48 (Arivaca/Amado) and go 3.5 miles south to the ranch. P.O. Box 636, Amado, 85645; 888-REXRANCH or 520-398-2914. Website: www. info@rexranch.com.**

Burro Inn—$$$–$$$$

So-named because gentle resident burros, Louie

and Andrew, are on hand to welcome guests. The inn, on a 12-acre plateau on top of Tubac Mountain, is surrounded by state forest land that is leased as open range to a working cattle ranch, so drive carefully once you're off the main road. The inn has four condolike two-room suites that sleep four, each with a wet bar, microwave, refrigerator (stocked with two carrots per day), phone, and color TV. There are remnants of the days when it was the site of Silo No. 7 in the 18-silo chain of Titan missiles that once crossed southern Arizona (see Museums and Historic Sites). The missile was completely dismantled in 1982 to comply with the SALT Treaty, but its owners are slowly excavating the dirt-filled, 10-story silo. A small pond, created to extinguish the fire that would have been caused if a missile had been launched, now holds water hibiscus. Located 1 mile west of I-19 at exit 40. **70 W. Burro Ln., P.O. Box 4188, Tubac, 85646-4188; 520-398-2281.**

Santa Rita Lodge Nature Resort—$$$

This quiet, secluded lodge is one of our favorite places for a weekend or a weeklong getaway. Situated above a stream in Madera Canyon at 4,800 feet elevation, units have tub and shower and color TV. Cabins accommodate two adults and two children, or four friendly adults; efficiency units with fireplaces are perfect for two adults. Both type of units have kitchens, so you can bring food in coolers, using outdoor barbecues at each unit and small decks overlooking the forest and creek. The nearest grocery store is about 13 miles away. Without ever leaving the cabin area, you can see noisy acorn woodpeckers and scrub jays, hummingbirds and nuthatches.

One of the neatest things about this lodge is its natural history program. Hikes, classes, and walks are conducted by local naturalists, recognized experts in their fields. Nature programs are scheduled regularly and may include archaeology, geology, astronomy, birding, and other topics for $15 per person; they last four to five hours, and include a light meal. Reservations essential. Bird walks Mar. 1–14 and June 1–Aug. 31, Mon., Wed., and Fri., leave at vari-

ous times; Mar. 15–May 31, daily every morning; cost is $12 per person. Take **exit 63 off I-19 and travel about 13 miles** to the lodge. **HC 70, Box 5444, Sahuarita, 85629; 520-625-8746. Website: www.santaritalodge.com.**

Tubac Country Inn—$$$

Just off Tubac's main drag, this pleasant blue and white wood-frame bed-and-breakfast truly looks like a country inn, even though it is just a block or two away from most of the interesting things in Tubac. Four suites open onto a friendly front porch. All have coffeemakers and fresh coffee, two have full kitchens, and two have wet bars, but none have phones. Rates include an in-room continental breakfast. Located at **Plaza and Burruel, Tubac, 85646; 520-398-3178.**

Where to Eat

Many restaurants are part of resorts. A number of interesting cafes in Tubac offer fare several notches above the chain eateries.

Tumacacori Restaurant—$$$

It has been here almost a decade, drawing its loyal clientele from Green Valley, Tubac, and Nogales, and attracting visitors that come to the mission just across the street. Small, homey, and family-run, it serves reasonably priced Greek food as well as Sonoran Mexican, an odd combination that somehow seems to work. Full cocktail service. Open Tues.–Sun., noon–8:00 P.M. Located **across from Tumacacori National Historic Site** (see Museums and Historic Sites), **Tubac. 520-398-9038.**

Burro Inn Restaurant—$$

This unpretentious place has huge, western-style, mesquite-broiled steaks and equally huge margaritas. If burro humor amuses you, take the time to read the captioned photos that line the walls. Open Wed.–Sat., 11:00 A.M.–7:00 P.M.; Sun., 11:00 A.M.–3:00 P.M. Located 1 mile west of I-19 at exit 40. **70 W. Burro Ln., Tubac; 520-398-2281.**

Historic ranch buildings at the Rex Ranch date back 170 years, yet have modern updates.

Tarantulas

Those hairy, scary creatures you see scurrying across quiet desert back roads are tarantulas, long a part of Indian lore and desert tales. You'll see the greatest number with the onset of southern Arizona's summer rains, usually late July–Aug., when males start actively pursuing a mate.

They may be the largest and hairiest spider in the United States, but their bite is not lethal. Their venomous reputation, and their name, date back to the 15th century when people sometimes suffered from a form of hysteria thought to be caused by the bite of a large wolf spider named after the town of Taranto in Puglia, Italy. The only cure for the afflicted one was to dance into a frenzy to purge the effects of the spider's bite. Modern-day medical professionals

have speculated that, once injected with the irritating venom of a tarantula, the gyrations of the dancer caused body sweat to dilute and wash away the toxin, thereby appearing to create a cure. The Italian folk dance called the tarantella is said to be named for this bizarre remedy.

The fuzzy arachnids don't spin webs to capture food. They seize their quarry by emerging cautiously from their burrows at night to pounce quickly on anything smaller than they are. The tarantula has a beaklike mouth from which it ejects a venom fatal to small creatures, along with enzymes that begin the digestive process. Thus disabled, hapless insects become a meal.

Tarantulas have been kept successfully as pets for many years. A female may live to

(cont.)

be as old as 30, and a male has a life span of about 10 years. If you held one in your hand, you'd expect it to weigh more than the half-ounce it does, because the 5-inch span of the hairy legs that extend from a 2-inch body makes it appear larger than it really is.

A tarantula spends most of its life in its burrow, which may be an abandoned animal hole or a remote ledge. Males don't leave the sheltered hollow until they are sexually mature, at about eight years of age. That's when you're most likely to see them scampering about the desert, so please don't deter them and put a damper on their romantic quest. Their mating process is complication enough. Although they don't spin webs for food-catching, they do create one for mating purposes. The male creates a small network of web material in which he deposits his sperm. He picks up the little bundle and puts it into two sacs in the female's abdomen. Apparently this is not a gesture that she appreciates, because she can viciously turn on her new suitor at any time during this process, possibly killing him.

Being a single mom doesn't seem to faze a female tarantula. She stores the little bundles of sperm for a number of weeks, then spins a silk sheet on which she lays up to 1,000 eggs. This may seem like a lot, but on average only two of the eggs will become mature spiders. Predation by small mammals like skunks, as well as birds, snakes, lizards, and frogs, takes its toll.

In six weeks, tiny white spiders hatch, staying with mother tarantula for up to a week, when they leave home (but stay in the neighborhood) to build burrows of their own. Tarantulas don't generally stray far from their original burrow, so if you see one, chances are that others are close by.

Tarantulas, naturally timid, try to run away if threatened, as will most wildlife. If cornered, a tarantula will try to frighten away the interloper by rearing up on its back legs and displaying its fangs, which are located quite far back in its throat. If it does bite, its venom has about the same effect on humans as a bee sting or mosquito bite. If you walk an area at dusk and spot large half-dollar-size holes in the ground, they probably belong to tarantulas. Hang around. They'll eventually come out to feed.

Services

There are clean public rest rooms with composting toilets in Tubac, off Tubac Rd. in the center of town.

Green Valley Chamber of Commerce

Staffed with helpful volunteers, it offers printed information on the area. Open May–Aug., Mon.–Fri., 9:00 A.M.–5:00 P.M.; Sept.–Apr., Mon.–Fri., 9:00 A.M.–5:00 P.M.; Sat., 9:00 A.M.–noon. 270 W. Continental Rd., No. 100, Green Valley, 85614; 800-858-5872, 520-625-7575, or 520-625-7594. Website: www.gvnews.com.

Tubac Chamber of Commerce

This is a small, all-volunteer chamber, so you'll probably get voice mail when you call. Things slow considerably in the summer, but someone always gets back to you if you leave a message. Send a self-addressed, stamped, business-size envelope and you'll receive information. P.O. Box 1866, Tubac, 85646; 520-398-2704. Website: www.tubacaz.com.

Ajo and Gila Bend

Just because it's located in the middle of nowhere, the amiable little town of Ajo gets short shrift in the visitor department. But it is well worth the time to linger. It is within easy striking distance of both Organ Pipe National Monument and Cabeza Prieta National Wildlife Refuge. Once thought of as just a place to pass through on the way to Rocky Point in Mexico, it now is becoming a destination of its own. Winter visitors swell its population from about 2,000 in summer to upward of 6,000 in winter.

There's no doubt that this was a copper mining town. Just look at the mounds of tailings, 2,400 acres of them, creating light vertical ridges that define Ajo's eastern border. After the mines shut down, retirees came, attracted by affordable housing, a low cost of living, and great sunny weather. Today the town centers around a tidy plaza with palm trees and benches. Everyone comes here to stretch out on the grass, since most homes have desert yards with few green lawns. A Catholic and a Protestant church overlook arched arcades that shelter shops and restaurants. Built in 1917, the plaza's red-tile-roof architecture is reminiscent of Spanish Colonial towns in Mexico. This look garnered it the role of a Mexican town in the 1972 motion picture *Pocket Money* with Lee Marvin and Paul Newman. The large, impressive building just off the plaza is Curley School. On the hill above the town is the hospital, closed since the mine shut down, and four small pastel homes that once housed doctors, nicknamed Four Little Angels for their lofty perch.

Lukeville is a little town south of Ajo adjacent to the Mexican border; it exists as a border crossing point and Immigration and Naturalization Service office. Recently a new duty-free store has been opened, and there is a campground with hookups and adjacent motel.

The town of Gila Bend, north of Ajo on I-8, is located at the point where the Gila River changes its southerly flow and turns to the west. Today, farmers cultivate more than 90,000 acres in the area, with alfalfa, cotton, wheat, barley, and a few experimental jojoba fields among the principal crops. You might wonder why this four-lane superhighway exists out here in the desert, apparently linking nothing but little agricultural towns. Its *raison d'etre* is that it goes all the way to San Diego on the California coast.

History

Although the word *ajo* (say "AH-ho") means "garlic" in Spanish, it is more likely that the town is named for the Tohono O'odham word that means "place of colored clay." Mining began in Ajo in 1911 with the discovery of a new leaching process and development of a dependable water supply. During its lifetime the mine, which employed about 1,500, yielded about 3 million tons of low-grade copper ore that produced about $8.4 billion in copper, as well as bits of gold, silver, and molybdenum. When the mine and smelter closed in 1985, Phelps Dodge, which owned just about the whole town, sold off its executives homes and the population plummeted. But, as did many Arizona mining towns, Ajo pulled itself together and prospered.

Father Eusebio Kino visited the spot now known as Gila Bend, once a Hohokam village, in 1699. A popular site for many cultures, the river supplied water for irrigation, thus assuring a food supply. In 1858 Gila Bend was established as a stage stop on the route between St. Louis and San Francisco, the Butterfield Trail.

Major Attractions

New Cornelia Mine

Standing at the chain-fenced overlook into the gaping mine pit gives a profound sense of how completely humans can revise a landscape. At one time, railroad tracks spiraled up the sides of the pit so that ore could be removed. It has been closed since 1985 because of falling copper prices. The pit is currently 1.5 miles wide and 1,100 feet deep with a vivid green lake at the bottom. The mine's mellifluous name is that of the wife of an early copper promoter. Today a small museum and satellite chamber of commerce at the mine overlook are staffed by volunteers, some with good stories to tell since they once were part of the mine workforce. Open winter months; hours vary. From the stoplight at the plaza, **take La Mina Rd. south about 0.75 mile** to the mine fence. 520-387-3778.

Cabeza Prieta National Wildlife Refuge

Managed by the U.S. Fish and Wildlife Service, this huge 860,000-acre refuge is a panorama of rugged mountains, lava flows, wide valleys, and sand dunes that shift and change with the sweep of winds across its broad expanse. It shares a 56-mile border with Mexico. The name means "black head" in Spanish, in reference to a promi-

Getting There
Gila Bend is 68 miles southwest of Phoenix at the junction of I-8 and Hwy. 85. Ajo is 42 miles south of Gila Bend on Hwy. 85, about 110 miles southwest of Phoenix and 131 miles west of Tucson.

nent lava-blackened granite peak within its boundaries. Established in 1939, it protects desert bighorn sheep, Sonoran pronghorns, and lesser long-nosed bats. You'll probably see lots of reptiles because lizards, rattlesnakes, and sidewinders (a type of rattlesnake) are comfortable in this hot, dry climate. The entire area is noted for inhospitable terrain, requiring careful planning and proper equipment to penetrate innermost areas.

Note: *Take caution.* Part of the refuge is within the Barry M. Goldwater Air Force Range and has been used for gunnery and bombing practice since World War II. Stuff that can hurt you may be lying around, or partially buried. If it looks dangerous, don't touch it. Make a note of where it is and let the refuge staff know. When "the range is hot," meaning there is air-to-air gunnery practice in airspace above parts of the refuge, you won't be allowed in. These schedules are known in advance, so call first. A small visitor center is located on the north edge of Ajo on Hwy. 85, where you must stop for permits. 1611 N. Second Ave., Ajo, 85321; 520-387-6483.

Organ Pipe Cactus National Monument

This may be the most under-appreciated national monument in the state, which is too bad because it encompasses an outstanding variety of Sonoran Desert plants and animals, preserving a major ecosystem in almost unspoiled condition. The largest national monument in the Lower 48 states, it is named for the stately

Organ Pipe Cactus National Monument near Ajo is home to this relative of the saguaro cactus.

cactus with arms that stem from a central ground-level base (unlike the saguaro, with arms that branch from a single large trunk), similar to pipes that serve a giant organ. The monument, and about an 80-mile additional radius, is U.S. habitat for the organ pipe, although the cactus is also common in the state of Sonora, Mexico. The park's south-facing slopes are liberally scattered with these great plants. May–July they produce delicate lavender-pink blossoms that open for a single night, then close forever. If pollinated by bats or moths, they produce a juicy fruit called *pithaya,* a favorite of cactus wrens. Other vegetation includes fuzzy-looking cholla, feathery mesquite, ironwood, prickly pear, paloverde, unmistakably scented creosote, spidery ocotillo, and countless wildflowers along washes and roadsides. For more on the monument, see Hiking, Scenic Drives, and Camping.

About 1.5 miles from the visitor center is a campground. Backcountry permits for primitive camping are available at the visitor center. The visitor center, located near the monument's entrance, is the best place to get information on

hiking conditions and scheduled programs. It has good "touch" exhibits that include small animal skeletons and portions of desert plants. Open daily, 8:00 A.M.–5:00 P.M. Located **22 miles south of Why on Hwy. 85. Route 1, Box 100, Ajo, 85321; 520-387-6849.** Website: www.nps.gov.

Tohono O'odham Reservation

The town of Sells sits in the southernmost corner of the Tohono O'odham Reservations, which include the Gila Bend and San Xavier Reservations. The reservation extends from Ajo on the west, sweeps south into Mexico, is bordered by the Baboquivari Mountains on the east, and ranges north to within a few miles of the city of Casa Grande just south of Phoenix. On the reservation's eastern edge, distinctive Baboquivari Peak is revered as the home of I'itoi, creator of the Papagos. Big landmarks on reservation land are Kitt Peak Observatory and San Xavier del Bac Mission (see Tucson chapter). The town of Sells, on Hwy. 86 between Ajo and Tucson, is the tribal capital.

Outdoor Activities

Hiking

Organ Pipe Cactus National Monument

Easy hiking trails near the visitor center are most enjoyable Oct.–Apr. when it isn't so hot. The 1-mile **Campground Perimeter Trail** is a good introduction to desert vegetation. The **Desert View Nature Trail,** a 1.2-mile loop, has great views and interpretive signs. The 2.6-mile, round-trip **Paloverde Trail** goes from the visitor center to the campground. For a workout, try tackling the **Bull Pasture Trail,** a tough 4 miles with considerable elevation gain. The payoff is a sweeping view of the valley below. Easier but equally rewarding is the **Victoria Mine Trail,** a 4.5-mile round trip that leads to the mine for which it's named. From the trails you can look south into Mexico. The visitor center is located **22 miles south of Why on Hwy.**

85. Route 1, Box 100, Ajo, 85321; 520-387-6849. Website: www.nps.gov.

Seeing and Doing

Museums and Historic Sites

Ajo Historical Museum

Once St. Catherine's Indian Mission, this little building now houses a re-created blacksmith shop, dentist office, and print shop as well as artifacts and photos from Ajo's mining days. Open daily, noon–4:00 P.M.; may be closed during some summer months, and winter hours are iffy because it is staffed by volunteers, so call first. Located **just beyond mine overlook** (see Major Attractions), **downhill to your right.** 520-387-7105.

Butterfield Trail

When you get into Gila Bend and stop at its museum, you'll find a replica of the early Butterfield Stage office in the museum. In 1858 the town was a stage stop on the route between St. Louis and San Francisco. The 2,800-mile trip took 25 days at an average speed of 5 miles per hour and cost $200 per person plus meals. **On I-80, about 4 miles east of Gila Bend,** a sign points out the Butterfield Trail.

Gila Bend Museum and Tourist Office

Here, displays of Hohokam pottery and Papago baskets tell of the hunters and trappers in pursuit of the "hairy dollar bill"—the beaver—that once was abundant along the fast-flowing Gila River. Other exhibits trace the town's Native American history and its connection with the railroad. You can pick up a driving tour map that directs you to the **Sanuc District** of the Tohono O'odam Nation and the former site of the ancient village. The map also guides you to the ruins of the old adobe **St. Michael's Catholic Church,** an Indian **ceremonial mound** that dates to the 900s, and the **Stout Hotel** at Pima and Capitol, built in 1929 and visited by Tom Mix, John Wayne, and Myrna Loy. Open daily, 8:00 A.M.–4:00 P.M. 644 **W. Pima St., Gila Bend,** 85337; 502-683-2002, fax 502-683-6430.

Painted Rocks Park

This Bureau of Land Management park protects extensive petroglyphs along a winding trail through a huge rock mound. The petroglyphs are accessible from Painted Rock Rd. on a 0.5-mile graded dirt road to Painted Rock Dam, which creates the largest flood-control reservoir in the state. The petroglyphs once served as a landmark for travelers along the Butterfield Stage route. There is camping in the park (see Camping). **Take I-8 west of Gila Bend 12.5 miles to exit 102 and continue north 10.7 miles to** Painted Rocks Park. For information call the **BLM Field Office (602-580-5500)** Mon.–Fri., 7:30 A.M.–4:15 P.M., or the **Gila Bend Chamber of Commerce (520-623-2002).**

Scenic Drives

Ajo Mountain Drive

This 21-mile, one-way loop through Organ Pipe Cactus National Monument (see Major Attractions) follows graded dirt and paved roads and is passable in a passenger car if you're careful. Don't cross washes if water is running through them. Pick up a road guide (50 cents) at the visitor center, fill your water bottles, and set out. The guide numbers correspond to clearly marked trail placards, pointing out types of plants, scenic views, and geologic formations. Don't miss the window rock at about 9.5 miles at milepost 13, formed by wind erosion and the expansion and contraction of freezing and thawing water. At milepost 15, Estes Canyon, there are picnic tables and solar toilets, but no water. The visitor center is located **22 miles south of Why on Hwy. 85.** Route 1, Box 100, Ajo, 85321; 520-387-6849. Website: www.nps.gov.

El Camino del Diablo (Hwy. of the Devil)

About 120 miles of this historic, dusty, and difficult route that links Mexico with California passes through the Cabeza Prieta Wildlife Refuge (see Major Attractions). The two-track trail requires a sturdy four-wheel-drive vehicle with high ground clearance. For safety and ecological reasons, no off-roading is permitted. You must stop for permits at the visitor center on the north edge of Ajo on Hwy. 85. Open Mon.–Fri., 7:30 A.M.–4:30 P.M.; closed from noon–1:00 P.M. for lunch. 1611 N. Second Ave., Ajo, 85321; 520-387-6483.

Tours

La Ruta de Sonora

This nonprofit company does genuine eco-tours that focus on the specifics of a region as seen through the eyes of local people. Three-day weekends explore the history, culture, biology, and landscapes of southwestern Arizona and northern Sonora. Three well-priced itineraries cover many hidden places, burrowing into an area's delightful secrets. If you like getting close to nature and different cultures, you'll love these low-key tours that leave by van from Tucson or Phoenix. 201 W. Esperanza Ave., Curley School, Rm. 2, P.O. Box 699, Ajo, 85321; 520-387-3499 or 800-806-0766. Website: www.laruta.org.

Will Nelson's Ajo Stage Line

An excellent way to explore the area comfortably and to cross into Mexico for a brief South of the Border experience is to hook up with Will. He guides day trips as far south as Puerto Peñasco, a developing resort city on the Gulf of California, and to El Pinacate, the ring of ancient volcanoes known to past Native Americans as the Stone People. He also does overnight camp outs, hiking treks, and fishing trips. A four-day/three-night trip covers the 17th-century Spanish missions established by Padre Kino. Call for availability and information on other trips that include California and Texas. 1041 Solana, Ajo, 85321; 800-942-1981 or 520-387-6467. Website: www.ajostageline.com.

Where to Stay

Bed-and-Breakfasts

Guest House Inn—$$$

Built in 1925 by Phelps Dodge for visiting company officials, it still reflects the desire to create a lasting impression with luxury furnishings and accommodations. There are four rooms with private baths. Full, cooked breakfast included. 700 Guest House Rd., Ajo, 85321; 520-387-6133. Website: www.wgn.net/~morris/ajo.

Mine Manager's House Bed and Breakfast—$$$

Voted one of the top 50 inns in America by *Inn Times,* the inn is poised on a hill that affords a 30-mile view. Built in 1919 for the manager of the New Cornelia Company and his family, it has five rooms with private baths. Rates include a full, cooked breakfast. 601 Greenway Dr., Ajo, 85321; 520-387-6505, fax 520-387-6508.

Motels

La Siesta Motel and RV Resort—$$

It offers modest rooms as well as camping spaces (see below). 2561 N. Hwy. 85, Ajo, 85321; 520-387-6569.

Camping

There are half a dozen places along Hwy. 85 to park your RV for one night or for an entire winter season, as many snowbirds do. **Ajo Heights RV Park** (2000 N. Hwy. 85, Ajo, 85321; 520-387-6796) has 32 large sites with full hookups, cable TV, and phones; many sites have great views. **Belly Acres** (2030 N. Hwy. 85, Ajo, 85321; 520-387-4365) has shade trees and spaces with patios, tables, and barbecue facilities. **La Siesta Motel and RV Resort** (2561 N. Hwy. 85, Ajo, 85321; 520-387-6569) offers spaces with full hookups, telephones, cable TV, pool, and tennis court. **Shadow Ridge RV Resort** (431 N. Second Ave./Hwy. 85, Ajo, 85321; 520-387-5055) gets top ratings from RV publications for its classy clubhouse, laundry room, and fitness center. It has 125 full hookup spaces plus overflow areas with electricity and TV.

Organ Pipe Cactus National Monument

About 1.5 miles from the visitor center, well-planned camping spaces with natural foliage have water, rest rooms, grills, tables, and a dump station, but no hookups. Expect to be visited by quail, roadrunners, cardinals, cottontails, and jackrabbits. Spaces are first-come, first-served. Located 22 miles south of Why on Hwy. 85. Route 1, Box 100, Ajo, 85321; 520-387-6849. Website: www.nps.gov.

Painted Rocks Park

There are 30 tent or RV sites, vault toilets, picnic areas, and fire grills but no showers. Take I-8 west of Gila Bend 12.5 miles to exit 102 and continue north 10.7 miles to Painted Rocks Park. For information call BLM Field Office (602-580-5500) Mon.–Fri., 7:30 A.M.–4:15 P.M., or Gila Bend Chamber of Commerce; 520-623-2002.

Where to Eat

Senor Sanchez—$$–$$$

This cheerful place is ideal for a frosty brew or a glass of vino, along with good Mexican food. Open daily, 11:00 A.M.–9:00 P.M. 663 Second Ave., Ajo; 520-387-6226.

Copper Kettle—$$

Good, basic food served buffet-style as well as from a regular menu. Located across from the Plaza Deli. Open Mon.–Sat., 7:00 A.M.–8:00 P.M. 23 Plaza St., Ajo; 520-387-7222.

Dago Joe's Family Restaurant—$–$$

Eating here is a sort of international grab bag, with steaks, Mexican, Italian, and seafood offered in a variety of dishes. Good selection of microbrews. Open Sun.–Fri., 11:00 A.M.–9:00 P.M.; Sat., 5:00 P.M.–9:00 P.M. May close Mon.–Wed. during the summer. 2055 N. Hwy. 85, Ajo; 520-387-6904.

Eat My Buns—$–$$

Wonderful fresh-from-the-oven breads, pastries, and donuts waft their wonderful aroma even before you're inside. Open Wed.–Sun., 5:30 A.M. until they sell out, they say. 932 Second Ave., Ajo; 520-387-2867.

Marcela's—$–$$

This new little restaurant and bakery, named for the owner's grandmother, serves made-from-scratch Mexican food as well as American dishes. If you've never tasted *machaca*, try it here. Homemade dried beef jerky is char-broiled, then stuffed into a burrito. Delicious! The bakery turns out *pan dulce*, cinnamon rolls, Mexican French bread, empanadas, and more. Open daily, 6:00 A.M.–8:00 P.M. 117 Dorsey St., Ajo; 520-387-4139.

Plaza Ice Cream & Deli—$

This is a traditional rest stop for travelers on their way to Rocky Point, the beach resort in Sonora, Mexico. In front of a onetime movie theater, umbrella tables sit under a shady arcade. Specialties are New York–style deli sandwiches (they're huge) and hand-dipped ice-cream treats, all at very modest prices. Owner Rose Sophy creates most of them herself. Open daily, 9:00 A.M.–5:00 P.M. 28 Plaza St., Ajo; 520-387-DELI.

Services

Traveling west on I-8 from the Phoenix area, at the point where Hwy. 85 converges with I-8, there is a rest area with a shaded table but little else.

Ajo Chamber of Commerce

Open Mon.–Fri., 9:00 A.M.–4:00 P.M. 321 Taladro, Ajo, 85321; 520-387-7742. Website: www.ajoinaz.com.

Gila Bend Tourist Office

Open daily, 8:00 A.M.–4:00 P.M. 644 W. Pima St., Gila Bend, 85337; 520-623-2002.

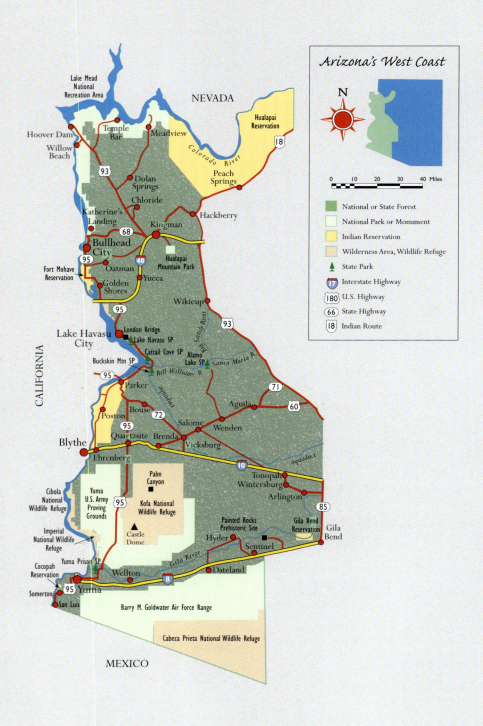

Arizona's West Coast

N

0	10	20	30	40	Miles	

National or State Forest
National Park or Monument
Indian Reservation
Wilderness Area, Wildlife Refuge
State Park
17 Interstate Highway
180 U.S. Highway
66 State Highway
18 Indian Route

NEVADA

Lake Mead National Recreation Area

Hoover Dam
Willow Beach
Temple Bar
Meadview
Hualapai Reservation
Colorado River
18
Peach Springs
93
Dolan Springs
Chloride
Katherine's Landing
Kingman
Hackberry
68
Bullhead City
95
Fort Mohave Reservation
Oatman
Yucca
Hualapai Mountain Park
40
Golden Shores
Wikieup
93
Sandy River
95
Lake Havasu City
London Bridge
Lake Havasu SP
Cattail Cove SP
Alamo Lake SP
Santa Maria R.
Buckskin Mtn SP
Bill Williams R.
Parker
Big Sandy River
Bouse
72
Salome
71
Aguila
60
Poston
95
Quartzsite
Brenda
Wenden
Blythe
Vicksburg
Ehrenberg
Palm Canyon
10
Tonopah
Wintersburg
Arlington
aqueduct
85
Cibola National Wildlife Refuge
Yuma U.S. Army Proving Grounds
Kofa National Wildlife Refuge
Painted Rocks Prehistoric Site
Gila Bend Reservation
Gila Bend
Imperial National Wildlife Refuge
Castle Dome
Hyder
Sentinel
Cocopah Reservation
Yuma Prison SP
Gila River
Somerton
Wellton
8
Dateland
95
Yuma
San Luis
Barry M. Goldwater Air Force Range
CALIFORNIA
Cabeza Prieta National Wildlife Refuge

MEXICO

Arizona's West Coast

*View from the Blue Water Resort in Parker, Arizona, shows the
Colorado River flanked by sunset-warmed cliffs.*

Yuma

On the banks of the Colorado River in Arizona's southwestern corner, Yuma often has the dubious distinction of being the hottest spot in the nation. At an elevation of just 138 feet, it gets less than 2 inches of rain per year. But with temperatures well under 100°F Nov.–May, the town has plenty of warm, sunny days that are wonderfully pleasant. They attract a huge snowbird population, with more than 20,000 RV spaces generally crammed full by the end of Jan., swelling Yuma's 60,000 population to more than 100,000.

Its riverside location makes it a prime agricultural center. Those tidy rows of green that stretch into the distance are lettuce. Iceberg, leaf, and Romaine cover more than 41,000 acres of desert adjacent to the Colorado River, securing the state's niche as the nation's number-two producer of lettuce, just behind California. Mid-Nov.–mid-Apr., about 95 percent of the lettuce consumed in the United States comes from Yuma and, on the other side of the Colorado, Imperial County, California. Planting begins in mid-Aug. with harvesting in full swing by early Nov.–Mar. Other crops you'll see include wheat, alfalfa, corn, peanuts, bell peppers, and cotton. The Marine Corps Air Station and Yuma Proving Grounds also add to the city's economy, which helps support the second largest K-Mart in the country.

Yuma is busy capitalizing on its rich history, still charmingly apparent in decades-old homes and commercial buildings. The whole town is awaiting federal approval as a National Heritage Area, and is well into a project that will create protected wetlands and host a birding festival.

History

Native Americans have farmed along the Colorado River near Yuma for centuries, with the Spanish showing up in the 1500s. Yuma became a river-crossing point and an important

steamship port, and the military used steamboats to transport wagons and mules, stagecoaches, and carriages. In 1877 the railroad arrived, further establishing the town's commercial value. When Laguna Dam was built upstream in 1909, the Colorado's now-controlled flow made it possible for commercial agricultural crops to flourish, but it was the military that made the biggest contribution to the city's ability to take hold in those brutal, pre-air-conditioning days (see Major Attractions). Soldiers were assigned here whether or not it was where they wanted to be, and ancillary services developed to support them.

Major Attractions

Yuma Crossing State Historic Park

One of the newest additions to the state park system, this 19-acre park celebrates 500 years of crossing the Colorado River between Arizona and California. At this point the river executes a particularly narrow bend that created an ideal place to ford, ferry, and, later, build a bridge.

The Southern Pacific Railroad built a bridge there, a version of which still stands, and a community grew up around the crossing. Native Americans, Spanish explorers, settlers, and miners on their way to California's 1849 Gold Rush have all contributed to the site's historic significance. Also part of the park, a refurbished U.S. Army Quartermaster Depot issued supplies to frontier forts. The mule barn, once housing 900 of the surefooted creatures as they transported munitions and food inland, has been restored, along with a storehouse for crates and barrels that traveled from the Gulf of California up the Colorado to Yuma. A 1910 Model T Ford, a 1931 Model A, and a 1907 Baldwin oil-fired steam engine donated by Southern Pacific are remnants of early river-crossing days. You can pick up a pamphlet at the visitor center for a self-guided tour, or call ahead for the schedule of ranger-guided tours. Small fee. Open Nov. 1–Apr. 30, daily, 9:00 A.M.–5:00 P.M.; May 1–Oct. 31, Thurs.–Mon., 9:00 A.M.–5:00 P.M.; closed Christmas and Thanksgiving. 201 N. Fourth Ave., Yuma, 85364; 520-329-0471. Website: www.pr.state.az.us.

Yuma Territorial Prison State Historic Park

A mile east of Yuma Crossing lies the most-visited historical park in the state system, attracting more than 100,000 visitors a year. In 1876, when seven inmates moved into two cells they had built themselves, this prison was on the cutting edge of penology. It had a library, hospital, tailor and shoe shops, blacksmith, and bakery. The first prison in the Arizona Territory, it was originally planned for Phoenix. But through early sleight-of-hand legislation it ended up in Yuma, expanding from two cells to hold a 30-bad-guy capacity to more than 400. The prison museum records transgressions of female as well as male prisoners. Unfaithful wives, robbers, and murderers did the crime and served the time. Recaptured escapees were made to wear a ball and chain. The chilling Dark Cell, a 15-foot-by-15-foot cave, along with a diet of bread and water, provided discipline. Because of

Getting There
Yuma is less than a three-hour drive from Phoenix. Take I-10 east toward Tucson (you're really going south at this point), and between Casa Grande and Eloy, transition to I-8 westbound, which goes east-west directly through Yuma. US 95 goes through Yuma north-south. Delta and Mesa Airlines serve Yuma from Phoenix and Los Angeles.

overcrowding, the prison was closed in 1909 and parts were converted to a high school. On Halloween, cells are rented to local businesses so costumed children can trick-or-treat. Rangers and volunteers in prison garb, locked in cells, portray former convicts. It's appropriate for a place that, some say, is filled with the ghosts of prisoners past. Small fee. Open daily, 8:00 A.M.–5:00 P.M., except Christmas Day. Located off I-8 and Giss Parkway. Box 10792, Yuma, 85366; 520-783-4771. Website: www.pr.state.az.us.

Festivals and Events

Gathering of the Gunfighers
early Jan.
This fun weekend festival includes skits and gunfights staged by authentically costumed re-enactors. Floozies and cowboys, sheriffs and preachers delight kids while teaching history and stressing gun safety. Held at Yuma Territorial Prison State Historic Park (see Major Attractions). 520-783-4771.

Outdoor Activities

Birding

Cibola National Wildlife Refuge
We absolutely love this refuge because of its

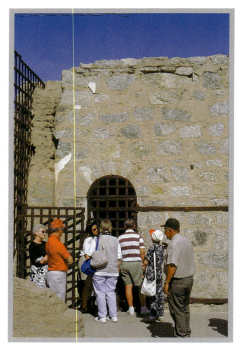

Now a state park, the Yuma Territorial Prison once held such shady Old West characters as Phin Clanton.

4-mile Canada Goose Loop. You drive your car slowly along the one-way gravel road, staying in the car so as not to frighten the geese, but getting very close to the fields where thousands of the dark gray birds are feeding. The loop is always open, but the time to see the geese is mid-Nov.–Feb., with peak numbers there Dec.–Jan. You'll probably also spot beautiful white snow geese, as well as impressive 4-foot sandhill cranes that follow the same migration routes. Hunting, fishing, and boating are allowed, but no camping. Located just north of Imperial National Wildlife Refuge (see below). From Yuma **take US 95 north to I-10, and take I-10 west to Neighbours Blvd. exit/exit 78 just west of Blythe, California, then head south about 18 miles. Cross over Cibola Bridge, back into Arizona; the visitor center, about 3.5 miles beyond the bridge, is on the right. Route 2, Box 138, Cibola, 85328; 520-857-3253.**

Imperial National Wildlife Refuge

This refuge hugs the Colorado River for about 30 miles along the California-Arizona border and encompasses a number of small lakes, providing rich riparian habitat for many species. Its 25,625 acres protect both desert and river ecosystems. During winter months (best time to visit because summers are excruciatingly hot), migrating waterfowl include marsh- and shore-birds using the lakes for winter stopovers. Located about 40 miles northeast of Yuma. **Take US 95 north from Yuma to Martinez Lake Rd. and follow signs to the visitor center. P.O. Box 72217, Martinez Lake, 85365; 520-783-3371.**

Golf

Many snowbirds come specifically to use the well-priced courses in Yuma, which *Golf Digest* magazine recently rated the seventh-best city in the country for golf. Thirteen well-tended courses bear this out. The 18-hole course at **Cocopah Bend (520-343-1663)** and the nine-hole, par 36 **Fortuna de Ray (520-342-4766)** connect with RV parks. You just walk next door. **Desert Hills Municipal Golf Course (520-341-0644)** has been recognized by *Golf Digest* as Arizona's Best Municipal Course. It has a par 72, 6,800-yard (blue tees) 18-hole layout. The 6,767-yard, par 72 course at **Mesa del Sol (520-342-1283)** has 18 championship holes designed by Arnold Palmer, on-course beverage service, and an upscale lounge and restaurant.

Hiking

Imperial National Wildlife Refuge

You can do a lot of things in this refuge along the Colorado River, like hunting, hiking, bird-watching, fishing, boating, and even water-skiing on two sections of the river. The **Painted Desert Trail**, a popular, easy walk through the Sonoran Desert, passes ancient lava flows, runs through dry washes, and provides views of beautifully colored rock formations. It takes about an hour to walk at a leisurely pace, with one fairly steep, but brief uphill. You can pick up a walking guide at the refuge office. Overnight camping is not permitted. **Take US 95 north from Yuma to Martinez Lake Rd. and follow signs to the visitor center,** which has natural-history exhibits and information for hiking, hunting, and boating. **P.O. Box 72217, Martinez Lake, 85365; 520-783-3371.**

Kofa National Wildlife Refuge

The refuge's name, Kofa, is a remnant from mining days, an acronym for King of Arizona Mine. Hiking is an excellent way to get to know the refuge, but watch for abandoned mine shafts and open pits. The **Palm Canyon Trail,** a 1-mile round-trip hike, has interesting plants along the way. Going is slow because of large rocks and a few steep scrambles. You'll see the palms for which the canyon is named (*Washingtonia filifera*) near the end of a side canyon to the north. You can hike up to them if you really want a workout. To get there, head **northeast on US 95, and once you're in the refuge, look for Palm Canyon to the right. Ten miles of dirt road lead to the canyon entrance.**

The southern boundary of the refuge is about 40 miles from Yuma on US 95 north. There are four clearly marked main refuge entrances along US 95. Stop for maps and information at the refuge office in Yuma. Open Mon.–Fri., 7:30 A.M.–4:30 P.M. **356 W. First St., P.O. Box 6290, Yuma, 85366-6290; 520-783-7861.**

Seeing and Doing

Scenic Drives

Imperial National Wildlife Refuge

You can drive your car on graded gravel **Red Cloud Mine Rd.** (if it's been raining, check at the visitor center for road conditions) to four lookout points that provide great views of the Colorado River and the Chocolate Mountains. The farthest lookout point, Smoke Tree Point, is at 4.2 miles. Beyond that, the road leaves the

refuge and winds through the U.S. Army's Yuma Proving Grounds, where you must stay on the road. It dead-ends in a refuge wilderness area with no facilities. The refuge is located north of the resort community of Martinez Lake. From Yuma take **US 95 north to Martinez Lake Rd. and follow signs to the visitor center. P.O. Box 72217, Martinez Lake, 85365; 520-783-3371.**

Shopping

Algodones, Baja California

It often comes as a surprise that you can be in Mexico 10 minutes after leaving your Yuma hotel. Park your vehicle in the large parking lot on the U.S. side and walk across the border. If you're staying less than 72 hours, a passport is not necessary, but a picture I.D. is a good idea. You're allowed to bring back $400 worth of merchandise per person, including a maximum of one quart of liquor and one carton of cigarettes.

It's immediately apparent from the signs that this is where U.S. residents come for low-cost surgery, dental work, and prescription drugs. "Buy $30 worth Tylenol, get a free Viagra sample" encourages one colorful sign. Among worthwhile shopping venues is **Curios la Paloma de Plata, on Calle 3a,** owned by English-speaking brothers who purvey stained and blown glass, ceramics, leather goods, and more. Street vendors display silver jewelry and knick-knacks, with bargaining expected as part of the fun. Algodones is so appreciative of its U.S. visitors that its two annual festivals are a Welcome Winter Visitors celebration in Dec., and a Thank You Festival in Mar.

Tours

BOAT TOURS

Colorado King I Paddle Boat

Leaving from the same point on the river as Yuma River Tours (see below), this replica stern-wheeler does relaxing, slow-moving cruises along the river. Seating on the upper deck is covered so you're protected from the sun. Reservations are a must because the schedule is pretty much determined by when there is a full boat. A recorded message tells you when the next available cruises will go. **520-782-2412.**

Yuma River Tours

An interesting, comfortable way to see the Imperial National Wildlife Refuge is via jet boat. You can join a three-, four-, or five-hour narrated tour to see petroglyphs, old ranch sites, and 1800s rock cabins. A stop at Lonesome Knolls reveals the spot where prospector Roy Morgan buried his dog, Lonesome. A headstone exhorts visitors to place a rock on the grave, which has resulted in an impressive cairn. This lovely riverside area is generally a picnic stop for the tour. A great variety of birds may be spotted along the river, commonly including double-crested cormorants, sandpipers, kingbirds, western grebes, and several varieties of herons. Winter months, Nov.–Mar., are best for seeing migratory birds. Senior's and children's rates are offered, and there is a minimum number of passengers per trip. Three-, five-, and seven-hour tours depart year-round from Fisher's Landing, 32 miles northeast of Yuma. **Take US 95 northeast to Martinez Lake Rd. Turn west and proceed 10 miles to Fisher's Landing.** The boat is moored behind Olsen's store. 1920 **Arizona Ave., Yuma, 85364; 520-783-4400. Website: www.yumarivertours.com.**

WALKING TOURS

To get a feel of the city's past, pick up a self-guided walking-tour map of historic downtown Yuma at the Convention & Visitors Bureau (see Services). It guides you to the art-deco **Yuma Theatre** on Main St., built in 1911, and the **Arizona Historical Society Century House Museum**, once the home of steamboat captain Andrew Mellon.

Wildlife Viewing

Kofa National Wildlife Refuge

Some people say they're hard pressed to find the beauty in this 665,400-acre desert refuge, but others absolutely revel in spotting a desert bighorn sheep or a sharp-shinned hawk. The sheep have a stable population of close to 1,000 within the refuge, enough so that it is a source for transplanting animals to other traditional sheep habitats that have lost their populations. Take binoculars for spotting them, because it's unlikely you'll get very close. Try early morning or evening around a water source, when the bighorns come down to drink, or you may catch a glimpse of one against the skyline at the top of Palm Canyon. Bird species in residence year-round are sharp-shinned and red-tailed hawks, Gambel's quail, western screech owl, Gila woodpecker, and its colorful look-alike, the gilded flicker. There are four clearly marked main refuge entrances along US 95. Stop for maps and information at the refuge office in Yuma. Open Mon.–Fri., 7:30 A.M.–4:30 P.M. **356 W. First St., P.O. Box 6290, Yuma, 85366-6290; 520-783-7861.**

Where to Stay

Chains include Comfort Inn, Days Inn, Holiday Inn Express, Motel 6, Super 8, and Travelodge.

Best Western Inn Suites—$$–$$$

Of the three Best Westerns in Yuma, we like this one because it has in-room coffeemakers, refrigerators stocked with juice and water, and microwaves with popcorn. You don't have to leave the room for that first caffeine jolt. A complimentary cocktail hour and an expansive breakfast buffet are included in the room rate. 1450 Castle Dome Rd., Yuma, 85366; 800-922-2034 or 520-783-8341.

Camping

There are no less than 84 RV and mobile home parks in Yuma, ranging from basic to luxury. Most are senior-friendly, catering to a mature crowd rather than families. Pick up a list from the Convention & Visitors Bureau (see Services).

Kofa National Wildlife Refuge

Though there no services anywhere in the refuge, you can camp pretty much anywhere you wish, for 14 days, but you must be more than 0.25 mile away from any water hole. There are four refuge entrances along US 95. Stop for maps and information at the refuge office in Yuma. Open Mon.–Fri., 7:30 A.M.–4:30 P.M. **356 W. First St., P.O. Box 6290, Yuma, 85366-6290; 520-783-7861.**

Where to Eat

The city has more than two dozen fast-food places and a good selection of Mexican restaurants, including **El Pappagallo, Don Quijote,** and the family-owned **Chretin's,** on S. 15th Ave.

Julieanna's—$$–$$$

At Yuma's most upscale eatery, prices are still reasonable for exceptionally good food. Fresh fish (yes, even in Yuma), steaks, and veal dishes, plus a great selection of luncheon salads make this place worth more than one visit. Open Mon.–Fri., 11:00 A.M.–3:00 P.M. and 4:30 P.M.–9:00 P.M.; Sat., 4:30 P.M.–9:00 P.M. **1951 W. 25th St.; 520-317-1961.**

La Fonda—$–$$

Still in its original location after 40 years, this wonderfully homey little restaurant serves chips and salsa even with breakfast, along with tumblers of fresh orange juice. Chimichangas and fajitas are specialties. If you ask nicely, Frank Ramos, the owner, will take you through the tortilla factory in back where workers handmake tortillas for the restaurant as well as other businesses. Open Mon.–Sat., 9:00 A.M.–4:00 P.M. **1095 S. Third St.; 520-783-6902.**

Lutes Casino—$–$$

The oldest continuing pool hall and domino parlor in the state, it has an almost Fellini-esque quality about it. You can't believe so much stuff has been crammed into one place without hampering the movements of the waitstaff. The 1901 building has housed an investment company, grocery store, and hotel. Although once rough and rowdy, today it has a family clientele, serving up giant burgers, sandwiches, tacos, burritos, and hot dogs washed down with beer or wine. The famous (or infamous) Especial, a combination cheeseburger and hot dog covered with hot sauce, has been known to singe the nose hair of even the hardiest eater. Best time to stop in is Sat. afternoon when the place is rockin'. You can tell the tourists; they're the ones walking around with beers, looking at all the stuff. Join in. Lute's loves it. Open Mon.–Sat., 9:00 A.M.–8:00 P.M.; Sun., 10:00 A.M.–6:00 P.M. **221 Main St.; 520-782-2192.** Website: www.lutescasino.com.

Services

Den of the Red Bear

A computer store and **cybercafe.** Two computers at $2 per hour. Open Mon.–Sat., 10:00 A.M.–8:00 P.M. **2801 S. Fourth Ave., No. 14; 520-344-1415.** Website: www.red-bear.com.

Yuma Convention & Visitors Bureau

Here you'll find good area information as well as sweatshirts and other items bearing the image of Henri, the elegant white egret that's the bureau's icon. Open winter, Mon.–Fri., 9:00 A.M.–6:00 P.M., Sat., 9 A.M.–4:00 P.M., and Sun., 10:00 A.M.–2:00 P.M.; summer, Mon.–Fri., 9:00 A.M.–5:00 P.M., Sat., 9 A.M.–4:00 P.M., and Sun., 10:00 A.M.–2:00 P.M. **377 S. Main St., Yuma, 85364; 520-783-0071.** Website: www.visityuma.com.

Quartzsite and Parker

Quartzsite is often simply a place to bypass quickly on the way to Palm Springs, California. However, it annually hosts 11 of the country's most important gem and mineral shows. Almost 2,000 vendors arrive in Nov.–Dec., settling in from colder climes to sell almost every product imaginable. Booths, trailers, stands, and cars along Business Loop 10 become seasonal shops.

Parker, a riverbank community of nearly 3,000, is beginning to rival Lake Havasu City, 38 miles to the north, as a fun-on-the-water capital. On the Colorado River Indian Reservation at an elevation of 450 feet, its current focus is year-round tourism, with snowbirds winging in from Washington and Oregon in force during winter months. More than 5,000 RV sites in nine parks accommodate this influx. A bridge crosses the Colorado to Earp, California, named for Wyatt, who locals joke was the area's first winter visitor. Aquatic recreation opportunities—speedboat racing, water skiing, swimming, kayaking, and canoeing, as well as fishing—are a powerful draw along the Parker Strip, a 16.5-mile stretch of river that extends from Parker Dam south to Headgate Dam. Banks on both sides of the river are lined with RV parks and manufactured homes, with a few notable upscale housing developments. In The Keys, laced with canals, homes can top $1 million.

History

Quartzsite is perhaps best known for Hadji Ali, a Syrian, who signed on as a camel driver for the U.S. Army in 1856. With a name anglicized to "Hi Jolly" to better fit local tongues, he was hired to herd desert pack animals ordered by then secretary of war Jefferson Davis; Davis believed camels could solve transport problems in the

desert Southwest. When the humped beasts proved incompatible with Army mules, Hadji Ali ended up with a small herd that he used in his guiding and prospecting business. He died in 1902. You can visit his grave at the Quartzsite Cemetery where a monument explains his history.

During World War II, close to 18,000 persons of Japanese ancestry, most of them U.S. citizens, were interned for more than three years in tarpaper barracks in the Poston area. A relic of the area's past is the Poston Memorial Monument, just west of the town of Poston.

Parker's history is evident in a nearby ghost town called Swansea, a source of rich copper ore in the mid-1800s. Swansea is a 45-minute ride on a dirt road from Parker, across the desert, but the remnants of many dwellings and shops make an interesting side trip. Parker's post office was established in 1876, and apparently was named for Captain Parker, an old-timer who lived with the Indians a few miles below the present town site. Not a great deal happened in this little place on the Colorado River Indian Reservation, even with the arrival of the Atchison, Topeka and Santa Fe Railroad in 1906. Parker was incorporated in 1948, relying on agriculture to sustain

Parker Dam, completed in 1938, forms Lake Havasu and creates an aquatic playground.

its economy. It took present-day tourism to make the state sit up and take notice of Parker and its scenic placement on the Colorado River.

Festivals and Events

Quartzsite Pow Wow

mid-Jan.

Known internationally as one of the world's largest gem and mineral shows, it attracts dealers (and bargain hunters) from all over the world. Part of January's Pow Wow are **Hi Jolly Daze,** named for Hadji Ali, a Syrian camel driver. 520-927-5600.

Another Dam Bike Race

last weekend of Feb.

Going strong since 1996 and one of the top eight bike races in the country, this popular event has attracted 36 Tour de France competitors as well as Jeannie Longo, a 12-time world champion who brought her entire team to participate. With substantial cash prizes, the three-day event includes a hill climb, criterium, and road race, in which more than 1,000 cyclists participate. Held **in Parker. 520-855-3553 or 888-733-7275. Website: www.anotherdamrace.com.**

La Paz County Park Swap Meet

Sats., Oct.–Mar.

More than 100 sellers gather at dawn at this park north of Parker to purvey everything from electronic equipment to antiques. Crowds of more than 4,000 generally spend the better part of the day cadging deals from vendors who figure bargaining is part of the game. Located **8 miles north of Parker on Hwy. 95 Business Route. 520-667-2069.**

Outdoor Activities

Birding

Bill Williams River Wildlife Refuge

This is an important and lovely habitat, since much of the indigenous cottonwood-willow forests along the lower Colorado have been wiped out by introduced salt cedar. The 6,000-acre refuge includes a marshy delta where the Bill Williams and lower Colorado Rivers meet, which is a sort of avian United Nations. At least 275 bird species, including visitors from South America and Canada, include Canada geese, tanagers, flycatchers, and the endangered Yuma clapper rail among frequent visitors during the winter. From Parker, **go 15 miles north on Hwy. 95 to unpaved Bill Williams River Rd.** north of Parker Dam just before the bridge. Leave your vehicle there, or drive the dirt road for a few miles, then continue on foot to the riparian habitat. 520-667-4144.

Boating

Parker's location on the Colorado, between Parker Dam on the north and Headgate Dam on the south, puts it at the lower end of a 16.5-mile-long aquatic recreation area called the Parker Strip that is fast becoming a prime Arizona West Coast destination. Parks, boat-launch ramps, marinas, and rental facilities for watersports equipment dot the shoreline. While Lake Havasu to the north is often gunwale-to-gunwale with boat traffic on a sunny summer weekend, Parker still has a less-crowded feel, but with plenty of waterfront restaurants and accommodations to take care of visitors. Sundance, Fox's, and The Roadrunner sometimes have boats three deep at their docks. In general, the water sports season runs Apr.–early Sept., after which river temperatures are too cold for all but the hardiest. For fun on the river, **River Parasail (520- 66-RIVER)** takes riders aloft from a winch-equipped boat, rents kayaks, and runs party cruises on a comfortable pontoon boat complete with drink-mixin' blender. The boat has a large barbecue and ice chests for guests' use.

Golf

Emerald Canyon Golf Course

Lauded by *Golf Digest* for its unusual layout and stunning surroundings as well as reasonable greens fees, this course offers a tricky 18 holes overlooking the Colorado River. Deep canyons, elevated tees, ravines, and sweeping vistas create fascinating play. The year-round desert course draws golfers nationwide for its beauty and top-notch facilities. Located **7.5 miles north of Parker on Hwy. 95 Business Route. 520-667-3366.**

Seeing and Doing

Museums and Historic Sites

Colorado Indian Tribes Museum and Library

Housed in a complex with tribal administra-tion offices, the museum explains a bit about the Mojave, Chemehuevi, Navajo, and Hopi cultures that all occupy the Colorado River Indian Reservation. Each, however, strives to retain its own culture and traditions. The museum contains the largest collection of Chemehuevi baskets in the world, Mojave pottery, Navajo jewelry, and Hopi kachina dolls. Open Mon.–Fri., 8:00 A.M.–1:00 P.M. and 2:00 P.M.–5:00 P.M. Located **at Four Corners, 1 mile south of Parker on Parker-Poston Rd. 520-669-1335 museum, 520-669-8262 library.**

Parker Dam

Built between 1934 and 1938, it is the barrier that forms Lake Havasu and is one of the dams built by the Bureau of Reclamation that helped bring the once-mighty Colorado River to its knees. Hwy. 95 crosses over it into California, where the power plant is located. The dam's main purpose is to store water for the Colorado River Aqueduct, which supplies southern California, and the Central Arizona Project aqueduct, which keeps water flowing to central and southern Arizona. The deepest dam in the world, 73 percent of its overall 320 feet lies below the original riverbed. Public parking, mostly on the California side, is available so you can get out of your car and walk across the dam for a good view of the downstream canyon. Viewing areas are open, but self-guided tours no longer are available. Located **about 17 miles northeast of Parker on Hwy. 95. 760-663-3712.**

Tyson Wells Stage Station Museum

The little museum is housed in an original adobe structure filled with mining and historical artifacts. Donations welcome. Open Wed.–Sun., 10:00 A.M.–4:00 P.M. Located on **Main St. 0.25 mile west of I-10 and US 95 junction in Quartzsite.** Watch for the brown Historical Marker sign. **520-629-5229.**

Scenic Drives

Parker Dam Rd. Backcountry Byway

The dam marks the north end of this scenic route

on the California side of the river. Established by the Bureau of Land Management, the 11-mile paved road parallels the Colorado River and can be part of an interesting loop if you cross back over to the Arizona side just south of Headgate Dam. You can stop and swim, fish, hike, and do some rockhounding. Information kiosks explain the forces that created the mountains 2 billion years ago when the earth's crustal plates collided. For information contact the **BLM Lake Havasu Field Office, 520-505-1200.**

Wagering

Blue Water Resort & Casino

A gaming enterprise of the Colorado River Indian Tribes, it's also the most upscale hostelry in the area (see Where to Stay). The low-key casino has 400 slots, a card room, and bingo room. The lounge has a big-screen TV, The Feast restaurant is open 24 hours and has well-priced buffets for all meals as well as table service, and a fine-dining area offers good steak and seafood. A dramatic five-story atrium overlooking the river encloses four swimming pools and a water slide. You can pilot your boat to the resort's private marina for a meal or a few hours of gaming. **11300 Resort Dr., Parker, 85344; 888-243-3360 or 520-669-7000. Website: www.bluewaterfun.com.**

Where to Stay

In Quartzsite there are a few chain motels, including a Hampton Inn and Comfort Inn, with more of a selection a half hour east in Blythe, California, or north in Parker. There's a Best Western, Budget Inn, and half a dozen other family-operated motels right in Parker. Call 520-667-2174 for a complete listing.

Arizona Shores—$$$

This motel has 11 modest rooms directly on the water. Each has two double beds, color TV, full kitchen with utensils, plus a boat slip. **9388 Riverside Dr., Parker, 85344; 520-667-2685.**

Blue Water Resort & Casino—$$$

This attractive resort has rooms with river and marina views. Lounge, 24-hour restaurant, and fine-dining area, plus four swimming pools and a water slide. Rates are seasonal, with best bargains during winter months. **11300 Resort Dr., Parker, 85344; 888-243-3360 or 520-669-7000. Website: www.bluewaterfun.com.**

Camping

In Quartzsite, almost a dozen well-priced RV parks fill up with snowbirds during winter months. There are more than 4,000 RV sites along the Parker Strip (includes the California side), as well as resorts that offer mobile-home rentals.

Buckskin Mountain State Park

This attractive park and its associate unit, River Island, have a variety of campsites with hookups. The site has rest rooms and showers, as well as a boat ramp, picnic area, gas dock, boat rentals, store, and adjacent hiking trails. **Buckskin** has 105 camping units; **River Island** has 22. Located **11 miles north of Parker** on the Colorado River. **520-667-3231.** Also try Alamo Lake State Park on the Bill Williams River; **520-669-2088. Website: www.pr.state.az.us.**

Havasu Springs Resort

It's hard to know how to categorize this multifaceted resort, because it has houseboat rentals, 45 motel rooms, 150 RV hookups in a campground with pool, and a restaurant, overlooking the river, that's open 7:00 A.M.–9:00 P.M. Located **0.5 mile north of Parker Dam** on Hwy. 95. **520-667-3361. Website: www.havasusprings.com.**

La Paz County Park

On one of the longest strips of waterfront, it has tent spaces, RV spaces with and without hookups, dry camping, and shade ramadas. A shallow lagoon is ideal for boat launching and fishing. Rest rooms and shower facilities are open year-round. Located **8 miles north of Parker. 520-667-2069.**

Where to Eat

McDonald's, Subway, Dairy Queen, a Chinese restaurant, a steak house, a yacht club (a bit of Quartzsite humor there), and a pizza place make up the Quartzsite dining scene. Kentucky Fried Chicken, Blimpies, McDonald's, Burger King, and Taco Bell, plus pizza and rib places, are easy to find in Parker.

Blue Willow Restaurant—$$$–$$$$

Inside the Blue Water Resort (see Wagering and Where to Stay), this fine-dining restaurant has an upscale menu with excellent New York strip steaks and prime rib as well as chef's special meat loaf and southern fried chicken. Open Wed.– Sun., 5:00 P.M.–9:00 P.M. **11300 Resort Dr., Parker; 520-669-7000. Website: www.blue waterfun.com.**

Paradise Cafe—$$–$$$

Full-service sit-down dining is offered in a cheerful environment, with barbecued ribs and chicken the house specialties. Lunch specials can be a real bargain. Open Mon.–Thurs., 11:00 A.M.–10:00 P.M.; Fri.–Sun., 11:00 A.M.–11:00 P.M. Located **14 miles north of Parker on Hwy. 95 at Parker Dam turnoff. 520-667-2404.**

Badenoch's on the River—$–$$

Riverfront casual best describes this pleasant outdoor place. Cool and airy in summer, enclosed and heated in winter, the menu includes omelets, burgers, sandwiches, and salads to linger over as you watch water skiers and boaters on the river. Open daily, 7:00 A.M.–9:00 P.M.; may be closed Dec. Located **3 miles upriver from Parker on Hwy. 95. 520-669-2681.**

Desert Bar (Nellie E. Saloon)—$

The main attraction of this quirky, friendly place is that getting there is half the fun. You jounce over a not-too-bad dirt road for about 4.5 miles, park near what appears to be a church, then sit at a copper-top bar on bar stools that sway from side to side. All this is, quite literally, in the middle of nowhere. The bar's electricity is solar-generated, stored in batteries and run through inverters. The "church" is a facade of solid steel that has been the site of a number of weddings. Although its primary function is not as an eatery, there is a snack bar with burgers and hot dogs. Open Labor Day–Memorial Day, Sat.–Sun., noon–sunset. Located **about 5 miles north of Parker; from Hwy. 95 take Cienega Springs Rd. exit and proceed about 4.5 miles to the bar.** No phone.

Services

Parker Area Chamber of Commerce

1217 California Ave., Parker, 85344; 520-669-2174 or 888-733-7275 for a free travel guide. Websites: www.coloradoriverinfo.com/parker and www.arizonaguide.com/parker.

Quartzsite Chamber of Commerce

Open Mon.–Fri., 9:00 A.M.–4:00 P.M., closed for lunch. 1495 Main Event Ln., P.O. Box 85, Quartzite, 85346; 520-927-5600. Website: www.quartzsitechamber.com.

Lake Havasu City

Less than 40 years old, Lake Havasu City is a sun-sparkled oasis, green with golf courses and gardens. Imaginative resorts cluster at lakeside, and good restaurants offer eclectic dining. Beyond city borders, the Sonoran Desert melts into the foothills of the Mojave Mountains on one side and the Chemehuevi on the other. The population has doubled within the last five years, and the number of annual visitors has tripled. The city's founder, Robert P. McCulloch, passed away in 1977, but a main thoroughfare named in his honor keeps his memory apparent in this "Blue Water Paradise," which is what Havasu means to the Mojave Indians.

History

In 1963 when chain-saw magnate McCulloch began constructing Lake Havasu City, the place was pretty dismal. A body of water formed when Parker Dam impounded the Colorado River was surrounded by dirt terraces bladed bare of trees and vegetation. A single spartan motel didn't do much to entice visitors. But McCulloch was a visionary. He promised a job with his company to anyone willing to relocate. Early guests were flown in on a four-motor Lockheed Constellation that landed on a rough, graded airstrip adjacent to the Nautical Inn. McCulloch hoped to entice them to purchase property, not a bad idea when lakeview lots sold for $5,000. But the new city languished. Phoenix newspaper articles joked about the "big mudhole," smugly pointing out that summer temperatures there topped even Phoenix's legendary heat. For almost two decades, Havasu's progress remained unremarkable, until the mid-1980s when the groundwork for this now-flourishing city and recreation area paid off.

Major Attractions

London Bridge

In 1971 the famed London Bridge came to Lake Havasu. A decade earlier, when the bridge was still British, it was discovered that the storied landmark was indeed, as the nursery rhyme declared, falling down, sinking into the Thames under the burden of increased traffic. For close to 2,000 years, since the Romans built a bridge across it in A.D. 43, the Thames was spanned by a bridge. The bridge now located in Lake Havasu was built in 1831 of granite quarried on Dartmoor and designed with five magnificent arches still in place today. When the bridge began its slow slide into the Thames in 1962, its British life was over.

Entrepreneurial Londoners put it on the market, and developer Robert McCulloch submitted the winning $2,460,000 bid. The bridge was dismantled; each piece was numbered when the bridge was disassembled. The pieces were transported to Long Beach, California, by boat, then trucked to Havasu at an additional

Getting There
Lake Havasu is about 208 miles northwest of Phoenix, about a 4-hour drive. Take I-10 west to AZ 95, and follow AZ 95 north through Parker to Lake Havasu City. You can also reach it from I-40 west of Kingman, driving south on Hwy. 95.

$4 million cost to McCulloch. Workers formed sand mounds along a 1-mile channel to the profile of each arch, and reassembled 10,000-plus granite blocks around them. As you pass under its arches, you can still see four-digit numbers painted on many of the blocks. The first indicate which span, the second number places it in its proper row, and the last two digits denote the block's position in the row. They removed the sand after construction, and diverted water from the lake, under the bridge, and back into the lake.

The bridge seems appropriate here in a Disneyesque sort of way, especially since the city of Lake Havasu was laid out by C. V. Wood, the man who designed Disneyland. But far from just a quirky anachronism, it attractively spans the lake, providing access to a small splotch of land called The Island and sheltering the shops of English Village at its mainland end.

Havasu National Wildlife Refuge

This is a truly beautiful refuge, especially if you see it during winter months when the river isn't clogged with boats. It is one of the most important riparian areas along the lower Colorado River, with more than 14,000 of its 44,000-plus acres designated as wilderness. Extending for 24 miles between Lake Havasu City and Needles, California, the refuge has for thousands of years supplied essential winter food for migrating geese, sandhill cranes, ducks, and other wildlife. The area's position on a major flyway makes it a prime viewing spot for the western grebe, great blue heron, and other migratory birds. Three hundred miles of shoreline, created by the Colorado River and its arms, shelter wading birds and shorebirds. The endangered Yuma clapper rail, southern bald eagle, and peregrine falcon all depend on the refuge for shelter and sustenance. In the area called Topock Marsh, there are large heron and egret rookeries. The marsh suffers the effects of high boat traffic, and during the busiest summer months wildlife may be difficult to spot. But be patient and try to visit during early morning hours, and you'll likely be rewarded with impressive sightings.

Within the refuge the soaring cliffs of 16-mile-long **Topock Gorge**, softened by centuries of eroding river water, look like large fists and giant dimpled kneecaps. Imaginative watchers of their random shapes can clearly see the eye of Stargazer Rock open and close as your boat passes by. Other discernable rock creatures include an alligator, fish, dolphin, hippo, gorilla, and praying Indian. Keen-eyed observers may catch a glimpse of desert bighorn sheep as the animals prowl the rocky ridges, sometimes drawn to the water's edge if drought conditions are severe. Near the waterline in some areas, ancient Indian petroglyphs are clearly visible. The gorge is closed to water skiing, camping, and open fires. Boaters are cautioned to pay close attention to two-way water traffic. For information contact **Refuge Manager, Havasu National Wildlife Refuge, 1406 Bailey Ave., No. B, P.O. Box 3009, Needles, CA 92363; 760-326-3853.**

Festivals and Events

There's something going on in this lively city almost every week. For a complete listing of events, contact the tourism bureau (see Services).

Hava Salsa Challenge

Apr.

Lake Havasu and its sister city, Ciudad Guzman in Mexico, get together for a multiday festival to share deep-pit barbecue, fry bread, tamales, tacos, arts and crafts, and performances by folkloric dancers and singers. "People's Choice" salsa judging is a highlight. In recent years the event has grown to include top-notch celebrity talent. 520-453-3444.

Skat-trak Jet Ski World Finals

Oct.

This aquatic event draws thousands of aficionados of these fast-paced personal watercraft. Book hotel rooms well in advance because this is one of the premier sporting events of the year. 520-453-3444.

London Bridge Seaplane Classic

early Nov.

At this in-the-air event for model radio-controlled floatplanes and seaplanes, you can watch earthbound "pilots" guide their planes to (hopefully) safe watery landings. Half the fun is looking at the beautifully handcrafted models. After owners put so much work into their planes, it might seem that they would be reluctant to launch their babies into the air and onto the water. But nope. Crashes and splashes are all part of the sport. Held **on the beach at Nautical Inn Resort. 520-855-2141.**

Outdoor Activities

Boating

Forty-five-mile-long Lake Havasu forms a human-created boundary between Arizona and California and also creates an extensive aquatic playground. Its waters chill to the mid-50s during winter months, but stay in the pleasant 80s from about mid-Apr. into early fall. A number of natural sand beaches are jumping-off points for windsurfing, jet skiing, sailing, canoeing, water skiing, fishing, and swimming.

Picnics are fun at the lake because there is so much pretty shoreline. A number of carry-out restaurants preclude you having to pack your own. **Rotary Beach Community Park** along the Colorado has shady picnic tables and beach-side volleyball sites, so many families come and spend the day. The beach here has a gentle, toddler-accessible slope.

HOUSEBOATING

Lake Havasu's placid waters and the coves and inlets along its irregular shoreline invite houseboaters, who find their floating condos a popular alternative to conventional hotel and resort accommodations. It's a leisurely way to explore in comfort. Most houseboats, at 46–52 feet about the size of a large motor home, come with standard-size beds, complete galleys, living rooms, and barbecue areas on deck, plus a lesson in captaining. Rentable for just a few days or a week, they're equipped with utensils, dishes, and linens, and can accommodate 10–12 guests. These apartments afloat adapt to your own leisurely ad-lib itinerary, allowing for frequent stops to explore nooks and crannies along the 45-mile-long lake. **H20 Houseboat Vacations, P.O. Box 2100, Havasu Lake, CA 92363; 800-242-2628 or 760-858-1008. Website: www. H20houseboats.com.**

Fishing

Houseboats provide a base from which anglers can pursue the wily trout, bass, bluegill, crappie, and catfish in Lake Havasu. You can launch your own boat from any of a number of public ramps and fish the river from shore or a craft, day or night, in any area that isn't posted. Fishing licenses and regulations are available at most marinas.

Golf

While winter months are glorious for getting in a round of golf, hitting the links in Havasu's 100°F-plus summer temperatures may sound like a bid for heatstroke. But many courses open at daylight so you can get in 18 holes and be home by 11:00 A.M., before temperatures reach their late-afternoon high. Most courses have lower fees after 2:00 P.M., and even lower rates closer to the end of the day.

London Bridge, brought to Arizona by chain-saw magnate Robert McCulloch as an attraction to draw residents, once spanned the Thames in London. It has found a second home in Lake Havasu City.

London Bridge Golf Club

Two par 71, semiprivate championship courses wind among lakes, palm trees, and lovely upscale homes. Almost every tee has a view of the lake. The East course is about 500 yards shorter than the West course, but the two are equally challenging. **London Bridge Golf Club, 2400 Club House Dr., Lake Havasu City, 86403; 520-855-2719.**

Nautical Inn Golf Course

This mainly flat 4,012-yard executive course is adjacent to the little motel originally constructed by McCulloch to house the guests he flew in as prospective buyers. You can walk over from the inn, which is **on McCulloch Blvd. on The Island. 520-855-5585.**

Seeing and Doing

Parks

Aquatic Center

This popular center is a good respite when even water-lovers need a break from the summer's 105°F sunshine. Colorful windsurfers hang from the ceiling, over "surf" in the wave pool that washes up on a cement "beach." It's all fringed with frankly fake palm trees sprouting plastic coconuts that periodically dump water on anyone underneath. A four-story water slide keeps kids busy, and a gently sloping shoreline-style entry accommodates the aquatic PVC wheelchair, available to anyone who needs it. Call for hours and swimming schedules; open swimming Mon.–Fri., 2:30 P.M.–5:00 P.M. **100 Park Ave., Lake Havasu City, 86403; 520-453-2687.**

Scenic Drives

FOUR-WHEEL-DRIVE TRIPS

Because it sits at the juncture of the Sonoran and Mojave Deserts, the area around Lake Havasu City has an amazing diversity of plant and animal life. Among the plants surviving in these arid conditions are the puffy smoke trees that look just like their name, yellow-flowering creosote bushes, red-blooming barrel cactus, and ocotillo. Chuckwallas, a type of desert lizard kept

The London Bridge Resort in Lake Havasu City overlooks the Colorado River and the famous bridge.

almost invisible by protective coloration, sometimes pose languidly on shaded ledges if visitors keep their distance and watch quietly. The phainopepla, a striking black cardinal-like bird, and the capricious roadrunner are commonly seen. It's not unusual to spot antelope, jackrabbits, and an occasional sidewinder rattlesnake working its way in S-shape squiggles across the road. If you're going out on your own, always observe posted signs, especially when you head off on old mining roads. Besides disturbing ancient Native American sites, you could be moving onto roads that are unsafe. Be sure you're carrying plenty of water.

Outback Offroad Adventures

For an interpretive look at fascinating aspects of the desert, you'll be picked up at your hotel in a custom 4-by-4 outfitted with roll bars and a shade top. Guide Dave Griffiths' knowledge of plants and animals makes it possible to see life where none seems to exist. Gold mines, ghost towns, native culture, and history are part of the adventure. The full- or half-day tours include snacks and cold drinks. **520-680-6151. Website: www.outbackadventures.com.**

Tours

BOAT TOURS

Bluewater Charters Jet Boat Tours

Nature lovers can catch a jet boat with view windows along the sides and in the roof for a three-hour cruise upriver to Havasu National Wildlife Refuge. Boats leave from the base of the London Bridge, cruise past petroglyphs and possibly bighorn sheep, and make a rest stop at Park Moabi. **P.O. Box 2032, Lake Havasu City, 86405; 888-855-7171 or 520-855-7171.**

Wagering

Havasu Landing Resort and Casino

You can challenge Lady Luck on the Chemehuevi Indian Reservation on the California side of the Colorado. Even though it's in a different state, it is very much a part of the Havasu scene. Games of chance (electronic only) include blackjack, bingo, lotto, and conventional slots. If you're not accustomed to the newest in slot machines, you may miss the sound of coins jingling out your reward when instead your winnings appear as a printed receipt. Take the slip of paper to the cashier and exchange it for the real thing. The *Colorado River Express* offers five daily, 20-minute shuttles between English Village underneath the London Bridge and the resort, which also has beaches, a restaurant, and a cocktail lounge. **P.O. Box 1707, Havasu Lake, CA 92363; 800-307-3610.**

Where to Stay

Among the chains, you'll find Super 8, Best Western, Days Inn, and Ramada in Lake Havasu City.

The London Bridge Resort—$$$

More than 100 acres of shops and restaurants keep guests busy at this castlelike place. With flags aflutter from crenelated turrets, it's a medieval castle transposed to the banks of the Colorado. Kids especially love it for its fantasy look. In the lobby is a replica of the elaborately decorated Gold State Coach, part of British coronation ceremonies in the 1800s. From its beach it's an easy launch into any number of water sports. The resort, whose rooms have kitchens and living rooms with sofa sleepers, recently has become a time-share. Reservations may be booked no more than 14 days out from time of arrival, except for holiday weekends, when some units may be available earlier. **1477 Queen's Bay Rd., Lake Havasu City, 86403; 800-624-7939 or 520-855-0888.**

Howard Johnson Lodge & Suites—$$–$$$

Located in town but with good lake and mountain views, this 47-room Hojos comes with refrigerator and microwave in all suites, which is why we list it here. If you're staying in for more than a night, it's always a bonus not to have to go somewhere to get morning coffee. Indoor spa and swimming pool. **335 London Bridge Rd., Lake Havasu City, 86403; 800-446-4656 or 520-453-4656. Website: www.hojo.com.**

Havasu Dunes Resort—$$

We particularly like this lovely site overlooking the lake because the one- and two-bedroom condos have complete kitchens, so we can settle in for a number of days, getting our groceries locally, without having to go out to eat for every meal. Each unit is set up with a well-furnished living room, TV, table and chairs for dining, and plenty of closet space. It has a pretty pool that hardly anyone seems to use. Nightly and weekly rentals. **620 Lake Havasu Ave. S., Lake Havasu City, 86403; 520-855-6626.**

Holiday Inn—$$

This is a bit different from many Holiday Inns because some of its 162 rooms have lake views and balconies that really put it in the resort category (ask when booking). All rooms have coffeemakers and refrigerators. The heated outdoor pool and spa overlook the lake. Things heat up after dark at the Reflections night club, where two dance floors generally are alive with gyrating dancers. Ask about special weekly and monthly rates. **245 London Bridge Rd., Lake Havasu City, 86403; 888-428-2465 or 520-855-4071. Website: www.basshotels.com.**

Nautical Inn—$$

Originally built by McCulloch when he was marketing Lake Havasu City, this resort's 120 guest rooms all recently have undergone a complete renovation. Located on The Island, across London Bridge, all rooms face the water. It has a small golf course, tennis courts, and laundry facilities. Cross the bridge and follow the main road. **1000 McCulloch Blvd., Lake Havasu City, 86403; 800-892-2141 or 520-855-2141. Website: www.nauticalinn.com**

Camping

Cattail Cove State Park Campground

There is not a lot of vegetation here, but you can camp literally feet from the water, a decided plus during hot summer months. More than 200 RV and tent sites are available on a first-come, first-served basis, with 150 sites accessible by boat. Located 15 miles south of Lake Havasu City, off Hwy. 95. 520-855-1223. Website: www.pr.state.az.us.

Havasu Landing Resort Campground

On the California side of the Colorado River, you can pitch a tent in a campground shaded by salt cedar within a minute or two of the water. Full-hookup sites with river views adjacent to the full-service marina may be reserved in advance. There is no vehicle crossing at Havasu Landing between the two states. When driving your RV from the Arizona side, you'll have to go north on I-40 to the town of Needles to cross the river, then return south on California US 95 to Havasu Landing. Campers and pedestrians can take the ferry that runs five times a day. **P.O. Box 1707, Havasu Lake, CA 92363; 760-858-4606.**

Lake Havasu State Park Campground

The park begins 2 miles north of London Bridge and extends for more than 40 miles along the shore. If you don't like desert camping, this place may not appeal to you. However, you'll be very close to the lake. Spaces are thoughtfully planned so that you're not on top of your neighbor, and there are paloverde trees and a cactus garden on the grounds. It has picnic tables, a swim area, and 75 first-come, first-served dry campsites, no hookups. There are 55 boat-access-only sites. From Lake Havasu City come **north on London Bridge Rd. 2 miles to the park entrance. 520-855-2784.** Website: www.pr.state.az.us.

Where to Eat

Eateries include the fun and funky as well as the truly elegant. The common denominator is that all are well priced, as are most attractions and facilities in Lake Havasu.

Bridgewater Cafe—$$$

This is a fairly classic place to eat because it overlooks the lake and all its activity. You can opt for dining alfresco on the terrace to get even closer to the action. You'll find a decent selection of mid-priced California wines. An opulent Sunday champagne brunch, offered seasonally, is a real crowd-pleaser. Open Mon.–Thurs., 7:00 A.M.–9:00 P.M.; Fri.–Sat., 7:00 A.M.–10:00 P.M. Located in **London Bridge Resort. 1477 Queen's Bay Rd.; 520-855-0888.**

London Bridge Brewery—$$

This English-style pub does a good job of replicating its U.K. counterparts. Service on the patio is offered during summer. Open Mon.–Thurs., 11:00 A.M.–9:00 P.M.; Fri.–Sun., 8:00 A.M.–9:00 P.M. Appropriately located in **English Village under London Bridge. 520-855-8782.**

Chico's Tacos—$

Locals come here for lunch. Situated "in town" and up the hill from the lake, this Baja-style taqueria has freshly prepared tacos for you to embellish from the fresh salsa bar according to your personal tolerance. It's also the place for a great margarita. Phone ahead and they'll have a bag of tacos waiting for you to pick up, to consume at one of the waterfront parks. Open Sun.–Thurs., 10:30 A.M.–9:00 P.M.; Fri.–Sat., 10:30 A.M.–10:00 P.M. Located in Basha's Center. 1641 McCulloch Blvd.; 520-680-7010.

Services

Lake Havasu Tourism Bureau

Call for a free vacation information packet. 314 **London Bridge Rd., Lake Havasu City, 86403; 800-242-8278 or 520-453-3444.** Website: www.arizonaguide.com/havasu.

Kingman

At an elevation of 3,336 feet, Kingman sits in a mining and cattle area in high desert surrounded by the Cerbat Mountains to the northwest, the Hualapais on the southeast, with the Black Mountains defining its southwest landscape. It is the jumping-off point for visits to Oatman, Lake Mead, and Hoover Dam. The town's railroad history carries on today, as more than 100 trains chug through in any 24-hour period. It isn't quite as disturbing as you might think, because 5 miles outside of Kingman the tracks split, permitting trains to pass, which means that two trains usually rumble through town within minutes of each other. If you listen, you can tell the difference between the musical *toot-toot* of Amtrak, which goes through twice a day, and the strident *blat-blat* of freight trains. The express stops here to change personnel. Kingman niches itself as being "The Heart of Old Route 66" because it lies on the longest stretch of the Mother Road, 158 miles, still in existence.

History

As do so many towns that developed during the late 1800s, Kingman owes its existence to the Atlantic and Pacific Railroad. When surveyor Lewis Kingman found a natural right-of-way, the line was built and the town of Kingman grew up around it. A park in the middle of town, built around 1927 steam engine No. 3759, now a historical monument, commemorates Kingman's locomotive history.

Andrew Timothy Devine, later known as Andy "Jingles" Devine to a movie-going public, grew up here, watching the horses and wagons along Front St. give way to automobiles as the street became Route 66. The portion that runs through the city and parallels Route 66 is called Andy Devine Ave. in honor of Kingman's native son. The downtown area has more than 60 buildings listed on the National Register of Historic Places. Clark Gable and Carole Lombard were married at the old courthouse here.

Festivals and Events

Route 66 Classic Car Rally & Show

late Apr.–early May

During this popular event, part of the whole weeklong Route 66 celebration, vehicles caravan along the old road. Events include a parade, bed races, a hot-air balloon glow, and music by a 1950s-style band. In recent years Martin Milner from the original Route 66 television series has put in an appearance at the Sat.-night barbecue. 520-769-2605.

Andy Devine Days

early Oct.

Until his demise in 1977, Andy Devine showed up for this three-day celebration that includes a PRCA rodeo, parade, and other festivities. 520-753-6106.

Outdoor Activities

Golf

Cerbat Cliffs Golf Course

Named for the bluffs that edge its western side, this high-desert year-round course is noted for its rocky challenges. If there's a breeze and you're at the Lava Loop, holes number 10, 11, and 12, you can be in a world of hurts because you can be blown into a bed of destructive rocks on either side of the fairway. Another hole, the short par 3 number eight, is completely surrounded by rock. The 18-hole course has bent-grass greens and a 71.9 rating from the blue tees. The Sand Trap restaurant serves three meals a day, and has wine and beer. **1001 Gates Ave., Kingman, 86401; 520-753-6593.**

Hiking

Hualapai Mountain County Park

Summer temperatures of about 78°F make this a favorite hiking and picnicking retreat for those escaping the heat of the Mojave Desert in California and the Lake Havasu area. Mixed forests of ponderosa, piñon pine, and scrub oak shelter a truly wonderful variety of bird life, not commonly seen in other parts of the state. If you've never watched the spectacular acorn woodpecker with his red cap, or the dramatic black-and-white downy woodpecker, this is the place to go. Located about 14 miles southeast of Kingman. **From I-40 take exit 51 to Stockton Hill Rd. south, which becomes Hualapai Mountain Rd. 877-757-0915.**

Seeing and Doing

Museums and Historic Sites

Bonelli House

Built in 1915, this family home is a good example of the Anglo-Territorial style of architecture popular in Arizona into the 1920s. Its

Getting There
From Lake Havasu City, drive north on Hwy. 95 to I-40 and head east to Kingman. From Williams and towns to the east, the quick way to get to Kingman is to stay on I-40 all the way. For a taste of history, however, veer off at Seligman and take old Route 66 through Hackberry and Peach Springs, named for the fruit trees planted there by early Mormon settlers. The road loops through the southernmost tip of the Hualapai Indian Reservation, the proposed site of a new gaming casino.

thick tufa stone (a porous limestone that makes up the Cerbat Mountains) walls and wide porches were early heat-beating features. The home is furnished with original family possessions as well as antiques appropriate to the period. Listed on the National Register of Historic Places. Open Thurs.–Mon., 1:00 P.M.–4:00 P.M. **430 E. King St, Kingman, 86401; 520-753-3195.**

Chloride

An old mining town (is there a town in this area that wasn't?) founded in 1862 with the discovery of silver in the Cerbat Mountains, Chloride is named for the ore that contains the precious metal. It's presently reincarnated as an artsy-craftsy place, a nice side trip from Kingman. The **old jail, Jim Fritz Museum,** and the **Silverbelle Playhouse** attest to a town not letting itself slip into oblivion. Once, more than 2,000 residents worked 75 area mines. The current population of 300 is a dedicated lot, with many fine artisans purveying their wares alongside antiques and collectibles in assorted shops and studios. Because this is a casual sort of place, you'll find store hours a bit iffy, but on weekends you'll usually find things open. It's probably the artistic influence that induces residents

Old cars of all vintages show up for the annual Route 66 Classic Car Show in Kingman.

ride, from Kingman take US 93 north 17 miles to the Chloride turnoff; head right (east) about 4 miles into town. Chloride Chamber of Commerce, P.O. Box 268, Chloride, 86431; 520-565-2204.

Hotel Beale

Although we currently consider this 1900 hotel an attraction, it may be just a matter of time until it is welcoming guests. The Beale is part of a restoration project that eventually will include the Andy Devine Celebrity Theatre and Old Town Meeting Hall. The plan is to renovate hotel rooms and provide a place to display memorabilia honoring Andy and his parents, Tom and Amy Devine, who acquired the Beale in 1906. Once a commercial center, here salesmen purveyed goods and services to Northern Arizona businessmen. The Beale changed ownership a number of times, and is presently in limbo. But it is on the National Register of Historic Places and if all you do is look at it from the outside, you'll get a sense of its history. 325 Andy Devine Ave., Kingman, 86401.

Mojave Museum of History and Arts

This little museum displays a one-third-size Santa Fe stagecoach outside and memorabilia from the life of Andy Devine, the perennial "good guy" actor who grew up in Kingman. It details his 176-movie career with posters and photos, and explains that as a child his larynx was pierced in an accident, giving him his characteristic scratchy voice. The museum also traces the area's Hualapai Indian history and the construction of Hoover Dam. The gift shop has a good selection of Kingman turquoise, locally quarried and prized for its spectacular color. Small admission. Open Mon.–Fri., 9:00 A.M.–5:00 P.M.; Sat.–Sun., 1:00 P.M.–5:00 P.M.; closed major holidays. 400 W. Beale St., Kingman, 86401; 520-753-3195.

Where to Stay

Coming into Kingman on I-40, get off at Andy

to turn old junk into yard art. Or, depending on your point of view, the art could still be junk. But it does add to the charm of this rustic little place.

Another example of its history, the **Chloride Fire Department** owns a custom-built 1939 Ford fire engine, along with a contemporary Mack fire truck. You might want to mail a card from the **local post office.** Established in 1862, it is said to be the oldest continuously operating mail facility in the state. In Chloride there are a couple of cafes, two saloons, a grocery store, one bed-and-breakfast, and an RV park.

Painted on sheer escarpments in the hills southeast of town are the **Purcell Murals,** remaining amazingly bright and colorful since they were created in 1966 and 1975. Although they remain open to interpretation, the artist-miner Roy Purcell called them "The Journey: Images from an Inward Search for Self." Take Tennessee Ave. out of town, then follow signs for about 1.5 miles to the murals. To reach Chlo-

Devine Ave. where the interstate crosses Route 66 to find lots of budget motels. They include Holiday Inn, Best Western, Motel 6, Budget Inn, Comfort Inn, Days Inn, Quality Inn, Super 8 and TraveLodge.

Hualapai Mountain Lodge and RV Park—$$–$$$

These six motel units and an RV park lie in Hualapai Mountain County Park (see Hiking and Camping) in the midst of a gorgeous ponderosa forest. Fourteen rustic cabins ($–$$) have beds, cooktop stove, and shower. Bring your own bedding, towels, cooking utensils, and dishes. In the lodge's award-winning restaurant, breakfast is cooked right at your table, sometimes with resident elk and mule deer watching through the picture windows. Reservations in summer are essential for both the dining room and lodge. Located **about 13 miles southeast of Kingman off County Rd. 147. Pine Lake, Star Route, Kingman, 86401; 520-757-3545.**

Hotel Brunswick—$–$$$

In addition to the proliferation of reliable chain motels along Route 66 and I-40, there is a new historic option. Next door to the Beale (see Museums and Historic Sites) and also listed on the National Register of Historic Places, this restored hostelry was built in 1909 to provide luxury accommodations for well-heeled miners and ranchers. The three-story hotel, constructed of locally quarried tufa stone, was the tallest building in the area. But by 1980, after countless renovations, the hotel was vacant and in decay. In 1994 a local couple took a look at the original architectural details such as the pressed-tin ceilings, mahogany wainscoting, and wood floors; hired an engineering team that pronounced it structurally sound; and set out on an ambitious renovation program. They reconstructed the balcony that runs the full length of the front, and decorated rooms with handmade quilts and antique furnishings. Subsequent owners have added phones and TVs to guest rooms.

The wide range of prices represents little $25 "cowboy" or "cowgirl" rooms that are com-

Mr. D'z in Kingman is a popular Route 66 eatery, with poodle-skirted waitresses and thick shakes.

fortably furnished with a single bed and shared bathroom down the hall, as well as large double rooms with private baths. The quietest rooms are near the back, away from the road and railroad tracks, but many guests say that train sounds in the night are welcome reminders of days past. **315 E. Andy Devine Ave., Kingman, 86401; 520-718-1800. Website: www.hotel-brunswick.com.**

Camping

Hualapai Mountain County Park

Within this remote, quiet park there are hiking trails and good bird-watching. Refreshing summer temperatures keep the 11 full-hookup RV spaces occupied most of the time. There are 70 tent campsites, with no facilities, scattered among the tall ponderosas. You can also park a small RV here. The steep road, although paved, can be tricky in winter because at the 6,000-foot-plus elevation there usually is snow. RV sites open May–Oct. only. Located **at end of County Rd. 147 about 13 miles southeast of Kingman. 877-757-0915 reservations (Mon.– Fri., 8:00 A.M.–5:00 P.M.) or 520-757-0915.**

Kingman KOA

Within the city limits of Kingman, yet quiet and off the highway, this well-kept park has 90 pull-through sites with hookups, and about a dozen tent spaces with tables and rest rooms nearby, as well as a convenience store and souvenir shop. The solar-heated pool is open mid-May–Oct. 15. From I-40, exit at Andy Devine Ave. (at McDonald's) and continue north on Andy Devine to Airway. Turn left onto Airway and continue about a mile to Roosevelt. Go right on Roosevelt to the campground. **3820 N. Roosevelt, Kingman, 86401-3298; 800-232-4397 or 520-757-4397.**

Where to Eat

There's no shortage of chain eateries and fast-food spots along Andy Devine Ave., but in the older part of town there are a few standouts.

Hubbs Cafe—$$$

Certified Angus beef carved into porterhouse, filet, and New York strip steaks is the draw at the newly restored crystal-and-tablecloth dining room in the Brunswick. It is one of the town's few fine-dining restaurants, yet has a casual atmosphere that invites jeans-clad cowboys as well as weary travelers. The lounge has live entertainment, beer, and wine and a player piano. Open Mon.–Sat., 11:00 A.M.–2:00 P.M. and 4:30 P.M.–9:00 P.M. Located in the Hotel Brunswick. **315 E. Andy Devine Ave.; 520-718-1800.**

El Palacio—$$

Good Mexican beer and cocktails are served in this large, friendly restaurant and cantina run by the Serrano family. Come with an appetite for the huge tostadas, tacos, and chiles rel-lenos, always on the menu. The historic, high-ceilinged building was once a drugstore that served townspeople and guests who came to the Brunswick and the Beale Hotels just one block away. Open daily, 11:00 A.M.–9:00 P.M. **401 E. Andy Devine Ave.; 520-718-0018.**

Mr. D'z Route 66 Diner—$–$$

The best place in town to watch traffic go by on Route 66, the pink and turquoise diner is straight out of the 1950s, with poodle-skirted waitresses, plastic booths, and lots of neon and chrome. Burgers and sandwiches are menu staples, as well as meat loaf with mashed potatoes and gravy, and chicken-fried steak. Open Tues.–Sun., 10:00 A.M.–5:00 P.M. Located at Route 66 and First St. **105 E. Andy Devine Ave.; 520-718-0066.**

Services

Historic Route 66 Association of Arizona

Open Mon–Sat., 9:00 A.M.–6:00 P.M.; Sun., 10:00 A.M.–2:00 P.M. **120 Andy Devine Ave., P.O. Box 66, Kingman, 86402; 520-753-5001.**

Kingman Powerhouse Visitor Center and Chamber of Commerce

Open daily, 9:00 A.M.–6:00 P.M. **120 W. Andy Devine, Kingman, 86402; 520-753-6106. Website: www.arizonaguide.com/visitkingman.**

Oatman

The little mountain town of Oatman, once a mining mecca, now is visited for its historic Route 66 sights and mining nostalgia. You can still see tailings mounded near town. Although the mine closed in 1942, it reopened in 1995 when gold prices soared. At full production it was running 500 tons of ore a day, producing 40,000 ounces of gold a year. The operation employed 135 miners at its peak. But alas, the mine closed again in 1998 when gold prices dropped below the $325-per-ounce benchmark that allows the mine to operate at a profit.

The Gold Road Mine is not idle, however (see Historic Sites), as tours are in full swing. Today the town depends largely on tourism for its economic base. Its population? "Around 150," joke locals, "unless you count the burros. Then it's more."

History

The stories of how Oatman, once called Vivian, got its name vary with the storyteller. One version says it was named for a family killed by Apaches in the 1850s. Another, possibly the most reliable, says that in 1851 a young girl named Olive Oatman was captured by Indians and held at Ollie Oatman Springs just north of town. She was rescued in 1857 near the current town site. Yet another story says it was named for the son of Olive Oatman, a Mojave Indian who became a successful miner. It doesn't much matter which you choose to believe because the town's appeal remains the same.

Founded in 1906 as a mining center, Oatman, first a tent city, within a decade turned into a boomtown of more than 10,000 industrious souls producing exceptionally rich gold ore. Prosperity was short-lived, however, and in 1924 United Eastern Mines permanently halted operations. What minimal mining continued was dealt a final blow in 1942 when even the few remaining mines were closed. The town seemed doomed.

But it was infused with new life when Route 66 made it a logical stop. It became the last oasis for migrants pushing westward before they headed out into the desolate Mojave Desert on their way to California. Bypassed in 1952 when Route 66 was rerouted through Yucca to alleviate traffic on the challenging mountain road, Oatman floundered a second time. But it hitched itself up by its bootstraps by developing into a historic destination, complete with plank sidewalks and tumbledown buildings.

Seeing and Doing

Historic Sites

A dozen or more burros freely roam the main street of Oatman, cadging handouts from willing tourists and posing for snapshots so long as they're being fed. These long-eared Eeyores, descendants of burros used by prospectors a century ago, now earn their living as crowd-pleasers.

On weekends Oatman really gears up, with gunfighters and golddiggers strolling Main St., "holding up" tour buses and perpetrating shotgun weddings.

Carole Lombard and Clark Gable spent part of their honeymoon at the little Oatman Hotel in Oatman.

Scenic Drives

Route 66 Scenic Byway

Located southwest of Kingman via Route 66, a designated scenic byway at this point, Oatman is approached by climbing through the Black Mountains along a series of stomach-lurching switchbacks. The quartz spire that interrupts the horizon in the distance is called Elephant's Tooth. At Sitgreaves Pass, named for 19th-century army topographic engineer Lt. Lorenzo Sitgreaves, who also gave his name to the national forest, the 3,652-foot elevation creates great views into Arizona, California, and Nevada. The scenery has lured filmmakers here to make *Foxfire, How the West Was Won,* and other less memorable flicks as well as countless commercials.

Getting There

Oatman is on Route 66, 25 miles southwest of Kingman and 30 miles southeast of Bullhead City.

Shopping

There are plenty of funky little shops and a number of classier establishments purveying trinkets and trivia as well as fine Indian crafts, leather goods, and stone jewelry. When spending time in Oatman, the best thing to do is try to find a parking spot wherever you can—no mean task on a holiday weekend. There's a parking lot on the left as you enter town from the east, and several smaller areas off the main drag. There are only four restaurants and no gas stations.

Tours

Gold Road Mine Tour

Until the Gold Road Mine reopens, visitors can take an hour-long tour of a genuine gold mine, led by real-life miners. Visitors walk about 0.13 mile with a guide into the original 1900 drift, at one point traveling directly beneath Route 66. At the "Glory Hole," black lights are used to highlight the gold vein structures. The mine contains enough known ore to run for at least three years, and additional prospecting indicates there may be enough to extend that to 10 years. Check before starting out to be sure tours are operating, because the minute gold hits $325 an ounce, the tour guides will once again turn into miners. Moderate fee. Tours daily, 10:00 A.M.–5:00 P.M. Located **2.5 miles east of Oatman on Route 66;** look for Gold Road Mine sign. **520-768-1600. Website: www. goldroadmine.com.**

Where to Stay

Oatman Hotel—$$

The only place to stay is a 1902 double-walled adobe building, one of the few two-story structures in town. Clark Gable and Carole Lombard spent their honeymoon here on Mar. 8, 1939. Legend has it that Gable, an inveterate poker player, returned often to sit in on games with local miners. The modest second-floor rooms have the bathroom down the hall. Enter through the gift shop on the first floor. Reservations essential during high-season winter months. **181 Main St., 86433; 520-768-4408.**

Services

Oatman Chamber of Commerce

There is no chamber office. This number rings in a small shop, and if the "chamber lady" is there, she'll help you, after she explains that she's the chamber president, but only because she slipped out of a meeting to get a cup of coffee at the wrong time. But don't hesitate to call. **P.O. Box 903, Oatman, 86433; 520-768-4274.**

Packrats

These scampering, bustling little mammals are found all over the Sonoran Desert. They may inhabit shallow caves or living cactuses. The spines discourage large predators, and the clever rat uses the plant for foot.

Packrats may build a home of "litter" called a midden, which can serve as home for generations. It's recognizable as a pile of desert brush, sticks, and leaves in a gently rounded mound that can be 6 feet or more across. By urinating on the outside, the rat creates an exterior surface that hardens into an armorlike shell, protecting the tunnels inside for hundreds of years. To examine one is to prowl through layers of history.

Human bones thousands of years old discovered in a midden helped place a culture in a particular area at a certain time. A packrat helped convict a lying husband of murdering his wife. The wife's wedding ring, lost when the husband dragged her corpse through a deserted thicket, was discovered in the midden. This led police to search the area for the woman's body. When it was found, the husband confessed.

One of the first sure signs you're being visited by a packrat is that small, shiny objects mysteriously disappear overnight. The ever-curious creature will pick up anything that strikes its fancy. Forks, jewelry, marbles, shiny coins, eyeglasses, keys, even pens and small perfume vials have been found in packrat middens. While on one of its foraging missions, the packrat may pick up an object, only to discard it when it finds another it likes better. This has given the animal the nickname trade rat, because the person who misses the eyeglasses may well find a teaspoon in its place.

Lake Mead Area

This long, skinny area has become one of the most popular water-sports and fishing destinations in the state. It includes more than 3,000 square miles of desert that borders on Lake Mead and Lake Mojave to the south. Both were created by damming the Colorado River, which flows almost 150 miles through the area beginning at Grand Canyon National Park. At Bullhead City, Davis Dam created Lake Mojave, while to the north Hoover Dam backs up Lake Mead. Both lakes generally follow the natural path of the Colorado, basically expanding it to overtake surrounding land. An amazing diversity of terrain ranges from a high of about 6,990 feet above sea level to 517 feet at the south end of Lake Mojave near Davis Dam.

Cleverly marketed as "Arizona's West Coast," what the area lacks in expansive stretches of water found on the nation's true West Coast in California, it makes up for in avid water enthusiasts who quite literally clog the river with boats and personal watercraft during the summer. That's about the only time the water temperature is warm enough to swim without a wet suit. Although spring and fall air temperatures are decidedly more pleasant, the water is icy.

Kingman is the hub for exploring this area; either head northwest on US 93 to visit Hoover Dam, or head west on Hwy. 68 to the south end of Lake Mead National Recreation Area, where three cities lie on the northeast edge of the Mojave Desert: Bullhead City is at the hub, just across from Laughlin, Nevada. **Bullhead City,** with a population of about 37,000, is linked to Laughlin, Nevada, by a bridge donated partially by Don Laughlin, its founder, who paid a portion of $3.5 million in 1987 for its construction. Bullhead City is home to many of the workers from the casinos across the river in Laughlin, where there is little permanent housing. **Katherine's Landing,** 6 miles northeast of Bullhead City, has a resort and marina, plus a small motel, store, restaurant, and lounge. On hot summer weekends the place is chockablock with boaters. **Laughlin, Nevada,** barely 30 years old, has nine hotel casinos without the Vegas price tag. There are more than 13,000 slots in Laughlin, ranging from nickel to sky's the limit.

History

Hoover Dam was completed in 1935 and named for Herbert Hoover, the 31st president of the United States. Sometimes called Boulder Dam, the name Hoover was made official by Congress in 1947. It took 16,400 men to build it, 96 of whom lost their lives to accidents and heat exhaustion. The party line is that the dam was constructed to control the Colorado, which was running amok because melting snow frequently swelled it to the point where spring and early summer floods destroyed property, crops, and lives. The production of hydroelectric power, so say the guides, was a secondary purpose. Yet 13 years before its completion, power had been parceled out to high bidders, with California getting 56 percent, Nevada 25 percent, and

Arizona 19 percent. Lake Mead National Recreation Area was established by President Lyndon Johnson in 1964, and is administered by the National Park Service.

Major Attractions

Hoover Dam

This dam has made Lake Mead one of the largest constructed lakes in the world. Its protracted length stretches 105 miles from Hoover Dam to Separation Canyon. With a maximum depth of 500 feet, its 550 miles of shoreline are broken by steep canyon walls, sheltered coves, and beaches. The massive structure of Hoover Dam straddles the Arizona-Nevada state line, holding back two years' flow of Colorado River water in Lake Mead.

The dam has been named one of America's Seven Modern Civil Engineering Wonders by the American Society of Civil Engineers for its arch gravity construction between the narrow walls of Black Canyon. It is 726.4 feet high and 45 feet wide at the top. When water is released, its temperature is a constant 52°F. Mammoth diversion channels, used to redirect the river during construction, are still part of dam tours. The dam has become such an attraction that a large parking structure had to be carved out of the canyon wall to accommodate cars, and a "snacketeria" has been built to provide sustenance. A 22-minute film shown at the visitor center, shot in the 1930s, presents an interesting background to the dam's construction.

Options for touring include a minimally priced **30-minute overview** that takes you through the dam; offered daily, 8:30 A.M.–5:45 P.M. The **Hard Hat Tour** (which we highly recommend to anyone seriously interested in dams) lasts about 60 minutes and covers about 1.25 walking miles. For $25 (you get to keep the dusty blue hard hat), you descend into the dam's interior. It is not for the claustrophobic, and is restricted to those eight and older. A dozen or so visitors at a time squeeze into an elevator for a 506-foot drop (yes, ears do pop) to the dam's pow-

Getting There
From Kingman, heading west on Hwy. 68, in about 30 miles you reach Katherine's Landing. Bullhead City is just south on Hwy. 95. Continuing 5 miles west on Hwy. 68 across the Arizona-Nevada border, where it becomes Hwy. 76, is Laughlin, Nevada. From Kingman, Hoover Dam is 80 miles northwest on US 93.
The Laughlin–Bullhead International Airport accommodates Boeing 727s, DC-10s, and MD-80s. America West Express flies into the airport on a scheduled basis.

erhouse for a close-up of eight-story-high generators. Dials and gauges installed when the dam was built, their function now replaced by computers, remain as interesting relics. The tour gives a look at intricately designed terrazzo floors created by Italian designers who replicated patterns found on Southwest Native American pottery. Workers use the three-wheeled bikes that you see leaning against walls and posts to quickly cover long distances within the dam. Both tours provide the humbling experience of being surrounded by billions of tons of cast concrete. Dam exhibits open daily, 8:00 P.M.–6:00 P.M. Located on US 93 80 miles northwest of Kingman. **Lower Colorado Dams Facilities Office, P.O. Box 60400, Boulder City, NV 89006; 702-294-3523 or 702-294-3524 (9:00 A.M.–3:00 P.M.).**

Davis Dam

This dam, which creates Lake Mojave, pales in size and drama by comparison with Hoover, but it gets a fair amount of traffic because it is one of the few places in the area to cross the Colorado other than at Hoover Dam, two hours north, or at Topock to the south where I-40 angles across. You can bring a picnic lunch to linger over at the ramadas along the river below

Hoover Dam creates Lake Mead, one of the most popular recreation areas on the Colorado River.

the dam. There is no set tour, but visitors can walk to the spillway gates overlooking the river for a pretty view. Open Mon.–Fri., 7:30 A.M.– 3:30 P.M. **520-754-3628.**

Outdoor Activities

Boating

A popular aquatic destination, **Bullhead City** offers water skiing, jet skiing, parasailing, and even sailboating. **Katherine's Landing** has a resort and marina with boat slips and rentals that include houseboats and personal watercraft. Launch ramp, swimmer-friendly beaches with barbecues, and picnic areas.

Fishing

Lake Mead

Fishing is a big attraction, with anglers gather-

ing for a number of major tournaments here each year. Striped bass, bluegill, crappie, and catfish are among the game fish regularly caught. In Meadview, guide service is available for fishing the lake and the Grand Canyon. Call **South Cove Guide Service, 888-564-2804.**

Lake Mojave

This roughly cigar-shaped lake south of Lake Mead extends for 67 miles along the length of the Colorado River. It has 45 square miles of surface area and is 4 miles across at its widest point in the Cottonwood Basin. Coyote, kit fox, desert bighorn sheep, and roadrunners are frequently sighted along the shores. Feral burros and horses as well as domestic livestock drink from the lake's clear waters. Enthusiastic anglers fish for naturally occurring game fish, regularly restocked. Species include cutthroat, rainbow and German brown trout, as well as bass, catfish, crappie, bluegill, and perch. Striper fishing is also excellent, say locals.

Seeing and Doing

Wagering

Spirit Mountain Casino (520-346-2000), on the Fort Mojave Indian Reservation 11 miles south of Bullhead City, has slot machines that satisfy the gaming instinct. **Laughlin, Nevada (800-452-8445),** has nine hotel casinos that offer low-stakes, low-key gambling, well-priced hotel rooms and buffets, and top-notch entertainment.

Where to Stay

Fun, themed hotels and casinos in Laughlin, Nevada, include **Ramada Express (800-383-6190)** with a Victorian railroad theme, *Colorado Belle* **(800-47-RIVER),** a river steamboat, and **Pioneer Hotel (800-634-3469),** with an Old West theme.

Themed hotels and low-stakes gambling draw Arizona visitors to Laughlin, Nevada, just over the state line.

The new Bay Shore Inn (702-299-9010) has 105 rooms on the bay along with a family picnic and barbecue area. Don Laughlin's Riverside Resort Hotel & Casino (1-800-227-3849 or 702-298-2535, www.riversideresort.com) has 1,400 rooms plus a 740-space RV park with full hookups. For the most expansive buffet on the river, go to the Edgewater Hotel & Casino (800-67-RIVER or 702-298-2453, www.edge water-casino.com.). Harrah's Laughlin Casino Hotel (800-447-8700 or 702-298-4600, www. harrahs.com/tour/tour_laughlin) has Laughlin's only soft sand beach.

Camping

Almost two dozen RV parks between Bullhead City and Laughlin, Nevada, verify the area as a popular winter escape, harboring as many as 15,000 snowbirds who migrate from colder climes for four to six months a year. The campground at Katherine Landing has 165 full hookups with spaces big enough to accommodate your boat.

Services

Bullhead Area Chamber of Commerce
1251 Hwy. 95, Bullhead City, 86429; 520-754-4121 or 800-987-7457, fax 520-754-551.

Laughlin Visitors Bureau
This helpful office provides information on entertainment and special events and will make room reservations. P.O. Box 502, Laughlin, NV 89029; 800-452-8445 or 702-298-3321. Website: www.visitlaughlin.com.

Index

About the Author and Photographer

Judy Wade and Bill Baker are a husband/wife writer/photographer team living in Phoenix. Judy earned a journalism degree from the University of Minnesota, and when she felt secure enough to quit her day job, she became a full-time freelancer. She currently writes for a number of national publications. In May 1997, she received the Arizona Press Women Sweepstakes Award, the highest creative honor the society bestows. She also received the Governor's Media Support Award "for providing extraordinary attention and/or support for Arizona's Tourism Industry through use of the media" for the state of Arizona. She is a contributor to *Travelers Tales: A Woman's World,* an anthology of women's travel experiences that won the 1996 Lowell Thomas Best Travel Book award. The Society of American Travel Writers Western Chapter awarded her a 1998 first place in its annual competition for a piece she wrote on hot air ballooning.

Bill, a communications major at Akron University, honed his photography skills in Akron, Ohio, as a retail fashion and product photographer. In the last ten years he has concentrated on travel photography, contributing to *Arizona Highroads, Cruise Travel, Valley Magazine, Physicians Travel & Meeting Guide* and other national publications. He is a member of the American Society of Media Photographers.

The Arizona Guide is the couple's second book for Fulcrum Publishing. It has been awarded a First Place for best nonfiction book in the 1999 Arizona Press Women and National Federation of Press Women creative competitions. It placed second in the Western Chapter of the Society of American Travel Writers 1999 competition. The critically acclaimed *Seasonal Guide to the Natural Year: A Month by Month Guide to Natural Events—Southern California and Baja* was published in 1997 and received a First Place award in the Travel Book category from the Arizona Press Women.

Explore the U.S.A.

with these new additions to Fulcrum Publishing's travel series!

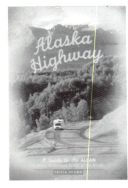

THE WORLD-FAMOUS ALASKA HIGHWAY
A Guide to the Alcan & Other Wilderness Roads of the North
Tricia Brown

Detailing routes, driving conditions, unique people, and all that awaits the adventurous traveler, this is a guide to some of the most beautiful places in all of North America.

ISBN 1-55591-446-2
6 x 9 • PB • 288 pages
90 full-color photographs • 6 full-color maps
$21.95

THE TEXAS GUIDE
Gary James

From the Red River Valley in the north to the Hill Country in the heart of the state to the Gulf Coast region, THE TEXAS GUIDE gives travelers a personal, detailed, and inviting look at the Lone Star State.

ISBN 1-55591-371-7
6 x 9 • PB • 400 pages
152 full-color photographs • 12 full-color maps
$21.95

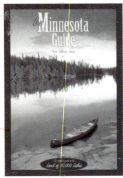

THE MINNESOTA GUIDE
Anne Gillespie Lewis

Third-generation Minnesotan Anne Gillespie Lewis weaves historical facts with practical information on local attractions, accommodations, restaurants, services, and countless recreational activities, sure to interest both residents and visitors alike.

ISBN 1-55591-362-8
6 x 9 • PB • 368 pages
80 full-color photographs • 9 full-color maps
$21.95

Coming Spring 2001! THE COLORADO GUIDE

Fifth Edition
Bruce Caughey & Dean Winstanley
**The best-selling guide to the Centennial State
now with full-color photographs and maps!**

BOOKS FROM THE WEST . . . BOOKS FOR THE WORLD

16100 TABLE MOUNTAIN PARKWAY • SUITE 300 • GOLDEN, CO 80403
800-992-2908 • FAX 800-726-7112 • WWW.FULCRUM-BOOKS.COM